Latin America and the Transports of Opera

 **PERFORMING LATIN AMERICAN & CARIBBEAN IDENTITIES**

Performing Latin American and Caribbean Identities

KATHRYN BISHOP-SANCHEZ, *series editor*

This series is a forum for scholarship that recognizes the critical role of performance in social, cultural, and political life. Geographically focused on the Caribbean and Latin America (including Latinidad in the United States) but wide-ranging in thematic scope, the series highlights how understandings of desire, gender, sexuality, race, the postcolonial, human rights, and citizenship, among other issues, have been explored and continue to evolve. Books in the series will examine performances by a variety of actors with under-represented and marginalized peoples getting particular (though not exclusive) focus. Studies of spectators or audiences are equally welcome as those of actors—whether literally performers or others whose behaviors can be interpreted that way. In order to create a rich dialogue, the series will include a variety of disciplinary approaches and methods as well as studies of diverse media, genres, and time periods.

Performing Latin American and Caribbean Identities is designed to appeal to scholars and students of these geographic regions who recognize that through the lens of performance (or what may alternatively be described as spectacle, ceremony, or collective ritual, among other descriptors) we can better understand pressing societal issues.

Other titles in the series:
Atenco Lives!: Filmmaking and Popular Struggle in Mexico by Livia K. Stone
Creating Carmen Miranda: Race, Camp, and Transnational Stardom by Kathryn Bishop-Sanchez
Living Quixote: Performative Activism in Contemporary Brazil and the Americas by Rogelio Minana

Latin America and the Transports of Opera

Fragments of a Transatlantic Discourse

ROBERTO IGNACIO DIAZ

Vanderbilt University Press
Nashville, Tennessee

Copyright 2023 by Vanderbilt University Press
All rights reserved
First printing 2023

Library of Congress Cataloging-in-Publication Data

Names: Díaz, Roberto Ignacio, 1960- author.
Title: Latin America and the transports of opera : fragments of a
  transatlantic discourse / Roberto Ignacio Díaz.
Description: Nashville : Vanderbilt University Press, 2023. | Series:
  Performing Latin American and Caribbean identities | Includes
  bibliographical references.
Identifiers: LCCN 2023034143 (print) | LCCN 2023034144 (ebook) | ISBN
  9780826506290 (paperback) | ISBN 9780826506306 (hardcover) | ISBN
  9780826506313 (epub) | ISBN 9780826506320 (pdf)
Subjects: LCSH: Opera--Latin America. | Latin America--In opera.
Classification: LCC ML1700 .D514 2023 (print) | LCC ML1700 (ebook) | DDC
  782.109--dc23/eng/20230801
LC record available at https://lccn.loc.gov/2023034143
LC ebook record available at https://lccn.loc.gov/2023034144

Front cover image: Maria Rosendorfsky as Asprano in Vivaldi's *Motezuma*, Theater Ulm, 2018; detail from a photograph by Jean-Marc Turmes. Used courtesy of the photographer.

*For Ana María Esteve
and James Stoecker*

CONTENTS

Acknowledgments   ix

	Introduction. Transatlantic Transports	1
1.	A Corpus of Fragments, I: Listening to Literature	13
2.	A Corpus of Fragments, II: Reading Operas	43
3.	Words by Calderón de la Barca: A Baroque Libretto in Lima	96
4.	Carpentier's Singing Moctezuma: A Neobaroque Novella in Vivaldi's Venice	136
5.	Havana and the Ghosts of Opera	169
6.	Henze and Gomes: Ghostly Testimonios in Copenhagen and Rio de Janeiro	209
7.	Adams and Catán: Magic and Realism in Houston and Paris	245
8.	The World in Buenos Aires: Cosmopolitans at the Teatro Colón	283
	Afterword. Caliban at the Royal Opera House	327

Notes   335
Bibliography   389
Index   405

ACKNOWLEDGMENTS

FOR THIS BOOK about transatlantic transports, I have been fortunate to count on institutions that supported multiple trips around Europe, Latin America, and the United States that allowed me to see, study, and write about the work of opera. The Rockefeller Foundation Bellagio Center hosted me at the Villa Serbelloni overlooking Lake Como, a collegial retreat where the writing of this book, so much of which concerns Italy, began to take shape. A liberal award from the Provost's Office at the University of Southern California underwrote visits to several countries where I presented my research, consulted archives and libraries, met opera professionals, toured opera houses, and attended multiple performances. USC's Dornsife College of Letters, Arts and Sciences provided yet more funding, including a generous grant from the Del Amo Foundation to fly to Spain for two audacious stagings of operas on the conquest of the Americas.

The transports in this book's title also concern the realm of affects, and I have felt buoyed by the openness, trust, patience and kindness that friends and colleagues have shown through the years. Lucille Kerr, Jorge Olivares, and Gustavo Pérez Firmat have always been there for me and endorsed my incipient project before many others did. Manfred Engelbert supported one of my first lectures about opera, focusing on Cuba, at Göttingen's Seminar für Romanische Philologie, a second version of which I read at the University of Southampton's Center for Transnational Studies, invited by

Jo Labanyi. Adriana Méndez Rodenas arranged a conference panel in Poitiers at which I first presented my views on Mercedes Merlin and the art of opera, followed by yet another conference organized by Carmen Vásquez in Amiens. Splendid musicians Mathias Friis-Hansen, Per Pålsson, and Kerstin Thiele welcomed me in Copenhagen and Oslo and vividly described their collaborative work in Henze's *El Cimarrón*. This incisive staging helped to refine my thinking about Latin America and opera, as I discussed in lectures at the University of Liverpool and the University of California, Los Angeles, invited by Lisa Shaw and Maarten Van Delden respectively. Jorge Volpi offered me a chance to speak on Verdi and Wagner in Latin America at the Festival Internacional Cervantino in Guanajuato. Elizabeth Dulanto de Miró Quesada guided me around Lima as I searched for signs of opera in the old viceregal capital, through whose ancient and modern crossings Fanny Schweig led me like only a dear friend can. In La Paz, Piotr Nawrot shared books along with insights into the rich musical history of eastern Bolivia, while Anna Lessa-Schmidt and Mary Cacheado Girondi greatly eased my visit to the Teatro Amazonas in Manaus. Mariano Siskind introduced me to Beatriz Sarlo, who kindly met with me in Buenos Aires to speak about her libretto on Victoria Ocampo. In Santiago de Chile, Matilde Romo de Pierrefeu and Bárbara Cortínez, true friends always, opened doors at the Teatro Municipal with their habitual grace and intelligence.

My colleagues in the Department of Latin American and Iberian Cultures at USC had faith in this project no matter how many years it took to complete. My gratitude to Natalie Belisle, Julien Gutiérrez-Albilla, Ronald Mendoza-de Jesús, Natalia Pérez, Samuel Steinberg, Sherry Velasco, and Erin Graff Zivin, who have crafted a benevolent community of scholars open to scholarship beyond disciplinary constraints. My gratitude as well to colleagues in the USC Department of Comparative Literature, especially Dominic Cheung, now retired, with whom I went to a memorable workshop on Cantonese opera in Hong Kong, and Karen Pinkus, who is no longer at USC but remains a loyal and meaningful friend. At Vanderbilt University Press, this book benefitted from the wise guidance of Zachary Gresham, who first showed an interested in the project, and the careful stewardship of Gianna Mosser, Joell Smith-Borne, and Katherine Feydash, who turned an unwieldy manuscript into a far more readable text. I am thankful to them for their dedication, and to the anonymous reviewers who offered perceptive readings and invaluable suggestions.

My gratitude as well to many friends who have been important actors in my operatic transports. Neil Walsh Soldevila took me to my first opera (with a young Plácido Domingo as Andrea Chénier) at the Teatro de la Universidad de Puerto Rico. Ray Green has been a superb source of wisdom about operas and singers and his beloved Teatro Real in Madrid, a city made even richer by the longstanding friendship of Johanna Damgaard Liander. Galina Bakhtiarova and I shared many an evening at the Los Angeles Opera, occupying the best seats a passion for opera can procure. Arthur Kolat took me to operas in Berlin and on a David Hockney-designed "Wagner Drive" in the Santa Monica Mountains, on which he is an expert. A fellow Bellagio resident, Cheryl Walker, later heard my lament at a South Pasadena café when it seemed this project might end in an ungodly twilight. Back in Italy, Héctor Febles and María Andrea Gauna welcomed me with love and friendship in their house near the Venetian lagoon; Héctor is now gone, but his benevolent reading of parts of this book, like so many of his words, still resound vividly with me. Ever since we met in snowy Massachusetts and for several decades now under the California sun, Verónica Cortínez has taught me how to love words precisely and make them mean exactly what they can; if there is anything good in this book, it owes much to her intelligence and sensibility.

A long time ago, one of my professors, Enrique Anderson Imbert, taught me that you should only write about what you love; this is one reason why I decided to write about opera. It also helps to be surrounded by love. In this long endeavor, I have been supported by my brother Juan Carlos, my sister Carmen María, and her husband, Joel. My niece Claudia, a traveler too, came to Paris and saw the library in the opulent opera house where my research keeps unfolding. Above all, my mother, Ana María Esteve, remains as steadfast a source of love now in Miami as she was decades ago when we first crossed the Atlantic from Havana via Gander to Madrid—a dramatic flight worthy of its own operatic libretto. Another fellow traveler, James Stoecker, has been with me on many a night at the opera from Austria to Australia, and he is a wise and loving companion every single day at our home in Los Angeles; as Verdi's Alfredo knew, love is the very breath of the universe.

Parts of this book were first published as articles or book chapters. "The Spirit of Cuba and the Ghost of Opera" appeared in *Symposium: A Quarterly Journal in Modern Literatures* 61, no. 1 (2007), https://doi.org/10.3200/SYMP.61.1.57-74, while "Transatlantic Deficits; or, Alberto Vilar at the Royal Opera House" came out in *Negotiating Difference in the Hispanic World: From Conquest to Globalisation* (Oxford: Wiley-Blackwell, 2011), edited by Eleni Kefala for the *Bulletin of Latin American Studies* book series; both texts have been rewritten for Chapter 5. "Daniel Catán's Butterflies; or, The Opera House in the Jungle" was published in *Opera, Exoticism and Visual Cultures* (Oxford: Peter Lang, 2015), edited by Hyunseon Lee and Naomi Segal; it is now part of Chapter 7. "Underground in Buenos Aires: A Chamber Opera at the Teatro Colón" first came out as a chapter in *Operatic Geographies: The Place of Opera and the Opera House* (Chicago: University of Chicago Press, 2019); it was rewritten for Chapter 8. My gratitude to all publishers for their permission to reuse these texts.

Introduction
Transatlantic Transports

THIS BOOK STEMS from an unusual measure of critical self-regard. Many years ago, I acquired a passion for opera, an art form that I had known only tangentially. Opera's ravishing sounds, stories, and spectacles took hold of me, becoming, as opera often does, an obsessive pursuit. I listened to recordings and attended live performances. Self-assuredly, I decided to research and write on the art of opera despite the fact that I was a scholar of Latin American literature and not a musicologist, and that Latin America, while a hotbed of musical creation, was not unanimously regarded as an operatic hub. Could I, with my circumscribed training, fruitfully indulge an avocation outside the established perimeters of my field? Would I have anything noteworthy to say about the literary convergence of Latin America and opera? Buoyed by my rapidly growing experience of the art form and the stimulating work of music scholars, I began to compile my own archive of Latin American and operatic junctures in which the principles of literary studies—most keenly, the scholarly practice of reading—might be critically and productively activated. Self-consciously, devotedly, this book delves into the affects at play when a venerable art form like opera travels to, and is read in, or from, a "new" place like Latin America, far removed from the birthplace of opera in "old" Europe.

The various objects in the archive of Latin America and opera yield a rich story of transports—motion and emotions—sailing back and forth, literally and metaphorically, across the Atlantic Ocean between Europe and the Americas. What ultimately emerges, I hope, is an argument that qualifies the well-guarded cultural limits of "Europe" and "Latin America." The operatic text—its composition, certainly, but its global stagings too—unsettles geographic, political, and scholarly confines. As opera travels, borders fall. Consider, for instance, one memorable night at the opera. In 1908, the new Teatro Colón opened in Buenos Aires with a performance of Verdi's *Aida*. One could regard that first show as yet another European imperial incursion in the so-called New World. The opera house, tellingly, is named after Christopher Columbus—not the first so-named venue in Buenos Aires, or the only one in Latin America. But one can view the new Colón's first *Aida* as a rapturous spectacle in which various cultures meet and perhaps clash, yet are ultimately reconciled and transformed. An Italian opera about ancient Egypt, famously commissioned for the Cairo opera house, works its magic in the physical and affective spaces of Argentina. Despite Verdi's nationality, an audience that surely included migrants of Italian descent, and an opera house organized along Italian principles, that first *Aida* at the Colón is no longer simply an Italian work as staged in any opera house in Italy. Its fervent transport to another land and the way it transports people there to a distinct realm of lofty theatrical practices and transcendent emotions underwrite, but also complicate, the ties that bind cultures across oceans and continents. As audiences in Buenos Aires take joyful possession of music and words through the performance of that famous European work, opera itself sheds its Old World lineage to become a spectacle for, and of, the world.

Before and after that night at the Colón, other stories of transports unfold as opera travels around the planet, especially in the Americas, a region whose diverse cultures are affectively intertwined with those of Europe in multiple ways. Sometimes these operatic encounters occur outside the hallowed precincts of traditional theaters, existing, for instance, as powerful literary texts. In Walt Whitman's "Italian Music in Dakota," the speaker is transfixed by the sounds of Bellini and Donizetti played by an imaginary army band in a remote land where the resonances of European music can be heard, even if they are faint:

> (Yet strangely fitting even here, meanings unknown before,
> Subtler than ever, more harmony, as if born here, related here,
> Not to the city's fresco'd rooms, not the audiences of the
>   opera house,
> Sounds, echoes, wandering strains, as really here at home,
> *Sonnambula*'s innocent love, trios with *Norma*'s anguish,
> And thy ecstatic chorus *Poliuto*;)[1]

The act of listening to those muted fragments of bel canto is placed in parentheses, almost as if opera did not exist, yet those sounds are infinitely moving and not merely a foreign thing. In fact, as opera finds a home in a new land, even its vague echoes may sound even richer than in their birthplace.

Whitman's poem is set in the US American West, but the emotions it describes resound with the experience of opera throughout much of Latin America. As it migrates across the Atlantic, the art form is reworked and recharged for new listeners and spectators. Whitman's audience is "Nature," which acknowledges "rapport however far remov'd" and "listens well pleas'd," but the poem's transports invoke, at least for me, all kinds of listeners situated far from Europe in the Americas. My Cuban grandmother, an old-fashioned lover of opera, would spend many Saturday afternoons by her old radio absorbing the sounds, echoes, and strains broadcast from the Metropolitan Opera House; she was surely not the only opera fan in the region, or the world, to do so. In Latin American narrative fiction, too, characters are affected by opera, even if they do not know exactly what it is. Thus Macabéa, the protagonist of Clarice Lispector's *A hora da estrela*, is suddenly moved to tears when she hears "Una furtiva lagrima" from Donizetti's *L'elisir d'amore* recorded by Enrico Caruso, an experience described as the only really beautiful thing in her modest life. In this hybrid ensemble of real people and literary creatures, we may also consider Latin America's opera workers, especially singers—flesh-and-blood persons who embody the characters of European opera for the sake of transporting others, including many operagoers in Europe, to imaginary realms. As they sing in theaters around the world, these artists renew the art of opera even as they make it their own.

The archive of Latin America and opera thus features a rich mix of cultural practices and products. It houses operatic works and performances but also literary and cinematic texts as well as such real-world habits as operagoing, record listening, and even grandiose acts of philanthropy. These multiple items encompass several centuries, places, and experiences. Latin America itself is of course hugely diverse, and variations in history and demographics obviously matter.[2] Grand opera in cosmopolitan Buenos Aires in the early twentieth century is a radically different experience from the short music dramas performed in the eighteenth century in the Jesuit mission towns of what is now Bolivia. Likewise, the Teatro Colón itself, so opulent when it opened in 1908, was an altered institution one hundred years later when the building's protracted renovation failed to be ready for centennial celebrations. Operatic composition, too, has greatly varied from country to country; many operas have been written in Argentina, but very few in some other places in Latin America. My notion of transports applies to the whole of Latin America, but the routes and reception of opera, as we will see, fluctuate widely across the region and remain relatively fragmented.[3] Likewise, Europe and European opera, too, are of course vastly heterogeneous, but this study foregrounds the commonalities of French and German culture, say, as perceived from across the ocean, or the notion that dissimilar music dramas by Monteverdi or Rameau, or Wagner and Tchaikovsky, may all be gathered under the grand rubric of European opera. Importantly, Latin America and Europe, bound by cultural norms and practices, should not be regarded as mutually exclusive opposites. Although the idea of transports may imply the importation of a foreign thing, opera for many in Latin America—consider, again, European migrants, but other persons as well—is not an alien experience. In fact, as opera arrives in Latin America and ravishes audiences, or as Latin American composers themselves craft their own works, or as Latin American authors thematize and scrutinize opera in their literary texts, the art form builds new followers and finds other homes, as the affects at play in Whitman's imaginary Dakota suggest. This rich and long process of naturalization, as it were, is what I seek to investigate in the manifold transports of opera that constitute my objects of inquiry.

This book contains eight chapters. The first two, conceptually interrelated, explore an archive of multiple, mostly textual convergences between Latin America and opera. Although they are not comprehensive historical narratives, these chapters seek to provide a background for the chapters that follow. The first chapter focuses on Latin American literature about opera, that is, works that have variously reflected on the art form. While scholars have paid attention to its role in several of these texts, a fuller vision and understanding of the significance of opera in Latin American cultural history emerges when works that relate to it are read together as one, albeit heterogeneous, literary family. This corpus includes such well-known texts as Estanislao del Campo's *El Fausto criollo*, the gauchesque poem that unfolds over a performance of Gounod's *Faust* in Buenos Aires, and a few poems by Rubén Darío, whose speaker passionately invokes Wagner's heroes. But there are also other novels, novellas, and memoirs that interimplicate the European operatic repertoire. If cultural and literary histories have not consistently paid attention to opera, then literature itself has much to say about its meanings in Latin America, showing that it is not simply a foreign concept but also an artistic experience that concerns some vital themes in the region's history: colonialism and nationhood; transatlantic relations and cosmopolitan aesthetics; and the intertwined discourses of gender, ethnicity, and modernity. Even canonical authors such as José Martí, universally identified with the call for cultural and political autonomy in "Nuestra América," his famous essay, also wrote works that elevate the place of opera as a practice in the region. In this context, it is also worth listening to what performing artists have said about their own crafts. As we will see, Alicia Alonso's words on ballet in Cuba resound with Jorge Luis Borges's discussion of the act of writing in Argentina in "El escritor argentino y la tradición," his well-known defense of creative freedom and thematic universality. Like Martí's,

Alonso's and Borges's arguments, when read with opera in mind, serve as stepping stones for imagining the potentials of the operatic craft for Latin America.

Conversely, the second chapter proposes a view of opera in which the practice of reading—operatic librettos but other texts as well—enriches our perception of opera as it engages with Latin America. My point of departure is Werner Herzog's *Fitzcarraldo*, the cinematic saga set in the Amazon rainforest, probably the best-known and most influential depiction in any medium of opera's adventurous passage to, and around, Latin America. The bulk of the chapter provides a wide-ranging overview of two distinct, yet connected bodies of operas. The first comprises European operas about the region, which frequently accentuate the exotic and the comical but also complicate and contest these stances. On the conquest of Mexico alone, it includes operas as dissimilar as Carl Heinrich Graun's *Montezuma*, with a libretto by Frederick the Great, and Wolfgang Rihm's *Die Eroberung von Mexico*, which resorts to texts by Antonin Artaud and Octavio Paz. The second body gathers operas written by Latin American composers—most famously Brazil's Carlos Gomes and Argentina's Alberto Ginastera, but many others as well—on subjects that often thematize the region, but also, as if heeding Borges's call for borderless creativity, eschew national subjects for stories that originate in Europe and elsewhere. Some recent works stand out as hybrid creations for their visions of Latin America from, and often for, the United States. They include *Ainadámar*, on the death of Federico García Lorca, by Osvaldo Golijov, a native of Argentina; and *Bel Canto*, set in Lima, by Jimmy López, originally from Peru. Like the rest of the book, this chapter also considers theatrical productions, masterminded by directors from various backgrounds, which refresh and enrich works that might otherwise be dismissed as predictable purveyors of problematic colonial discourses.

The remaining six chapters are organized in roughly chronological order from the early eighteenth century to the first two decades of the twenty-first. They provide close readings of operas and fiction created mostly in Latin America and Europe, but also in the

United States, as well as analyses of some notable episodes in the art form's history in the region.

The third and fourth chapters specifically examine the intricacies of opera in the viceregal period through the shifting lenses of baroque and neobaroque practices and discourses, which define much Latin American literary and cultural history. My analysis starts with Tomás de Torrejón y Velasco's *La púrpura de la rosa* (1701), the first opera performed in the so-called New World. Its richly poetical libretto, by Pedro Calderón de la Barca, retells the myth of Venus and Adonis, which, of course, has everything to do with European literary practices but less, at least at face value, with Latin America. Written originally for an opera composed decades earlier in Madrid, Calderón's libretto was revived for a new work at the viceregal court in Lima. The next chapter considers Alejo Carpentier's *Concierto barroco* (1974), a novella that reimagines the creation of Antonio Vivaldi's *Motezuma* (1733), yet another tale of conquest, through the eyes of a Mexican traveler troubled by the work's exoticist misrepresentations.

In the case of *La púrpura de la rosa*, I seek to read Calderón de la Barca's libretto not just as a European play but also as a forward-looking text whose mythological plot, as alien as it appears, allows for the opera's resignification as an important work in Peruvian and Latin American literary cultures. My objective is not to rehearse taxonomic categories but to test the possibilities of rereading the libretto, perhaps preposterously, as a living creation that may mean different things depending on the literary networks within which it is considered. In these intertextual filiations, theories of the baroque and neobaroque by twentieth-century authors such as José Lezama Lima and Severo Sarduy—or Carpentier, for that matter—provide a powerful imaginative apparatus. They help to reforge Torrejón y Velasco's Spanish creation as a Latin American cultural product and to recast Latin America as a region in which, through the work of reading, the spectral coloniality of opera may be replayed as a natural event, both eerily foreign and uncannily familiar. The chapter ends by briefly considering the so-called mission operas, variously created and performed by, and for, Jesuits and natives in the *reducciones* of what is now Bolivia; these hybrid texts take into account native audiences as they implant European forms in a new place.

Similarly, Carpentier's textual interimplication of Vivaldi's baroque opera in his own neobaroque novella suggests an original framework for reevaluating opera's exotic proclivities. What may first appear as historical errors to be dispelled or corrected can be reread and reimagined as fictional flights that serve to craft and uphold new transatlantic cultural configurations for Europe and Africa as well as the Americas. The novella may seem at first yet another postcolonial instance of writing back to the empire, but its argument for the analysis of cultural history, anchored to Carpentier's expansive cartography of the baroque, closely intertwined with his vision of the marvelous real, is far more complex. In the fictional logic of *Concierto barroco*, the colonial enterprise, while undeniably brutal, sets the ground for the rise of new cosmopolitan forms, such as jazz, and for the reappraisal not just of *Motezuma* but of European opera more broadly as a corpus that richly and productively engages with Latin American history.

Several episodes related to opera in Cuba—its ghostly apparitions through the island's history—are the subject of the fifth chapter. Despite its colonial status under Spain, mid-nineteenth-century Havana became a hub of operatic production in the Americas. Italian opera companies performed at the grand Teatro Tacón and went on to tour the United States. If only fleetingly through the transports of opera, Havana could see itself on a par with the metropolitan centers of Europe. An unlikely episode in Cuba's filiation with opera concerns the legend of Pedro Figueredo's "La bayamesa." The patriotic song, which became the national anthem, contains some music supposedly inspired by "Non più andrai," the aria in Mozart's *Le nozze di Figaro*. That the ironic tune reincarnates in Cuba as a serious martial hymn serves as a key for analyzing the discourses of masculinity and homosexuality, connected with the Cuban Revolution, in Tomás Gutiérrez Alea and Juan Carlos Tabío's film *Fresa y chocolate*, and in Reinaldo Arenas's novel *El color del verano*. Returning to the nineteenth century, the chapter also analyzes

Madame Malibran, by Mercedes Merlin, the Cuban French author. In the widely read life of the celebrated French-born singer of Spanish descent, operatic culture emerges obliquely as a space for viewing issues of race and ethnicity in Europe and the Americas. The chapter ends by looking at Alberto Vilar, the Cuban American businessman who, at the turn of the twenty-first century, became known as the most generous philanthropist in the history of opera. One of his most prominent gifts, a pledge of £10 million to London's Royal Opera House in 1999, resulted in the naming of the Vilar Floral Hall, the theater's iron-and-glass atrium. After failure to complete payment, Vilar's name, in yet another spectral figuration of Latin America and opera, was removed from that prestigious space.

The real-life and fictional characters who appear in this account of Cuba and opera are most clearly linked with the island's European ethnic legacy. Yet opera, easily regarded as a white art form in Cuba and elsewhere, engages in depicting other races and even appears to give a voice to, or even sing for, black and other nonwhite subjects. But can opera, so tightly conjoined with European canons, speak for marginalized groups? In this, Latin America's rich body of testimonial literature may offer a valuable lesson for reading opera. The sixth chapter analyzes two music dramas whose eponymous heroes are nonwhite enslaved men: *Lo schiavo*, by the celebrated Carlos Gomes, first performed in Rio de Janeiro in 1889 to an Italian libretto; and *El Cimarrón*, composed in Havana in the 1960s by Hans Werner Henze, who set a series of German texts by Hans Magnus Enzensberger, who in turn was inspired by Miguel Barnet's *Biografía de un cimarrón* (1966), the now-classic testimonio of Esteban Montejo. The chapter looks first at Henze's *El Cimarrón* and the story of its black protagonist, a runaway slave who at the age of 103 recounts his life to Barnet. How should we read the words of a German poet, who cites the text of a white ethnologist, who in turn transcribes a black man's oral discourse? A possible response stems from a 2009 staging of *El Cimarrón* at the Royal Danish Theater. Shunning exoticism, Lars Kaalund and Mia Stensgaard's production of Henze's "recital for four musicians" builds on the interethnic collaboration among three Scandinavian instrumentalists and Sir Willard White, the Jamaican British baritone—yet another story of transatlantic passages in which cultures are intertwined, as in *Concierto barroco*, by their partaking equally onstage in the act of musical storytelling. The workings of testimonio appear also in Gomes's *Lo schiavo* more perceptibly if read and heard retroactively from Henze's music drama. Gomes, who had left Brazil to study and work in Italy, achieved triumph at Milan's La Scala in the age of Verdi. His early *Il guarany* adapted José de Alencar's classic novel of sixteenth-century Brazil, but Gomes mostly worked with librettos on European themes, returning to his country's history only later with the tale of an enslaved man. Contrary to traditional perceptions of slavery in Brazil, the protagonist of *Lo schiavo* is not an Afro-descendant, but an indigenous person; in this, the composer followed the conventions of Italian opera, which eschewed black characters. But the opera is dedicated to Princess Isabel, who as regent had signed the law proclaiming the abolition of slavery—a gesture that, along with Gomes's evocative music, allows, after all, for the toils and aspirations of persons of African descent to become legible and audible.

The pleasures and perils of magical realism are at the center of the seventh chapter, which explores the uses of Latin American literature on the global stages of opera. My focus is on two works written around the turn of the twenty-first century. The first is John Adams's *El Niño* (2000), a "Nativity oratorio" but also, arguably, a kind of opera whose libretto, assembled by Peter Sellars, integrates texts by poets from the Latin American literary canon, especially Rosario Castellanos, along with texts from other parts of the world. Speaking to multicultural societies such as that of the United States, Adams and Sellars's collaboration tells the story of two births: that of Jesus and that of a Latino child in California. The second work is Daniel Catán's *Florencia en el Amazonas* (1996), the first opera commissioned from a Mexican composer by a major company in the United States, the Houston Grand Opera. Chronicling a Latin American soprano's river journey to the Manaus opera house, the work, a milestone in Catán's career, has been revived many times. Reportedly, though, Catán had wanted to set a tale by Isak Dinesen, but Houston preferred a libretto that showcased the kind of magical realism often expected from Latin American authors. A realist, Catán purveyed the requested magic, whereas Adams freely resorted to poetry from all over. Nonetheless, *Florencia en el Amazonas* provides a dramatic meditation on the transactions between creative freedom and metropolitan exigencies. The chapter concludes with a brief analysis of Sor Juana Inés de la Cruz as a central character in Louis Andriessen's *Theater of the World* (2016), seen in Los Angeles and Amsterdam. In this work, the region's literature matters for itself and not for what it may conjure up about Latin America for the sake of European and North American spectators seeking difference.

The last chapter focuses on two Argentine authors, Manuel Mujica Lainez and Victoria Ocampo, whose literary careers and public endeavors were closely linked to the Teatro Colón. Mujica Lainez's *El gran teatro* (1980), a novel set around a staging of Wagner's *Parsifal* at the storied opera house in the 1940s, is an ideal text for viewing the workings of opera as both practice and metaphor in Buenos Aires. Mirroring the opera, one of the subplots in Mujica Lainez's text also concerns the vexations of desire—same-sex eroticism, in the novel's case. The chronicling of an extramarital affair is the central episode in Victoria Ocampo's *La rama de Salzburgo* (1981), an autobiographical work partly set during yet another performance of *Parsifal* at the Colón. A woman who resisted gender strictures, Ocampo herself also became the subject of a chamber opera staged at the Centro de Experimentación del Teatro Colón: *V.O.* (2013), with music by Martín Bauer and libretto by Beatriz Sarlo. Given Sarlo's work as a critic and cultural theorist (including essays on Ocampo's life and writings) and Bauer's as composer and advocate of contemporary music in Buenos Aires, *V.O.* is especially valuable for appraising the role of opera in Argentina's negotiations with the practices and discourses of modern life.

Finally, the book's afterword considers Thomas Adès's *The Tempest* (2004), an opera based on Shakespeare's play, premiered at the Royal Opera House. At first glance, the libretto by Meredith Oakes appears to efface the postcolonial readings of Caliban, key in Latin American and Caribbean arguments about European discourses on those regions. Yet on closer examination, Adès's Caliban, sung by a white English tenor yet tacitly informed by such works, emerges as a tragic figure who speaks ethically for the entire planet. In the new millennium, signs of Latin America's own cultural history could be seen and heard at a house at the center of the world of opera.

Like many operas, this book is animated by the spirit of an ancient myth. As if replicating the tale of Europa, the Phoenician princess abducted from her homeland and transported to the shores of what will be a new continent, the transports of opera in Latin America may also appear to be a story of rape and rapture in the various archaic or modern senses of those two interconnected words: a seizure by force, physical assault, spatial displacement, sheer ecstasy. Trembling as she is carried off to distant shores, Europa, as rendered by Titian or Rembrandt (or, for that matter, a Latin American artist like Fernando Botero, or a poet like Julián del Casal), looks up fearfully and expectantly as the white bull snatches her from her birthplace, as if sensing the mystery of a life to come in a still-unknown world—a newly born land. A series of comparable feelings surfaces as one regards the various journeys of opera across the Atlantic Ocean as a by-product of imperial conquests—except, this time around, the myth of ravished Europa is transmuted into the imperial rigors of rapacious Europe. The old continent seizes the so-called New World and plunders its history and stories to fabricate its operas; the potent art of European opera fearlessly implants itself as a superior cultural practice in that pillaged land; people fall for the grandeur of the genre and the glories of its creators; singers sing those songs. Yet this is only one possible way of conceiving the powerful and passionate union of Latin America and opera. The various chapters that follow, as they delve into Latin America and its ties with Europe inside and through the art of opera, tell a more nuanced and complicated story of these vexing transatlantic specters and amorous liaisons.

1 A Corpus of Fragments, I

Listening to Literature

THE CULTURAL HISTORY of Latin America and opera is made up of fragments—an archive that houses a multiplicity of items, including, as I seek to show in this chapter, a wide range of literary texts written by authors from the region. These disparate elements can be critically assembled into an argument that addresses the status of Latin America in the realm of opera. Although literary scholars have explored the verbal dimensions of Latin American music, they have tended to focus not so much on opera but on popular genres such as tango, bolero, salsa, and the protest song.[1] The established discussion about literature has mostly overlooked the fact that operas, even if they are first and foremost a musical creation, also contain words and tell stories; they are a form of drama, with characters and events, akin to other kinds of storytelling normally dissected under the purview of literary studies. But if scholars have mostly disregarded librettos, literary authors, in contrast, have crafted eloquent works that engage in dialogue with opera's music and tales, comment on its social prestige or its transatlantic crossings, or expound on what it has to say about nationhood, gender, sexuality, and ethnicity. Stretching from the mid-nineteenth century to the present day, these texts, mostly fiction and poetry, enrich the cultural history of Latin America by granting the transports of opera—its ties with Europe, the emotions it provokes—a more visible and audible role.

The reasons for the relative absence of opera in the region's literary scholarship are understandable. Besides the widespread view that opera is only a musical genre, it is easy to regard it as an elitist and pretentious, if not downright exclusionary, practice. For some literary historians and critics, opera surely rises as an uncomfortable and unredeemable symptom of Europhilia—an instance of the shallow cosmopolitanism that Mariano Siskind questions in José Rodó's negative judgment of Rubén Darío's foreign-sounding lyrical poetry: "a shorthand for supposedly elitist, denationalizing, apolitical, antipopular, uprooted, Francophile, queer, displaced, and mobile forces in the literary field."[2] The absence of a strong Iberian connection matters too. The librettos in the operatic repertoire are mostly in Italian, German, or French but rarely in Spanish or Portuguese, let alone the region's indigenous languages. Likewise, opera's plotlines often invoke European mythologies and histories—gods, monarchs, star-crossed lovers—as well as the myth of Europe itself, so influential in the cultural history of Latin America, yet so easily dismissed as foreign despite its seductiveness. In imagining the ideal opera fanatic in the United States, a construct that also resounds with visions of operagoers in Latin America, David Littlejohn underscores the importance of European culture in many operas. This fan should be, "if not Eurocentric, at least Europe oriented and more than usually interested in the European past. It would help if he were at least an amateur student of the history, literature, and art of Western Europe. . . . Typically, the settings and stage designs of standard repertory operas evoke, or were originally intended to evoke, European castles and cathedrals, European cities and towns, European mountain and valley landscapes."[3] Even operas set in other parts of the world most often evoke those far-flung regions through confident European eyes, as if Europe, broadly understood, were opera's default prism for viewing others.

Musicologists who study the region's rich musical culture and history, including the composition and performance of opera, have often focused on these multiple transatlantic connections. Writing about Rio de Janeiro in the nineteenth century, Cristina Magaldi, for instance, underscores the construction of "a complex web of internal identification and cultural associations" that perceives Europe, especially its metropolitan centers, as the site and source of modernity. At the heart of this network, Magaldi posits the experience of music as a powerful form of transport:

> Because of its uncanny ability to help people pretend they are somewhere else, music played a pivotal role in this process.... By attending an opera or a concert in which European music prevailed, or by composing or performing homemade European-style music, Rio de Janeiro residents could share with those in European centers of power, namely Paris and London, the ownership of something that for them represented "civilization" and "modernity." At the same time, by immersing themselves in the music arriving from Europe, Cariocas avoided the general feeling of being left out on the periphery, and shunned the prospect of "not being" European. In sum, European music served some Cariocas well in their attempts to disguise the sharp, local distinctions between "here" and "there."[4]

To be sure, if many residents of imperial Rio de Janeiro were extreme Europhiles, the whole spectrum of music drama or theatrical music in Latin America is certainly far more complex. As Rogério Budasz shows in great detail, the onstage uses of music in Brazil alone encompass multiple genres and practices, including Jesuit morality plays introduced in the sixteenth century, Portuguese operas in the eighteenth century, and much more. Budasz's diverse archive also shows how transatlantic cultural routes, traveling in both directions across the ocean, reveal signs of resemblance and difference between Europe and the so-called New World: "The circulation of scores, texts and artists between Portugal and Brazil provides evidence of a shared theatrical culture.... Yet performances were not always identical. On paper, the colony was united under one king, one language and one religion, but local factors determined differences in terms of casting, vocal qualities, aesthetic paradigms, sense of humor, linguistic usage, and even interactions with indigenous and African culture and languages."[5]

Since the nineteenth century, the centers of culture have shifted from Europe to elsewhere, and other media, most saliently cinema, have emerged to challenge the central status of music. Yet the kinds of affects and practices that Magaldi and Budasz investigate are still discernible. Opera in Latin America, certainly in many cities, is still often an event at which members of an audience perform their own metropolitan affinities. They may be far from the centers of the West, but as literary works often show, opera is a noble endeavor whereby, majestically, opera lovers may aurally and visually reach out across the Atlantic and touch, if only through a fleeting spectacle, some prestigious sites of European civilization. They incidentally do not need to be wealthy to enjoy opera, for despite accusations of elitism, opera can also work its exalted magic on recordings, over the airwaves, or by means of various gadgets. They can be transported by "Celeste Aida" even if they have never heard it performed live against a background of Orientalist pyramids on a real stage.

To complicate the full appreciation of opera in the region, the international discussion about the art form has often elided Latin American works. As Malena Kuss states, opera's master narratives do not serve the region's composers or their works particularly well.[6] The seven volumes of *Pipers Enzyklopädie des Musiktheaters* include entries on a substantial number of Latin American operas; two chapters of *History of Opera*, edited by Stanley Sadie, contain sections by Kuss focusing on Latin America; and Kuss's "Das lateinamerikanische Libretto," included in *Die Musik in Geschichte und Gegenwart*, is a rich survey of opera (not just librettos) in the region.[7] But *A Short History of Opera*, for instance, dismisses operatic composition in Latin America as essentially "an off-shoot of Italian and Spanish opera,"[8] and *The New Grove Book of Operas*, described as "the world's definitive single volume of opera reference" on its dust jacket, includes only one work from the region: Alberto Ginastera's *Bomarzo*.[9] Likewise, *A History of Opera*, a more recent tome, contains no references to Latin American operas except for a brief mention of two works—Ginastera's *Don Rodrigo* and Heitor Villa-Lobos's *Yerma*—in a list of ten twentieth-century "high-profile disasters."[10]

To explain the relative scholarly invisibility of Latin American opera, one may cite the dearth of works written by composers from the region in the international repertoire. Even Carlos Gomes, so prominent in Italy and elsewhere in the last decades of the nineteenth century, is no longer that well known outside of his native Brazil. His once-popular operas are now rarities that have virtually fallen off the international map of opera seasons and festivals. In the twentieth century, Ginastera's musical artistry is undoubted, but his fame does not equal that of, say, Jorge Luis Borges or Gabriel García Márquez in the literary field.

There is also the enormous weight of popular music from the region. The relative inaudibility of Latin American opera composers also appears to reflect well-entrenched trends in the global division of musical labor. While Latin America's popular rhythms are world-famous, the region's art music remains virtually concealed. Carol A. Hess quotes Leonard Bernstein, who, in 1962, comically encouraged the audience in his Young People's Concerts in New York to move beyond bossa nova: "We mustn't begin to think that all Latin American music is chuck-a-chuck-a-chuck-a dance music. Not by a long shot. Our Latin neighbors have produced a very impressive number of serious symphonic composers who have succeeded in preserving the folk flavor of their own countries while at the same time expanding their music into what we think of as universal art."[11] Hess also cites the US vice president Hubert Humphrey, who, at a reception held in the Argentine embassy in Washington after the world premiere of Ginastera's *Bomarzo* in 1967, found the opera untypically "difficult, discordant and different."[12] When it comes to opera, even those improbable works that have garnered a measure of "distinction," as Humphrey quickly adds about *Bomarzo*, continue to elicit a sense of geographical puzzlement. Ginastera's challenging score is indeed a surprise after the easy rhythms of, say, Antônio Carlos Jobim and Vinícius de Moraes's "The Girl from Ipanema," which had won the Grammy for Record of the Year in 1965.

Well before either Latin America (or the United States, for that matter) played any significant role in operatic creation or performace, the very European art of opera, though cumbersome to produce, became an early instance of sustained cultural traffic among continents. At play in these journeys is the status of non-European locations as civilized parts of the world, fluent in the lingua franca of art, as Gonzalo Aguilar puts it: "In its way across the world, opera became an artistic and cultural koyné with a relatively limited repertoire which circulated through the 'civilized' cities of the globe (or cities which were civilized through its circulation), and which generated not only an art form but also a series of multiple interpellations (social, urban, cultural)."[13] Through much of the nineteenth century, foreign troupes sailed from Europe to the main cities of Latin America, playing a crucial role in the history of international musical contacts and the global circuits of opera. John Rosselli documents an Italian troupe, for instance, that traveled with the Portuguese royal family to Rio de Janeiro during the Napoleonic Wars, some of whose singers would reach the River Plate.[14] Rosselli also describes three general routes along which opera companies toured the Americas during much of the nineteenth century.[15] One circuit might comprise Rio de Janeiro, Montevideo, and Buenos Aires, as well as other cities in Brazil, Uruguay, and Argentina; a second itinerary took in the Caribbean and the United States, with engagements in Havana but also New Orleans and New York or cities like St. Louis and Cincinnati; and a third route traveled along the Pacific, from San Francisco in the north to Valparaíso and Santiago de Chile in the south—two cities that, in turn, were also connected via the stormy waters near Cape Horn with the circuit along South America's Atlantic coast. Rosselli also documents singers who undertook their own ambitious tours. The soprano Teresa Schieroni and the contralto Margherita Garaviglia, for instance, performed in Buenos Aires in 1829 and Valparaíso and Santiago in 1830–1831, then traveled to Macau in 1833, continuing supposedly all the way to Calcutta.[16]

Importantly, the richness of these transoceanic voyages often confounds the binary thinking of Latin America and Europe as mere opposites. Opera artists often belonged to intercontinental networks, and as Aníbal Enrique Cetrangolo shows, Italian musicians who performed at the premiere of *Aida* in Cairo were later engaged in orchestras for *Aida* in Rio de Janeiro and Buenos Aires; some of them "would then go on to leave a lasting imprint in the musical destiny of Argentina."[17] Moreover, Latin American locations could act at times as key platforms for European artists. Most famously, perhaps, is the case of Arturo Toscanini, whose unplanned debut at the age of nineteen as conductor of *Aida* in Rio's Teatro Imperial Dom Pedro II would soon became the stuff of legend.[18]

In these operatic journeys, a few Latin American capitals played pivotal roles. Much of the Romantic bel canto repertoire, for instance, was first performed in the United States by Italian opera companies based in Havana. As John Dizikes recounts, one of these companies took *Ernani* to New York in 1847, the first opera by Verdi staged in the country.[19] According to Rosselli, an "unusually gifted" Italian company traveled to Havana after the 1848 revolutions; some of its members decided to stay there, or in Central America, for several years.[20] But geography was a real challenge. Traveling from one Latin American city to another might have required a transatlantic crossing; as late as 1878, a group of singers in Havana could reach Rio de Janeiro and Buenos Aires only via Liverpool, Le Havre or Bordeaux.[21] As Schieroni and Garaviglia sailed around the planet, or as the Italian performers of the Havana opera companies toured North American cities, they triggered multiple forms of cosmopolitan transports. Musicians got to see firsthand the world's diverse cultures, even as they brought to local audiences a prestigious and rapturous art form from their own distant part of the planet.

An esteemed form of operatic trophy was embodied in the iconic European singers who performed in various Latin American capitals. Enrico Caruso's travels in the region were closely watched by both the local and international press. In Buenos Aires, at the old Teatro de la Ópera in 1899, he performed the established repertoire and also sang his only role in a non-European opera: the Inca protagonist of *Yupanki*, by Arturo Berutti, the Argentine composer.[22] At times, newspaper reports went beyond the singer's artistry to invoke, at least tangentially, a discourse about Latin America as a region marked by extravagance—lands as operatic as opera itself. Upon Caruso's return from a tour of Argentina and Brazil in 1917 on which he earned $6,666.00 for each of his forty performances, the *New York Times* ran a story entitled "Caruso Returns with South American Gold."[23] Shortly thereafter, in 1920, when the tenor survived an explosion during a performance of *Aida* in Havana, the same newspaper printed the news on its front page: "Bomb Exploded at Caruso Performance; Six Injured in Havana Opera Panic."[24] Local audiences held sway. Decades later, singing the role of Norma at Mexico City's Palacio de Bellas Artes in 1950, Maria Callas was told how much the city's operagoers loved high notes, so "she interpolated in the Act I finale a sustained full-throated D."[25] Absence could hurt. About to leave Buenos Aires, Elisabeth Schwarzkopf finds her path at the airport covered by flowers, and one of her admirers, a young man, crying as he realizes he may never see her perform in person again. Upon seeing his desperate tears, the soprano walks back across the runway to console her fan with a tender rendition of "Non piangere" from Puccini's *Turandot*.[26] Indeed, the man's lachrymose lament unfolds at the juncture of geographic and emotional deprivation: all transports are spent.[27]

At the heart of it all is the sound of opera. While my study is anchored on literary studies, it is not hard to argue for the primacy of music over words in opera. Indeed, even when considered from a literary viewpoint, what makes opera different from other kinds of storytelling is that characters sing, and that the narrative itself is carried by the work of music. In opera, as Joseph Kerman puts it, "the dramatist is the composer."[28] Yet music's import is only relative; opera also contains words that ought to be analyzed with the same tools deployed for other kinds of narratives. Rejecting the dismissal of librettos as banal, David J. Levin, for one, argues for the need of not only reading the words, but, importantly, recognizing how they are "an erratic player" among the codes of opera: "if we look (or listen) a bit more closely, we can perceive the shifting, restless quality of the words, how they take off and respond not necessarily just to the music, but by, from, and to themselves."[29] Deeming words as variously and incessantly significant complicates the cultural and social implications of opera, as my own reading of

Calderón's libretto for Torrejón y Velasco's *La púrpura de la rosa* in Chapter 3 seeks to show.

In this verbal turn, the lessons of feminist and postcolonial theory, among other critical stances, have shown opera to be a more ambiguous, interesting and complex space. A focus on words serves to tease out opera's explicit and complicated engagement with history and the larger world. In the case of Latin America, the reading of opera affords an especially powerful, even paradoxical, lesson for cultural history. If multiple European operas appear simply to chronicle the region's history from the one-sided viewpoint of imperial powers, a close analysis of librettos may tell a richer story in which continents and cultures are bound by cultural ties more powerful—and often less malign—than it traditionally appears to be the case. As we shall see, Alejo Carpentier's metafictional liaisons with Vivaldi's *Motezuma* is one such case. The art of opera may thus emerge not just as a foreign thing, but as a practice that modulates prescriptions of cultural autonomy and facile thinking about nations. In Europe, too, new concept-driven productions have also resulted in performances where imperial histories and the art of opera itself are contested, underscoring the ties that unite cultures around the globe as audiences confront their own discursive privilege by heeding other versions of history. As European opera travels back to its birthplace, lessons from the rest of the world often qualify and alter the meanings of the old tunes.

Words of Alicia Alonso and José Martí

Before surveying Latin American literature about opera, a brief textual exchange on the work of Cuban ballet may provide a distinctive viewpoint for evaluating the status of European performing arts in the region, so often pulled asunder by the divergent claims of nationalism and cosmopolitanism. It involves Alicia Alonso, the world-famous ballerina who founded and directed the Ballet Nacional de Cuba with the support of the Cuban Revolution. In all this, José Martí, often regarded as one of the leaders of Latin American cultural and political autonomy, will also have much to say about how art forms such as opera may be approached in countries still haunted by Europe's imperial regimes.

Visiting Lima in 1982, Alonso was asked by a journalist a series of slightly accusatory questions on the appropriateness of European ballet—specifically *Giselle*, which featured Alonso's signature role—for nations whose citizens were mostly of mixed, indigenous, or African descent.[30] What relation could there be between an art form crafted for European elites and Cuba's own culture? What could the ghostly Wilis in Adolphe Adam's work say to Yemayá and Ochún in the Afro-Cuban pantheon, or to Andean mountain spirits—and what could the latter say back to the former? Somewhat defensively, Alonso provides an expansive response in which she considers these queries from several angles, invoking the origins of classical ballet in folk dances as well as the need to seize the art of ballet from privileged groups and bring it to larger audiences. First, however, she reminds the journalist that European culture too is part of the framework of Latin America's mestizo nations. Moreover, Alonso argues, if the imperial legacy is ultimately unavoidable, the corporal and spiritual sameness of people around the world justifies the suitability of ballet for the region—or anywhere else, for that matter. Like intelligence and emotions, she says, anatomy is essentially the same in Latin Americans and Europeans. While she then qualifies the purported universality of ballet by bringing up the existence of national schools, including that of Cuba, her stated belief in the shared physical and emotional makeup of humans is a rare declaration of cosmopolitan principles in cultures often defined by stalwart nationalism.[31]

One might be tempted to dismiss Alonso's apology for ballet as an artist's self-justification, or a mere act of will, yet its implications for the reading of opera are worth considering. While nations and people are of course not identical, the art of ballet, despite its European origin, foregrounds the ties that bind all humans—a postulate that is equally valid for opera as well. What Alonso says about ballet and the body also resounds with opera and the human voice. If ballet can ultimately be a common, even welcome, pursuit in Latin American culture and not an elitist, extraneous thing, so too can the art of opera, regardless of ethnicity, social status, or a nation's political state of affairs. Underscoring cosmopolitan sameness, Alonso's argument impacts the meanings and uses of identity, a cherished concept in much of the discourse about Latin America. By focusing on the similarities among all humans, she retrieves the etymology of identity—its root in *idem*, "the same"—and diminishes the role of otherness in thinking about cultures and nations.

In literary studies, issues of cultural identity continue to be hotly debated and contested. Indeed, literature is one of the fields in which relations between Latin America and other parts of the world, especially Europe, have been vigorously investigated and theorized. But some readers of Latin American literature may readily sense that Alonso's defense of artistic freedom resonates with Jorge Luis Borges's argument in "El escritor argentino y la tradición," in which he calls for a vision of Argentine authors free of nationalist requirements and open instead to all the cultures of the world. As he puts it, "nuestro patrimonio es el universo" ("the universe is our birthright").[32] In Borges's eyes, an Argentine author should not be afraid to eschew the local for the universal. Just like no one would fault Shakespeare for setting his plays in Italy, or Racine for finding sources in Greek mythology, Argentine authors—and, by extension, Latin American creators in any medium—should be free to craft works on any subject they please and still retain their status as Argentine authors.

Consider, for instance, *modernismo*, conventionally regarded as the first literary movement born in Latin America to transform writing in Spain. Its rise in the last decades of the nineteenth century and into the twentieth coincided with the opening of major opera houses around the region. Consider, specifically, the writings of José Martí, for whom cultural liberation, again, was a necessary step in the search for true political sovereignty, free from the authority of Europe and the increasingly dangerous United States. In "Nuestra América" ("Our America"), his signature essay and a highpoint of political *modernismo* published in 1891, Martí employs a sartorial metaphor to convey and condemn what he decries as the appetite of Latin American elites for foreign things: "Éramos una máscara, con los calzones de Inglaterra, el chaleco parisiense, el chaquetón de Norteamérica y la montera de España" ("We were a whole fancy dress ball, in English trousers, a Parisian waistcoat, a North American overcoat, and a Spanish bullfighter's hat").[33] Beyond the inventory of suspect metropolitan fashions, Martí's invocation of *máscara*, which may mean *masked ball* or *masquerader* or simply a *mask*, transforms the elective affinities of cultural consumption into a kind of artifice-laden performance that unfolds in real life. A passion for brilliant European forms may result in ostentatious mimicry—a dishonorable pageant of sorts. Inspired by Martí, one can easily imagine a night at the opera in a Latin American city where enraptured members of the audience appear to shun the national in favor of the foreign—in love with the drama onstage and their own ensuant performance. No aphorisms from "Nuestra América" will make them recoil from the dramas of Orpheus and Ariadne sung rapturously in other tongues, or the orchestral clamors of Mozart and Wagner, or from their own well-accoutred roles in what may be perceived as a troubling pageant.

More broadly, Martí's metaphorical masks resonate with Theodor Adorno's observations in "Bourgeois Opera" on the exalted status of the art form among members of that social class: "It would be appropriate to consider opera as the specifically bourgeois genre which, in the midst and with the means of a world bereft of magic, paradoxically endeavors to preserve the magical element of art."[34] Many aspects of the operatic experience in Latin America may also be regarded as a function of class, as Hans Werner Henze, for one, brings up: "Italian conductors who worked in Cuba during the Batista dictatorship say they had never seen anywhere in the world such a sea of jewels and mink coats as in the Havana opera house."[35] The region's peripheral status vis-à-vis Europe may justify a reformulation of Adorno's terms. In Latin America, one might consider opera as the specifically bourgeois genre which, in a world removed from its mythical origins on the other side of the Atlantic, uncannily seeks to reach the magical allure of European art. The reverberation of European opera, then, deploys its outlandish artistry—a siren song full of perils and pleasures seducing audiences in a region that is both a part of the West and also distinct from it. Opera emerges as a privileged site for viewing the ambivalent positioning of a certain Latin American ethos (surely not the only one) vis-à-vis the familiar yet alien patterns of European culture. In over three hundred years of existence in the region, opera often resounds with perilous imperial echoes. Yet it is precisely the uncanny status of the art form that may well be the source of opera's fascination for some Latin Americans. A ghostly masquerader itself, opera crosses the Atlantic as part of a story of transports, landing repeatedly in a region ravished by ghostly empires, yet faithfully enrapturing its lovers through its arts.

That image, however, supports only a limited argument about opera in Latin America. Despite what narrow readings of "Nuestra América" might argue, the status of European arts and letters in Martí's multiple works is far from simple. Other essays, chronicles and reviews written for newspapers and journals across the Americas reveal a sustained passion for performances and performers of European works, including opera. He praises, for instance, Adelina Patti, the celebrated soprano, as a "criatura canora, de cristal hecha y plata" (singing creature made of crystal and silver), describing her voice as "promesa de otros mundos" (a promise of other worlds).[36] Texts that deal with subjects other than music also tell a richer story. Indeed, Cuban readers, who generally revere the author for his valiant and tragic struggle for independence from Spain, are often more familiar with less clearly political works, such as "Los zapaticos de rosa" (The Little Pink Shoes). The children's poem—easily dismissed as a minor, if endearing, text—tells the story of a young girl named Pilar, who, during the course of a day at the beach, leaves her family for a walk on the sand and meets another girl, who appears to be sick and is sadly barefoot. Affected by what she witnesses, Pilar gives the other girl her own pink shoes—a tender, even theatrical, performance of good deeds. Perhaps because of its charitable message and spirited verses, Cuban children are often taught to recite the poem by heart. The speaker's diction in "Los zapaticos de rosa" sounds at times conversational and rather local; the suffix *-ico* signals the diminutive in only a few countries, while the word *espejuelos* (eyeglasses) is typically used only in the Spanish-speaking Caribbean. To describe Pilar's beach paraphernalia, the speaker uses the phrase "con aro, balde y paleta" (with her hoop, bucket and pail),[37] which, in Cuba, has become an idiom that signifies enthusiasm and readiness, denoting Martí's hold over national mores and speech.

Yet the plot, if one may call it that, of "Los zapaticos de rosa" is not obviously set on any of Cuba's tropical beaches, but on some unspecified seashore—a cosmopolitan locale, one feels, where women from various nations shed tears upon learning of Pilar's act of kindness: "Se vio sacar los pañuelos / A una rusa y a una inglesa; / El aya de la francesa / Se quitó los espejuelos" (193; A Russian woman and an Englishwoman were seen taking their handkerchiefs out; the French girl's nursemaid removed her glasses).[38] Dedicated to one "mademoiselle Marie,"[39] the poem first appeared in *La Edad de Oro*, a children's magazine edited by Martí in New York (where he lived), limited to four issues between July and October 1889, which defined itself as "publicación mensual de recreo e instrucción dedicada a los niños de América" (a monthly entertainment and educational publication dedicated to the children of the Americas). If in "Nuestra América" Martí famously calls for Latin Americans to rethink their cultural priorities—to study, for instance, the history of the Incas over that of ancient Greece—texts specifically devoted to the region, such as an essay on Bartolomé de las Casas, are rare in the magazine. In fact, much of *La Edad de Oro* deals with Europe, a choice presumably dictated by the perceived universality and prestige of its arts and letters, and on the natural germaneness of European culture and Latin America.[40]

Viewed in this context, it comes as no surprise that Martí's Pilar, as she walks to the beach before temporarily shedding her well-heeled status, should ask her mother an unexpected question about monarchy: "¡Dí, mamá! / ¿Tú sabes qué cosa es reina?" (189; Say, mother, do you know what a queen is?). Pilar's mother does not answer her daughter's query, and both characters move on literally and figuratively, but it remains rather odd that Martí's literary creature—a model, arguably, for the children of the Americas reading the magazine—should be intrigued about a concept associated with ancient regimes rather than the free republics discussed in "Nuestra América." Pilar's ignorance of the meaning of *reina* may denote that she is not a European child, or simply too young, but her curiosity bespeaks the long reach and prestige of transatlantic symbols in the Latin American imagination. If Pilar is anything like the real-world readers of *La Edad de Oro*, she will learn much about the arts of Europe in the magazine. For one, she will be duly impressed with the miniature portraits of opera composers in "Músicos, poetas y pintores" (Musicians, Poets, and Painters), an essay in the August 1889 issue.[41] The musicians, part of a long inventory of European creators in the magazine, are ostensibly included as exemplary figures for the upbringing of children in Latin America. Carl Maria von Weber, one reads, crafted his first opera when he was just fourteen, and Domenico Cimarosa did so when he was nineteen. The early years of the ever-popular Gioachino Rossini are encapsulated in a few concise but authoritative sentences, and we learn that his father played the trombone and his mother was a singer for a troupe of traveling actors; also a singer himself, the boy eventually lost his voice, but by the age of twenty-one he had become the famous composer of *Tancredi*, an opera. The illustrious surnames lovingly invoked in *La Edad de Oro* vaunt a golden aura even as they assert the European bonds, as Alicia Alonso would have it, of Latin American culture. Borges, too, might find nothing amiss in the text's foreign affinities.

But, to complicate matters, the actual text of "Músicos, poetas y pintores" stems quite literally from Europe. Like five other works (two poems and three stories) written by Martí for *La Edad de Oro*, the essay is a translation from a work in another language: a section of "Great Young Men," the third chapter of *Life and Labour, or Characteristics of Men of Industry, Culture and Genius* (1887), by Samuel Smiles, the Scottish author and reformer. In this passage from English to Spanish, or from Britain to the Americas, Martí's thoughts on translation—yet another kind of transport—provide a revealing key for conceptualizing European culture in a region like Latin America.[42]

Placing the six translated texts featured in *La Edad de Oro* alongside Martí's previous Spanish versions of Victor Hugo's "Mes fils" (1874) and Helen Hunt Jackson's *Ramona* (1884), Roberto Fernández Retamar cites Martí's notion of *transpensar* versus *traducir*, which Martí elaborates in his own introductory notes to the Hugo translation. If *traducir* can be understood simply as *transcribir*, or to transcribe, from one tongue to another, Martí calls for *transpensar*, a neologism that can be rendered only awkwardly (alas!) as "to trans-think"—a concept that seeks to account for translation's veritable work. To further expound this idea, he also makes up the verb *impensar*, which could be translated as "in-thinking" or "thinking inside." Beyond the specific character of each language, the translator must inhabit the mind of Hugo to transport Hugo from one tongue to another. Passionately, lovingly, Martí views the act of translation—the literal and affective transport of words and works from one language to another—as a chameleonic endeavor, an authorial mirroring whereby the foreign is esteemed for what it may bring to one's own cultural realm. In his essay, Fernández Retamar deploys the image of a Spanish-language house for French. Close to Martí's thinking, the metaphor is valuable not only for what it says about Martí, but also for creating a critical space for opera—or opera houses, literal and figurative—in Latin America. While it is not difficult to come up with good reasons for excluding the art form from traditional constructions of culture in the region, an argument can also be made for wanting to create an adequate habitation for opera in a place where, if one heeds these various lessons regarding the seemingly foreign, the whole world should be regarded as part of its own cultural legacy.

None of this means, of course, that Martí should now be perceived as a clichéd cosmopolitan intent in mimicking all aspects of European culture. Elsewhere, in other poems bearing such titles as "Príncipe enano" (Dwarf King), "Mi reyecillo" (My Little King) or "Los dos príncipes" (The Two Princes, written after an "idea" in Helen Hunt Jackson's "The Prince Is Dead"), regal and princely motifs linked with Europe emerge almost seductively, if only to be, at times, powerfully indicted. This is the case of "La imagen del rey"

(The King's Image), included in *Versos sencillos*: "La imagen del rey, por ley, / Lleva el papel del Estado: / El niño fue fusilado / Por los fusiles del rey. / Festejar el santo es ley / Del rey: y en la fiesta santa / ¡La hermana del niño canta / Ante la imagen del rey!" (The image of the king, by law, carries the role of the State: the boy was shot with the king's guns. To celebrate a saint's day is the king's law. At the saintly feast, the boy's sister sings before the king's image).[43] The poem tells a story of ruthlessness. The king not only orders the execution of an innocent child, but also forces the victim's sister to sing in front of the royal portrait. Further, the poem also narrates the frightful metamorphosis of the tyrant's body into a visual image in front of which the young girl must subserviently perform. The textual link between the king's pictorial representation and the girl's vocal display—a command performance of the most abusive kind—is poignant; instead of rising as a clear proclamation of freedom, singing is bound with the visible symbols of absolute power.

Cautiously, I bring this up because, viewed from a certain angle, the art of opera in Latin America may be perceived as mere songs to far-off sovereigns, performed not only by those onstage but also, tacitly, by acquiescing audiences transported by the arts of Europe. Like Alonso in the grand roles of European ballet, Latin American singers play an important role in these emotional flights. Ángela Peralta (1845–1883), the soprano known as the "Mexican Nightingale," sang in Italy and in such far-flung cities as Cairo and St. Petersburg, while Antonio Paoli (1871–1946), the famed Puerto Rican tenor, was decorated by several European royal houses. Chile's Ramón Vinay (1912–1996) became famous as Verdi's Otello and sang Wagner at Bayreuth, while Peru's Luigi Alva (1927) shone in Haydn and Mozart roles as well as the bel canto repertory and had a prestigious recording career. There are many other examples. It would be rare to find a season in numerous opera houses in Europe and the United States where a singer from Latin America or of Latin American descent does not perform. One may see these performances as forms of collusion, but they are undoubtedly an expression of enchantment and an act of incantation—haunting forms of transport and ravishment through which borders between cultures come down. Literature in Latin America often explores these transcultural passages.

Latin American Literature and the Sounding of Opera

The work of opera richly pervades multiple Latin American literary texts. Authors have often found opera to be a lofty cultural practice through which it is possible to dissect issues of nation and coloniality, or race, ethnicity and class, or gender, sexuality and modernity—or various intersections thereof. In their treatment of European composers, the view of opera as a sign of the foreign, or of Latin America as a peripheral region of the West, often prevails. Yet, if one reads and listens closely, the literature of opera often complicates any binary oppositions. Despite its extraterritorial qualities, opera emerges also as a domestic element, even as Latin American cultural history becomes richer through the acknowledgment and exploration of those transports that trigger powerful reactions in authors, characters and readers alike.

Possibly the best-known literary work to base its plotline on the experience of opera is Estanislao del Campo's *Fausto: Impresiones del gaucho Anastasio el Pollo en la representación de esta ópera* (1866), the narrative poem that helped to establish Argentina's national literature even as it played a major role in the rise of the gauchesque genre in the River Plate countries. Commonly known as *El Fausto criollo,* the text is the tale of a sagacious gaucho, Anastasio, who attends a performance of Gounod's *Faust* in Buenos Aires and candidly describes what he sees and hears. (Ginastera's *Obertura para el Fausto criollo* is inspired by the poem.) Employing the rural diction mimicked by city-dwelling gauchesque authors, Anastasio comments on the spectacle of opera patrons congregating at the old Teatro Colón as he tries to purchase his own ticket: "Como a eso de la oración, / Aura cuatro o cinco noches, / Vide una fila de coches / Contra el tiatro de Colón. / La gente en el corredor, / Como hacienda amontonada, / Pujaba desesperada / Por llegar al mostrador" ("Nights back, I was roamin' around this town, / Sort of takin' stock here and there, / When I came on a string of coaches drawn /

Outside of a slap-up theatre, / That I see'd by the sign was called Colón. / The folks that had come were pilin' down, / And crowdin' like crazy through the door / To a counter set 'cross the corridor").[44] An obvious first reaction to Anastasio's account might be to remark on the gaucho's status as a cultural and linguistic outsider vis-à-vis both opera and operagoers; as he buys his *dentrada* (ticket), he does not sound like the urban elites attending the performance. His uncouth speech is also far removed from opera's mellifluousness, as some would imagine it. Yet he too, mistaking all the business on stage for reality, is moved at least occasionally by opera's ravishing sounds, as when Marguerite, sitting at the spinning wheel, intones her famous aria "Il ne revient pas," sung in Italian:

> Al rato el lienzo subió
> Y deshecha y lagrimiando
> Contra una máquina hilando,
> La rubia se apareció.
> La pobre dentró a quejarse
> Tan amargamente allí,
> Que yo a mis ojos sentí
> Dos lágrimas asomarse. (33)

> When after a bit they raised the screen,
> There was the gal again,
> All untidy, workin' a spinnin'-machine,
> And cryin' now and then.
> She'd had a raw deal, so it appears,
> And as she went puttin' us wise,
> Before I could think to swallow my tears,
> I was oozin' at the eyes. (61)

For a character who does not understand the libretto's foreign words, Anastasio's transport, albeit brief, exemplifies the long, if fleeting, reach of opera's work.

But who does opera belong to in the newly constituted Argentine Republic? Does it even belong there? Can its artifice take root in

Argentina—become somehow natural, as the speaker of Whitman's "Italian Music in Dakota" would have it? As several critics show, the workings of del Campo's text are more intricate than Anastasio's plainspoken narrative of a night at the opera might at first suggest. Enrique Anderson Imbert reads the effects of irony to include not only the inexperienced gaucho but also the elite members of the audience, who thought of themselves as European but were as marginal to a city like Paris as the gauchos were to the Teatro Colón.[45] For Nancy Vogeley, "the poem is an early example of a developing Argentine literary style, but the humor also ridicules the rustic in his first contact with European civilization."[46] Going further, Josefina Ludmer views the opera house, unlike the public square in the poem, as an exclusive space where European culture "se representa" (is represented)—which can mean it is "depicted" or "illustrated" as well as "presented again" and "performed."[47] In Ludmer's nuanced reading, the plot of Gounod's *Faust* and its various correspondences in the story line of del Campo's *Fausto* allow for the emergence of a double mockery—or as she puts it, a symbolic revenge in which Anastasio is derided as well as the gauchesque genre itself (230). The art of opera is ridden with artifice, but so, one may conclude, is poetry that seeks to depict Argentine types and mores.

If del Campo's text presents a character who views opera as an unusual and semi-illegible spectacle, Eugenio Cambaceres's *Sin rumbo* (1885), a classic novel of Argentine naturalism, focuses by contrast on a jaded young man for whom the art form, like other urban cultural practices, is a routine spectacle—yet another element in a world mostly devoid of newness and excitement. A rich estancia owner equally at home in Buenos Aires, Andrés engages in a passionate affair with Marietta Amorini, an Italian soprano performing the title role in *Aida* at the old Teatro Colón. The choice of Verdi's opera is significant for readers of postcolonial theory, for its history and subject are central to the discussion about opera in peripheral locations outside of Europe. *Aida* was famously commissioned by Egypt's Khedive Ismail for the opening of the new Cairo opera house, a context that, as Edward Said argues, underscored the work's Orientalism even as it underwrote a desire to give Cairo a European face.⁴⁸ In the case of Cambaceres's Buenos Aires, the city's metropolitan status is secured partly by the prestige of its operatic culture, admiringly described by the character of Solari, an Italy-born impresario, who equates the old Colón to La Scala.⁴⁹ The city's assembly of operatic talents coexists with other signs of modernity; yet another Italian character, the soprano's husband, remarks on the busyness of shoppers and streetcars circulating among modern buildings. One may view Solari's praise of Buenos Aires as ironic or even self-serving; he, after all, seeks to please Andrés. Yet the novel's image of Buenos Aires conveys its assertive self-fashioning as a world-class city while Andrés himself emerges as a cosmopolitan Argentine who, unlike Anastasio el Pollo, masters the codes of opera as well as any "civilized" man in Europe.

In Latin America's poetic discourse about modernity, no composer arguably boasts a status as exalted as that of Richard Wagner. Likewise, no Latin American author has been more powerfully seduced by Wagner's persona and craft than Rubén Darío, the central figure of Spanish American *modernismo* who wrote various poems that invoke Lohengrin and Parsifal, the great Wagnerian protagonists. In the preface to an anthology of the Nicaraguan poet's travel chronicles, Graciela Montaldo labels Darío an "extreme cosmopolitan."⁵⁰ Indeed, his writings attest to a veritable fascination with scenes of European culture, both historical and contemporary, which he lovingly re-creates in *Azul* (1888) and *Prosas profanas* (1896), his early poetry collections. Later "philosophical" or "political" poems, such as "Lo fatal" and "A Roosevelt," appear in countless anthologies and occupy an important place in the region's literary canon. But many readers may be better acquainted with the euphonious "Sonatina," from *Prosas profanas*, the subject of which is a delicately crafted blue-eyed princess—an improbable figure in Latin America. As the title indicates, Darío's text posits itself as music, and in fact, one may well listen to its words—it is often memorized and declaimed—as if it were a musical piece, perhaps a cantata or even a miniature opera, relishing a splendid soundscape without making much sense of the actual verbal fabric or even the unfolding story. Like an exoticist music drama condensed into forty-eight fourteen-syllable lines, "Sonatina" vaguely recounts a princess's tribulations: "La princesa está triste. . . . ¿qué tendrá la princesa? / Los suspiros se escapan de su boca de fresa, / que ha perdido la risa, que ha perdido el color" ("The Princess is sad. What ails the Princess? / Nothing but sighs escape from her lips, / which have lost their smile and their strawberry red. / The Princess is pale in her golden chair, / the keys of her harpsichord gather dust, / and a flower, forgotten, droops in its vase").[51] If the verses swiftly invoke an Orientalist geography—places like Golconda and pearl-rich Ormus are mentioned—the princess's fantastic palace is full of items redolent of European fairy tales and myths, including "los cisnes unánimes en el lago de azur" ("the [unanimous] swans reflected on the azure lake"). She may have nothing to do with Latin America, yet her sweet tale of sadness and longing stands as one of the classic poems in the region, transporting readers to a lyrical realm that, like many an opera, is far removed from the real world.

In the melodic workings of *Prosas profanas*, the reader encounters yet more graceful white swans whose source may be the improbable fantasies of Wagnerian opera. But these literary creatures are not to be taken as mere imports. In the logic of Darío's poetic thinking about cultural transports, the seemingly alien swans belong as much to him as they do to Wagner, and they express a new sensibility all his own. In "Divagación," before the swans appear, the speaker lustfully evokes a series of spatially and temporally distant cultures: "¿Vienes? Me llega aquí, pues que suspiras, / un soplo de las mágicas fragancias / que hicieron los delirios de las liras / en las Grecias, las Romas y las Francias" (Are you coming? There reaches me here, as you sigh, / a breath of the magic fragrances / that raptured the lyres / in places such as Greece, Rome and France).[52] Later on, meditating on the content of his dreamscapes, the speaker posits his preference for one culture's revival of another over the original source itself: "Amo más que la Grecia de los griegos / la Grecia de la Francia, porque en Francia, al eco de las Risas y los Juegos, / su más dulce licor Venus escancia" (93; I love, more than the Greece of the Greeks, / France's Greece, because in France, amid the echo of Laughter and Games, / Venus pours its sweetest liquor). This brief story of contacts and permutations provides a key for making sense of Darío's foreign leanings and loans. As soon as European objects are possessed and displayed by his craft, they become part of Latin America's cultural history—and the objects themselves are transformed and enriched. Thus, the speaker imagines new formations: "¿O un amor alemán?—que no han sentido / jamás los alemanes" (94; or a German love—which Germans / have never felt). The phrase stresses the split between the creation and reception of cultural products. What the German nation makes will be *felt* differently by others, and those others, through their own feelings, will then possess Germany. Besides allusions to Goethe, Heine, and other creators, the speaker's German passions materialize in the hero of Wagner's *Lohengrin*: "Y sobre el agua azul el caballero / Lohengrín; y su cisne, cual si fuese / un cincelado témpano viajero, / con su cuello enmarcado en forma de S" (94; And on the blue water, the knight / Lohengrin; and his swan, as if it were / a traveling chiseled iceberg, / with its neck framed in the shape of an S). In "El cisne," yet another poem from *Prosas profanas*, the speaker alludes to "el acento del Cisne wagneriano" ("the voice of the Wagnerian swan") and places under its white wings nothing less than "la nueva Poesía" ("the new Poetry"), whose leader, in the Spanish-speaking world, is none other than Darío himself.[53]

How should one "feel" Darío's Wagner—Lohengrin and Parsifal, as we shall see later—in Latin America? The poet's aesthetic affinity for this chapter of European opera is not without its complications. If in some of his poems the spirit of Wagner is linked with a powerful vision of Western aesthetic modernity, Darío's sensibilities are at times allied with a view of the arts from which non-European groups are excluded. The whiteness of the swan's wings may just be a biological fact, but in the context of the poet's lyrical axioms in "Palabras liminares" (the preface of *Prosas profanas*), it resounds within a racial discourse tinged with irony, if not contempt, for the indigenous and African legacy in his native region, including his own family background. Not shunning polemic, the poet writes: "¿Hay en mi sangre alguna gota de sangre de África, o de indio chorotega o nagrandano? Pudiera ser, a despecho de mis manos de marqués: más he aquí que veréis en mis versos princesas, reyes, cosas imperiales, visiones de países lejanos o imposibles: ¡qué queréis!, yo detesto la vida y el tiempo en que me tocó nacer; y a un presidente de República no podré saludarle en el idioma en que te cantaría a ti, ¡oh Halagabal! de cuya corte—oro, seda, mármol—me acuerdo en sueños) (Is there some drop of Africa's blood, or of Chorotega or Nagrandan Indian [indigenous peoples of Nicaragua], in my blood? It could be, despite my having the hands of a marquis: but, in my verses, lo and behold princesses, monarchs, imperial things, visions of distant or impossible countries: what can I say! I detest the life and times in which I was born; and I could not greet a republic's president in the same language in which I would sing to you, oh Elagabalus!, whose court—gold, silk, marble—I remember in dreams).[54] Darío's dramatis personae and luxurious accoutrements denote a literary world in which the ethnic complexities of his country are summarily dismissed. That his own poetry, in turn, should at times be regarded as alien to the region comes as no surprise.

Yet beyond race, Darío's Wagnerian allusions seek not simply to import into Latin America the themes of European mythologies and operas but also to mimic what Wagner, as a preeminent artist, crafted in his own milieu. His desire is to establish a new world of poetry that can rise above the utilitarian proclivities of the age.[55] As Cathy L. Jrade explains, Darío's "nueva Poesía" brings forth purity and eternal perfection: "In this context, Wagner is converted into the epitome of the artist whose work is able to usher in a new day for all humanity."[56] This, as Jrade argues, is clearly evident in some well-known lines from "El cisne," the sonnet cited earlier:

> Fue en una hora divina para el género humano.
> El cisne antes cantaba sólo para morir.
> Cuando se oyó el acento del Cisne wagneriano
> fue en medio de una aurora, fue para revivir.[57]

> It happened in a divine hour for the human race.
> The swan, before, had only sung to die.
> When the voice of the Wagnerian swan was heard,
> it was amidst a dawning day, he sang to live again.[58]

The new life that Darío's Wagnerian swan proclaims at sunrise indeed signals a new day as well for poetry in Spanish. After all, Darío, imitated by others, helped recraft Spanish verse, and *modernismo* itself, despite (or at least in part because of) its extraterritorial affinities, was arguably the first major literary contribution from Latin America to poetry in Spanish. Its meters and themes were soon embraced by poets everywhere, including Spain. What Wagner wrought for the transformation of European opera, Darío crafted and advanced in the realm of Spanish-language poetry.

Despite the problematic dismissal of his own mixed ethnicity in the "Palabras liminares," Darío does not exclude the indigenous world of the Americas from his poetic vision. Rather, in an interesting—and literal—parenthesis, he states that the continent's native poetry can be found only in its vanished pre-Hispanic civilizations: "(Si hay poesía en nuestra América ella está en las cosas viejas: en Palenke y Utatlán, en el indio legendario y el inca sensual y fino, y en el gran Moctezuma de la silla de oro. Lo demás es tuyo, demócrata Walt Whitman)" (If there is any poetry in our America, it resides in old things: in Palenque and Utatlán, in the legendary Indian and the sensual and elegant Inca, and in the great Montezuma of the golden throne. The rest is all yours, democratic Walt Whitman).[59] Darío crafts indigenous people as elements in a world that no longer exists—a legendary world that has been replaced by such mundane characters as a republic's president. Curiously, the aristocratic figures that inhabit Darío's poems most often hark back to Versailles and other exalted European locations and periods; likewise, his epigrammatic mention of indigenous peoples focuses on their status as actors from a long-vanished world. In this, he unwittingly recalls European composers of opera who tell stories about the New World and other far-flung regions—Vivaldi's *Motezuma* readily springs to mind—precisely in part for their value as emblems of distant spaces and times.[60]

Besides the celebrated Palenque and the less well-known Utatlán, the "Palabras liminares" mention only one other Latin America location: the capital of Argentina. In a minuscule one-phrase paragraph to which nothing, apparently, needs to be added by way of explanation, the speaker simply proclaims: "Buenos Aires:

Cosmópolis." In Darío's cultural cartography, the city in Latin America most clearly linked with modernity is Buenos Aires, which he first visited in 1893. On the occasion of the country's centennial in 1910, Darío composed the long "Canto a la Argentina," which contains powerful images in praise of Buenos Aires, especially its port and industries, as well as the immigrant groups that turned the city into a worldly metropolis. Indeed, by 1914, just six years after the opening of the new Teatro Colón, 50 percent of the residents of Buenos Aires had been born abroad, mostly in Spain, Italy, and other European nations; many of them, as Claudio Benzecry shows, played a role in the continued rise of opera at the Teatro Colón and other venues.[61] If Darío's engagement with opera, through Wagner, appears to be assertively textual, his poetry embraces also a vibrant city in which opera is not just a literary trope but a real-life passionate pursuit.

Darío is hardly the only Latin American poet enthralled by Wagner's operatic universe. Ricardo Jaimes Freyre—the Bolivian *modernista* and cofounder, with Darío, of *Revista de América* in Buenos Aires—published *Castalia bárbara* (1899), the first section of which contains thirteen poems inspired by Nordic mythology. The last lines of "El Walhalla," the tenth poem in the cycle, deploy images that resound with Wagner's operatic Valkyries: "Hay besos y risas. / Y un cráneo lleno / de hidromiel, en donde apagan, / abrasados por la fiebre, su sed los guerreros muertos" (There are kisses and laughter, and a skull full of mead from which the dead warriors, burning with fever, quench their thirst).[62] This is surely an outlandish vision, yet an absolutely domesticated one if Wagner and opera are viewed as recurrent elements in Latin American literary culture.[63]

Wagner's mighty aura reappears in two twentieth-century Argentine texts to which I return in Chapter 8: Manuel Mujica Lainez's *El gran teatro* (1980), a novel whose plot unfolds entirely during a staging of Wagner's *Parsifal* at the Teatro Colón; and Victoria Ocampo's *La rama de Salzburgo* (1981), the third volume of her autobiography, in which yet another performance of *Parsifal* at the Colón frames an important episode in a story of forbidden love. *Parsifal* resurfaces once again in the title and plot of Jorge Volpi's *En busca de Klingsor* (1999), a historical novel set mostly in Germany that chronicles the search for Hitler's top scientist after World War II. A Mexican writer, Volpi transports his own act of writing to the very center of European affairs—an act of cosmopolitanism through which Latin American authors are free to represent Europe, just like many European authors in the past had depicted Latin America. The cultural history of opera informs Volpi's narrative lexicon as organically as any other subject, including those more readily recognized as Mexican or Latin American.

A similar sense of worldliness linked with the art of opera appears in Carlos Fuentes's *Instinto de Inez* (2000), a novel with a dual plotline. One story concerns a man and woman living in Paleolithic times who communicate with each other through what appears to be song and an incipient language. The second chronicles the encounters between a famous conductor, Gabriel Atlan-Ferrara, and a Mexican opera singer, Inez Rosenzweig, who changes her name to Inez Prada to advance her operatic career. The love affair between conductor and singer develops intermittently around performances of Hector Berlioz's *La Damnation de Faust* in various times and places—London, 1940; Mexico City, 1949; and finally London, again, in 1967—and is later recalled by Atlan-Ferrara as a nonagenarian living in Salzburg. The choice of Berlioz's masterpiece is significant in the context of Latin American works about opera, as it, too, retells the legend of Faust just a few years before Gounod's opera, featured in *El Fausto criollo*. Though very different in tone and fabric, del Campo's narrative poem and Fuentes's novel are both tales of Latin America's relatively peripheral status in the world of opera. In the first wartime staging of Berlioz's work in London, Inez is a member of the chorus, but her powerful voice soars above those of her fellow singers, audibly signaling her as a truly gifted artist, yet also an oddity in the musical culture of a European city.

As the plot progresses, Inez's stature as a world-class performer rises, but so does a sense of Mexico as less than a central player on the operatic stage. The novel dwells on the difficulty of transporting opera across the Atlantic, as seen in the fraught history of Mexico City's main lyric stage that it tells: "Afuera, el Palacio de Bellas

Artes era un gran pastel de bodas imaginado por un arquitecto italiano, Adamo Boari, seguramente para que el edificio mexicano fuese la novia del monumento romano al rey Vittorio Emmanuele: el matrimonio se consumaría entre sábanas de merengue y falos de mármol e hímenes de cristal, sólo que en 1916 el arquitecto salió huyendo de la Revolución, horrorizado de que su sueño de encaje fuese pisoteado por las caballadas de Zapata y Villa" ("Outside, the Palacio de Bellas Artes was a great wedding cake conceived by an Italian architect, Adamo Boari, surely with the idea that the Mexican building would be the bride of Rome's monument to King Vittorio Emanuele: the wedding would have been consummated with marble phalluses and crystal hymens between meringue sheets, except that in 1916 Boari fled from the Revolution, horrified that the lace of his dream was being trampled by horses of Zapata's and Villa's troops").[64] In an episode that mirrors the violence committed against the splendid building, Atlan-Ferrara is brutally attacked by Inéz's lover as he ventures out into the nearby Alameda Central. The act appears as an attempt to banish both the conductor and the art of opera—foreign usurpers of sorts—from the land. In fact, the fantastic liaison between the Palacio de Bellas Artes and the Vittorio Emanuele monument, couched in gendered metaphors, invokes the language often used to narrate the conquest of Mexico as a rape by Europe. If Fuentes's well-tempered words create a new planetary cartography over which opera reigns as an art form without borders, its home in ravished Latin America remains unstable.

Elsewhere, Fuentes's own authorial persona revels in his own experience of the art of opera. In "How I Wrote One of My Books," an essay in *Myself with Others* (1988), the novelist retroactively identifies seven events that led to the writing of *Aura* (1962), his early novella on love, time, and death. One is his memory of Maria Callas in the role of Verdi's Violetta in Mexico City in the 1950s, a performance whose highlight is "the unbelievable, unfathomable, profoundly disturbing voice of Maria Callas in the death scene of *La Traviata*."[65] Importantly, the novelist's act of remembrance is triggered by an encounter with the singer at a dinner party in Paris just a few days before her death in September 1977. Proudly, Fuentes emerges as a full-blown cosmopolitan: the famed Latin American author transported by his own celebrity to the heart of the Old World, where he dines with the consecrated soprano, whose voice and artistry had once upon a time transported him to create a literary work of his own. Indeed, *Aura* is a tale of raptures whose rather operatic plot unfolds in Mexico and France, flaunting long passages in French, as if to denote the author's seamless mastery of both European and Latin American cultural history.

If Fuentes broaches the subject of opera as a sign of transcultural expertise, other Latin American works—and at least one film, adapted from a literary text—invoke the art form as they investigate specific social and political issues. The life of Carlos Gomes is the subject of Rubem Fonseca's *O selvagem da ópera* (1994), a novel that, in the guise of a cinematic project, follows the composer from the imperial court of Rio de Janeiro to Italy as he negotiates the status of Brazil in his music. César Aira's *Canto castrato* (1984) is a historical novel set in the eighteenth century in various parts of Europe. An episode in Reinaldo Arenas's *El color del verano* (1991) concerns the Comtesse Merlin, the Cuban French author; Merlin, who was a well-regarded singer too, sang parts of Bellini's *Norma* during a return visit from France to her native Havana, a performance that Arenas sarcastically reworks in his novel. Yet another novel about Cuba and opera, Mayra Montero's *Como un mensajero tuyo* (1998), reimagines the aftermath of Caruso's famous performance of *Aida* in Havana in 1919, cut short by an explosion, and adapts Verdi's Orientalism to explore Cuba's ethnic diversity, especially the lives of Chinese immigrants.[66] Based on the novella by Senel Paz, the film *Fresa y chocolate* (1993), by Tomás Gutiérrez Alea and Juan Carlos Tabío, juxtaposes opera and nation; the character of David, who blindly supports the Cuban Revolution, learns to appreciate opera from his friend Diego, a gay man who opposes the country's forbidding regime. (We return to several of these works in Chapter 5, whose focus is Cuba.) Yet another text about opera's convergence with homosexuality is Pablo Simonetti's *La razón de los amantes* (2007), a novel in which *Tosca* frames the tale of a married man who discovers he loves another man in a country, Chile, whose restrictive social codes resound with the political repression portrayed in Puccini's opera. Most recently, the Mexican tenor Rolando Villazón published *Mozart en bicicleta* (2021), the playful tale of a young Mexican singer in Salzburg, which, as a sign of the singer's standing in European operatic culture, first appeared in German as *Mozart auf dem Fahrrad* (2020).

But arguably the most insightful meditation on fiction and opera in Latin America is Alejo Carpentier's *Concierto barroco* (1974), the self-reflexive tale of a Mexican traveler—an eighteenth-century criollo—who embarks on a grand tour of Europe and ends up meeting Antonio Vivaldi just in time for carnival in Venice. The traveler decides to dress up as Montezuma, and his outlandish mask and costume inspire the composer to write an opera about the conquest of Mexico. It is a work the traveler despises. After the first performance, he furiously confronts the composer, proclaiming: "False, false, false, all false!"[67] Yet the lessons of Carpentier's text have little to do with historical precision or the redressing of wrongs. Flagrantly violating historical truth and thereby mirroring Vivaldi and Giusti's own work, the novella's characters unrealistically witness Wagner's funeral procession along the Grand Canal and picnic by Stravinsky's grave on the Isola di San Michele. Wagner and Stravinsky are dead, but there is no time for mourning. The last chapter rapidly traverses time, and Filomeno, the traveler's Afro-Cuban servant, arrives in twentieth-century Paris to attend a concert by Louis Armstrong. The jazz master's trumpet—an instrument as ancient as the Bible, played also in Handel's *Messiah* and by musicians in Cuba or the United States—emerges not only as the text's leitmotif but also as an audible sign of the spatial and temporal continuum among the cultures of Europe, Africa, and the Americas. I return to the novella in Chapter 4.

Like Carpentier's fictional trumpet, the argument this book seeks to make also focuses on the journeys of cultural products from one place to another and across the centuries—not only the spaces and times in which operas are composed and their plots unfold but also the cities on both sides of the Atlantic where these operas continue to be reimagined and performed onstage and on the pages of literary works.

2 A Corpus of Fragments, II
Reading Operas

WHEN ONE THINKS of Latin America alongside the art of opera, the sights and sounds from Werner Herzog's *Fitzcarraldo* (1982) are likely to suggest themselves before anything else. Set in the heart of the Amazon rainforest, the film chronicles the purported difficulty of opera's transports to, and in, a far-flung part of the world. In the first scene, a man and a woman, elegantly dressed but disheveled after what appears to have been a grueling journey, arrive by boat at the sumptuous riverside opera house in Manaus just in time to catch the surreal finale of a performance of Verdi's *Ernani* featuring Enrico Caruso and a lip-synching Sarah Bernhardt. In reality, Manaus's opera house—with its impressive dome covered with yellow and green ceramic tiles, the colors of the Brazilian flag—is located a few blocks from the Negro River, and Caruso never sang in that remote location, plus Bernhardt was not even an opera singer. But as Richard Leppert notes, "epic-quality improbability constitutes the film's cultural logic," and both Caruso and Bernhardt (who is played by a cross-dressed male actor) are key elements in the fantastic tale in which history and fiction seamlessly merge, branding opera in Latin America, or at least some parts thereof, as a kind of extravagant folly.[1]

Remarkably, much of the discourse about the real Teatro Amazonas resounds with Herzog's imaginings. Earlier, Eduardo Galeano had placed Caruso singing there as the deplorable edifice opened to the public: "The Amazonas theater, a baroque monument in triumphantly poor taste, is the chief symbol of the vertigo of wealth at the beginning of our century. Caruso navigated the river through the jungle to sing to Manaus's inhabitants for a kingly fee on opening night. Pavlova, who was supposed to dance there, could not get beyond Belem but sent her apologies."[2] Alain Pacquier also envisioned Caruso traveling by river to sing at the first night of a theater whose faux-baroque architecture was in terrible bad taste—a symbol of rubber-baron megalomania.[3] But Herzog remains the most powerful artisan behind the lasting myth of Caruso at the tropical opera house. In a BBC report on the opera house as an imported sign of "the grandeur of Europe," Benjamin Ramm notes "a degree of historical accuracy" in the film, namely, that the first performance at the Teatro Amazonas, of Ponchielli's *La Gioconda*, "featured Caruso."[4] Derek Malcolm falls into a similar trap as he reviews *Burden of Dream*, Les Blank's documentary on Herzog's film: "*Fitzcarraldo* is the true story of the attempt by an arguably mad Irishman called Fitzgerald to build an opera house in the Amazon."[5] In reality, as Joshua Lund concludes, Carlos Fermín Fitzcarrald, the man on whom Herzog's Brian Sweeney Fitzgerald is modeled, probably did not care much for opera, let alone the erection of new opera houses in the rainforest.[6] Not surprisingly, the historian Mário Ypiranga Monteiro feels the urge to separate fact from fiction in his chronicle of the Teatro Amazonas, decrying what he regards as Herzog's cinematic vulgarity.[7] Even now, some viewers may suspend disbelief and see the film as a credible document of Latin American excess. Herzog's imagination is a reminder of the pleasures and perils of writing about a region often represented in fantasy-rich narrative modalities.

Yet when it comes to the Teatro Amazonas, both truth and fiction are strange. Inaugurated in 1897 at the height of the rubber boom, the theater is easily perceived as the gawdy by-product of an industry that gave Manaus enormous wealth. As Lund argues, Herzog's film is less about opera than it is about capitalism—the "capitalist irrational"—with the theater rising as "the symbol of incalculable social and economic inequality: the counterpoint of obscene luxury and material poverty that amazed Herzog himself when he first visited Manaus."[8] Having the opera house as its hub, the city fashioned itself as a prestigious outpost of Western civilization and came to be called—what else?—"a Paris das selvas," or "the Paris of the jungles." Indeed, Manaus built its opera house with an eye to the other side of the Atlantic. Its architecture mirrors that of the great European theaters, and as tour guides at the opera house remind visitors, even the local woods used in its building were sent to Portugal to be carved and then shipped back to Brazil—yet another iteration of the long colonial exchange of raw materials for finished goods.[9] In the film, Fitzcarraldo learns that the wealthy citizens of Manaus send their laundry to Lisbon because the local water is not deemed pure enough for washing their clothes. This real-life transport of laundry to Europe did actually happen—a way for the clothes of local elites to stroll through foreign capitals even if their owners never traveled abroad, as José Seráfico would have it.[10] Ana Maria Daou explains how citizens also benefited from a streetcar system, street paving, a sewer and electricity network, and telegraph lines under the river, and how the opera house, specifically, emerged as part of a project to construct secular spaces to educate the mind and ennoble the spirit; attending operatic performances became both a symbol of refined taste and a sign of distinction.[11] But by the time Elizabeth Bishop visited Manaus in 1960, circumstances had changed, as she writes to Robert Lowell: "Rubber collapsed completely just after that there the Opera house stands, huge, magnificent, art-nouveau-ish, with the town dwindled to nothing around it, and the Rio Negro rolling magnificently below."[12] And yet, as Bishop would have it, "it is quite lovely inside."[13]

Much of Herzog's film deals with Fitzcarraldo's colossal efforts to build a railway that will eventually yield the capital needed to build yet another opera house elsewhere in the jungle—in Iquitos, Peru, where he lives. The audacious engineering project requires nothing less than hauling a steamship over a mountain. In a gesture redolent of imperial exploitation, Fitzcarraldo charges mostly indigenous men with this excruciating task. Ultimately, he fails to build the opera house and must resort to technology (a gramophone and shellac discs) to bring the ravishing sounds of European opera—what Leppert calls the "acoustic sublime" (112)—to Iquitos.[14] It matters that all this is fiction, for it exposes the transatlantic history of opera not only as Latin America's desire for European art forms and lifestyles but also as Europe's own fascination with the mythical spaces and outlandish history of the so-called New World. In Julian Barnes's *Flaubert's Parrot* (1984), the narrator critiques the themes and tropes of fiction set in "South America," inevitably viewed through the prism of what sounds like magical realism: "Ah, the daiquiri bird which incubates its eggs on the wing; ah, the fredonna tree whose roots grow at the tips of its branches, and whose fibres assist the hunchback to impregnate by telepathy the haughty wife of the hacienda owner; ah, the opera house now overgrown by jungle."[15] In such discursive creations, Latin America mimics the Old World, though imperfectly; the civilizing emblem of the opera house ends up, after all, being devoured by the forces of nature. In this context, Herzog's film—elliptically alluded to, perhaps, in Barnes's enumeration of South American things—is yet another link in a long and illustrious chain of European works that reveal as much about the world they seek to describe as they do about the invention of those depictions and the practices of their consumption.[16]

The real Teatro Amazonas has a complicated history of its own. Monteiro's study has a section on the theater's "apogee" from 1897 to 1908, followed by its "decadence," as if confirming the implausibility of sustaining the institution of opera in a location such as the Brazilian rainforest. Significantly, Monteiro speeds through almost four decades of history, from 1937 to 1971, during which not much took place inside the hallowed interior except for the occasional performance by a touring company.[17] His notion of a crisis of high culture that includes opera is hardly exceptional. As we will see, part of the discourse about the Teatro Colón, Buenos Aires's storied opera house, also fluctuates between the proclamation of a golden age—or more than one—and subsequent declarations that much, if not all, has been lost. Indeed, the junction of Latin America and opera is far richer and more diverse—less exotic, and more prosaic and complex—than one may at first suspect from Herzog's film or the hyperbolic gestures of rubber barons.

Beyond Herzog and the opera house in the jungle, the archive of operatic texts that travels back and forth, literally and figuratively, across the Atlantic Ocean is often far more prosaic yet formidably diverse. Drawing on the work of both musicologists and literary scholars, the survey of opera that follows considers two large bodies of work. The first gathers operas about Latin America written mostly by European composers, often featuring exotic or comical plots. The second collects operas by Latin American composers on diverse subjects: the region itself, for sure, but also many other things, as if heeding Borges's discussion of the universe as birthright. In this survey, the United States plays a salient, at times imperious, role; American composers, like many Europeans, have taken Latin America as their subject, and their Latin American peers have often thrived in the United States. A few of the European operas discussed here belong to the international repertoire, but many other works are rarities, often unseen since their premieres and accessible only through partial recordings or in musicological accounts. Yet taken together, these operas amount to a substantial and rich body of works. What follows is not meant as a comprehensive history of these two traditions (if one could call them that) but as a potential background for the arguments that emerge in subsequent chapters as Latin America and opera variously intersect.

European and US Operas: Plots from Latin America

Unfolding in various historical periods and geographic locations, the corpus of operas about Latin America composed in Europe, plus a few in the United States, is far more heterogeneous than one might expect. Featuring visions of exotic charms and political comicality, not devoid of clichés and misconceptions, these works also include nuanced depictions of shared human experience—the notion that people are essentially the same across geographic and cultural boundaries. The patterns or formulas that some of these works deploy are often found in operas about other non-European locations. What we now call Latin America is first and foremost one of those "various Elsewheres," which, as Ralph P. Locke shows, Western music helped to conceptualize even as ideas about those unfamiliar lands and peoples contributed to the development of music in Europe and, to some extent, its colonies around the world.[18] Indeed, besides the so-called Orient—the subject of such operas as Mozart's *Die Entführung aus dem Serail* and Verdi's *Aida*, or Delibes's *Lakmé* and Puccini's *Madama Butterfly*—composers have looked most often to the Americas for extraordinary customs, outlandish topographies, and dizzying historical junctures.[19]

It would be easy to dismiss many of these operas as misrepresentations—elements in a discourse whereby Europe asserts its supremacy over other parts of the world. But careful readings reveal a more complex landscape. As Herbert Lindenberger suggests, a creative approach to these often troublesome works would seek a fuller critical engagement with the aesthetic and historical contexts in which they were created and first staged.[20] Given a natural inclination to disregard or denounce Eurocentric works, this might be a thorny proposition for Latin American cultural history or literary studies. Yet as I will argue, the sharp European inflections of opera may not seem entirely prejudicial if one takes into account the ambiguous and complex verbal and musical arguments that many of these works ultimately deploy. Close readings of these old operas can tease out the cultural assumptions on which they rest, divulging more about Europe than the regions they purport to depict. Other operas about Latin America will even prove more culturally nuanced and aesthetically complex than one might expect. Moreover, the colonial underpinnings of even the most recalcitrant Eurocentric works are often contested by productions that may be regarded as decolonial in both theory and practice.

In these arguments, the various codes of opera—musical, verbal, theatrical—all matter. Starting in the seventeenth century, some early works that concern the native cultures of the Americas—rare works overall no longer performed—are closely related to dance. In France, as Michael V. Pisani recounts, Jean-Baptiste Lully crafted music for court ballets that sought to represent the diverse peoples of the world. *L'Amour malade* (1657), performed at the Louvre, contained a Peruvian sequence that featured twelve sunburned "Indians," men and women, carrying umbrellas. According to Pisani, they are "the first New World inhabitants represented on a European stage with music by a major composer."[21] The libretto by Francesco Buti, as Olivia Bloechl argues, "does support an exotic interpretation of their music, as an expression appropriate to intemperate peoples and climates," as one can see in this description she cites: "Ces Indiens que nous voyons / Apres que le soleil a noircy leurs visages / Eviter avec soin l'ardeur de ses rayons, / Ne nous paroissent pas trop sages" ("These Indians that we see / Carefully avoiding the ardor of the sun's rays / After it has already blackened their faces / Do not seem very wise to us").[22] In England, William Davenant's *The Cruelty of the Spaniards in Peru* (1658) and *The History of Sir Francis Drake* (1659) are two masques that incorporated singing as well as dancing and acting. The music has not been preserved, but the words tell a story in which Spanish colonialism, as Richard Frohock explains, is condemned even as the English are lauded as "defenders of Native American interests"—a music drama that says more about intra-European obsessions than anything else.[23]

One early semioperatic work about the Americas still performed rather frequently is Henry Purcell's *The Indian Queen* (1695). Based on a dramatic work by Sir Robert Howard and John Dryden first staged in 1664, the musical play chronicles the madcap story of Zempoalla, a Mexican queen fighting an invasion by Peruvians, led by a warrior improbably named Montezuma, who in turn discovers that he is the son of yet another queen whose throne has been usurped by Zempoalla herself. The plot, which Curtis Price describes as a "historically and geographically preposterous story," is unusual for not featuring any European characters.[24] Composed at the end of Purcell's life, *The Indian Queen* appears to be unfinished. This lack of a conclusion, along with its outrageous misrepresentations, has prompted creative reinterpretations. Guillermo Gómez-Peña, the Chicano performance artist, reconceived the work for the Long Beach Opera in 1998 as *La Indian Queen*, and Peter Sellars substantially rescripted the text for Madrid's Teatro Real (as well as the English National Opera and Russia's Perm Opera and Ballet

Theater) in 2013, a version also seen in Salzburg in 2023. Writing for the *Los Angeles Times*, Jan Breslauer described Gómez-Peña's production as part of a spectacle that concerned the Spanish conquest as much as it did Hollywood's views of Latin America and the politics of Mexico at the century's end: "A dance troupe of blue-skinned Carmen Mirandas is trapped in a bamboo cage. And an array of other characters sport garb ranging from Zapatista ski masks and exotic 'native' headdresses to full-on 17th century British court regalia. They speak a dizzying mix of Spanish, English, Spanglish, Old English and an array of California dialects from surfer dude to Valley gal."[25] Likewise, Sellars galvanized the work's potential to address the conquest of the Americas from the viewpoint of contemporary sensibilities. Explicitly critiquing the violent acts that bind Latin America to Spain, the production displayed paintings by Gronk, the Chicano artist, and inserted passages from *La niña blanca y los pájaros sin pies* (1992), a novel by the Nicaraguan author Rosario Aguilar, into Howard and Dryden's archaic libretto.[26] Instead of silencing the work for its obviously defective approach to history, both Gómez-Peña and Sellars preserve Purcell's sumptuous music (and add other musics by Purcell, in Sellars's case) even as they review and revise the problematic libretto by crafting audacious stagings that expound their own critical evaluation of conquest.

Later European operas about Latin America often focus on the first encounters between the Spanish conquistadors and the indigenous peoples of the Americas. Jürgen Maehder has documented close to seventy musical works written and performed from the turn of the seventeenth century to 1992 that variously deal with confrontations between Europe and the so-called New World.[27] Most of these operas are now true rarities, never or hardly ever performed. While some of them are devoted to Christopher Columbus, no historical figure has drawn as much attention as Moctezuma, the so-called emperor of the so-called Aztecs, whose tragic downfall could transport audiences anywhere.[28] Indeed, Francesco Algarotti's *Saggio sopra l'opera in musica* (1755), a sophisticated and often cited treatise that underwent multiple editions in Italian and other languages, deemed the conquest of Mexico an ideal subject for opera.

In the third Italian edition (1763), Algarotti praises the librettos by Pietro Metastasio on the mythical subjects of Dido and Achilles, because they allow, amid highly passionate scenes, the staging of splendid feasts and spectacular conflagrations. These theatrical extravagances, he suggests, could also inform operas on the vanquished Aztec emperor—a strange and grand plot that calls for magnificent and unfamiliar things to be deployed in order to contrast Spaniards and Mexicans on their first encounter. As Algarotti puts it, audiences are transported to a new world by the power of music, dance, and stagecraft.[29]

The best-known opera about the dramatic conquest of Tenochtitlán is probably Antonio Vivaldi's *Motezuma* (1733), with a libretto by Alvise Giusti. Its plotline features, among other imaginative flights, a romance between Cortés's brother and Montezuma's daughter. At face value, Vivaldi's opera seems to rest on the assumption that Europe and the indigenous world of the Americas are essentially each other's opposites. Yet as Pierpaolo Polzonetti observes, Giusti's libretto eschews a single-minded pro-Spanish perspective and affords the possibility of reading "contrasting interpretations" of the conquest.[30] Building on these often ignored nuances, Alejo Carpentier's *Concierto barroco*, which I study in Chapter 4, makes the most of the interconnected cultural histories of the Atlantic, especially musical contacts, to dispel rigid notions of otherness.

Lessons of a common human experience similarly inform Carl Heinrich Graun's *Montezuma* (1755), which has a libretto by Frederick II of Prussia—at whose court, not coincidentally, Algarotti resided for a number of years. As Polzonetti explains, Frederick imagined the Mexican ruler as an enlightened monarch such as himself.[31] In his opening recitative, Montezuma describes an ideal king and kingdom to one of his officials: "Si, mio Tezeuco, il Messico è felice. Frutto di quella libertà, che, unita alla prudenza, al solo fren soggiace delle leggi, ch'io stesso sono il primo ad osservare; il popol mio di stabil gaudio e bel riposi abbonda, e il mio poter su l'amor suo si fonda" ("Yes, my Tezeuco, Mexico is happy, being in league with judiciousness, that is only subject to the control of those laws that I myself observe first; my people enjoy a reliable fortune and plenty of sweet peace, and my power is founded on their love").[32] Cortés, by contrast, is reprehensible. But Frederick's receptive posture was soon challenged. From 1765 to 1781, eight other composers working in six Italian cities set to music yet another libretto on the conquest of Mexico, this one by Vittorio Amedeo Cigna-Santi.[33] As Polzonetti explains, this version "corrected the progressive standpoint of Frederick's subject and rehabilitated the moral stature of Hernán Cortés."[34] Cigna-Santi's version became better known than both Giusti's and Frederick's librettos. One setting, by Niccolò Zingarelli, first performed at Naples's Teatro San Carlo in 1781, even traveled north to Eszterháza Palace, in present-day Hungary, where Joseph Haydn reworked it yet again by adding music by a few other composers.[35]

Yet another work on Moctezuma is Gaspare Spontini's *Fernand Cortez, ou La conquête du Mexique*, which went through four different versions, in French and German, between its 1809 premiere and 1832.[36] Adopting certain clichés about native peoples, the libretto by Étienne de Jouy and Joseph-Alphonse Esménard features an evil high priest and a potential human sacrifice—that of Amazily, Moctezuma's niece. But as the opera concludes, she is saved and, in yet another interethnic romantic twist, united to Cortez himself. Importantly, as Pisani notes, *Fernand Cortez* was the first European musical work to feature indigenous instruments from the Americas: percussion in the orchestra pit and onstage dancers playing the Mexican *ayacachtli* (gourds) as well as tambourines and cymbals.[37] Miriam K. Whaples quotes Spontini's own words of instruction to a performer—a dancer who must strike the instrument known as *ajacatzily* ad libitum; as Whaples notes, "Since the instrument in question is a gourd or pottery rattle, we may wonder why it was to be struck; but efforts at authenticity could only go so far."[38] Disregarding the allure of historical exactitude, a staging of *Fernand Cortez* at the Maggio Musicale Fiorentino in 2019 opted instead, as the director Cecilia Ligorio viewed it, to delve into the opera's dual challenge: to respect Spontini's heroic portrayal of Cortés and to acknowledge the conquest as "one of the darkest and bloodiest episodes" of modern history.[39] The character of Moralez, Cortés's soldier, questions the veracity of official history as he writes his own personal memories, seen projected onstage. As the opera comes to an end, the audience considers Moralez's final judgment as he asks himself where truth is in the story and realizes that the conquest originated not in valor but in deceit. Even as Spontini's grand music resounds, Spain's grandiose epic is debated and deflated.

Indeed, attempts to tell a different kind of history appear in multiple later operas about the conquest from the mid-twentieth century to the present. Librettos sometimes use several languages, including Nahuatl, suggesting the possibility of viewing and narrating Moctezuma's story from different cultural perspectives. Roger Sessions's *Montezuma* (1964), first performed at Berlin's Deutsche Oper, features an English-language libretto by Giuseppe Antonio Borgese that contains phrases in Nahuatl, Latin, and Spanish, while the libretto for Lorenzo Ferrero's *La Conquista* (2005), which premiered at Prague's National Theater, is written in English, Spanish, and Nahuatl. Despite its nod to Mexico's languages, Sessions's opera partly deploys exoticist practices to represent the indigenous world. As W. Anthony Sheppard observes, the scene of the Spanish auto de fé lacks any sign of musical exoticism, but the depiction of a sacrifice, by contrast, contains an Aztec Teponaxtli slit drum as well as percussion instruments of Chinese origin.[40] An American, Sessions partly resorts to remote Asia to craft a non-Western sound to evoke neighboring Mexico. Then again, Martin Brody underscores Sessions's status as a non-European composer as a key for evaluating the opera: "In its concern with cultural assimilation and conflict and the ambiguous relations between colonizers and colonized, *Montezuma* seems to reflect Sessions's own predicament as an American composer coming to terms with European musical culture."[41] Andrea Olmstead partly blames the libretto's use of Nahuatl for the opera's lack of success. Besides the unusual narrative structure—the opera is told as the reminiscences of Bernal Díaz del Castillo, Hernán Cortés's soldier—the phonetics of the indigenous language complicate the act of singing. For Olmstead, librettos in any language should avoid "words with many consonants," which is impossible to do in Nahuatl: "But historical accuracy in

Montezuma necessitates the repeated use of Aztec proper names such as 'Quetzalcoatl,' 'Cuahetemoc,' and 'Tenochtitlan' that are inherently difficult to sing and hear. Many Aztec names end with the syllable '-atl.' The narrator complains ironically, 'O my shackled tongue'—while trying to pronounce the names of the volcanoes 'Popcatepetl' [*sic*], 'Citlaltepetl' and 'Ixtaccihuatl.'"[42] As we shall see, Carpentier's fictional Vivaldi in *Concierto barroco* also blames the sounds of Nahuatl to justify the brazen alteration of indigenous names in Giusti's libretto.

Premiered in Hamburg for the fifth centennial of Columbus's first landfall in the Americas, Wolfgang Rihm's *Die Eroberung von Mexiko* (1992) treats Moctezuma and the historical record more audaciously than previous works. It contains an anonymous Nahuatl song and the Spanish-language text of Octavio Paz's "Raíz del hombre" (1937) in its German-language libretto, written by Rihm himself, who adapted Antonin Artaud's *La Conquête du Méxique* (1932). The role of Moctezuma (Montezuma in the work) is performed by a woman, which recalls the practice of feminizing other cultures observed in many European depictions of conquered peoples. But the overall treatment of gender is actually more complex than that. Informed by the writings of Tzvetan Todorov and Jacques Lacan, Alastair Williams suggests that Rihm undercuts the male-female binary by crafting a work in which Moctezuma "ceases to be a human subject, in any standard sense of the term, [and] becomes dispersed into the musical fabric."[43] The music itself, though, as W. Anthony Sheppard notes, relies on the conventions of exoticist opera, with percussion representing native drums from the start and music for Moctezuma that conforms to certain musical clichés about non-European cultures. That Malinche is incarnated by a mute dancer is also a complicated choice for Sheppard: "In this opera, the subaltern does not speak much."[44] Indeed, for the benevolent claims of an opera such as Rihm's to work, Sheppard postulates the need for "an audience sophisticated enough to see through or ignore the clear signs of orientalist representation" (807). In this, an important key is the music's interaction with the libretto itself.

If Giusti, Vivaldi's librettist, took as his source a chronicle by Antonio de Solís, who had never been to the Americas, Rihm's citation of Mexican texts secures a space for other affects and worldviews. Specifically, the workings of Paz's poetry—cited four times, at the end of each act—informs the opera's musical and verbal exploration of the concepts of self and other through the fictional interaction of Cortés and Moctezuma as the battling leaders. For Williams, both men inhabit "incompatible sign systems," yet Rihm's score searches for "a form of intersubjective understanding" between them.[45] As the opera reaches its denouement, the "Spanish" baritone and the "Mexican" soprano together sing the last verse of Paz's poem. The two voices attempt to acknowledge each other but do so, beyond ethnic differences, with "a solemnity appropriate for words attesting the underlying loneliness of death" (270). Paz's lines, translated into German, are indeed somber:

Unter diesem Tod, Liebe, glückhaft und stumm,
gibt es keine Adern, keine Haut, kein Blut,
sondern nur der einsamen Tod;
tobende Stille,
ewig, umrißlos,
unerschöpfliche Liebe, der Tod entströmt.[46]

Under this death, love, fortunate and mute,
there are no veins, no skin, no blood,
but only lonely death;
raging silence
eternal, shapeless,
inexhaustible love, from which death emanates.

The fact that the libretto's last lines are by a Mexican poet is not simply a gesture of cultural inclusion; it is the musical acknowledgment of the worth and work of Latin American literature. In Rihm's opera, an author from that part of the world happens to offer a more powerful understanding not just of the conquest of Mexico but also, more broadly, of the archetypes of cultural encounter.[47]

In a staging of *Die Eroberung von Mexico* conceived by Pierre Audi for Madrid's Teatro Real in 2013, as the music began and the lights went out, a large faction of bodies, rushed down the central aisle of the theater, startling the audience. Playing violent conquistadors, the men wielded swords as they ran toward the stage. Facing the audience there rose a vibrant preconquest urban scene, as if Tenochtitlán had been transported to Europe, or as if the Aztecs had taken active possession—or were the original inhabitants—of the hallowed precincts of the opera house. Audi's vision began by spatially unleashing the power of European opera to side with the defeated natives. Musicians occupied and played in the royal box, as if to banish from the house those figures representing the crown under whose auspices the conquest of Mexico had taken place. If the indigenous peoples onstage remained exotic creatures, they also stood peacefully for the fruits of civilization, including opera. As the piece unfolded, the words of Octavio Paz were projected for the audience to read in the original Spanish—each of the four stanzas a theatrically deployed text whereby a voice from Latin America could make itself plainly legible and understood. The staging also featured a Malinche dressed in Japanese garb. Although some critics were puzzled by the juxtaposition of Asia and Latin America, it might have been possible—at least for some members of a purportedly sophisticated audience, as Sheppard would have it—to view and read the character's costume as a demonstration of the interchangeability of cultural stereotypes.[48] On those nights at the opera, the conquest of Mexico uncannily crossed the Atlantic and lay siege to Madrid through Audi's bold theatrical vision.[49]

Besides works on the conquest of Mexico, a good number of European operas unfold in other parts of Latin America, but the extent to which these settings truly matter remains an open question in some cases. Consider, for instance, Gaetano Donizetti's *Il furioso all'isola di San Domingo* (1833), vaguely inspired by an episode in the first part of Cervantes's *Don Quixote*, transposed from Spain's Sierra Morena to the Antilles. The libretto, by Jacopo Ferretti, does little to depict the island where the action unfolds with any kind of specificity, while Donizetti's score remains resolutely within the conventions of Italian bel canto. As if to profit from the outlandish location, the story of the ireful Cardenio is intertwined with that of Kaidamà, an enslaved man described both as *moro* (Moor) and *negro* (black). A tragicomic Caliban-like figure, Kaidamà protests the physical and mental abuse to which Cardenio and other characters subject him. He is also "a figure of pathos," as William Ashbrook would have it.[50] A whip, seen or mentioned several times almost as a leitmotif, resounds indeed with the history of slavery in the Caribbean. Yet the plot focuses mostly on the protagonist's amatory entanglements with Eleonora. As the opera progresses, Cardenio regains his reason and asks Kaidamà for forgiveness, but it all ends with the couple's decision to return to Spain. The island of San Domingo is left behind as if it had never existed.

In the eighteenth and nineteenth centuries, Peru was, besides Mexico, virtually the only location in Spain's American dominions often represented in European opera. In Paris, Jean-Philippe Rameau devoted the second of the four *entrées* of *Les Indes galantes* (1735), an *opéra-ballet*, to the tale of "Les Incas du Pérou," which, like Purcell's and Vivaldi's earlier works, focuses on war and love. To the rivalry between two male characters—the Spaniard Don Carlos and the Peruvian Huascar—for the affection of Phani, an Inca princess, Rameau adds an exotic "Invocation et hymne du soleil," about sun worshiping, sung by Huascar. There is also a volcano eruption, a turn of events marked by great theatricality. It ends badly for the maleficent Huascar, who is crushed by molten rock, thereby allowing the romance between Don Carlos and Phani to bloom. Beyond the spectacle, Sylvie Bouissou argues that Louis Fuzelier, Rameau's librettist, is mostly interested in observing the volcano as a natural phenomenon; in this, he shares the Enlightenment's scientific inclinations.[51] Not unlike an old *ballet des nations*, the complete four-act opera mixes the Peruvian tale with three other stories from around the world: "Le Turc généreux," the tale of European captives in Ottoman lands; "Les Fleurs," set in Persia; and "Les Sauvages," in which a Frenchman and a Spaniard compete for the love of a native North American princess, who ends up choosing Adario, an indigenous man. Challenging, arguably, the notion of

European superiority, Rameau's overarching vision takes in much of the non-European world in what amounts to a global display of intertwined amatory sentiments. In the case of the two *entrées* that take place in the Americas, as it also happens in some of the Moctezuma operas, the love stories between European men and indigenous women herald the onset, or at least the possibility, of *mestizaje*. Vivaldi and Rameau postulate, if only through their exoticist plotlines, the latent power of love to erase binary conceptualizations of race.[52]

The notion of *mestizaje* as the potential outcome of interracial desire, or as a factual historical reality, reappears in the two operas by Giuseppe Verdi that concern Peru. Freely adapted by Salvatore Cammarano from Voltaire's *Alzire, ou les Américains* (1736), published just a year after the premiere of *Les Indes galantes*, the plot of *Alzira* (1845) revolves around three romantically interlinked characters: Gusmano, the Spanish governor; Zamoro, a native Peruvian leader; and Alzira, a local chieftains' daughter, whom both men love. The labyrinthine plot culminates in a highly dramatic final scene. As Gusmano and Alzira are about to be married, Zamoro, dressed as a Spanish soldier, wounds his rival with a dagger. As he dies, Gusmano pardons Zamoro and encourages him to marry Alzira, who in fact loves her fellow Peruvian and had acquiesced to marry Gusmano only to spare Zamoro's life. The true love shared by the Peruvian characters thus cancels the prospect of *mestizaje*.[53] Interestingly, the first performance of *Alzira* in the Americas took place at Lima's Teatro Principal as early as 1850, less than five years after its premiere at Naples's San Carlo in 1845. In 2018, as if to reassert the cultural ties that bind Latin America and Europe, the work was restaged in a coproduction by Lima's Gran Teatro Nacional, Bilbao's Asociación Bilbaína de Amigos de la Ópera, and the Opéra Royal de Wallonie-Liège in Belgium. Writing about the Lima staging, Pablo Macalupú-Cumpén analyzes the work of director Jean Pierre Gamarra, who included audio testimonies by indigenous persons from Peru's Comisión de la Verdad y Reconciliación, charged with investigating terrorism between 1980 and 2000. As Macalupú-Cumpén puts it, the concept effectively resignified

Verdi's early opera by connecting it to the concerns of a modern Peruvian audience.[54]

Another interethnic love story involving Peru and Spain is the subject of Verdi's *La forza del destino* (1862; revised in 1869), which features a libretto adapted from the Duque de Rivas's *Don Álvaro o la fuerza del sino* (1835) by Francesco Maria Piave, later revised by Antonio Ghislanzoni.[55] In this much better known work, the romantic lead, Don Alvaro, is of mixed European and indigenous descent; his mother, like Rameau's Phani and Verdi's own Alzira, is also an Inca princess. Unfolding in Spain and Italy, this is a story of miscegenation that concerns both Alvaro's ethnic origin and his status in Europe. The initial conflict—the rejection of Alvaro by the Marchese de Calatrava, Leonora's authoritarian father—stems exclusively from Don Alvaro's background. As early as the first scene, Calatrava describes his daughter's suitor as "lo straniero" ("the foreigner") and imprecates him by invoking his mixed origin: "la condotta vostra / da troppo abbietta origine / uscito vi dimostra" ("Your behavior shows the kind of gutter stock you come from").[56] Begging Leonora to elope with him, Alvaro mentions his own origins as he invokes the Christian sacrament of matrimony: "Pronti destrieri di già ne attendono; / un sacerdote ne aspetta all'ara... / Vieni, d'amore in sen ripara / che Dio dal cielo benedirà! / E quando il sole, nume dell'India, / di mia regale stirpe signore, / il mondo innondi del suo splendore, / sposi, o diletta, ne troverà" (32; "Swift horses are standing by for us; / a priest is waiting at the altar . . . / Come, rest within these arms of mine / and enjoy the blessing of Heaven. / By the time the Sun, Lord of the Indies, / the founder of my royal house, / bathes the world in his splendor, / oh, my beloved, he will find us married" 32). There are no other allusions to syncretism in the opera, but Alvaro himself narrates the story of his mixed parentage in the arioso at the start of the third act. His Spanish father had married the last native princess in the hope of overthrowing the yoke of Spain, but this led to suffering instead: "I miei parenti sognarono un trono, / e li destò la scure!" (76; "My parents dreamed of a throne, / but the axe awoke them"). The political story, though, remains undeveloped, and the opera largely unfolds as yet another

Verdian tragic family tale of patriarchal rights and duties. Yet as the opera comes to an end, Carlo di Vargas, Leonora's brother, brings up Alvaro's "macchia del tuo stemma" ("ignoble stock") again, to which the Peruvian angrily ripostes: "Desso splende più che gemma" (121; "My lineage is as bright as jewels"). Confusing the terms used for African and indigenous miscegenation, Carlo replies, "Sangue il tinge di mulatto" (121; "Your blood has a mulatto tinge to it"). Alvaro meets the accusation with claims of mendacity.

Indeed, it would be tempting to dismiss Verdi and his librettists' treatment of Don Alvaro's interracial status as shallow. Even the exoticism of earlier operas about the Americas—or of Verdi's *Aida*, premiered shortly after *La forza del destino* in 1871—is absent from this tale set in Europe. Yet the opera tacitly concerns the cultural makeup of Latin America and the long reach of European forms and norms. Despite his mixed lineage and birth on the other side of the world, or the malevolence with which Carlo persecutes him, Alvaro strikes spectators as not much of a foreigner on Spanish soil. He camouflages his ethnic difference rather effectively through much of the plot, apparently passing for a typical Spaniard at home on the other side of the Atlantic from where he was born. The comical Fra Melitone reports describing him as a "mulatto" (114) and an "Indian selvaggio" (115; "wild Indian") terms that trigger Alvaro's outrage. But elsewhere in the opera, the foreigner, if that's what he is, blends in without any difficulty. Ultimately, Alvaro's otherness is a matter of a family's prejudice, for the stranger from Peru masters the cultural codes of Europe as well as any other character. Significantly, unlike many operas about transatlantic contacts, *La forza del destino* is not set at the time of the conquest and its upheavals, but later, in the eighteenth century, when Spain's viceroyalties in the Americas were an integral part of a Western cultural network. The libretto is of course silent on the matter, but Don Alvaro is probably the first operatic character from what is now Latin America whom it would not be hard to imagine attending and understanding the performance of a European opera. In his familiarity with European forms, he is altogether distinct from other American characters whose experience of the West's cultural matrix is limited to the people and practices transported to their native lands. Alvaro may be a persecuted mixed-race person, but he is not a cultural outsider; he may hail from far-flung Peru and fleetingly invoke sun worshiping and even be dismissed as *lo straniero*, but he is not a stranger in Verdi's world. When he and Carlo join their voices in final duet, the famous "Invano, Alvaro," the power of their shared destiny surely resounds as magnificently as Alvaro's ancestry in another world.

Also set in Peru but more entangled with its cultural and political history than Verdi's two operas, Carlo Enrico Pasta's *Atahualpa* (1875) returns to the 1530s to chronicle the imprisonment and execution of the last Inca sovereign by Francisco Pizarro at the onset of the conquest. One may read Pasta's version of Atahualpa's plight as yet another Italian opera set in an outlandish location; the libretto, after all, was crafted by none other than Ghislanzoni, who had worked on the revision of *La forza del destino* and written the words for Verdi's *Aida*. Yet as Malena Kuss notes, the drama emerges as the thoughtful confrontation between two complex characters who stand for different faiths: Atahualpa, heroic yet repentful; and Pizarro, aware of the atrocities committed in the name of Spain.[57] Born in Milan, Pasta was a longtime resident of Lima, where he flourished as a composer of zarzuelas for local theaters. *Atahualpa* premiered in Genoa in 1875 and was staged in Lima in 1877, becoming, as Robert Stevenson notes, the first opera on the conquest of Peru ever seen in the country.[58] A Spanish version of the libretto was printed in Lima the same year of the opera's first staging in the city, which suggests a veritable interest in the work among Peruvians. Religion is a central subject. In a highly dramatic moment, Valverde, a Dominican friar, raises a crucifix in front of Atahualpa, who sings against the uncanny object and praises his own religious practices, in Italian: "No! non è dio chi l'umile / Spoglia mortal vestia . . . / Chi in croce al par d'un reprobo / Per man dell'uom peria.—/ Il nume che qui adorasi / Di rai fulgenti è adorno, / Egli ravviva il giorno, / Del ciel, degli astri è il Re" (No! The man who wore this humble mortal flesh, who died on a cross beside a criminal by the hand of man, was no god. The deity adored here is adorned with bright sunrays; he revives the day; he is the King of heaven and the stars).[59] Don Alvaro's passing reference to sun worshiping in Verdi's opera is rather tame in comparison with Atahualpa's plainly non-Christian beliefs.

Yet Atahualpa's otherness is subtly qualified in the fourth act. Just as the Inca sovereign is to be executed, Soto—a Spanish officer in love with Cora, Atahualpa's niece—addresses Pizarro and Valverde, censuring their actions before the Spanish troops. But Atahualpa reveals his own affection for the Spanish officer, calling him "straniero amico" (63; foreign friend). Finally, in the last scene, desperate Cora kills herself, singing "con accento profetico" (with a prophetic accent) these remarkable words: "Ah! del popolo redento / Risuonar già l'inno io sento; / No . . . dei liberi la terra / Non fia schiava agl'oppressor!" (70; Oh, I can already hear the hymn of this redeemed people resound; no, the land of the free should not be slave to the oppressors!). As Cora dies, in an anachronistic musical turn, the exultant notes of the Peruvian national anthem, composed by José Bernardo Alcedo centuries after the conquest, are clearly heard as part of Pasta's score, sung by a chorus. These republican sounds foretell Peru's independence; as Kuss describes it, the musical ending denotes a sense of history linked to the hope of liberation for Atahualpa's people.[60] From this angle, the opera's denunciation of the conquest may be perceived as a typical allusion to the Spanish black legend, a discourse whose best-known operatic formulation is Verdi's *Don Carlos* (1867), first performed in Paris not long before Pasta and Ghislanzoni's composition. Italian operagoers in Genoa might have sympathized with the anti-Spanish sentiments, but in Lima, *Atahualpa* must have struck a nationalist chord never heard before on the operatic stage.

Indeed, the opera might be unique in its overarching vision of history—from the start of colonial rule to, if only briefly and proleptically, the Peruvian republic. It is a story told both in music and words. The original Italian version of Ghislanzoni's libretto is preceded by a short essay titled "Cenni storici," which briefly recounts the history of Peru, describing massacres and the imposition of Christianity by Spain and concluding with a mention of how the population of the Inca Empire was reduced from twenty-four million people to just around two million after the Spanish invasion—all of which led to independence from Spain's barbarian rule in 1822.[61] The Spanish-language version of the libretto lacks a historical introduction but ends with a footnote that explains the patriotic strains of the national anthem heard as the opera comes to an end. In 2013, *Atahualpa* was revived in a concert version for Lima's Festival Internacional de Ópera Alejandro Granda, which honors the renowned Peruvian tenor. As if to underwrite its nationalist credentials, the opera was performed at the Gran Teatro Nacional and featured both the Orquesta Sinfónica Nacional and the Coro Nacional del Perú. The Spanish words in the final chorus of *Atahualpa* are all about liberty: "Al hermano vengarémos / Como libres vivirémos / Ó en la lucha morirémos / Maldiciendo al opresor" (40; "We will vindicate our brother, we will live like free men, or die in the struggle"). So too are the initial words of Peru's national anthem: "¡Somos libres, seámoslo siempre, seámoslo siempre!" ("We are free, let's always be free, let's always be free!"). At least briefly, the opera summons up a sense of Latin American nationalism.

Yet these lofty ideals glorified in *Atahualpa* are gainsaid in other texts about the region—Peru and other countries, real or imaginary—in which opera and Latin America are metaphorically conjoined to denote hopeless political failure. In some works, Latin America appears not just as an incongruous place, as seen in some of the "discovery" and conquest operas, but as a site of inordinate strife after independence. The operatic often becomes entangled with the comical, and this sense of high drama resides not only in the actual fabric of music theater but also in some prominent literary works that resort to images of opera as they craft their own imaginary Latin Americas.

Consider, for instance, Joseph Conrad's *Nostromo* (1904). Set in the fictional republic of Costaguana, which borders the Pacific Ocean and boasts a famous volcano, Conrad's tale is one of the most complex novels about Latin American governance and mores written by a European author. One of its characters, Martin Decoud, a local man educated in France, comments on conflict and corruption in Costaguana by resorting to an operatic metaphor: "Imagine an atmosphere of opera-bouffe in which all the comic business of stage statesmen, brigands, etc., etc., all their farcical stealing, intriguing, and stabbing is done in dead earnest. It is screamingly funny, the blood flows all the time, and the actors believe themselves to be influencing the fate of the universe. Of course, government in general, any government anywhere, is a thing of exquisite comicality to a discerning mind; but really we Spanish-Americans do overstep the bounds."[62]

Indeed, the political intrigues of Conrad's Costaguana would not be out of place in a full-blown comic opera on an actual stage. Decoud's self-deprecating speech brings to mind the German term *Operettenstaat*, which typically invokes a nation, real or imaginary, small in size, whose political life is both absurd and facetious, such as one would encounter in an opéra bouffe, the emphatically humorous genre, or in an operetta, the lighter form of opera that is interspersed with dialogue. The fictional grand duchy of Jacques Offenbach's *La Grande-Duchesse de Gérolstein* (1867) and Pontevedro, the Balkan principality from which some of the characters in Franz Lehár's *Die lustige Witwe* (1905) hail, readily come to mind. Belying the import of the little country beyond its own borders, characters in an *Operettenstaat* might wear ostentatious costumes and uniforms and engage, as characters in Conrad's Costaguana do, in highly theatrical actions. Gérolstein and Pontevedro are of course situated somewhere in Europe, but they hardly represent the whole continent; their Latin American counterparts, in contrast, seem to occupy a more prominent place, if nothing else because fictional works about the region, literary or operatic, are simply less numerous.

In fiction about Latin America, comic-opera theatricality merges at times with the entrenched stereotype of the banana republic, deployed to refer to small countries in Central America and the Caribbean. O. Henry's *Cabbages and Kings* (1904), the series of interrelated short stories in which the term was actually coined, is set in fictional Anchuria, which the narrator describes as a "small, maritime banana republic."[63] The reader learns that Anchuria is hardly unique but one of many comical yet troubled countries—and there are operatic connections. Sarcastically, the narrator states: "The little *opéra-bouffe* nations play at government and intrigue until some day a big, silent gunboat glides into the offing and warns them not to break their toys" (9). One of Anchuria's foreign residents is Doña Isabel Guilbert, "the young American opera singer" (4); another, a man named Felipe, is appointed admiral of a one-boat navy, a newly created rank for which he designs a bizarre costume: "a pitiful semblance of a military uniform—a pair of red trousers, a dingy blue short jacket heavily ornamented with gold braid, and an old fatigue cap that must have been cast away by one of the British soldiers on one of his coasting voyages" (138). There is opulence in Offenbach's Pontevedro, but the natives of Anchuria must conform to a degraded version thereof in their own comic-opera nation. Latin American authors, for their part, have also cited these clichéd images to deplore corruption and abuse, invoking, once again, images of opera. In "La United Fruit Co.," included in *Canto general* (1950), Pablo Neruda, for one, unites banana republics and opera buffa in denouncing imperial and commercial ventures: "United Fruit Inc. / reserved for itself the juiciest, / the central seaboard of my land, / America's sweet waist. / It rebaptized its lands / the 'Banana Republics,' / and upon the slumbering corpses, / upon the restless heroes / who conquered renown, / freedom and flags, / it established the comic opera."[64] But unlike Conrad's and O. Henry's narrators, who chronicle imaginary lands, Neruda's speaker enumerates a series of historical dictators, such as Rafael Trujillo, linking them with flies attracted to both blood and marmalade, a bittersweet image that suggests both comedy and tragedy.[65]

Aspects of such absurd calamities become visible and audible in actual music dramas set in Latin America. Probably best known is Offenbach's *La Périchole* (1868), which is indeed labeled an "opéra bouffe."[66] Set in eighteenth-century Lima, the libretto, by Henri Meilhac and Ludovic Halévy, focuses on the actress Micaela Villegas. Known in Spanish as "la Perricholi," she was the lover of Manuel Amat y Junient, who ruled Peru as viceroy from 1761 to 1776. Georgine Balk attributes the choice of Peru not only to its distance from Europe but also to issues in the larger Spanish Atlantic world, including the French occupation of Mexico and the then-recent breakout of a revolution in Spain, plus the fact that Napoleon III's wife, Eugénie, was Spanish.[67] A clear allusion to the conquest appears in the first act's "Marche indienne," which introduces "L'Espagnol et la jeune Indienne," a ballad sung by La Périchole and her lover, Piquillo, and is, in effect, a story within a story. Meilhac and Halévy's plot does not explicitly chronicle an interethnic romance, but the short ballad, like other works about the Americas, concerns the possible union of a Spaniard and an indigenous woman, framed by conquest and the notion of European supremacy: "Le conquérant dit à la jeune Indienne: / 'Tu vois, Fatma, que je suis ton vainqueur / Mais ma vertu doit respecter la tienne / Et ce respect arrête mon ardeur. / Va dire, enfant, à ta tribu sauvage, / Que l' étranger qui foule ici son sol, / A pour devise 'Abstinence et courage'! / On sait aimer, quand on est Espagnol! ("The victor says to the Indian girl: / 'As you see, Fatma, you are in my power. / But I am virtuous enough to respect your virtue. / And this respect puts a check in my ardour. / Go tell your primitive tribe, my child, / That the foreigner who has made a foothold in their land / Has 'Abstinence and courage' for his motto: / And a Spaniard knows how to love'").[68] As it turns out, the Indian girl falls in love with the conqueror, which leads to the birth of a child, who placidly sleeps under a sunshade and whose parents proudly proclaim, "Il grandira, car il est Espagnol" (34; "He will thrive, for he is a Spaniard"). If one is reminded of Verdi's Don Alvaro's downfall as a result of his mixed-race condition, one cannot but wonder at the ballad's pronouncement. But this is, after all, the realm of opéra bouffe, where nothing, even the unsavory consequences of empire, needs to be taken seriously. Delightful melodies sweeten historical culpability and racial prejudice.

Offenbach's operetta is not about an *Operettenstaat* to the extent that Peru in the eighteenth century was not an independent nation or a small place. Yet the plot of *La Périchole* focuses on the comicality that surrounds absolute power in a location that, despite its geographical vastness, functions like a tiny fiefdom. Don Andrés de Ribeira, the viceroy, forces La Périchole to marry another man so that she can be his mistress without raising suspicion. That this man is Piquillo, whom La Périchole loves, is just happenstance, but it softens the idea of authoritarian rule even as it turn the fictional viceroyalty into a land of amusements. A sense of the comical also ensues as characters act and sing as pairs or groups, mimicking each other: the two notaries, the three cousins, the four ladies-in-waiting. Most effectively, Offenbach's tuneful music, with such famous numbers as the voluptuous "O mon cher amant, je te jure" and the flirtatious "Griserie" (Tipsy), mollifies the story of abuse with the veneer of merriment.

Meilhac and Halévy adapted *La Périchole* from *La Carrosse du Saint-Sacrement* (1829), a one-act play by Prosper Mérimée, and they went on to collaborate on the libretto of Georges Bizet's *Carmen* (1875), also based, of course, on Mérimée's novella. Conceived and presented as an opéra comique, Bizet's plot is set in Andalusia, but Carmen's sensuous "Habanera," as its name indicates, has Cuban roots, which suggests yet another tale of transports across the Atlantic.[69] The musical conflation of Seville and Havana is natural given the powerful cultural and musical ties binding Cuba and Spain, but it also fits the French Romantic vision of the land beyond the Pyrenees as an exotic, not quite European land. A similar merging occurs in *La Périchole* when various Iberian wines—Jerez, Malaga, Madeira, and Alicante—are melodiously inventoried, or when Piquillo calls La Périchole "my lovely Andalusian girl" (41), as if prefiguring Carmen, who, like Offenbach's heroine, could also be derided using Piquillo's words: "the most captivating of women, and at the same time the falsest!" (95).[70] The line cited above, "A Spaniard knows how to love" (33), further signals the semantic fusion of eroticism with Spain and its imperial possessions.[71]

Yet another example of an operetta about comicality and Latin American politics is Kurt Weill's *Der Kuhhandel* (1935), set on an imaginary Caribbean island that, like the real-world Hispaniola, is divided into two republics, Santa Maria and Utqua. When the work was revived by Berlin's Komische Oper in 2013, the company's brochure described it as "Kurt Weills spritzige Operette über die Liebe in einer Bananenrepublik, eine Satire in bester Offenbach-Manier"

(Kurt Weill's lively operetta about love in a banana republic, a satire in the best Offenbach style).[72] Robert Vambery's wonderfully convoluted libretto deploys a series of clichés about the region's history, including an American arms dealer, a corrupt press, a peace-loving president forced into war, an abusive general named Conchaz, and, inevitably, a coup d'état. At the center of it all, two lovers, Juan and Juanita, struggle to stay alive. When the regime confiscates Juan's cow, his livelihood, Juanita decides to become a prostitute. As tragically realistic as it may sound, Santa Maria, like other operetta lands, is an imaginary place where all can end well. In a highly dramatic scene, Juan, refusing to swear loyalty to General Conchaz, slaps him in the face and is arrested. Suddenly, the dictator finds out that the newly purchased weapons are rusty and therefore unusable, and he decides to make peace with neighboring Utqua. Juan avoids execution and is able to marry Juanita.

As Jürgen Schebera explains, the plot of *Der Kuhhandel* resonates with historical events. A few years before the work's composition, Rafael Trujillo had seized power in the Dominican Republic, and an incident in the Chaco War had involved the sale of armaments to both Bolivia and Paraguay.[73] Against this real-world context, beyond operatic clichés redolent of Offenbach, Weill's vivacious music and Vambery's sharp words may be heard and read as powerful indictments of authoritarianism—in Latin America as well as Europe. As Schebera adds, Hitler had risen to power in Germany in 1933, and both Weill and Vambery were émigrés living in Paris at the time. The words of "Juan's Lied" in the second act wittily encapsulate the workings of any oppressive and warmongering state: "Ich habe eine Kuh gehabt, ich hab' die Kuh nicht mehr. Ich hab' dafür Gott helfe mir, jetzt einen Maschinengewehr. . . . Zuhause meine Mutter hat weder Milch noch Butter und leidet große Not. Es gibt da eine Frage noch, die läßt mir keine Ruh. Wer hatte vorher das Maschinengewehr, und wer hast jetzt meine Kuh" ("I once had a cow. I have the cow no more. God help me, I have now a machine-gun. . . . At home my mother has neither milk nor butter and is suffering great need. There is still one question that leaves me no rest: who previously had the machine-gun, and who now has my cow").⁷⁴ Juan's lament may be dismissed as part and parcel of a comical discourse about Latin American political disarray, yet it is also an earnest call for social justice beyond the specificity of any region's borders.

Indeed, to claim an exclusive link between Latin America and the practices of opéra bouffe would be an overstatement. After all, not all comic operas unfold in Latin America, and Offenbach himself, for one, set his many other works elsewhere. *Orphée aux enfers* (1858), the first opéra bouffe, and *La belle Hélène* (1864) parody classical mythology, while *La Grande-Duchesse de Gérolstein* (1867), as mentioned earlier, takes place in a fictional country somewhere in central Europe. There is even a series of opéra bouffes (plus other kinds of operas) set in Europe by Reynaldo Hahn, who was born in Caracas but lived in France for most of his life. His best-known operetta, *Ciboulette* (1923), takes place partly at Les Halles, the old Paris food market, and its drawn-out plot—the love affair between a market woman and a nobleman—situates the work, at least initially, in an emphatically French milieu.⁷⁵ Then again, as Rubén Gallo shows, *Ciboulette* also obliquely concerns Latin America—or at least Hahn's status as a non-French composer and, therefore, an ostensible purveyor of exotic rhythms such as those of Georges Bizet, in which, again, Spanish and Latin American traits appear to merge. When Ciboulette, mimicking Carmen, disguises herself as Conchita Ciboulero, Hahn's music acquires a recognizable southern sound, a transformation that Gallo connects to Hahn's toils in French musical life: "After fifty years composing like a respectable Frenchman, Reynaldo pastiched Spanish music to accompany this character in Latin drag, dressed in mantillas and donning a pair of castanets. If Ciboulette cross-dresses as a Spanish seductress, Reynaldo cross-dresses as composer of boleros."⁷⁶ That Hahn's musical metamorphosis can be read as parody, as Gallo does, confirms nonetheless a lasting connection between opéra bouffe and places like Latin America. As if to commemorate these transatlantic bonds, mezzo-soprano Susan Graham's recording of French operetta includes ten arias—out of a total of seventeen—by either Hahn or Moisés Simons.⁷⁷ Born in Havana and best known for his international hit

"El manisero," Simons lived for a few years in France and was the composer of *Toi, c'est moi* (1934), set in Paris and on Princesse, yet another imaginary Caribbean island.[78]

Despite the prominence of works built on exoticism or comicality, not all depictions of Latin America in European opera fit neatly within those rubrics. A case in point is Hans Werner Henze's *El Cimarrón* (1970), a music drama that retells the story of the runaway slave chronicled in Miguel Barnet's *Biografía de un cimarrón*, to which I return in Chapter 6. Yet another European who turned to Latin American literature for a dramatic story is Peter Eötvös, the Hungarian composer who adapted *Del amor y otros demonios* (1994), Gabriel García Márquez's novel of religion, forbidden passion, and demonic possession in eighteenth-century Cartagena de Indias. Commissioned by the Glyndebourne Festival Opera and BBC Radio 3 and premiered in 2008, Eötvös's *Love and Other Demons* set a libretto by Kornél Hamvai, who underscored the cultural plurality of the Caribbean region. A tetralingual text, the libretto is mostly in English, but it also includes Spanish and Latin as well as Yoruba, the language of the enslaved characters of African descent. While Eötvös praised what he termed García Márquez's "polysemic manner," the opera itself was actually devoid of any facile imitations of the author's magical realism—a fact that some critics regretted.[79] Yet the opera's uprootedness, if one agrees with Andrew Clements, may also emerge as a positive ejection of exoticism and local color. By not magnifying García Márquez's uses of fantasy, *Love and Other Demons* avoided turning into yet another ersatz depiction of bizarre customs.[80]

In the first decades of the twenty-first century, other composers and librettists have looked at Latin American literary culture in search of operatic subjects. Inspired by Jorge Luis Borges's "La biblioteca de Babel" (1941), *Babel* (2011), a chamber opera by the German-Icelandic composer Steingrímur Rohloff and the Danish librettist Morten Søndergaard, was premiered in Copenhagen in 2011. "Una venganza," a short story in Isabel Allende's *Cuentos de Eva Luna*, is the source of Lee Holdridge's *Dulce Rosa* (2013), premiered in Los Angeles and later staged in Montevideo. Aspects of Reinaldo

Arenas's autobiography *Antes que anochezca* (1992) have become the subject of two operas: *Cuba Libre* (2005), by the Chinese composer Cong Su, produced in Erfurt, Germany; and *Before Night Falls* (2010), by Jorge Martín, a Cuban American composer. Martín's opera was staged at the Fort Worth Opera, which also produced Daniel Krozier's *With Blood, with Ink* (2014), on the life of Sor Juana Inés de la Cruz, who is also a character in Louis Andriessen's *Theater of the World* (2016), co-commissioned by the Los Angeles Philharmonic and the Dutch National Opera. Also in Amsterdam, Micha Hamel's *Caruso a Cuba* (2019) featured an Italian-language libretto by the composer that adapted Mayra Montero's *Como un mensajero tuyo* (1998), a novel that freely imagines Caruso's adventures in and near Havana after an explosion during a performance of *Aida*. Straddling oratorio and opera, and drawing on works by Latin American authors from various periods, John Adams composed *El Niño* (2000) and *The Gospel according to the Other Mary* (2012), which transpose the account of Christ's Nativity and Passion, respectively, to Latino communities in Southern California. Commissioned by four major opera companies in Europe and the United States, Thomas Adès's *The Exterminating Angel* (2016) adapts Luis Buñuel's Mexican film *El ángel exterminador*; the work is set in an unnamed Spanish-speaking city. Yet another opera, *Buenos Aires* (2014), a chamber work by the Danish composer Simon Steen-Andersen, while not based on any specific literary text, features scenes of kidnapping and torture that allude to Argentina's history of dictatorship even as it reflects on the nature of music drama. I shall return to Adams's *El Niño* and, briefly, Andriessen's *Theater of the World* in Chapter 7.

Singularly positioned is *El último sueño de Frida y Diego* (2022), premiered at the San Diego Opera and seen soon thereafter at the San Francisco Opera and the Los Angeles Opera. Defying easy national taxonomies, it was composed by Gabriela Lena Frank, born in California of Lithuanian-Jewish and Peruvian-Chinese descent, to a libretto in Spanish by Nilo Cruz, the Cuban American playwright. The story, set on the Día de los Muertos in 1957, focuses on Frida Kahlo's return from the underworld to see her husband, Diego Rivera, once again. Other characters include Leonardo, an actor who impersonates Greta Garbo, as well as Catrina, the guardian of the dead. Because of the diverse background of its creators, its subject matter, and the language in which it was performed, it is possible to view Frank and Cruz's collaboration as a pan-American opera, the rare work that easily spans cultural and political borders.

Consider, last, *Hopscotch*, an opera by six composers and librettists performed in the streets of Los Angeles under the direction of Yuval Sharon.[81] Freely inspired by Julio Cortázar's *Rayuela*, the Latin American Boom classic set in Paris and Buenos Aires, Sharon transposes the text's fabric—or threads thereof—to Los Angeles. Like the novel (if one can call it that), whose readers are authorized by an authorial voice to read its 155 chapters in whichever order they prefer, *Hopscotch* features a nonlinear narrative in which each member of the audience is asked to collaborate in assembling the work's various pieces. It is a story of love and death, which, in a nod to traditional accounts of the birth of opera in Florence, recalls the myth of Orpheus and Euridice, as told by Peri or Monteverdi. The protagonists are a woman named Lucha and a man called Jameson. If his name vaguely implicates Fredric Jameson and the realm of critical theory, hers is explicitly connected to an actual person, as the book-length program distributed at each performance made clear: "*Hopscotch*'s protagonist, Lucha, is named after Lucha Reyes, the Guadalajaran born singer and actress, Reyes is considered the mother of ranchera music, traditionally a single guitarist and a sole singer."[82] While *Rayuela* often focuses on characters as they walk, *Hopscotch* is all about the automobile. Defined as "an opera for twenty-four cars," it was performed at various sites around the city to which audience members were driven in limousines, inside of which the plot also continued to unfold. Depending on the route they were assigned (there were three), spectators would visit various sites in downtown Los Angeles, Chinatown, and Boyle Heights, a predominantly Latino district where a statue of Lucha Reyes happens to be located. Provided occasionally with cameras, the limousine passengers were also instructed to shoot whatever they chose at each scene for the sake of nonpaying spectators watching the opera on numerous screens at a "central hub," thereby contributing to the work's creation and fulfilling Cortázar's authorial call for audience collaboration.[83] Adopting the narrative stance of the text and adapting its spirit to tell the story of an uncommonly resilient Latina protagonist—*lucha* happens to mean "struggle"—in a predominantly Spanish-speaking metropolis, *Hopscotch* is an innovative blend of Latin America and opera. Importantly, just as Cortázar's *Rayuela* reformulates the form of the novel and the concepts of author and reader, Sharon's *Hopscotch* questions a series of cultural axioms and operatic principles: the smug prestige of the traditional opera house; the certitude of characters and plotlines; and even the established limits between different parts of the world, especially Latin America and its others.

Latin American Operas: Empires and the Universe

The first performance of an opera in what is now Latin America took place on December 19, 1701, when Tomás Torrejón y Velasco's *La púrpura de la rosa* was first staged at Lima's viceregal palace to commemorate Philip V's eighteenth birthday. The young king had recently ascended the throne of Spain as the first monarch of the new Bourbon dynasty, and as Louise K. Stein and other musicologists have explained, the composition and performance of the splendid music drama was closely connected to a desire to firm up the new dynasty in the viceroyalty of Peru. For his libretto, Torrejón y Velasco resorted to a play by Pedro Calderón de la Barca on the myth of Venus and Adonis, a subject that may initially strike modern listeners and readers as indisputably foreign to the region. That Torrejón y Velasco had been born in Spain and that the sound of his score was uncompromisingly European, coupled with the fact that he set to music a text by a Spanish playwright who had never set foot in the New World, are other facts that support the view that the inception of opera in Latin America was inextricably bound to the plays and ploys of empire. To complicate matters, the libretto had been previously set to music by another composer, Juan Hidalgo, and first performed in Madrid in 1660 as part of yet another royal commemoration. In its Lima afterlife, Calderón's libretto is preceded by an anonymous loa, or short play, written in Peru that serves as a prologue to the main text. As I discuss in Chapter 3, it is nonetheless possible to see in Calderón's version of the myth—if one reads his words closely—a story that engages in dialogue if not with Peru itself, at least with some of the discourses at the heart of identity-thinking in Latin America, especially those of the baroque and the neobaroque.

A sense of opera's seeming extraterritoriality also tinges the evaluation of other works composed and staged in the region during the eighteenth and nineteenth centuries. Its music now lost, Manuel de Zumaya's *La Partenope* was performed at the viceregal palace in Mexico City on May 1, 1711, or even earlier.[84] Like *La púrpura de la rosa*, the work fulfilled a dynastic function: to commemorate the feast of St. Philip in honor of Philip V. Unlike Torrejón y Velasco, though, Zumaya was born in the Americas and is therefore more naturally at home in what we may now call the corpus of Mexican and Latin American art music. But Zumaya set a text written by an Italian librettist, Silvio Stampiglia, which, as if to assert its impeccable European credentials, was also later employed by George Frideric Handel for his own *Partenope*, performed in London in 1730. As Stein and José Máximo Leza point out, the Mexico City libretto contains a Spanish translation that may have been done by Zumaya himself and employed in the actual performance (248–49). Stevenson notes that *La Partenope* was seen in Mexico City the same year in which Handel staged his first Italian opera in London; in contrast, in eighteenth-century English North America, "nothing so ambitious as a Handel opera was ever attempted, even during his heyday in London."[85] While Zumaya's operatic music remains lost, his work has not been absent from the operatic stage. In 2010, the year of Mexico's bicentennial, Claudio Valdés Kuri, director of Mexico City's Teatro de Ciertos Habitantes, staged a radically new version of Graun's *Montezuma*. In what might be heard as attempt to move beyond the apparent impasse of Eurocentric discourses, the opera ended with a musical piece by Zumaya inserted for the occasion, performed on both sides of the Atlantic Ocean.[86]

Altogether different from Torrejón y Velasco's and Zumaya's works, the case of the Jesuit mission operas written and staged in what is now eastern Bolivia is singularly interesting. Three such works, powerfully concise, are still at least partly preserved: *San Ignacio* (ca. 1720), written in Spanish; *San Francisco Xavier* (ca. 1720–1740), with a libretto in Chiquitano, the language of the Chiquito indigenous people; and *El justo y el pastor*, also in Chiquitano, but extant only in fragments. Scholars have not ascertained the extent to which native musicians actively participated in the creation and performance of these works, but Piotr Nawrot, who has researched and reconstructed this musical corpus, views their authorship as a product of interethnic artistic collaboration. Thematically, the mission operas are clearly part and parcel of the process of Christian evangelization, while their musical structure is devoid of any traits recognizable as native. Yet if one accepts Nawrot's broader argument that the music dramas are distinct from anything composed in Europe, it is not difficult to see how these sacred works belong in the Latin American musical archive more clearly than they do in that of any other operatic tradition. Indeed, the notion of archive resounds quite literally in the case of these works, as the physical preservation and transmission of the scores took place in the very same region—a handful of small, remote villages—where they were created and performed. Devotedly safeguarded by native copyists into the twentieth century, along with hundreds of other compositions in a plethora of musical genres, the mission operas stand as a clear emblem of cultural hybridity at work in an art form often deemed as foreign in Latin America.

After independence in the early nineteenth century, Latin American composers wrote operas whose plots more often than not eschewed national themes and employed librettos in languages other than Spanish or Portuguese. In fact, European operas were staged far more frequently in the region than any local works. In Mexico, to cite one example, Italian operas were routinely performed, yet works by native composers were few, and those that did get written typically lack any obvious traits—musical or literary—that could easily distinguish them from their European counterparts.[87] One such work is Melesio Morales's *Ildegonda* (1866), whose run-of-the-mill, Italian-language libretto, by Temistocle Solera, recounts, in the manner of many European operas of the period, a story set in medieval times—in this case, thirteenth-century Lombardy. As if to heighten these non-Mexican affinities and the ties that bound Latin America to European culture and politics, the work's premiere, at Mexico City's aptly named Gran Teatro Imperial, counted with the patronage of Emperor Maximilian and his consort, Charlotte of Belgium, who had arrived in the city from Europe only in 1864. Yet despite these links, the premiere was also a victory for nationalism; members of the city's Club Filarmónico rowdily interrupted a performance of Verdi's *Un ballo in maschera* to demand the staging of Morales's work, which the impresario Annibale Biacchi, an Italian, had vetoed by claiming that a work by a Mexican composer constituted a financial risk.[88]

It might be tempting simply to dismiss *Ildegonda* as an opera that has little or nothing to say about Mexico. Yet the foreign materials in the work's fabric, plus the fact that it was also performed in Florence in 1869, make *Ildegonda*, as Anna Ochs argues, a valuable text for analyzing the project to fashion Mexico as an essentially European nation.[89] That a Mexican composer could write an opera on an Italian subject, and that the work could be staged in Italy itself, the birthplace of opera, was reportedly cheered by some as a veritable national triumph. As Ramón Pulido Granata recounts it, *Ildegonda* was a great success at its Florence premiere, and shouts of "¡Viva México; viva Juárez!" resounded in the theater.[90] That Benito Juárez, Maximilian's opponent and a man of indigenous descent, should have been hailed during a performance in Italy of an Italian-language opera by a Mexican composer sponsored by a foreign-born monarch is surely a sign of the competing affects surrounding nationalism and opera in Latin America. On the one hand, the art form exemplifies the prestige and, indeed, supremacy of Europe over the region even after independence. On the other, to master opera by staging it, or even contributing to its repertory, enhances a nation's sense of progress and modernity—its real or potential standing as the equal of Europe but also, notwithstanding those transatlantic bonds, its relative autonomy.[91]

One Mexican work, though, explicitly connected with the nation's history is Aniceto Ortega del Villar's *Guatimotzín* (1871), first performed at Mexico City's Gran Teatro Nacional, as the Gran Teatro Imperial was called following the restoration of republican governance. The opera is yet another setting of the Spanish conquest, but Ortega del Villar's version, with a libretto by José Tomás de Cuéllar, differs from those of European composers like Vivaldi or Graun by focusing not on Moctezuma but on Cuauhtémoc, who succeeded Cuitláhuac, Moctezuma's younger brother, as Mexica ruler. Viewed as a hero for leading an insurrection against Cortés, Cuauhtémoc emerges in Ortega del Villar's opera as a brave figure of resistance. In its contestation of the Spanish conquest, *Guatimotzín* resembles Pasta's *Atahualpa*, likewise composed in the 1870s. The nationalist viewpoint is also powerfully supported by the fact that Ortega del Villar, unlike Pasta, employed Mexican melodies in his score. As Stevenson notes, the rhythm of *tzotzopizahuac*, a native dance, is used in the music associated with Hernán Cortés's Tlaxcalan allies; the opera was such a success that Ortega del Villar was hailed as Mexico's Glinka.[92] But as Malena Kuss explains, the musical nativism of the "Danza tlaxcalteca" is expressed through "Mexico's regional folklore of Ibero-American roots" and not, as one might expect, through its Amerindian traditions.[93] Oddly, the work was praised both for its magnificent depiction of Mexican history, a judgment resonant with Algarotti's musings about operas on the conquest, and for its purported historical accuracy.[94] Thus, Ortega appears to merge the best of both worlds: an imposing spectacle as was customary in European operas, but also the sense of cultural autonomy befitting a country that was certainly not a mere offspring of Europe.

Although the series of ravishing Italian operas staged in Mexico after independence stands out for their "very foreignness" (288), as Nancy Vogeley would have it, a work like *Guatimozín* tells a more complicated story of transports in which music itself plays a specifically local role. Examining, again, the contrapuntal combination of a European waltz and the *tzotzopizahuac*, Kuss notes how this "national substance" is limited to a dance number and does not truly advance the drama. Yet, she adds, the composer nevertheless "inaugurates the possibility of a national opera": "While being himself in a language which is foreign, Ortega is also himself in a language which is native. . . . The delicious juxtaposition of foreign and native is not Italian, it is Mexican."[95] Kuss's point is well taken, as it foregrounds Ortega del Villar's originality, if not his "authenticity," while bringing out the story of *mestizaje* at the heart of the region's cultural history. Then again, as compelling as the concept of *mestizaje* may be, it is not all there is in Latin America, nor should it be described uncritically as the touchstone of regional creativity in the arts. As one looks at the many operas crafted in the region since the nineteenth century to the present, it becomes clear that the inclusion of "nativistic," to use Kuss's term, or otherwise "national" musical or verbal elements has not been deemed essential by many composers. In fact, almost a century and a half after Ortega del Villar's innovative work, it can be argued that Latin American operas very often lack any self-evident literary or musical signs of nation or region. In this, composers, unwittingly or not, embrace Borges's famous argument about universality in "El escritor argentino y la tradición," seen in Chapter 1.

Also since the early 1870s, albeit intermittently and without becoming firmly or permanently established in the international repertory, a few Latin American composers have left their imprint not only on their national stages but also on those of Europe and, more recently, the United States. The most celebrated case is no doubt that of Antonio Carlos Gomes, whose works achieved great success throughout Italy and much of the world in the last third of the nineteenth century. Although his first opera, *A noite do castelo* (1861), set to music a Lusophone text based on a Portuguese novel, Gomes employed Italian-language librettos and followed the musical and theatrical conventions of Italian operas. Indeed, as Durval Cesetti recalls, Gomes "could be facetiously nicknamed 'the greatest Brazilian composer of Italian opera.'"[96] As for *Il guarany*, Gomes's signature opera, Duval asks: "is it merely an entertainment intentionally designed to please both Italians (with its exoticism) and Brazilians (with its Italian flavor)?"[97] Far more complex than Cesetti's witty, insightful remarks would suggest, Gomes's eight well-constructed and musically powerful operas constitute a distinguished chapter in the history of Latin American opera. Five of Gomes's operas are set in Europe and one, *Condor* (1891), in Samarkand, but two of them, *Il guarany* and *Lo schiavo,* unfold in Gomes's birthplace and resound with discourses on race and nationhood, including the aesthetic uses of *indianismo*, in Brazilian literature of the time.[98]

Based on José de Alencar's canonical novel *O guarani* (1857), set around Rio de Janeiro in 1560, *Il guarany* (1870) garnered much praise at La Scala upon its premiere, including, as the legend would have it, from none other than Verdi, who reportedly said, "Questo giovane comincia da dove finisco io!" (This young man is taking up where I let off!).[99] Nowadays, the work's overture—the "Protofonia"—is often described as Brazil's second national anthem. Like other European operas about the Americas, or like Verdi and Ghislanzoni's exoticist *Aida*—to which Gomes's work, staged a few months earlier, is often compared—*Il guarany* also focuses on an interracial romance, but in this case, the two lovers do not hail from far-flung and alien lands, like Aida and Radamès. Much closer to Gomes's Brazil in space if not in time, Cecilia is the daughter of a Portuguese nobleman, Antonio de Mariz, while Peri is the son a Guarani chieftain. The couple, then, appears to stand for two of the three predominant ethnic groups—people of indigenous and European, but not African, descent—in Brazil's ethnic makeup at the time. Although two Portuguese men are in love with Cecilia, it is Peri whom she cares for. In the opera's last scene, Peri renounces his own gods and is baptized as a Christian by Don Antonio himself. Just before a terrible explosion that causes much death and destruction, the two young lovers manage to escape to Rio de Janeiro, heralding in their conjectural union an ethnically mixed future, perhaps, for the Brazilian nation.[100]

Jorge Coli describes the opera's euphoric first night at Rio de Janeiro's Teatro Lírico Fluminense in December 1870, just months after the Milan premiere. Despite, again, the work's indebtedness to Italian opera and its foreign-language libretto, the audience, which included Emperor Pedro II, exploded in "ovações delirantes" (delirious ovations) as the curtain fell.[101] The singers were costumed as Indians and sang in Italian against an exotic backdrop, but as Coli explains, audiences self-identified with a work based on a Brazilian novel. As Maria Alice Volpe argues, *Il guarany* resounded with Brazilian spectators not because of its "exoticist appeal," which swayed audiences in such distant sites as Moscow and St. Petersburg, nor as a patriotic response to the esteem in which it was held abroad, but rather because Gomes's work was the rare operatic expression of the narratives of national identity fostered by the "official culture" of the Brazilian Second Empire.[102] Accusations of foreignness aimed at the opera—so Italian, so strange—can arguably be tempered by the resoluteness with which Gomes took up and developed a subject meaningful to Brazilian and, by extension, other Latin American audiences. More than a century later, the symbolic import of *Il guarany* was underwritten yet again when it inaugurated Plácido Domingo's general directorship of the Washington National Opera in 1996—a production staged by Werner Herzog.[103]

The treatment of race is hardly predictable in Gomes's operas. One wonders also about the absence of characters of African descent in his other best-known work, *Lo schiavo* (1888), whose protagonist is actually an indigenous man, seemingly obfuscating the long history of black slavery in the nation. The original story—the outline for a libretto, in Portuguese, by Alfredo d'Escragnolle Taunay, a Brazilian author—featured a black slave, but the actual Italian text by Rodolfo Paravicini, which Gomes ended up setting, transformed the enslaved man into an indigenous character to conform to the "scenic necessities" of Italian opera, as Gerard Béhague notes.[104] In a telling gesture, Gomes dedicated the opera to Princess Isabel, who, as regent, had recently signed the Lei Áurea, which proclaimed the abolition of slavery in Brazil on May 13, 1888. As I discuss in Chapter 6, the composer's words in the dedication suggest that the opera, along with Gomes's orchestral music, ought to be interpreted in the context of that momentous event in the nation's history. Moreover, Gomes's acknowledgment of Brazil's African roots is audible in his use of the *batuque* rhythm in the "Dansa dos Tamoios" in the second act; the orchestra's use of native instruments is, as Kuss notes, the only nationalist musical reference in the composer's operas.[105]

Gomes's European-themed operas, whose musical scores and librettos eschew any signs of Brazil, are further examples of transatlantic collaboration. Ghislanzoni, who, as mentioned earlier, had written the words for Verdi's *Aida* and would do the same for Pasta's *Atahualpa*, also crafted the libretto for Gomes's *Fosca* (1873), a tale of pirates set in medieval Istria and Venice, and that of *Salvator Rosa* (1874), which chronicles the baroque painter's role in an insurrection against Spanish Habsburg rule in Naples.[106] Considered by some to be Gomes's masterpiece, *Fosca* suffers from a conventional plot, but it is a musically ingenious work in which the composer deploys practices learned from Wagner, such as the leitmotif. Although the opera was still created under Verdi's clout, Gomes nonetheless proved himself to be much more than just a brilliant imitator of Italian formulas.[107] In Brazil, his achievements are sometimes regarded as a story of lost opportunities and thwarted modernity, with a vast array of culprits such as conservative audiences, who initially disregarded Wagner, and Maria Teresa, the empress consort, who had meddled in Emperor Pedro II's wish that the young Gomes study in Germany.[108] Nonetheless, the composer's vigorous oeuvre—its Italian triumphs, stature in Brazil, and occasional revivals in other parts of the world—remains virtually unparalleled in Latin American operatic history to this day.

The intertwined issues of exoticism, nationalism, and modernity, all so clear in Gomes's oeuvre, are evident also in other countries beyond Brazil. Writing on the idea of national opera in Argentina, including the larger context of opera as a global commodity, Gonzalo Aguilar underscores the concept of synchronicity—the notion that, despite what might be expected, cultural forms sometimes do arrive and develop in peripheral regions such as Latin America at the same time as in places reputed to be the world's art centers. For Aguilar, this is the case of Arturo Berutti's *Pampa*, first performed at Buenos Aires's Teatro de la Ópera in 1897. Three of Berutti's operas had been staged in Milan and Turin, including *Evangelina* (1893), based on Longfellow's poem, and *Tarass Bulba* (1895), adapted from the novel by Gogol. *Pampa*, his first work set in his native country, is often regarded as Argentina's first national opera because of its subject matter, the tale of a gaucho named Juan Moreira, who is in turn the eponymous hero of a novel and play by Eduardo Gutiérrez. That the libretto, by Guido Borra, was written in Italian and rendered the name of Juan Moreira as Giovanni Moreira was not an impediment to the work's positive reception by many Argentine operagoers. As Aguilar describes it, the premiere of *Pampa* was a momentous occasion. Members of the Buenos Aires elite, including two former presidents, were in the audience, and the press reviewed the work extensively and passionately. Yet even though Berutti received numerous curtain calls after each performance, aspects of the opera struck the wrong note, such as Borra's words for an aria sung by a *payador*, the revered creator of popular gaucho poetry: "Era un giorno una donzella / Graziossima e gentil; / Era fresca ed era bella / Come rosa dell'April" (Once upon a time, there was a very pretty and gentle maiden; she was as fresh and beautiful as a rose in April).[109] If the allusion to the Northern Hemisphere's spring could be excused on the ground that the opera might one day be performed in Europe, the overall view of *Pampa* as an Argentine work was negative, as Aguilar notes: "The spectators discovered that the national, once brought to the opera, was transformed into an unbearable exoticism."[110] If Gomes's nods to the conventions of Italian opera were not a barrier to the enthusiastic reception of his works in Brazil, the same cannot be said of Berutti's attempt to write an Argentine opera.[111]

Nonetheless, despite its questionable status as an Argentine opera, *Pampa* succeeded at being readily perceived as a sign of modernity—an eminently contemporary work. As Aguilar recounts, less than a year after its 1890 premiere in Rome, Pietro Mascagni's *Cavalleria rusticana* had made its way to Buenos Aires, where it was staged in February 1891. Mascagni's work introduced the new aesthetics of operatic *verismo*, which sought to infuse the art of opera with the lessons of literary naturalism, to what was arguably Latin America's most sophisticated operatic audience. Mindful of these new practices, Berutti was able to achieve a sense of synchronicity with European opera by crafting *Pampa* as a work that could also be regarded as *verista*. Like some of the best-known operas of the new school, the plot of *Pampa* unfolded in a rural setting, which also fit Berutti's plan for creating a national opera for Argentina, at least in theory. As Aguilar notes, the opera was a successful fusion: "*Verismo* permitted the composer to respond to various demands: to the modernizing demands for synchronization with the new styles coming out of Europe, to the demands of the national elite with their fervent *criollismo*, and the metropolitan demands that assigned a place of privilege to particularities in the new *verismo* style" (89). Though not widely seen as an altogether credible national work, *Pampa* invoked a kind of operatic modernity such as Gomes had previously achieved, if only temporarily, in his own transatlantic practice of opera.[112]

Besides the works by prominent composers inventoried thus far, many more operas were certainly written across the region; in some countries, in fact, the number of locally composed works was not insubstantial. In the course of the twentieth century, opera composition was abundant in Argentina; at the new Teatro Colón alone, Kuss identifies forty-seven works by twenty-eight Argentine composers premiered between the first season in 1908 through the 1970s—and she calculates that, until around 1980, some two hundred operas were composed in Buenos Aires and other parts of the country.[113] These operas make up an impressively diverse corpus, as Kuss's scholarship on Argentine opera also shows. Carlos López Buchardo's *Il sogno di Alma* (1914), for instance, has an Italian-language libretto and a dreamlike plotline featuring a queen, a prince, peasants, a forest, and a castle; but the very popular *El matrero* (1929), by Felipe Boero, deploys the nativist diction of gauchesque poetry, plus some fragments in Guarani at the onset of the third act.[114] Kuss also refers to Luiz Heitor Corrêa de Azevedo's 1938 catalog, which lists ninety-seven operas by Brazilian composers, as well Robert Stevenson's research, which accounts for nineteen operas by thirteen composers written in Mexico by the early twentieth century.[115] In a study of Mexican opera published in 2002, Octavio Sosa lists 197 titles, starting with Zumaya's now-lost *La Partenope* and including such diverse works as Gustavo Río Escalante's *Xtabay*, described as a Maya opera and performed in Mérida in 1924, and Julio Estrada's *Pedro Páramo*, an "ópera radiofónica" (radio opera).[116] The composition of opera has been long sustained in Cuba, a smaller country, where Jorge Antonio González records numerous foreign- and native-born composers writing new works.[117] These operas range from Giovanni Battista Bottesini's *Colón en Cuba* (1848), whose libretto by Ramón de Palma dramatizes the indigenous people's submission to Columbus upon his landfall in 1492, to Héctor Angulo's *Ibeyi Añá* (1969), a chamber opera based on one of Lydia Cabrera's *Cuentos negros de Cuba*. Whether these various works have a theatrical future remains an open question, but there are signs of renewed vitality for reviving at least part of the region's little-known operatic legacy. In 2022, for instance, Chile's Colectivo de Ópera Nacional sponsored a concert that Gonzalo Cuadra, a scholar and musician, described as the first gala performance of Chilean opera ever. Broadcast online, it showcased arias from operas composed between 1898 and the present. Drawing on multiple literary sources and historical episodes set in Chile and elsewhere, the featured operas employed librettos in Spanish, Italian, and even German, revealing, yet again, the rich, if understudied, transatlantic dialogue of Latin America's operatic culture.[118]

Around the mid-twentieth century, several Latin American opera composers, in a flourish of cosmopolitanism, began again to be heard in Europe and, for the first time, the United States as well. One such case is Argentina's Juan José Castro. His *Proserpina e lo straniero* won the Verdi Prize in a competition whose jury was presided by Stravinsky, made it to La Scala in 1952, and was revived as *Proserpina y el extranjero* at the Colón in 1960. Setting a libretto by Omar del Carlo rendered in Italian by Eugenio Montale, Castro adapted the myth of Persephone by transposing it to a brothel in the outskirts of Buenos Aires. The music, as Kuss explains, included "motivic material characterizing conceptual abstractions" as well as "elements from the urban popular tradition" heard in Marfa's milonga in the first act.[119]

While the United States emerged as a welcoming location, it was nonetheless a complicated musical scene for the writing and staging of Latin American operas. Carol A. Hess analyzes the careers of the composers sometimes grouped together as the Big Three of Latin American art music: Mexico's Carlos Chávez, Brazil's Heitor Villa-Lobos, and Argentina's Alberto Ginastera.[120] They all wrote for the operatic stage and did so for at least some period of time in New York and other American cities, even as they led active careers in their native countries. But as Hess argues, each of them had to find his own way to fulfill the task of writing musical works—not just operas—variously heard as "different" or "universal," or something in between, in the context of Pan-Americanism and the Cold War. Carlos Chávez, for instance, composed an opera on a libretto by the highly esteemed Chester Kallman inspired by a tale from Boccaccio's *Decameron*; emphatically cosmopolitan, *Panfilo and Laureatta* was first staged in New York in 1957. He later revised the opera, employing librettos in English and Spanish and renaming it *Love Propitiated* (1959) and *El amor propiciado* (1963)—and yet again, as *Los visitantes* (1968) and *The Visitors* (1973).[121] As Stevenson explains, Chávez belonged to a social class that "regarded opera as a Mexican composer's highest aspiration," which may explain the persistent revisions of the work for over twenty years.[122]

Some of Heitor Villa-Lobos's operatic works, too, had hemispheric projections. Even if, as Lisa M. Peppercorn argues, Villa-Lobos did not value the musical stage, he did complete four rather heterogeneous works.[123] Two of these were first performed at Rio de Janeiro's Teatro Municipal: *Izaht*, the Puccini-like melodrama of a gypsy girl who works for a gangster band in Paris and falls in love with an aristocrat (1958); and *A menina das nuvens* (1960), a fairy tale about a young girl taken by birds to live in the clouds.[124] A third work was premiered in Los Angeles in 1947: *Magdalena*, a collaboration with George Forrest and Robert Wright, who wrote the words and drew on various musical pieces by Villa-Lobos. Set along the eponymous river in Colombia, the work has been described as an operetta but also, by Hess, as an "American musical."[125] But Villa-Lobos's best-known stage work is arguably *Yerma*, with a libretto by the composer himself that follows almost verbatim the text of Federico García Lorca's play. Commissioned by the Department of Drama at Sarah Lawrence College, the work was supposed to have set an English-language libretto by Alastair Read and Hugh Ross, who taught at the college, but Villa-Lobos, who did not know English, opted for García Lorca's original text instead. Staged only posthumously in 1971 by the Santa Fe Opera, the work attracted a large audience from various countries because of its double status, in Ross's words, "as one of the only Spanish operas and a South American work as well."[126]

In the twentieth century, Alberto Ginastera is no doubt the Latin American opera composer whose international fame most closely approximates that of Gomes decades earlier. Despite the radical modernity of his musical idiom, Ginastera's three operas treat European historical themes in a fashion that recalls the repertoire of grand opera; as Gilbert Chase and Lionel Salter put it, "Penderecki may hover in the pit, but the spirit of Verdi watches in the wings."[127] Reversing the transatlantic journey of European operas set in the New World, the Argentine composer extracted his own operatic hyphen- plot-lines from medieval Spain and Renaissance Italy. The highly literary librettos he employed were the work of distinguished authors.

All three of Ginastera's operas have an illustrious, albeit intermittent and at times thorny, performance history. Set in eight-century Toledo just before the Muslim invasion of the Iberian Peninsula, *Don Rodrigo* (1964) set to music a libretto by Alejandro Casona, the Spanish playwright. Originally performed at the Teatro Colón, it enjoyed a celebrated North American premiere two years later, when it inaugurated the New York State Theater at Lincoln Center with a young Plácido Domingo in the title role. Far more controversial—in Argentina, at least—was *Bomarzo* (1967), a tragic story of lovelessness and cruelty chronicling the life of Pier Francesco Orsini, the Italian nobleman who built the Parco dei Mostri in Bomarzo, near Viterbo, in the sixteenth century. The opera was based on a historical novel (1962) by Manuel Mujica Lainez, who also wrote the libretto. After its premiere by the Opera Society of Washington in 1966 and another staging in 1967 by the New York City Opera, *Bomarzo* was banned in Argentina; the country's president, with the support of the archbishop of Buenos Aires and other public figures, declared its content obscene. Informed by psychoanalytic discourse, the plot openly engages with sexuality, containing, as Hess puts it, "cross-dressing, parental abuse, poisoning, at least one humiliating encounter with a prostitute, various occult ceremonies, an orgy, and the hint of a homosexual relationship with a mute slave, Adul."[128] Yet as a New York critic remarked, if some in the audience came to the opera "licking their lips," *Bomarzo* was "small time compared to . . . *Lulu* or *Il Trovatore*, for that matter."[129] Nonetheless, as Esteban Buch argues in a book devoted to the so-called Bomarzo affair (as the US embassy in Buenos Aires branded the events in a confidential communiqué), the act of censorship led to the rise of *Bomarzo* as a cause célèbre, even after its belated staging at the Colón in 1972.[130] Disavowing his troubles in Argentina and signaling his lofty status as a world-class composer, Ginastera's third opera, *Beatrix Cenci* (1971), with a libretto by Alberto Girri and the Scottish-Argentine author William Shand, had a highly visible premiere in the United States; also set in sixteenth-century Italy, it was the first opera staged at Washington's Kennedy Center for the Performing Arts.

The question nonetheless emerges whether any of these mid-twentieth-century works, written in diverse musical styles and treating a variety of subjects, succeeded in creating a recognizable Latin American operatic tradition. Does the international status of these composers match that of poets and fiction writers in the region, such as Borges and Pablo Neruda, to name just two, who came to world prominence in the mid-twentieth century? Is there anything in opera akin to the narrative fiction of the Latin American Boom in the 1960s and 1970s? An anecdote might shed some light on at least one composer's international aspirations. Writing about Villa-Lobos, Peppercorn refers to an "extraordinary news-item" in a Brazilian publication that preceded the staging of *A menina das nuvens* in Rio de Janeiro in 1960. Probably generated by Villa-Lobos himself, the story matters not for its veracity (it appears to have none), but as an extreme, if sardonic, instance of one Latin American composer's desire for opera fame in "far-off horizons": "For this year's season the Metropolitan Opera House of New York commissioned an opera by Villa-Lobos who invited the writer Lucia Benedetti to write the libretto. *A Menina das Nuvens*—a work by two Brazilians—will have as female interpreter the Italian soprano Renata Tebaldi. The authors will receive US$ 500.000 from the Metropolitan without prejudicing their authors' performing rights. Maestro Villa-Lobos will rehearse and conduct his opera. Likewise La Scala in Milan, the Operas in Paris, Berlin and London will include in their season this year *A Menina das Nuvens*" (179). Nothing of the sort ever materialized for the charming opera; its transatlantic transports, mixed with the notion of monetary gain and the name of a revered soprano, were just the figment of somebody's imagination.[131]

Even for Ginastera, a lasting position in the international repertory has also eluded his works. An article by William Robin in the *New York Times* in 2016, the centennial of the composer's birth, retrieved his lofty standing in the original review of *Don Rodrigo*—"an audience that contained seemingly everybody in New York music, philanthropy and society"—only to focus on efforts by various institutions to salvage his works.[132] Although there was a new production of *Beatrix Cenci* at the Colón in 2016 and one of *Bomarzo* at Madrid's Teatro Real in 2017, directed by Pierre Audi and co-commissioned with the Dutch National Opera, the fact remains that Ginastera's operas, like those of many twentieth-century composers, remain at least for now premature rarities of sorts.

While Ginastera's plots shun Argentina and his scores deploy a diverse range of modern practices not readily associated with Latin America, works by other composers feature stories and musical idioms more easily seen and heard as local or regional. One such work is *María de Buenos Aires* (1968), by Astor Piazzolla, who set a libretto by Horacio Ferrer. Labeled by its creators as *tango operita*—which might be rendered as a tango that is also a little opera—the work remains difficult to classify. Bernardo Illari, for one, resists facile readings that view *María de Buenos Aires* as a history of tango or María as an allegory of the city, underscoring that it is an "operita en tango," a little opera played in tango, a musical form conscious of both its legacy and its renewability in a modern city like

Buenos Aires in the 1960s.[133] Despite its uncertain status as opera, the work remains popular as part of operatic seasons around the world. Predictably, opera companies typically focus on the composer's ability to showcase his native country even as directors refashion it according to their own views of Argentina. Staging the work for the Long Beach Opera in 2012, Andreas Mitisek linked Piazzola's music with the Dirty War of the late 1970s and early 1980s, the violent period in which the production was set: "Taking the tango to its most brutal extreme, the 'Dirty War' was a dance of torture, covered in blood, and danced by the highest echelons of society and power."[134] If Mitisek's emphasis on violence risks typecasting Latin America, it also turns the work into a tool for expounding on aspects of the region's political history.

Other experiments in music drama variously show and shun the specificity of Latin America. Mauricio Kagel, the Argentine composer who spent much of his career in Germany, crafted audacious stage works that, while pushing the genre's limits, may still be described as operas. The best known of these works is probably *Staatstheater* (1967–1970), commissioned by the Hamburg Staatsoper. A radical and humorous creation, it seeks to dismantle operatic conventions by reducing the plot to brief interactions of players with objects on the stage. Eight of its nine sections, like chapters in Julio Cortázar's *Rayuela*, may be performed in whichever order is preferred. Yet another work, *Mare nostrum* (1973–1975, and revised in 1997), first staged in Berlin, boasts a long subtitle that reveals the comical postcolonial thrust of its story: "Entdeckung, Befriedung und Konversion des Mittelmeerraumes durch einem Stamm aus Amazonien" (Discovery, Pacification, and Conversion of the Mediterranean Region by a Tribe from Amazonia). The subject of *Mare nostrum* is indeed the reverse "discovery" of Europe by the Americas, which allows spectators, arguably, to regard it as a Latin American work. In fact, its playful inversion of Columbus's voyage is also an ironical reflection on the long European tradition of operas about the conquest of the so-called New World. As David Sawer explains, Kagel offers in *Mare nostrum* (as well as in *Kantrimiusik*, which deals with folk music) "a personal commentary on misrepresentation and mishearing."[135] But even outside these thematic and ideological signs, the fact remains that Kagel's status as an Argentine (or Argentine German) composer should ensure the possible evaluation of all his works as elements in the cultural history of his native country and region—regardless of how his forms and themes might depart from what is normally regarded as Latin American. After all, to work in Europe and employ librettos written in languages other than Spanish and Portuguese on subjects that have little or nothing to do with Latin America was what Carlos Gomes, for one, did. Obviously, Gomes and Kagel composed their music dramas in different theatrical cultures; postmodern practices are radically distinct from the conventions of La Scala in the nineteenth century. But it may well be argued that Kagel's German-language scripts—in *Aus Deutschland* (1981), subtitled *Lieder-Oper*—mirror the Italian-language librettos that Gomes set to music a century earlier. John Cage once comically asserted that the best European composer was an Argentine named Kagel—a paradoxical statement that nonetheless underwrites the complicated ties that bind the cultures of the Atlantic world.[136]

In the global practice of opera, the United States remains a central site for Latin American composers, who, not infrequently, are called upon to create new works expected to mirror the exotic region to the south. The most successful of these is Daniel Catán's *Florencia en el Amazonas* (1996), which, as if taking cues from *Fitzcarraldo*, tells the story of a Latin American soprano who journeys by steamboat to the mythical opera house in Manaus. Premiered at the Houston Grand Opera as the first commission from a Mexican composer by a major American opera company, the work has been revived numerous times in both Europe and the Americas, signaling a lasting presence in the international repertory. (I return to *Florencia en el Amazonas* and other operas by Catán in Chapter 7.) In the United States, the growing visibility of Latin America in works by Catán and other composers, either native or born elsewhere, is intrinsically linked to migration and demographic changes. Two recent operas with connections to the region's history are Osvaldo Golijov's *Ainadámar*, originally created for the Tanglewood Music

Festival in 2003, and Jimmy López's *Bel Canto*, premiered at the Lyric Opera of Chicago in 2015. Although substantially different, both works exemplify the notion that opera in the United States is an art form that takes into account the nation's multicultural fabric, including creators and audiences with Latin American roots. Aware of its local and hemispheric neighbors, both works appear to argue tacitly that those engaged in the enterprise of opera must listen to and speak for the growing cultural plurality of the United States.

Born in Argentina of Eastern European descent, Golijov is an immigrant, and his librettist for *Ainadámar*, the Asian American playwright David Henry Hwang, is yet another creator familiar with stories of geographic displacements like the events chronicled in the opera. That Golijov translated Hwang's English-language text into Spanish, the language in which *Ainadámar* is performed, is yet another episode in opera's history of transcultural passages. In 2000, before writing *Ainadámar*, Golijov had achieved much critical success with *La Pasión según San Marcos* in Germany and elsewhere. One of four oratorios commissioned by the Internationale Bachakademie Stuttgart to mark the 250th anniversary of Bach's death, Golijov's *Pasión*, which some have also viewed as an opera, joyously deployed Latin American and Caribbean rhythms and dances (among other kinds of music) in a powerful permutation of a genre typically perceived as European. Against this background of musical and theatrical innovation, *Ainadámar* emerged as a milestone in Golijov's development as a Latin American composer of global import.

Set on both sides of the Atlantic, the opera chronicles the murder of Federico García Lorca at a place called Ainadámar, near Granada, in 1936. The story, told partly through flashbacks, also concerns the death of Margarita Xirgu, the famed Catalan actress who had often worked with García Lorca, just before a performance of the playwright's *Mariana Pineda* at Montevideo's Teatro Solís in 1969. Golijov's score was critically praised for its artful reworking of Spanish and Latin American music: an alluring instance of cultural convergences beyond the well-trodden history of war and conquest that had attracted previous composers. As Yayoi Everett explains, the score of *Ainadámar* evokes the music of three civilizations—Christian, Muslim, and Jewish—and is full of references to flamenco even as it incorporates "lighter song forms" such as the Cuban rumba.[137] After its Tanglewood premiere, Golijov's *Ainadámar* was revised for Santa Fe Opera in 2005. The new production, revived at Madrid's Teatro Real in 2012, was staged by Peter Sellars, who used paintings by Gronk, the Chicano artist from Los Angeles, for the sets. At the end of the show, Sellars opened up the back of the stage so that the audience could see the adjoining Plaza de Isabel II—a theatrical gesture that meant not only the opening of the self-enclosed realm of opera to the city but also the public announcement of the arrival of an opera from the Americas in the midst of a European capital.[138] That the work tells the story of a dead Andalusian poet as recalled by a Catalan actor in Montevideo, and is set to music by an Argentine composer of Eastern European descent working in the United States with a libretto written by an Asian American author, complicates and enriches the traditional routes of opera. Vivaldi had "journeyed" to Mexico to bring the story of Moctezuma to Europe, but cosmopolitan Golijov re-creates García Lorca in the multicultural Americas and sails with him "back" to the so-called Old World.

Indeed, partly because it is the work of Hwang, the libretto of *Ainadámar* signals the resolutely non-European status of the work—and, more broadly, of opera at the turn of the twenty-first century. In *M. Butterfly* (1988), the playwright had laid out an incisive argument against operatic discourses that misuse other cultures, exemplified by *Madama Butterfly*. That Hwang and Golijov would collaborate on an opera of their own that treats the life of García Lorca and Xirgu simply as that of an artist, outside the parameters of ethnic clichés and expectations, is both a change of heart and a declaration of independence. This notion of opera as a global form and practice is also at play in the various other librettos that Hwang has written, most notably the text of *Alice in Wonderland*, by Unsuk Chin, the Berlin-based Korean composer, which premiered at Munich's Bayerische Staatsoper in 2007 under the baton of Kent Nagano, the Asian American conductor. As they move literally and figuratively from one part of the planet to another, artists such as

Golijov, Hwang, Chin, and Nagano make opera speak and sing for various parts of the world beyond Europe.[139]

The story of Jimmy López's *Bel Canto* is to a great extent the work of Latin Americans. An immigrant from Peru, López set to music a libretto by Nilo Cruz, the Pulitzer Prize–winning Cuban American playwright, who in turn based his multilingual text on the bestselling novel by Ann Patchett (2001). The original story takes place during a hostage crisis at an embassy in a nameless Latin American capital city that sounds like Lima: "Father Arguedas explained to Gen, who explained to Mr. Hosokawa, that what they were looking at in the hours they spent staring at the window was called *garúa*, which was more than mist and less than drizzle and hung woolly and gray over the city in which they were now compelled to stay."[140] The opera, by contrast, redefines the setting explicitly as Peru. Against the interchangeability of spaces in works about Latin America, López foregrounds the historical and political concreteness of his own native country. As he stated in an online guide to the opera, López remembered the actual hostage crisis and wanted to introduce "a dose of history" in the opera version—"to throw in a phrase here and there, suggesting what's going on in the negotiations, or . . . the interests of each character. We have a lot of little hints that complement the story, for anyone interested in . . . further research, they will understand those references."[141] Cruz, in turn, crafted a libretto parts of which were not in English, but in Spanish, French, Japanese, Russian, Italian, German, Latin, and Quechua. This linguistic plurality, which reflects the national and ethnic origins of the characters held at the embassy, surpasses the three or four languages in the librettos of Sessions's *Montezuma* or Eötvös's *Love and Other Demons*, and it also suggests an all-encompassing approach to the global ambitions of opera. Giusti's libretto for Vivaldi's *Motezuma* was assertively monolingual, whereas Cruz's text boldly takes into account the planet's rich linguistic diversity.[142]

Even a random survey of other operas written by composers linked with Latin America since the 1990s reveals a rich multiplicity of musical styles, subjects, and even technologies. As in the past, some operas adapt literary works by the region's authors, including texts by Jorge Luis Borges, often associated with a kind of cosmopolitanism free of the local color that opera has typically favored. Based on Borges's "El milagro secreto" and staged at Karlsruhe's Zentrum für Kunst und Medientechnologie, *Los enemigos* (1997) is a chamber opera by Mesías Maiguashca, an Ecuadorean living in Germany. Composers also adapt texts from other parts of the world. Such is the case of Tania León, the Cuban American composer of *Scourge of Hyacinths* (1994), based on a radio play by Nigeria's Wole Soyinka and originally commissioned as a chamber opera for the Munich Biennale; a longer version, staged by Robert Wilson, was first performed at the Grand Théâtre de Genève in 1999.[143] Aspects of Afro-Cuban culture inspired *Ebbó* (1998), a chamber opera oratorio by Louis Aguirre, a Cuban who lives in Denmark; an online production was created in 2021 by Yelaine Rodríguez, a Dominican American artist. Yet other works are prompted by historical or current events, including natural disasters. León herself is writing an opera about racial integration at Central High School in Little Rock, Arkansas, and Sebastián Errázuriz's *Viento blanco* (2008), performed at Santiago de Chile's Teatro Municipal, chronicles the tragic deaths of forty-five soldiers caught in a blizzard in the Andes in 2005.[144] Errázuriz also composed *Patagonia* (2022), coproduced by the Teatro Biobío and the Teatro del Lago in southern Chile, and focusing on the first encounter between the Aónikenk indigenous people and Magellan's crew. Gabriela Ortiz's *Únicamente la verdad* (2010), first staged at Indiana University and Mexico City and reprised as *Camila la tejana—Only the Truth* at Long Beach Opera, is a video opera about the semilegendary heroine of a popular *narcocorrido*. Also related to violence in Mexico is Marcela Rodríguez's *Bola negra: El musical de Ciudad Juárez* (2013), with a libretto by the composer and Mario Bellatin, the fiction writer, who also performed as an actor at the opera's premiere at Guanajuato's Festival Internacional Cervantino. Setting a libretto by the American filmmaker Charles Koppelman and staged in Havana, Roberto Valera's *Cubanacán, revolución de las formas* (2015) chronicles the architect Ricardo Porro's design of the nation's new art schools after the revolution; Fidel Castro and Che Guevara share the scene as they play golf. An example of transatlantic collaboration is *Stefan and Lotte in Paradise* (2012), by Marcos Lucas and Alan Edward Williams, composers from Brazil and Britain, respectively. Staged at the University of Salford, in England, it considers the deaths by suicide of Stefan Zweig and his wife, Charlotte Altmann, in Petrópolis, near Rio de Janeiro, where they had sought refuge from Nazism. Also inspired by a literary figure whose life unfolded on both sides of the Atlantic, Martín Bauer and Beatriz Sarlo's *V.O.*, which I discuss in Chapter 8, is a chamber opera about Victoria Ocampo.

Like a specter, Herzog's *Fitzcarraldo* returns again as a seemingly indelible sign of Latin America's convergence with opera. But this time the jungle's operatic resonances are crafted by the region's own creators. First performed in Buenos Aires at the Centro de Experimentación del Teatro Colón in 2014, *Hércules en el Matto Grosso*, with music by Esteban Insinger and libretto by Pola Oloixarac, revisits the Brazilian wilderness in yet another expedition by Europeans: Hercules Florence, the French Brazilian photography pioneer; and the Baron von Langsdorff, the German Russian naturalist and diplomat. Written mostly in Portuguese, but also in German and Quechua, the libretto chronicles the journeys of both men as they confront anacondas, tropical fevers, and madness. Against this indomitable natural world, Florence's experimentation with the reproduction of images, which he terms *photographia*, transforms the cultural history and depictions of the region. Regardless of whether *Hércules en el Matto Grosso* or any of these other new operas becomes a lasting work in the operatic repertoire, the diverse nature of these compositions is a sign of opera's vitality in Latin America.

3 Words by Calderón de la Barca

A Baroque Libretto in Lima

AT THE TURN of the twenty-first century, when compact discs were a popular object of consumption, an opera lover browsing through new arrivals at a record shop might have been surprised by a title showcased as "the first opera in the New World" (fig. 1). Judging from the words on the CD's cover, the work, surely a rarity, held the promise of an undiscovered soundscape: "Sung to the lively rhythms of South American dances, with a colorful Spanish continuo-band of harp, guitars and percussion." Perhaps most enticing—or most exotic—was the featured image: a landscape of giant leaves; a half-hidden black ape; a starfish-like object shining in the sky like a sun; and in the foreground, two dark-skinned women, both nude—one of them recumbent, her companion gently caressing her. As it turns out, the picture is a close, though not exact, reproduction of Frida Kahlo's painting *Two Nudes in a Forest*, also known as *The Earth Itself* or *My Nanny and I*. One might wonder what a modern image by Kahlo has to do with Tomás de Torrejón y Velasco's *La púrpura de la rosa*, indeed the first opera ever performed in the Americas, in Lima in 1701. Curiously absent from the CD's cover are the names of the composer and his librettist, Pedro Calderón de la Barca. Both men are consigned to the back, as if Kahlo's nameless visual signature were all that was necessary to assert

FIGURE 1. *CD cover for Tomás de Torrejón y Velasco's La púrpura de la rosa,* Deutsche Harmonia Mundi, 1999.

the opera's New World credentials—its difference, its provenance from an Elsewhere, as Ralph P. Locke would have it. The passion-filled image, along with few wisely chosen catchphrases, might suffice to sell the work as an outlandish commodity to the most jaded global listener of opera searching for new transports.

Kahlo, of course, is a Latin American icon, and one can easily imagine why Deutsche Harmonia Mundi, the German label that produced the recording in 1999, would have chosen an image by her to lure browsers and sell as many CD sets as possible, which is, after all, what record labels do.[1] Yet the choice of Kahlo—and in particular, this oil painting on metal displaying the two nude women in the jungle—implies a story larger than marketing. Torrejón y Velasco's opera recounts the myth of Venus and Adonis, and Kahlo's imagination matches the erotic intensity of the old classical myth, one in which nature too plays a prominent role. That Kahlo's two figures are women speaks obliquely, unwittingly, to the fact that female singers, following Spanish operatic conventions, perform the lovers' roles in the opera. That these figures have dark-skinned bodies may be seen a sign of opera's rebirth in a new land, a part of the world in which the idea of *mestizaje* has been at the center of much thinking about identity. Albeit anachronistic and, arguably, clichéd, Kahlo's image may well be, then, a valuable first key for listening to this opera more than three centuries after its composition. If not "Latin American" in the strict sense, Torrejón y Velasco and Calderón's work remains the inaugural work in the operatic history of what we now call Latin America; listeners, readers, spectators, and even promoters might be excused if, seduced by natural or manufactured signs of the region, they choose to go even further and regard *La púrpura de la rosa* as a Latin American work.

From a purely musical standpoint, Kahlo should not be needed to sell the opera. As Robert Stevenson, who first edited the manuscript score in 1971, asserts, the work is "no mere historical curiosity" but rather "an artistic accomplishment of the first water."[2] Yet as others have argued, the Latin American connection is not unproblematic. This first example of European music drama across the Atlantic Ocean is first and foremost an act of transplantation in which the new land—the new landscape—is mostly a background. Like Octavio Paz, who speaks of "a transplanted literature" to describe the connections between the works of Sor Juana Inés de la Cruz and Spanish baroque poetical practices, Louise K. Stein similarly invokes a botanical analogy to describe Torrejón y Velasco's creation: "Opera in its Hispanic guise thus arrived in the New World in the same way that many other 'innovations' had before it. It was a European implantation. If Spaniards in the New World believed that the 'only civilized diet was the European one,' Calderón's text of *La púrpura de la rosa*, a well-worn symbol of Spanish dynastic celebration, was like an Old World crop planted suddenly in a foreign landscape to provide the Spanish and criollo elites at the viceregal court with European cultural nutrition."[3]

In an essay written for yet another recording of the opera (by the label K617), Bernardo Illari underscores the work's extraterritoriality, deploying a taxonomical gesture that questions its connection with Peru. While Torrejón y Velasco's score may have been written in Lima, Illari points out that the music is not Peruvian and laments that Peru itself has been carefully erased from it: "una ausencia que está dolorosamente presente" (an absence that is painfully present).[4] Illari's rhetoric is factual; as Stein and other musicologists have shown, the music follows the nascent Spanish operatic practices of the seventeenth century.[5] The composer himself, who was chapel master of Lima's cathedral, had been born in Spain, whereas the libretto is by one of Spain's eminent early modern playwrights. To complicate matters, Calderón's words had previously been set to music (now lost) a few decades earlier by another Spanish composer, Juan Hidalgo, in Madrid.[6] Yet as my analysis of the libretto seeks to show, I am persuaded that one may also read, regard, and rethink the opera's mythological spectacle, despite its apparent foreignness, as a full-blown element in the culture of colonial Spanish America—indeed, as a Latin American work as much at home (or not) in the region as, say, Sor Juana Inés de la Cruz's sonnets, closely modeled on those of Luis de Góngora and other Spanish baroque poets, or even the works linked with the Latin American neobaroque of the twentieth century.[7]

A focus on the words of Calderón's libretto, I argue, reveals a baroque sensibility commonplace in what we now call Latin America; even as the libretto looks back at the literature of Spain, it may be seen, if only through the transformative power of reading, as concerning the future as well. I am interested in the permutation that takes place when we read the libretto not simply as serving Torrejón y Velasco's music but as "an erratic player," as David J. Levin, cited earlier, would have it.[8] The meaning of Calderón's words shift when placed in literary contexts resolutely connected with the Latin American baroque. Specifically, some keys may be found in the rich verbal corpus crafted by authors such as Alejo Carpentier, José Lezama Lima, and Severo Sarduy, in which baroque artifice, recast as the neobaroque, emerges as a site of cultural hybridity, often viewed as a Latin American response to, and contestation of, imperial power. Writing about Lezama Lima, the Cuban neobaroque author who coined the term *contraconquista* (counterconquest) to describe how artists in Latin America adopt and adapt the European baroque as a "retort to the colonizers," Lois Parkinson Zamora and Monika Kaup bring up what one could call the temporal flights of this "New World Baroque"—its capacity to retrieve older works and tease out their hybridity for readers removed from the period when they were created.[9] Parkinson Zamora and Kaup underscore the baroque's transcultural time travels: "Most twentieth-century theories of the New World Baroque celebrate cultural *mestizaje* and artistic resistance to colonizing norms, thus reclaiming histories and traditions and refashioning them for present use. The capacity of the Baroque to overarch contradictions and include oppositions has made it particularly useful for theorizing the hybridity of Latin American cultural products."[10] The notion that the past can be remodeled from, and for, other historical periods is particularly relevant for thinking about opera, whose librettos acquire new meanings when theatrically re-created for new audiences situated elsewhere in time and space. (In fact, librettos, often set in earlier historical periods, may themselves creatively reconstruct the past without any directorial input.)

Importantly, Calderón's verbal intricacy, with its focus on convoluted birth and incompleteness, suggests a more nuanced and productive manner for thinking about cultural products in the Americas than exclusionary classifications would allow. Having died in Madrid in 1681 without ever traversing the Atlantic, Calderón is of course an unwitting player in this story of opera's origins in Latin America.[11] Yet the playwright's afterlife as a librettist in viceregal Lima concerns not only the journeys of Spanish cultural forms to a new land but also their potential resignification, beyond imperial hierarchies, as new cultural contexts with different horizons of expectation emerge. Like other forms of music and drama, opera is reborn with every new performance of a whole work and—why not?—every new reading of the libretto as one listens to a recording.[12] Reinterpreting Calderón's words in the new transatlantic world it now inhabits allows for the recasting of Torrejón y Velasco's soundscape as a rich and resonant, if vexatious, Latin American creation.

Rereading Calderón's inaugural text also provides a key for analyzing yet another form of music drama that flourished in viceregal South America: the "Jesuit" operas, written by anonymous composers and performed for and by the indigenous peoples of what is now eastern Bolivia. Like *La púrpura de la rosa,* these mission operas—*San Ignacio* and *San Francisco Xavier* are the only two fully extant works—can also be read fruitfully through the lens crafted by the discourses on baroque aesthetics in the New World. Mixing messages, the operas take into account the native cultures—for instance, by using Chiquitano, an indigenous language, in the libretto of *San Francisco Xavier*—even as they seek to beguile native audiences into the confines of a Christian imperial system.[13] On the cover of the K617 recording, *San Ignacio* is tantalizingly described as "L'Opéra perdu des missions Jésuites de l'Amazonie" ("the lost opera of the Jesuit missions of Amazonia"), an archaeological find that, like *La púrpura de la rosa*, is also available for listeners around the world. Writing in the CD's booklet, Illari shies away this time from any pronouncement of foreignness, labeling the work "un opéra de l'altérité" (an opera of alterity).[14] Indeed, there is much that bespeaks otherness in the short music drama, not the least its composition and performance in a remote jungle location. But the cover's chosen toponym, *Amazonia*, conjures up the ghost of Herzog's Fitzcarraldo and his mythical opera house, yet another citation of the cinematic story that defines for some the extravagant convergence of Latin America and opera. Yet these works, despite their initial outlandishness, exemplify the long reach of European cultural forms outside of their native continent—very far, in fact, from Florence, the purported birthplace of opera, and Prato, hometown of Domenico Zipoli, the Jesuit composer who may have collaborated in the creation of *San Ignacio*.[15] In Bolivia, the vibrant afterlife of the mission operas, part of a vast corpus of other works composed in the region, is closely linked now to the Festival Internacional de Música Renacentista y Barroca Americana, which, along with recordings, plays a vital role in preserving this musical corpus.[16]

As we saw in Chapter 2, stories of colonial Peru are not infrequent in eighteenth- and nineteenth-century European operas. It is the setting for one of the four acts in Rameau's *Les Indes galantes* as well as for Verdi's *Alzira,* Pasta's *Atahualpa,* and Offenbach's *La Périchole*; it is also the homeland of Don Alvaro in Verdi's *La forza del destino.* Peru is also briefly mentioned in Lorenzo Da Ponte's libretto for Mozart's *Così fan tutte* (1790). As the first act comes to a riotous end, Dorabella and Fiordiligi, worried because their lovers, Ferrando and Guglielmo, have suddenly fainted, welcome Despina, who pretends to be a physician; grateful for the doctor's ministrations, the sisters lovingly sing together: "Ah, questo medico vale un Perù" ("Ah, this doctor is worth a fortune").[17] Peru's mineral wealth was proverbial, but in Da Ponte's text, the toponym almost unnoticeably becomes associated with a sense of the miraculous (the lovers are cured), invoking as well a measure of dramatic irony: Despina, Ferrando, and Guglielmo, as well as the audience, all know the fainting and healing are a farce. But what is Peru's worth in the global circulation of opera? What can Peru be exchanged for? What can *La púrpura de la rosa* contribute to the real and metaphoric value of Peru in opera? And what role, really, can a painting by Frida Kahlo, who is not even Peruvian, play in all this?

At the Viceregal Palace: Two Worlds

Opera's arrival in what we now call Latin America in 1701 was a belated affair. Well over a century had passed since the genre's purported birth in Italy at the turn of the seventeenth century. By that time, other European cultural forms, including genres related to opera such as drama and certain forms of musical theater, had already traversed the ocean and established themselves in the New World.[18] When opera finally arrived, its official advent was singularly polished and triumphant. Held at the viceregal palace in Lima, the first performance of *La púrpura de la rosa* was planned as a grand spectacle, as befit its royal connections. The first setting of Calderón's libretto to music by Juan Hidalgo, performed at Madrid's Palacio del Buen Retiro in 1660, had been part of the festivities marking the betrothal of the Infanta María Teresa, daughter of Spain's Philip IV, to Louis XIV of France.[19] In 1680, Hidalgo's opera was revived to celebrate yet another royal wedding, that of Charles II and Marie Louise d'Orléans. Forty-one years after Hidalgo's composition, the creation of Torrejón y Velasco's new setting of *La púrpura de la rosa* in an important, if far-flung, city of the Spanish Empire could be seen as a magnificent victory of European cultural forms—or, less benevolently, as an emblem of imperial authority over another part of the world whose native cultures survived the conquest, but were violently transformed. Besides its royal lineage, the work explicitly proclaimed its adherence not to the land where it was staged but to the Spanish crown and its proxies in a city that had been founded by Francisco Pizarro in 1535 and named the Ciudad de los Reyes. Those kings were the New Testament figures commemorated on the feast of the Epiphany (the city's foundation was decreed on January 6), but given Lima's prominent status in the political and ecclesiastical hierarchies of empire, one is tempted to conflate the biblical monarchs with the absolutist crowns of Europe ruling over the land.

The viceroy, Melchor Portocarrero Lasso de la Vega, Conde de Monclova, decided to stage *La púrpura de la rosa* to celebrate the eighteenth birthday of a new king, Philip V, as well as the dawn of the Bourbon dynasty in Spain.[20] The first words in the opera's manuscript, preserved at Lima's Biblioteca Nacional, declare these regal bonds in solemnly authoritative language. They are cited and translated in the Deutsche Harmonia Mundi recording of the opera: "Musical drama, fiesta with which the most excellent Count of Monclova, Viceroy, Governor, and Captain General of the Kingdoms of Peru, Tierra Firme, and Chile, celebrated the eighteenth birthday of our King Philip V, & composed in music by Don Tomás Torrejón de Velasco, Chapelmaster of the Holy Cathedral of the City of Kings, in the Year 1701."[21] This title page was obviously not written by Calderón, but it functions as an imposing paratext, a verbal key that, placed before the old libretto, virtually determines the opera's reception as a tool of empire—a vast geographical domain, for, as the reader is explicitly reminded, it encompassed three "kingdoms" and extended all the way south to remote Chile.

The work of Lima's *La púrpura de la rosa* as imperial spectacle is further declared and reinforced by the anonymous loa, or short play, written explicitly for this occasion and performed before

Calderón's text.²² In its one scene, astronomy and mythology merge symbolically in praise of the Spanish monarchy. The slight plot revolves around the birth of a new planet, Mars, announced in highly baroque language powerfully sung by a chorus: "De la esfera luciente / del fuego, los rayos / dorados, anuncios / del sol, sin incendios / que abrasan, alumbran / el día que nace / el planeta mayor" (46; "From the shining sphere / of fire, the golden rays / heralds of the sun, / without fires that burn, / light the day on / which the greatest planet is born"). Mars, the fifth planet and also the powerful god of war, stands as a symbol of Philip V, the new monarch. If Spain was an empire over which the sun did not set, the new dynasty would shine on with luminous power. El Tiempo (Time), an allegorical figure, cryptically alludes to a new light and life that can be seen in the skies: "Ya el Tiempo a tu duda ofrece, / clara luz que incierta vio / antes que fuese una vida / término a su esplendor" (46; "Now Time offers your doubts / a clear light, yet uncertain, that he saw / even before a new life / was the cause of its new splendour" 46). Upon learning of the bright birth of Mars, the muses Calliope and Terpsichore enter the stage, followed by Urania, who wonders about the nature and meaning of this sudden apparition in her celestial dominion. The chorus describes the presence of Mars, "de dos mundos superior" (46; "ruler of two worlds" 46), while yet another allegorical figure, España, relates the new planet to the new king, extolling the rise of the new dynasty: "La siempre invencible España / la corona le ofreció, / porque a su obediencia diese / quilates su obligación" (46; "Ever invincible Spain / offered him the crown, / so that her obedience will yield / carats to her obligation" 46). The loa soon concludes with the proclamation of Philip's greatness by the chorus, which enthusiastically sings several times the phrases, "¡Viva, Felipe, viva! ¡Viva el sucesor!" (46; "Long live Philip! Long live the successor!" 46). As Stein and others have argued, the loa makes it clear that the conflicts of succession are now over, and that a new dynasty is firmly enthroned.²³

But one can tease out other readings from this scene. Despite its brevity, the loa also includes two consequential, if brief, allusions to the imperial territories where the work is staged. Predictably, the chorus casts the empire as the new monarch's loyal servant and source of fame: "puesto a sus plantas, / seguro afianza / su eterno blasón" (46; "placed at his feet / loyally assures / his eternal glory" 46). Straightforwardly, it also asserts that Philip was born in another part of the world, to the east of Peru: "¡Viva Felipo, / y su nombre aclame / el clarín de la fama veloz, / por invencible, / por justo y benigno, / desde el oriente / de su formación!" (46; "Long live Philip! / and may the trumpet / of speedy Fame acclaim / his name as invincible, / just, and kind, / from the Eastern hemisphere / of his birth!" 46). These words may sound like stock phrases deployed on official occasions, yet in this intensely baroque realm, the loa's sung words hold other potential meanings as they publicly and explicitly remark on Philip's birth on the other side of the Atlantic—on a continent to the east of Peru. Like the sun, the new king, appearing in the guise of a new planet, is a radiant entity, but "el oriente"—not just an astronomical reference or an etymological link with the temporal concept of birth—marks Peru's geographical distance from Spain and perhaps obliquely the existence of a separate and distinct cultural makeup. We do not know who the author of the loa was, but the fact that it must have been written in Peru offers the tantalizing possibility of reading its imagery, at least tentatively, as a proclamation of an incipient cultural autonomy.

The implications of the loa for the libretto's potential reception in Latin America are in fact long-reaching. By the turn of the eighteenth century, authors from both Peru and the viceroyalty of New Spain—the Inca Garcilaso de la Vega (living in Spain) and Sor Juana Inés de la Cruz and Carlos de Sigüenza y Góngora in Mexico City, but others as well—had expressed and praised the cultural specificity of the countries in which they were born. In contrast, what is at work in this opera is less direct or concrete, but potentially just as powerful. Though written by a Spanish playwright long dead, the libretto may be newly interpreted by heeding the loa's prompt in its discourse about two worlds. This reading would disclose the libretto's inadvertent chronicle of its own rebirth—or partial birth, as I will argue—in Peru. If Mars, as the loa's chorus powerfully sings, is the ruler of two worlds, one must at least wonder what, beyond mere physical distance, may distinguish one such world from the other—or, for that matter, Torrejón y Velasco's Lima-specific setting of Calderón from Hidalgo's in Madrid. To consider *La púrpura de la rosa* as a fortuitous Latin American work, as I propose here, may be dismissed as anachrony—a willful act of reading. But my critical gesture takes into account the view that the work of opera is never finished. Each new reading or staging of a dramatic text can foreground meanings that may not have been obvious to the original audience but that have always been there and may crystallize, as it were, with the passage of time.

Indeed, these reimaginings of the old work from a belated standpoint may well constitute yet another kind of transport—a temporal movement—beyond the importation of a cultural product or the rapture it may trigger. The libretto, muted into insignificance, as it often happens in opera, by brilliant and overpowering music, can be read and reread from another period to retrieve a series of latent meanings. Indeed, Calderón, or his ghostly avatar in Lima, speaks to some of the core issues in the continent's cultural history, especially the relation of the arts to European forms, the workings and uses of baroque aesthetics, and the privileged status of hybridity. If this first opera may be read, and then heard and reheard, as an important element in the cultural histories of Peru and Latin America, it is due not to any explicit act of subversion in the score or libretto but to the fact that spectators and listeners can sense in its rich verbal fabric and mythological plot a potential story of transculturation. Despite the odds, the entity we now call Latin America resounds through the words. Uncannily, Peru, too, becomes audible. The strangeness of Calderón's libretto performs its own oblique tale of rebirth, whereby *La púrpura de la rosa* becomes not just "the first opera performed in the New World," as Deutsche Harmonia Mundi would have it, but an opera responsive to the discourses that now function as cultural cornerstones for Latin America.

Reading and viewing European seventeenth-century works intemporally through the discursive prisms of the baroque and neobaroque in Latin American culture is not unprecedented. In her study of Caravaggio and Latino artists in the United States, Mieke

Bal posits that, after viewing the baroque visuality of Ana Mendieta and Rafael Serrano, one cannot behold the Italian baroque master with the same eyes. Bal prefaces her introduction to *Quoting Caravaggio* with a citation from T. S. Eliot's "Tradition and the Individual Talent" (1919): "Whoever has approved this idea of order . . . will not find it preposterous that the past should be altered by the present as much as the present is directed by the past."[24] Bal's critical gesture, then, is not merely anachronistic, but, as she would have it, also preposterous—an audacious convergence of both "pre" and "post." Writing on a work by Ken Aptekar that copies fragments from a seventeenth-century piece, she explains her approach: "Such revisions of baroque art neither collapse past and present, as in an ill-conceived presentism, nor objectify the past and bring it within our grasp, as in a problematic positivist historicism. They do, however, demonstrate a possible way of dealing with 'the past today.' This reversal, which puts what came chronologically first ('pre-') as an aftereffect behind ('post') its later recycling, is what I would call a *preposterous history*. In other ways, it is a way of 'doing history' that carries productive uncertainties and illuminating highlights—a vision of how to re-vision the Baroque" (6–7). One can speculate about the reactions of those men and women who attended the opera's first performance in viceregal Lima. Similarly, one can also imagine the expectations of other listeners or spectators for whom *La púrpura de la rosa* may emerge belatedly as a work not only crafted in Latin America but also more richly meaningful if read within the region's rich cultural history.

But how can one make the emphatically European notes and verses of *La púrpura de la rosa* sound and read as part of this locally grounded archive? Cultural contexts, scholarly discourses and musical practices matter. One may, for instance, eschew rigid prescriptions of what identity, community, or nation ought to be. In fact, musicologists have tended to avoid narrow labels, describing the opera broadly as an important milestone in the musical history of the "New World" or as a major landmark within a Hispanic—not simply Spanish—musical and dramatic tradition that flourished on both sides of the Atlantic. Instead of calling it either Peruvian or Spanish, Stevenson views it as part and parcel of two interlinked developments: "seventeenth-century Spanish musical spectacle" and the "origins of the Peruvian lyric stage."[25] Likewise, Stein underwrites its location in both hemispheres, describing it as a "natively Hispanic opera," distinct from the Italian operatic tradition that would eventually prevail in Spain, and stressing how "perhaps, its extraordinary lyricism, strikingly panconsonant harmony, and overtly seductive rhythms sing of a Hispanic identity."[26] Importantly, Stein, who also served as the DHM recording's artistic adviser and dramaturge, brings up the role that transatlantic musical practices had to play in the work's creation: "In Lima in 1701, it would have been impossible to perform the opera without the skilled leadership of local musicians whose performances were traditionally based in improvisation. Europeans who traveled to the New World commented especially on the magnificent improvisations of the local players."[27] In this, Torrejón y Velasco's Lima may correspond to what Geoffrey Baker calls "the resounding city," a counterpart to Ángel Rama's lettered city. Animated by musical performance and thus surpassing Rama's logocentrism, this auditory formulation of the city includes not only Europeans and their descendants but indigenous and African musicians as well. Like other scholars who underscore colonial hybridity, Baker links the resounding city's ethnic expansiveness to the practices of the baroque.[28]

Contemporary musicians, too, tend to accept the view of *La púrpura de la rosa* as the product of two worlds. The conductor Andrew Lawrence-King, who also contributes an essay to the Deutsche Harmonia Mundi booklet, stresses the local: "Torrejón's setting calls for only two male singers, and he entirely avoids the italianate *stile recitativo*. Instead, the poetry is declaimed in strophic songs over a colourful Spanish continuo-accompaniment of harp, guitars and percussion, with choruses sung to the lively rhythms of South American dances."[29] The K617 recording, which contains the essay by Illari in which he laments the opera's purported deletion of Peru, also features an interview with the conductor Gabriel Garrido in which he is asked a precise question regarding the first performance of the work: "Did the integrated Indians as well as the Spanish settlers take part in the production of our opera?"[30] Without needing to provide any concrete evidence, Garrido responds quite simply, "Yes," thereby recasting the performance, if not the work itself, as a hybrid affair in a mestizo city.[31] He then embarks on a protracted journey through several centuries of musical creation and performance in both Spain and colonial Spanish America in which the baroque propels transatlantic exchanges even as it fosters a supranational community and, in his words, "the idea of blending" as well as "the force of symbiosis."[32] Although neither Lawrence-King nor Garrido mention hybridity (or transculturation) explicitly, it is clear that both artists view *La púrpura de la rosa* as a work in which the cultural plurality of the New World can, or ought to, be heard. Interestingly, when the University of Sheffield staged the opera in 2003 under Lawrence-King's musical direction—in effect, the work's British premiere—it counted with the support of both the Peruvian and Spanish embassies in London.[33]

But let's read Calderón's words. Beyond the acknowledgment by musicologists and musicians of a semishared transatlantic musical culture, a key for interpreting *La púrpura de la rosa* as a Latin American creation may be found, as I said, in the uncanny texture of Calderón's words, heard or read after the Peruvian loa. For Stein, the viceroy's choice of this libretto to celebrate the accession of the first Bourbon king to the Spanish throne at a time of war makes political sense because of its use in an "earlier royal and pro-French associations, as well as its pacifist message."[34] But if the act of reviving in South America a text written for the court in Madrid may seem a nostalgic embrace of mid-seventeenth century Spain, the plot and language of *La púrpura de la rosa* also concern the future of Latin American culture as well—or, more accurately, the act of thinking about culture in Latin America.

Speculatively, in the eyes and ears of some of those original spectators of 1701, the story unfolding onstage must have seemed to come from another world, and in some measure, it did: another palace, in faraway Spain; another royal celebration; the archives of classical mythology. Had we been there, we would have seen and heard Venus chasing a wild beast, and young Adonis rescuing her from danger, and the goddess's four loving nymphs, and then Mars, Bellona, and the child Amor, as well as one soldier, one villager, and two comic rustics, plus various allegorical figures named Envidia (Envy), Temor (Fear), Sospecha (Suspicion), and Ira (Anger), who guard the grotto where Desengaño (Disillusion), an old man with a name redolent of Spanish baroque discourses, spends his days. Moving from forest to garden to dark grotto, the players act and sing a story that hardly conforms to the codes of dramatic realism. But this is not surprising in opera; after all, song, rather than speech, already contradicts what normally happens in real life. In this mythological spectacle, song was emitted mostly by female actors singing at a very high vocal range, and this included the ultravirile roles of Mars and the soldier.

The score, in the tradition of seventeenth-century musical drama, featured a lament, as one encounters in the operas of Monteverdi.[35] Upon discovering the dead body of Adonis among some flowers, Venus addresses her plaintive words to Mars, and as the myth prescribes it, the story ends with the young lover's metamorphosis into a dazzling rose tinted with his blood. But Calderón's highly erotic version has a joyful ending. As Amor tells us, Jupiter wants the two lovers to be reunited forever as stars: "De esa derramada sangre / quiere que una flor se forme, / y que de aquella se vistan / roja púrpura las flores, / para que en tierra y en cielo / estrella, y flor, se coloquen: / a cuya causa, subiendo / donde entrambos se coronen, / verás que, desde este día, / con la nueva luz de Adonis, / sale la estrella de Venus / al tiempo que el sol se pone" (106; "From this spilled blood [Jupiter] wishes to create a flower, and from it as well, the flowers would be dressed in blood-red, so that on earth and in the heavens star and flower might be placed together; and so they ascend to where they are crowned together, and you will see that, from this day, with the new light of Adonis, the star of Venus comes forth just as the sun sets" 106). The work fails to revive ancient Greek tragedy, as Florentine humanists had sought to do more than a century earlier; instead, as traditional (if incomplete) accounts of the birth of opera would have it, they invented a new art form. But Calderón's libretto nevertheless embraces the classical world, ascertaining the enduring power of myth and, arguably, giving it new meanings to generate the birth of Latin American opera.

Like other dramas by Calderón, *La púrpura de la rosa* has an enigmatic title, labyrinthine syntax, and brilliantly difficult images; the whole text is loaded with baroque artifice. This, as I mentioned earlier, is hardly foreign to the practice of writing in New Spain and Peru. Sor Juana's writings deploy the conventions of the Spanish baroque, but a poem like "Primero sueño" or a play like *Los empeños de una casa* is typically read as part of Latin American literature. Other works by Sor Juana, such as the loa for *El divino Narciso*, even thematize the cultural repercussions of the conquest by resorting to baroque literary conventions. The case of *La púrpura de la rosa* is different. Neither Calderón not Torrejón y Velasco, as we saw, were natives of the New World (although the composer spent most of his life in Peru). Moreover, the genre of opera, seldom performed in colonial times, cannot easily be regarded as part of any sustained artistic tradition in colonial Latin America—a generic isolation that may be seen as an impediment to inserting the opera into the discourse about cultural continuity in the region. Further, Calderón's libretto complicates the well-entrenched idea of national or regional communities as homogeneous, or at least coherent, spaces. Then again, images in Calderón's dramas suggest a contrary view of the matter—a new potentiality. Nations like Peru, or regions like Latin America, may yet emerge as baroque realms branded by conflict, difficulty, elusiveness, and even absence—a vacancy of sorts, arguably, but a latently powerful condition that the various arts, through their ever-changing array of significations, endlessly reformulate and replenish.

Calderón's text easily seduces readers through the poetic vigor of its words, especially after the loa's homespun diction.[36] Consider, for instance, Adonis's speech to Venus in the opera's first scene. Having saved her life, but wary of her beauty and status as the mother of dangerous Amor, Adonis attempts to flee. But before he can do so, Venus demands to know who he is. In an aria of sorts,

Adonis sings about his own birth and parents and what he perceives to be his star-crossed future in matters of love:

> Quien de aborrecido hijo
> tan desde luego nació
> de sus padres, que aún en ellos
> no supo qué era afición.
> Mirra mi madre lo diga,
> pues apenas me engendró
> cuando, en odio del concepto,
> hurto de amante traición,
> su mismo padre mi vida,
> y su vida abandonó,
> tanto, que la dio la muerte;
> cuya mísera aflicción
> en sus últimos alientos
> los dioses compadeció,
> convirtiéndola en un árbol,
> de cuyo llorado humor,
> guardando el nombre de Mirra,
> nací bastardo embrión,
> maldecido de mis padres,
> y con tan gran maldición
> como que de amor muera.
> Considere tu atención,
> si en mi horóscopo primero
> aborto de un tronco soy,
> si después llevo tras mí
> el heredado temor
> de que de amor muera, puedo
> no aborrecer el amor. (52)

> He who was born such a hated son
> even by his parents
> that even in them
> he did not know affection.

Myrrah my mother could tell you,
since hardly was I engendered, when
in hatred of the very act of my conception
(the spoils of loving treachery),
her own father abandoned
my life and hers,
so utterly that he killed her.
Her miserable affliction was such
that in her last gasps
the gods took pity on her
transforming her into a tree,
from whose weeping moisture,
preserving the name of myrrh,
I was born a bastard embryo,
cursed by my own parents,
and with a heavy curse to the effect
that I should die of love.
Consider carefully your attention,
for if in my natal horoscope
I am the aborted offspring of a tree,
and if later I carry with me,
the inherited terror
that I should die from love,
I cannot but hate love. (52)

Adonis goes on to explain his decision to abandon contact with others and embrace solitude in the mountains. The offspring of a troubled liaison, he fears a beautiful being like Venus more than he does any wild animal: he risks falling in love with her, which is, of course, what happens. In his own eyes, Adonis is almost a beast. As he admits to Venus, anyone who sees him hunting in the wild has trouble deciding whether he is "la caza, o el cazador" ("the prey or the hunter"). Despite his bodily perfection, which has seduced a goddess, Adonis's story underwrites his wildness and strangeness. He may be, as one of the nymphs puts it to Mars, "un bello, airoso, galán garzón" (56; "a beautiful, fleet, and gallant young man"

56), but as Venus herself states, he is also a "montaraz adalid" (66; "uncouth chief, born of the hills" 66).

Beyond the allure of these opulent verses, Adonis's halfway condition between human and a lesser form of being—an entity seemingly in the making, as is so common in Calderón's dramas—resounds with critical approaches to the baroque in Hispanic letters. Consider Roberto González Echevarría's insightful linkage of the hybrid and the monstrous in *La vida es sueño*. In his argument, Rosaura, "dressed simultaneously as a man and a woman, is a portent, a marvel, a monster."[37] Segismundo, too, is a monster not because of "his being a fierce or beastly man, but of his having been *born* beast and man" (89, his italics). Analyzing other plays by Calderón, such as *El monstruo de los jardines* and *La hija del aire*, González Echevarría concludes: "The outward appearance of Calderón's monsters, then, clearly reflects that they are figures in transition, in flux, mixed beings in the process of assuming a definite shape. As they are all young, products of supernatural births, and exiled from society until they undergo certain trials, the monsters are figures in a rite of passage, of initiation."[38] Calderón, of course, never suspected that *La púrpura de la rosa* would be transported to the viceregal court of Lima, so reading Adonis's self-description in the colonial context might be, again, dismissed as preposterous. Yet as González Echevarría also notes, the most powerful vision of the monster in Calderón happens to be the attempt to describe a Spanish vessel by Guacolda, an Inca princess in *La aurora en Copacabana*, which is the playwright's sole text set in the Americas. Beholding the object she deems "un raro asombro" (a rare astonishment), Guacolda seeks to define it by variously calling it "escollo que navega" (rock that sails), "preñada nube" (pregnant cloud), "marino pez" (marine fish), and "velera ave" (sailing bird), but none of these concepts accurately describes her vision, which leads her to conclude that what she sees approaching the land is a monster "de tal extrañeza" (of such strangeness) that it can also be deemed "aborto de mar y viento" ("aborted offspring of sea and wind"). Regarded halfway between the animate and the inanimate, Calderón's baroque vessel imagines the amazement of those who witnessed the birth of a new world in which Europeans and native Americans faced each other and would eventually merge, even as new cultural patterns developed. These hybrid images also resound with Sor Juana's diction in the loa to *El divino Narciso*, where the character of América, an indigenous figure, is startled to see what readers and spectators can surely identify as Spanish soldiers on horseback: "¿Qué Centauros monstrüosos / contra mis gentes militan?" ("What are these Centaurs, man and horse, / that now my followers assail?").[39] Strangely, América does not know what a horse is, yet she is fluent in the language of classical mythology.

Read in this context of baroque hybridity, Adonis's strangeness is reinforced by his self-description as a "bastardo embrión" (bastard embryo) and "aborto de un tronco" (aborted offspring of a tree), and by his focus on his own unnatural birth from the incestuous and violent union of Myrrah and her father Cyniras. Turned into a tree by Aphrodite, Myrrah gives birth to Adonis, who is then bathed by nymphs in myrrh, which are really his mother's tears—yet another strangely hybrid thing. Loving such a human being, Venus seems to suggest, is to wander into a new kind of amatory experience. Moments before finding Adonis asleep in the woods, she conveys her astonishment that she could be in love with such a being:

> ¿Qué género de ansia,
> altos montes, decid,
> qué especie de penar,
> linaje de sentir,
> en el que en mí ha engendrado
> haber llegado a oír
> baldones del amor
> a espíritu tan vil
> que su deidad infama? (62)

> What kind of anxiety,
> oh vast mountains, tell me,
> what kind of sorrow,
> what family of feeling, is this one

> that has been engendered in me
> from having come to hear
> love insulted
> in such a vulgar spirit
> that its deity is infamed? (62)

The phrase *linaje de sentir* is remarkable because it suggests that Venus's passion not only lies outside the conventions to which she is accustomed but is, in fact, an unlikely, even unnatural, affect. Adonis stems from another world and to fall in love with him, therefore, is to enter a new realm or, as the text's English translation wisely explicates, a different "family of feelings." Aware of his own difference, Adonis himself fights the effects of his unnatural birth, and instead of avoiding Venus, he seeks to domesticate his innate impulses: "Como al verte sabré / forzar y reprimir / aquel amenazado / influjo en que nací" (68; "Upon seeing you, I'll know / to force and repress / that threatening / influence under which I was born" 68). The oddity of their union has been made audible a few minutes before when, in a rare moment, strangely fusing their voices, Venus and Adonis sing together a few lines: "¡Ay de mí! / ... Si hallo el descanso donde le perdí. / ... Que me da muerte a quien la vida dí" (64; "Ah, alas! / ... if I can find peace where I lost it / ... for she to whom I gave life kills me" 64).

Although neither Adonis's self-definition nor the tale of his convoluted ancestry neatly coincide with the specific meanings attached to hybridity in the discourse about culture in Latin America, there is a powerful consonance between the character's story of a violent birth and the original clash whereby the civilization of Europe meets its New World counterpart. This, again, is an anachronistic position and a forced reading, yet I am seduced by what seems to be a natural affinity between Calderón's language for Adonis and the way some authors chronicle the origins and growth of Latin American cultures. These narratives of illegitimacy, impurity, and mixture emerge in the arts in a great number of forms, many of which are traditionally classified as baroque. Regardless of whether theories of the New World baroque are valid analyses or mere flights of literary or critical imagination, what matters here is the potential impact of their echoes for reading and viewing *La púrpura de la rosa* not as a text about Latin America, which it is not, or a text from Latin America, which it is only to a certain extent, but as a text for Latin America, an opera that subtly contains the prospect of naturalizing itself—of being natural despite, or through, its artifice—in a new land as it attains new meanings for local readers and spectators.

The tale's denouement, which is the same in Hidalgo's Madrid setting of 1660 and Torrejón's Lima version of 1701, may well invoke different significations in Spain or Peru, depending on how one relates Calderón's words to other texts and literary systems. At the end of the opera, when Venus and Adonis are reunited as stars, Mars sings about how this magical event occurs "al tiempo que se ve el sol / entre pardos arreboles, / y la enemiga del día / su negro manto descoge" (106, 108; "as the sun sets / among crimson clouds / and the enemy of the day / unfolds its black mantle"). The setting sun at the end of the opera is powerfully suggestive. Although the anonymous loa had begun by mentioning Philip V's origin in the east, *La púrpura de la rosa* concludes as the sun sets to the west, a transit that may be read as an acknowledgment, brief but not insignificant, of mythology's arrival in another part of the world across the ocean from Europe. What might be regarded as mere astronomical precision from a strict European viewpoint turns into a story of birth on the other side of the Atlantic. Transported to a new land, the old classical tales of metamorphosis, like this version of the myth of Adonis, are not just instruments of empire but also the seed of new cultural creations.

Indeed, if one juxtaposes and compares the symbolic uses of mythology in the anonymous loa and Calderón's libretto, there emerges an essentially contradictory story. This oblique clash is especially significant in the case of Mars, associated with Philip V in the loa, but mostly a negative character, the antagonist of Venus and Adonis, in the rest of the opera. As he confronts Venus suspecting that she has found a new lover, Mars reminds her of his own prowess in war, an attribute that, in the loa, had made the analogy between god and king altogether decorous but that now makes the god—and by extension, perhaps, Philip V himself—sound and resound as a potentially terrifying oppressor: "¿Ves el militar estruendo, / ves el bélico rumor con que me aclaman las lides / por su más guerrero dios?" (54; "Do you hear the martial noise, do you see the warlike furor / with which the battles acclaim me / as their greatest warrior god?" 54). Line by line, Calderón's poetry accentuates Mars's violent temper not only by relating the god to a lexicon of war—*militar, bélico, lides, guerrero*—but also by noting the actions of war with highly audible, even thunderous, signs: *estruendo, rumor*, and *aclamar*. If the god's ferocity is partially belied by a female singer's sweet envoicing of him in Torrejón y Velasco's harmonious score, then the action onstage clearly underscores his terrifying presence. Before exiting the stage, after threats from the god, Venus exclaims, "Muerta voy" (54; "I'm done for!" 54), while three of her nymphs refuse to answer his interrogation and leave their fourth companion, Libia, alone with him. Angrily, Mars demands that Libia confess what she knows about Venus and Adonis: "Dime qué ha sido, o la muerte. . ." (56; "Tell me what has happened, or death" 54). If there is a certain comical levity about these exchanges—one suspects, rightly, that no real damage will be caused by the god—the fact remains that Calderón's plot and diction qualify the loa's deferential association of Philip V and Mars.

Indeed, the powerful god of the loa succumbs to passion in the opera. Even as he is praised by the crowd—we hear "¡Marte viva!" once again—he confesses to Belona his own weakness: "Mejor, Belona, fuera, / decir la aclamación que Marte muera, / pues aunque de blasones / vitorioso en Egnido me corones / de Delfos, ¿qué ha importado, / si en Chipre estoy a una ilusión postrado, cuyos vanos recelos / ni celos son, ni dejan de ser celos?" (72; "It would be better, Belona, / to announce that Mars would die! / For, although you proclaim me / emblazoned with victory in Cnidus, / and crowned in Delphi, what does that matter, / when in Cyprus I am prostrate before an illusion, / whose vain misgivings are not jealous, but do not refrain from jealousy either?" 72). Later, upon seeing the child Amor, jealous Mars becomes something of a laughingstock, as when he anxiously exclaims, "¡Tenedle, que es el amor!" (76; "Catch him, for he is Love!" 76). It is also easy to be amused when Celfa deflates the imperious god by addressing him as "Señor Martes" (96; "Mr. Tuesday 96).

Finally, as the opera comes to an end and Adonis is changed into a new star by Jupiter, the audience is reminded of the celestial apparition seen in the loa: the rise of Philip V announced through the emergence of the fifth planet, Mars. Is it possible to say, then, that the bright star of Adonis somehow outshines or even usurps the primacy of the Spanish king, metaphorically entangled with Mars? In the Hidalgo setting of 1660, Mars was simply Mars, but a permutation takes place in Torrejón y Velasco's setting of 1701. The Peruvian loa imbues Mars with kingly associations, and these, in turn, filter into Calderón's text with new meanings and, most importantly, a certain measure of ambiguity. Given hybrid Adonis's hierarchical inferiority and Mars's regal bellicosity, a modern listener and reader may potentially surmise in the opera a tale analogous to that of the Spanish conquest; in this regard, one could conceivably envision a staging that would boost the parallels between the loa's and Calderón's two versions of Mars. From a strictly historical viewpoint, one cannot go as far as reading into this any kind of seditious intent, yet it is still remarkable that an anonymous loa written in Peru can subtly open the door to a permutation, even if minimal, in what Calderón's words may mean in this part of the Spanish Empire.

Yet another change potentially brought about by the loa's words concerns the subtle presence of other gods, such as Apollo, who is alluded to, and Jupiter, who ultimately decides the plot's exultant denouement.[40] After the four nymphs' exit and just before Bellona is about to enter the stage, amid drums and trumpets, voices are heard singing in martial honor of two gods: "¡Arma, arma! ¡Guerra, guerra! / ¡Viva Marte! ¡Viva el Sol! (56; "To arms, to arms, to war, to war! / Long live Mars! Long live the Sun!" 54). The singers' powerful acclamation mirrors that heard in the loa, but if those initial cheers sung by a formal chorus had praised one man alone, the young Philip V, the excitement heard at this juncture brings into being a formal duplication: far from being the absolute ruler, Mars must share the opera's soundscape with Apollo. In this uncanny doubling, the singular status of Mars yields to yet another god, Jupiter, who, as we saw, decides the outcome of the play. The presence of two gods recalls Severo Sarduy's invocation of the ellipse, where the notion of one center, proper of the circle, gives way to two centers, which, as Rolando Pérez and others have noted, Sarduy adopts from Kepler: "the circle is described around some fixed center, but the ellipse, which is the figure of the planetary, is described around two centers."[41] If, when everything is said and done, Jupiter rules above all gods and determines the opera's happy ending, one wonders about the status of the loa's enthusiastic association of Mars and Philip V in this baroque cosmology. Does the ineptness of the god of war cancel the loa's analogy, or should one simply ignore this double deployment of Mars? Spectators, after all, may have forgotten the loa by the time they reach the opera's end. Yet the ultimate consequences of the initial analogy are still there to be pondered and expounded, even if my appraisal is dismissed as one opera lover's private echo chamber in which words and music quirkily resound.

Indeed, the fact remains that much of the work's score or libretto—including, arguably, some of its most seductive passages—has little or nothing to do explicitly or implicitly with Peru or Latin America. Consider, for instance, the protracted episode at Desengaño's grotto, where music of preternatural beauty augments the libretto's uncanny imagery. The verses in question seek to convey and elucidate the universal sentiment of jealousy. Infuriated because Venus loves Adonis, Mars pursues Amor, who ends up hiding by the grotto as he seeks to flee. Upon seeing the dark, cavernous interior, Mars's melancholy singing intensifies the bleakness of Calderón's words:

> la escasa luz que dispensa
> el torpe bostezo que entreabre la gruta,
> porque el sol, que de miedo no pasa,
> de lejos la acecha, aun más que la alumbra,
> melancólico espacio diviso
> de negras paredes, que teas ahuman,
> colgadas de grillos, cadenas y lazos,
> trofeos que infaman, deidad que no ilustran. (78)

> In the scarce light shed by
> the grotesquely yawning opening of the grotto,
> for the sun, out of fear never enters here,
> so that the distant light hides more than it illumines,
> I divine a melancholy space
> with black walls lit by smoking torches,
> hung with chains, shackles, and ropes:
> trophies that disgrace, rather than honour a god. (78)

Inside the grotto, as the libretto states, one can hear "la música en tono triste" (78; "sad music is heard" 78), at which point four allegorical figures emerge from within, each of them carrying an object to represent various aspects of jealousy. Singing one after the other, each figure tries to explain the grotto's mystery: "Esta es de los celos. . . / La mísera cárcel. . . / Adonde de Amor. . . / Siempre paran las fugas" (80; "This jealousy's / miserable jail. . . / . . .where Love's escapes / . . .always comes to an end" 80).

The libretto specifies that all four figures are dressed in black and wear small masks; each of them also carries an object, the emotional meaning of which is explored with complex baroque diction and great lyrical intensity as they reflect on the concept of jealousy. Temor carries a torch, which she puts off as she sings about the links among trust and seeing: "Yo soy aquel miedo que tiene el que ama / de cuanto achacosa es cualquier hermosura; / y así, tropezando en primeros temores, / le sirvo la luz, / y déjole a escuras, / porque busca con ella su daño, y luego le pesa de hallar lo que busca" (80; "I am that Fear which the lover has, / that every beauty is full of flaws, / and thus, as he stumbles over the first fears, / I serve him a light, / then leave him in darkness, / because with it he seeks his own harm, and later regrets to find that which he sought" 80). She is followed by Sospecha, who carries a telescope that stands for a magnified perception of things: "Que artificioso este antojo de vidrio, / creciendo los grados a cuanto presuma, / represente de un álamo un monte, / de un átomo un mar, de una gota una lluvia" (82; "That the artifice of these glasses, / enlarging the focus to however much as one imagines, / could show a poplar-tree to be a mountain, / an atom an ocean, or a mere drip of water a rainstorm" 80). Envidia, too, explains the snake she carries in terms of chilling multiplication: "Y yo, que siguiendo antojos de aumento, / doy luego por ciertas ajenas fortunas, / anudando un áspid a otro, / de Envidia en mi seno les doy la cicuta" (82; "And I come later, following through magnifying glasses / what I see of certain fortunes of others, adding one snake to another, / I feed them hemlock from the envy of my breast" 80). Finally, Ira's dagger is explained as an emblem of revenge: "Con que, a la Envidia siguiendo la Ira, / los áspides que ella enlaza, y anuda, / en víboras yo convierto de acero, / que para venganza afilen sus puntas" (82; "So that, with Anger following Envy, / the asps that she entwines and feeds, / I convert into vipers of iron, / that sharpen their points for vengeance" 80). The strangeness of Calderón's images cannot be overestimated, and one can well conceive of a staging where all four objects are dramatically foregrounded to convey and delve into the psychological nuances of jealousy. What is remarkable in the allegorical display is that nothing, really, can be related to the specificities of Latin American cultures. Indeed, because of its general nature, this exploration of jealousy underscores the fact that the opera's most intensely felt subject is the concept of passion and that any thematic connections between *La púrpura de la rosa* and the place it was first performed—despite my argument heretofore—may well be figments of an odd critical imagination.

Yet the arts in Latin America—including, certainly, many important creations by painters, sculptors, and writers from the colonial period—do not perforce bear the imprint of anything one may explicitly recognize as regional or, speaking from an anachronistic viewpoint, as national. This is the case, of course, of Sor Juana, whose loa for *El divino Narciso* treats the issue of religion in the New World, but whose sonnets, to name only one aspect of her large literary corpus, show nothing that would indicate to readers that they should be read or labeled as Mexican, or even as the work of an author whom we now call Mexican. Indeed, the sonnets boast poetic practices that originated in Spain, crossed the Atlantic, and became part of the literary culture of such places as Lima and Mexico City without displaying any signs of the local—except, paratextually, the signatures of authors whom we now place, in a retroactive gesture, in the national and regional canons of literature. In Calderón's case, beyond his foreignness and imperial bonds, an accidental afterlife as a librettist in colonial Lima tells a story of uncanny intertwinings. Calderón's unexpected apparition at the inception of opera in the New World harkens back inevitably to European cultural forms associated with the violent colonial history of Latin American, a fact difficult to ignore even if one brings up the role of the native loa in the reading of the libretto. But when it comes to its status within a community's artistic canons, opera has an advantage over other forms of literature, such as fiction and poetry. Because opera is first and foremost a dramatic form, a work like *La púrpura de la rosa* can in effect be partially reborn, or in a sense rewritten, every time that it is newly performed. In this sense, each new staging is a chance to rethink and reconceive the opera for new audiences, who can then see and hear aspects of the work—such as the double status of Mars in the loa and Calderón's text—that would otherwise remain invisible and inaudible.

Since the 1990s, several productions and, as we have seen, recordings of *La púrpura de la rosa* have worked to bring about the opera's naturalization for Latin American culture. While recordings deploy such paratexts as images, blurbs, and essays by scholars and artists, the critical process on stage may be achieved through visual and dramatic means. Productions at the Grand Théâtre de Genève and Madrid's Teatro de la Zarzuela (1999), the University of Sheffield (2003), and the Musikfestspiele Potsdam Sanssouci (2015) have amplified the opera's ties with the New World for spectators and listeners. At Potsdam, for instance, the festival website described the work as a "Barockoper mit Latinoflair" (baroque opera with Latino flair), which included two characters dressed in what Jean-François Lattarico described as "Peruvian costumes"—a traditional hat and an extravagantly colorful chullo—plus some theatrical makeup sadly reminiscent of blackface in yet another character. A measure of inventiveness, if not pure invention, also marks the presentation of the two audio recordings referred to in this chapter. The first set, produced by K617 for its collection *Les Chemins du Baroque*, contains the essay by Illari and the interview with Gabriel Garrido quoted earlier.⁴² It makes sense, then, that the cover for *Chemins du Baroque* feature a photograph from the Geneva and Madrid productions that shows not only Adonis's mythical red rose but also, dancing around it, four women dressed in seemingly traditional Latin American garments. Arguably, opera recordings, focusing as they do on the music, may appear to erase opera's theatrical visuality, which Theodor Adorno praises in his short essay "Opera and the Long-Playing Record." Adorno refers to a recording of Mozart's *Le nozze di Figaro*, which frees the work from the predictability of stage production: "The music of *Figaro* is of truly incomparable quality, but every staging of *Figaro* with powdered ladies and gentlemen, with the page and the white rococo salon, resembles the praline box, not to mention the *Rosenkavalier* and the silver rose."⁴³ Adorno's point is well taken, but the visual aspects of opera, even if minimal in the context of audio recordings, can tease out a work's meanings by making listeners see, quite literally, what may not be all that obvious in the work's other codes, thus influencing a listener's reception thereof.

In this visual realm, the reworking of the image by Kahlo in the recording of *La púrpura de la rosa* by Deutsche Harmonia Mundi is especially productive. Oddly, against common practice in opera recordings, the set's booklet does not contain a synopsis of the work. But this absence may benefit the work's implications for Latin America, as it might prompt more listeners than usual to actually read the libretto in order to follow closely the baroque spirals of Calderón's version of the myth of Venus and Adonis—or to read instead, searching for the plot, the two essays the booklet does include, quoted earlier, by Stein on the hybrid nature of local musical practices and by Lawrence-King on the work's Spanish and Spanish-American rhythms. Beyond these scholarly and artistic insights into the pan-Hispanic status of *La púrpura de la rosa*, one may focus, again, on the recording's visual surface, an especially significant paratext that serves as a creative retrieval of the work for Latin American culture.

In this, the history of painting plays a vital role, especially in baroque thinking about the hierarchy of the senses. Calderón, for one, held painting in high esteem, fervently defending its practitioners in "Deposición en favor de los profesores de la pintura" (1677), where he places "la Óptica" above "la Música": "pues si ella [la Música] tiene por objeto suspender el espíritu a cláusulas sonoras, a no menos acordes cláusulas le suspende la Pintura con las ventajas que lleva el sentido de la vista al del oído" (because if she [Music] has as its objective to suspend the spirit to sonorous clauses, Painting does no less to harmonious clauses, with the advantages that the sense of sight has over that of hearing).[44] Further, Calderón underwrites the power of painting to make present or real that which is not: "Pues sabiendo que es un manchado lino de minerales y licores, hace creer (o cuando no le crea que lo dude) que se ve presente lo historiado y real lo fabuloso" (720; Because knowing itself to be linen stained with minerals and liquids, it makes one believe [or if not believe, at least suspect] that the historical is seen to be present, and the fabulous to be real). Indeed, if we choose to see things through Calderón's eyes, the vehement eroticism of his verbal depiction of the lovers can indeed be made to seem "real" in paintings of the subject, as one can see, for instance, on Paolo Veronese's *Venus and Adonis*, now housed in the Museo Nacional del Prado but part of the royal collection in the mid-seventeenth century.[45]

In Veronese's work, handsome Adonis sleeps on Venus's lap, but the goddess is pensive—the melancholy moment just before the young mortal sets out on the hunt whose outcome will be his own death. The viewer also sees two elegant hounds, one held by Amor and the other peacefully sleeping; a luxurious fabric covers the goddess's legs, richly colored, just like Adonis's orange garment and the surrounding leaves, clouds, and sky. An earlier recording of the opera, by Nuova Era (1990), reproduces on its own cover a detail of Veronese's picture, a brilliant work but one whose choice, in this context, is perhaps altogether predictable. By visually linking *La púrpura de la rosa* with a work by a prestigious Venetian old master, the Nuova Era recording tacitly underscores the European lineage of opera—a long line of artists that can transport the listener from Calderón and Torrejón y Velasco back to Veronese and other painters who, in turn, had found a canonical source for their vision of Venus and Adonis in Ovid's *Metamorphoses*. In the case of Veronese's painting, specifically, the body of Adonis mimics the sculpted figure of Endymion on a sepulchre at Rome's Basilica di San Giovanni in Laterano. Moreover, that the painting belonged to Philip IV, father of María Teresa, for whose betrothal to Louis XIV Calderón's libretto was originally written, can only magnify the ties that bind *La púrpura de la rosa* to Europe's royal houses. If musically the Nuova Era recording violates the practices of seventeenth-century Spanish opera—Adonis, for instance, is sung by a tenor—its visual presentation hearkens back to the European cultural and political context in which the opera's music and libretto were first authored.

Audaciously, as we saw, the Deutsche Harmonia Mundi cover reproduces instead its own version of Kahlo's *Two Nudes in the Forest*. As in Veronese's *Venus and Adonis*, whose composition Kahlo's image seems to mimic, the listener confronts two highly eroticized naked bodies, one of which places a hand on her recumbent companion. Transposed onto *La púrpura de la rosa*, Kahlo's lovers stand for Venus and Adonis, and the fact that these two figures are women may be surprising yet, as mentioned, consonant with Torrejón y Velasco's score, where the two mythic lovers' roles are also sung by women. But Kahlo's bodies, unlike anything one finds in the opera, suggest different races and mysterious landscapes—diverse skin tones set against a harsh backdrop where enormous leaves grow next to what looks like a barren desert. A world apart, or so it seems, from Veronese's obedient hounds, the black visage of a strange monkey peers from among the leaves. Resurfacing on the disc's cover, surveying the lovers in repose, could this be Amor himself transposed to another world, envisioned by Kahlo? The figure that seems to stand for Adonis has a light-skinned body, but Venus has undergone a metamorphosis whereby she is an indigenous red-brown woman. She sits on what seems to be a rebozo, the traditional shawl worn by Mexican women, as red as the mythical rose's blood.[46] On the box-set cover, but absent from the original painting, a pink and white star, not unlike a strange eight-tentacled starfish out of water, has magically appeared, shining in the sky above. In the context of Calderón's libretto, one readily identifies the star with Adonis's ultimate transformation—"la nueva luz de Adonis" (106; "the new light of Adonis" 106)—or else, perhaps, menacingly, with Mars, the fifth planet related to Philip V in the loa.

At first glance, again, Deutsche Harmonia Mundi's colorful cover may appear to be yet another instance of capitalizing on Kahlo's iconic status—the Mexican artist will likely sell more records than Veronese—or yet another example of fetishizing Latin American otherness; using this image may recall some facile, even crude, blurbs found sometimes on the covers of translated novels or on the plastic cases of DVD films.[47] But one may also view the paratextual deployment of Kahlo's lovers as an attempt to inscribe hybridity in the opera and thereby represent a region whose indigenous and mestizo cultures are now visible—or, to put it differently, as a Latin American site in which *La púrpura de la rosa* resounds not as a venerable creation from the past but as a living text that may, or be made to, speak to new readers and spectators. Yet despite this rush of vitality, the amorous liaison between Kahlo's Venus and Adonis is a poignant affair, for Adonis is dead, a metaphorical impediment for the ongoing workings of hybridity. Then again, this uncanny coloring of European visuality may well emerge as a faithful vision of the opera's contradictory status in the cultural fashioning of Latin America. By projecting a presence that is in fact not there, the cover image highlights the artificiality of desperately seeking what cannot be found. Any effort to bring out an invisible presence will result only in exposing an absence that refuses to go away, a failure that may cause the opera's silence on the New World to resound even more sorrowfully to those desirous of hearing the sounds of another, more ancient Peru—a dream, if you will.

Yet Calderón's writings delicately account for the presence of absence, a space of ruins where one may imagine a truer, if always elusive, always prospective, vision of the region's face. A gradual apparition is, after all, how he views the birth of painting in the "Deposición": "Salían de bañarse en el mar unos muchachos, y hallándose desnudos en su orilla, notaron cuán parecidos los semejaba el sol de el arena; y traviesamente jugando, empezó el uno a seguir con el dedo los perfiles de la sombra de otro" (718; Some young men were coming out of the ocean after swimming, and finding themselves naked on the shore, they noticed how much the sun made them resemble the sand; and playing mischievously, one of them began to trace with his finger the contours of someone else's shadow). Out of the artist's playful appreciation of shadows and similarities, Calderón traces the development of painting as it becomes the perfect art known by his contemporaries:

> y así, siguiendo a porfiadas instancias de su idea en repetidas líneas las grabadas señas del informe embrión que le ofreció la playa, le fue perficionando hasta lograrle parecido. Y como es fácil hallar la senda que hay desde lo inventado a lo añadido, siguieron otros su dictamen, que a emiendas del estudio y mejoras del tiempo creció a la suma estimación en que hoy se halla. De modo que para argumento de ser la pintura inspirado numen de sobrenatural aliento, baste saber que fuese su primer taller la luz, su primer bosquejo la sombra, su primer lámina la arena, su primer pincel el dedo, su primer artífice la joven travesura de un acaso. (718)

> And thus, urged by the stubborn demands of his idea of tracing the repeated lines, he went over the imprinted marks of the shapeless embryo which the beach offered him, perfecting it until achieving a resemblance. And since it is easy to find the path that goes from invention to addition, others emulated his ruling, which, amended by study and improved with time, rose to the supreme esteem in which it is held today. So in order to demonstrate that painting is a deity animated by otherworldly inspiration, let it suffice to know that light was its first workshop, shadow its first sketch, sand its first sheet, a finger its first brush, and the youthful mischief of chance its first maker.

Interpreted in the context of the baroque, and projected onto the long trajectory of *La púrpura de la rosa* from Lima's viceregal palace to a digital recording at the turn of the new millennium, Calderón's renewed invocation of an amorphous embryo resounds with the potential of the colonial *fiesta cantada* to become a full-blown Latin American opera. An artist tinkers with an image—retraces its contours—until little by little it resembles its real-world referent. Yet what matters here is not so much the ultimate triumph of verisimilitude or sameness or identity, but the protracted and playful process whereby incipient forms can be made to resemble an ideal model. The slowly forming figure brings to mind not only Adonis's self-description as a "bastardo embrión" (52; "bastard embryo") and "aborto de un tronco" (52; "aborted offspring of a tree") but also his ultimate metamorphosis into a free and radiant star. The rose of Adonis is stained with blood, yet it goes on blooming, like the constantly shifting forms of Latin American culture.

A Detour in the Jesuit Missions: All Worlds Lead to Rome

Before the creation of *La púrpura de la rosa*—indeed, before the arrival of Europeans in the Americas—there had been staged performances in what is now Peru, which, after the conquest, merged occasionally with European theatrical practices. According to the Inca Garcilaso's *Comentarios reales*, members of Christian orders, especially the Jesuits, drew on native performers for their evangelizing message. In Lima, a play on the Eucharist written in both Spanish and Quechua, performed by indigenous people, reportedly contained singing that transported the colonizers and transformed their cultural prejudices: "and they sang the songs so sweetly that many Spaniards wept with pleasure and joy to see the grace and skill and wit of the little Indians, and changed the opinions they had hitherto held that they were uncouth, stupid, and clumsy."[48] That performance is irretrievably lost, and its musical component may not have amounted to anything we would effortlessly regard as opera, but Garcilaso's memory thereof constitutes an important initial gesture in the history of music drama in Latin America. If the city of Cuzco, as Garcilaso famously proclaims in the preface of his magnum opus, was "formerly the Rome in that empire" (4)—or "otra Roma en aquel imperio,"[49] as the Spanish original would have it—the existence of music drama in the two far-flung capitals,

Cuzco and Rome, may be seen as an important bond between both parts of the world.

A century after Garcilaso, Domenico Zipoli, an Italian composer and organist from Prato, Italy, settled in Córdoba, present-day Argentina, in 1717, and wrote music for the indigenous population, whose talents for performance were celebrated even at the Vatican.[50] Zipoli's many compositions, as well as the plethora of sacred music written by other European and indigenous composers in the *reducciones*, the Jesuit mission towns in South America, stand as a powerful convergence of art, religion, and politics. Vanished for the most part from public performance after the expulsion of the Jesuits from Spanish lands in 1767, this rich musical corpus, as I mentioned earlier, made a comeback in the second half of the twentieth century through the efforts of scholars such as Robert Stevenson and Piotr Nawrot, who retrieved and published musical scores that had been out of view for generations.

In the past few decades, recordings made in Europe and Latin America and performances on various continents have expanded the audience of these works, including two music dramas. Boasting a sweet musicality and minimalist plots, *San Francisco Xavier* and *San Ignacio*—reconstructed by Nawrot and Bernardo Illari, respectively, and conducted by Gabriel Garrido for two separate French-produced recordings—stand in contrast, structurally and thematically, to the complex European theatrical practices at the heart of *La púrpura de la rosa*. Nawrot underscores their uniqueness. Although no autochthonous musical themes, rhythms, or instruments have been detected, their sacred subject, vocal arrangements, and language choice bespeak the culture of the *reducciones*. Despite the absence of any concrete evidence to show the extent to which indigenous persons participated in the works' composition, Nawrot concludes that they could not have been mere spectators, but active participants in their creation.[51] In all, the survival and revival of the two operas are a riveting episode in the long history of transculturation in Latin America; this is no longer merely music drama transplanted from Spain, but rather a homespun creation designed for local audiences under imperial rule. As Leonardo J. Waisman notes, their musical practices were "clear manifestations of the norms of order and discipline that Spaniards considered essential to urban life and to civilization."⁵² Rural *reducciones* were not cities, Weisman adds. Yet if one heeds Geoffrey Baker's concept for the urban in colonial Latin America, the multiethnic nature of musical performance arguably turns those small places into resounding towns.

Consider *San Ignacio*. Its unique structure fulfills the specific needs of a work whose aim is to evangelize the indigenous peoples, an audience far removed from any center of European culture. As Illari argues, *San Ignacio* is indeed an opera of alterity, but its otherness does not stem from autochthonous melodies or any kind of contrived local color. What makes *San Ignacio* different from other works is the extent to which the musical score and libretto actually transform—or "rejects," as Illari would have it—certain conventions of European operas or oratorios for the sake of a local audience.⁵³ In his view, the indigenous peoples would not have understood the highly formalistic codes of eighteenth-century opera seria; to perform something in the style of those long works staged in Italy or Spain would have impeded the transmission of the evangelizing message. (One might add that opera buffa would surely not have been an apt vehicle for conveying a saint's life.) Illari stops short of calling *San Ignacio* a Bolivian or Latin American work, but he highlights its colonial otherness not through an inclusion of the local, but persuasively, through the erasure of specific European patterns that turn it into "otra ópera"—another kind of opera, one whose otherness depends on its deletion of European codes.⁵⁴ Thus, to ensure the attention and interest of the indigenous audience, the work has a better balance of solos and ensembles, shorter arias da capo—no seemingly endless singing of the same words—and no subplots, and its characters are less "living beings" than "abstractions, symbolic stereotypes, radically good or evil."⁵⁵ Nonetheless, Illari underscores the subaltern role of the indigenous people in the opera's workings:

> *San Ignacio*, as an emblem of Jesuitical activity, acquires many values. On the one hand, it shows us that there is room for the

Other, including within the most stubbornly Eurocentric frame, and the most openly colonialist political system. The characteristics of the work were adapted to the Other, to whom it was meant. On the other hand, it recalls us that a cultural event could hardly ignore the prevailing Eurocentrism and colonialism, especially if it allowed an opening to the presence of the Other. The opera was a political and ideological, but also cultural propaganda, supported by all the Jesuitical strength. Indeed, the Other possesses a space in this work allowing him to renounce what was the essential of his alterity: religion, ethical values and principles opposed to Catholicism, economical and political independence, social organisation. (55–56)

Indeed, to read and listen to the mission operas outside the broad critical paradigm of European hegemony and indigenous subalternity remains a challenge. Can one extract *San Ignacio* from the old familiar story of empire and religion to focus on other aspects of the work? And if so, what remains valuable in that particular work?

Again, it is easy to view the minimal story line of *San Ignacio* as a straightforward story of conversion. The plot, such as it is, obliquely concerns, even mirrors, the activities of the Jesuits, devoted followers of the real-life Ignacio de Loyola and Francisco Javier, among the indigenous peoples, the opera's intended audience. At the work's end, after the spectators have witnessed San Ignacio's mystical yearnings and battle with a demon, the story turns toward San Francisco Javier, to whom San Ignacio announces he must depart for Asia: "Al Oriente, hijo, el cielo te destina, / y que vayas es voluntad divina" ("To the Orient, son, heaven destines you, and for you to go is divine will").[56] San Francisco Javier asks, then, what he will do there, to which San Ignacio replies: "De Jesús propagarás la milicia / contra la ceguedad, y la malicia, / sacando de las fauces del infierno, / tanto gentil que vive sin gobierno" (25; "You will expand God's army against blindness and evil, removing from the jaws of hell so many gentiles living without law"). Although the non-Christians to whom San Ignacio alludes are purportedly those whom San Francisco Javier will convert in Asia's Far East, the zeal of evangelization, as Zipoli's dictum can only remind one, reverberates in the context of the indigenous peoples of South America. The saint's response is, naturally, to welcome the task which he has been assigned: "Pasa ligera, oh navecilla, / el mar profundo, / que mi alma espera ya ver / la orilla del otro mundo" (25; "Cross lightly, oh little ship, the deep sea, for my soul awaits to see the shores of the other world"). But what is this other world that he sings about? Where is it located and how can one be transported to it?

The phrase "el otro mundo" normally refers in Spanish to the afterlife; in fact, as the audience would know, Francisco Javier would die a martyr's death—on Sanchwan, an island off the coast of mainland China, to where he was traveling in order to continue his mission to evangelize others. But in a literal context of ships and deep seas, the phrase can also invoke, if one so chooses, the existence of other "worlds"—other cultures—in other parts of the "world." In the same spirit that the loa to *La púrpura de la rosa* had described Mars as "de dos mundos superior" (46; "ruler of two worlds" 46)—thereby acknowledging the distance separating Spain and its colonies and, tacitly, the expanding geography of opera on both sides of the Atlantic—*San Ignacio* points to other journeys to other parts of the world.

All roads lead to Rome—that "otro Cuzco"—and there one finds another Jesuit opera whose subject contains a whirlwind trip around the world. Performed at the Jesuits' Roman College in 1622 as part of the canonization celebration for Ignatius and Francis Xavier, the *Apotheosis sive Consecratio Sanctorum Ignatii et Francisci Xaverii* had music by Johannes Hieronymus (Giovanni Girolamo) Kapsberger, a Venetian composer of German descent, and a libretto, in Latin, by Orazio Grassi, a Jesuit priest. The opera's five acts chronicle the journeys of both Ignacio and Francisco Javier through various lands in Europe (Spain, Portugal, France, Italy) and Asia (Palestine, India, China, Japan), by featuring characters who stand as personifications of those other places. At the onset of act 2, India appears and sings about pearls for Francis Xavier: "Divitis Ponti generosa partu / Luce concharum saxa discolori / Dona Francisci cumulamus aris / Indica pubes" ("Let the Indian youth amass on the altars of Francis gifts of pearls, ennobled by their birth in the rich Pontus, and marked with mussels' variegated stripes").⁵⁷ As Victor Anand Coelho observes, India in the *Apotheosis* is variously subordinated, feminized, and sexualized, while pearls, along with gold, emerge as "symbols both of the Orient and maritime abundance."⁵⁸ (Centuries later, in yet another operatic iteration of colonialist discourses, India and pearls would again cohabit the stage in Bizet's *Les Pêcheurs de perles*.) Because neither Ignacio nor Francisco Javier ever set foot in the Americas, no land in the Western Hemisphere is a character in the opera's global order, but India, seen in an engraving depicting the original performance, wears a feathered crown that, in the eyes of Ralph P. Locke, "may have been inspired by headdresses of another kind of 'Indian': the natives of the New World."⁵⁹ The character of India refers then, as Locke observes, to the concrete struggles between the Portuguese and the Mughals, while Japan, in act 3, recalls the presence of Xavier as a missionary on its land, and China, in act 4, laments not having the saint's relics, as he died before setting foot on its shores.

Against such literary and visual discourses of otherness, the South American *San Ignacio* stands out as an almost abstract creation, shying away from depicting specific cultures; its characters, such as they are, live in a stateless universe. Compared to other works based on the interactions of Christian Europe with other parts of the world, this opera is a virtual tabula rasa; imperial bonds and religious trappings are inevitable, but there are no feathered crowns, no *indios*. In short, the Americas are not represented, and this virtual absence may just allow listeners and readers to imagine more freely another kind of world, one in which Europe's others can perhaps represent themselves. As for *San Francisco Xavier*, with its Chiquitano-language libretto, listeners who cannot understand those words—a subset surely comprising most operagoers on the planet—will probably sense that other tongue with a measure of strangeness. In Garrido's recording, the opera begins with a text described as "Llamado a la fiesta" ("The call to celebrate") full of relatively familiar words in Latin: "Canite, plaudite, / exsultate omnes. [. . .] Haec est dies quam / fecit Dominus" ("Sing, dance, shout and rejoice all. . . . For this is the day the Lord has made").[60] Later, after several arias and a minuet, San Xavier, as he is called, sings: "Aub'apaezo îriabo roma, / aub'apaezo cînîmanasma, / aub'apaezo oxima tañama" (22; "There are so many to be baptised, by being converted they become great," 23). For those of us who do not know the language, it is hard to determine the specific lexical, morphological and syntactical workings of each of these written signs, but anyone who is all eyes, or all ears, will surely repair on "roma"—Rome, Cuzco's peer—as written (in lowercase) and sung in the middle of the verse. The word may certainly be seen as yet another sign of European intrusion into the subaltern culture, but we can may also perceive it as a familiar sound rendered both new and other in this opera's uncanny South American context.

4 Carpentier's Singing Moctezuma

A Neobaroque Novella in Vivaldi's Venice

THE COVER OF THE COMPACT DISC set is mostly blue (fig. 2). The recumbent figure, crafted of pale stone, lies underwater, sunken in a sandy seabed, perhaps the victim of a shipwreck or a natural catastrophe, or the violence of war. It is a chacmool, the enigmatic Mesoamerican sculpture that some archaeologists believe may have depicted a sacrificial victim, holding a receptacle that contained hearts after the execution of human sacrifices.[1] An accident may have befallen this particular chacmool, for it looks at us, global listeners of opera, not from a museum or some other kind of shelter, but from an uncanny submarine dwelling. The photograph, by Mark Lewis, was first used in an advertising campaign for tourism in Cozumel, promising a mix of "the splendor of the most beautiful beaches in the Caribbean with the mysticism of the Mayan culture."[2] That the image should also appear on the cover of a compact disc—an operatic recording—might be startling, but not altogether unexpected. Theodor Adorno describes opera as "a bourgeois vacation spot," which explains, for instance, opera's uninvolvement with the social conflicts of the nineteenth century.[3] Nonetheless, the sculpture can make you think about the clashes and struggles

FIGURE 2. CD cover for Antonio Vivaldi's *Motezuma*, Archiv Production (Deutsche Grammophon), image by Mark Lewis.

that have besieged lands that opera has actually often depicted if only from a safe historical distance.

If you look again, the chacmool may appear not to be undersea, but dropped mysteriously in a dark and snowy landscape, as if it had been taken across the ocean to another latitude in a wintry space, maybe in Europe. It is from there, of course, that men had come to conquer the ancient civilizations for which the chacmool stands as a powerful icon. The impression of snow is not unwarranted, for this is a boreal European product—the cover of the Archiv Produktion recording of Antonio Vivaldi's *Motezuma*, with Alan Curtis conducting Il Complesso Barocco. First performed in November 1733 at the Teatro Sant'Angelo in Venice, the opera itself, if listened to and read from a certain angle, appears to unfold as a narrative of cultural appropriation, a creative act whereby cold and distant Europe reserves for itself the right to chronicle its legendary transatlantic exploits, which is what European institutions such as opera houses and museums often do. After all, the Weltmuseum Wien, once known as the Museum für Völkerkunde and just a short walk from the old Hapsburg capital's illustrious Staatsoper, still houses yet another famous Mesoamerican icon: Moctezuma's splendid headdress, which Mexico has claimed and failed to recover. Although that object's origin and provenance have not been ascertained, its astonishing feathers, mostly quetzal mounted in gold and jewels, stand as an emblem of plunder—not unlike the series of operas where the so-called emperor of the so-called Aztecs is made to sing the story of his own demise in front and for the sake of victorious others. In this context of forced spectacle, the aqueous or niveous chacmool is not just a beguiling symbol of indigenous cultures but also a poignant sign of their ultimate ruin.

Discussions of aesthetic value may not always stand as a central concern of Latin American cultural history, but I bring up the material splendor of the chacmool and Moctezuma's headdress because the established discourse about opera, in contrast, upholds the art form's sheer beauty—the power of music to take listeners to places, or make them feel emotions, to which they rarely have access. Deadly silent, the chacmool on the cover prefigures nonetheless the gorgeous musical score to which Vivaldi set the emperor's tragic story. In the debate about the primacy of words or music, as old as the art form itself, most people would agree that the transports of opera stem typically not from a libretto's words but from the effect of voices and instruments. As compelling as fictional Motezuma's tale may be, to many, what matters most in the work is Vivaldi's resplendent notes, and one wonders to what extent the opera's historical setting matters at all—or is even, quite literally, understood. As Paul Robinson and others have argued, there is much about the art form that conspires against the intelligibility, let alone the real appreciation, of opera's verbal code. Regardless of whether a libretto is written, or even rendered, in a language familiar to the audience, operatic singing tends to defy comprehensibility by its very nature. Concerned first and foremost with the necessity of projecting their unamplified voices over loud, at times thunderous, orchestras, even singers with perfect diction cannot always enunciate so clearly as to be fully understood by all.[4] The difficulty is compounded when several performers sing different words simultaneously, as happens in the famous sextet in Donizetti's *Lucia di Lammermoor*. Yet even if listeners do not know what an opera's plot is about or what the libretto's words say, they will agree on the magnificence of opera's musical fabric—the transports it triggers. Writing about Mozart in *A History of Opera* (2012), Carolyn Abbate and Roger Parker recall the scene in Frank Darabont's film *The Shawshank Redemption* (1994) in which a group of incarcerated men suddenly perceive the sound of operatic singing played over the prison's loudspeaker system. Not knowing what he is listening to (it happens to be a scene from the third act of *Le nozze di Figaro*), yet moved to his core, the prisoner played by Morgan Freeman exclaims:

> I have no idea to this day what those Italian ladies were singing about. Truth is, I don't want to know. Some things are best left unsaid. I'd like to think they were singing about something so beautiful, it can't be expressed in words, and makes your heart ache because of it. I tell you, those voices soared higher and farther than anybody in a gray place dares to dream. It was like some beautiful bird flapped into our drab little cage and made those walls dissolve away, and for the briefest of moments, every last man in Shawshank felt free.[5]

The prisoner's words eloquently describe the sense of rapture that ensues from listening to the power of the human voice in opera. Beyond plotlines, such lofty singing will transport and set you free, if only momentarily.

But what happens when we do pay attention to the story, which nowadays can happen rather effortlessly through supertitles and easily available librettos? More specifically, how should one react when the sung words, as is the case in Vivaldi's opera, concern a people's historic loss of freedom? How can Moctezuma's voice soar higher and farther when he is presented as defeated and trapped? How can he, a subaltern, sing, if agents from the victorious culture have chosen words and music for him? Should Vivaldi's setting of a seemingly Eurocentric libretto, by Alvise Giusti, be dismissed as yet another discursive mishmash of imperial hegemony and exoticism? Does the fallen emperor's sung lament have something to say, specifically, to audiences in Mexico and the rest of Latin America? As I rehearse answers to these old questions, I rely on the possible narrative lessons of Alejo Carpentier's *Concierto barroco* (1974), a fast-moving novella that deploys the tools of fiction and the workings of the baroque to examine the pleasures and perils of writing operas in Europe about other parts of the world. Set mostly in the eighteenth century, the intricate text of *Concierto barroco* mirrors the baroque gestures of Vivaldi's opera as it wistfully invents a Mexican criollo's journey from his home in Coyoacán to Venice, where he meets Vivaldi and accidentally inspires the composition of *Motezuma*. The traveler is at first angry at the libretto's purported misappropriation of Mexican history. Yet Carpentier's antirealist plot tempers the reader's evaluation of the traveler's anger by underscoring the common ties that bind cultures, including opera and other forms of music, on both sides of the Atlantic.[6] Culture itself, I argue, emerges as a complex tapestry whose threads exultantly unite both blatant exoticism and claims of cosmopolitan thinking, even as certain rigid Latin American conceptualizations of national and regional identity become unraveled.

The questions around Vivaldi's *Motezuma* and Carpentier's *Concierto barroco* that I seek to answer resound with some of the concerns of postcolonial theory. In the field of opera, as elsewhere, they also echo the work of feminist critics. I, for one, am persuaded by Catherine Clément's argument that operatic plots, especially in the nineteenth century, are morbidly obsessed with the tragic death of its heroines—the undoing of women, as Clément would have it in the title of her groundbreaking study. If male characters die too, it is the women—Norma, Lucia, Violetta, Gilda, Carmen, Mimì, Tosca, or Butterfly—who appear to do so most frequently and spectacularly. As we shall see, the role of Vivaldi's Motezuma, undone by the conquest, defeated by Spanish men, was performed by a countertenor in an unusual staging of the opera in Montecarlo in 1992, a musical pasticcio that may be easily heard as a tale of emasculation. A crucial aspect of Clément's analysis concerns not only the goings-on onstage but also the emotions in the audience's hearts and minds—the pleasure an operagoer, often a woman, may feel witnessing the lyrical deaths of female characters performed by women. Transposed to an opera such as *Motezuma*, these affects may also surface in Mexican or Latin American listeners or spectators as the tragic story of Motezuma unfolds couched in sublime music. In opera, as Clément writes, the singing prevails: "Oh voices, sublime voices, high, clear voices, how you make one forget the words you sing! How beautiful is suffering's melody, how good it feels to suffer an agreeable little sorrow, scratching the surface of the soul to give it depth, without really hurting it."[7] Likewise, when the curtain rises in the first act on the beaten Motezuma and he sings, one may forget the story of cultural devastation mostly inaudible in the plot. As David Vickers, for one, has argued, Giusti's libretto is neutral in that "neither the so-called civilized Europeans nor the supposedly barbaric savages occupy the high moral ground."[8] The music itself, as Steffen Voss puts it, "is free of the barbarisms that were often adopted by baroque and classical composers for the portrayal of exotic locales," and Motezuma and Mitrena, his wife, sing music of "tragic grandeur."[9] Nonetheless, this is the story of a vanquished people—and yet historical sorrow gives way to aesthetic enchantment. One may just be seduced by the sound of Motezuma's powerful, if utterly tragic, voice. If the emperor must suffer and be defeated at every performance of the work, or if the history of Mexico as seen onstage or heard on headphones is so terribly deformed that it offends some, there is not much that audience members can effectively do—except, perhaps, be transported by the workings of opera, like Clément reports herself to be even as the heroine dies, yet again, in the darkened theater.

Near the end of her book's "Prelude," Clément declares that the addressee of her fervent argument—"my passion," as she calls it—is none other than a man.[10] She invokes the image of her young son, who has not yet spent a night at the opera, but who in all likelihood will eventually do: "This is for him too so that, when the time comes, he will love differently; so that the music and the words will be clear to him; so that his pleasure will be all the greater because he can understand the opera's story and history, and that of past centuries."[11] The ravishments of opera must certainly be preserved, but they will sustain a different kind of affect for spectators and listeners in a world yet to come. In Clément's vision, the operatic event will be enriched and redeemed through a mindful knowledge of the history of opera and the role that women have played, or been assigned, in it. This is an experience not unlike the double consciousness which Edward Said postulates when he advises readers not to ignore the history of imperialism behind, say, a novel by Jane Austen, whose sentimental plot they will surely enjoy. It is also, in effect, the argument of Carpentier's novella about *Motezuma* in Venice. To find an opera's plot reprehensible is easy, but that judgment is only a fragment of the multiple emotions and arguments the mighty European spectacle triggers and deploys.

The Novelist Reads a Libretto: A New World Anew

In Carpentier's *Concierto barroco*, there is an episode that one may regard as highly operatic, and not just because it takes place on a fictional night at the opera. The nameless protagonist—a criollo, or descendant of Spaniards—undertakes a grand tour of Europe, arriving in Venice in time for carnival and the opera season. Brightly costumed as Moctezuma, he meets Antonio Vivaldi, who inquires about his birthplace and is drawn by the traveler's baroque account of the conquest of Mexico, as he perceives it:

> una larga historia que el fraile, ya muy metido en vinos, vio como la historia de un rey de escarabajos gigantes—algo de escarabajo tenía, en efecto, el peto verde, escamado, reluciente, del narrador—, que había vivido no hacía tanto tiempo, si se pensaba bien, entre volcanes y templos, lagos y teocallis, dueño de un imperio que le fuera arrebatado por un puñado de españoles osados, con ayuda de una india, enamorada del jefe de los invasores.[12]

> a lengthy tale which the priest, already deep in his cups, took to be about a king of giant beetles—the narrator's glossy, green, squamous breastplate did, in fact, resemble a beetle's—who had lived

not so long ago, when one considered it, among temples, lakes, and *teocallis*, the ruler of an empire that was wrested from him by a handful of bold Spaniards with the help of an Indian woman who was in love with the chief of the invaders.[13]

The composer's evaluation of his new acquaintance's exotic, dramatic tale is fast and clear. Imagining a stage full of trapdoors and levitations, earthquakes and monsters, he concludes: "Buen asunto; buen asunto para una ópera" (36; "Good story. Good theme for an opera" 70). As simple as the fictional composer's motivation sounds, the reasons for the historical Vivaldi and Giusti's choice of Moctezuma as a subject matter are far more complex, ranging from the perception of powerful affinities with Tenochtitlan as a city of canals and bridges, like Venice itself, to the potential significance of Moctezuma in the European political context, especially in relation to Spanish imperialism.[14] But Carpentier's fictional logic is far more direct: it is first and foremost a spectacular tale. The opera is expeditiously composed and performed, and the Mexican traveler is not pleased with *Motezuma* at its premiere. Witnessing the opera's brazen reworking of the major event in his country's history, he confronts the fictional Vivaldi and resoundingly proclaims: "¡Falso, falso, falso; todo falso!" (68; "False, false, false, all false!" 114).

Sure enough, there is much that is historically not true, or simply concocted, in Giusti's libretto, as the criollo's ensuing recitation makes it clear. For one, the historical Moctezuma could not have had a wife like the woman portrayed in the opera, nor was there ever a god worshiped in central Mexico under the Spanish-sounding name of Huchilobos.[15] In his own defense, Vivaldi ripostes by invoking Antonio de Solís's chronicle *Historia de la conquista de México* (1684) as the trustworthy source for Giusti's libretto and, more persuasively, by emphasizing the artistic needs of music drama. After the Mexican traveler admits that the so-called Huchilobos must be none other than Huitzilopochtli, Vivaldi explains why they could not have used the deity's original name in Nahuatl—or any other word in that phonetically challenging language: "¿Y usted cree que hay modo para cantar *eso*? Todo, en la crónica de Solís, es trabalenguas.

Continuo trabalenguas: Iztapalapa, Goazocoalco, Xicalango, Tlaxcala, Magiscatzin, Qualpopoca, Xicotencatl ... Me los he aprendido como ejercicio de articulación. Pero ... ¿a quién, carajo, se le habrá ocurrido inventar semejante idioma?" (69; "And do you think it's possible to sing a word like that? Everything in Solís's chronicle is a tongue twister. Nothing but tongue twisters all the way through: Iztlapalapa, Goazocoalco, Xicalango, Tlaxcala, Magiscatzin, Qualpopoca, Xicotencatl ... I learned them by heart to use as an articulation exercise. But ... to whom, dammit, did it ever occur to invent such a language?" 115). If Italian tacitly emerges as a most musical tongue, Nahuatl is branded as essentially unsingable.[16] Crucially, the criollo's mother language is really Spanish; he is, after all, an important personage attached to the viceregal capital. In Mexico he may feel no special regard for the indigenous peoples, but in Europe he develops a strong identification with the pre-Hispanic world—a cultural permutation reinforced yet ironized by the narrator's calling him "Montezuma," plain and simple, in this episode. For carnival, the criollo, a cosmopolitan sojourner, had put on the emperor's mask, an act that one may view as a profession of self-exoticism.[17] In fact, it is the costume's bizarreness that first catches Vivaldi's attention. That much of Giusti's knowledge about the conquest of Mexico derives from a book written by a Spaniard who never set foot in the Americas does not strike Vivaldi as an impediment for the composition of an opera; at the same time, paradoxically, it is the European opera that awakens the criollo's patriotic sentiment.

Vivaldi and Giusti's version of Moctezuma's story, as recounted by Carpentier, fits preposterously with Francesco Algarotti's suggestion, mentioned in Chapter 2, that the conquest of Mexico could be a particularly rich subject for opera because of its inherent potentiality for a magnificent spectacle, which derives from "la grandezza, come per la stranezza e novità dell'azione" (the grandiosity as well as strangeness and novelty of the plot).[18] Indeed, Miriam K. Whaples notes a similar appreciation of outlandishness in many European musical works about non-European peoples, which she broadly describes as an "endless Arabian Nights entertainment."[19] These include operas set in the New World as well as the various figurations of the *Türkenoper*, the German eighteenth-century term for any Orientalist opera. Whaples summarizes their plot and general structure: "Nothing of any lasting import could happen there; its people—so long as they were not actually fighting one's armies or besieging one's cities—were imaginary creatures whose deeds and words could be edifying or farcical, as one chose. Their principal occupation was to inhabit unusual landscapes and architecture and to wear astonishing costumes. Often they would dance" (3).[20] European creators and audiences admire Moctezuma not because they know much about him, but because his undoing at the hand of a small Spanish army can be transformed into grand drama.[21] Yet, a kind of knowledge may nonetheless be derived from Carpentier's fictional meditation on European exoticist practices, and it is a lesson that concerns the ties that bind the world's diverse cultures and become audible in the realm of music.

In Montesquieu's *Les Lettres persanes* (1721), a classic tale of critical exoticism, Parisians famously wondered how anybody could be a Persian, and there is a related series of questions at play in *Concierto barroco*. Although Carpentier's European characters never go as far as doubting that one can be a Mexican, the operations and implications of exoticism in Vivaldi's opera are, at least at face value, open to their own series of questions. Again, how can European opera represent an alien culture that it hardly knows, or knows only through inadequate sources? More poignantly, how should spectators with a stake in the matter listen to opera's misrepresentations of their own culture and world? If baroque opera deals with untruths, as Carpentier's Vivaldi freely admits, what are the consequences of these imaginative retellings of history for us as modern spectators, listeners, or readers? More broadly, what lesson can narrative fiction impart for the reading of opera? Carpentier's transatlantic traveler, in an unwitting postcolonial gesture of sorts, stresses the intertwining issues of empire and gender. He deplores, for instance, Giusti's libretto's erasure of Malinche, the legendary interpreter, as well as the fact that Teutile, one of Moctezuma's generals in Solís's chronicle, resurfaces as a woman, the emperor's daughter, who, to make matters worse, treacherously falls in love with Ramiro, the younger brother of Hernán Cortés. The Mexican protagonist, viewing both the gender permutation as well as the intercultural romance with a mixture of wounded masculinity and incipient nationalism, asks, "¿Y esa Teutile que se nos vuelve hembra?" (69; "And what about that Teutile being turned into a female?" 115). Speaking like a true man of the operatic stage, Vivaldi replies, "Tiene un nombre pronunciable, que puede darse a una mujer" (69; "He had a pronounceable name we could use for a woman" 115). The composer's quip is surely witty, but this is a sensitive issue for the traveler and, one suspects, some of Carpentier's readers, especially those accustomed to seeing his neobaroque novels and stories as a heartfelt defense of the specificities of Latin American cultural history.

On a first level, *Concierto barroco* may be read as yet another instance of Latin America's literary charge against European discourses that have repeatedly altered or devalued the vanquished indigenous cultures and the world that emerged upon their downfall. A textual defense of one's culture against representations perceived as inaccurate or unjust may of course are of course to be found in many other parts of the world. In literature as well as opera, these representations include not only specific turns of events in certain stories, such as Pinkerton's abuse of Cio-Cio-San in *Madama Butterfly*, but also a broader discourse—the process, for instance, whereby Puccini, following other European creators, feminizes the so-called Orient in his opera. As both a replay of and riposte to this discourse, consider the various gendered interplays of East and West in David Henry Hwang's *M. Butterfly* (1988); Gallimard, a French diplomat, falls in love with Song, a Chinese male spy, whom he believes to be a woman, because, as the play would have it, entrenched cultural stereotypes predispose Europeans to view Asia and Asians as feminine.[22] In the case of the Americas, one observes a similar trope as early as Columbus's logbook and letters, where, as Margarita Zamora has shown, the sign "Indies" implies a "gendered difference."[23] In fact, much of modern Latin American fiction, including other texts by Carpentier, may be read as rewritings of colonial works in which the Americas, to paraphrase the

Mexican traveler's words, are depicted through falsehoods. Carpentier's *El arpa y la sombra* (1979), to cite one such word, reinterprets Columbus from what might be termed a decolonial posture; that this new chronicle props itself on historical inaccuracies is actually a device that calls attention to the multiple errors, to say the least, generated by Columbus himself.

Against this background, *Concierto barroco* itself emerges as a far more subtle and intricate meditation on the claims and vagaries of representation than the traveler's protestations would suggest. First, not all misrepresentations appear to be deemed equally offensive. A large painting by an Italian artist of "el máximo acontecimiento en la historia del país" (11; "the most transcendent event in the country's history" 35), depicting Moctezuma, Cortés, Malinche, and others, hangs proudly in the criollo's house in Mexico despite all its historical blunders: "Allí, un Montezuma entre romano y azteca, algo César tocado con plumas de quetzal, aparecía sentado en un trono cuyo estilo era mixto de pontificio y michoacano, bajo un palio levantado por dos partesanas, teniendo a su lado, de pie, un indeciso Cuauhtémoc con cara de joven Telémaco que tuviese los ojos un poco almendrados" (11; "Montezuma was portrayed as part Roman and part Aztec—a Caesar with quetzal-feather headdress seated on a throne, its style a hybrid of Vatican and Tarascan Indian—beneath a canopy held aloft between two halberds, a vague-looking Cuauhtemoc with the face of a young Telemachus, eyes slightly almond-shaped, standing beside him" 35). Significantly, as we shall see, Carpentier's own text incurs in a series of misreadings, misrepresentations and just plain falsehoods which make Vivaldi and Giusti's equivocations pale in comparison.

In this transcultural context in which both Europe and Latin America point mirrors at each other across the ocean, I am intrigued by the apparent influence the novella is credited for having in the afterlife of Vivaldi's opera, by which I mean not only the libretto's ghostly appearance in the pages of Carpentier's text but also, surprisingly, an atypical revival of Giusti's libretto on the European stage in 1992. At the time Carpentier wrote his novella, in the 1970s, Vivaldi's music for the opera was lost and only Giusti's words remained. In fact, not until 2005, after a substantial part of Vivaldi's score was rediscovered, were audiences able to listen once again to much of the original work. Against all theories about the primacy of music in opera, it was the plot alone that inspired and informed Carpentier's fictional text. Reading *Concierto barroco*, in turn, prompted French musicologist and conductor Jean-Claude Malgoire to "resurrect" *Motezuma* by setting Giusti's libretto to a series of "musics" taken from various other compositions—operas as well as concerts—by Vivaldi. For Malgoire, resetting Giusti's words was not a mere postmodern act of recycling or a pastiche in the broad sense of the word, but rather it was a new and contemporary instance of pasticcio, that is, the common practice in baroque operatic culture of adapting previous music for use in new librettos. Handel had done it in *Rinaldo*, Vivaldi in *Tamerlano*, and Malgoire, centuries later in a neobaroque gesture of sorts, does it in *Motezuma*. More recently, in 2011, the Metropolitan Opera House commissioned a pasticcio of its own, *The Enchanted Island,* which deployed musics by Handel, Rameau, and Vivaldi to tell a story that combined elements from the plots of Shakespeare's *A Midsummer Night's Dream* and *The Tempest*; the work boasted its own postcolonial repercussions, including the belated onstage creation of Sycorax, Caliban's mother. Malgoire's *Montezuma* premiered at the Printemps des Arts of Montecarlo in May 1992. In the booklet for the performance's recording (by Astrée), Malgoire praises Vivaldi's operatic genius but dedicates his work to Carpentier: "to the great Cuban writer, who proved to be such a convincing ambassador to the last emperor of Mexico in his novel."[24] Malgoire's creation, then, is intended to honor the voices of Latin America, a literary culture where authors, besides writing about their countries, have often occupied political and diplomatic posts, and where an author's work is often perceived as a multipronged representation, in the literary and civic sense of the word.

Despite Malgoire's encomium, one wonders about the true effect of Carpentier's fictional ambassadorship of Montezuma when first listening to the emperor's voice in the Montecarlo pasticcio. Closely following the libretto's directions, the curtain rises on a scene of military devastation: "Part of the Mexican lagoon separating the Imperial Palace from the Spanish encampment, with a magnificent bridge on two levels. Signs of a recent battle."[25] In this landscape after the conquest, Montezuma intones his lament: "Son vinto, eterni Dei! Tutto in un giorno lo splendor de' miei fasti, e l'alta Gloria del valor Messican cade svenata. [. . .] Sposa . . . Figlia . . . Grandezze . . . Sudditi . . . un dardo vibrate nel mio sen" (90; "I am vanquished, eternal Gods! In a single day, all my splendour and the glory of Mexico and its valour fall in bloody battle" 91). The voice that sings Montezuma is that of Dominique Visse, the French countertenor, and one is easily seduced by the female-sounding male voice. But as Pierpaolo Polzonetti explains, the countertenor's voice "can have an alienating effect on modern audiences who are aware of, but not perfectly accustomed to, the early opera practice of assigning male roles to either castrato singers or women."[26] How, then, does one listen to this high-pitched voice in the context of Carpentier's assigned role as Montezuma's representative? How does one interpret this seemingly emasculated voice?

In Malgoire's re-creation of Vivaldi's work, the countertenor's throat resonates in multiple ways, none of which completely mutes the other; rather, the uncanny sound becomes audible in a chamber of echoes that replays various episodes of the not-always-harmonious history of European opera. The most obvious echo—the most audible one—is the legacy of the castrati, whose mutilated bodies, victims of the practice of orchidectomy, yielded sounds of incredible beauty as they sang some of the major roles of baroque opera. Moctezuma's emasculation, if that is what it is, might be yet another episode in the discourse about genocide and extinction in the conquest of the Americas. As Martha Feldman puts it, "the castrato's nonprocreative status has a distinctive place within critical boundaries of patriarchy, and . . . it is no coincidence that castrating boys for music became a going concern in Italy during the very period when patriliny hardened into a norm."[27] If the arrival of Europeans in the New World signals the imposition of new cultural markings, including surnames, on the indigenous peoples, the musical range of Moctezuma's plaint needs no words to invoke that history. But if one listens to Malgoire's countertenor voice as just an act of musical archaeology, then one may choose to remember that, during the seventeenth and eighteenth centuries, roles written for the alto castrato voice included such European male heroes as Julius Caesar and Orlando. Indeed, as Roger Covell states, when it comes to baroque opera, "we need to discard the notion of voice register related to virility."[28] Yet for modern audiences first hearing the sound of Malgoire's emperor, the question of queerness in very high male voices posed in the subtitle of Ulrich Linke's "Vokaler Gender Trouble: Wie queer sind sehr hohe Männerstimme?"— which considers the voices of castrati as well as countertenors— is altogether relevant.[29] Simply put, as Polzonetti shows, there is an implicit "feminization of Motezuma" in Malgoire's choice of music sources; the emperor's first aria, for instance, is an adaptation of Vivaldi's *Amor hai vinto*, a cantata for soprano and basso continuo.[30] In audible contrast to the countertenor's sound, it is telling that Malgoire's Fernando, or Hernán Cortés, is sung by a baritone, whose powerful masculine voice is imperiously juxtaposed to Montezuma's female resonances.

Besides the conventions of eighteenth-century Venetian opera at play in Malgoire's pasticcio, the countertenor's voice has its own history in recent operatic culture. Countertenors perform many of the roles originally written for castrati and long interpreted by mezzo-sopranos, but modern composers have written new works that feature these increasingly sophisticated voices. Between 1960 and 2010, Linke identifies more than two hundred operas that include one or more countertenors, including works by Benjamin Britten, Györgi Ligeti, John Adams, Peter Eötvös, and Unsuk Chin. One of these operas is Bernhard Lang's *Montezuma—Fallender Adler*, premiered in Mannheim in 2010 with, not surprisingly, a countertenor in the title role. In Linke's analysis, not all countertenor roles are queer; others are metaphysical, transcendental, or uncanny, while, exceptionally, even some queer characters are performed by other kinds of singers—Reinaldo Arenas in Cong Su's *Cuba Libre* (2005), as Linke notes, is sung by a tenor. Generally speaking, though, countertenors sing the roles of characters who may be viewed as "other" or "strange"—or, in Linke's conceptualization, distant, alienated, absurd, transported, uncanny, or outside of space and time.[31] An article in *Opera Now* once described countertenors as "beautiful freaks," and this may well be an accurate description of Montezuma in Malgoire's pasticcio, for it underscores the voice's artful oddity and outlandishness. Images of the opera's first staging at Montecarlo show the Mexican emperor all dressed in feathers, a rara avis of sorts, a picture of exoticism that could have been only magnified by the queer register, if you will, of the countertenor's voice, an alluring blend of masculine and feminine that can also be seen as postmodern fascination with androgyny and, more broadly, with the instability of gender constructs.[32] In this context, then, one may listen to Malgoire's choice of the countertenor as a marriage of baroque conventions and postmodern practices whereby the pasticcio emerges as an uncanny musical text that is both old and new—a text in which opera exhibits its own past even as it seeks to assert itself as an art form of the present.

But, again, what about Carpentier's ambassadorship of Montezuma? Can one regard Malgoire's creation, in turn, as a faithful musical representation of Carpentier's fictional text, as the conductor purports it to be? An answer may be found in the interplay of truth and untruth in the pasticcio. Writing about this belated revival, or resurrection, of Vivaldi's work, Blas Matamoro observes that it can be regarded as both true and false; as if following the fanciful temporal disposition of *Concierto barroco*, Malgoire's work allows the hearing of Vivaldi's opera—falsified, as it were, yet provided with authentic music by Vivaldi.[33] The music is really by Vivaldi, even if it is not the music that Vivaldi composed for this particular libretto. Malgoire himself speaks of a previous attempt at a pasticcio of Handel, a practice that results in what he calls "false operas," a concept that he then extends to all modern stagings of opera seria: "the fact that the work is a real one, a false one or a 'false-real' one does not alter the fact that a modern-day audience no longer has the same way of listening to and apprehending a performance, of whatever kind."[34] Conscious of modern sensibilities, the booklet for Malgoire's recording also contains an essay by

Serge Gruzinski titled "The Spanish Invasion: The Mexican Version," which attempts to retrieve the viewpoint of Moctezuma even as it celebrates the transcultural fusions of Spanish America's baroque: "the culture of the conquerors eventually merged with the culture of the defeated; the interbreeding of Whites, Indians and Blacks produced a new world: Baroque Mexico, with its stunning images, festivities and music."[35] Carpentier, one of the foremost theorists of the New World baroque, could not have said it better himself, and Gruzinski's paratext helps to positively reframe Malgoire's complicated representation of the Cuban author.

Then again, *Concierto barroco* is not just a defense of Latin American forms and patterns, nor a critique of Vivaldi's and Giusti's historical inaccuracies, but an intricate meditation on the status of truth and falsehood in fictional works and cultural theories. In many ways, Carpentier's text dovetails with Said's *Orientalism* and its theoretical offspring, as well as with much fiction from around the postcolonial world: it, too, writes back to an empire. Yet its lesson in reading resonates most specifically in the textual realm of *Motezuma*—Vivaldi's and Giusti's original work as well as Malgoire's pasticcio. Indeed, Carpentier's novella questions the authority of imperial discourses, but it does so not through corrections, but by tactically deploying the same historical imprecision—the same kind of errors—that it critiques. In this sense, the best antidote to a misrepresentation, the text suggests, is yet another misrepresentation, and indeed *Concierto barroco* abounds in these, especially anachronies, as if to defy the temporal rigors of the discipline of history. Incredibly, the novella's eighteenth-century characters, who include not only Vivaldi but also Handel and Domenico Scarlatti, suddenly witness Wagner's funeral cortege along the Grand Canal in 1883, and behold Stravinsky's tomb on the Isola di San Michele, no matter that Stravinsky died more than two centuries after the time when the novella begins. To justify the obvious historical inaccuracies in *Motezuma*, Vivaldi tells the Mexican traveler, "La ópera no es cosa de historiadores" (68; "The opera is none of the business of historians" 114). Indeed, a similar vision of opera's counterhistorical audacity is deployed apropos *Der Ring des Nibelungen*, whose fantastic plot is vaguely alluded to when Carpentier's characters observe the transport of Wagner's coffin: "Parece que escribía operas extrañas, enormes, donde salían dragones, caballos volantes, gnomos y titanes, y hasta sirenas puestas a cantar en el fondo de un río" (56; "It seems he wrote strange, colossal operas with dragons, flying horses, dwarves, Titans, and even Sirens put to sing at the bottom of a river" 98). Despite their Nordic origin, Wagner's assertively antirealist plotlines are not unlike Carpentier's own practice of fiction in Latin America—*lo real maravilloso* (the marvelous real), as he termed it—in which verisimilitude is stretched to include other viewpoints that defy reason or logic.[36] By the same token, if one looks at the tampering with European history in Carpentier's text, one may conclude that fiction and history are contradictory endeavors—and that fictional forms, whether literary or operatic, are in no way a lesser form of representation because of their notable breaches of historical fact.

Ultimately, however, it is a matter not so much of how authors write opera or fiction, but of how one reads those stories. With irony, *Concierto barroco* exposes the credulity of readers, including those who stand for Latin America, when the Mexican traveler, having read (or at least heard) of Shakespeare's *Hamlet*, describes Denmark from Havana in exotic terms as "la lejana Dinamarca donde las reinas, como es sabido, hacen asesinar a sus esposos mediante venenos que, cual música de infernal poder, habrá de entrarles por las orejas" (20; "distant Denmark where the queens, as is well known, have their husbands murdered by poisons which, like music with infernal powers, must enter through the ear" 49). A European kingdom emerges as barbaric and, indeed, exotic, but such generalizations stemming from stories people tell or read are ultimately revealed as risible. Upon hearing from Vivaldi that the king of Denmark is traveling in Venice, the Mexican traveler, yet again deploying his talent for misreading, proudly proclaims that there cannot be any kings in Denmark because "allí todo está podrido, los reyes mueren por unos venenos que les echan en los oídos, y los príncipes se vuelven locos de tantos fantasmas como aparecen en los castillos, acabando por jugar con calaveras como los chamacos mexicanos en día de Fieles Difuntos" (38; "everything is rotten there, the kings die of poison that's poured into their ears, and the princes are driven crazy by all the ghosts that appear in the castles and end up playing with skulls, like Mexican kids on the Day of the Dead" 73). The analogy between Hamlet and Mexican children matters greatly within the text's logic, because it reveals how Europe and the Americas routinely misrepresent and misread each other, or even themselves, by appealing to the outlandish. The novella's apology for the New World is closely linked with an incongruous rumination on the limits of both fiction's and opera's claims on historical truth, a sign to readers as well as spectators that they should take their representations with a grain of salt instead of summarily dismissing them as falsehoods. Vivaldi and Giusti as well as Carpentier and Malgoire emerge, then, as latter-day believers in Sir Philip Sidney, who in *The Defence of Poesy* reminds readers that the poet "nothing affirms, and therefore never lieth."[37] If some authors depart from Sidney by citing "authorities" and "other histories" (235)—which, according to Sidney, poets never do—they do so while wearing the ironic signs of "untruth" quite visibly, or audibly, on their sleeves. When Carpentier's Vivaldi knows who Wagner and Stravinsky were, or when opera's "Motezuma" has a daughter who falls in love with the conqueror's brother, one can affirm that fiction and opera are traveling under Sidney's "great passport of poetry" (215), the invisible document that stands for the freedom of creators to invent whatever stories they please, no matter how "false" their tones or undertones might be.

Yet one wonders what any of this may do for the afterlife of Moctezuma—not the character in Vivaldi's opera or Carpentier's novella or Malgoire's pasticcio, but the real man who lived and died at the time of what we now simply call the conquest of Mexico. How can we, five centuries after all that bloodshed, make his vanquished voice reach us, perhaps transport us? In this, paradoxically, opera's sounding of Moctezuma by means of a countertenor's voice may be the most beguiling of all possible revivals, not because Moctezuma should be in any way emasculated but because a countertenor's uncanny sound bespeaks a long history of cruelty and collapse that resonates with post-conquest accounts of pre-Hispanic civilizations. If one regards Moctezuma as the paragon of all that was lost through the arrival on these shores of violent men from Europe, then one may find a parallel story in the lives of the castrati, for they too, as children sacrificed to the vocal arts, were the victims of a world in which they mattered first and foremost as objects to be consumed for the sake of others. Because there are no longer any castrati around to sing the roles written for them, Patrick Barbier speaks of an "undeniable void" that opera seeks to fill in various, often polemical ways.[38] Indeed, one may ask, how can one recover the voice of the castrati when they are no longer around? Likewise, how can one sing like Moctezuma when his voice, too, cannot be retrieved no matter how desperately we search for it? As the curtain rises on the stage and the emperor's lament fills the void, we can sense the presence of worlds lost forever, but that opera extravagantly continues to invoke. Through the workings of opera, we can begin to sound those melancholy realms whose substance seems reduced to absence.

Absence, however, can sometimes be repaired, and this happened, at least partially, at the dawn of the millennium as a direct outcome of the end of the Cold War. After World War II, the archive of Berlin's Sing-Akademie, a major repository of musical materials, had been taken to Kyiv, where it was rediscovered after the collapse of the Soviet Union and, in 1999, returned to Germany. Among the manuscripts, there was one amazing operatic find: a substantial portion of Vivaldi's score for *Motezuma*. The uncanny restoration of the old music, suddenly new again, led to the opera's revival on the modern stage. In 2005, a concert version of the opera was performed in Rotterdam, followed shortly thereafter by a staging in Düsseldorf, and yet another at Schwetzingen Palace near Heidelberg, which then traveled to several cities in Mexico. The audio recording whose cover I examined earlier was made in 2006, followed by a video recording of a production at the Teatro Comunale di Ferrara, also with Alan Curtis leading Il Complesso Barocco.

Surprisingly, the work's unearthing yielded an important vocal revelation: the role of Moctezuma, weirdly sung by a countertenor in Malgoire's pasticcio, had really been composed for a bass baritone, whereas that of Fernando, or Hernán Cortés, had been written for a soprano castrato. In the context of baroque opera, there is only so much that one can say about this role reversal of sorts. But the change in the emperor's and the conquistador's voices may well sound to modern ears as a lovely, if delayed, operatic version of Moctezuma's revenge—a performance in which the main European character now happens to sound more feminine than his Mexican rival. There is of course nothing wrong in a female-sounding man, but the implications of these voices confute any facile distribution of gender and power in operatic designs. Just like a castrato's sound does not disprove a character's masculinity, a lower register does not necessarily signify a kind of supremacy.

Reflecting the historical record over vocal gender insinuations, the premiere of *Motezuma* in the United States, at Long Beach Opera in 2009, opened with a scene in which the defeated emperor walked around a room in a museum housing glass-encased pre-Columbian artifacts. To audiences unfamiliar with the practices of baroque opera, Motezuma, played by a baritone, may have sounded more powerful than Fernando (Cortés), performed by a countertenor. But trapped in a cold modern space where objects from his ancient culture were displayed for the pleasure of others, Motezuma appeared yet again as a victim of a commanding and violent European gaze.[39] A different approach informed the premiere of *Motezuma* in Mexico City in 2007. Writing about those first performances at the Palacio de Bellas Artes in the city where the opera unfolds, the historian Matthew Restall stresses how "the 'Conquest of Mexico' has never ceased to be a topic of entertainment, debate, celebration and conflict," and he views the opera as part of a discourse "indulging in a fantasy that European colonial expansion was about romance, with happy endings that might act as metaphors for civilization's joyful triumph over barbarism."[40] Restall describes the alterations made by artists and historians to Vivaldi and Giusti's "romantic-comedy plot" for those performances at Bellas Artes: "Some phrases in Nahuatl were added, and some pre-Columbian instruments were included. The Mexican violinist Samuel Máynez Champion, in consultation with the venerable Mexican historians Alfredo López Austin and Miguel León-Portilla, made plot adjustments, muting the original opera's happy ending with reminders to audiences of Montezuma's tragic death."[41] While not misrepresented, Vivaldi and Giusti's version of the events stood corrected in Mexico City.

As if seeking to overcome history's continental divisions, Carpentier's text juxtaposes a cultural geography all of its own, a literary and musical remapping in which the cultures of the Atlantic—Europe and the Americas but also Africa and its diaspora—reemerge not as possessing their own discrete sounds but as voices that come together in literal and figurative concerts. In this, the character of Filomeno, the Mexican traveler's black servant, performs, quite literally, a crucial role. Hired by his master in Regla, a town across the bay from Havana associated with Afro-Cuban culture, Filomeno is a musician whose marginal position animates an important subplot in which music, as invoked by words, tells its own story of cultural affinities and even unity. Upon meeting the traveler, Filomeno recounts to him the plot of Silvestre de Balboa's *Espejo de paciencia* (1608), the narrative poem traditionally read and regarded as the inaugural text of Cuban literature and often cited for its early description of music-making on the island.[42] With gusto, Filomeno enumerates the various instruments played during a two-day festivity in Balboa's poem: flutes, pipes of Pan, rebecs, bugles, tambourines, and "hasta unas *tipinaguas*, de las que hacen los indios con calabazos—porque, en aquel universal concierto se mezclaron músicos de Castilla y de Canarias, criollos y mestizos, naboríes y negros" (25; "even *tipinaguas*, drums fashioned by Indians from gourds—since in that general concert there took part musicians of Castile and the Canaries, criollos and mestizos, *naboríes* and Negroes" 25). The Mexican traveler is astounded by the mere notion of African-inflected music, which he repudiates in no uncertain terms: "¡Imposible armonía! ¡Nunca se hubiese visto semejante disparate, pues mal pueden amaridarse las viejas y nobles melodías del romance, las sutiles mudanzas y diferencias de los buenos maestros, con la bárbara algarabía que arman los negros, cuando se hacen de sonajas, marugas y tambores!" (25; "An impossible harmony!

Never could such folly have occurred, for the noble old melodies of the romance and the subtle modulations and variations of good maestros would have married ill with the barbarous racket raised by Negroes when they set to work with their rattles, maracas, and drums!" 55). In his racist review of a concert he never even attended, he deploys a lexicon that tinges the practices of *mestizaje* and transculturation with danger and negativity. The strange verb *amaridarse*, "to marry," sounds somehow less reputable than *casarse*, the more common term. Likewise, *algarabía*, translated as "racket," is the Spanish formulation of the Arabic word for *Arabic*; despite its implicit invocation of what for many is the positive history of cultural fusion that took place in Spain before 1492, its connotations in this passage are altogether censorious.

Besides expressing his antipathy for the kind of music described by Filomeno, the Mexican traveler goes as far as doubting the veracity of *Espejo de paciencia* as a source for learning about the past: "y gran embustero me parece que sería el tal Balboa" (25; "and what a great liar that Balboa must have been" 55). In Venice, too, as we saw, he will accuse Vivaldi and Giusti of producing an untruthful account of the history of Mexico. Yet the evidence is everywhere around him that the arts, especially music, tell their own unequivocal story of contacts across cultures. The outcome of these relations is really an unstoppable string of endless acts of creation that, as Sidney would have it, never affirm and therefore never lie; it is all art. Against any skepticism, Filomeno's own musical experiences—first in Havana and later in Venice and Paris, where, in yet another anachrony, he attends a concert by Louis Armstrong as the novella reaches its end—concern a baroque marriage of sounds that belong nowhere because they belong everywhere. At the Ospedale della Pietà, the charitable institution for girls and women with which the historical Vivaldi was involved as a teacher and composer for almost four decades, a concert like the one orchestrated, literally and figuratively, by Filomeno had never been heard before. It takes place at the height of carnival, and in Rabelaisian and Bakhtinian furor, Handel plays the organ, Domenico Scarlatti the harpsichord, and Vivaldi himself the violin. They are joined by seventy women on a variety of instruments, plus, finally, Filomeno himself, carrying spoons and rolling pins that he turns into percussive tools, creating "tales ocurrencias de ritmos, de síncopes, de acentos encontrados, que, por espacio de treinta y dos compases lo dejaron solo para que improvisara" (43–44; "such prodigies of rhythm, syncopation, and complex patterns that he was given a thirty-two-bar chorus all to himself" 80). Transported by the new soundscape that Filomeno, the master musician and custodian of multiple kinds of music, has conceived and produced, the canonical European composers can only exclaim "¡Magnífico!" (44; "Stupendous!" 80). Shortly afterward, amid much merry music-making, a conga line is formed, presided by the Mexican traveler himself in his Moctezuma costume. The performance is key to understanding the fictional logic of cultural fusion. As González Echevarría notes: "The heterogeneous, the amalgam, is also an abandonment of the notion of origins; instead it is in itself an origin, a new beginning—it is already the future contained in the beginning."[43] But what, exactly, is being born as this literary baroque concert resounds on?

If fiction were the business of historians, all this music making at the Ospedale della Pietà could simply be dismissed as false. But Carpentier's novella deals in untruths to suggest another, perhaps truer, method for interpreting—indeed, birthing—culture beyond the well-guarded limits of racial, national and continental categories. In this argument, yet another musical instrument, the trumpet, works as a powerful leitmotif for sensing the latent unity of the cultures that thrive on both sides of the Atlantic. The eighth and last chapter in the text is headed by an epigraph taken from 1 Corinthians 15:52: "Y sonará la trompeta" (73; "And the trumpet shall sound," 120). Having made up his mind to return to his home in Coyoacán as soon as possible, the Mexican traveler visits a music shop where works by Scarlatti, Vivaldi, and Handel happen to be for sale. These masterpieces of European baroque music, as we would now view them, will be presents for his friends back home in Mexico. Although he intends to remain in Europe, Filomeno has accompanied his master to the shop, where, rummaging through the scores, he finds a copy of Handel's *Messiah*. Once again, the novella engages in an anachrony: this fictional event takes place just after the premiere of Vivaldi's *Motezuma* in 1733, yet Handel will not compose his famous oratorio until 1741, after living in London for several decades. As befits Carpentier's text, temporality once again is no constraint for imaginative flights. Fervently, Filomeno starts to read Handel's score and deems it admirable, remarking on the bass aria for solo trumpet and strings, in the third part, which sets the verses from Corinthians:

> *The trumpet shall sound*
> *and the dead shall be raised*
> *incorruptible, incorruptible*
> *and we shall be changed,*
> *and we shall be changed!*
> *The trumpet shall sound,*
> *The trumpet shall sound!* (78, his italics; 125)

If the Mexican traveler is deaf to this music, Filomeno, by contrast, is in tune even with its Anglophone textuality—and even with another English word invented much later in North America to describe music created by persons of African descent: "estas palabras que parecen cosas de *spiritual*" (78; "there are words that look like a spiritual or something" 125; Carpentier's italics).

The biblical discourse about change and transformation resounds with Filomeno as he contemplates his life to come in another European city: "En París me llamarán *Monsieur Philomène*, así, con P.H. y un hermoso acento grave en la 'e.' En La Habana sólo sería 'el negrito Filomeno'" (79, Carpentier's italics; "In Paris, I'll be known as *Monsieur Philomène*. Like that, with a *Ph* and a beautiful grave accent over the *e*. In Havana, they'll just call me 'the Negro, Filomeno'" 126). In Paris, too, as the novel comes to an end, he will hear Armstrong's trumpet "en un enérgico *strike-up* de deslumbrantes variaciones sobre el tema de *I Can't Give You Anything But Love, Baby*—nuevo concierto barroco al que, por inesperado portento, vinieron a mezclarse, caídas de una claraboya, las horas dadas por los moros de la torre del Orologio" (83; "in a glorious jamming of 'I Can't Give You Anything But Love, Baby' with dazzling variations—a new baroque concerto into which, dropping through a skylight by marvelous fortuity, there blended the hours rung out by the Moors of the Orologio Tower" 131). The ancient Mediterranean trumpet that the British Handel invokes in *Messiah* crosses the Atlantic. In its new life in the Americas, coupled with other instruments and rhythms, most resonantly the musics of Africa, the trumpet becomes a major element in the birth of such rhythms as jazz—a new musical form that, in turn, sails back, as it were, to Europe, and in Paris, through Armstrong's prodigious playing, transforms the immemorial sense of time on St. Mark's Square in the heart of Venice.

Whether it can be accurately described as baroque or not, jazz emerges as the ultimate item in Carpentier's catalog of transoceanic transports, a precious array of works and practices that may be easily associated with a cosmopolitan view of things. Indeed, as *Concierto barroco* appears to argue, the movement of people across cultures has the capacity to transform the world. From the first page, in which the Mexican traveler packs a series of silver objects to take on his grand tour of Europe, the text underscores the importance of cultural artifacts. The element of silver matters not as a raw material to be extracted from mines for the wealth of other nations but as an element that can be crafted into things—the artifacts of culture—that express one's own history. In the text's first paragraph, as he lists the silver objects of colonial Mexico that will be transported to Europe, Carpentier displays a carefully crafted prose that verbally mirrors the complexity of baroque design: "De plata los delgados cuchillos, los finos tenedores; de plata los platos donde un árbol de plata labrada en la concavidad de sus platas recogía el jugo de los asados; de plata los platos fruteros, de tres bandejas redondas, coronadas por una granada de plata; de plata los jarros de vino amartillados por los trabajadores de la plata; de plata los platos pescaderos con su pargo de plata hinchado sobre un entrelazamiento de algas; de plata los saleros, de plata los cascanueces, de plata los cubiletes, de plata las cucharillas con adorno de iniciales" (9; "Of silver the slender knives, the delicate forks; of silver the salvers with silver trees chased in the silver of the hollows for collecting the gravy of roasts; of silver the triple-tiered fruit trays of three round dishes crowned by silver pomegranates; of silver the wine flagons hammered by craftsmen in silver; of silver the fish platters, a porgy of silver lying plumply on a seaweed lattice; of silver the saltcellars, of silver the nutcrackers, of silver the goblets, of silver the teaspoons engraved with initials" 33). Again, whether one chooses to catalog this as baroque or neobaroque or something else altogether, Carpentier's style exhibits the same kind of unnaturalness as one can easily find in the practices of baroque opera. For one, a sentence constructed on repetition—"de plata" and "los platos," with the *p-l-t* alliteration, or the patterned absence of verbs and the hyperbaton—recalls somehow the baroque aria da capo, in which the singing of two verses is followed by the repetition of the first verse, with multiple challenging iterations of the same phrases. The brief lines in Motezuma's initial recitative, "Gl'oltraggi della sorte" (The ravages of destiny), take a full three minutes to perform, while the seven lines in "Là sull'eterna sponda" (There on the eternal shore), sung by Mitrena, the emperor's wife, take more than six. If the aria da capo showcases the stratospheric reaches to which the human voice can rise, Carpentier's challenging twists and turns likewise exemplify the limitless potential of language.

However, against these formal parallels between words and music, if one ponders yet again the misrepresentations that troubled the Mexican traveler, it is not difficult to view Vivaldi and Giusti's use of the Moctezuma story as yet another instance of imperial exploitation in which Europeans comb the so-called New World for raw materials—raw silver—that they will then rework for their own sake. In the novella's last chapter, as he lays out the reasons for his return to New Spain, the traveler, adopting now a postcolonial stance of sorts, reveals how much he, despite being of Spanish descent and against all historical evidence, would have wanted the Mexicans to defeat the Spaniards in *Motezuma*. He also reveals a sense of jealousy on seeing the singer Massimiliano Miller taking over—in fact, impersonating—the historical Moctezuma. His reaction reactivates the questions of who possesses Mexico and to whom Moctezuma belongs. For the traveler, as his carefully italicized statement reveals, crossing the ocean has been a lesson in self-knowledge: "*A veces es necesario alejarse de las cosas*, poner un mar de por medio, *para ver las cosas de cerca*" (76, his italics; "*It is sometimes necessary to distance yourself from things*, to put an ocean in between, *in order to get a close look at them*" 123). Indeed, physical and cultural distance affords a new angle from which to regard oneself and reconceptualize one's own place in the world. Yet the truth of the matter is rather more complex than the traveler acknowledges in his lament. Traversing the ocean is a powerful metaphor, but arguably, what opens the traveler's eyes and ears is Moctezuma's apparition in a spectacle where Europeans, once again and with every performance, conquer the space and time of a distant world. Then again, if one listens to Vivaldi's music and reads the words in Giusti's libretto on the key provided by Filomeno's sounding of things, *Motezuma* is no longer just an Italian opera of the baroque age, but a powerful, if ambivalent, element in the transatlantic systems of culture. In the end, Moctezuma and *Motezuma* belong as much to Europe as they do to the Americas, and vice versa.

The Novelist Writes to His Mother: Origins and Ends of Exoticism

But what if we choose the opposite view and read *Concierto barroco* to tease out the signs through which the text's uncritical view of hybridity becomes complicit with the logic of the imperial discourse? From the start of his literary career, first as an essayist and then an incipient novelist in the 1920s and 1930s, Carpentier appeals to New World cultural products to seduce European audiences, asserting difference over commonality. In a letter written from Paris to Lina Valmont, his mother in Havana whom he calls Toutouche, he requests an illustration of St. Lazarus made by Afro-Cuban religious practitioners. It will be used by the publishers of *Documents*, the surrealist art journal edited by Georges Bataille. What matters, he insists almost conversationally, is the illustration's capacity to shock through novelty, contrast, and even ugliness:

> Tú sabes cómo son: unas litografías muy malas, de unos cincuenta centímetros de alto, sobre papel abrillantado, que representan a

San Lázaro cubierto de vendas, sostenido por *muletas*, con unos perros que le lamen las heridas. Son las que hay en casa de todos los negros. Si encuentras una, envíamela, pero acuérdate de una cosa: mándame *la más espantosa, la más bárbara, la más fea* que puedas encontrar. Como es para ilustrar una cosa de carácter un tanto etnográfico, explicando las virtudes que los negros atribuyen a San Lázaro, hace falta que sea una cosa verdaderamente salvaje, como alguna que he visto.[44]

You know what they're like: those very bad lithographs, about fifty centimeters high, on glossy paper, depicting St. Lazarus covered with bandages, resting on *crutches*, with a few dogs licking his wounds. All blacks have them in their houses. If you find one, send it to me, but just remember one thing: send me *the most frightening, barbaric and ugly one* you can find. Since it's meant to illustrate something of a slightly ethnographic nature, explaining the virtues attributed to St. Lazarus by blacks, it's necessary for it to be a really wild thing, like one or two that I have seen.

Young Carpentier's urgent request, albeit crude and hyperbolic, resounds with the literary project in which the author emerges as a collector of wondrous Latin American items. As he posits in his famous preface to *El reino de este mundo*, where he develops the concept of *lo real maravilloso* or "the marvelous real," Latin American novelists can find subjects for their craft of fiction by looking around and seizing on the astounding nature and history of their own part of the world. In Haiti, where the novel is set, Carpentier observes a culture born from contacts between French colonial settlers and enslaved persons of African descent—a new world unlike anything one might find in old Europe. Carpentier's fictional oeuvre affords a remarkably sophisticated vision of Latin America, but works such as *Los pasos perdidos* and *El siglo de las luces*, not to mention *Concierto barroco*, ultimately depend on at least a certain measure of exoticism to convey the region's specificity and, arguably, to persuade an international readership of its worth and originality as a literary subject. In that regard, Carpentier's own project, though historically rigorous, profits from a similar sense of spectacle at play in Vivaldi and Giusti's operatic creation of Moctezuma. To say that Carpentier capitalized on Latin America's difference might be overstating it, but like his own fictional Vivaldi, the novelist, too, knew about the business of art.

Beyond his literary career, Carpentier was an accomplished musicologist and music critic. He wrote an opera libretto of his own and authored *La música en Cuba* (1946), regarded as a revelatory study of several centuries of music culture on the island. When it came time to writing his own libretto for *Manita en el suelo* (1931), a puppet opera crafted in collaboration with Alejandro García Caturla, he took care to create a text that engaged Cuba's racial and religious diversity but avoided any kind of overt exoticism. As Malena Kuss shows, the short work's cosmopolitan affinities did not obscure the Cuban connections. García Caturla marked his modernist musical language with the popular rhythms of *rumba*, *son*, and *danzón*, while Carpentier, entrenched in European surrealism, was inspired by the story of the Virgin of Charity, Cuba's Catholic patron saint, and drew on the historical figure of Manuel Cañamazo, the eponymous Manita en el Suelo ("Long Arms")—a *ñáñigo*, or member of the Abakuá, an Afro-Cuban secret society—and other characters and visual elements from "popular mythology."[45] Carpentier's earlier description of the visual culture of Cubans of African descent, potentially exploitative, yields to a rich vision of their rituals and an appreciation of the aesthetic potential of black culture for an opera about Cuba. Music and libretto embrace the island's European legacy as well; Kuss, for one, identifies plot points that recall Monteverdi's *L'Orfeo* and sounds that echo Stravinsky's neoclassical works. All in all, García Caturla and Carpentier successfully crafted a work that eschews the worst forms of nationalism and exoticism, emerging instead simply as an original Cuban and Latin American operatic piece.[46]

But where does all this leave Vivaldi's conquest of Mexico, its operatic Aztecs and Spaniards singing mightily onstage or online? How should we listen to that sound after reading Carpentier? Consider, for instance, Mitrena's first aria, intoned just after she has handed her daughter, Teutile, a dagger—the same instrument that Motezuma has given her with precise instructions: "Questo ti serva / di strumento a mostrar il tuo gran core, / e prima ch'il traditore / stringa le destre di servil catena, / passa il cor della figlia e poi ti svena" (31; "May this serve / as the means of proving your great courage: / before the traitor / puts you in chains as slave, / pierce your daughter's hearts, then kill yourself" 31). These brutal words may be interpreted as signs of indigenous barbarism, but they are also, quite generically, the ravishing stuff of opera. When Mitrena raises her voice, she sings a mother's inconsolable words:

> Là sull'eterna sponda
> d'orrida e flebil onda,
> ombra seguace or ora sì, m'avrai.
> Quanto sia il mio tormento,
> figlia mia, non ti rammento;
> mira la doglia in me,
> pensa all'amor per te, quanto t'amai. (33)

> There on the eternal shore
> of the sad and dreadful river
> like a shadow following you, yes, there I shall be too.
> How I do suffer,
> my daughter, I need to remind you;
> look upon my sorrow, think of the love
> I bear you, and of how much I have loved you. (33)

In all likelihood, though, some spectators or listeners, sitting in a darkened theater or linked to powerful headphones at home, may just close their eyes and become enraptured by the mezzo-soprano's sublime voice, ignoring the words she sings. Like Clément, they will know how suffering's melody can be beautiful; Mitrena and Teutile, along with Motezuma himself and the rest of the Aztecs and Spaniards, may vanish, for this song might well not be about them, but about the power of music and the human voice to rise above any and all conflagrations.

As it turns out, the music Mitrena sings here is not what Vivaldi originally created for the aria; that section of the score remains lost. This poignant moment was recomposed by Alessandro Ciccolini by taking an aria from Vivaldi's own *Farnace*, first performed in 1727, as his model. That aspects of Tamiri's "Combattono quest'alma" should resound in Mitrena's "Là sull'eterna sponda" makes dramatic sense, as Tamiri too is a mother and has been instructed by Farnace, king of Pontus on the Black Sea, to kill their son and then to kill herself. Not coincidentally, the roles of both Mitrena and Tamiri were performed by Anna Girò, who, as Steffen Voss notes, specialized in tragic roles containing "short, affecting or dramatic arias and accompagnato recitatives with strong contrasts of emotion, where she could display her histrionic talents."[47] In *Concierto barroco*, Girò appears briefly; she is described as Vivaldi's mistress, but it is her stage persona that tells the story of European opera's geographic and historic appropriations: "Y aparece la Emperatriz con traje entre Semíramis y dama del Ticiano, guapa y valiente mujer" (61; "And enter the Empress costumed as a combination Semiramis and Titian subject, a brave and beautiful woman" 65). On the one hand, Girò's hybrid aspect (Venetian plus something else) recalls the portrait of Montezuma (part Aztec and part Roman, as we saw) in the criollo's house; on the other hand, as Voss explains, Carpentier's allusion to Semiramis, the Assyrian queen, is insightful, for Mexico must have appeared to Vivaldi and his European contemporaries "like a fairytale land," which then allowed Mitrena to appear as "an Amazon-like warrior queen, which would have been very unlikely for a classical Western heroine."[48] While Mitrena emerges as clearly non-European, it is possible also to view her as interchangeable with heroines from other parts of the world, somehow effacing her specifically Mexican status.[49]

This is, yet again, a story of transports. You may close your eyes and just listen to Mitrena for her beautiful song, but you, like Clément's operagoer of the future, may also want to know the story and the history of opera, and of this particular opera in which Europeans inscribe the long reach of their culture in a distant land. As the plot comes to an end, there is much singing about the end of military conflict. Fernando demands that Motezuma swear allegiance to the Spanish monarch, upon which, in exchange, his brother Ramiro will marry Teutile. That these characters were invented by Giusti only underscores the imaginative flights whereby the conquest of Mexico must have a happy ending of sorts. Mitrena and Motezuma sing last; she speaks of love, while he praises the Christian "gods" and announces the rebirth of his native land: "Cade il Messico è ver, ma poi risorge" (92; "Mexico falls, it is true, but then it rises again" 92). The chorus has the final say, with words of harmony about matrimony and the new royal couple. No one mentions it, but these transatlantic imperial liaisons are bound to end with stories of ethnic and cultural *mestizaje* never seen before, which is, after all, the ravishing core of Alejo Carpentier's own neobaroque works.

5 Havana and the Ghosts of Opera

THE STORY THIS CHAPTER seeks to tell concerns mostly the cultural history of Cuba, but its origins lie on the other side of the Atlantic—on the stage of Vienna's Burgtheater. There, on May 1, 1786, the curtain rises for the first time on *Le nozze di Figaro*, and Mozart's sublime music pervades the air. The opera's characters—aristocrats and commoners—play out an intricate plot where the social and the amatory converge. The French Revolution is just three years away, but this is opera; ancient regimes, at least in fictional Seville, are still firmly in place, and the audience is seduced by the music and the words. Figaro is about to marry Susanna, but Figaro's master, the Conte di Almaviva, desires that young woman for himself, scheming to revive the droit du seigneur. To complicate matters, Almaviva's own wife, the Contessa, is loved by a young man named Cherubino, sung by a mezzo-soprano. The Count, a jealous man wielding absolute power, wants to eliminate his rival from the picture, so he orders the boy to leave the castle and join his regiment. Just before the curtain drops on act 1, Figaro bows to his master and mockingly bids farewell to androgynous Cherubino by singing "Non più andrai," a splendid military-sounding aria. The words by Lorenzo Da Ponte, who adapted Beaumarchais's original play, seek to inspire fear in the frail youth even as they deride his apparent ineptitude for the manly arts of war:

Non più andrai, farfallone amoroso,
notte e giorno d'intorno girando
delle belle turbando il riposo,
Narcisetto, Adoncino d'amor, ecc.
Non più avrai questi bei pennacchini,
quel cappello leggiero e galante,
quella chioma, quell'aria brillante
quel vermiglio donnesco color. . . .
Tra guerrieri poffar Bacco!
Gran mustacchi, stretto sacco,
schioppo in spalla, sciabola al fianco,
collo dritto, muso franco,
o un gran casco, o un gran turbante,
molto onor, poco contante,
ed invece del fandango,
una marcia per il fango,
per montagne, per valloni,
colle nevi, e i solleoni,
al concerto di tromboni,
di bombarde, di cannoni,
che le palle in tutti i tuoni
all'orecchio fan fischiar.
Cherubino alla vittoria,
alla gloria militar!

No more, amorous moth, will you flutter
night and day, flitting here, flitting there,
disturbing the rest of the ladies,
Little godling, Adonis of love!
No more will plumes your head adorn,
or this cap so gay and jaunty,
flowing locks and air so dashing,
cheeks as pink as any girl's! . . .
With the soldiers, by Jove!
Wide moustaches, tight tunic,
gun on shoulder, sword at side,
straight of back, sincere expression

big helmet or a large turban,
lots of glory, not much gold.
Instead of dancing the fandango,
you'll be marching through the mud,
over mountains, through deep valleys
chilled by snow, or scorched by sun,
to the sound of the blunderbus,
and the bombards, and the cannons
thundering with mighty roar,
Bullets whistling past your ears.
Cherubino, on to victory,
On to glory in the wars![1]

As Figaro concludes the aria in his powerful baritone voice, the libretto specifies that all characters are to leave the stage to the sound of a military march. In many productions of the opera, everyone troops out, performing the role of soldiers; Cherubino must do so too, dismayed at the sartorial and acoustic calamities, not to mention the perils of combat, that loom ahead. Figaro is traditionally viewed as standing for social change; he is, after all, the hero of the play which, as the story goes, Napoleon defined as the first shot in the French Revolution. But the truth remains that, at the end of act 1, his commanding voice terrorizes Cherubino. A corrupt aristocrat may have conscripted the boy, but it is Figaro's hypermasculine tones that reverberate confidently while the mezzo-soprano stands soundless and helpless as the curtain drops. In Mozart's opera, though, all conflicts are ultimately resolved. The Conte and Contessa make up, and Cherubino, for all his fears, never goes off to war. As befits a masterpiece of the Enlightenment, all is forgiven, and the glorious music of *Le Nozze di Figaro* tells a story whose denouement is an exalted reconciliation.[2]

Many decades later, in a rather unlikely turn of events, distant echoes of Mozart's music traverse the ocean and signal the beginning of a real war. The year is 1868, and we are in Oriente, Cuba's easternmost province, at the onset of a bloody ten-year military conflict against Spain's colonial domination. On October 10, on a sugar plantation named La Demajagua, Carlos Manuel de Céspedes solemnly proclaims Cuba's independence and frees the people he enslaved. Ten days later, in the main church in the nearby city of Bayamo, a patriotic song composed by Pedro, or Perucho, Figueredo is publicly performed for the first time. This song will eventually become the official anthem of the Republic of Cuba. Known sometimes as "Al combate," after its first words, but also "La bayamesa," in imitation of "La Marseillaise," the song exhibits a peculiarity. Some of its lofty notes are said to mimic those of Mozart's "Non più andrai," a musical gesture in which, at least initially, one may perceive an outlandish intersection of Cuban nationalism with the very European realm of opera. The song's words are, of course, very different, closer to the deadly serious verses of "La Marseillaise" than to Da Ponte's playful aria. War, portrayed as a rough occupation in *Le nozze di Figaro*, portends real death in Figueredo's composition:

> Al combate, corred, bayameses,
> que la Patria os contempla orgullosa;
> no temáis una muerte gloriosa,
> que morir por la Patria es vivir.
> En cadenas vivir, es vivir
> en oprobio y afrentas sumido.
> ¡Del clarín escuchad el sonido,
> a las armas, valientes, corred!

> Hasten to battle, men of Bayamo,
> the Fatherland looks proudly to you;
> Fear not a glorious death,
> for to die for the Fatherland is to live.
> To live in chains is to live
> in shame and ignominy.
> Hear the clarion call,
> hasten to arms, brave men!

The song's call to arms was followed by veritable battles not only in that long war, which the Cubans lost, but also during the War of Independence from 1895 to 1898, which resulted in victory—tampered, however, by US interventionism and Cuba's own democratic failings. If all ends well in *Le nozze di Figaro*, the island's history may easily be seen as one of ongoing conflict and struggle well into the twenty-first century.

Whether "La bayamesa" actually stems from "Non più andrai" cannot be proved beyond any reasonable doubt; indeed, its general musical structure closely resembles the strains of much military, or military-sounding, music.[3] Nevertheless, Cubans have tended to believe that the patriotic song that eventually became their national anthem did originate in Mozart's musical universe. If there is some confusion as to which aria—or even as to which opera—the aria belongs to, it may be because Mozart himself quotes "Non più andrai" in the final scene of *Don Giovanni*, as the opera's eponymous hero awaits the arrival of the commendatore, yet another European music drama.[4] But the legendary Mozart connection is routinely invoked. In 2018, speaking on Radio Rebelde, the broadcasting service founded by Che Guevara at a time of revolutionary fervor, the musicologist Jesús Gómez Cairo, who wrote a book on "La bayamesa," answered a question on the anthem's "aliento mozartiano" (Mozartian inspiration) by saying that Figueredo's borrowings, such as they were, could have been meant as an implicit homage to "el joven viejo Mozart" (young old Mozart) or emerged as "un fenómeno casi inconsciente" (an almost unconscious phenomenon); in any event, said Gómez Cairo, the borrowings must be regarded not as a compositional shortcoming but simply as a sign of Figueredo's excellent musical culture—at the heart of which, one may add, lies the island's European legacy and relations.[5]

But what interests me here is not so much the musical echoes of comical "Non più andrai" in solemn "La bayamesa," but a less audible permutation that concerns the aria's words and the opera's plot. The song's origin in *Le nozze di Figaro*, even if partial and unproven, tacitly raises the issue of Cuba's relationship with Spain and the rest of Europe. When Figaro, the former barber of Seville, sings "Non più andrai," he speaks and acts for the Conte di Almaviva, a Spanish grandee. What to make, then, of the fact that the nationalist strains of "La bayamesa" may bear a connection with an aria that somehow bespeaks imperial authoritarianism? And how to view the opera's comical turns of events? If "Non più andrai" sounds like a parody of military music, Figueredo's song, with its invocation of *combate* and *armas*, would present itself by contrast as an earnest combat march. What prompts some listeners to hear in Mozart's ironic celebration of "gloria militar" a link with Figueredo's tragically martial "morir por la patria es vivir" remains a mystery, but one may see in this passage an aspect of Cuba that the discourse about the nation at times conceals. Specifically, Figueredo's perceived musical gesture seems to reverse the central thesis in Jorge Mañach's *Indagación del choteo* (1928; *An Inquiry into Choteo*), the influential essay on the so-called national character. In his inquiry into the idea of *choteo*—that is, the way nothing, especially perhaps high culture, seems to be taken seriously in Cuba—Mañach defines the country as "a land totally devoid of gravity, etiquette, and distance."[6] A literary performance of *choteo* aimed at the canons of European art music, for instance, appears in Guillermo Cabrera Infante's *Tres tristes tigres* (1967), the highly experimental text now deemed a classic of Cuban and Latin American narrative fiction. Johann Sebastian Bach is targeted in a section entitled "Bachata." The word recalls the composer's name and rhymes nicely with such terms as *cantata* and *sonata*, but in Cuba's lexicon *bachata* denotes a boisterous celebration—not exactly the well-tempered performances typically associated with Bach's art of music. Driving in a convertible along Havana's seaside promenade in the frenzied years preceding the Cuban Revolution, Cabrera Infante's three main characters listen to a baroque work on the radio and one of them wonders aloud:

> Bach, Juan Sebastián, el barroco marido fornicante de la reveladora Ana Magdalena, el padre contrapuntístico de su armonioso hijo Carl Friedrich Emmanuel, el ciego de Bonn, el sordo de Lepanto, el manco maravilloso, el autor de ese manual de todo preso espiritual, El Arte de La Fuga [. . .]. ¿Qué diría el viejo Bacho si supiera que su música viaja por el Malecón de La Habana, en el trópico, a sesenta y cinco kilómetros por hora?[7]

Bach, Johann Sebastian, the baroque bang-up husband of the revealing Anna Magdalena B., the contrapuntal father of a harmonious son, the blind man of Bonn, the deaf man of Lepanto, the one-handed wonder, the author of that instruction emanuel, *The Art of the Fugue*. . . . What would the old boy Bach say if he knew that his own music was speeding along the Malecón of Havana, in the tropics, at sixty miles an hour?[8]

That the piece they are listening to is eventually revealed to be by Vivaldi and not Bach, or that the physical ailments of Cervantes and Beethoven are mixed up, is met with a playful dictum: "Chico [. . .] la cultura en el trópico" (298; "Culture in the tropics, *chico!*" 322). All is confused, all is confounded, but nothing in the end really matters, except perhaps the pleasures of substitution and wordplay. Mañach would surely recognize the fictional characters' repartee, for he claims that "everything in Cuba has the laughter of its light, the lightness of its clothes, the frankness of its homes open to passing curiosity" (82). His conclusion is equally ironic: "We are in the perfect republic" (83).

Yet Mañach's linkage of laughter and lightness with the spirit of Cuba, if such a thing may be said to exist, is belied by the Mozart-centered listening of Figueredo's anthem. In its replacement with bloodshed and death, "La bayamesa" may sound and operate like the opposite of *choteo*. Then again, it is also possible to hear the faint echoes of "Non più andrai" as a more intricate, if unwitting, form of the same phenomenon. After all, to base a solemn air on a funny aria, and to sing it at the birth of a nation—a dramatic watershed in what will become Cuba's imperfect republic—may be seen as a derision of military life no less pointed than that of *Le nozze di Figaro*. Reverse *choteo*, one may argue, is perhaps the ultimate form of Cuban *choteo*. Not surprisingly, the anthem itself has on occasion become the target of comical misreadings whereby *corred*, the imperative form of a highly dignified *vosotros*, is taken to signify not "run to battle" but simply and quite inelegantly "run away!"[9]

But what if we compare the phrases that Figueredo deploys in "La bayamesa" as he calls his fellow countrymen to arms with the words in Da Ponte's libretto with which Figaro threatens Cherubino? I am especially intrigued by the first lines of both aria and anthem—the odd passage from the opera's *farfallone*, which one may literally render in Spanish as *mariposón*, a slang term for homosexual in Cuba, into the anthem's manly *bayameses*. This is a curious metamorphosis, especially if one takes into account the various ways discourses of Cuban nationhood often censure, if not altogether silence, signs of homosexuality.[10] My critical gesture is of course both anachronistic and idiosyncratic, for there is no historical record to prove that Figueredo—or, for that matter, any of the brave men of Bayamo called to arms—might have been at all conscious of Cherubino's gender bendings, which *farfallone* seems to invoke; or, more generally, of the many ties that many now believe bind many gay men and opera.[11] But my focus is less on the anthem's authorship than on the possible reception of this national icon and, more generally, of opera as an art form and cultural practice in Cuba when the uncanny legacy of Mozart in Figueredo is purposefully retrieved and reimagined. Indeed, the workings of "La bayamesa" may turn out to be an ideal site for exploring how Cuban nationalism plays out Freud's *unheimlich*, those familiar yet strange elements that are repressed but that ominously keep coming back to haunt an individual or, arguably, even a national community.[12]

In some late twentieth-century Cuban works—*Fresa y chocolate* (1993), the film by Tomás Gutiérrez Alea and Juan Carlos Tabío made on the island, as well as *El color del verano* (1991), the novel by Reinaldo Arenas written in exile—one witnesses opera's return to Cuba. This new transport, though, is not at first a festive occasion, for opera reappears most obviously—most audibly—as a kind of acoustic menace, a sign of strangeness and even foreignness. Yet the ghost of opera is an odd figure, for even as it exposes certain insecurities in the national spirit, it operates in a truly revolutionary manner, working to recast homosexuality not as a moral vice or a dangerous national threat but simply as yet another element in a diverse—ethnically, sexually, politically—Cuban nation. In Senel Paz's *El lobo, el bosque y el hombre nuevo* (1991), the novella on which *Fresa y chocolate* is based and whose title invokes Che

Guevara's concept of the "new man," David, the heterosexual narrator, succinctly links queer subjects with disloyalty to the Cuban Revolution; after all, he believes it is both the nature and the original sin of "los maricones" (faggots) to be treasonous.[13] The idea of same-sex desire as perilously counterrevolutionary, and of cultural products such as opera as telltale signs thereof, taints Diego, the gay protagonist. David will come to reject this notion through his friendship with Diego, a story of reconciliation in which opera plays a small but critical role.

To tell and investigate this story in which the transports of opera expose and suture the complexities of the Cuban nation, this chapter considers both history and fiction. I bring up, again, operatic Figaro and Cherubino (and their antecedents in Beaumarchais) and focus more extensively on literary and cinematic David and Diego. But I also find a lesson in two historical figures whose life journeys unfold most visibly as exiles from Cuba: Mercedes Merlin, the nineteenth century Cuban French author who hosted a distinguished musical salon in mid-nineteenth-century Paris and wrote an opera singer's biography, and Alberto Vilar, the Cuban American philanthropist who lived and worked in New York and infamously donated funds he lacked to opera companies and other musical endeavors around the world. In yet another mélange of history and fiction, I also convene the fantastic Condesa de Merlín, a parodic version of the real author, invented by Arenas for two of his novels. Haunting these assorted personages is the spirit of Mozart, who appears again most audibly as the chapter comes to an end.

The Nation and the Countess's Throat

For a small country in the Americas, the history of opera in Cuba is rather long and illustrious. In the mid-nineteenth century, Havana became a major center of operatic fervor and activity, a fact that may seem surprising if one remembers that, when it comes to music, Cuba is considered first and foremost as the birthplace of popular rhythms. Indeed, if we limit our listening of music in Cuba to that which is created by Cubans, one can easily argue that opera is just not an important genre. In this, Cuba would be like most other places, in which writing operas is a somewhat rare pursuit. But if we look at the history of musical performance instead of composition, Havana soon emerges as one of the operatic capitals of the Americas, at least for a time. Some of the lasting works of the Italian bel canto repertoire, for instance, may have had their Western Hemisphere premieres in Havana. As Enrique Río Prado notes, these include Rossini's *L'italiana in Algeri* and *Semiramide*, Donizetti's *Lucia di Lammermoor* and *Roberto Devereux*, and Bellini's *Norma* and *I puritani*.[14] Río Prado also states that seventeen of Verdi's operas were performed in Havana shortly after their Italian premieres, which encouraged local audiences to refer to their city as the philharmonic capital of the New World.[15] One milestone is November 18, 1846, when Verdi's *Ernani* was staged at the Teatro Tacón—the first production of an opera by Verdi, then a rising star, in Spanish America, and only the second outside of Europe, following its performance in Rio de Janeiro just five months earlier.[16] A review in the *Faro Industrial de la Habana* records the audience's excitement at that inaugural night; all seats were sold out, and even the standing sections were full. If we examine the performance history of Verdi's early repertoire, we find that, in fact, five of his operas were staged at the Tacón before anywhere else in the Americas. Indeed, the importance of opera in Havana, as well as the prominence of Havana for the practice of opera on this side of the Atlantic, cannot be overestimated. It was, for instance, one of several Italian opera companies based in Havana that introduced Verdi to the United States, on an 1847 tour that the *New York Herald* praised in glowing terms: "The most finished and excellent company that has ever visited this city, . . . the largest and most completely appointed and equipped."[17]

Yet by the turn of the twentieth century, even as Verdi's long career came to an end, the center of opera in the region had shifted elsewhere; most of the composer's last works were first staged in Buenos Aires. After that, at least on one occasion, opera in Cuba unexpectedly reached famously fearsome proportions. In 1920, a bomb exploded at Havana's Teatro Nacional during a performance of *Aida* that featured none other than Enrico Caruso, whose fees in Cuba were said to be the highest he had received thus far in his career, an emblem of the wealth and self-assurance of Havana's bourgeoisie.[18] But other links between Cuba and opera are far more subtle. The "Habanera" in Bizet's *Carmen*, for instance, first sung in Paris in 1875 even as the Ten Years' War devastated the island, originated in an Afro-Cuban rhythm.[19] In fact, the *habanera* itself—sometimes incorrectly rendered in English as *habañera*, diacritically reinforcing its foreignness—stems from the *danza habanera*, or Havana dance, a vibrant instance of transatlantic transculturation that still persists.[20]

It is not difficult to imagine an operagoer from Cuba, watching a performance of *Le nozze di Figaro* or listening to or viewing a recording of it, responding to "Non più andrai" on several levels. Besides the glorious music—this is, after all, Mozart and the art of opera at their loftiest—there is the semihidden Cuban connection, a little story that may be heard as a meditation on Cuba's self-fashioning. What if the operagoer, in an act of musical will, decides to trace in the unfolding plot a key for understanding Cuba—its autocratic politics, its views of gender and even sexual orientation? Mozart's opera, like Beaumarchais's play, is a clear indictment of autocratic rule. In *Le Mariage de Figaro* (1778), the words that Da Ponte later reworks for "Non più andrai" vividly depict Chérubin's fortunes if he ends up joining the Count's regiment. Figaro says with much irony: "Adieu, mon petit Chérubin. Tu vas mener un train de vie bien différent, mon enfant : dame! tu ne rôderas plus tout le jour au quartier des femmes; [. . .] un grand fusil bien lourd; tourne à droite, tourne à gauche, en avant, marche à la gloire; et ne va pas broncher en chemin; à moins qu'un bon coup de feu" ("Goodbye, my dear Cherubin. You are going to a very different life. . . . No more running around with the girls. Soldiers of the Queen, by Gad! Just think off'em, . . . weighed down with their muskets, right turn, left wheel, forward march! On to the field of glory and no flinching in the way—unless a round of shot").[21] The female characters in the play fear the prospect of Chérubin's demise, and Suzanne responds, "Fi donc, l'horreur!," while the Comtesse exclaims, "Quel pronostic!"[22]

But because the play is a comedy, we do not need to worry about Chérubin's foretold death; it will not take place. Figueredo's song, though, is a different matter. Given that a real war is about to begin when "La bayamesa" is first publicly performed, a phrase such as "morir por la patria es vivir" is no joke but a truly ominous version of Horace's "dulce et decorum est pro patria mori." In Mozart's aria, Figaro sings threats at the top of his lungs, "ed invece del fandango, una marcia per il fango"; Cherubino's life will no longer be occupied with a lively Spanish dance but will rather be an endless march through the mud. In Figueredo's text, there is no mention of *fango*, yet it is clear that the ensuing war will not be a walk in the park. That *fango* is the same word in Italian and Spanish may make Mozart and Da Ponte's silent reverberation in Figueredo's patriotic song even more jarring.

The Figaro connection, then, may afford a new angle from which to reflect on a troublesome aspect of Cuban cultural and political history: the view of homosexuality as a perilous form of unmanliness, foreignness, treason, and madness. In this narrative of the anthem's origin in *Le nozze di Figaro*, one must remark on the aria's view of Cherubino's boyishness as a formulation of androgyny—he may be madly in love with the Contessa di Almaviva, but the role of Cherubino is sung by a woman, likened in "Non più andrai" to a self-loving Narcissus, obsessed with his coiffure, big hat and feathers, and boasting a "donnesco vermiglio color"—or, as one record liner notes' English-language translation would have it, "cheeks as pink as a girl's."[23] Cuban opera fans listening to "Non più andrai" in the darkened theater may at times feel tempted to stand up and salute the Cuban anthem; by the same token, when they hear the martial strains of "La bayamesa," they might not help thinking of Cherubino's operatic travesty, a repressed lineage whose ghostly return may be troubling, unless one is willing to admit the uncanny temper of nations. As I indicated before, "Al combate" is also known as "La bayamesa," a title that echoes "La Marseillaise" and, by so doing, the European filiation of Cuban revolutionary struggles (and of much Cuban culture in general), but it is one whose feminine gendering somehow hushes the hypermasculinity of "La bayamesa" and allows for a more inclusive, and therefore undoubtedly happier, republic to emerge from the shadows.

But let's return, with opera, to Cuba. It's Havana in 1979, just shortly before the Mariel boatlift of 1980, when thousands of gay men, among many other Cubans, left the island for the United States. The setting is a grand building in the old heart of Havana, a city marked by architectural decay. Music is playing, and it's the voice of Maria Callas, singing an aria from Verdi's *Trovatore*, an opera that, like so many other operas, recounts the tale of a woman's undoing at the hands of patriarchal authority. *Il trovatore* is indeed a most operatic opera, boasting a plot that an old edition of *The Metropolitan Book of the Opera* describes as "a story of unrelenting revenge, with sorcery, poisoning, dueling, abductions, stake-burnings, a beheading, and fratricide cropping at every turn."[24] In *The Mambo Kings Play Songs of Love* (1989), the Pulitzer Prize–winning novel by Oscar Hijuelos, the Cuban man in New York who listens obsessively to the same mambo record is a man who desires women. But in *Fresa y chocolate*, the man in Havana who listens to Callas is Diego, and he is trying to seduce another man, David, who is not only straight but a fervent revolutionary as well. Having invited David to his apartment, Diego plays an opera cassette for him. As we can see and hear in this scene, Diego's life abounds in numerous and dangerous signs of the foreign. One of his walls is decorated with Cuban icons such as an image of the Virgin of Charity and a portrait of José Martí (who, as if heeding "La bayamesa," died on the battlefield in 1895 fighting against Spain). But Diego's tastes are largely eclectic and cosmopolitan—from his preference for tea (presented as a British custom) and foreign phrases to his love of Donne's and Cavafy's poetry. In this, a passion for opera emerges as a seditious emotion. Diego's worship of Callas, specifically, is both a personal and a political gesture, as he openly confesses when he follows his praise for Callas's voice with his wish for other kinds of expression in Cuba: "Dios mío, qué voz, ¿por qué esta isla no da una voz así, eh? Con la falta que nos hace otra voz" ("My God, what a voice. Why can't this island give us such a voice? We have such a great need for another voice").[25] One may hear his words as a lament for the fact that Cuba has not produced an operatic genius as grand as Callas but also as an oblique demand for democratic reform. Indeed, the rest of the film centers on Diego's attempt to remake revolutionary Cuba into a civil society where all Cubans, including those who happen to be gay, will enjoy political freedom. Significantly, Callas's aria in the film is "D'amor sull'ali rosee," which the character of Leonora sings in a prison cell, where her love for Manrico has taken her. Like the movie we are watching, *Il trovatore* is very much a tale of passion and politics where injustice and incarceration are all too real. If opera is typically seen as a repository of bourgeois propriety, there is another side to opera as the singer's voice pierces silence in protest and rebellion.

In *The Queen's Throat*, Koestenbaum comes up with twelve reasons that explain the gay cult of Callas, and one of these is the singer's ability to express fury at the wrongs that have been unjustly inflicted on one.[26] It is suitable, then, that Diego, who is mad at the injustices of the Cuban state, be transported by Callas's voice. One can hear in Diego's love of Callas an act of rebellion as well as a major revelation, for the sounds that emanate from the diva's throat may be read not only as a sign of Diego's location outside of the Cuban body politic but also as a display of how a passion for opera may herald a story of dangerous liaisons, one that involves a risky flirtation with foreign cultural forms and civic pluralism. That Diego is homosexual brands him as a potential outlaw, a rebel, but this note of suspicion also tinges the art of opera itself, easily viewed as a bourgeois, foreign, reactionary, decadent, and ultimately frivolous avocation. In Diego's devoted listening of Callas, one can hear, then, an indictment not only of the Cuban state, but also of the narrowly patriarchal versions of the nation that the Cuban Revolution has at times promoted, especially against homosexuals.[27]

Diego's affects find an echo in the voice of Callas because, as Koestenbaum argues, she also had an ear for passion and peril, as seen in some of the very difficult bel canto roles that she helped to revive. Finding Mozart "boring," Callas opted for such Romantic heroines as Bellini's Norma and Donizetti's Lucia.[28] Indeed, the most exalted moment in *Lucia di Lammermoor* is the so-called mad scene, in which the heroine, after a forced marriage at her brother's behest, invokes the brief periods of time spent with the man she loves—a forbidden passion. As she sings her last aria in a state of hallucination, Lucia's soaring notes stop producing recognizable words and transform into florid vocalization—an unintelligible discourse. Lucia cannot speak because she is mad; that Diego himself is mad as well as a *loca*—as one of the Cuban slang terms for homosexual would have it—makes his veneration of Callas's voice particularly telling, for therein lies a tale of literal and figurative madness. Lucia has lost her mind, but Diego is mad in the other sense of the word; he is furious at the way he is treated. Both characters sing, or scream, at the top of their lungs. If Lucia's madness lacks words, Diego's cry is distinctly verbal, even lucid, and it is precisely the clarity of his rage that makes him dangerous to the end. Opera's notes may be sublime, but there is no sublimation for Diego, not even through art's highest notes; he states the foibles of his nation all too explicitly. Life is elsewhere, then, and this outside locus becomes real for Diego, who, to prevent his own undoing at the hands of the state, departs from Cuba into exile as the film reaches its melancholy denouement. The madwoman Lucia leaves the stage to die, while Diego, the angry opera queen, the *loca*, the silenced hero, exits the picture—and the nation—for good. Before he leaves, though, he has shown his friend David not only another view of the Revolution but also another side of opera, one in which grandeur, rebellion, and freedom are jointly audible. In a scene halfway through the film, David sits alone in his room listening to the radio. As he tunes into various stations, one can barely distinguish an official-sounding voice that says the word *nacional*; seconds later, as he moves the dial, we hear the voice of Maria Callas, sounding very far, singing again her aria from *Trovatore*. Affected by the voice's eloquence, David decides to revise a collection of short stories he has been writing. He shows it to Diego, forging a new bond of intimacy and solidarity that rises above the rawness of politics and finds expression in the arts.[29]

    As I review my progress from Mozart's *farfallone* or *mariposón* to Figueredo's *bayameses*, and from Callas's madness to Diego's fury as a *loca*, I fear this argument might be dismissed as a series of philological twists and turns signifying nothing, or perhaps just as a strange chamber of faint echoes with only myself in it. Can the ties between "Non più andrai" and "La bayamesa" be established without any doubt? And even if they can, do they ring for others the same way they do for me? Moreover, as I speak of *Fresa y chocolate* and its arguably problematic depiction of the homosexual subject, I suspect that opera may resound unpleasantly as just another element in what Enrico Mario Santí calls the film's "melodrama" or "efecto musical," and Paul Julian Smith describes as its "fatal fascination with bourgeois decadence."[30] Yet Cuban literature, for one, contains other stories in which opera and homosexuality merge to reflect on and redefine Cuban nationhood. The sounds of opera are not always audible in Cuba, but they are there to be sounded, as it were, by those who hear them.

This is where another countess—not opera's Contessa di Almaviva, but the real-life Comtesse Merlin—enters the stage. A frequently muted figure in Cuban letters, María de las Mercedes Santa Cruz y Montalvo, better known as the Condesa de Merlín or Comtesse Merlin, or simply Mercedes Merlin, was born in Havana in 1789 but lived in Paris for most of her life. Merlin wrote exclusively in French, although often, and quite passionately, her subject was Cuba, or herself and Cuba: childhood memoirs, in *Mes douze premières années* (1831), or the detailed narrative of her one voyage back to the native land, in *La Havane* (1844).[31] Beyond literature, Merlin's principal pursuit in life was music. Not only did she host one of the most celebrated musical salons in Paris during the Romantic age, frequented by Rossini and Chopin, she also wrote a widely read biography of Maria Malibran, the famous mezzo-soprano. Merlin herself was a talented singer. During her visit to Havana in 1840, she gave a concert in which she sang several passages from Bellini's *Norma*, an opera whose main role, as mentioned earlier, became one of Callas's greatest. It is interesting to note, also, that Callas always carried a portrait of Malibran with her—one of only two portraits found in her possession when she died.[32] At this point, it is fair to wonder what this dead divas' society may have to do with Cuba beyond Merlin's filiation with Malibran, but *Norma* may well be yet another key in a furtive narrative from which Cuba may rise not just as a comical opera-buffa country but, fearlessly, as a veritable republic of opera—among many other kinds of music and many other things.

Significantly, the Countess's throat—her outlandish French, her very high notes—has resurfaced most audibly in the works of Reinaldo Arenas, in such novels as *La loma del Ángel* (1987) and *El color del verano* (1991), where Merlin appears not so much as a character who writes but as one who sings.[33] Much can be said about *El color del verano*, but suffice it to remark here on its boundless exaltation of opera's puissance. If opera is an art of excess—an extravagant art, as Herbert Lindenberger would have it—then Arenas's text rewrites Merlin's concert in Havana in an operatic but also grotesque manner: he removes the aristocratic soprano from the concert hall and places her in the middle of a homosexual orgy in a men's public urinal. Against this coarse background, the Countess stages her own private revival of Bellini's masterpiece, a performance the narrator exalts, quite operatically: "Ninguna Norma alcanzará jamás la altura y el rigor, el sentido armónico y el matiz dramático, que María de las Mercedes de Santa Cruz le insufló a esa ópera en aquel gigantesco urinario. La magia inundaba todo el palacio; la Condesa de Merlin volvía a triunfar" ("No other *Norma* will ever achieve the heights of perfection, harmonic complexity, and dramatic depths breathed into it that night by María de las Mercedes Santa Cruz y Montalvo in that monster men's room. The magic flooded every inch of the palace; the Condesa de Merlín had triumphed yet again").[34] This, to say the least, is not the customary rendition of "Casta diva"; Arenas's scatological revival of *Norma* in Havana surpasses the wildest stagings of the work (or even the listening to baroque music in Cabrera Infante's "Bachata"). That Norma also happens to be one of Callas's signature roles is a meaningful coincidence, for the opera chronicles a woman's fury at a man's betrayal, while she herself, a sexual transgressor, is accused of treason. Norma, as lovers of Callas well know, is a Druid high priestess in love with Pollione, the Roman consul who occupies Norma's country. Her passion for the enemy leads to her death, but her reputation is restored before her people and she is ultimately described, in Felice Romani's libretto, as a "sublime donna" (sublime woman)—a belated yet valuable redemption pronounced by Pollione himself.[35] Speaking through Merlin's imagined voice as eloquently as she herself sings through his words, Arenas conjures up a fictional universe disfigured by madness, but one whose sublime flashes of magic tell another story of Cuba in which inaudible voices may yet be heard. Merlin's lyrical inscription in Havana, like Arenas's own, is only textual, but therein lies the redemptive power of art, be it literary or musical. Beyond the temporal confines of history, art may help recompose the way a nation views itself.

But what about Merlin's own writings? Readers who approach the works of Mercedes Merlin simply from the viewpoint of Cuban literary culture may find it rather surprising that her best-known work should have been *Madame Malibran* (1838), where she virtually ignores Cuba. The subject of this long book is the short life of the famous mezzo-soprano, who died tragically at the height of her fame following a horseback riding accident near Manchester, England. Born in Paris of Spanish descent, Malibran lived in the United States and traveled across much of Europe, but she, unlike Merlin, her friend and biographer, had no personal bonds with Latin America.[36] In most of her other books, Merlin proclaims her Cuban connection with passion and intelligence, but as she writes on Malibran, her first-person narrator's voice undergoes a literary permutation in which the writer strikes the notes of a full-blown French author. Her colonial homeland is rendered virtually invisible in favor of metropolitan milieus, and she writes with an aplomb presumably acquired at her musical salon on the old rue de Bondy as she hosted renowned composers and select music lovers. Yet Merlin's authorship of Malibran's biography says as much about the singer's life as about the less evident ties that bind the art of opera and non-European lands like Cuba—a story in which Malibran's Spanish ancestry and Merlin's literal and literary transatlantic journeys converge.

A singer herself, as mentioned earlier, who enjoyed the fine reputation that Arenas exploits in his fiction, Merlin remains first and foremost a woman of letters for most Cuban readers. Yet her place in the Cuban literary corpus has not always been secure; Gastón Baquero, for instance, dismissed her authorship with a fierce boutade: "una cubana escritora no es siempre una escritora cubana" (a Cuban who writes is not always a Cuban writer).[37] This act of exclusion seems unwittingly reasserted in *Madame Malibran*, where Merlin fashions herself as a citizen of Paris and an authority on opera, that most European of art forms, and where Europe itself emerges as the privileged space of music and culture. Yet if one takes into account both Merlin's and Malibran's multilingual transatlantic lives, Europe appears in fact to be quite small and limiting, even provincial. Like the art of opera that it describes, *Madame Malibran* is avowedly supranational as it chronicles the story of two essentially foreign women who come together in a strange tale without borders. This is also a story that brings up the travels of race and ethnicity to contest the idea of opera as just a European art form belonging only to Europeans.

If one reads Merlin's autobiographical texts, it is easy to picture her as a young girl in a lovely colonial house in Havana or as a resplendent hostess in a Paris salon. Yet an equally clear emblem of her literary career is situated somewhere in the middle of the Atlantic Ocean, a geographical space as well as a symbolic location for the transport of peoples and cultural forms among Europe, Africa, and the Americas. In April 1840, Merlin boarded the steamship SS *Great Western* from Bristol to New York, her first stop on a journey whose final destination would be Havana and its literary outcome *La Havane*, an engrossing travel narrative. The steamship belonged to the Great Western Railway, the company linking London with the west of England, which played a notable role in the history of maritime transport and, tangentially, European literature. Although it also had masts and sails, the SS *Great Western* was designed to be the first steamship with regularly scheduled service from Europe to North America. This fact was a milestone not just for naval engineering but for business competition as well, given that the British and American Steam Navigation Company had built the SS *Sirius* with the intention of becoming the first company to cross the Atlantic by steamship. In a gesture full of drama, the race across the Atlantic ended with victory for the *Sirius* as its crew, seeing that coal was running low, decided to burn the cabin furnishings and mast. A similar crisis is recounted in Jules Verne's *Le Tour du monde en 80 jours* (1873), when Phileas Fogg requests from Captain Andrew Speedy to burn anything made of wood in order to reach Liverpool, and Europe, thereby completing his journey back to London on time.

Yet Merlin depicts her real-life crossing not as a modern feat of technology but as a Romantic sentimental journey in which fear and courage do battle with each other. As storms hit the *Great Western* en route to New York, she writes a letter to her daughter, Madame Gentien de Dissay, dramatically describing how she lay on the bridge exposed to wind, rain, and fog—the waves crashing against the ship, her heart beating only because of her love for her child. Yet much about the trip is a far more prosaic affair than the lofty tones of passages such as this would imply. Onboard, Merlin's eyes and ears perceive the great movement of people and cultures between Europe and the Americas. She records passengers of multiple nationalities and ethnicities who speak diverse tongues and occasionally attempt to communicate in a strange *Sprachmischung* that contrasts with the book's otherwise spotless French. This is the case of an Englishman and a Spaniard whose quarrel about the placement of a hatbox on deck the author skillfully transcribes: "'Vos était remarquablement stioupid' . . . 'Y vuesa merced es un malcriado' . . . 'Cet homme . . . avé une très-irreverencious manner . . . Jé défendé vos de paalé davantadge!—taisez-vos, tutte suite, tutte!' . . . 'Hérético dou diable!—Caramba!. . . que si jè mè lève!'" ("You are remarkably stupid," "And your honor has no manners," "This man has a very irreverent manner," "I forbid you to say anything else; shut up right now!," "I forbid you to say anything else; good gracious, I'm not about to stand up!").[38] The richly phonetic notation of the travelers' interlingual diction is perhaps to be expected in a translingual author receptive to linguistic quirks; it is also a sign of cosmopolitanism in an aristocrat who had long resided in various capitals.[39] Merlin's gaze includes may kinds of persons, including members of operatic troupes, like Malibran and her family, or people of African descent, some of whom are also travelers on the *Great Western*.

Among the passengers on board the *Great Western* is Fanny Elssler, the dancer born in Vienna whose fame across Europe has now led to a tour of the United States that would last through 1842. If steam navigation and other technological advancements shorten geographical distance, they also contribute to the speedy transport of cultural practices and products. Elssler's crossing is not only an emblem of the multiple ties that bind both sides of the Atlantic but also clear evidence of an aesthetic impulse in which the performing arts, including opera and ballet, emerge as visible and privileged signs of cosmopolitan modernity: raptures that can be transported across the ocean. In the midst of the heated discussion, the cantankerous Englishman, whom Merlin identifies vaguely as Lord M., finds himself unexpectedly in front of Elssler. The author attentively describes the English passenger's expressed admiration for the dancer, which stems from her physical beauty but may also be related to the prestige of an international artist who travels from city to city deploying a ravishing art.

Elssler's journey to the United States is a noteworthy chapter in that country's cultural history. (She would also perform in Cuba on a second transatlantic tour.) It reprises the crossing of a troupe of opera performers a few years earlier, in 1825, when a family of singers, including Maria Malibran, left Europe for New York. There they enchanted the public with a performance of Rossini's *Il barbiere di Siviglia*, the first Italian opera staged in a city that until then had only known English-language musical theater.[40] Malibran's father was Manuel García, the famous tenor from Seville for whom Rossini had composed the role of Almaviva; in America, he was an operatic pioneer. García's associate in New York was none other than Lorenzo Da Ponte, who decades earlier had written the librettos for Mozart's *Le nozze di Figaro* and for *Don Giovanni* and *Così fan tutte* as well. An immigrant in the United States, he became the first professor of Italian at Columbia University and was involved, in 1833, with the Italian Opera House, the first building in the country designed specifically for performing operas. In New York, with Da Ponte himself in the audience, the Garcías performed *Don Giovanni*, the first staging of an opera by Mozart in

North America—yet another milestone in transatlantic cultural relations. Dizikes vividly chronicles the Garcías' visit to New York; the book's first scene, in fact, describes an Anglophone audience beholding a scene set on a square in Seville and listening to a tenor singing Rossini's work in a language, Italian, that most of them could not understand.[41]

After thirty-nine performances of nine different works (in Dizikes's account), Manuel García left with his family, save Maria, for Mexico. She would remain in the United States until November 1827, when, after marrying François Eugène Malibran, a Frenchman who had become an American citizen, she returned to Europe to embark on her own triumphant singing career. Maria's transports—her indefatigable tours across Europe, her rapturous voice, her transmutation into an opera legend—are the focus of Merlin's *Maria Malibran*. Published in two volumes in Brussels in 1838 (as well as in Paris that same year as the longest section of Merlin's *Loisirs d'une femme du monde*), Malibran's biography became an instant bestseller, with German, English and Italian translations and adaptations appearing shortly after its publication. In 1839, Georg Lotz published in Leipzig *Maria Malibran als Weib und Künstlerin, nebst Characterzügen und Anecdoten aus ihrem Leben*, by the Gräfin von Merlin, while in 1840 *La Malibran* appeared in Milan. There must have been also much demand for the book from English-speaking readers. The first edition of *Memoirs of Madame Malibran, with a Selection of Her Correspondence and Notices of the Musical Drama in England*, published by Henry Colburn in London in 1840, was followed by a second edition, in 1844, which contained a long anonymous foreword on the "Progress of the Italian Opera in England Previous to the Performances of Malibran," a title that elevates the young singer's career into a milestone for the art form also in Britain. Across the Atlantic, the book was published as *Memoirs and Letters of Madame Malibran* in Philadelphia in 1840 and reviewed favorably by Edgar Allan Poe in *Burton's Gentleman's Magazine*: "The memoirs now published by the Countess de Merlin, an intimate friend of the cantatrice, belong to the best order of biography, and convey a vivid picture of their subject. We conscientiously recommend them as the most interesting reminiscences of the day. They abound in just reflection, and amusing anecdote; evincing, moreover, a poetical, as well as an artistical, sense of music and song."[42]

Merlin's biography has not been republished since the mid-nineteenth century, nor has there ever been a Spanish translation. But a fictional version partly chronicling the book's composition was the subject of a film by Sacha Guitry, *La Malibran* (1943), with Géori Boué in the singer's role, Jean Cocteau in that of Alfred de Musset, and Suzy Prim as the Comtesse Merlin herself. The film is in fact structured around Merlin's research for the biography; learning of the death of Maria as the film begins, she decides to visit a number of people who knew her, including Musset and Alphonse de Lamartine, as well as Maria's father and husband. While Merlin's Cuban birth is not mentioned, her authorial role as the singer's biographer is at the center of the film. This, I believe, is Merlin's only cinematic portrayal to date, but it is not her only apparition as a fictional character.[43] Balzac had mentioned her in *Béatrix* (1839) and she had previously inspired the character of the Marquise de San-Réal in *La fille aux yeux d'or* (1835), two works in *Scènes de la vie parisienne*, before resurfacing, as seen earlier, in the works of Reinaldo Arenas. As in Guitry's film, the text of *Madame Malibran* matters for its analysis of the singer's career and its depiction of Romantic musical culture and also for what it says of Merlin's shifting practice of writing. As Claire Martin points out, the book is as much a biography of Malibran as it is Merlin's own autobiography of sorts.[44]

In *Madame Malibran*, Merlin's cosmopolitan experiences mirror those of her subject's life. Maria's artistic debut in Paris in 1823, at the age of fifteen, takes place at her salon for an audience that hailed from several countries in two continents. Two of Merlin's Cuban relatives—Nicolás de Peñalver y Cárdenas and his wife, María de la Concepción, to whom Rossini had dedicated a wedding cantata—were there. Rossini himself had just arrived in Paris at the time, a period when, in Merlin's mordant words, the art of song had been diminished. As they searched for a contralto to perform the piece, Manuel García, volunteered his daughter, Maria, whom he, according to the author, had been hiding away, just like a miser hides his treasure. Merlin's phrase insinuates García's severity toward his own daughter, as well as the role that she herself would play in the young singer's career. In her telling, Maria is presented by her father—and introduced in the text—as a kind of musical offering for Merlin; it will be from the author's Paris salon that the girl's prodigious voice will first soar in front of a public audience and then cross the Atlantic soon thereafter to perform in various cities in the United States before returning to Europe, a continent she will crisscross as the greatest singer of the age. Almost immediately after the scene at the salon, the biography also becomes its own travel narrative—a detailed story about the geographic and affective transports of opera. Maria is in London and then in New York, where readers witness dramatic multilingual scenes that define the transatlantic lives and times of both women. In a vivid episode, the text recounts in French the performance of an Italian opera in an English-speaking city where a desperate cry in Spanish is heard. It is the last act of Rossini's *Otello* (1816), and Maria is singing the role of Desdemona; her father incarnates the Moor of Venice, and he is about to kill her with a dagger that she knows to be real because she had seen him purchase it. When she feels her father's dagger on her breast, Maria desperately screams, in Spanish: "Papa! Papa . . . *por Dios, no me mate!*" (Dad, dad, by God, please do not kill me).[45] Merlin needs to explain the meaning of the phrase in a note, while Maria remarks that the audience, unable to distinguish between Romance languages, took her sudden panic for superb acting, assuming the Spanish words were part of the Italian libretto.[46] Maria's alarm remains imperceptible on the American stage, while Merlin's French readers require a translation to understand the horror, or humor, of what took place on a New York stage; such are the pleasures and perils of opera and multilingualism in Merlin's overpowering account of the transports of opera.

According to Merlin, Maria spoke four or five languages perfectly and, having traveled through much of Europe, had also adopted the customs of several nations. Apparently, though, Merlin exaggerated Maria's linguistic skills as well as the extent of her journeys;

in the United States she did not travel much farther than New York, while her purported multilingualism, as April Fitzlyon explains, was a sign of her multiple habitations: "From the age of three, she was to be a traveller, a nomad; she was never really to belong to any country. Although Spanish, she was never to visit Spain. Born in France, she spoke Spanish at home, and French and Italian outside it. She was a good linguist, and later learned English well; but she never spoke any language perfectly. She was always to be rootless."[47] This extraterritorial condition by which languages and nations variously overlap accounts for the natural affinity between Malibran and Merlin. It is the author who welcomes the singer, who felt isolated, into her house upon her return to Paris; when they sing a duet together, Malibran tears up because Merlin's artistry reminds her of her father's Spanish school. A bilingual sign marks their friendship, as can be seen in a letter from Maria to Mercedes written mostly in French, except for the heartfelt valediction: "Adieu, je vous embrasse de tout mon cœur. Je tâcherai d'être chez vous un peu après neuf heures du soir, ou avant si faire se peut. Maria, *que sus bellos y dulces carrillos besa con amor y respeto*" (1:261, her italics; Good-bye, I embrace you will all my heart. I will try to be at your home a little after nine this evening, or earlier if possible. Maria, who kisses your beautiful and sweet cheeks with love and respect). Epistolary intimacy results not from the quick announcement of a rendezvous, but from the trusting deployment of a shared tongue learned by the singer in a Spanish household and by the writer far away and long ago in Havana.

Although *Madame Malibran* is the story of a woman's life, what triggers the biography is Maria's premature death in Manchester on September 23, 1836, five months after an equestrian accident during a hunt in London. Her injuries, the cause of which she hides to her husband, the Belgian violinist Charles de Bériot, are frightful. Ignoring her pain, the devoted artist decides not to cancel her performance on the evening of the accident. A medical lapse, this marks the undoing of Maria Malibran, a woman as tragic as those heroines whom she had envoiced through the grandeur of her voice. According to Poe, Merlin, as a biographer, fails to understand the real ties between the singer's art and her death: "She seems never to approach the full truth. She never reflects that the *reason* of her friend's speedy decease was but a condition of her rapturous life. No thinking person, hearing her sing, would have doubted that she would die in the spring of her days."[48] Poe's evaluation might not be medically accurate, but Merlin plays down the exceptionality of her friend's singing by trying, for instance, to find the origin of her passions not in her personal character, but, rather generically, in her Spanish roots, a "blood" she imagines marked by Africa and Arab Spain. Despite her own birth elsewhere, or perhaps because of it, Merlin's minute description of Malibran's visage echoes the racialized discourses of European Orientalism: "D'ailleurs, ce goût d'activité et de mouvement allait à la merveille à sa nature arabe-espagnole; car si l'on observe bien, il y avait en elle plus d'africain que d'européen. Par exemple, une partie de ses traits, la grandeur de sa bouche, l'épaisseur de ses lèvres, ses yeux lorsqu'il étaient animés par l'indignation, ses formes minces, grêles, et pourtant si fortes, si agiles, si adroites: tout en elle décelait la race africaine. Si nous la suivons dans ses habitudes, nous retrouverons encore mieux les traces d'une origine étrangère à l'Europe" (2:110–11; Besides, this taste for activity and movement went wonderfully with her Arab-Spanish nature; for, if one observes well, there was more African than European in her. For instance, part of her traits, the size of her mouth, the thickness of her lips, her eyes when stirred by indignation, her forms, thin and slender yet so strong, agile and skillful—everything in her revealed the African race. If we observe her habits, we will find traces of a non-European origin even more clearly).

Merlin's deployment of race is, of course, troublesome, opening as many questions as it answers. Malibran died well before the premiere of *Carmen* in 1875, but Merlin seems to view in her a persona not unlike that of Bizet's heroine: a gypsy whose ethnicity sets her apart from other characters in the opera, and whose first aria, the "Habanera," sounds out a non-European world. Dramatically, Merlin brings up once again Malibran's unusual physical prowess as a form of alterity: horseback riding through hills and valleys, traveling all day and night in the middle of winter, sitting next to a carriage's coachman at the height of summer, swimming in the ocean, and skating on ice. These actions are signs that "le sang qui coulait dans ses veines n'était pas tout à fait européen" (2:115–16; the blood that ran in her veins was not quite European). Yet by depicting the great Malibran as possessing an alien lineage, Merlin's rhetoric effectively retrieves the art of opera for other parts of the world. In reality, even though she does not succeed in telling "the whole truth" as contemplated by Poe, Merlin, who knows her friend well, underscores the ties that link Malibran's artistry with a life journey not unlike her own, difficult to pin down within a typical French or European paradigm.

Despite her enormous vitality, Malibran's voice inevitably vanished as her body perished; neither life nor art were long. But the legend survives, certainly among opera singers like Callas, as mentioned earlier. Another famous mezzo-soprano, Cecilia Bartoli, collects objects that belonged to Malibran, including letters, manuscripts, posters, and stage jewelry. To commemorate the bicentennial of the singer's birth in 1808, the Cecilia Bartoli Foundation sponsored an exhibition of the collection that, as if following in Malibran's footsteps, toured eight European countries. In the absence of any recordings of Maria's voice, Bartoli also studied the singer's repertory and undertook, with other musicians and musicologists, a close reading of the original scores of Italian bel canto, including music composed for Malibran, played on antique instruments, to reanimate the sound of the singer's long-vanished voice. The outcome of this research was *Maria* (2007), a recording in which Bartoli performs works from the Romantic canon and compositions by Manuel García, such as "Yo que soy contrabandista" and "E non lo vedo," an aria from his opera *La figlia dell'aria* (1826), created in New York, as well as pieces written by Maria herself, including "Rataplan" and "Prendi, per me sei libero," an alternate aria for Donizetti's *L'elisir d'amore* (1832).[49] The video recording included in the compact disc's "special edition" captures Bartoli as she examines the manuscript of *Norma*, sings "Casta diva," and explains the advantages of having a mezzo-soprano's voice, such as hers and that of Malibran (whom she calls a "megastar"), to tackle the challenges of Bellini's grand aria. Both the audio and video recordings of *Maria* are included in a book on whose cover the names of both singers merge uncannily as *Maria Cecilia Bartoli*. Mournfully, the book features numerous photographs of Bartoli posing by Malibran's portraits, items of furniture that belonged to her, and even her death mask. It also contains epistolary fragments, including fragments of letters from Maria to Giuditta Pasta; Rossini to Pauline Viardot, Maria's sister; Joaquina García, her mother, to George Sand; and Bellini to Maria, in which he expresses his devotion to her.

As it gathers these ghostly fragments of the singer's life, the book seeks to answer the simple yet impossibly ambitious question with which it begins: "What was Maria Malibran, scion of the illustrious García family, really like?"[50] To this end, passages from Merlin's biography are cited to shed light on Maria's own musical works, a little-known aspect of her career that Bartoli wishes to underscore: "Maria had a great facility in composition, and we are acquainted with a number of airs and romances of her authorship which attest to that. As a rule, these pieces are original in character, at once tender and brilliant. She never sold any of them, intending them as presents for her friends or charity."[51] Merlin is also invoked to explain a lithograph made in Naples in 1835, entitled "Caduta della Malibran" and placed in the book under large letters proclaiming "Pig Stops Prima Donna!": "at a place where coaches have great difficulty getting through the crowds, a pig was having its throat cut in the middle of the road. It escaped from the hands of its executioners and rushed at the feet of the horses that were drawing our artist's carriage. . . . Maria was knocked down, twisted her right elbow and wrist, and fell in a faint on the pavement[52]" These excerpts are cited in the original French and rendered in English, German, and Italian, a tetralingual deployment easily regarded as part and parcel of the globalized revival of Romantic musical culture that Bartoli's activities, including the touring exhibition, sought to accomplish—but also a tacit acknowledgment of Malibran's cosmopolitan life and career. Merlin's textual apparition is marginal, yet considering the bonds of friendship that linked both author and singer, the brief emergence of those words in the passionate context of *Maria* powerfully captures and revives the spirit of *Madame Malibran*. After all, both Merlin's writing and Bartoli's singing seek to bestow a kind of eternity on a ravishing voice that death silenced all too early.

Merlin ends her biography by describing a lofty monument that will be erected to her friend's memory in Ixelles, near Brussels. It will be a white marble statue, illuminated by one sunray and surrounded by shadows—an apparition likened to a fantastic thought or a poet's dream (2:144). An English version corrects the chapel's location even as it invokes the slightly more modern image of the public for whom Malibran was a goddess, a diva: "A chapel is about to be erected over her tomb at Lacken, and her bust is to be placed in it. At that sacred shrine let her admirers devoutly kneel, and, while offering up a prayer, let them recal [*sic*], as a beautiful dream, the tones of the one idolised Malibran!"[53] In the first decade of the twenty-first century, those admirers include Cecilia Bartoli, yet another diva whose practice of singing can now resound with the vanished mezzo-soprano's voice. The silence of the grave, however, resembles most closely the writing of Mercedes Merlin, whose soundless voice is also a personal monument to Maria Malibran's grandeur.

Malibran emerges in Merlin's biography as a democratic spirit—her singing not just a sublime pursuit but also, diligently, a woman's hard-earned sustenance. It is also not difficult to read in the story of the singer's journeys across Europe and the Atlantic a kind of cosmopolitanism in whose practices various cultures come into contact and, to some extent, artfully merge.[54] Yet the history of traffic across the Atlantic also includes, of course, tales of division and conflict. Some of these, such as the story of Lord M. and his harsh words with a fellow passenger from Spain, are minor. But others are part and parcel of the history of the African diaspora. Also on the *Great Western*, in the middle of the ocean, Merlin's *La Havane* tells yet another story of a thorny bilingual exchange, viewed this time through a racial lens. A storm is rocking the ship and her cabin is flooded. She asks for help and a valet quickly appears, whom she describes as a tall and ugly black man, scary to behold. He does not speak French, so she resorts to pantomime, pointing to the water under her bed. A broken-up dialogue laboriously ensues, and Merlin records her own imperious words:

> —*To-morrow*,—me dit-il tranquillement.
> —Demain!—Sainte Vierge!—Mais que deviendrai-je d'ici là!—Demain!—Non, tout de suite, à l'instant même!—
> Et le nègre de répéter en grommelant:
> —*To-morrow*.—
> En vain je tâchai de le persuader par de bonnes paroles; il ne me comprenait pas, et me répétait avec une impassibilité barbare:
> —*To-morrow*.— (1:43; her italics)

> "Tomorrow," he told me calmly.
> "Tomorrow! Holy virgin! But what will happen to me until then? Tomorrow! No, right away, this very instant!"
> And the black man kept mumbling:
> "Tomorrow."
> I kept in vain trying to persuade him with good reasons. He did not understand me, and kept repeating with barbarian impassibility:
> "Tomorrow."

In this brief interlingual encounter, the literal role and symbolic status of the Atlantic in the slave trade comes to the fore. The waters through which Merlin sails back to Havana, the city where she will perform Bellini's sublime music at a concert held in a relative's palace, is the same ocean through which Europeans transported Africans to places like Cuba. Further, the business of opera in Cuba was closely connected with the profits of slavery; Merlin herself supported the institution.[55] Receptive to Malibran's purported Arab and African lineage, she does not extend the same openness to the black valet. The English-speaking man cannot be understood; he remains out of bounds—a muted figure and an uncanny apparition, and also, implicitly, a racialized subaltern whose connections with Merlin's cosmopolitan cultural practices, including the performing arts, seem nonexistent.

As it travels to Cuba, Merlin's art of opera appears to remains very much an exclusivist pursuit—a realm in which the island's European stock rules supreme. Yet one morning in Havana, an astounding voice awakens the sleeping countess. It is the voice of an enslaved young woman who sings an aria from Bellini's *Il pirata*. Merlin describes this voice as "juste, etendue et pure" (1:340; in tune, expansive and pure) and posits that, were the singer ever to be seen on a stage in Paris, her copper skin would be a welcome change from the lilies and roses of habitual performers. There is of course no record of that lovely voice ever reaching European audiences— or local ones, for that matter. But Merlin's brief transport augured a different racial conceptualization for the art form, a subject to which I return in the next chapter.

The Undoing of Alberto Vilar and the Phantom of W. A. Mozart

It is, if nothing else, a grand and tragic operatic tale. On a day in November in the year 1999, in the center of London, Elizabeth, the Queen Mother, graciously renamed the iron-and-glass atrium at Covent Garden's Royal Opera House as the Vilar Floral Hall. The designation came about in gratitude to Alberto Vilar, the Cuban American investor who, in the late twentieth century, became known as the most generous philanthropist in the history of opera, with colossal and highly publicized donations to various companies on both sides of the Atlantic, from St. Petersburg and Vienna to Los Angeles and New York.[56] One of Vilar's most visible gifts was his pledge of ten million pounds to Covent Garden, which resulted in the naming of the Vilar Floral Hall. As the Royal Opera's foyer and bar area, this is an ideal site, before performances and during intermissions, for the social aspects of operagoing such as eating and drinking, or seeing and being seen.[57] Sadly, after Vilar's financial collapse and subsequent failure to complete payment on his promised gift, his name was removed—"reluctantly," according to the press release—from the Floral Hall, as well as from the

Vilar Young Artists Program, which the investor had also previously funded.[58] This was to be the least of Vilar's problems; convicted of fraud in New York in 2008, he would be released from prison in 2018, only to die in reduced circumstances in 2021. But this public lapse from grace is not just a journalistic story of misdoings and undoing. Vilar's progress from hero to rake is marked by pathos; seeking to possess the art of opera by attempting to buy a protagonist's role for himself, he is deprived of the transports—a dizzying story of motion and emotions—that he so cherished.

My focus here is the short-lived visibility of Vilar's name in Covent Garden not just as an episode in the history of philanthropy, or as a melodramatic case-study in vanity and excess, but as an extreme tale in the transatlantic yarn of European and North American and Latin American relations—a story in which the so-called New World, personified in Vilar's extravagant deeds, seeks to compensate for its self-perceived cultural insufficiencies through the public display of wealth. Money could buy him consideration, if not love, in the exclusive world of opera. One can imagine Vilar, who lived in New York and proclaimed Havana as his birthplace, as a new figuration of Christopher Newman, the hero of Henry James's *The American* (1877), who, seeking the kind of art and culture that only the Old World can offer, reclines on a divan in the very center of the Louvre's Salon Carré, carrying a Baedeker guidebook and opera glasses.[59] For Vilar, though, there was no need of the latter artifact at the Metropolitan Opera House, for he would habitually sit in the theater's first row to have the closest view of the stage and so that everyone would know where he could be found, performing his own role as the loftiest patron and possessing the hallowed spaces of opera. As if channeling the lessons of Adorno's "Bourgeois Opera," he told Allan Kozinn, of the *New York Times*, in 2000: "I adore the Met, there's no question about that.... I go into that place, and I get goose pimples. Wow, this is the Met! My rich friends laugh at me, because I sit in the same seat every night, in the first row. A101, that's my seat. I want to watch the conductor, the pit, the stage. Not only that, I hold court. My friends come up. They know where I am."[60] If the Queen Mother looked diminutive in the photograph taken with Vilar that graced an intimate corner of the Floral Hall, it may well have been due less to her height than to the donor's own majestic self-aggrandizement.

According to Norman Lebrecht in his rather polemical history of the Royal Opera House, the story of Britain's premier company mirrors that of the nation in whose capital it resides: "In manners and morals, habits and hobbies, attitudes and ambitions, England changed fundamentally in the second half of the twentieth century. The upheavals were most visible in demographics and wealth distribution. In 1946, any nonwhite face at Covent Garden would certainly have belonged to a North American soldier or a Latin American diplomat. By 1996, opera appealed to Londoners of Asian and Caribbean descent."[61] Although one would be hard-pressed to view the naming of the Vilar Floral Hall after a rich Cuban American philanthropist as a major chapter in the history of race and ethnicity in Britain, one can still read the uncanny apparition of Vilar's name through the house as a significant, albeit mostly symbolic, development in the globalization of operatic culture, a realm in which Europe still plays a leading role. For an art form typically viewed as trapped in the past, the association of Vilar with its future could spell only doom for some. Indeed, reporting on the Salzburg Festival for the *Times* of London in 2000, Rodney Milnes had referred to large donations by the "ubiquitous Alberto Vilar" while declaring, "It's starting to look as though the future of opera will depend on the whim of a Cuban American stockmarket investor with a love of music."[62] In 2006, as Vilar's legal troubles mounted, John Allison would write an article for *The Telegraph* titled "Opera Moneybags Faces the Music" in which Vilar was depicted as a social and artistic climber: "Money—or, rather, the promise of money—was the only thing Vilar had to offer. As I remember from sitting next to him at a Covent Garden lunch I attended reluctantly some years ago, there can be few more boring men on this planet. Supporting an art form he loved in an unsophisticated, childlike fashion gave him entrée into a world of excitement."[63] Whether a real passion of opera was his main motivation for philanthropy, or what the art form may have truly meant for him, is elided from the discussion.

If Allison diminishes Vilar's generosity by reducing him to a "would-be opera philanthropist"—after all, Vilar did end up contributing more than four million pounds to the Royal Opera alone—the truth remains that Vilar's prominence and pronouncements often resounded with a certain measure of New World moral superiority. He chastised European, including British, millionaires for not donating enough money to the arts, and complained that some governments did not acknowledge his bequests with sufficient enthusiasm. Speaking to Robert Hilferty, he deplored that, in Salzburg, the president of Austria failed to recognize him after a performance of *Ariadne auf Naxos* for which he had paid: "He did not even say, 'We have the biggest donor of this place in our midst. We thank him. Wouldn't it be nice if everyone followed his example?' Didn't say a word . . . That's a mistake. That is an *absolute mistake*."[64] Speaking to the *Times* of London before addressing the Association of British Orchestras in Liverpool, Vilar expressed his opinion that the British elite were less generous with their wealth than their American counterparts. The article was titled "Rich Told: Get Your Hand in Your Pocket," a phrase mirrored by the *Guardian* in its own article on the interview, by Sarah Gaines: "Britain's Super-Rich Are Miserly, Says Philanthropist."[65] If Lord Joffe, chair of the Giving Campaign, defended Vilar in a letter to the *Times* editor by stating, "Sir, Alberto Vilar is to be congratulated not only on his generosity, but on opening up a debate which needs to take place," others replied by pointing out important examples of British philanthropy as well as different taxation laws in the United Kingdom and the United States.[66]

The convoluted story of Vilar's actual and putative philanthropy has been analyzed in greatest detail by James B. Stewart in "The Opera Lover," an article for the *New Yorker* that appeared in February 2006, several months after the removal of his name from the Floral Hall. The phrase "opera lover" to describe Vilar is fitting, for his is very much a story of ardor. At the height of his wealth and fame, he was said to attend as many as one hundred performances of opera every year, some fifty at New York's Met and the rest at other venues on both sides of the Atlantic. His passion resulted in phenomenal displays of wealth. Stewart recounts how Vilar himself told the *New York Times* in 2000 that his donations made him "the largest supporter of classical music, opera and ballet in the world" and how *Forbes* magazine reported that his donations between 1996 and 1999 amounted to three hundred million dollars—"a largess," in the words of Stewart, "reminiscent of the projects of the mad King Ludwig II of Bavaria."[67] Indeed, the comparison with an extravagant European monarch is also fitting. Much has been written on Vilar's operatic ego, specifically, his desire to see his name and person acknowledged everywhere he contributed money. In his eyes, donations were not just a matter of capital, but an artistic gesture both part of the show and worthy of applause. In Salzburg and St. Petersburg, his photograph appeared in programs, while in Los Angeles and Washington he was recognized onstage for his donations. He told the *New Yorker*, "You look . . . at the program for, say, *The Marriage of Figaro* and it starts with 'Libretto by. . .' Well, who cares who wrote the libretto? How about the guy who wrote the check?"[68] He complained to Johanna Fiedler about the treatment of donors by the Met as "second-class citizens": "What makes me less important than Plácido Domingo? Why shouldn't I take curtain calls?"[69] Philanthropy, for him, was not an anonymous avocation but a public performance and an instrument for achieving recognition in the operatic history of many countries. Ultimately, his desire to inscribe himself in the annals of opera complicated the established discussion; to the roles of composers, librettists, performers, and designers, Vilar, like a belated sovereign of sorts, aggregated the figure of the patron.

In this search for operatic grandeur, the so-called Old World is at the center of things. While Vilar's gifts focused on New York and other cities in the United States, he often proclaimed his own elective affinities for Europe, as he tells Lebrecht: "I happen to be a Cuban refugee, . . . I landed in the States and I didn't like it. I came to Europe as a student, and it was one of those infatuations. London in the late 1960s and '70s had some of the best music. So I have been coming to Covent Garden all my life. Plus, I used to take tours from here to Russia and discovered the quality of their art."[70] This devotion to European cultural forms becomes visible in his New York apartment through a series of artifacts that invoke Mozart and Austria. Hilferty enumerates these operatic objects: "It's the life-size statue of a young violin-toting Mozart, his back turned defiantly to Donald Trump's 90-story Trump Tower across the ether. And the imposing bronze of Don Ottavio, from Wolfgang-Amadeus's *Don Giovanni*. And the miniature facsimiles of the Metropolitan Opera's Austrian crystal chandeliers glittering above the dining-room table. Oh, and the frescoes overhead, copies of the rococo paintings in Salzburg's famed Mozarteum concert hall."[71] Whether or not Vilar's decorative choices unwittingly mirrored the excessive lavishness often associated with his Manhattan neighbor remains an open question, but they are nonetheless a testament to his passion for opera.

Besides his declarations of love for European musical culture, Vilar's Cuban roots run as a leitmotif through his own public accounts of his life as well as in what others write about him. As if invoking the story initiated in Mozart's "Non più andrai" and its metamorphosis into the Cuban anthem, Vilar's self-fashioning concerns patriarchy, patriotism, and masculinity. A longtime resident of New York, Vilar appears first and foremost as a Cuban American immigrant. Fiedler, for instance, relates what one may now read as the standard version of Vilar's life, the origins of which are tinged with a measure of exoticism and visions of the ancien régime ambiance of his childhood in prerevolutionary Havana, redolent of old money, lost after Castro and regained in the United States: Vilar's father had owned a sugar plantation in Cuba, and the family had fled the Cuban Revolution as penniless refugees.[72] The young Alberto had come to New York believing that the United States would not tolerate Castro's regime in its own backyard. While he waited out Castro, he joined Citibank as a trainee in their overseas division. About the time he realizes that Cuba was not going to change, he tired of banking and moved to London, where he began his career as an investor. A poignant side of the Cuban story concerns paternal rejection of the son's interest in music and the arts. When young Alberto wanted a violin, his father refused, which, according to Vilar, stemmed from cultural prejudices about gender roles. When the boy expressed his wish to play that instrument, his father is said to have replied, "Cuban men do not play the violin."[73]

An upshot of Vilar's downfall from the hallowed spaces of opera has been the strange twilight of his Cuban origins. Stewart writes in the *New Yorker* about the discovery by Vilar's fiancée, Karen Painter, that the philanthropist was born not in Havana but in East Orange, New Jersey. In Stewart's account, Vilar's melodramatic tales of Cuba unravel as spectacularly as his finances: "According to others who have known him well, most of the life story Vilar had laid claim to was fiction. Although his father was indeed Cuban, his mother was Irish American, and he never lived in Cuba. The father worked for a sugar company with offices in Havana."[74] When confronted with the apparent embellishments in his biography, Vilar backed off "the more colorful aspects, including the claim that he lived in Cuba and that the family had fled the Castro revolution."[75] Allison put it more bluntly in the *Telegraph*: "All that can be said with any certainty is that Vilar is a fantasist of the first order, with stories of a childhood in Cuba and an early flight from Castro's revolution. It now appears that he was born 'Albert' in New Jersey."[76] Even as the name of Vilar, the cosmopolitan capitalist, disappeared from the operatic centers of the world, Cuba vanished from his biography, and the elegant and rather old-fashioned figure of the Cuban American philanthropist turned in the public eye into a ungraceful character from an unglamorous corner of the United States. His newly unhyphenated persona—just American—became yet another element in a story of unfulfilled promises and glaring untruths, as if only American money could buy the kind of love that the Cuban American opera lover once possessed. As Vilar exited the stage, like Cherubino and Merlin before him, Cuba too faded away with the other ghosts of opera.

But let's return, with opera, to Cuba. Decades earlier, back in Senel Paz's fictional Havana, Diego, upon taking David to his apartment in the old part of the city, proudly and seductively describes his opera collection, which holds original recordings by Maria Malibran, Teresa Stratas, Renata Tebaldi, and "la Callas" (22). Having died before the invention of the phonograph, Malibran, of course, could never have recorded anything, and many years would pass before Cecilia Bartoli would attempt to revive the mezzo-soprano's voice. How, then, should one interpret Diego's enthusiastic invocation of the dead singer's name? Is it simply an oversight on the author's part, or is Diego trying to test David's knowledge, or is someone—Paz, Diego—engaged in some form of mild *choteo*, as Mañach would have it? Or may we, as readers from another time period, opt for a singularly unrealistic interpretation, one that would elevate anachrony? As the story comes to an end and Diego is about to leave his hometown for another city abroad, he continues to add more titles to David's list of must-read authors, including yet another dead figure. Diego's language, absolutely conversational, paints a picture of Merlin as if she were alive and well and just living elsewhere: "No olvides a la Condesa de Merlín, empieza a investigarla. Entre esa mujer y tú, se va a producir un encuentro que dará que hablar" (56; "Don't forget the Comtesse Merlin; you should start researching her now. Your encounter with that woman will result in much talk"). Merlin, the virtually forgotten writer, and Malibran, the impossible recording artist, are both at the heart of Diego's own private literary and musical canon. As he leaves Havana, those nineteenth-century revenants continue to resound almost inaudibly in the nation's echo chambers, a place where Cuba itself, a nation left behind, is as ghostly as opera.

But how should this story end? In 1870, two years after the first public performance of "La bayamesa," as war raged against Spain, Perucho Figueredo was captured by the Spanish army and taken to Santiago de Cuba. Charged with treason, he was offered an official pardon on the condition that he never again fight against Spain. Figueredo refused and, soon after, like Cavaradossi in Puccini's *Tosca*, was executed by firing. His last words were reported to be, "Morir por la Patria es vivir" (to die for the Fatherland is to live). On a first level, Figueredo's undoing may well be seen as the clear embodiment of Cuba's defeat in the Ten Years' War, which Spain won. Then again, one knows that Figueredo's death was hardly the end of Cuba's struggle for liberty and independence—just like *Le nozze di Figaro* does not conclude with "Non più andrai" at the end of act 1. No one knows how things will turn out for the Republic of Cuba, but one may want to go back to that original stage in Vienna in search of a musical key.

Mozart's opera has a happy, if melancholy, ending, in which reconciliation, at least temporarily, triumphs above all.[77] In this, the Contessa di Almaviva plays a key role even as she sings some of opera's most poignant music. After the last notes of "Non più andrai" have died, the curtain rises again. It is act 2, and we behold the Contessa's profound solitude as she intones "Porgi, amor," whose music and words lament a lover's betrayal and contemplate the solace of death: "O mi rendi il mio tesoro, / o mi lascia almen morir" (124; "To my arms restore my loved one / or vouchsafe that I may die" 125). By act 3, when she sings "Dove sono," she still regrets how "i bei momenti di dolcezza e di piacer" (222; "the happy moments / of sweetness and of pleasure" 224) have given way to tears and pain. But as the aria ends, she hopes that discord will fade and harmony be restored, and this is exactly what happens as the opera concludes.[78] In act 4, after all the comic business of stage is done, all the intriguing, the Conte di Almaviva understands the extent of his guilt and, kneeling before his wife, begs for forgiveness. "Contessa, perdono" (284; "My lady, forgive me" 285), he sings, and she lovingly replies, "Più docile io sono, / E dico di sí" (284; "More amenable am I, and I do" 285). Words, words, words, one may protest, and these, quite frankly, are not very inspired. But opera is much more than just words, and here, if one listens to Mozart's lofty notes, one witnesses a moment of real transformation in which music makes us believe in pardon and new beginnings.[79] Or, as *The New Grove Book of Operas* would have it, "The humbled Count's prayer for forgiveness, and her loving response, build into a radiant hymn before the brilliant conclusion brings down the curtain on the crazy day."[80] But can the real world reflect the affects of the stage? Can the passionate history of Cuba really take its cue from an opera's last act and be transformed?

Cuba's national anthem, of course, is all about brave men about to enter combat and meet perhaps a glorious death, and one is easily tempted to close one's ears at the song's end. But if one so chooses, one may secretly perform "La bayamesa" as part of a larger story, one that remains inaudible but not unimaginable and whose happy ending may well mirror the luminous finale of Mozart's opera. By stressing those faint echoes of hope, one can perhaps listen again to Figueredo's song with new ears, as it were, and by so doing imagine that every single time voices rise to sing the national anthem, one can hear the ghostly return of opera to Cuba. This may well be a fantasy, but one worth imagining, for the phantom of opera, if acknowledged without fear in all its outlandish domesticity, may yet proclaim a happier story for a troubled nation.

6   Henze and Gomes

Ghostly Testimonios in
Copenhagen and Rio de Janeiro

THE STORY THIS CHAPTER seeks to tell concerns the practice of slavery and its afterlife in music drama. My focus is on two theatrical performances, separated by more than a century and the Atlantic Ocean, unfolding on two stages rich in regal associations: Rio de Janeiro's Theatro Imperial Dom Pedro II, in 1889, and Copenhagen's Royal Danish Theater, in 2009. But the most dramatic event in this story, while unrepresented in the operas, lies vaguely in the oceanic vastness between Africa and the lands of the Western Hemisphere. The key to understanding what follows—its initial emblem—may well be the Middle Passage, one of whose outcomes, as Paul Gilroy and others have shown, is the unending tale of transcultural contacts and creations among Africa, Europe, and the Americas. Although these diasporic voyages remain untold and unsung, their sequels activate and animate the two music dramas I consider here.

The first is Carlos Gomes's *Lo schiavo* (1889), with a libretto in Italian by Rodolfo Paravicini, who adapted the outline of a story, presumably in Portuguese, by Alfredo d'Escragnolle Taunay, the Brazilian author. Moving the plot from the early nineteenth century back to the sixteenth, Paravicini also altered the race of the opera's protagonist. Taunay and Gomes had conceived the eponymous Slave as a man of partial African descent, but their mixed-race Ricardo became indigenous Iberè; in this, Paravicini sought to uphold the conventions of the Italian operatic stage, on which black bodies were not to be seen. The second work is *El Cimarrón* (1970), a dramatic piece composed by Hans Werner Henze, who set a German-language text by Hans Magnus Enzensberger. Both men were inspired by *Biografía de un cimarrón* (1966), the now-canonical testimonial novel by Miguel Barnet, who in turn had crafted his own text by listening to, recording, and editing the words, in Spanish, of Esteban Montejo, a former runaway slave whose ancestors had been taken to Cuba from Africa. As the story goes, Barnet, trained as an ethnographer, read about Montejo in a magazine article that featured Cuban men and women who had reached the age of one hundred. In most paratextual presentations of *El Cimarrón*, both Enzensberger and Barnet share credits for the libretto, as in the booklet for the recording by Wergo: "Text from the book by Miguel Barnet. Translated and adapted for music by Hans Magnus Enzensberger."[1] Montejo's name, though, is missing, and his personal narrative is presented under the generic appellation of *cimarrón*, or runaway slave—one of several permutations that Montejo's oral discourse undergoes as it becomes a written text in the hands of Barnet and, in turn, a music drama through the collaboration between Henze and Enzensberger.

Subject to the demands of the global stage, performances of *El Cimarrón* often undergo yet another linguistic change, whereby Enzensberger's German text is sung in English. This was the case of the 2009 production at the Royal Danish Theater, a staging on which I focus for what it reveals about the challenges of theatrical collaborations that seek to represent an almost indescribable experience: the trials of a real person who spent years as an enslaved man. Retroactively, the Copenhagen production serves as a kind of prism through which to look back at the premiere of Gomes's opera at Rio de Janeiro's Theatro Imperial 120 years earlier. These variously translingual and transatlantic histories concern yet again the notion of transports in the multiple senses of the word: the lofty emotions triggered by music dramas; but also, in these two cases, the literal act, undertaken by European traders, of conveying men and women by ship across the ocean from Africa to be sold in places like Brazil and Cuba, which were, incidentally, the last two countries in the Americas to abolish slavery. The idea of transports speaks as well to the cultural traffic among continents—the hazardous voyages of opera and its creators and subjects from one city to another in order to tell their tales.

A measure of skepticism is unavoidable. What, if anything, remains in productions of these music dramas that accounts for the experience of slavery invoked in their titles? Can Henze's and Gomes's heroes convey the intrinsic brutality of their own tales as they sing for audiences likely to be privileged and culturally distant as well? Can these dramatic figures—singing in other languages, circumscribed by theatrical conventions—vocally express the dangers, toils, and snares in their stories, which surely inspired composers and librettists, who also surely intended to move audiences in diverse places? These transatlantic journeys, I argue, may be regarded as subtle acts of transculturation as well as powerful instances of cosmopolitanism, by which I mean the notion that all human beings belong to one single planetary community—and that, indeed, the enslaved figure can sing his own story, despite multiple obstacles, with the help of a friendly congregation of artists.[2]

As I think about these works, a series of questions emerge that resound with the idea of black opera as described and analyzed by Naomi André. Although her focus is on the operatic cultures of the United States and South Africa, André's insights provide a valuable paradigm for reading the transatlantic workings of opera and race in the creation and performance of Gomes's and Henze's music dramas. André underscores the long lineage of segregation and exoticism in the plotlines and stagings of traditional operas about non-European characters. Two canonical works by Giuseppe Verdi stand out: *Aida*, which André, following in the critical footsteps of Edward Said, views as "a made-up story with little knowledge of the historical Egyptians and Ethiopians," having "no reference to living Egyptians and Ethiopians during the late nineteenth century," and *Otello*, which has "little connection to the real lives of North Africans . . . living in European settings."[3] As is well known, the roles of both Aida and Otello have typically been performed by singers in blackface, as if to showcase how "little" opera producers have paid attention to the scruples of people of color. Yet as a believer in the power of opera despite its far-reaching historical aggressions, André counterposes the concept of "shadow opera," a critical posture that reanimates and broadens the art form by bringing up black perspectives and focusing, among other things, on how black performers and spectators experience both the traditional repertoire and newer works. André's objects of study are reworkings of Bizet's *Carmen* in operatic films such as *Carmen Jones* and *U-Carmen eKhayelitsha*, and contemporary operas on black historical figures, such as Sally Hemings and Winnie Madikizela-Mandela. But she also asks larger historical questions about the art form. Optimistically, André describes opera as a "flexible and capacious genre" that can transcend the strictures of mainstream opera: "with the participation of black composers and librettists behind the scenes, black bodies and black stories embodied on the stage, and black audience members interpreting the performance, opera compellingly expresses multiple vantage points that have not been previously engaged."[4] Black opera, an idea that Mercedes Merlin, as seen in Chapter 5, could hardly believe in, richly flourishes in the twenty-first century. In an example that concerns both the United States and Latin America, André mentions Tania León, the Cuban American composer who, at the time of André's writing, was working on a libretto by Thulani Davis about the integration of Central High School, in Little Rock, Arkansas.

Yet when it comes to *Lo schiavo* and *El Cimarrón*, to speak of shadow opera is not a self-evident proposition. For one, the composers and librettists of these works are not black, and neither is the majority of the mainstream audiences for which they are typically performed. But Latin American testimonial writing may provide a conceptual framework for viewing the complicated workings of shadow opera in the cultural history of the Atlantic. A testimonio involves a collaboration between someone whose access to the act of writing faces great obstacles and someone else—an experienced author or scholar—who knows how to navigate the requirements of literary culture with ease. In the case of *Biografía de un cimarrón*, Montejo narrates orally the story of his own life, but Barnet is engaged, in the various meanings of the term, in listening to his words and crafting a stylized text that reaches multiple readers. In many testimonios, as well as in the two music dramas discussed here, the notion of engagement surpasses mere contractual obligation and resounds with the ethical claims of *littérature engagée*. André, too, writes about an "engaged musicology"—a scholarly practice that, for instance, can listen to the voice of Leontyne Price, the revered black American soprano, and hear in that voice not only Aida's tribulations but also Price's own "body and experiences": "Revealed in this voice is the childhood in Mississippi during the 1930s and 1940s; the proud and puzzled receptions of her operatic singing by her family, community, and audiences around the world; the comments she must have endured. As the regal and long-suffering Aida, Price was the African American singer whose voice fit the character perfectly; in this role she proved so many people wrong for their bigotry and violence. And she made so many things right for those of us who have fallen in love with opera."[5] Works engaged in denouncing prejudice, *Lo schiavo* and *El Cimarrón* seek to give a voice to the plight of their protagonists through words and music. Because of its literary source, Henze's drama requires and even facilitates interpretations that take into account the principles of testimonial writing. But Gomes's opera, so intertwined with the operatic practices of Verdi and other nineteenth-century Italian composers, is harder to relate to a genre that only developed much later under different circumstances. But despite the conventional libretto, Gomes's orchestral music, plus a few words he wrote about the opera, make it possible to perceive in Iberè's voice the bodies and experiences of black enslaved persons. Read and heard after a performance of *El Cimarrón*, *Lo schiavo* can operate effectively as a shadow testimonio.

The Runaway Slave Sings His Life

At the start of the new operatic season in the fall of 2009, four gifted musicians, equipped with numerous musical instruments and, in one case, the sheer power of the human voice, performed Henze's

El Cimarrón at Copenhagen's Royal Danish Theater. This was not the new Operaen, inaugurated in 2005 across the water from Amalienborg Palace, but the so-called Gamle Scene or Old Stage, at Kongens Nytorv, which opened in 1874 on the same site where theaters had stood since the eighteenth century. As its website describes it, the Royal Theater is the storied venue to which "the 14-year-old fairytale storyteller Hans Christian Andersen devoted his early ambition," and which Søren Kierkegaard regarded as Denmark's "one theater."[6] The ultimate passage of Montejo's tale from a veteran soldiers' home in tropical Cuba to this august theatrical venue in a Nordic capital is complex, but that transatlantic story may well be said to begin and end with two men from the Caribbean united as one figure.

The first man is Esteban Montejo himself, born a slave in Cuba in 1860 and a witness to many of the key events in the history of his country: the abolition of slavery in 1886; the War of Independence, lasting from 1895 to 1898; the often tumultuous decades of the Cuban republic; and the storied revolution that came to power in 1959. Montejo died in 1973 at the age of 113, and his fame was a product of his unusual longevity and powerful life story. The second man, also a black person from the Caribbean, is Sir Willard White, the British baritone born in Jamaica in 1946, the son of a dockworker, and a student at the Jamaican School of Music and the Juilliard School. One of the great opera singers of our times, White was appointed commander of the Order of the British Empire in 1995, receiving a knighthood in the Queen's birthday honors list in 2004. Although his career began at Juilliard in 1971 in the role of the runaway slave Jim in Hall Overton's operatic version of *Huckleberry Finn*, most of White's career has had little or nothing to do with depictions of race or slavery. He has sung much of the classic bass-baritone repertoire in operas by composers from Monteverdi and Handel to Wagner and Puccini, performing as well in rarely produced twentieth-century works. This includes the memorable staging of Messiaen's *Saint François d'Assise* at the War Memorial Opera House in San Francisco, where he sang the title role.

Interpreting Montejo, White literally and powerfully envoiced Barnet's written text. But the passage from Havana to Copenhagen hardly took place in a straight line, involving instead, as is typically the case with stage work, a number of artists charged with various creative tasks. Besides Barnet, who wrote the original text, and Henze and Enzensberger, who collaborated on the musical work, there were also other artists in Copenhagen who supported White's performance and helped Montejo's story become alive through images and sounds. Directed by Lars Kaalund and staged by him and Mia Stensgaard, *El Cimarrón* also featured the work of percussionist Mathias Friis-Hansen, guitarist Per Pålsson, and flutist Kerstin Thiele. These five white European artists, plus White on center stage, transported the story of Montejo from Cuba into a very different kind of space, thereby chronicling—or more precisely, performing—a tale of transatlantic relations that concerns Africa and the Americas as much as Europe, the old birthplace of opera.

But what kind of transports are these? What kind of passage? Visiting Cuba in the 1960s after the triumph of the Cuban Revolution, Graham Greene, who only a few years earlier had published *Our Man in Havana*, read and praised Barnet's *Biografía de un cimarron* for its originality: "There wasn't a book like this before, and it is quite improbable it will be repeated."[7] Barnet's text still occupies a salient place in the literary and cultural history of Cuba and Latin America as one of the texts that created the genre now known as *testimonio* or *novela testimonio* or *novela testimonial*. The triple terminology is indicative of the genre's perceived fluctuations between fiction and nonfiction. Although *Biografía de un cimarrón* was first published in 1966 by Cuba's Instituto de Etnología y Folklore as an ethnographer's work, the book is now typically read as a novel by literary scholars. The process of its composition, which Barnet himself recounts in the book's introduction, serves as a meaningful entry into the text's shifting status. What first drew his attention to Montejo, instead of other centenaries profiled in the magazine article, was the personal story. Barnet describes Montejo's life as "interesting," which unwittingly invokes Henry James's well-known prescription for the genre of the novel in "The Art of Fiction": "The only obligation to which in advance we may hold a novel, without incurring the accusation of being arbitrary, is that it be interesting."[8] The adjective, then, is an early sign of the modification in the text's perceived genre from ethnographic report to narrative fiction—a creative text now read mostly as a full-blown novel. As it turns out, the young ethnographer's attention is soon displaced from his scholarly focus on Africa-connected religious practices in Cuba, the subject of his first interviews with Montejo, to the man's wholly absorbing life journey. In this, too, Barnet engages James's vision of the novel as a genre that freely seeks to "reproduce life": "It lives upon exercise, and the very meaning of exercise is freedom."[9] As Abraham Acosta explains, Barnet's theoretical writings on testimonio resound with Mario Vargas Llosa's privileging of creative fiction, in which "stylistic, imaginative and perhaps even fantastical conventions" prevail.[10] Aware of the craft of writing, Barnet makes early on the authorial decision to compose a first-person narrative that will preserve Montejo's spontaneous orality, including words and idioms typical of his speech; even the English translation of the text contains a glossary of Cuban words. Exercising freedom, Barnet's search for a precise textual representation of Montejo's voice is not just an ethnographic or linguistic challenge, but as the text lapses into what may read like a novel, it is also the sign of an author's search for the literary form that will best express the protagonist's rich life experience.

Most conversations, Barnet reveals, were recorded on tape, but not all, which implies that his task was not only transcribing Montejo's actual words but also, crucially, remembering details and recreating his subject's verbal style. While at first Montejo, eyewitness and storyteller, appears to Barnet, editor and writer, as somewhat surly, the two men soon develop what Barnet describes as a normal conversational rhythm.[11] As Montejo labors to recall long-lost aspects of the past, Barnet's own recollection of the process implies a Proustian sense of memory; a word or an idea would unexpectedly lead them (or "us," as he puts it) to worthwhile digressions (16–17). But while Barnet employs the first-person plural to describe their fraternal collaboration, what eventually emerges from the text is a picture of Montejo as a solitary and lonely human being. He fights for such collective endeavors as the War of Independence and the

Cuban Revolution, but he is his own man; Barnet, therefore, underscores his sense of individualism, willful and rebellious personality, and reserved distrustfulness (19). These qualities of Montejo's temperament reappear vividly in Henze's musical adaptation and, specifically, in the Copenhagen staging, which visually preserves the runaway slave's sense of separateness and isolation. In Henze's piece, Montejo is the only character, and even though three other players—the flutist, guitarist, and percussionist—work together side by side with him in crafting a stunning soundscape for the protagonist's epic story, Willard White sings alone. In Copenhagen, he was the only singer onstage, the only black person, the only human voice.

Much has been written on the workings and trappings of testimonio, but theoretical claims about the genre may not clearly fit Henze's musical work or opera in general; conversely, how the singing voice, or music in general, may in turn qualify or alter the critical discourse on testimonio is an open question. The discussion about testimonio has focused on various issues pertaining to the practices of ethnography and the concept of voice. Whose voice does one follow in the text? Whose voice prevails, and is therefore heeded, in the structuring of the tale? In the case of *Biografía de un cimarrón*, is it simply Montejo who speaks and Barnet who writes? What can one make of the fact, emphasized by Elzbieta Sklodowska and other scholars, that some of Latin America's most visible examples of testimonio depend on collaboration between two individuals belonging to different cultural groups of unequal social standing? Who shapes and controls the singing in *El Cimarrón*? What about the Europeans writing music, providing foreign words, and playing various instruments? If, on the one hand, Barnet and Montejo are both citizens of revolutionary Cuba, a system that seeks to end class and racial divisions, the fact remains that Barnet, the white man of letters, ultimately determines and controls the textual record of Montejo's own life story. But Barnet, too, as his words are adapted to another medium by others, must stand back and read or listen to a text that is no longer his own.

Identifying the concepts of ventriloquism and heteroglossia in *El Cimarrón*, Sklodowska highlights the ethnographer's awareness of what she calls a non-Afro-Cuban virtual reader for whom the text provides such tools as a glossary of Afro-Cuban terms, including the names of Yoruba deities, food, dances, rituals, and idioms.[12] Sklodowska also analyzes Elisabeth Burgos's collaboration with Rigoberta Menchú in *Me llamo Rigoberta Menchú y así me nació la conciencia*, the famously controversial testimonio, noting the fissures between the editor's and the eyewitness's discourse that result in a struggle between dissonant voices. Through the workings of research and writing, an eyewitness's account—Menchú's as well as Montejo's—is "transculturated," and the text itself can be read as the discursive representation of an intercultural encounter.[13] Roberto González Echevarría, exploring the role of ethnography in Latin American narratives, connects Barnet's practice of writing to a long lineage that hearkens back to such colonial chroniclers as Bernardino de Sahagún and Felipe Guaman Poma de Ayala. He also brings up the fact, easily missed, that Montejo himself, as he speaks with Barnet, becomes an ethnographer of sorts, describing the various immigrant groups, from Galicians and natives of the Canary Islands to Turkish and Chinese people, whom he encounters in Cuba.[14] As we shall see, Montejo's detailed remarks on the music and dance of persons from different parts of the world living in Cuba may play an unwitting role in interpreting Henze's musical adaptation of Barnet's text and Kaalund's vision of Henze's work. Delicately, obliquely, Henze's composition and its theatrical realization in Copenhagen appear to tell their own ethnomusicological history of Cuba and the Atlantic world, one in which Montejo's observations can function as verbal keys for the reception of the work.

But can the runaway slave speak or, moreover, sing? How is he empowered, or not, onstage? It is certainly possible to find theoretical liabilities in Barnet's and Henze's appropriation of Montejo's tale. Yet as the anthropologist Stephan Palmié notes, Barnet at least does not hide his role as editor, and texts such as his, despite their flaws, may yet be the best way to preserve an enslaved person's recollections. Remarking on the well-trodden impasses of postcolonial theory, Palmié asks: "If Montejo's case seems to exemplify [Gayatri Chakravorty] Spivak's dictum that 'the subaltern cannot speak' except in the distorting language of those who would deign to give him or her 'voice,' we need to ask: How then could there possibly be a 'memory' of slavery? For Montejo's case is obviously not an isolated one."[15] Palmié mentions a visit to Montejo in the winter of 1967–1968 by the Jamaican writer Andrew Salkey, who must have been, according to Palmié, "one of the last ever to record a conversation with a person who remembered once having been a slave in a New World plantation society."[16] Unexpectedly, the anthropologist's meditation on Salkey's visit is mournfully literary: "Montejo's death in 1973 was to mark a historical juncture: the end of an era, by then of more than 400 years' duration, when the term slavery could still designate the contents of autobiographic remembrance. We will never know who may have been the last victim of New World racial slavery alive after Montejo's death. But it is clear that with his or her passing, the experience of slavery likewise passed out of 'living memory.'"[17] One thing remains, though, and that is the access that texts such as slave narratives, or testimonios, can afford into the content of a dead person's memory—just a residue, perhaps, but a valuable one.

As it contemplates the passage of time, Palmié's melancholy is almost Borgesian in tone. In "The Witness," for instance, Borges's narrator imagines the last man in England who still remembers the practices of pre-Christian religion: "Before dawn he will die, and in him will die, never to return, the last eye-witness of those pagan rites; the world will be a little poorer when this Saxon dies."[18] Borges's minimal plot, albeit assertively fictional, suggests, at least in theory, the possibility of preserving at least some aspects of a lost world from absolute oblivion. Likewise, Henze and Enzensberger's work, by resorting to Barnet's chronicle of Montejo's life, salvages at least some memories of the runaway slave. The words, sounds, and images deployed on a stage in Denmark can effectively transport an audience, if only partially and fleetingly, across time and space to Esteban Montejo's now-vanished life and times.

Politically committed to the Cuban Revolution like other European artists and intellectuals, Henze spent several months in Havana on two separate visits in 1969 and 1970. Even before these trips, he had shown his support for left-leaning movements by composing *Das Floß der Medusa*, an oratorio written as a requiem for Che Guevara that chronicles the saga of the *Méduse*, the French frigate that sank off the Atlantic coast of Africa and became the subject of Théodore Géricault's iconic *The Raft of the Meduse*. The work's premiere, scheduled for Hamburg in 1968, was canceled after a controversial red flag was placed onstage. Things went more peacefully at the University of Havana in 1969, when Henze conducted the first performance of his Sixth Symphony for an audience he described as "consisting largely of soldiers of the revolutionary army, sons of workers, students from the University of Havana."[19] In his words, the symphony builds on the "experiences of a bourgeois who had been writing music to the ruling class for twenty years to compose against the bourgeoisie. Instead of nostalgia and skepticism I wanted affirmation, direct avowal of revolution."[20] Indeed, the work, scored for two large chamber orchestras, incorporates the song of the Vietnamese Liberation Front as well as improvisations on Latin American folk music and the *son*, the popular Cuban dance rhythm of a previous era. Whether the traditional *son* can be heard as nostalgic in the fabric of the Sixth Symphony surely depends on each individual listener, but it is hard to overestimate the vibrant encounter between Henze and Cuba, which reached a milestone in the story of Esteban Montejo. With Barnet's help, Henze met Montejo; shortly after this visit, he started working on *El Cimarrón*. The composer remarked on the strength and dignity of his subject; he "was then 107 years old, tall as a tree, walked slowly and upright, his eyes were lively, he radiated dignity and seemed well aware that he was a historical personage."[21] If Henze later parted company with the Cuban Revolution, *El Cimarrón* and other compositions remain formidable musical testaments to a fervid period in the shared cultural history of Latin America and Europe.

After returning to Europe, Henze's involvement with Cuba continued to exert an influence in his creative process, at least through the early 1970s. *El Cimarrón* was first performed at the Berlin Philharmonic and the Aldeburgh Festival in 1970. He then wrote *La Cubana oder Ein Leben für die Kunst* (1973). Also featuring a libretto by Enzensberger, this new music drama was based on Barnet's second book, *La canción de Rachel* (1969), yet another *novela testimonial*, on the life of a vaudeville actress in Havana in the early decades of the twentieth century. In London in 1974, taking sides with those who had become disenchanted with the Cuban Revolution, Henze premiered *Voices*, a song cycle for mezzo-soprano and tenor that set to music two poems by Heberto Padilla, including "Los poetas cubanos ya no sueñan," from the collection *Final del juego*. The book, critical of the revolution, had triggered Padilla's arrest in 1971 for subversive activities; this, in turn, had led over thirty European and Latin American intellectuals, including Enzensberger, to write a public letter to Fidel Castro in support of Padilla.[22]

Enzensberger too was in Cuba in the 1960s, met Montejo, and praised Barnet's ability to turn the former slave, who had no access to the traditional tools of literature, into an author—to lead Montejo to an act of speech, as it were: "Der Schriftsteller wird zum Agenten und zum Sprachrohr dessen, mit dem er spricht: er bringt den Cimarrón zum Sprechen und macht ihn zum Autor seiner eigenen Geschichte" (The writer becomes agent and spokesman of the one with whom he speaks; he makes the Cimarrón speak and makes him the author of his own story).[23] The joint allusion to speech and authorship matters not only for what it reveals about Barnet's and Montejo's interaction and Enzensberger's view thereof but also for what it may indirectly say about Henze's belief in music's ability to approximate and communicate as actual language—in other words, the possibility of a musical work by a German composer to operate as its own testimonio for a Cuban runaway slave. In a musicological analysis of *El Cimarrón*, Ivanka Stoianova quotes Henze from an article titled "Musica impura—Musik als Sprache," in which he states: "What I should like to achieve is that the music becomes language; that music should not remain in a musical vacuum, where emotion is mirrored, uncontrolled, and depleted. Music should be understood as speech."[24] If operas and other kinds of musical theater have frequently been regarded as a space where music, through its sheer physical volume, can drown and silence words, Henze's recital for four musicians, in contrast, seeks to function as an actual form of language. Stoianova explains Henze's thinking: "Music must abandon the purist ideas so carefully cultivated by the avant-garde musical research from the 1950s to 70s, and improve its power to communicate, by adopting enunciation techniques common to other languages but traditionally considered as outside the parameters of music.[25]" But can Henze be right? Can his music make Esteban Montejo speak? Going even further, can Montejo be heard as the author of his own music drama as he emits his own story onstage?

For Stoianova, Henze's objectives are realized in *El Cimarrón* more successfully than in any other of his works—a positive outcome connected inherently to its status as musical theater. Words are obviously key: "The interaction of the verbal sounds bearing linguistic significance, vocal and instrumental noise, and visual gesture on stage creates impure signs which are dense, substantial, full of meaning and affect. At a time of militant avant-gardism and of the search for purity in musical language, Henze declared, 'My music is *impura*. It does not wish to be abstract or pure; it is impure.'"[26] Henze's elevation of impurity to an ars poetica of sorts, besides allowing his own music to overcome what Stoianova, citing him, calls "muteness," resounds with much of the established discussion about hybridity at the heart of much thinking about culture in Cuba and Latin America. It also mirrors some of the practices of testimonio—a mixed genre in which the sense of authorship is blended and even fluctuates, as the two competing titles of Barnet's text in English translation suggest: *Autobiography of a Runaway Slave* and *Biography of a Runaway Slave*. Henze and Enzensberger's full title, *El cimarrón: Autobiographie des geflohenen Sklaven Esteban Montejo*, replaces Barnet's indefinite article, *un* (a) with the definite genitive article, *des* (of the), thereby making it the story of one specific man. In the program of the Copenhagen production, the work even has two separate subtitles: "Den bortløbne slave," which means "the runaway slave" and may be intended simply as a translation of the Spanish original, and "Esteban Montejos selvbiografi," which appears to elevate the protagonist's entire life, not just the fact he was a *cimarrón*. Like Barnet's text, Henze's adaptation is also the search for a narrative form through which Montejo can tell the story of his life, as any author would. In this regard, it is not altogether surprising that *The New Grove Dictionary of Opera* erroneously states that Henze's *El cimarrón* is based on Esteban Montejo's *The Biography of a Runaway Slave*, erasing Barnet's authorial role. Indeed, when compared to Barnet's original text (if one may call it so), Henze's and Enzensberger's version clearly enhances Montejo's authorial position by not bearing any explicit textual marks of Barnet's work. The ethnographer's introduction is deleted, and one hears only Esteban sing and speak his impure tale.

Esteban's singing, though, is highly literary. He tells his story by means of fifteen lyrical texts composed by Enzensberger, a structure that departs from the more prosaic workmanship of the original work.[27] Barnet's table of contents divides the text into five discrete parts: an introduction; sections titled "Slavery," "The Abolition of Slavery," and "The War of Independence"; and a glossary. The introduction and glossary signal the anthropologist's mediation, with a structuring drive that is also detectable in the headings of the three middle parts constituting the bulk of the text. Take, for instance, "The War of Independence"; the title sounds highly official and therefore can be read as part and parcel of Barnet's scholarly proclivities, but its only subtitle, "Life during the War" reflects Montejo's less formal storytelling. Enzensberger's short titles, in contrast, reinforce literariness by abstracting specific motifs, themes, and events—everything from "Die Welt" (The World) and "Die Sklaverei" (Slavery) to "Die Flucht" (Escape), "Die Schlacht von Mal Tiempo" (The Battle of Mal Tiempo) and, last, "Das Messer" (The Knife—or The Machete, as some versions, perhaps with an eye to local color, render it). German-proficient listeners will be able to understand rather easily the clear prose style of "Die Welt," the first section of the work. Because of the immediacy of the first-person pronoun, they will also perceive Esteban as the simple lyrical chronicler of his own story: "Früher, in der Zeit der Sklaverei, habe ich oft in den Himmel geschaut. Die Farbe des Himmels gefällt mir sehr. Einmal hat er sich verfärbt wie eine Kohlenglut und es gab eine entsetzliche Dürre" ("Back then, in the days of slavery, often I stood looking into the sky. Its beautiful color was good to see. Once the sky began to glow just like a burning coal. After that there was a terrible dry spell").[28] In Henze's search for verbal clarity, the form of Esteban's singing matters too. Partly conceived to be rendered as *Sprechgesang*, the protagonist's utterances are closer to speech and other nonmusical utterances than most operatic arias. As a review by Wolfgang Becker-Carsten of the work's premiere in Berlin puts it, "The black singer William Pearson handled a vocal range which stretched from bass baritone to countertenor, and made use of all techniques that can be produced by mouth and vocal cords, including humming and laughing, speaking, whispering, screaming, and singing."[29] Edward Greenfield, reviewing the first performance at Aldeburgh, also observes that the baritone uses "every kind of vocalization from falsetto to Indian war-whoop, but mainly sticks to Henze's brand of sing-speech."[30]

Enzensberger's words and Henze's musical setting tell a story that intimately connects with the island of Cuba and, more broadly, the Atlantic world. The fact that they crossed the ocean, met with Barnet and Montejo in person, and crafted a thoughtful music drama based on what they read and heard allows them to stand, as I have argued, as credible witnesses of the life of one formerly enslaved man. But what about the next group of people in the work's progress—the listeners and spectators who receive the work by means of audio recordings or actual performances? What kind of testimony does *El cimarrón* manage to convey? As we saw earlier, Adorno, writing about opera and the long-playing record, praises the possibility of listening to Mozart or Strauss without the theatrical clichés of an actual production. A listener may solely perceive the music and perhaps the words: Enzensberger's libretto, in German or in translation, which recalls Barnet's text, who cites Montejo himself. But what happens when listeners or readers of imageless opera witness the work onstage—when *El Cimarrón* suddenly materializes at the Royal Danish Theater, and they, operagoers now, sitting in the dark, sheltered in the plush nineteenth-century interior, are enraptured by words and sounds but also by the curious goings-on onstage, the theatrical testimony of a black man whose ancestors were brutally carried from Africa to the Americas? What happens when that man's life story, now in the form of music drama, is transported back across that same ocean, but instead of traveling to his ancestors' continent, it makes landfall in the so-called Old World, the very heart of Europe, the birthplace of opera, the origin and end of the triangular slave trade? Stomu Yamashta, the percussionist in the first performances of *El Cimarrón*, writes about the reactions of different audiences in London and Spoleto. For him, people who experience intolerance and social prejudice—or as he puts it in English in the middle of a German text, "people who know"—can feel that this music speaks directly to them.[31] Although Yamashta's remarks are proffered without any actual evidence, the reported feeling is still worth taking into account as Montejo's life story travels from place to place.

Denmark was the first nation to abolish the slave trade, but its colonies in the Caribbean—St. Thomas, St. Croix, and St. John, now the US Virgin Islands—preserved slavery until 1848. One hundred sixty-one years later, *El Cimarrón* at the Royal Danish Theater had little or nothing to say directly about the enslaved people of the Danish West Indies, yet tacitly building on the historical context and regal venue, the staging proved to be an insightful meditation on how the performing arts can speak, even in an impure fashion, for those who, like Montejo, lack the traditional means to tell their own stories. Kaalund and Stensgaard's work intelligently laid bare the process of representing a man, now absent, who had once been enslaved. The set was mostly minimalist; instead of numerous actors or dancers as other productions of the work sometimes feature, only the four musicians invoked in Henze's subtitle could be heard and seen. The music making, just as Henze's score calls for, rose as an oblique story of transculturation. The percussion, flute, and guitar could resound with the discourse about race and music that Montejo, through Barnet, elaborates in *Biografía de un cimarrón*. Montejo's amateur ethnomusicology offers a key for listening to and thinking about Henze's music. Reminiscing about Sunday celebrations at sugar plantations, for instance, he calls them *el tambor* (the drum). Percussion seemed to prevail over everything else, and it was linked with the musical practices of people of African descent, and not, for instance, Chinese migrants, another important ethnic group in nineteenth-century Cuba. As González Echevarría observes, Montejo typecasts the races as he evokes those festive gatherings of long ago: "Sundays were the noisiest days on the plantation. I don't know where the slaves found the energy. The biggest fiestas during slavery too place on that day of the week. There were plantations where the drum began at noon or at one.... I noticed that the ones who were least involved were the Chinese. Those bastards didn't have an ear for the drums. They were standoffish. It was that they thought a lot. In my opinion they thought more than the blacks. Nobody paid them any mind. And folks just went on with their dances."[32] Montejo goes on to describe one of those dances, called *yuka*, in detail: "In the *yuka* three drums were played: *la caja*, *la mula*, and the *cachimbo*, which was the littlest.... *Yuka* was danced in pairs, and the movements were dramatic. Sometimes they swooped like birds, and it even seemed like they were going to fly they moved so fast" (18). He focuses also on the music-making of people of French descent, who, transculturated, sang in "patois" and played on two large drums as the crowd moved to a dance called "the French Dance" (20). After speaking of the *guajiros*, peasants often of largely Spanish descent, he notes again important musical differences that he ascribes to race, including the musical instruments played for singing and dancing: "As I understand it, at that time the *guajiros* made music using only a guitar. Later, around the year 1890, they played *danzones* on those Pianolas with accordions and gourds. But the white man has always had music different from the black. White man's music has no drum at all. Tasteless" (20).

But to what extent should Montejo's race-specific observations be taken into account as one listens to Henze's score? Is percussion "black" and the guitar "white"? And if so, what color, if any, is the flute? And how should one interpret the fact that both the guitarist and flutist in Henze's *El Cimarrón* are at times called on to play percussion instruments as well? Is there a story of hybridity in all this that a perceptive staging can effectively enhance?

Indeed, at the Royal Theater in Copenhagen, listening to and watching the four musicians of Henze's recital playing together, a spectator familiar with Barnet's text or, more generally, with certain discourses about music in Cuba could not fail to see and hear a history of transculturation that concerns the Americas and Europe as well. The dramatic uses of percussion onstage were particularly gripping for their possible meanings in a transatlantic history of music and race. Inevitably, an old issue comes up: what import, if any, should one ascribe to a performer's ethnicity? The question, of course, is a long standing one in opera, having already been asked and answered many times in various forms. Was Leontyne Price an ideal Aida because she, like Verdi's heroine, was not white? Conversely, was she less suitable, at least in theory, to sing, say, the role of Leonora in *La forza del destino*, which she did magnificently? Should it be an ethical decision, as many believe, that Madama Butterfly be performed only by Japanese, or at least East Asian, sopranos? If so, how should race function as one evaluates the work of Maria Callas or Renata Tebaldi in that supremely Orientalist role? Perversely, could their European origin be the ideal vehicle to expose the offensive stereotype crafted by Puccini and others? Because sound matters more than image in the visually nonrealistic art of opera, audiences are typically expected to be or become color-blind; the mature Plácido Domingo can portray young Parsifal, say, as convincingly as Willard White can play a young Italian when he sang the role of Francis of Assisi in Messiaen's opera.[33]

But what happens in a music drama whose plot is intrinsically connected to a person's blackness and, more broadly, to the longstanding history of race in the Atlantic world? Because he is a black man and was born in Jamaica, Cuba's neighbor, it is not difficult to regard Willard White as an ideal Esteban.[34] Yet beyond those biographical and ethnic bonds, White's universally acknowledged artistry would presumably have been enough to cast him in the role. In opera, then, race seems to appear and disappear as both a meaningful and a meaningless category. In the Copenhagen staging, the audience could focus as well on Mathias Friis-Hansen, the percussionist—a tall blond man who stood mostly behind White, whose own physical stature was equally commanding. Playing their own part in a theatrical experience successively crafted by Montejo, Barnet, Enzensberger, Henze, Kaalund, Stensgaard, and others, the moving bodies of White and Friis-Hansen, different yet alike, played out an insightful and liberating story about the cultural ties and intertwining histories that bind all peoples because, but also regardless, of race.

The Copenhagen *Cimarrón* was engrossing both musically and theatrically. A proliferation of diverse instruments crowded the stage, as if announcing from the start what Leo Brouwer, the Cuban composer and musician who played the guitar in the inaugural performances of the work in Berlin and Aldeburgh, noted early on about the work: all of Cuba is there.[35] At the Royal Danish Theater, the staging was simple; a tree trunk placed horizontally, for instance, suggested the forest where Esteban seeks refuge, altered later by its vertical repositioning against an image of rich vegetation projected upstage (fig. 3). As we will see, the musicians themselves, even as they played the complex score, acted discrete parts. Echoing some of the reviews of the work's premieres in 1970, Gregers Dirckinck-Holmfeld praised the protagonist's self-expression through both song and speech, commenting as well, suggestively, on the difficulty of telling the sounds produced by White himself apart from those that came from the percussionist's work, as if those instrumental reverberations also emerged from the singer's lips.[36]

Indeed, the musical and physical interplay, even fusion, between White and Friis-Hansen was especially remarkable as the plot unfolded. Consider the ninth scene, titled "The Machines," which centers on Cuba's notoriously cruel sugar industry. Blacks, freed from slavery, have become exploited laborers, and whites—in this case, foreign engineers mostly from the "England or America" (27)— still hold unequal power. Here, strikingly, there is a permutation in Friis-Hansen's stage role. No longer merely the percussionist who masterfully plays various instruments, he impersonates, if only briefly, one of the various disreputable characters in Cuban history recalled by Montejo, near whom he now stands. Indeed, his suit and light-colored hat, alongside the physical interaction with White, suggest that he is one of the foreign engineers who came to the tropical island with new machines that, as the libretto would have it, signaled "amazing progress" but also brought "a lot of hate and injustice" (29) (fig. 4). Friis-Hansen's role, moving quickly onstage,

FIGURE 3. Per Pålsson, Willard White, Mathias Friis-Hansen and Kerstin Thiele in Hans Werner Henze's *El Cimarrón*, Royal Danish Opera, 2009. Photo by Per Morten Abrahamsen.

is double. For a few seconds, his body incarnates an engineer, Montejo's foil, but then, almost simultaneously, it also creates some of the powerful music that accompanies and supports White as he performs his song of protest. Significantly, Friis-Hansen's potent drumming, at least for spectators familiar with histories of musical instruments in Cuba, or with Montejo's testimony thereof, invokes the long-standing cultural presence of Africa on the island. Then again, this powerful sound cannot be described simply as African or Cuban; after all, percussion is also a vital tool in European art music. Friis-Hansen's playing, then, is an element interwoven with much else in a work that concerns multiple cultural locations and various kinds of transports across the ocean.

In other scenes, Pålsson and Thiele don light-colored hats too, along with Friis-Hansen. In "Escape," the fourth scene, White's Esteban remembers the sufferings of slavery, associated with a hat-wearing figure, and his decision to run away: "What could be worse than working in the fields? That was like being in hell! I kept my eyes on the overseer, that son of a bitch, I watched him closely. He never took his hat off" (23). Again, the hats act as a sartorial bond

FIGURE 4. Mathias Friis-Hansen and Willard White in Hans Werner Henze's *El Cimarrón*, Royal Danish Opera, 2009. Photo by Per Morten Abrahamsen.

between the three musicians and a history of exploitation, yet the playing provides the vivid musical scaffolding for White's furious words. That this formidable soundscape includes Pålsson's guitar, which members of the audience might readily hear as an acoustic symbol of Spain, is yet another mixed-up sign in the musical hodgepodge of Cuban music, which inspired Henze. In the eighth scene, "Women," Esteban recounts his many liaisons with "every kind of girl there is: soft ones and dark ones" and, most especially, Ana, "one of those most attractive mulberry-colored mulatto girls" (27). That this catalog aria is accompanied by Thiele's flute might well denote the European modulation that is also an element in Cuba's and Latin America's own histories of *mestizaje*. In yet another twist, that Pålsson and Thiele occasionally forsake their guitar and flute to play sundry percussion instruments suggests the erratic routes of cultural *mestizaje* and artistic collaboration: mixture above purity, as Henze would have it.

A story that begins with the Middle Passage and unfolds in Cuba moves to Europe and moves audiences in Copenhagen, where musicians perform a recital whose principal emblem may be the kaleidoscopic sign of transculturation. Indeed, one can also hear the sounds of such hybrid Cuban rhythms as the *habanera* and the *rumba* throughout Henze's score. Although one might be tempted to dismiss these borrowings as cultural appropriation or simply part and parcel of Europe's musical flirtation with exoticism, akin to Bizet's "Habanera" or Puccini's use of the pentatonic scale in *Madama Butterfly*, the outcome is arguably far more complex. As the runaway slave sings and figures resembling engineers or overseers play along onstage, an operagoer can imagine the many twists and turns of transatlantic traffic. It is undoubtedly a disgraceful history, but also, as Filomeno's musical work suggests in Carpentier's fictional tale, it generates an ever-expanding archive of stories that continues to trigger wonderfully mixed, blatantly impure creations and sentiments in culture and the arts.

Unlike Henze's work, yet mirroring Barnet's text, the Copenhagen *Cimarrón* goes beyond recounting Montejo's biography to expose and meditate on the process of telling someone else's tale. Barnet describes his writing method in his introduction. Likewise, Kaalund's production engages in self-reflection through the visual fabric of the staging itself. In the scenes titled "The Cimarrón" and "Slavery," a cameraman appears onstage to film White's body, projecting his face and chained hands simultaneously on a large screen over the stage. The cameraman stands as a visible emblem of all those who have sought to chronicle Montejo's life. Not unlike a paparazzo, who regards and records the pain of others, he intrudes into Montejo's privacy, but even as he gazes on the other man's physicality and records his sung and spoken testimony, the audience notes exactly what's going on; they see who is looking at whom, and for what malicious or benevolent purpose the camera is acting. The viewing of the cameraman's viewing of Montejo occurs even as the audience views what the camera views. The audience sees a suffering body onstage but also sees its passage into representation;

or to put it differently, the audience sees a body in chains but also sees the mouth that sings and speaks that body's history (fig 5). Like a theatrical version of Velázquez's *Las Meninas*, this double act of displaying and self-displaying exposes not only the making of the testimony—its artifice, if you will—but also the narrative material therein: slavery, to quote Palmié, as the content of autobiographical remembrance. The huge box that White slowly drags across the stage, a physical emblem of his forced labor, becomes the background against which his laboring body is laboriously projected. In the afterlife of slavery, the act of remembering that brutal institution appears, then, intrinsically connected to the flesh-and-blood figure in which memory itself can be located. From this angle, the act of regaining the past, and the past regained, are one and the same.

Above the proscenium of the Royal Theater in Copenhagen, established with royal patronage in 1748 when slavery gripped much of the world, including the Danish West Indies, there is an inscription that solemnly reads, "EI BLOT TIL LYST"—"not for pleasure alone." A material reminder that the performing arts should transcend mere entertainment or even aesthetic satisfaction, the words instruct operagoers to see and hear more than they might at first perceive; they perhaps can learn something from those works that unfold in front of them.[37] Indeed, as pleasing as the performances of *El Cimarrón* in September 2009 were, Kaalund and Stengaard's production schooled the audience on the history of Cuba and the inhumanity of slavery, and also on the ethical returns of testimonial collaboration. By performing Henze's recital, the four musicians exemplified the lessons of working and witnessing together, making the theater's opulent interior, traditionally devoted to European arts, a space in which the stories of others—Europe's others—could also be read through the work of opera.

But what about other possible reading and lessons? Can these tales of hybridity be regarded uncritically? What if one foregrounds Henze's and Enzensberger's work as an appropriation of Esteban's biography, like Vivaldi and Giusti did with Montezuma two centuries earlier, for their own self-regard? Or is this harsh judgment

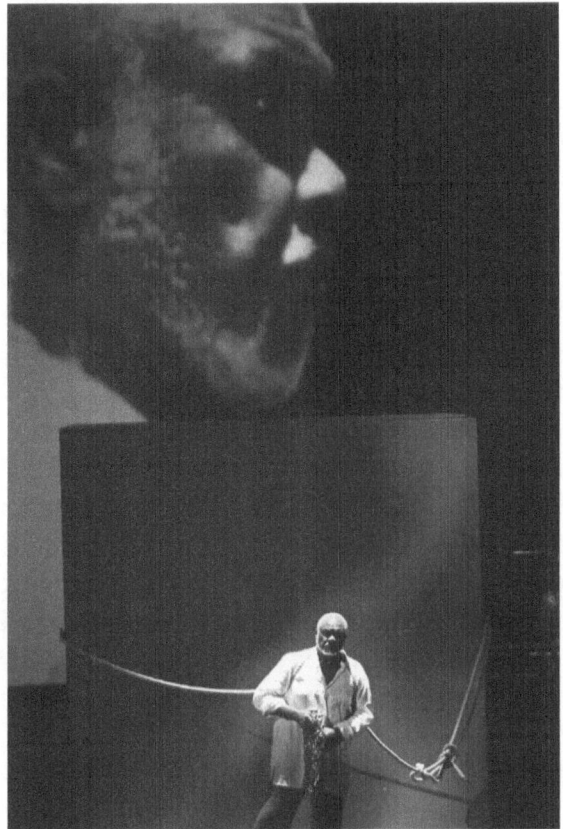

FIGURE 5. Willard White in Hans Werner Henze's *El Cimarrón*, Royal Danish Opera, 2009. Photo by Per Morten Abrahamsen.

belied by the affects and effects of the hero's voice, rising above it all? What would Esteban Montejo say about all this stage business—if he could speak? Reading *El Cimarrón* in Copenhagen along with *Lo schiavo* in Rio de Janeiro provides yet another angle from which to consider, if not solve, these questions.

The Composer Writes to the Princess

Like *El Cimarrón*, *Lo schiavo* is built on the intertwined workings of adaptation and translation. Just as Enzensberger took Barnet's Spanish-language text and turned it into a dramatic piece in German,

Rodolfo Paravicini transformed a Portuguese-language sketch by Alfredo d'Escragnolle Taunay into a full-blown Italian libretto. At face value, these linguistic passages share a common cultural and geographic itinerary. They are stories of enslaved persons written by white authors from Latin America—the protagonist's compatriots—and subsequently reworked by European writers, who must meet their own aesthetic demands. Paravicini's modifications are more extreme than those of Enzensberger, as he not only switched the original language in which the story was conceived but also, as mentioned earlier, moved the action from 1801 to back to 1567, changed the nationality of one of the two main female character, and (more radically) transformed Taunay's Afro-descendant hero, the mixed-race Ricardo, into an indigenous character, Iberè, of the Tamoio people. Both tales are intrinsically different also in that Esteban's story, through its several narrative iterations, ultimately hearkens back to a historical figure, whereas Taunay's Ricardo and Paravicini's Iberè are fictional creatures. Yet the multiple texts in which they appear surely share a common objective, at least in the eyes and ears of some of their cocreators: to bear witness to the plight of enslaved persons.[38]

But to what extent is *Lo schiavo* an effective testimony of slavery? In what way are audiences transported by the work's plotline and music? Operagoers familiar with the history of race and enslavement in Brazil may be taken aback by the protagonist's ethnic metamorphosis. Luiz Gonzaga de Aguiar, writing about the opera's genesis for a recording's booklet, ironically asks and answers several questions: "Escravidão indígena? Quando? Como? Por que? Como sabemos, pela História do Brasil, os nossos índios jamais se deixaram escravizar" (Indigenous slavery? When? How? Why? As we all know, according to the History of Brazil, our Indians never let themselves be enslaved).[39] This rhetoric echoes the astounded words of the Mexican traveler in *Concierto barroco* who levels accusations of falsehood at Vivaldi and Giusti's operatic distortions of his country's history. Opera, of course, has frequently amended historical facts to serve its own dramatic purposes, but the racial liberties in Paravicini's libretto appear, at least at face value, far more consequential, even troubling. Although indigenous slavery did occur in Brazil, the institution affected mostly people of African descent. Moreover, the sixteenth-century setting also allows opera to overlook that the fact that abolition was at the center of the nation's concerns at the time when it was being composed.

Published by Ricordi in Milan, the libretto described the work as a "dramma lirico in 4 atti di Alfredo Taunay e Rodolfo Paravicini" (lyrical drama in four acts by Alfredo Taunay and Rodolfo Paravicini). But the Brazilian author, despite being credited before his Italian collaborator, was not altogether pleased with the changes to which his sketch was subjected. As Maria Alice Volpe argues, the libretto by Antonio Scalvini for Gomes's earlier *Il guarany* had differed in some minor (albeit significant) ways from Alencar's *O guarani*, the novel that it adapted, yet Peri's indigenous ethnicity had been the Brazilian novelist's own choice. By contrast, the crucial changes in *Lo schiavo* were designed by Europeans for the sake of non-Brazilian audiences—and then remitted to Brazil, yet another episode in the transatlantic history of New World raw materials and Old World craftsmanship, if not craftiness. The changes had too much import for Taunay, an author who had forcefully supported abolition, to remain silent. Ironically defining himself as a man of letters somewhat knowledgeable of his country, he decries "as esquisitices, anacronismos e extravagantes confusões históricas e étnicas infiltradas num modestíssimo escorço de libreto, ás pressas por mim delineado, no dia da partida de Carlos Gomes para a Europa, ao findar 1880" (the oddities, anachronisms, and extravagant historical and ethnic confusions filtered into a most modest sketch for a libretto, hastily outlined by me, on the day Carlos Gomes departed for Europe at the end of 1880).[40] In later published versions of the libretto, though, the actual role of each author in the making of the text is stated more precisely. For instance, the title page in the booklet for the live "historical recording" of *Lo schiavo* at Rio de Janeiro's Teatro Municipal in 1959 states that the libreto is by Rodolfo Paravicini, which in turn is based on a sketch by the Viscount of Taunay—an authorial demotion that at least absolves Taunay from the grievous historical lapses.[41] Significantly, the booklet also states under the two authors' names that the opera is "Dedicada à Princesa Isabel" ("Dedicated to Princess Isabel"), a paratext that allows well-informed listeners to retrieve Brazil's black history and possibly read, or hear, Taunay's suppressed plot—not in the opera's verbal fabric, where one might expect it but, as Volpe's scholarship suggests, in the long wordless stretches of symphonic music composed by Gomes for his opera. Isabel's silent role, I argue, speaks volumes too.

Gomes's dedication to the Princess Imperial, as she was known, came in the form of a letter written in Milan on July 29, 1888, her birthday. The composer's words are first and foremost an expression of gratitude for Isabel's decision, as regent, to sign the Lei Áurea, whereby slavery had been abolished less than three months earlier on May 13, 1888. Supremely respectful, circumlocutory, Gomes's florid words are worth citing in full for what they obliquely reveal about the composer's reading of his own opera and the potential work of *Lo schiavo* in documenting the social and ethnic hierarchies of Brazil:

> Senhora, digne-se Vossa Alteza acolher este drama no qual um brasileiro tentou representar o nobre caráter de um indígena escravizado. Na memorável data de 13 de maio, em prol de muitos semelhantes ao protagonista deste drama, Vossa Alteza, com ânimo gentil e patriótico, teve a glória de transmudar o cativeiro em eterna alegria da liberdade. Assim, a palavra Escravo no Brasil, pertence simplesmente à legenda do passado. É, pois, em sinal de profunda gratidão e homenagem que, como artista brasileiro, tenho a subida honra de dedicar este meu trabalho à Excelsa Princesa, em quem o Brasil reverencia o mesmo alto espírito, a mesma grandeza de ânimo de D. Pedro II, e eu a mesma generosa proteção que me glorio de haver recebido do Augusto Pai de Vossa Alteza Imperial. Hoje, 29 de julho, dia em que o Brasil saúda o aniversário da Augusta Regente, levo aos pés de Vossa Alteza este Escravo, talvez tão pobre como milhares de outros, que abençoam a Vossa Alteza na mesma efusão de reconhecimento com que sou de Vossa Alteza Imperial, súdito fiel e reverente.[42]

Madam, Your Highness, please be kind enough to welcome this drama in which a Brazilian man tried to represent the noble character of an enslaved native. On the memorable date of May 13, for the welfare of many persons who resemble the protagonist of this drama, Your Highness, with a gentle and patriotic spirit, took the glorious step of transmuting captivity into the eternal bliss of freedom. Thus, the word Slave simply belongs now to the legends of the past. It is therefore as a sign of profound gratitude and tribute that I, as a Brazilian artist, have the deep honor of dedicating this work of mine to the Sublime Princess in whom Brazil reveres the same lofty spirit and greatness of mind of Dom Pedro I, August Father of Your Imperial Highness, whose same generous protection I am honored to have received. Today, July 29, the day in which Brazil salutes the August Regent on her birthday, I lift to the feet of Your Highness this Slave, perhaps as poor as thousands of others, who bless Your Highness with the same effusive recognition that I, a faithful and reverent subject, feel for Your Imperial Highness.

The epistolary dedication elevates Isabel, as recipient of letter and opera, to the position of privileged reader and spectator. *Lo schiavo* would receive its world premiere at the Teatro Imperial Pedro II in September 1889, and although Isabel could not be at the performance because of a death in the family, her royal person, through the composer's dedication, remains intertwined with the opera.[43] Gomes's words, reassessed in the context of the military coup that would put an end to the Empire of Brazil and establish a republic only a few weeks later, also ring as a swan song of sorts for the longstanding bonds between European monarchies and the realm of opera in Latin America. As we saw, the first operatic performance in the Americas, that of Torrejón y Velasco's *La púrpura de la rosa* at the viceregal palace in Lima in 1701, honored the eighteenth birthday of Philip V, who had just ascended the Spanish throne as the first king of the Bourbon dynasty; almost two centuries later, the first staging of *Lo schiavo*, an emblematic work by Latin America's preeminent opera composer, appears to bid farewell to the House of Braganza, under whose patronage—especially that of Pedro II, the Teatro Imperial's namesake—opera had been transported to and flourished on those new shores.[44]

The opera that Gomes describes from Milan deals explicitly with Brazil and invokes the history of slavery in the country. But the dedication to Isabel shies away from presenting *Lo schiavo* as a work that faithfully chronicles the lives of enslaved persons or advocates explicitly for a better future for Brazilians. Instead, as one might expect from an experienced artist, Gomes's language stresses the permutation of the historical into the fictional. The first sentence brings up the opera's option for an "indígena escravizado" while proclaiming shortly thereafter that the title itself, rendered "back" in Portuguese as "Escravo," belongs to the past—an anteriority, importantly, that is not prosaic "history" but the stuff of "legend." By the grace of her signature, he suggests, Isabel rescues enslaved Brazilians from a painful reality and relocates them in a romantic realm of bygone make-believe. This transformation is augured by Gomes himself when setting to music the impossible story of his own enslaved Iberè, first conceived as Ricardo. As he reflects on the finished work, Gomes invokes once again "este Escravo"—the opera, his creation, but also its protagonist, his own creature—pointedly remarking on "its," or rather "his," poverty. If at first the reader assumes that the allusion to poverty is just Gomes's deployment of the *topos modestiae* (akin to that of Bach, say, in his *Musikalisches Opfer*, dedicated to Frederick the Great), that reading undergoes forthwith a prompt correction. This Slave is not an opera; he is not even a character: he is a virtual person, like the thousands of other poor Brazilians who, in Gomes's imperial imaginings, bless and laud the real-life princess whose signature secured their freedom. The adjective *semelhantes*, which contains the ideas of similitude, is also the word invoked to refer to one's fellow human beings; Gomes's indigenous protagonist and Brazil's newly liberated black person may then be regarded as one and the same as other Brazilians—their equals.

Although his focus is literature, Gérard Genette's analysis of dedications is also relevant for opera, an art form whose works are also presented through the adscription of a title and various other paratexts. In the case of a public dedication, the author proclaims some kind of relation—intellectual, aesthetic, political, and so on—with the recipient. To inscribe someone's name revives the ancient practice of invoking the muse. Further, Genette suggests, inspiration is also a form of authorship: "'For So-and-So' always involves some element of 'By So-and-So.' The dedicatee is always in some way responsible for the work that is dedicated to him and to which he brings, willy-nilly, a little of his support and therefore participation. This little is not nothing: is it necessary to bring to mind again that the Latin for 'guarantor' is *auctor*?"[45] In the case of Princess Isabel, it might be farfetched to regard her as Gomes's coauthor, yet it is not impossible to read her imperial signature on the Lei Áurea as a final flourish of sorts in the corpus of antiabolitionist writings by many Brazilian writers, including the Viscount of Taunay, who had long focused on the struggles of enslaved persons. As the opera's recipient, Isabel's name prompts the temporal retrieval of *Lo schiavo* as a relevant contemporary work that tells the tale not just of its indigenous protagonist but also, obliquely, the history of those persons of African descent who have just gained their freedom in Brazil. If you know how to listen in a certain way, Gomes's testimony may be as powerful, arguably, as that of Barnet's and Henze and Enzensberger's texts, in which Esteban Montejo can appear more clearly to voice his own tale.

But what tale of freedom does *Lo schiavo* tell? Despite its singular name, its largely melodramatic plot focuses on four emotionally intertwined characters: Iberè, the enslaved Tamoio; Americo, who frees Iberè, his friend; Ilàra, who loves and is loved by Americo, and for whom Iberè, too, has feelings; and the Condessa de Boissy, a French noblewoman, romantically interested in Americo. The quartet's fortunes are largely controlled by the Conde Rodrigo, who, to thwart the love of his son Americo for Ilàra, forces her to marry Iberè. Remarkably, long before the opera reaches its climax, neither Iberè nor Ilàra are any longer enslaved. As if mirroring Princess Isabel's abolitionist deeds, the Condessa de Boissy purchases a number of slaves, including Iberè and Ilàra, with the sole purpose of liberating them, which happens at the end of act 2, an action preceded by much elevated singing about freedom and a happier future: "Lo sguardo in me fissate, / E la fronte che già pensosa e triste / Verso la terra era chinata, alzate, / Perchè liberi siete! / In voi ritorna il dritto umano, andate: / Che il ciel vi benedica / E la fortuna amica / Sorrida sempre a voi" (Fix your eyes on me, and lift your forehead, which leaned brooding and sad to the ground, because you are free! The rights of humans return to you. Heaven bless you, and gracious fortune always smile on you).[46] While the Contessa's motives appear somewhat self-serving, the splendor of Gomes's music elevates her character to the grandeur befitting such a momentous occasion. Ironically, it is Iberè who, after being liberated twice from slavery, is undone by the plot's political twists and turns. Angry that his affection for Ilàra is unrequited and hers for Americo remains as strong as ever, he organizes an indigenous rebellion against the Portuguese. Yet moved by the enduring love between Ilàra and Americo, who has earlier been captured by the Tamoios, Iberè allows the two lovers to escape, upon which he decides to kill himself.

If at face value *Lo schiavo* appears to eschew the plight of enslaved persons in Brazil, this impression stems from Paravicini's deletion of black characters and from the convoluted amatory plot whose tragic denouement hinges on the fate of Americo and Ilàra's love and not on Iberè's own subaltern condition. As much as it is a tale of slavery, the opera is also a story of friendship and fraternity between the two male protagonists, who sadly happen to love the same woman. Then again, if one rises above the libretto and listens to the orchestral sound, as Maria Alice Volpe does, in the context of Brazilian cultural history—not only literature and music, but other arts as well—one may yet hear how Gomes's score subtly concerns the drama of African enslavement in the country and portends its termination, even as it melancholically suggests the difficulties ahead. In this, music narrates the story that words are simply not allowed to tell.

Indeed, the absence of words is replenished by the fluent speechlessness of music. Gomes's musical score speaks, as it were, for the erasure of both Taunay's plotline and the actual history of slavery in

Brazil. To view how the composer becomes the tale's cryptic dramatist, I am persuaded by Volpe's argument about Gomes's embrace and deployment of landscape as a musical idea. As she demonstrates, musical landscape, derived from both literature and painting, emerges as a nationalist topos in the earlier *Il guarany*, but far more potently in *Lo schiavo*, especially in "Alvorada" (Dawn), the symphonic prelude to act 4. While some of the opera's arias have achieved a measure of fame—"Quando nascesti tu," for instance, sung by Americo in act 2 and recorded early on by Enrico Caruso and Beniamino Gigli—the most often performed section of *Lo schiavo* possibly remains the wordless "Alvorada," in which Gomes seeks to re-create the song of various species of native birds as heard in a tropical landscape at sunrise. In a sense, these sounds complement the stage directions of the Italian libretto, which call for outlandish visual images of a country whose nature is distinctly non-European. The set design for the first act makes this visible: "Alberi di cocco, banane, palmizi, sparsi per la scena—e pittorescamente distribuiti sui campi. Nel vastissimo sfondo le piantagioni de canne di zucchero. Più in là le foreste vergini. Fanno poi corona al grandioso paesaggio le altissime montagne in distanza" (20; coconut, banana and palm trees, scattered around the stage and picturesquely spread over the fields. Sugar plantations in the vast background. Virgin forests beyond. Very tall mountains crown the grandiose landscape). But detailed inventories of nature, which reoccur in the remaining three acts, are a two-pronged device. The scene may recall, for instance, foreign depictions of Brazil by Dutch seventeenth-century painters such as Albert Eckhout and Hans Potter, but it also speaks to the nationalist debates at the Academia Imperial de Belas Artes and elsewhere, which, as Volpe notes, elevated landscape and genre painting into ideal forms for Brazilian art. What is openly exotic for Europeans emerges, then, as simply a habitat of their own for local artists in search of visions of the nation. Gomes would learn much from these pictorial lessons, as Volpe points out: "Only after landscape had become a critical issue in the nationalization of Brazilian painting did Gomes concern himself with evoking Brazilian birds, forests, sunrise, hills, and so forth."[47] As one listens to "Alvorada," one can picture a virtual image of Brazil crafted by its Romantic landscape artists, a powerful vision transposed into sounds by the nation's foremost composer, an heir to Verdi but also a viewer and reader of local artists and authors.

Importantly, for spectators of *Lo schiavo* familiar with depictions of landscape in Brazilian literature, "Alvorada" also calmly invokes authors and works that played a role in the struggle for the liberation of enslaved Afro-descendant persons. Specifically, Volpe cites Antônio de Castro Alves, whose *Os escravos* (1883) had linked the image of sunrise with the promise of emancipation, as a "direct influence" in Gomes. Indeed, the poem "América" postulates the link between sunrise and a better future, and so do such images in "O século" as "o sol do porvir" (" the sun of the future") and "a aurora da redenção" ("the dawn of redemption"). Also cited by Volpe is "Ao romper d'alva," which "elaborates on the sound and visual effects of poetic language by contrasting the sounds of Brazilian Edenic forest with slavery's irons."[48] Sensing the promise of emancipation in the splendor of nature, the cited poem also contains a rhetorical question that, in my eyes, is worth considering in the context of opera and testimonial writing. Addressing the Christian god, the speaker hearkens in the forest a metaphorical orchestra: "Oh! Deus! não ouves dentre a imensa orquestra / Que a natureza virgem manda em festa, / Soberba, senhoril, / Um grito que soluça, aflito, vivo, / O retinir dos ferros do cativo, / Um som discorde e vil?" ("O God! Don't you hear amidst this immense orchestra joyfully sounded by the virgin, mighty and superb nature, and afflicted and sobbing cry, the clang of captive irons, a vile and harsh chord").[49] Faithful Christians at the premiere in Rio de Janeiro in 1889 may have answered the question affirmatively; slavery, by the grace of God, had indeed come to an end.

But we may wonder about other audience members, past and future, less in tune with the memories of Alves's work and that of other abolitionist authors, including the Viscount of Taunay, whose antislavery writings were far more direct than his sketch for *Lo schiavo*. Can it be possible for others to detect and read a meaningful story of black enslavement—a shadow opera, as André might put it—amid the sweet notes of orchestral birds in "Alvorada"? This too may stand as a rhetorical question, except that Gomes's opera, despite its old-fashioned conventions, remains a living text. Spectators, listeners, and readers can approach *Lo schiavo* and renovate its lessons from their own horizons of expectation, which will surely include black slavery as a historical fact.

Ironically, despite the various changes imposed by Paravicini to conform to what he thought his compatriots wanted, the opera was not performed in Italy until 2019. Recognizing Gomes's work on both sides of the Atlantic, this first Italian *Schiavo* was partly sponsored by the Brazilian embassy in Rome and coproduced by both the Festival Amazonas de Ópera in Manaus and the Teatro Lirico di Cagliari, which described the work on its website as a beautiful musical rarity. In Rio de Janeiro, *Lo schiavo* has been staged more frequently than any other national opera with the exception of *Il guarany*. To celebrate the 180th anniversary of Gomes's birth, the Teatro Municipal commissioned a new staging of the work, employing for the first time ever the opera's full score, revised for the occasion by Roberto Duarte under the auspices of the Fundação Nacional de Artes (Funarte). For this momentous production, Duarte and Francesco Maestrini, the stage director, told Márvio dos Anjos of *O Globo* that they considered whether to "africanizar ou não o enredo, ainda mais diante das discussões de nossos dias" (Africanize the plot or not, especially in the light of current discussions).[50] Their priority, though, was to remain as faithful to Gomes's original as possible, but, while Paravicini's libretto stood unchanged, Duarte and Maestrini did at least acknowledge the possibility of a "releitura abolicionista" ("abolitionist rereading"). Indeed, one may conceive of future stagings of the opera that visibly underscore its untold tale of black slavery, thereby making palpable now what was then a repressed testimony.

Preposterously, one may also imagine an operagoer who comes belatedly to old *Lo schiavo* from a newer operatic culture that heeds the lessons of such works as Henze's *El cimarrón*. This operagoer, real or illusory, will surely fathom a plot whose invisible and inaudible black enslaved persons may yet be seen and heard in the rapturous musical passages crafted by Gomes. If words cannot tell this history, music will—or at least music will stand for the impossibility of telling it. What cannot be said, music can nobly attempt to represent.

7 Adams and Catán

Magic and Realism in Houston and Paris

AROUND THE TURN of the twenty-first century, two new music dramas variously linked to the Latin American literary tradition were performed in several cities around the world. Informed by the themes of magical realism, Daniel Catán's *Florencia en el Amazonas* (1996) was commissioned by the Houston Grand Opera, where it was premiered, and two other companies in the United States. John Adams's *El Niño* (2000), an oratorio often seen as an opera, debuted at the Théâtre du Châtelet in Paris using a libretto by Peter Sellars that showcased texts by poets from Mexico, Nicaragua and Chile. That both Catán's and Adams's works were chosen for the Metropolitan Opera House's 2023-24 season, aiming to showcase contemporary opera, is a sign of the vitality of Latin American literature on the global operatic stage. But not all stage works appear to be created equally. Adams, born in Massachusetts and a resident of California (where Catán, born in Mexico, also lived) seems to have worked unfettered by any kind of cultural constraints, crafting his own literary and musical vision of Latin America as he chronicled the Nativity and the birth of a Latino child in Southern California. Indeed, *El Niño* celebrated the region's literary corpus, especially the poetry of Rosario Castellanos, even as it brought attention to the historical plight of migrants from the region in the United States.

By contrast, Catán, who wrote his own libretto for *Florencia en el Amazonas*, was asked to operate within a narrower and more predictable idea of Latin American literature, stuck in magical realism. Whereas Adams's carte blanche appears to be a sign of metropolitan privilege, the limits placed on Catán's practice speak to the creative challenges of writing Latin American operas for audiences around the world. With a little help from butterflies, I argue, Catán was able nonetheless to overcome and even profit from any strictures.

What are these strictures? Consider, for instance, yet another night at the opera—a festive occasion in Houston on which a new work by Catán, written several years after *Florencia en el Amazonas*, was staged for the first time. Set in an imaginary magic-rich Caribbean republic, *Salsipuedes: A Tale of Love, War and Anchovies* (2004) employed the English version of a libretto written in Spanish by Eliseo Alberto and Francisco Hinojosa, authors from Cuba and Mexico respectively. The plot recalls the amatory and military complications of Mozart's *Così fan tutte*, but all the comic business taking place in Salsipuedes, an island nation, replicates and parodies the intertwining tropes of *Operettenstaaten* and banana republics. Indeed, Catán's Salsipuedes—whose dictator, General García, declares war on Hitler's Germany but sells anchovies to the Germans—appears to be a good neighbor of Joseph Conrad's Costaguana and O. Henry's Anchuria. Surprisingly, the "atmosphere of opera-bouffe" and "exquisite comicality" that Conrad deploys in his fictional republic, seen in Chapter 2, was not limited to the stage on the night when *Salsipuedes* received its world premiere but materialized eagerly elsewhere through the opera house. As part of its fiftieth anniversary, Houston Grand Opera celebrated its Latin American connections by crafting an offstage performance that preceded the actual show. Opera patrons and staff were encouraged to shed the long-established solemnity of operagoing and play out instead some of the clichés associated with the sultry latitudes of places like Salsipuedes. As D. L. Groover described it in a review: "There are ushers sporting tropical wear, salsa demonstrations in the grand foyer, palm tree shadows reflecting off lobby walls, a 'cruise' photographer and even a trained monkey. If you arrive in a

Hawaiian shirt or anything approximating island garb, you'll get a free chilled mojito. And we're informed that it's okay to dance in the aisles."[1] While Catán's vibrant work captured the complex origins of Caribbean music ("rhythms and melodic ideas from Europe, the Middle East, Spain and Africa," as a story on National Public Radio put it a few years later), much that was enacted on- and off-stage invoked a commonplace vision of the world to the south of the United States.[2]

This was not the first time that the Houston Grand Opera had assigned Catán a specific place in a rather predictable Latin American cultural cartography. For *Florencia en el Amazonas* (commissioned jointly with the Los Angeles Opera and the Seattle Opera), Catán, born in Mexico City and educated in Britain and the United States, reportedly expressed his wish to compose an opera based on a tale by Isak Dinesen. But Houston had a problem with that cosmopolitan choice and suggested instead that he craft a work that could be readily recognized as Latin American, preferably using a libretto by Gabriel García Márquez—or, in the master's absence, a text that at least deployed the formulas of his signature magic-realist mode.[3] García Márquez was unavailable at the time, so the task fell to Marcela Fuentes-Beráin, whom news clips and programs variously described as the author's pupil or protégée. García Márquez did agree to supervise the project, so both composer and librettist met up on several occasions with the novelist, who offered alternatives and suggestions. When all was said and done, though, the Spanish-language libretto that Catán ended up setting, with its apparent indebtedness to episodes and motifs in *Cien años de soledad* (1967) and *El amor en los tiempos del cólera* (1985), was regarded by some reviewers as a pale imitation of García Marquez's fiction or, at best, a competent pastiche thereof.[4] Marc Swed, writing for the *Los Angeles Times*, lamented Fuentes-Berain's mechanical craft: "She's a screenwriter and playwright, assigned to create Márquezian characters and transfer his magic realism, that quality of representing the wondrous adventures of a psyche by ineffable little weirdnesses in the surrounding world, to the stage. Instead she spells out the characters and their relationships as if the libretto were a set of Cliffs Notes for a García Márquez novel."⁵ Predictably, the opera's tale of a soprano traveling on a steamboat to the Manaus opera house also recalled the extravagant vision of European opera in the South American rainforest consecrated by Herzog's *Fitzcarraldo*.⁶ And yet the continuous presence of *Florencia en el Amazonas* on stages across the United States, Europe and Latin America itself denotes its status as a singularly successful opera by a composer from the Global South.

Catán's career after his first US-sponsored opera replays the work of magical realism as a stand-in for Latin America in the global cartographies of the novel. Surveying and analyzing the conceptual development of world literature, Mariano Siskind identifies a double movement in which magical realism plays a complicated role. On the one hand, there is "the postulation of world literature as an even playing field that makes possible an idealistic sense of parity among the literatures of the world—in other words, world literature as an equalizing discourse that rights the wrongs of cultural imperialism and/or economic globalization"; on the other hand, it is possible to observe "an *expressive* logic according to which some works convey the historical or aesthetic experience of their cultures of origins and, therefore, become part of a world literature composed of a plurality of global particularities."⁷ In Siskind's analysis, one book, *Cien años de soledad*, emerges as "a global bestseller [that] came to represent and express what a large portion of the world's literary public assumed to be the essence of Latin American culture and social history."⁸ That the Houston Grand Opera should have suggested García Márquez as librettist to Catán is opera's response to the same equalizing and expressive logic that Siskind perceives in the literary field. There is a place for Latin American operatic creations, but their contours, as it happens with narrative fiction, are often restricted according to preestablished expectations.

There are pleasures and perils in these cultural traffics. The fact that Latin American authors have seen their stories and practices filter into operas performed globally suggests a coming of age for the region. No longer passive objects of the European gaze, Latin Americans can also speak and, indeed, compose in their own voices.

But even as Catán gained a new level of visibility, certain formulations affected, perhaps even compromised, the fabric of his work in the United States and, to some extent, Europe as well. Catán's next opera after *Salsipuedes* was was yet another quintessential Latin American fantasy. A transatlantic project from the start, *Il Postino*, which turned out to be his last opera, was commissioned by the Los Angeles Opera and coproduced with Vienna's Theater an der Wien in 2010 and Paris's Théâtre du Châtelet in 2011. Many spectators were probably familiar with the opera's plotline, which Catán (who also wrote the libretto) took from Michael Radford's popular film, *Il Postino* (1994), whose plot, in turn, had been adapted from Antonio Skármeta's *Ardiente paciencia* (1985), a novel that stemmed from a previous film also titled *Ardiente paciencia* (1983), also directed by Skármeta. The Latin American literary connections were rich; both Radford's film and Catán's opera originated in a Chilean film and novel that chronicled the fictional friendship between Pablo Neruda and a young mailman. Skármeta's story is set on Isla Negra, where the poet had a house, and Radford's film moves the plot to an Italian island on which Neruda arrives as an exile; Catán follows Radford's lead.

Presenting a passionate story with a rather conventional political subplot, *Il Postino* bears much in common with operas from an earlier era, especially Italian works from the turn of the twentieth century. Indeed, Catán's music has often been likened to that of Puccini, and the libretto's focus on the power of art, plus its tragic denouement, bring to mind both *Tosca* and *La rondine*. Profiting from these familiar traits as well as the star power of Plácido Domingo in the role of Neruda, *Il Postino* turned out to be an unqualified success with audiences in Southern California, including spectators of Latin American descent keen on a Spanish-language libretto. To see yet another work in that language staged in both the United States and Europe was for Catán yet another crucial step in creating a strong Spanish-language operatic tradition, a personal mission of his.[9] But a general sense that the opera was a product of recycling could not be avoided—a feeling that its status as a Latin American work was deftly prefabricated, being as it was an adaptation of an adaptation of an adaptation. Reviewing the opera's run in Vienna for the *New York Times*, George Loomis summarized the mixed reaction of the European press: "The *Frankfurter Allgemeine Zeitung* called it 'a triumph,' but *Die Presse* found that the story, about the Chilean poet Pablo Neruda and his unlikely mentoring of a young mailman, was 'smothered in operatic sugar-icing.' The word 'kitsch' cropped up in more than one review."[10] For Loomis, Catán's music, while not explicitly Latin American, stuck too closely to an antique model of opera—pleasurable, but sounding "a lot" like Puccini and deploying an "ersatz quality." While he mentions the composer's education at Princeton under Milton Babbitt and Benjamin Boretz, "two stalwarts of musical modernism," Loomis observes that Catán "chose a very different artistic path."[11]

Il Postino was staged just a few months before Catán's untimely death in 2011. At the time, he was working on a new opera, *Meet John Doe*, based on Frank Capra's film with Gary Cooper and Barbara Stanwyck; the libretto, also by Catán, was written directly in English. Sadly, the work remained unfinished, but its commission, by the University of Texas's Butler School of Music in Austin, may be seen as the ultimate act of naturalization. The Mexican composer was at last no longer required to represent his ethnic origin but free to create something else: an opera set in his adopted country, adapted from a classic Hollywood film that had nothing to do with Latin America. One can only speculate about Catán's development as an opera composer had he lived longer, but it is interesting to see how *Meet John Doe* somehow mirrors the start of his opera career in Mexico City. In his hometown, Catán had written *Encuentro en el ocaso*, a chamber opera performed at the Teatro de la Ciudad in 1980, which was followed by *La hija de Rappaccini*, premiered at the Palacio de Bellas Artes in 1991 and staged at the San Diego Opera in 1994. Disregarding national borders and local color, *La hija de Rappaccini* was based on a short play by Octavio Paz, who in turn had adapted Nathaniel Hawthorne's story "Rappaccini's Daughter."[12] That a New England tale set in Padua would end up as the first Mexican opera performed (if not commissioned) by a major company in the United States can easily be regarded as a sign of creative freedom and cultural openness. Shunning exoticism,

San Diego took a gamble on Catán's borderless imaginings, and it paid off.[13] Reviewers praised the choice of *La hija de Rappaccini* as a breakthrough in operatic programming, lamenting, if anything, that it had taken so long to happen, but not that the opera lacked a specifically Mexican or Latin American texture. Catán's score at times invokes non-European sound worlds, but it is not the music of Mexico, as might be expected, but rather that of Asia, where Catán had spent some time before composing the work.[14] As if impervious to the constraints later imposed by such constructs as "world literature" and "world music," Catán was worldly before he was anything else. So, too, was Adams in *El Niño*, whose uses of Latin American literature I examine before returning to Catán's *Florencia en el Amazonas*.

A United States Libretto: Annunciations of Latin American Poetry

A creator at home on both sides of the Atlantic, John Adams is the rare American composer whose operas travel around the world with relative frequency, qualifying the emphatically European content of the international repertoire.[15] In *Hallelujah Junction*, his 2008 autobiography, Adams recounts a personal journey to Paris to witness the premiere of a new work. In the days preceding the staging of *El Niño* at the Théâtre du Châtelet in December 2000, "while Paris was decorating its streets and shops for Christmas," the composer knows himself to be in a city whose cultural and material history speaks directly to the timeless subject of his work: birth and, more specifically, the Nativity of Jesus.[16] A modern-day flâneur, he reflects on the ties that bind his new composition to the cultural and physical legacy of Christianity in Paris: "It was indeed possible to walk out of rehearsal and cross the bridge onto the Ile de la Cité and wonder into Notre Dame cathedral to stare in wonderment at the medieval statuary and pictures of Mary with her newborn on her lap."[17] There are of course many cathedrals and churches dedicated to Mary the world over, but Adams, an artist from the Americas, faces Notre-Dame de Paris knowing that artistic glory in that city is an uncommonly prestigious achievement.

That *El Niño* tells a new New World version of an old Old World tale is a remarkable reversal of the traditional routes of music drama. The piece recounts a millennial story from the Gospels but offers a plot twist that stems from the other side of the Atlantic—indeed, from the edge of the Pacific. The story that Adams and his co-librettist, Peter Sellars, recount is the tale of the birth of Jesus and also that of a nameless child born unto a Latino migrant couple at home, yet unhoused, in Southern California. Besides alluding to the child Jesus, the title also invokes the El Niño weather phenomenon in the Pacific Ocean, which, as Erwan Dianteill observes, links western South America to California through the hazards of climatology and was particularly strong in the winter of 1997–1998.[18] The work's generic filiation itself is novel; as Susan McClary puts it, *El Niño* is an instance of "an idiosyncratic genre of music theater" that Sellars, through his scenario, helped create.[19] Its association with opera is nonetheless strengthened by continued performances as part of operatic seasons in New York and elsewhere.

Technology preserves the birth of Adams's work at its world premiere. One can watch the DVD of *El Niño* at the Châtelet over and over again or listen to the CD of those first performances—or download either the video or audio version to any number of devices. Yet even before those recordings are played, there is another work in an older medium that is worth examining for its role in Adams's and Sellars's multicultural agency and agenda. A colorful presence on the CD's cover, the image features symbols and pigments that tell yet another New World story—an Old World story too—that concerns the historical ties binding the Americas and Europe. *Mujer de mucha enagua: Pa'ti Xicana* is a serigraph by Yreina D. Cervántez, a Chicana artist, adapted for the cover as a powerful paratextual marking of the cultural region invoked in *El Niño*.[20]

The image looks simple, yet its various elements make up a system of opaque Mexican signs (fig. 6). Most salient are the figures of a woman and two children on the left. A handkerchief hides her face, recalling the portrait of a Zapatista leader and, by extension, the struggle for social justice in Mexico. She wears a white apron, suggesting domestic employment, but the apron bears an unlikely

FIGURE 6. *Mujer de Mucha Enagua: PA TI' XICANA*, serigraph, Yreina D. Cervantez, ©1999.

inscription, as does her blue skirt. Although she might be someone's nanny, she also holds a baby and clutches the hand of a young girl, who in turn hugs a doll, as if mirroring the woman's posture; the two children may well be the woman's own. Just below the girl, to the right, is the profile of a head whose contours suggest a Mesoamerican sculpture or painting. One can see the silhouette of six small blue hands on the right, with fingers placed in various positions, plus a larger brown hand in the middle, whose fingers in turn convey a salutation or a valediction, or perhaps request viewers simply to stop and reflect on what they see. The image is indeed arresting; a spiral marks the palm of the disembodied hand, and its broad wrist appears to be tattooed or inscribed, for those pointed incisions seem to be letters and words. Next to the elusive signs, as if to clarify that we are in fact seeing—if not deciphering—a piece of writing, there appears a feathered pen, held by yet another hand, belonging to yet another woman. Readers of Latin American literature may know this person, wearing a nun's habit: Sor Juana Inés de la Cruz, whose face also appears on the Mexican peso. But not all that we see here fits Sor Juana's iconic image. For one, the front of her habit, a black surface in the original portrait, is covered with yet more letters and words. On her breast rests the large oval visage of a woman. The original portrait of Sor Juana shows a picture of the Annunciation, but here it is replaced by the black-and-white photograph of yet another woman. Few viewers might know it, but this is Rosario Castellanos, the twentieth-century novelist, poet, and essayist—yet another canonical figure, albeit less well known abroad than Sor Juana, in Mexican literary and cultural history.

For an image full of inscriptions denoting centuries of writing in Mexico, it is somewhat ironic that the only words one can effortlessly read on the CD cover are the non-Mexican names linked to the recording, produced by Nonesuch. This is, after all, a cultural artifact that the intriguing image is meant to represent and, one surmises, help to sell to music lovers as it travels around the world. The white words announce that this is John Adams's *El Niño*; that it features singers Lorraine Hunt Lieberson, Dawn Upshaw, and Willard White; and that Kent Nagano conducted the work. These names, well known to many opera lovers, are hardly provincial, for each invokes a world larger than the United States, where Adams lives and the work was composed. Nagano, the Asian American conductor, has held highly visible posts at opera companies in Los Angeles and Munich, while White—who, as we saw, sang the role of the Cuban runaway slave in Henze's *El Cimarrón* in Copenhagen—is a Jamaican British bass baritone who, like the American soprano Upshaw, is internationally renowned, as was the American mezzo-soprano Hunt Lieberson before her death. As for Adams himself, his operas, some of which are at times described (and dismissed) as "CNN operas," are hardly local affairs but powerful musical explorations of the place of Americans in the world and, more recently, of people from other nations in the United States.[21] *Nixon in China* (1987) dramatizes the initial rapprochement between Washington and Beijing; *The Death of Klinghoffer* (1991) chronicles the murder of a Jewish American man by Palestinian terrorists on a cruise ship; *Doctor Atomic* (2005) delves into Robert Oppenheimer's misgivings before the nuclear attack on Hiroshima; and *Girls of the*

Golden West (2017) follows migrants from various parts of the world in Gold Rush San Francisco. On the first page of the CD booklet of *El Niño*, listeners learn that the world-famous Peter Sellars directed the work's first production, and that, in yet another international twist, Nagano conducted the Deutsches Symphonie-Orchester Berlin. Printed on both the cover and in the booklet, these celebrated names make up a collective cosmopolitan signature that validates the work's aesthetic worth.

Seen against these European and North American credentials, the imprint of Mexican literary and visual culture on the cover poses its own set of questions. Are these signs of Latin America just a bit of color denoting mystery and exoticism? What story of their own might they tell? How indispensable are they as one interprets the work? As fetching as the image is, its elements are superseded by names from elsewhere; at least at first glance, they also remain only poorly visible and, unless one gets a magnifying glass, virtually illegible as well. Yet they are there, not signifying nothing. Rich visual hints of other cultures are not rare in recordings of operas linked with parts of the world regarded as outlandish, and, as we saw, their meanings are often complex. Cover images for recordings of Torrejón y Velasco's *La púrpura de la rosa* and Vivaldi's *Montezuma* may appear to recycle certain clichéd images—a portrait of Frida Kahlo, a Maya sculpture—as if to brand the operas they represent as seductively exotic. Yet they also serve to tease out the multiple affects at play in the transatlantic journey of those operas. One may argue that such images are not the composer's work and should therefore not be overinterpreted as one evaluates the actual musical creation. But even after the near obsolescence of CDs, images are often the first thing a consumer sees when approaching a recording, and Cervántez's adapted serigraph still presents *El Niño* on YouTube and music-streaming services. Besides signaling Adams's engagement with Mexican history and culture, the serigraph's deployment may also be seen as a device for revealing and concealing, like the veiled woman on the left.

Underscoring the importance of the serigraph, the CD booklet contains an essay by Cervántez herself that serves as yet another paratext through which the meanings of Adams's music drama may be pondered. The artist starts by explaining the title of her work, which has two parts, the subject of the image and its intended viewers: "In Mexico when you speak of 'una mujer de mucha enagua,' translated literally as a 'woman with a lot of petticoat,' you are talking about a woman of strength, courage and integrity. The phrase has been used to describe women Zapatistas and their political activism and displays of military skill. In my serigraph, I am adopting this metaphor to represent all women united in a struggle for a better life. The second half of the title, *PA'TI XICANA*, is a dedication to my sister Xicana/Latinas in the US who have their own brand of activism."[22]

Cervántez then explains some details that may not be obvious in the serigraph's visual and literary references. She starts with the three female images. The woman on the left is indeed meant to invoke Comandante Ramona, a Zapatista leader, and the words on her apron come from the Mayan *Popol Vuh*; Sor Juana speaks in Nahuatl and invokes Tonantzin, the mother goddess; and Castellanos is defined as a "daughter of Chiapas," while lines from her poem, "Madre india," are printed on Sor Juana's habit. Various Native American symbols are explained too, shedding light on the relevance of non-European forms in Cervántez's artistic practice. The six enigmatic blue hands on the right turn out to be Mayan hand mudras "done in the compositional style of Mayan stelae reliefs," while, below right, a tiny figure also in blue is "la mujer que simboliza fecundidad" (woman, who symbolizes fecundity).[23] Cervántez ascribes a specific meaning to this concept: "In this instance, fecundity represents creativity/creation, the engendering of fertile ideas, and the actualization of dreams."[24] By reading Cervántez, a window is opened into the realm of *mestizaje*; indigenous and European signs mix and interact in a hybrid culture whose forms and affects are often taken to be the defining core of Mexico and Latin America.[25]

Should the public, then, building on the cues offered by the cover and the essay, perceive *El Niño* as a mestizo creation of sorts? When asked by Thomas May to define "the driving force" behind the work, Sellars stressed his relationship with Latino artists in

California as a source of inspiration but also, implicitly, as evidence of an acquired transcultural knowledge that he can convey to audiences less familiar with that other culture: "Nothing at all prepared me for John saying he wanted to do the birth of Jesus! . . . Meanwhile, in those years I had begun working very closely with artists in East Los Angeles, making shows that were both in Spanish and English: with the poet Gloria Alvarez, the painter Gronk, and the painter Yreina Cervantes [sic] (whose work profoundly influenced *El Niño* and is on the cover of the record). For me it's an ongoing commitment to do works in both Spanish and English that reflect the cultural and demographic realities of the state of California."[26]

In the DVD booklet, Cervántez is mentioned under the rubric of "Artistic Collaboration." But oddly, the tiny blue figure that she herself associates with the act of creation, and which can be seen clearly in the original serigraph, is rendered virtually invisible by the CD cover's assertive graphic design, which practically erases it by circumscribing it with the letter O at the end of *El Niño*. While in Cervántez's eyes her own serigraph is dedicated to Chicana women, the opera it serves may be addressing other people—another audience. But who and where are they? What do they see and read as they listen to this work that appears to speak about, or for, people from Mexico and Latin America? What is the status of those creators from other parts of the world in this new work crafted mostly by non–Latin Americans and premiered in Europe? Should one simply agree with Dianteill, who views *El Niño*—its musical fabric, classically trained performers, vanguard-leaning audiences—as a globalized yet essentially non-multicultural work? How else can one regard these cultural and affective transports?[27]

Overlooking the stated recipients of Cervántez's image, Adams dedicated *El Niño* to Sellars, his longtime collaborator—a paratextual gesture that honors Sellars's agency as an ambassador for, if not a member of, other cultural groups. Not unlike Miguel Barnet on behalf of Esteban Montejo in *Biografía de un cimarrón*, Sellars acts as a powerful mediator between other people's words and new audiences they may otherwise be deprived of. However, that Sellars, through Adams's dedication, is also the privileged recipient of the work bespeaks a self-contained circle, or a self-referential circulation, in which other possible actors, including Latin Americans, may be rendered less visible or less audible. An uncanny author- and reader-like figure, then, Sellars appears to stand as a central creative entity behind *El Niño*, notwithstanding the absence of his name on the cover.

At its premiere, *El Niño* sought nevertheless to assert its status as a secular *Messiah* for a multicultural and closely connected world. Adams himself had stated his wish to compose a piece on the subject of birth; as he tells it, the birth of his daughter was nothing short of a miracle: "There were four people in the room, and then there were five."[28] Appealing to an experience common to all humankind, *El Niño* transforms the Christian myth by recasting Jesus, Mary, and Joseph as members of a Latino immigrant family in California. Not only is the biblical story turned into a contemporary tale, the traditional Western accoutrements of Christmas are also ejected from the stage, as Bernard Holland remarks in his review of the work's American premiere in San Francisco in early 2001: "*El Niño* dispenses with camels in the desert, tipsy British carolers in the snow and the images from Currier & Ives. Its Joseph and Mary are Latino teenagers seeking shelter on the freeways, public beaches and parking lots of Southern California."[29] Importantly, the nontraditional libretto, by Adams and Sellars, consists of texts from diverse literary practices and linguistic traditions—English, Spanish, and Latin—classified in the booklet along two categories: early English anonymous poems, texts from the Wakefield Mystery Plays, Martin Luther, the King James Bible, and the New Testament Apocrypha, as well as poems by Rosario Castellanos, Gabriela Mistral, Hildegard von Bingen, Sor Juana Inés de la Cruz, Rubén Darío, and Vicente Huidobro.[30]

More questions, then, emerge. To what extent can *El Niño* be regarded as a work not just about but also by and for Latin Americans? What does the inclusion of five authors from the region—Castellanos, Mistral, Sor Juana, Darío, and Huidobro—say about the work of Latin American literary culture in the creation of opera? What does the dead writers' society convoked by the co-librettists say about the authorship of operas for the global stage? Whose voices are productively read and heard as Adams sets to music Sellars's literary offerings? Who speaks, as it were, when singers and dancers perform the collage-like text of *El Niño* onstage? These questions are not posed explicitly in *El Niño*, but they matter for an analysis of its Latin American literary connections, especially taking into account Adams's sustained readings of Edward Said, which Mathieu Duplay remarks on in his analysis of the work. For Duplay, Adams must be at least obliquely concerned with the statement by Marx in *The Eighteenth Brumaire of Louis Bonaparte*, cited by Said as an epigraph in *Orientalism*: "They cannot represent themselves; they must be represented."[31] Who, exactly, "they" are (or not) in the case of *El Niño* is yet another query to consider in Adams's formidable creative engagement with a Spanish-language poetical corpus. Persuasively, Duplay argues that *El Niño* can be heard not as part of a discourse aimed at overpowering Spanish-speaking America but rather as an opera in which binaries, largely through Castellanos's texts, are dissolved. Yet as we will see, this is not the only possible assessment of Adams's absorption of Mexican poetry, especially if one reads *El Niño* in the larger context of other operas linked to Latin America, such as *Florencia en el Amazonas*.

Reviewers of the Paris premiere praised the works by Latin American authors convened in the libretto, especially the four texts by Castellanos—the most numerous by a single author—sung by Hunt Lieberson and Upshaw. Indeed, the poet's voice plays a substantial role in *El Niño*. If Cervántez's serigraph replaces the beloved European depiction of the Annunciation—the ever-present Mary and Gabriel—with a photograph of Castellanos, the poet's "La anunciación" complements and vastly expands the New Testament story as chronicled in "The Play of the Annunciation" from Martial Rose's version of the fifteenth-century Wakefield Mystery Plays. In this regard, the affects at play in *El Niño*, departing from the values linked to habitual readings of the biblical story, stem powerfully from Castellanos's reflections on motherhood and other subjects.

In Sellars's staging, the Wakefield Mystery Play is performed not by two actors playing Mary and Gabriel, but by a soprano, Upshaw, who sings Mary's part, and three countertenors and a dancer who jointly personify the archangel. In the scene titled "Hail, Mary, Gracious!" Mary gracefully bows to Gabriel's announcement that she will be the mother of God by singing the play's lovingly phrased assent and assertion of faith: "My lord's love will I not withstand, / I am his maiden at his hand. / And in his fold. / Gabriel, I believe that God will bring / To pass with me each several thing / As thou hast told" (39). But then she sings the lines of Castellanos's "La anunciación," which features, by contrast, a plaintive voice—that of Mary, or any other expectant mother—who beholds with concern the future birth of a son—Jesus, or any other child. The poem's images resonate with the story of creation in Genesis and recall the sensual undertones of the Song of Songs, but they also include a word, *llagas* (wounds), that ominously foresees Christ's death. In the last two stanzas, the speaker dramatically addresses her yet unborn child with passionate words that complicate the wonders of the Annunciation by prefiguring the Crucifixion in the mother's own body:

> He aquí que te anuncias.
> Entre contradictorios ángeles te aproximas,
> como una suave música te viertes,
> como un vaso de aromas y de bálsamos.
> Por humilde me exaltas. Tu mirada,
> benévola, transforma
> mis llagas en ardientes esplendores.
> He aquí que te acercas y me encuentras
> rodeada de plegarias como de hogueras altas. (41)

> And here you are, announcing yourself.
> Among contradictory angels you approach,
> pouring yourself like gentle music,
> like a glassful of balms and aromas.
> You praise my humility. Your gaze,
> benevolent, transforms
> my wounds to fiery splendors.
> And now you approach and find me
> surrounded by prayer as if by high flames.

As the poem ends, the speaker casts herself once again as a woman who, like Mary, is told she will have a child, but also as a person whose metaphorical wounds might recall those of Christ even as she ends up surrounded by fire—a martyr-like figure not unlike Joan of Arc. Significantly, Castellanos's nuanced rewriting of the Scriptures centers on a woman's complicated affects—a powerful enactment of Adams's stated wish that his work on birth should have a feminine viewpoint.

Another poem by Castellanos, "Se habla de Gabriel," invokes the physical and psychological demands of pregnancy, childbirth and motherhood. (Gabriel is the name shared by the archangel and Castellanos's own son.) Yet another text, "Memorial por Tlatelolco," dedicated to the students massacred in Mexico City in 1968, is performed right after a verse from the Gospel of Matthew on Herod's slaying of the children of Bethlehem, thereby juxtaposing two episodes—one from the New Testament and another from twentieth-century Mexican history—that can be read as stories of maternal sorrow. Not just simple updates, Castellanos's texts amplify the old stories by exploring present-day issues related to women's bodies as well as social justice. Specifically, "Memorial de Tlatelolco," as Duplay explains, functions almost as an operatic aria by contributing to the drama's unfolding and to characterization.[32] Indeed, the character singing these words can be perceived as an individual, not a generic or impersonal voice.

Finally, a fourth poem, "Una palmera," is sung as *El Niño* comes to an end. Its rich lines are interpolated with a narrative passage from the Gospel of Pseudo-Matthew, which, like the poem, also concerns a palm tree. In the ancient tale, Joseph, Mary, and Jesus rest on their flight to Egypt. Joseph is afraid that they will run out of water, upon which the child, invoking Pseudo-Matthew, addresses the palm tree under which they have been resting: "Open a water course beneath your roots which is hidden in the earth, and from it let flow waters to satisfy you" (65). As the miracle unfolds, a chorus sings words from Castellanos's poem: "Señora de los vientos, / garza de la llanura, / cuando te meces canta / tu cintura" (66; "Lady of the winds, / heron of the plains, / when you sway / your waist sings" 66). The interpolation of both texts completes the musical and theatrical merging of the old Nativity story with the shared human experience of birth. As soloists and chorus sing the intermingled words of Pseudo-Matthew and those of Castellanos, Sellars's film shows intermittent images of palm trees in urban and rural California.[33] The last word in the libretto is in fact the last line in Castellanos's "Una palmera": *poesía* (66). Meaning both "poetry" and a "poem," this is yet another textual sign of the importance of literary creation—and of Spanish-language writing—in the makeup of *El Niño*.

Indeed, besides the story of a Latino family, Adams and Sellars's libretto may be read as a lovingly curated survey of Latin American poetry. In a 2001 interview with Ken Ueno, Adams revealed how his own knowledge of that literary corpus was virtually inexistent: "Like most Americans, I knew only certain well-known names in Latin-American literature: Carlos Fuentes, Gabriel García Márquez, Pablo Neruda. I didn't know these women poets."[34] Adams writes about the transformative power of Spanish in California and how he learned the language in order to set the Spanish-speaking texts to music.[35] In a tacitly didactic gesture, the five authors whose poems appear in *El Niño* exemplify major schools and periods of poetry in Latin America: Sor Juana, writing in Mexico City in the second half of the seventeenth century, is one of the lasting authors of the transnational baroque; Darío, born in Nicaragua, is one of the founders of Spanish American *modernismo*, credited for renewing the forms and themes of Spanish-language poetry, and Huidobro, from Chile, is a major avant-garde figure; Mistral, also from Chile, was the first Latin American author to be awarded the Nobel Prize for Literature; and Castellanos played a major role in both the literary field and diplomacy, serving as Mexico's ambassador in Israel until her accidental death in Tel Aviv in 1974. Interestingly, most of the first reviewers of *El Niño* had more to say about the three women authors, as if heeding Adams's call for a female-inflected vision of childbirth or learning the lessons of Cervántez's woman-centered serigraph. When all was said and done, Latin American poetic culture is well served, elegantly represented and lovingly proffered by Adams's gorgeous setting of Sellars's chosen readings.

Sellars emerges, then, not only as Adams's main collaborator but also as an authority on all things Latin American in the creation and performance of *El Niño*. Apart from the libretto's assemblage, his main contribution to *El Niño* was the film projected onstage behind the singers and dancers, whom he also directed. Foregrounding the streetscapes and landscapes of Southern California and the bodies of the young Latino couple unto whom a child is born, the film contests the classic European representations of the birth of Jesus by adding a complicated, somewhat confusing visual story. As the performance begins, the audience sees onstage a palm tree and a Christmas tree, both made of small lights; choral singers dressed in red; the soprano singing the role of Mary, wearing a plaid shirt; and the three countertenors, standing in for Gabriel, also colorfully attired. In the film, a young woman sits in the passenger seat of a car, driven at night in the rain; then, a woman sits at a table by a lamp, reminiscent of Georges de la Tour's images of Mary Magdalene, her hands projected near a ceiling fan; then a man stands in a bedroom with his arms lifted to suggest a cross. The film is paused, and a real-life dancer mimicking the man's cross-like posture—they are one and the same performer—appears onstage behind the soprano and the countertenors. And this is only the beginning; the "Hail, Mary, Gracious" scene is derived from "The Play of the Annunciation," with yet more images projected behind the figures onstage.

Although praised by some, many reviewers reproved Sellars's film, expressing reservations both on artistic and political grounds. In *Hallelujah Junction*, Adams himself takes issue with the film, calling it "full of charm," but noting it competes with the music and the singers' acting onstage.[36] Beyond aesthetics, others paint Sellars as an unduly conspicuous figure in his endeavors to speak for others. Bernard Holland describes the director's multifaceted job with a measure of irony: "This is a Nativity not only cast with minority figures but told from the woman's point of view. Mr. Sellars takes his usual role as honorary member and emotional spokesman for the oppressed and the slighted. It must gall him at times to be so showered with attention and success."[37] If these ironic views are speculative, they nonetheless foreground the question of Sellars as an overly fervent agent in making the plight of others visible and audible, entangling political engagement and aesthetic value. Yet Holland himself confirms Sellars's effective work in promoting some of the authors featured in *El Niño*; he praises Castellanos's poems for their "evocations of pregnancy" and "hair-raising beauty."[38] This auspicious judgment was shared by other critics and, one can imagine, audience members who otherwise would not have been readers of the poet's works—or, for that matter, of the four other Latin American poets included in the libretto. Despite Holland's scruples, as it conflates the story of a Latino father, mother, and child with the biblical narrative of the Holy Family, *El Niño* also lays out a strong vision of equality and fraternity for a place like California, or a multicultural nation like the United States—a lesson, if you will, that also speaks to Europe, the cradle of old operas about Latin America and a new home for people from the Global South. Without a sociologist's toolbox, it is difficult to gauge whether the outcomes of these acts of hospitality are large or small, but it is possible to sense the dramatic power of *El Niño* in recasting cultural history within an expansive and welcoming cultural framework.

As one evaluates the affects and effects of Adams's spacious cultural geography, a meaningful analogy may be found in the climate phenomenon officially known as the El Niño Southern Oscillation. Writing about the origins of his piece, Adams himself recalls how El Niño hit the coast of California in 1997 and somehow brought the lands of the Pacific closer together, producing such amazing things as the sighting of tropical fish swimming as far north as Alaska.[39] Like those fish inhabiting strange waters, the multiple creators convoked in *El Niño* tell a story of wondrous interconnectedness among the multiple cultures of the Americas. If Adams remains an all-powerful Zeus-like figure or the chief meteorologist in this enterprise, his hospitable craft floats marvelously in part because he turns his curious eyes to fellow creatures from the hemisphere's southern latitudes.

Yet behind the openhearted zeal of *El Niño*, there is also a troubling story of asymmetry in regard to liberty and power in the realm of opera. Working from a position of privilege, the creative team headed by Adams and Sellars exerts unrestricted freedom to decide on the subject and tenor of the piece. A Mexican composer like Daniel Catán, though, is expected to create operas that bespeak links to his native land, but Adams and Sellars, as American artists, can freely roam the hemisphere—indeed, the world—hunting for other peoples' stories, which they can then subsume into their own. This argument should not be construed as an accusation of cultural appropriation. New art, after all, is often inspired by preexisting works without much regard to borders; adapting, citing, recasting, or redeploying the words of others also empowers the original texts, transporting them, arguably, to a more visible place full of new readers. But this is a story of unequal opportunities. The seemingly multicultural fabric of *El Niño* shows how the world of opera is free and wide for some but not so much for others.

A decade later, Adams created yet another work—oratorio or opera—of biblical proportions, premiered not in a Parisian theater but at Walt Disney Concert Hall in Los Angeles. First seen in a concert version in 2012 and revised for a staged performance in 2013, *The Gospel according to the Other Mary* chronicled the public life of Jesus leading to the Crucifixion and Resurrection. If *El Niño* had been a response to Handel's *Messiah*, the new work, as critics observed, was Adams's opera-like version of Bach's *Passions*. The *Gospel*, too, had a Latin American focus. Again, the biblical story was transported to Southern California—a spectacle animated by migrants from other parts of the world, including Gustavo Dudamel, the passionate conductor from Venezuela who led the Los Angeles Philharmonic Orchestra and the Los Angeles Master Chorale for the evening. Once again, the libretto, crafted solely by Sellars, sought to tell a familiar story through the eyes of others, this time the censured and censored Mary Magdalene. Once again, the libretto was built on a diverse array of works, including two poems by Darío and Castellanos. And once again, when a recording came out, a colorful CD cover displayed the composer's and conductor's names and credited the orchestra and chorus even as it boasted an image readily identifiable as, or of, Latin America. As the booklet explains, the image is a photograph by Evelyn Henn of *Resurrection of the Green*

Planet, a 1990 mural by Ernesto de la Loza located in the Boyle Heights district of Los Angeles. The exact address, on Breed Street at César E. Chávez Avenue, is also provided, perhaps for the sake of anyone interested in seeing the original—or of anyone, one can also imagine, doubtful of the work's actual provenance. As they listen to Adams's terrific music on their headphones, listeners can take it that vision of Los Angeles and be transported to what for many surely would be a strange urban landscape. In de la Loza's mural, they can see two women encircled by roses. A white car is parked in front of the mural, but they can also see, placed more or less discreetly in the lower right corner, the yellow logos of Deutsche Grammophon, whose representation of Adams's work no doubt ensures the consumption of the music, words and images all over the world.

A Latin American Libretto: Metamorphoses in the Amazon

Read from a certain angle, Daniel Catán's *Florencia en el Amazonas* is an opera about opera—or an opera about the pleasures and perils of composing Latin American operas in a globalized age. Since its commission by three major opera companies in the United States, *Florencia en el Amazonas* has become one of the most successful Latin American operas ever written, comparable to Carlos Gomes's works at La Scala in the 1870s. Catán's opera was premiered in Houston in October 1996 in a production by Francesca Zambello, which traveled to Los Angeles in 1997 and Seattle in 1998. A concert version was performed in Mexico City and Manaus, Brazil, while excerpts and an orchestral suite were played in Bogotá, Colombia. The work was revived in Houston in 2001 and Seattle in 2005, had its European premiere in Heidelberg in 2006, received new stagings at the Cincinnati Opera in 2008 and Opera Colorado in 2012, was performed at several universities in the United States, and, in 2016, at Lincoln Center's Rose Theater, by the New York City Opera, followed by other productions at the Lyric Opera of Chicago in 2021 and the Metropolitan Opera House in 2023.[40] In 2018, a staged production finally reached the Teatro Amazonas in Manaus, which plays a central role in the plot. In an era when new operas often fall quickly into oblivion, the performance history of *Florencia en el Amazonas*, as well as a recording of it released in 2002, are evidence of a potent example of music drama.

Yet the story of Catán's rise within the American operatic establishment has not been not devoid of a certain measure of ambivalence. Within these constraints, *Florencia en el Amazonas* can be read as a powerful meditation on the intricate ties that bind Latin America and the art of opera—and, more generally, on the challenges of being a Latin American composer on the global stage. To explore these questions, my focus is on the work's delicately self-reflexive plot: the melodramatic tale of a renowned South American soprano's river journey from the port of Leticia, Colombia, to the grand opera house in Manaus, where she hopes to be reunited with her lover, a butterfly hunter. The soprano is named Florencia, invoking the city of opera's birth, and the music she sings hearkens back to the art form's European canon; Catán is often compared to Debussy, Puccini, and Ravel. The plot recalls the enduring implications of exoticism for composing operas about Latin America. In this, Florencia's apparent metamorphosis into a butterfly at the opera's denouement is especially significant. If Catán's opera engages in the practices of many European operas set in far-flung locations, its complex amalgam of literary, musical, and visual sources ultimately queries and transcends the colonialist lineage of much operatic exoticism. Some of the opera's self-assertive work hinges on the wings of the incarnated butterfly that overshadows everything at the end of Zambello's inaugural production.

In what one might call the cultural history of *Lepidoptera*, and especially in the chapter pertaining to Latin American relations with other parts of the world, there is one episode that strikes me as particularly revealing. It took place in London, at 52 Tavistock Square where, in October 1935, Virginia Woolf received a glass box full of colorful Brazilian butterflies. The outlandish gift came from Victoria Ocampo, who modestly called herself one of Woolf's "common readers" but who, in Buenos Aires just a few years earlier, had founded *Sur*, which would become Latin America's top literary journal as well as one of the foremost publishing houses in the

Spanish-speaking world. In her thank-you letter to Ocampo after receiving the glass-encased butterflies, Woolf describes the rather operatic scene in which two mysterious foreign ladies wearing veils delivered the precious object: "they pressed into my hand a large parcel, murmured some musical but unintelligible remarks about 'giving it into your hands' and vanished. It took me at least ten minutes to realise that this was your present of South American butterflies."[41] Not devoid of a certain Nabokovian playfulness, this transport of butterflies by an Argentine reader for an English author has attracted attention from critics for what it seems to disclose about the friendship between the two women of letters and, more generally, about the nature of cultural exchanges between Latin America and Europe—or, if you will, from the Global South to the metropolitan north. Anyone who has read Ocampo's essays on Woolf can attest to Victoria's unqualified reverence for all of Virginia's writings, some of which, including *Orlando* (1928) and *A Room of One's Own* (1929), she asked her friend Jorge Luis Borges to translate into Spanish; indeed, the influence of Borges's version of the former work in Latin American letters cannot be exaggerated.[42] But if Ocampo esteemed Woolf's work, the English novelist could not respond in kind. Not knowing Spanish, Woolf was unable to read almost anything written by her friend from Buenos Aires, although she at least knew of her short volume on Dante, written originally in French, plus a number of essays that Victoria, who spoke English fluently from childhood, translated for the sake of her friend in London.[43]

But beyond these stories of books, one is seduced by the gift of butterflies and intrigued by their possible meaning in the story of the two women's friendship. One may surmise this in a letter by Woolf to Ocampo in which she freely imagines Argentina as a beautiful, if strange, country: "How remote and sunk in time and space you seem, over there, in the vast—what d'you call them—those immense blue grey lands with the wild cattle and the pampas grass and the butterflies? Every time I go out of my door I make up another picture of South America: and no doubt you'd be surprised if you could see yourself in your house as I arrange it. It is always grilling hot, and there is a moth alighted in a silver flower."[44]

In this fictional landscape, it is striking to see Woolf's openly willful, even manipulative gaze "arranging" things, including Victoria, according to certain expectations of exoticism candidly devoid of true knowledge. According to Ocampo, one possible source for the butterfly-filled pampas may well have been Charles Darwin, who in *The Voyage of the Beagle* (1839) describes his encounter with the "insects," as he rather unpoetically calls the butterflies, in the southern part of Buenos Aires province: "One evening, when we were about ten miles from the Bay of San Blas, vast numbers of butterflies, in bands or flocks of countless myriads, extended as far as the eye could range. Even by the aid of a telescope it was not possible to see a space free from butterflies. The seamen cried out 'it was snowing butterflies,' and such in fact was the appearance."[45] Although Darwin identifies most of the butterflies as being similar to the *Colias edusa*, quite common in England, their profuse South American cousins, as Ocampo suggests, may well have remained in Woolf's mind as a sign of the extraordinary character of the antipodes. Woolf had, of course, set her first novel *The Voyage Out* (1915) in a fictional South American country that bore little resemblance to the real-world continent, at least in the eyes of W. H. Hudson, who, before settling in London, had spent the first forty years of his life on the Argentine pampas.[46] It comes as no surprise, then, that Woolf should regard Ocampo's world with a novelist's eyes—or that *The Voyage Out* should feature at least one yellow butterfly at a significant turn in the protagonist's story.[47]

In these intersections of real and fictional butterflies, what interests me most is Victoria's somewhat ironic acquiescence or subtle complacency—one might even say encouragement—regarding Virginia's own private Argentina, a gesture not unlike that of Catán, perhaps, upon deciding to heed Houston's call for an opera full of Latin American things. It does not matter much to Ocampo that the picture created by Woolf gainsays her country's self-fashioning as a modern, civilized place. Writing more than forty years after their first meeting in London, Ocampo affectionately recalls the author's epistolary inventions: "Me hablaba en sus cartas de nuestras inmensas llanuras de un verde azulado ¿Cómo se llaman?—agregaba entre paréntesis. Han de ser impresionantes, como el ganado salvaje, decía. Y yo pensaba al leerla: ¡Santo Dios! Con el trabajo que les ha costado a nuestros estancieros criar vacas, toros, caballos, carneros dignos de figurar junto a los mejores de Inglaterra (de donde muchos provienen). Pero si te divierte imaginar las cosas así, Virginia, no me opongo. Ganado salvaje, hierbas verde azulado de la pampa, mariposas revoloteando en el aire. Virginia creaba una Argentina a su paladar" (Virginia spoke to me in her letters of our immense bluish green plains. What are they called—she would add parenthetically. They must be quite impressive, like the wild cattle, she would say. And I would think as I read her: Dear God! With all the efforts our ranchers have gone through to raise cows, bulls, horses and sheep worthy of standing side by side with the best of England [where many of them come from]. But if it amuses you to imagine everything like that, Virginia, I'm not opposed. Wild cattle, the bluish green grasses of the pampas, butterflies fluttering in the air . . . Virginia created an Argentina that fit her own tastes).[48]

In fact, Virginia's musings seem to have a life of their own, as one can see many years later in Quentin Bell's hyperbolic remarks to Antonio Bivar, a Brazilian journalist, in 1996: "Virginia Woolf's notions concerning Latin America were grotesque; she had a friend, Victoria Ocampo, from Buenos Aires, who had to explain to her that the Argentine was not a great forest with alligators, butterflies as big as vultures, and natives pursued by pumas."[49] If this is not quite how Woolf describes Argentina in her letters to Ocampo, Bell's amplification does resonate with what Virginia notes in her diary after having met Victoria for the first time at an exhibition of Man Ray photographs on Bedford Square in 1934. Virginia finds in Victoria a human type supposedly identified and classified by Roger Fry and writes in her diary that she has met "a South American Vasta—was that what Roger called those opulent millionaires from Buenos Aires," and she goes on to depict her not only as a dweller in an exuberant land but also as a kind of astonishing fruit, a curious fusion of nature and culture: "she was very ripe & rich; with pearls at her ears, as if a large moth had laid clusters of eggs; the colour of an apricot under glass; eyes I think brightened by some cosmetic; but there we stood and talked, in French, & English, about the Estancia, the great white rooms, the cactuses, the gardenias, the wealth & opulence of South America."[50] As Fiona G. Parrott aptly describes it, the Argentine woman, despite her fluency in all matters British and European, is an "other" of sorts: "Ocampo, like the exhibition photographs, is on display for Woolf who observes her through the lens of an Old World colonist."[51] A few days after their first meeting, Victoria sends her new friend a bouquet of orchids known as butterflies, which Virginia acknowledges thus: "And I must compare you to a butterfly if you send me these gorgeous purple butterflies. I opened the box and thought 'this is what a garden in South America looks like.'"[52]

But what does a garden—or broadly speaking, nature—in South America look like? The question is of course rhetorical, but the fact is that Latin American authors, as well as writers from other parts of the world, have long produced minute descriptions of that supposedly brave new world. A case in point in the local literary canon is that of Andrés Bello, the Venezuelan author who, while living in London in the 1820s, wrote "Silva a la agricultura de la zona tórrida," whose long neoclassical verses seek to represent the bounty of the tropical regions by carefully depicting such things as bananas, coffee, and sugarcane. Indeed, much of Latin American literature may be read as the story of an engagement with the continent's natural world, whose perceived extravagance sets it apart from Europe and even North America. Several of the most enduring works of narrative fiction from the 1920s and 1930s belong to the modality termed *novela de la tierra*, an example of which is José Eustasio Rivera's *La vorágine* (1924), at the end of which the protagonist and his companions vanish forever in the thick of the South American jungle—a denouement that, as we will see, resounds at the end of *Florencia en el Amazonas*.[53] If Woolf depicts a garden when she writes to Ocampo about her imaginary Argentina, the truth of the matter is that those artificial, delicate spaces are far less common in the discourse about Latin America than various forms of wilderness, from the Amazon rainforest to the desolate plains of Patagonia. As Carlos Fuentes remarked, it is easy to picture Heine singing to a domesticated Rhine, or Goethe searching for peace in the Alps, but when it comes to Latin American fiction, the prevailing image, at least through the mid-twentieth century, is that of terrifying jungles and mountain ranges.[54]

In the context of Latin American literary culture, it is not strange, then, that Catán's opera should be set along the Amazon, a picturesque location where the street vendors, in the words of the libretto, "ofrecen su mercancía, rica en texturas y colores; granos, frutas, verduras, animales; polvos y aceites; ópalos, esmeraldas y plata" ("offer their wares, rich in textures and colors; grains, fruits, vegetables, animals; powders and oils; opals, emeralds and silver").[55] The chorus of street vendors happily proffers such odd items as love potions and an alligator, while Florencia herself, whose face is covered in a mysterious silk scarf, describes the river in her first aria as "un lodazal de anacondas" (24; "a quagmire of snakes"). Indeed, even if Fuentes's dictum about the perception of nature in Latin America may be dismissed as a sweeping statement, it is clear from the start of *Florencia en el Amazonas* that we are no longer in the waterscape of, say, *Das Rheingold*. Yet the excess of the landscape—its rich, untamed life, dear to authors traveling the world in search of new botanical or zoological experiences—seems to resound with operatic undertones. Darwin, for instance, upon first landing in South America near Salvador de Bahia, is ecstatic: "The day has passed delightfully. Delight itself, however, is a weak term to express the feelings of a naturalist who, for the first time, has wandered by himself in a Brazilian forest. The elegance of the grasses, the novelty of the parasitical plants, the beauty of the flowers, the glossy green of the foliage, but above all the general luxuriance of the vegetation, filled me with admiration."[56] Twice in *The Voyage of the Beagle*, he resorts to musical and theatrical metaphors to describe his awe at the grandeur of nature. Entering what he calls a "noble forest" above Rio de Janeiro, he beholds the unusual topography and luxuriant vegetation: "At this elevation the landscape attains its most brilliant tint; and every form, every shade, so completely surpasses in magnificence all that the European has ever beheld in his own country, that he knows not how to express his feelings.

The general effect frequently recalled to my mind the gayest scenery of the Opera-house or the great theatres."[57] High in the Andes, master of all he surveys, he sums up his lyrical description of sky, valleys, and ruins by invoking Handel: "I felt glad that I was alone; it was like watching a thunderstorm, or hearing in full orchestra a chorus of the Messiah."[58]

Darwin's textual conflation of nature and culture is hardly unique; indeed, it may well be one of the continent's emblems, as one observes in the fictional bit of literary criticism offered by the narrator of Julian Barnes's *Flaubert's Parrot* (1984), quoted in Chapter 2. In that narrator's composite vision of the fictional South America of contemporary writers, one can easily identify a range of rather bizarre motifs that bespeak a clichéd image of the wondrous continent, including an opera house in the jungle. His focus on such strange things as impregnation by telepathy, seemingly presented as normal, can be read as in ironical indictment of magical realism, in turn closely linked, by means of the uncanny fredonna tree, with a naturalist's discourse not unlike that of Darwin. Indeed, magical-realist authors such as García Márquez, like belated naturalists, often foreground the oddities of the natural world by inventing such phenomena as the cloud of yellow butterflies that temporarily invades Macondo in *One Hundred Years of Solitude*, an episode whose strongest intertext may well be *The Voyage of the Beagle*.[59] Significantly, Barnes's sundry list of themes and tropes acknowledges the existence of a mass audience for works set in South America; such phrases as "package-tour baroque" and the "daiquiri bird" invoke the pleasures of tourism in the tropics, thereby equating the act of writing and the practice of reading with the production and consumption of exotic delights such as one might find in some jungle bazaar—or on cinema screens or operatic stages delightfully exhibiting or mysteriously invoking such items as the opera house virtually devoured by the jungle.[60]

Indeed, in this marketplace of cultural products, it is interesting that Barnes's closing image should be that of the opera house in the jungle, an allusion, perhaps, to the subtle textual antecedent in Darwin, but more likely to Herzog's *Fitzcarraldo*. As he surveys Rio from a mountaintop, Darwin invokes grand theaters as metaphors for the splendor of nature, but Herzog's lens, as seen in Chapter 2, focuses on the folly of wanting to dream up opera houses in Latin America's material world. "I want the opera house! I want my opera house! I want my opera!" Fitzcarraldo (played by Klaus Kinski) passionately proclaims from the top of a church tower, below which one sees a town, a river, and a jungle. His plan is to exploit the rubber tree, *Hevea brasiliensis*, to raise enough money to build a new opera house in Iquitos, Peru, where Caruso will be invited to sing; but the region's wild topography defeats him. Regardless of whether it was Catán, Fuentes-Berain, or even García Márquez who came up with the idea of an opera about a river journey eastward to the Manaus opera house, which is how Herzog's film begins, it is almost impossible to watch *Florencia en el Amazonas* and not think of *Fitzcarraldo*—even though Catán had not seen the film before composing the opera.[61] For one thing, the steamboat on which the opera's seven passengers travel may be named *El Dorado*, alluding to a much older story about the New World, but visually it really resembles the steamship *Molly Aida* in Herzog's film. Indeed, the art of copying—of reproducing what already exists elsewhere—lies at the heart of both Herzog's film and Catán's opera. *Fitzcarraldo* is not about the Manaus theater specifically; it is about erecting a similarly grandiose house elsewhere in the jungle. Likewise, Catán's plot is not about the opera house itself either but about reaching it again—recovering it, if you will—so that the opera's protagonist, Florencia Grimaldi, who is both a famous soprano and a native of that part of the world, may sing there. If the opera house in Manaus stands as a monument to the long reach of European culture, both *Fitzcarraldo* and *Florencia en el Amazonas* seek to negotiate the theater's absence—the fact that the grand opera house cannot be easily duplicated or reconstituted in the ungodly wilderness of the South American jungle. Fitzcarraldo desperately seeks to build an opera house that will mirror what exists elsewhere; Florencia and her fellow passengers must fight the river's stormy waters and, upon reaching Manaus, a cholera epidemic right out of García Márquez's *El amor en los tiempos del cólera*.

Against this cultural background, *Florencia en el Amazonas* may be seen, heard, and read as a reflection on the origins of opera and its possible translation, both physical and metaphorical, to Latin America, a continent whose literary authors and visual artists have gained a place in the Western canon but whose classical composers have yet to produce any truly lasting contribution to the international operatic repertoire. The name of Florencia invokes the place where operas were first created; her surname, Grimaldi, which at first may ring as a glossy allusion to Monaco's ruling house, also alludes obliquely, perhaps, to the aristocratic family name in Verdi's *Simon Boccanegra*. The protagonist's name, then, links opera and Europe as a semantic pair. Having triumphed all over the world through her singing, Florencia Grimaldi now travels in the Amazon hoping to be reunited with her lover, Cristóbal, the butterfly hunter, even as she sings the majestic notes of opera in the heart of the South American continent.

But this highly romantic plot—and there are two additional love stories onboard the *El Dorado*—also brings to mind the plot of other operas set in exotic locations. In the program notes for the Albany recording of *Florencia en el Amazonas*, Efraín Kristal perceptively refers to Cristóbal as Florencia's "Papageno of the Amazon," yet the butterfly hunter resounds with other meanings that may be muted in Mozart's bird catcher.[62] First and foremost, I believe, there is the story of Puccini's *Madama Butterfly* (1904), whose libretto buys into the pleasures of Orientalism even as it exposes its perils. Catán's Cristóbal never appears onstage, and there is no evidence whatsoever to argue that he resembles Puccini's Pinkerton in his attitude to women, but the fact that he is a butterfly hunter reminds one of Cio-Cio-San's mournful exclamation, in the act 1 love duet: "Dicon ch'oltre mare / Se cade in man dell'uom / Ogni farfalla d'uno spillo / È trafitta / Ed in tavola infitta!" ("They say that overseas / if it should fall into the hands of man / a butterfly is struck through / with a pin / and fixed to a board!").[63] Cio-Cio-San's ominous vision of butterfly collecting, an act in which Pinkerton metaphorically engages, alludes to the taxonomical zeal of natural historians, often part and parcel of the story of European colonial practices. In this context, yet another name in Catán's opera seems meaningful; not much is revealed about Florencia's lover, but that his first name recalls that of Christopher Columbus resounds with imperial histories and transatlantic transports of culture. Fuentes-Berain's libretto forgoes any actual explanation of what this butterfly hunter's mission is—the recording's synopsis mentions he is in search of the Emerald Muse, a mythical butterfly, but it does not explain why—so one may wonder whether Cristóbal's job is to gather *Lepidoptera* to advance the study of natural history, or simply, more prosaically, to fill glass boxes such as the one Victoria Ocampo presented to Virginia Woolf. One thing is clear: the idea of butterfly hunting leads directly to the final image in *Florencia en el Amazonas*, in which the famous diva turns into a huge butterfly majestically presiding over the stage before the curtain falls.

Ironically, perhaps, when Catán's opera first made it to the Teatro Amazonas in Manaus, it was only in a concert version. But had members of the audience wanted to see a swarm of butterflies, they could have viewed the delicate blue creatures depicted by Domenico De Angelis, an Italian, in the opera house's Salão Nobre (Noble Room). Yet the gigantic Emerald Muse was nowhere to be seen. Florencia had finally arrived, or returned, to the opera house in the jungle, but under what guise was the art form born in Florence fully present there?

The history of opera, akin to the life of butterflies, is full of metamorphoses, but arguably few of these bodily alterations are as colossal as Florencia's sprouting of huge green wings at the end of Catán's opera—a mad lepidopterist's dream or an impossible chapter in the natural history of Latin America. As the *El Dorado* reaches Manaus, it is announced that cholera has spread through the city, whereupon the captain decides not to disembark. Unaware that Florencia Grimaldi is on board and that her performance at the opera house will therefore not take place, the passengers are disappointed they will miss the recital for which they have endured a difficult journey through the jungle. But Florencia is devastated that she will not meet Cristóbal, and she sings, briefly invoking the violent ending of Rivera's *La vorágine*: "¿Dónde estás, Cristóbal? ¿Vine aquí para perderte de nuevo? ¿Te arrebató otra vez la selva voraz? ¿Por qué te siento cerca?" (72–73; "Where are you, Cristóbal? Did I come all this way just to lose you again? Has the voracious jungle taken you from me once more? Why do I feel you near?" 72–73). Indeed, what follows in Florencia's final aria are words that express the metaphorical and ultimately literal bond of song, love, and the natural world. She sings:

> Escúchame, Cristóbal
> mi voz vuela hacia ti
> como un ave y se cierne
> sobre el amor del mundo.
> De ti nació mi canto.
> De entre tus manos
> que en sueños y despiertas
> veneran mariposas. (73)

> Hear me, Cristóbal
> My voice soars toward you
> like a bird and spreads its wings
> sheltering the world's love.
> My voice was born in you
> from your hands
> which asleep or awake
> dream of wondrous butterflies. (73)

After these words, in this final vision, Florencia and Cristóbal are reunited or, as the record liner's synopsis has it, "Florencia's spirit drifts toward Cristóbal in a mystical union."[64] And then—as audiences across several cities in the United States saw—the giant butterfly appears in the flesh on stage (fig. 7).

But how should one regard the spectacular apparition of the uncanny butterfly? Is it simply yet another instance of metropolitan-required exoticism, or could one view it, perhaps, with other eyes? Florencia first appears on stage with her face covered by a silk scarf, an object whose nature and fabric belong in any cultural history of

FIGURE 7. Houston Grand Opera production of Daniel Catán's *Florencia en el Amazonas*. Photo by Lynn Lane.

Lepidoptera and in many a story of transcultural exchanges. Indeed, Florencia's first aria, whose self-reflexivity recalls Tosca's meditation about her musical work in "Vissi d'arte," relates her own singing to love and butterflies: "De la pasión brotó mi voz / Cristóbal / como aquella mariposa / que buscabas en la selva" (24; "From this passion my voice was born, / Cristóbal, / like that butterfly / you sought in the jungle" 24). But if these initial images may strike one as rather empty words to please an audience in search of outlandish pleasures, to view the butterfly's strange materiality may be a way of peering into opera's exoticist practices and metaphors in all their nakedness. The sheer size of this lofty butterfly, with its wings seemingly marked by eerie, cartilage-like lines, standing higher than the audience and masterfully surveying everything, reworks and resists the delicate associations of Puccini's archetypal vision of women in other cultures. Unlike Cio-Cio-San, Catán's Florencia is not the meek operatic heroine undone by man's cruelty; instead, avoiding the collector's pin and board, she soars above it all and, in a daring act of will, seems to be reunited forever with the butterfly hunter of her dreams. Passion gives a voice to the silk-covered Florencia, and the soaring butterfly may signify her everlasting apotheosis.

Beyond the stage, the image of the butterfly, reproduced on myriad posters advertising the opera and on the record's cover, has become the visual icon of *Florencia en el Amazonas*, signaling as well yet another belated Latin American arrival on the operatic stage. In fact, an issue of the popular *Opera News* features a review of the work's first staging in Cincinnati, by Charles H. Parsons, which calls Catán's work "a musical triumph" even as it underscores its emblematic visuality: "The opera has an interesting story, music of great lyric beauty and a gorgeous orchestration. The production was the original 1996 Houston Grand Opera staging by Francesca Zambello, ... complete with Florencia's mesmerizing transformation into a giant butterfly during her 'Brazilian Liebestod'"[65] Florencia is certainly no Isolde, but the butterfly's visual impact may signal a breakthrough. Like a modern-day Victoria Ocampo who sends friends to London bearing gifts of butterflies, Catán creates an enduring work easily recognizable as Latin American. All things considered, this musical offering from the antipodes is also about empowerment, and the opera's giant butterfly rises commandingly as an important milestone in the evolution of operatic composition and performance.

Words by Sor Juana

Soaring bodies like that of Catán's butterfly are visible in other operas staged around the world, but in music dramas connected with Latin America, none might be loftier than the character of Sor Juana Inés de la Cruz in Louis Andriessen's *Theater of the World* (2016). Jointly commissioned by the Los Angeles Philharmonic and the Dutch National Opera, Andriessen's vertiginous work disregards the certainties of political engagement or the bounties of magical realism to imagine instead the life of Athanasius Kircher, the German Jesuit polymath of the seventeenth century who had a strong Latin American connection. A hemisphere away at a convent in Mexico City, Sor Juana fervently read Kircher's works. Andriessen's title is inspired by Pedro Calderón de la Barca's play, *El gran teatro del mundo*, and his rather baroque plot pursues Kircher, along with Pope Innocent XI and a character named Boy, on fast-paced journeys through ancient civilizations, including

Egypt, Babylon—the Tower of Babel—and China, linked with the the Netherlands' United East India Company.[66] In the last scene, following Kircher's death, Voltaire, Descartes, Goethe, and Leibnitz are conjoined in the figure of Nachwelt, or Posterity. But the character who commands both plot and stage is habit-clad Sor Juana as she sings her own verses in the original Spanish as part of yet another multilingual libretto, by Helmut Krausser, in which English and German prevail, but also Italian, French and Latin, with spoken sections in Middle Dutch. The libretto engages audaciously in bilingual and trilingual forms of *Sprachmischung*, especially German, English, and Italian, but Sor Juana sings her own unmixed brand of baroque Spanish, difficult and grand.

Andriessen's music drama enacts, then, a round-trip cultural journey; as Kircher's works travel to the New World and seduce scholars there, so Sor Juana's words are now reread and redeployed to help structure a new European composition.[67] Erudite and electrifying, Kircher's books, such as *Oedipus Aegyptiacus* (1652–1654), arrived in New Spain and found their way into Sor Juana's cell and library, leaving their imprint on her writings and worldview. If one heeds Octavio Paz's eloquent description, Sor Juana's ardent reading of Kircher may be regarded as a kind of transport: "Through Kircher, an orthodox author, she glimpsed the vast territories that stretched beyond the boundaries drawn by the Church. Territories at once real and chimerical: an abstract Egypt dotted with obelisks incised with magic signs and mathematical formulas, pedantic enigmas, and scientific instruments."[68] Such concepts and objects reappear in Sor Juana's "Primero sueño," the abstruse poem whose speaker probes the idea of knowledge, confounding readers with labyrinthine images of ascension from its first lines: "Piramidal, funesta, de la tierra / nacida sombra, al Cielo encaminaba / de vanos obeliscos punta altiva, / escalar pretendiendo las estrellas" ("Pyramidal, doleful, mournful shadow / born of the earth, the haughty culmination / of vain obelisks thrust toward the Heavens, / attempting to ascend and touch the Stars").[69] In Andriessen's work, Kircher arrives in Egypt, a territory both real and chimerical, alongside Pope Innocent XI, who sings: "Vedo una piramide. Sfingi. E obelischi" ("I see a pyramid. And sphinxes. And obelisks").[70] Besides influencing her literary works, Kircher also occupies a central place in Sor Juana's iconography; as Paz mentions, his name can be read on the spines of some of the books that encircle the nun's body in her famous portrait (175).[71] If Kircher's name is legible in that image, Sor Juana's poetry becomes audible and her portrait visible in this opera devoted to the Jesuit's life.

Indeed, both Sor Juana's words and persona find new meanings in *Theater of the World*. Like a powerful archangel (Gabriel and Michael are mentioned in the libretto), the soprano playing the author appears high onstage, alone, enclosed by an actual frame, as if replicating the iconic portrait also adapted by Cervántez's serigraph and used for Adams's *El Niño*. Powerfully, on six occasions, Sor Juana sings verses from "Primero sueño." The words can be interpreted in the context of Kircher's writings, but now they inform and define Andriessen and Krausser's operatic work. In the first scene, Kircher is in the ancient Roman cemetery by St. Peter's in Rome while Sor Juana sings "from the proscenium box, far away, so to say, from Mexico": "El sueño todo, en fin lo poseía: / todo, en fin, el silencio lo ocupaba: / aún el ladrón dormía: / aún el amante no se desvelaba" ("Sleep, at last, possesses all: / silence, occupies all: / the thief sleeps, / even the restless lover"). As the plot unfolds, Sor Juana, turning into a transatlantic traveler, eventually descends to interact with Kircher onstage, becoming for him, as John Henken puts it, "a sort of platonic intercontinental lover."[72] Other reviewers shared this view of the poet's dramatic centrality. For Damjan Rakonjac, she is "the only bit of salvific sincerity" in a work hampered by irony and defamiliarization, while for Marc Swed, she becomes Kircher's "spiritual guide and conscience" and "the real vocal soul of the opera," saving the work from its excesses: "several scenes end no longer as grotesqueries in the thrall of Andriessen's unearthly settings of her ethereal lyrics."[73]

In the opera, Innocent XI asks Kircher whether there was ever a woman in his life; Kircher's words elevate Sor Juana into a distant, yet intimate soulmate: "In Mexiko gäb es jemand, die meiner würdig wäre. Sie schrieb mir. Eine Nonne, eine Dichterin von großer Kraft und Eleganz" ("Word is that there is a woman in Mexico, who would be worthy of me. She wrote to me. A nun, a poet of great virtue and elegance"). Right after this heartfelt declaration, the orchestra plays what sounds like Mexican folk music, but Andriessen's exotic playfulness quickly dissolves as Sor Juana becomes visible and sings verses alluding to the steganographic mirror, one of Kircher's inventions: "Así linterna mágica, pintadas / representa fingidas / en la blanca pared varias figuras, / de la sombra no menos ayudadas / que de la luz" ("Thus, a magic lantern / projects onto a blank wall / various false, painted figures, / produced no less by shadow / than by light"). Inert on the painting, Sor Juana stirs seductively in the opera, the sleeves of her habit not unlike a butterfly's wings. Her sung words soar, and so does the drama whose center she fully inhabits. Toward the end of her life, the historical Sor Juana, undone by the ecclesiastical hierarchy of New Spain, renounces the practice of writing; her operatic reincarnation, in contrast, grants her poetry the power to uplift new audiences.

As the opera reaches its denouement, the four European philosophers evaluate Kircher's legacy, but it is Sor Juana who sings the last words. This time it is a few lines from the last stanza of "Primero sueño," in which the speaker, after an entire night spent passionately cogitating on knowledge, describes the arrival of sunrise in her own part of the world, "[mientras nuestro hemisferio] la dorada / ilustraba del Sol madeja hermosa, / que con luz judiciosa / [. . .] repartiendo / a las cosas visibles sus colores."[74] Andriessen's score does not actually set the first three words, but they are nonetheless included, in brackets, in the libretto, retrieving a geographical location also conveyed in the English translation by John Campion: "While the golden Sun / adorns our Hemisphere / with skeins of judicious light / dispensing their colors / to visible things."[75] As the sun rises and both the poem and the opera come to an end somewhere across the Atlantic from Europe, Andriessen's transcontinental time travel helps reimagine Latin America not as exotic location or a region seeking political redemption, but simply as yet another part of the world whose writers can speak as equals to animate the work of opera.

8 The World in Buenos Aires
Cosmopolitans at the Teatro Colón

ON THE NIGHT OF MAY 25, 1908, the Teatro Colón in Buenos Aires opened its doors for the first time, and the men and women of the almighty Argentine oligarchy—many of whom were ardent believers in the art of opera—must have listened with varying degrees of rapture as singers and orchestra executed the revered notes of Verdi's *Aida*. Sitting in posh dark-red-velvet seats, not far from the opulent brilliance of the Salón Dorado and the solemn marble heads of eight European opera composers in the Salón de los Bustos, beholding the tragic story of Radamès and his Ethiopian lover unfold in front of them, the operagoers could have imagined themselves transported to ancient Egypt, but also, quite naturally, to the heart of Europe—a city like Paris or London or Vienna. They may have been geographically removed from those cultural centers, but the majesty of opera carried them aurally and visually across the Atlantic Ocean. Audience members of Italian descent, a substantial group in Argentina, might perhaps feel a bond with the old country—or imagine they had never left. From its very first seasons, a series of distinguished world-class singers and conductors traveled to Buenos Aires to perform at the Colón, and audiences in the antipodean metropolis—a geographical periphery—could see themselves resituated in a center of their own, for the capital of Argentina had little to envy other modern cities. The Teatro Colón would soon become one of the great opera houses of the twentieth century, and while its prestige may now not be untarnished, its status as an operatic icon remains as powerful as ever.[1]

My focus here is less on the Colón as a grand architectural and theatrical wonder than on its potential as a site for thinking about the real and symbolic ties that bind opera with the experience of modernity in Buenos Aires. Perhaps more fervently than its Latin American peers, the city has valued its synchronicity, real or potential, with the places in Europe (and North America) with which it often compares itself. Indeed, as Alan Gilbert would have it, growing prosperity in the early twentieth century meant that "Buenos Aires began to transform itself into the first European city in Latin America"—by which Gilbert, writing from a transatlantic viewpoint, means a modern city whose development encompassed technology and culture: "Electricity and water systems were improved and major port works began. City beautification included the building of wide avenues, most notably the *Avenida de Mayo*, intended to rival the *Champs Elysées*. An electric tramway was opened in 1897 and, in 1913, the region's first underground railway—the *subte*. The city's elite aspired to turn Buenos Aires into one of the world's main cultural centres and after its opening in 1908 the Colón theatre became a regular stop for top opera singers."[2]

Yet despite this kind of growth, urban and cultural modernization was incomplete. As Beatriz Sarlo argues in *Una modernidad periférica* (1988), the city's modernity in the 1920s and 1930s, was "mixed"; the culture of intellectuals—writers and artists—was a blend of opposites in which European practices were tempered by local conditions, while the avant-garde coexisted with regionalism, and traditionalism with a spirit of renewal. Sarlo calls Buenos Aires "el gran escenario latinoamericano de una *cultura de mezclas*" (the great Latin American stage for a culture of mixings), a phrase that not only invokes the notion of hybridity, central for thinking about culture in the region, but also generates a vision of the city in which a qualified modernity is a kind of performance.[3] Writing about music and the intellectuals linked to *Sur*, the journal edited by Victoria Ocampo from 1930 through much of the twentieth century, Pablo Gianera speaks of an unfinished modernity, a picture that also implies a complicated history of transports; as European music arrives on the River Plate, it receives a mixed welcome.[4] At face value, the Teatro Colón, like much else in Buenos Aires, may validate the widespread view of the city simply as an extension of Europe. A closer look, though, reveals a different kind of modernity, less imitative and very much its own distinct chapter in cultural history, including the art of opera.

To investigate what opera itself, along with its literary imaginings, may have to say about these notions of modernity, periphery and inconclusiveness, I focus on two works that circle around the venerable spaces and lofty status of the Teatro Colón: *El gran teatro*, a novel by Manuel Mujica Lainez; and *V.O.*, a chamber opera about Victoria Ocampo written by Sarlo and set to music by Martín Bauer. Staged at the Centro de Experimentación del Teatro Colón, Sarlo's libretto reenacts Ocampo's passionate liaisons with culture, especially Stravinsky's music, as well as a critical amatory episode in her life. *V.O.* itself also suggests a vision of music drama that resist the burdensome grandiosity of operatic culture, sometimes linked with social class and snobbery, which is in turn one of the main subjects in Mujica Lainez's fictional depiction of the house. Indeed, *El gran teatro* relies on the venerable history of the Colón for its own ironic tale of social mores, which exposes the cracks in the city's modern self-formulations and in the opera house's own practices, akin at times to immutable objects in a museum. Notably, the novel unfolds during a performance of *Parsifal* at the Colón, and so does a remarkable section of Ocampo's *La rama de Salzburgo*, an autobiographical text that I also take into account in my analysis of *V.O.* As we will see, Wagner's dark story of sexual desire functions as a key for elucidating the visions of modernity in Buenos Aires obliquely crafted in the texts.

Through their passionate and erudite engagement with the practices and symbols of the European operatic canon, Mujica Lainez, Ocampo, and even Sarlo emerge as boldly cosmopolitan actors. As in the various "episodes" that Gonzalo Aguilar dissects in his analysis of esthetic cosmopolitanism in Argentina, these writers' opera tales should not be dismissed as elitist or uprooted but should be read closely for what they reveal about the rich place of the art form in the national ethos.⁵ A chamber of echoes, opera, so natural yet so foreign there, resounds uncannily with Argentina's filial bonds with Europe and its sovereign status as a land of its own.

Desiring Wagner: A Novel by Manuel Mujica Lainez

The opera house that Manuel Mujica Lainez dubs "the grand theater" in the novel surely deserved the appellation. With its perfect acoustics, superior theatrical standards, and loyal audiences well versed in the art of opera, the Teatro Colón became one of the world's most prominent houses soon after its opening night. In 1949, still early in her career, Maria Callas made her debut at the Colón singing the role of Turandot, followed by Norma and Aida. The engagement was considered a milestone for the singer because, as Michael Scott points out, the Colón was regarded then as part of an exclusive sextet of operatic venues—along with New York's Metropolitan Opera House, Milan's Teatro alla Scala, London's Royal Opera House, the Vienna Staatsoper, and the Paris Opéra—that routinely presented the most brilliant programs.⁶ If austral Buenos Aires was very distant from the other five cities, all located in the Northern Hemisphere, the reversed seasons allowed theater regularly to welcome many of the world's most highly regarded singers and conductors. Indeed, a roster of those artists who worked at the Colón through much of the twentieth century easily reads as a Who's Who of stellar performers. Titta Ruffo, the Italian baritone, sang ten roles in the inaugural season, and Boris Chaliapin, the Russian bass, did three that same year, while such legendary names as Amelita Galli-Curci, Nellie Melba, Luisa Tetrazzini, Tito Schipa, Enrico Caruso, and Beniamino Gigli had all performed at the Colón by 1919. Thereafter the list also includes, besides Callas, most of the operatic stars of the following decades: Kirsten Flagstad, Birgit Nilsson, Renata Tebaldi, Elisabeth Schwarzkopf, Régine Crespin, Beverly Sills, Montserrat Caballé, Plácido Domingo, Luciano Pavarotti. A few important opera composers, too, conducted their works at the Colón, including Camille Saint-Saëns in 1916, Pietro Mascagni in 1922, and Richard Strauss in 1920 and 1923.[7] Symphonic and ballet programs were often equally brilliant, and Arturo Toscanini, who conducted fifteen of the seventeen operas performed at the Colón in the 1912 season (as well as concerts through the early 1940s), is famously said to have proclaimed, "This is the first and best organized theater in the world."[8] The opera house where *El gran teatro* unfolds is indeed as solid and magnificent as its real-life model, but the carefully crafted plot reveals also the social fissures in the grand edifice.

If the complicated history of the Colón is not directly alluded to in Mujica Lainez's novel, it is nonetheless a rich background against which the fictional goings-on make better sense. In later decades, certainly by the 1970s when the novel was published, political problems and labor disputes had forced the cancellation of performances and even one entire season, but the opera house continued to function, as it still does, as a splendid space for the importation and display of operatic trophies from Europe. Opera contributed visibly to Buenos Aires's position as a cosmopolitan outpost of European cultural forms—or as the subtitle of a French-language book about the city would have it, a *port de l'Extrême Europe*.[9] The ever-current management crafted seasons in which new works by important composers were often performed shortly after their European premieres. At least in the realm of opera, if not in other aspects of life, the Argentine public enjoyed what could hardly be considered isolation. By means of opera, the cosmopolitan citizens of Buenos Aires could access Europe's treasure trove of stories—classical myths, historical episodes, tales of distant lands, modern chronicles—and the city itself partook of the cultural authority vested in the Old World, becoming, as the cliché goes, the most European city in the Americas.

Yet aspects of the history of the Colón, from its first night onward, also point to the unsteady position of Latin America in operatic culture and, similarly, that of opera in the region's cultural history. When the old Colón shut down in 1888, the plan was to build its replacement in time for a glorious inauguration on

October 12, 1892, the fourth centennial of Columbus's first landfall in the Americas. As it turned out, construction was delayed for several years. When the new theater finally opened, the occasion was recast to commemorate the ninety-eighth anniversary of Argentina's declaration of independence. The 1810 Revolución de Mayo was invoked and the national anthem played before the orchestra undertook *Aida* on that first night, but the ghost of Europe, signaling both pleasures and perils, haunted the hallowed precincts. The name of the Colón memorialized the so-called discoverer, while its edifice, a pile of various French and Italian styles, summoned the phantoms of grand European opera even as Argentina partly receded into the background.[10] In that first season, seventeen different operas were performed, but only one, Héctor Panizza's *Aurora*, was the work of an Argentine composer. In fact, *Aurora* had been chosen as the opera to be performed on the inaugural night, but its score was not be finished in time, delaying its premiere until September 5, a few months into the season. Even then, Europe was a strong presence in the opera. The subject of *Aurora* was a tragic love story set in Córdoba at the time of Argentina's independence, but it was sung in Italian. A local author, Héctor Quesada, furnished a national angle to the plot, but the words were written by Luigi Illica, who, along with Giuseppe Giacosa, had collaborated with Puccini on the librettos of *La bohème*, *Tosca*, and *Madama Butterfly*. Illica's involvement signaled the prominence of the Argentine operatic stage and its deep cultural ties with Italy; Panizza himself was the son of an Italian musician who spent many years as a conductor in Milan, besides London and New York. But the fact that *Aurora* was not sung in Spanish until 1945 may be an index of opera's dissonance when confronted with discourses about the nation and the region that underscore nativist strains. Since then, the Colón has staged more operas by local composers than any other theater in the Americas,[11] but this fact may not fully dispel the notion of opera as broadly a foreign practice.

The inaugural performance of *Aida* also recalls the history of European imperial relations with other parts of the world. As mentioned earlier, Said argues that Verdi's opera, commissioned by

Egypt's Khedive Ismail for the first night of a new opera house in Cairo facing the European-inspired side of the city, serves to "confirm the Orient as an essentially exotic, distant, and antique place in which Europeans can mount certain shows of force."[12] From the viewpoint of demography and urbanism, Buenos Aires in 1908 was far closer to Europe than Cairo could have been, and the staging of *Aida* at the Colón might be interpreted as the brandishing of trophies by Europeans, or their descendants, on a land that they had also once conquered and over which their cultural forms still ruled. *Aida*, of course, is about Egypt, not Argentina, but its Orientalism recalls other discourses that have posited Latin America as distinct from, and inferior to, Europe. It is a complicated story. Surveying the Colón's architecture, Alberto Bellucci links the grand Egyptian sets of *Aida* on that first night to the theater's own grandeur: "The monumental pharaonic sets displayed onstage that night for a triumphal Verdian *Aida* . . . were an adequate reflection of this building, equally colossal, now making its début as a venue for the operatic and social calendar of Buenos Aires."[13] The city could show off its strong ties with European countries by staging its own powerful vision of ancient Egypt—a mimicked Orientalism but one in which material grandness could still bespeak modernity and cultural self-assurance. Yet there emerges a more complex game of mutual reflections than the literal monument Bellucci observes. The Colón mirrored Europe, but the last-minute choice of Verdi's masterpiece for its opening night also exposes a certain resemblance between Buenos Aires and Cairo. Foreshadowing the belatedness of *Aurora* at the Colón, the opera commissioned for Cairo was not ready in time for opening night, so another work by Verdi, *Rigoletto*, was performed instead. Almost four decades later, Verdi's Egyptian opera traversed the Atlantic Ocean and became the inaugural work elsewhere—in yet another theatrical game of replications and replacements in far-flung locations of what we now call the Global South.

Beyond that first accidental *Aida*, the history of opera in Argentina has been markedly different from that of Egypt. The Khedivial Opera House burned to the ground in 1971, while the Teatro Colón, despite its difficulties, reached its centennial in 2008. Nonetheless, a sense of melancholy and disappointment marked the celebrations, as the renovation master plan fell substantially behind schedule and the theater itself remained closed for its own festivities. Ironically, the idea of restaging *Aida* yet again on May 20, 2008, was no more successful than the expected premiere of *Aurora* had been a century before. And yet the Colón's palatial architecture and decoration, which the theater's website proudly showcases, continue to tell a story of literal and figurative transports. An icon of Buenos Aires, the theater is visited by national and foreign tourists on well-attended tours. There is all that marble from Italy and Portugal brought to downtown Buenos Aires to erect the Colón. There are the glass windows in the Salón Dorado—reminiscent of Versailles and Schönbrunn, according to the website—that silently illustrate the myth of Apollo and the legend of Sapho. And there are also, in the Salón de los Bustos, the sculpted effigies of eight European composers—Beethoven, Bellini, Bizet, Gounod, Mozart, Rossini, Verdi, and Wagner—whose consecrated works continue to charm operagoers who may live in another continent yet feel very much at home in those distant worlds.

Of the eight composers honored in the Salón de los Bustos, Wagner stands most potently at the center of Mujica Lainez's work. Likewise, the staging of the composer's long, challenging works denote the Colón's stature as a world-class opera house and, more recently, for its declining fortunes. A brief account of performances of the four operas that make up *Der Ring des Nibelungen* sheds light on this tale of magnificence and subsequent contraction. The Colón staged *Siegfried* in 1908, its inaugural season, followed by *Das Rheingold* and *Die Walküre* in 1910, and *Götterdämmerung*, conducted by Toscanini, in 1912. By 1922, it imported its first complete *Ring,* featuring the Vienna Philharmonic Orchestra led by Felix Weingartner. Another cycle followed in 1931, under Otto Klemperer; then again in 1935, under the same conductor; in 1947, under Erich Kleiber; and yet again in 1962 and 1967. Like few other theaters in the Americas, the Colón's productions of the *Ring* counted with some of the great Wagnerian singers of the twentieth century: Lauritz Melchior sang

Siegmund and Siegfried in 1931; Kirsten Flagstad was Brünnhilde in a stand-alone *Götterdammerung* with Kleiber in 1948; Hans Hotter was Gunther in that same production, and Wotan in *Die Walküre* in 1960 and in the 1962 cycle; and Birgit Nilsson sang Brünnhilde in both the 1962 and 1967 cycles. Writing about the completion of yet another *Ring* cycle in 1998, begun in 1995, Enzo Valenti Ferro composes a self-congratulatory note, arguing for the Colón the kind of Wagnerian exploits that just a handful of theaters in Germany, including Bayreuth, could achieve.[14] One may dismiss Ferro's boast as yet another sign of Argentina's perceived self-importance—its delusions of grandeur, to quote the title of a collected volume of essays on the nation.[15] His pride, seen in the context of the country's various economic crises and the Colón's own protracted troubles, may also be taken as an oblique acknowledgment of Buenos Aires's operatic dimming at the turn of the millennium.

To celebrate Wagner's bicentennial in 2013, the Colón decided to present a shortened version of the tetralogy. The Colón *Ring*, as it came to be called, was viewed by some as a sign that Latin America's grandest opera house had fully entered an era of diminished expectations. Katharina Wagner, the composer's granddaughter, praised the renovated Colón for its glamour and technological innovations, and Deutsche-Welle, which became the Colón's "exclusive media partner," reported brightly on the abridged work, calling the seven-hour version a "one-of-a-kind project" that allowed the staging of Wagner's "powerful music drama" in just one day.[16] But Pablo Bardin, reviewing the production for the *Buenos Aires Herald*, lamented its staging in the grand opera house: "What a pity that it was dubbed 'Colón-Ring,' for now our theater has its institutional stamp attached to a sorry fiasco."[17] If the Colón remains the preeminent symbol of opera in Latin America, it may be due less to its latest seasons than to the legend of its first few decades.

What can fiction, then, say about the almost mythical standing of the Teatro Colón? Unfolding during a staging of Wagner's *Parsifal*, Mujica Lainez's *El gran teatro* (1979) fusions Buenos Aires, opera and the Colón itself into an image of culture in which the burden of tradition, as Sarlo suggests, qualifies, if not overwhelms, the axioms and habits of modernity. The Colón was, after all, the opera house that as late as the mid-1960s had banned an opera, Alberto Ginastera's *Bomarzo*, for its treatment of sexuality. Mujica Lainez, who wrote the novel on which the opera is based as well as the libretto, deplored the act of censorship, as he told Barnard L. Collier, of the *New York Times*: "I am at the center of an absurd storm . . . I have gone from a state of astonishment to ironical amusement to fury and combativeness and now to melancholy and sadness."[18] Ginastera's musical idiom was altogether avant-garde, but the opera's dazzling modernity was defeated by the ultraconservative mores of patriarchal Argentina. Significantly, *El gran teatro* is dedicated to Ginastera himself and to Jeannette Arata de Erize, who presided the prestigious Mozarteum Argentino and attended the premiere of *Bomarzo* in Washington, as well as to Oscar Araiz, who choreographed the various dances, including its *ballet erótico*, performed when the opera was finally produced in Buenos Aires in 1972. Written just a few years after these events, *El gran teatro* opens under repression's shadow. Its exploration of Argentine customs and manners, including the real or affected ravishments of opera, tacitly invokes and recasts Sarlo's argument about Buenos Aires's peripheral modernity.

At face value, it is possible to read the novel as the narrative counterpart of an essay by Jorge Aráoz Badí, who celebrates the rituals of opera and operagoing in the glossy bilingual commemorative book about the Colón published in 2000, quoted earlier: "As the operatic capital of Latin America, Buenos Aires reached the end of the nineteenth century with seven halls devoted to the widest possible spectrum of shows. When the new Colón Theatre opened in 1908, besides confirming that leadership, it was understood to be recognition of the refined taste developed by Argentine audiences."[19] Indeed, a substantial portion of Mujica Lainez's tale delights in describing the theater's architectural splendor and enumerating its operatic glories as tokens of civilization in Buenos Aires. In the novel's opening scene, Salvador, a fifteen-year-old boy from a rural part of the country visiting his patrician family in the city arrives at the Colón on a rainy evening and is struck by the sheer luxury of the place: marble and gold, columns, and balustrades . . . Playing on the word's etymological connection with silver, the narrator describes the breathtaking interior as "aquel mundo de argentina magnificencia" (that world of argentine magnificence).[20] The theater's luxury is a reminder of the country's seemingly unlimited wealth at the time of its construction. The physical transport of marble from Italy and Portugal precedes the lyrical raptures of European opera. But if the narrator's minute description resounds with a measure of haughtiness, it is also part and parcel of Mujica Lainez's satirical tale in which members of the city's elite and a few other Argentines play out their own sense of self-importance. Notably, one of the sculptures mentioned in the novel's opening scene is that of Gounod's Marguerite, an unspoken invocation of Estanislao del Campo's *Fausto criollo*, the narrative poem in which, as seen in Chapter 1, a gaucho named Anastasio accidentally attends a performance of Gounod's *Faust*. Feeling shy and inapt, Salvador pretends to study the statue even as he seeks to hide it behind it—as much of an outsider as his literary precursor, the gaucho protagonist of del Campo's tale. As it happens, most characters, including those who act as the Colón's owners, will turn out to be far more indecorous than either Anastasio or Salvador, opera's outsiders.

Proudly displaying his intimate knowledge of operatic tradition, the narrator also focuses on the Colón's high musical standards by listing the specific kind and number of instruments needed for playing the score of *Parsifal* (27). The almost pedantic inventory of architectural features and musical instruments bespeaks a vision of Argentina as not only a repository of European forms but also a country wealthy enough to possess the tools required to faithfully reproduce the legacy of Europe on its side of the Atlantic. Even on the stage, as the opera unfolds, the narrator focuses on the Colón's sense of tradition. Two young singers, playing the young squires whose voices are heard sporadically as Gurnemanz intones his long account of the story's background, emerge briefly as the novel's focalizers, trembling with fear and joy because their voices are about to resound in "el primer teatro de la América del Sur, quizás el más bello del mundo" (59; South America's principal theater, perhaps the most beautiful in the world). A sense of awe envelops virtually every inch of Mujica Lainez's Colón—from the vestibule to the orchestra pit and the stage itself. But this vision becomes far more complicated as the narrator's glance detours from architecture and operatic culture to focus on the multiple characters playing their own melodramas in the theater that evening.

Published in the late 1970s, *El gran teatro* takes place during World War II, a historical period whose fictional uses are at least twofold. The war serves as the background for one of the various subplots in the novel: the latent rivalry between a distinguished British couple (a naturalist and an actress) sitting at the mayor's box on one side of the proscenium, and an equally eminent German prince, representing the Third Reich on a land-purchasing mission, who takes in the opera from the presidential box, on the other side of the stage. More importantly, the temporal framework suggests a melancholy reading of the Teatro Colón; after all, the work of the opera house was far more brilliant then than three decades later.[21] As readers grasp that *El gran teatro* may in fact be read as a historical novel of the not so distant past, yet another rearrangement subtly takes place. The wartime Colón was one of the liveliest opera houses in the world, but at the time of the novel's publication during what came to be known as the Dirty War, the house was at risk of falling off the global map of opera. The novel's last line alludes somewhat wistfully to future performances of *Parsifal* (298). The narrator correctly states that the opera was staged again at the Colón in various seasons after World War II, but the question of the theater's unbroken greatness, if not its grandeur (the adjective *gran* implies both concepts) remains open.[22] Borges's "A Manuel Mujica Lainez," a poem written in 1974 and collected in *La moneda de hierro* (1976), speaks to the passing of old glories by casting Argentina as a vanishing fatherland. The speaker alludes nostalgically to a bygone era of knives and bravery, which resounds with Borges's themes, and then laments the end of Mujica Lainez's own "versión de la patria, con sus fastos y brillos" ("version of the fatherland, its splendid flourish").[23] The sonnet, like the novel, addresses the issue of cultural impermanence. Does the Colón remain truly great in a city and country that are now significantly altered, or does it lose its lavishness and brilliance?

It is not difficult to sense in the omniscient narrator a persona not unlike that of the novel's all-knowing author—an insider possessing boundless authority over the story of the Colón and its patrons. Like the voice that guides the readers into the lives and times of multiple characters against the spatial and temporal axes of the opulent edifice, Mujica Lainez was well positioned to write about the opera house with what might be described as a proprietor's insight. He was indeed, as Claudio Benzecry would have it, "the paradigmatic writer of the Colón."[24] Besides writing the libretto for Ginastera's *Bomarzo*, he also contributed the main text of *Vida y gloria del Teatro Colón* (1983), a book featuring photographs by Aldo Sessi. He even left an imprint on the theater's décor; after learning that Marc Chagall had painted a new ceiling for Paris's Palais Garnier, he suggested that Antonio Soldi do the same for the Colón's dome. Yet despite these long-standing affective and professional bonds with the theater, the novel is an incisive satire aimed at the well-heeled members of the audience, who are there mostly for reasons that have little or nothing to do with the art of opera, especially such a demanding work as Wagner's very long last opera.

The novel's plot unfolds mostly around the elegant boxes and orchestra section where most of the characters are seated—locations from which they can espy each other with far more interest than the spectacle of *Parsifal* can muster in most of them. The words of Vittorio Meano, the architect who took over the design of the Colón after Francesco Tamburini's death in 1890, resound with those private spectacles variously related to family ties, financial concerns, and flirtatious gestures on which the novel, as if mirroring life, focuses. For Meano, the Italian-style horseshoe would help members of the audience to see one another and be seen, especially "la gentil corona de bellas señoras, primer adorno y atractivo de toda sala teatral" (the gentle garland of beautiful ladies, prime ornament and attraction of any theater).[25] One of the novel's epigraphs, taken from Heinrich Heine's *Florentische Nächte,* echoes Meano's words: "Va usted ahora a menudo a la Ópera, y creo, Max, que va usted más a ver que oír" (9; You often go to the Opera, and I think, Max, you go in order to see rather than hear). As if taking his cue from both the Italian architect and the German author, the narrator—a voyeur of sorts—views his characters viewing other characters, but his act of vision goes even further. As if mimicking their superficial attitudes, the narrator lingers on facades, portraying clothes with as much precision as he does the theater's architecture, but rather brutally, he also exposes the inner turmoil of the splendidly dressed, coiffed and bejeweled operagoers.

The focus on fashion acts often as a window into a character's mind. The novel's first lines, for instance, capture Salvador's insecurity as he arrives at the opulent Colón knowing all too well that his overcoat is inelegant. Hiding behind the columns, the young man takes off his light gray garment even though he is feeling very cold (13). If he self-consciously hides his ostensible sartorial deficiency, Amelia Zúñiga de Castro, his great-grandmother's cousin, by contrast, displays her dazzling vestments as she imperiously enters the hall with a retinue of family and friends; the performance has already begun, and two people are needed to help her take off a velvet cape decorated with ermine (52–53). As for María Zúñiga de Gonzálvez, Salvador's grandmother, she too shows up impeccably dressed, adorned by her most precious possession, an important motif in the plot: an old necklace incrusted diamonds and emeralds that belonged to the cousins' ancestor, a vicereine of Mexico. The narrator describes the two octogenarians by resorting to regal or episcopal analogies. Not only does Amelia wear ermine, like a queen would, her male companions are quaintly and ironically described as "pajes caudatarios" (53; train-bearing pages), like the clerics holding a bishop's long robes. As for María, we learn that people simply used to say that she "parece un reina" (24; looks like a queen). In fact, both Amelia and María are referred to as queens of Buenos Aires society (60), even if María's financial position is weaker than ever before. Not surprisingly, Amelia deploys her opera glasses to look at María, who in turn directs hers on Amelia. The reader can regard the cousins, as impressive as the onstage drama, as they perform their own intertwined spectacles in the darkened auditorium. Much of the novel's plot centers, quite operatically, on their ancient rivalry—the question of who would inherit the vicereine's necklace and the love affair between Amelia's husband and María, the source of a long-standing quarrel. As readers take in the twists and turns of both women's erotic and material affairs, it is not difficult to view their rich dresses as costumes akin to those worn onstage, or their life stories as antiquated melodramas such as one would find in an old opera plot.[26]

The narrator's diction is old-fashioned and opulent, not unlike the objects he painstakingly describes or the inflated verbiage of an operatic libretto. As one considers this style, along with the characters and events of *El gran teatro*, it is possible to conclude that the voice telling the story belongs to an entity fully at home not only at the Colón, but also in Amelia and María's narrow world. After all, at least at face value, the narrator appears to partake of the social prejudices some characters flaunt. When Salvador meets his great-grandmother in the family box, he colloquially says to her, "¡Cuánta gente ha venido al Colón!" (So many people have come to the Colón); she reprimands him, "No *al* Colón, sino *a* Colón" (33, emphasis in original; Not *to the* Colón, but *to* Colón). Describing her as "irónica" (33; ironic), the satire-prone narrator appears to agree with her and views Salvador's innocent remark as a terrible, if endearing, faux pas. Amelia later adds, "*Nosotros* decimos a Colón" (33, emphasis in original; *We* say to Colón). A quick study, Salvador reflects on the probable existence of a social circle to which his family and a few others belong: "*Nosotros* —pensaba—, *nosotros* significará los Gonzálvez y los Zúñiga. Y habrá otros más. Los que no decimos *al* Colón (que es como se debe decir) sino *a Colón* (que es como *nosotros* debemos decir). ¿Por qué? ¿Quiénes somos *nosotros*? ¿Debemos decirlo así para distinguirnos? ¿Es una clave? ¿Hablamos nosotros en clave?" (33–34, emphasis in original; "*We*," he thinks, "*we* must mean the Gonzálvez and the Zúñigas. And there must be others. Those of us who do not say *to the* Colón, which is how one should say, but *to* Colón, which is how *we* should say. Why? Who are *we*? Should we say it like that in order to distinguish ourselves? Is it a code? Do we speak in code?"). Besides omniscience, the narrator flaunts his mastery of an elite's coded sociolect.

Mimicking those exclusionary prejudices, the narrator's most patent disdain is aimed at a character known only as El Sapo (the Toad), a literature professor from an unnamed provincial city. The professor wants to make the most of his soirée at the Colón by meeting as many members of the Buenos Aires elite as possible and collecting as many anecdotes as he can as trophies to display for his acquaintances back home. Like Salvador, whom he attempts to befriend, he exclaims, "¡Cuánta gente ha venido al Colón!" (32; So many people have come to the Colón!). But unlike the young man, El Sapo remains very much a pathetic caricature (28). His main objective through the evening is to secure an invitation to a ball—the social event of the season—that Amelia will be hosting for her granddaughter, Bebé. Surreptitiously, El Sapo manages to meet Bebé, who is also at the Colón, and she kindly invites him to the ball to the dismay of others, who suspect him to be an interloper. The event, as the reader learns in the novel's epilogue, is ultimately canceled because of Amelia's sudden death shortly after the performance of *Parsifal*. If El Sapo cannot have his fabulous ball, neither can other audience members for whom the opera had been mostly the obligatory prelude to a magnificent gathering. Indeed, the prospect of Bebé's ball, repeatedly foreseen from the shifting perspective of various characters, functions as a leitmotif of sorts for the novel's ironic dissection of social status and aspirations.

Beyond El Sapo, the narrator's deployment of metaphors inspired by the natural world also touches the conductor, who is called El Hongo (the Mushroom) because of the shape of his head, as well as the entire audience, described as birds of variously colored feathers exhibited in a golden cage. The narrator, prone to enumerations, lists the avian species they resemble: cardinals, hummingbirds, pheasants, toucans, macaws, falcons, ravens, and starlings (28). A group of characters whom the narrator explicitly derides are the Capris, a rich landowning family of Italian descent whose social climbing leads them also to the Colón. Unfamiliar with the consecrated practice of not applauding at the end of the first act of *Parsifal*, which Wagner described as a *Bühnenweihfestspiel* (festival play for the consecration of the stage) and not a traditional operatic spectacle, the Capris begin to clap as more experienced members of the audience disapprove (88). In yet another sign of class difference, Ambrosio, the Capris' paterfamilias, dislikes Wagner and blatantly expresses his enthusiasm for a more popular, if less exalted, repertoire, such as Leoncavallo's *Pagliacci* and Mascagni's *Cavalleria rusticana* (89). He then proceeds to reminisce about a performance of *Pagliacci* with Enrico Caruso in the role of Canio that he had attended over thirty years earlier, before becoming wealthy. The narrator links Ambrosio's enthusiasm to his nonpatrician Italian immigrant origins (89). In his case, a passion for opera does not denote cultural refinement but ethnic heritage.[27] As it turns out, various members of the Buenos Aires elite also find Wagner's music dreadful and would rather attend an Italian opera. Such is the case of María Zúñiga, who after the long performance of *Parsifal*, admits her preference for Puccini, a contemporary of Ambrosio Capri's beloved Leoncavallo (234). María's cautious remark counters the established view of Wagner's highbrow creations as the ultimate expression of the art of opera, including the Colón's self-congratulatory discourse on its Wagnerian trophies.

How, then, should one read the aesthetic affinity between a Zúñiga and a Capri, especially if considering the exalted role of *Parsifal* through much of the text? The narrator zealously recounts the plot of the opera, explaining its musical structures and place in Wagner's oeuvre. The text itself is constructed along the lines of the opera's performance: an *entrada* (entrance) and *salida* (exit) frame three *actos* (acts), which in turn are divided by two *entreactos* (intermissions). As the overture begins, the narrator seeks to articulate the possible raptures the music may elicit in the spectators. Yet on this night at the opera, members of the Colón audience remain indifferent (51–52). Indeed, Wagner's music, in this fictional journey to the most illustrious opera house in the antipodes, fails to transport all listeners. As the plot unfolds, the various reasons many characters are attending *Parsifal* that evening are revealed to be essentially unrelated to the art of opera. The Gonzálvez clan, headed by María, is on the verge of economic collapse; they are at the Colón so that Alejandro, María's handsome grandson, can court Tina Capri, Ambrosio's daughter. As it turns out, the Capris, who hold a large fortune, have acquired most of El Fortín, the Gonzálvezes' estancia; if Alejandro marries Tina, his family's financial position will vastly improve. Unbeknownst to his grandmother, Alejandro is homosexual—as Salvador discovers when his older cousin secretly grabs his hand in the darkened box. María, too, has her own secret. The shining diamonds and emeralds in the vicereine's necklace are fake; the real jewels have been sold to pay for her numerous debts incurred by her womanizing son, Javier, Alejandro's father.

What, then, is the value of Wagner's opera in Mujica Lainez's tale? Members of the Gonzálvez family care little for the performance because of they are immersed in a melodrama of their own. Not without irony, the fictional plot in which they play such sorrowful parts recalls the traditional Italian operas favored by Ambrosio Capri and María Zúñiga herself. The story of two rival queens resound with Donizetti's *Maria Stuarda* or, more broadly, with tales of competing women in Bellini's *Norma* or Verdi's *Don Carlos*. Upon closer analysis, the secretive drama at the Colón reveals itself to be, in fact, also rather Wagnerian. Discreetly, various aspects in the plot of *El gran teatro* resound with narrative situations in Wagner's works. Like *Parsifal* itself, the novel contains a story of desire and sin, especially as it pertains to Alejandro; like *Tristan und Isolde*, it is also a tale of adultery and betrayal, that of María and Amelia's husband; further, the chronicle of the impecunious Gonzálvez clan desperately seeking to save what remains of El Fortín recalls the tale of Valhalla in *Der Ring des Nibelungen*. If there are no flames at the end of *El gran teatro*, as in *Götterdämmerung*, one may still read the novel's denouement as the twilight of a class whose rule over Argentine society is indeed about to eclipse. The powerful elite that once saw Wagner's operas staged with such brilliance in Buenos Aires may need to travel back in time to revisit the history of the Colón, like Mujica Lainez does in the novel, to retrieve and experience what those lofty transports were like.

The text's sense of opera as a cultural practice past its prime appears to echo, as seen earlier, some of Adorno's arguments about the art form. In "Bourgeois Opera," he posits that Alban Berg's unfinished instrumentation of *Lulu* "says something about the genre."[28] That a great modern composer cannot complete his own score does not bode well for the art form: "Opera has been in a precarious situation since the moment when the high bourgeois society which supported it in its fully developed form has ceased to exist."[29] For Adorno, the art form can no longer please the newcomer, who did not learn from childhood "to be bowled over by opera and to respect its outrageous impositions"; nor the "intellectually advanced public," who is "almost no longer capable of responding immediately or spontaneously to a limited store of works, which have long since sunk into the living-room treasure-chests of the petite bourgeoisie, like Raphael's paintings, abused through innumerable reproductions."[30] Powerfully, Adorno likens opera to yet another retrospective institution: "In fact, opera corresponds to a great extent to the museum, even in the sense of the latter's positive function, which is to help something threatened by muteness to survive. Taken together, what happens on the operatic stage is usually like a museum of bygone images and gestures, to which a retrospective need clings."[31] If Adorno's words may be belied by the expansion of the art form in decades after his essay was written (or the vitality of many museums), some of his views may yet serve as keys for interpreting the value of opera in Mujica Lainez's text.

Indeed, the notion that opera and the museum may be fundamentally related becomes easy to argue if one focuses, again, on the narrator's storytelling. As we saw, his diction and prejudices imply a mindset at home in Amelia and María's traditional world of luxury and privilege. It is also a voice that appears to be in love with, even in awe of, the archives of European culture, whose contents it summons up by engaging in feverish enumerations of proper names and common nouns whose provenance is explicitly the other side of the Atlantic. Indeed, the opening scene follows young Salvador as he timidly views the old musical instruments housed in the Colón's lobby, all lovingly listed just as the instruments needed for the *Parsifal* orchestra will later be (16).³² Consider as well the description of Flaminia, a character referred to throughout the novel as "la Dama de la Linterna" (the Lady of the Flashlight) because she carries such a tool to read the libretto during the performance. Her odd appellation triggers a parenthetical free association of related personages by the narrator: the Lady of the Unicorn, Rossini's Donna del Lago, and the Belle Dame Sans Merci (187–88). That a parenthesis can contain such an inventory of famous literary, visual, and operatic figurations of "Dama," plus references to various art forms, defines a narrative modality intent on displaying its mastery of an imported culture. In the same vein, two women sitting at the Colón are said to resemble a series of mythological entities: Eros, the Sphinx, Nike, Melusine, and others (119). As if indulging explicitly in Adorno's association of opera and the museum, the text is also punctuated by the names of European galleries: the Victoria and Albert Museum and the British Museum (84), the Musée Grévin (113), the Musée de Cluny (126), and others. Each of these names stands not only for a specific museum itself but also for all the things that it may house within its walls—a relentless proliferation of European cultural accomplishments.

Perhaps the most vital of the narrator's enumerations occurs in the "Primer entreacto," as he describes what two young people, Luis Moro and Clara Musto, discover as they walk around the theater. As it happens, they are among the few characters in the novel truly enraptured by *Parsifal*. Sitting in a less costly upper section, they have just met and seem to like each other. Luis, who writes poetry, had decided to attend the performance because he knew that Alejandro, his former lover, would be there. Unexpectedly, Wagner's opera takes possession of him, and the narrator describes what amounts to physical rapture; breathlessly, Luis closes his eyes, grows pale, thinks he is running out of air, and his pulse is altered (77). During the intermission, as they walk around the theater, Luis and Clara happen on the inscribed list of opera titles favored at the time of the theater's opening in 1908. After they find "Parsifali," the Italian version of Wagner's title, they read other names, an archaic-sounding, overwhelmingly European list that the narrator, in yet another enumerative impulse, fervently records: "Ione, Orfeo, Falstaff, Ebrea, Fidelio,

Freischutz, Carmen, Sonambula, Aida, Guarani, Lucia, Tannhauser, Otello, Salome, Thais, Barbieri ... Manon, Bohème, Ugonotti, Traviata, Valli, Walkiria, Safo, Rienzi, Favorita, Mignon, Rigoletto, Marta, Werter, Mose, Lohengrin, Hamlet, Mefistofele, Dinhora, Hamlet, Profeta, Fausto" (135). As they slowly come into sight, the names invoke the ghostly status of opera—a genre from the past or from theatrical seasons long vanished—whose death is forestalled by its power to still haunt and possess at least a few living spectators.

Back in his seat, transported by Wagner's art, Luis is stirred to write a poem about the opera—no longer a museum piece but a living text that can move others to create yet more art. The narrator lyrically describes the opera's birthing of the poem as an ascension from the stage to a section in the house where the city's elite is absent: "Como si viniese dentro de una pálida nube, y como si esa nube ascendiera del proscenio donde Parsifal seguía arrodillado, el poema subió hasta él, hasta la altura de la galería teatral, flotando, formándose y diluyéndose" (260; As if enveloped in a pale cloud, and as if that cloud ascended from the proscenium where Parsifal was still kneeling, the poem climbed to him, up to the theater's gallery, floating, taking shape, and diluting itself). The reader follows closely the creation of the text as Luis, at three different moments, inscribes and revises the poem's thirteen lines in the opera program. The fragments finally come together as the performance is about to conclude, and Luis reads his own handwritten draft scrolled over the prosaic advertisement for an Omega watch. The poem is titled "Parsifal," and its last few lines may be interpreted as the speaker's realization and acknowledgment that he and his lover, whose gender is unspecified in the Spanish text, will not share their lives:

> Así veré hundirse
> la lluvia del nombre que me amaba,
> la audaz batalla que perdí en sus brazos
> y el temor de no ser, a su lado,
> el abrigo del fuego en los inviernos,
> la paz y el silencio
>   en las noches que se acercan.[33] (282–83)

Thus I will see, as they sink,
the rain of the name that loved me,
the brave battle I lost in his arms
and the fear of not being, beside him,
the shelter of fire in winter,
peace and silence
in the coming nights.

Although grammatically ambiguous, the second cited line, in which "nombre" sounds very much like "hombre," suggests that Luis is daring enough to write, if not speak, his passion.

Indeed, it is possible to read Luis's poem in the context of his short-lived affair with Alejandro as well as the larger story of *Parsifal*, which is, after all, a tale of desire and healing. As the narrator suggests, most audience members do not know all aspects of the opera's plot, such as Klingsor's self-castration, rendered euphemistically as "un nefando pecado" (160; a loathsome sin) in the program.[34] But Luis grasps the opera's full implications; even though he is a novice, his sensibility allows him to have a far richer understanding of Wagner's art, an experience through which his amatory malady will be made well by the act of writing. He may be socially marginal vis-à-vis other characters in the novel, yet he emerges as a privileged spectator and, arguably, the true inheritor and redeemer of opera's exalted past—more of a savior than Salvador himself, whose destiny, despite his name, does not quite match that of Parsifal.[35] The narrative comes to an end without any prolepsis into Luis's affective life, but his operatic introspection portends the story of another kind of sexuality in which freedom, a sign of modernity, may loosen the burden of accepted beliefs and received conventions.[36]

In Latin American literary culture, writing inspired by Wagner, such as Mujica Lainez's novel and Luis's poem within it, can appear as traces of the ghost of Rubén Darío, the *modernista* master who, as we saw in Chapter 1, composed laudative poems about Lohengrin and Parsifal. Specifically, Darío's "Parsifal," a sonnet, picks up on the musical and liturgical dimensions of Wagner's drama: "Violines de los ángeles divinos, / sones de las sagradas catedrales, /

incensarios en que arden nuestros males, / sacrificio inmortal de hostias y vinos" (Violins of divine angels, sounds of sacred cathedrals, censers where our ills burn, immortal sacrifice of hosts and wines).[37] Its concluding lines entreat readers to behold Parsifal's body, underscoring his source's theatrical lineage: "¡Mirad que pasa el rubio caballero / mirad que pasa, silencioso y fiero, / el loco luminoso: Parsifal!" (964; Look at the blond knight passing by, look how he passes by, silent and fierce, the luminous madman: Parsifal!).[38] Like many other poems by Darío, the Wagner texts may be read as brilliant episodes in Latin America's long history of cosmopolitanism, especially because of opera's habitual status as a European import. Yet those works—Darío's as well as Mujica Lainez's own embedded "Parsifal"—reveal an understanding of Wagner that naturalizes his art and, by extension, the realm of opera for Latin American literature and cultural history. Unlike the characters of *El gran teatro* who tolerate *Parsifal* but remain unperturbed by what takes place on stage, the speakers of those poems, by passionately engaging with the work's tales and motifs, suggest a modernity far more reaching than what a frivolous night at the opera might imply. The art form is no longer a site of foreignness passively imported and consumed; it is a corpus that can be activated for the creation of new Latin American forms and texts.[39] In the case of *El gran teatro*, opera ceases to be a mere museum piece to become a fertile locus of creation. If the narrator's recitations of names read as items in a reverential archive of European culture, Luis's poem is evidence of the fruitful bonds that link both sides of the Atlantic through the work of opera.[40]

Notably, the only other character in the novel with a real passion for Wagner and the art of opera is a jeweler identified as "el Orfebre" (the Goldsmith), a highly cultivated septuagenarian described as a worldly Jew of Genoese descent (108). Despite his wealth, the Orfebre is, like Luis, a marginal figure; while much appreciated by the Buenos Aires upper crust because of his craft, he is not truly one of them. During the first intermission, noticing that something does not look quite right in María Zúñiga's necklace, he approaches her box only to discover that the famous diamonds and emeralds are in fact counterfeit. The city's elite is not what it seems and the

Orfebre, a lover of antiques hoping one day to curate an exhibition of traditional jewelry at the Museo de Arte Decorativo, feels exceptionally betrayed. Beyond his professional expertise, he possesses a deep-rooted knowledge of European operatic culture; in Germany, as he recounts to a ballet dancer also in the audience, he would often attend the festival at Bayreuth. One memory is proffered as a cherished symbol of an older European culture: "Frau Wagner llegaba puntualmente, erguida, de negro, con su gran sombrero de paja negra, abierta la sombrilla gris, en un break colosal del cual tiraba una yunta de caballos blancos, como si llegase en carroza, y el ensayo empezaba minutos después" (224–25; Frau Wagner would arrive punctually, upright, with a large black straw hat, in a huge carriage pulled by a team of white horses, as if she were arriving in a chariot, and the rehearsal would begin minutes later). Defined by the narrator as a cosmopolitan, the Orfebre, despite his dyed beard, emerges as an arbiter of authenticity—the most direct link to a rich cultural tradition that the Colón has indeed managed to transport to the other side of the world but that appears to have lost some of its luster.

Several decades later, in 2011, the Fundación Teatro Colón and the Fundación Manuel Mujica Lainez jointly published an illustrated edition of *El gran teatro*. Besides a few pages of the author's notes for the novel, including a diagram of the main auditorium marking where characters should be sitting, plus new drawings by Sophie le Comte of spectators (most prominently El Sapo) humorously portrayed as animals, the book also contains sketches by Héctor Basaldúa created for the sets of the *Parsifal* production chronicled in the novel as well as photographs by Gustavo Luque that vividly capture the theater's magnificent architecture. That the book could be purchased at the renovated Colón's gift shop may strike some at first as an ironic cooption of Mujica Lainez's satire by the very institution whose most distinguished patrons—or at least some of them—are depicted as lacking any real engagement with one of opera's top composers.

One wonders, then, to what extent the novel's ironic approach to the transports of opera in Buenos Aires might be superseded by text's metamorphosis into a rather glamorous coffee-table book. In fact, from a certain angle, the luxurious tome stands as yet another museum piece—an homage to an anteriority long foregone. Yet its very existence also speaks to Mujica Lainez's power to extend the life of opera beyond the confines of the theater and the temporal duration of any performance. A photograph by Luque of the empty red-and-gold auditorium exists side by side with the author's own black-and-white diagram of his characters' seating arrangements, which in turn is amplified by le Comte's witty drawing of the novelist's figures morphed into animals. In a letter to Oscar Monesterolo partially reproduced on the last page of the illustrated edition, Mujica Lainez celebrates having finished his novel the day before. The book, he says, is odd and original, and he congratulates himself that no one had thought of writing a novel that takes place in the course of one night at the Colón (224). Fortunately, this is not just a novel set inside the theater, but also, more powerfully, a picture of the theater and its visitors dissected by the novelist's tools. As it so often happens in fiction, what begins as a vision of the real ends up as a complex artifact and a valuable source of knowledge.

The Undoing of Opera: Citations of Victoria Ocampo and Beatriz Sarlo

Despite the troubles through its now centenary history, the Teatro Colón remains a steadfast purveyor of the grand tradition of European opera and, though not as often, the rich corpus of operas by Argentine composers. But there are of course new works too. Among the latter is *V.O.*, a chamber opera with music by Martín Bauer and libretto by Beatriz Sarlo. Premiered in 2013 and revived in 2014, with an orchestra made up of just six strings, a piano, and percussion, and a plot that unfolds in one act with fourteen fast-moving scenes, Bauer and Sarlo's creation succinctly chronicles the life of Victoria Ocampo, author, publisher, and passionate promotes of cultural exchanges. Like other members of the prominent social class to which she belonged, Ocampo regularly attended performances at the Colón, but that was hardly the extent of her involvement with the theater. In the 1930s, she was a member of its board of directors, and on one occasion in 1934, she was also a performer, playing the speaker's role in the Latin American premiere of Igor Stravinsky's *Perséphone*. Moreover, she often wrote eloquently about what she saw and heard at the theater. That she should have turned into the subject of a music drama staged there may be seen as a homecoming of sorts but also, arguably, as an oblique meditation on modernity and the work of opera in the cultural history of Argentina.

Unassuming and discreetly self-reflexive, *V.O.* explores Ocampo's ardent liaisons with the forms of modern art, especially the music of Stravinsky, who was also a friend. Significantly, it was not produced on the opera house's main stage as part of its world-class opera season, but at the Centro de Experimentación del Teatro Colón, a venue with a curious double status. The CETC is a nucleus for theatrical innovation, but it is also a peripheral entity. Its activities do not include the traditional repertory for which the Colón is best known, and even its physical location in the building, far from the plush main hall, can be seen as modest and marginal. In this context, even as it invokes Ocampo's engagement with culture, *V.O.* may be read as a new and powerful act in Sarlo's sustained analysis of Argentina's own kind of modernity. As she argues it in a chapter of *Una modernidad periférica* titled "Decir y no decir: Erotismo y represión," which also examines the work of Norah Lange and Alfonsina Storni, Ocampo, despite her privileged social status, was deprived of real and symbolic freedoms—intellectual, sexual, emotional.[41] This struggle ends only in 1931, when Ocampo founds *Sur* and becomes a cultural leader in Argentina—and when, in Sarlo's words, she also begins to reign over her own body with "la libertad de los hombres" (87; the freedom of men). By acting out Ocampo's literary progress and feminist endeavors in an opera produced both under the aegis of and inside the Colón, Sarlo's libretto vividly performs the symbolic elevation of a figure often hastily dismissed as just a wealthy woman with interesting, often European, contacts.

In a review, Pablo Gianera praised Bauer and Sarlo's affirmative representation of Ocampo's life and deployment of Stravinskian grace, charm, and intelligence.[42] The libretto itself, Gianera rightly observes, could not have existed were it not for Sarlo's earlier critical work on Ocampo, rendered now on a fervent analytical note; it allows spectators to feel an intellectual passion for its subject. Gianera's focus on *amor* matters because it brings to the fore the creative bonds that tie *V.O.* to a network of creators that include not only Ocampo and Stravinsky (as well as other figures from the past) but also Bauer and Sarlo themselves. Although my focus is on the libretto, one should note Bauer's leading role not only as composer but also as longtime director of the Ciclos de Conciertos de Música Contemporánea at the Teatro San Martín, a position of great influence in shaping and supporting an appreciation for modern works among music lovers in Buenos Aires. Likewise, Sarlo's critical writings on Ocampo have played a major role in raising the perceived worth of an author whose works, including multiple essays and a six-volume autobiography, have often been regarded as minor.

In fact, I am persuaded that Sarlo's analyses are key for understanding the themes and structure of the libretto, and also that the words of *V.O.* go deeper as a critical tool. They enact, quite literally, Sarlo's vision of her subject by duplicating what she identifies as the defining trait of Ocampo's writings: the practice of citation. Sarlo's longest and most substantial study of Ocampo, included in *La máquina cultural* (1998), is titled "Victoria Ocampo o el amor de la cita" (Victoria Ocampo or the Love of Citation). This is a suggestive phrase for what it says about the author's craft, marked (or marred, for some) by the words of others, and for what it says about Bauer and Sarlo's opera. The libretto, for one, cites Ocampo's own words as well as her citations of other authors' words.[43] That Sarlo should be so close to Ocampo's text might tempt one, perhaps, to dismiss *V.O.* as overly partial to its subject's own self-fashioning. But in fact, Sarlo's libretto, prompted and assisted by Bauer's music, is a balanced presentation of Ocampo's intellectual pursuits. If as Catherine Clément famously argued, women in opera are often undone through plots that inexorably lead to their violent deaths, as can be seen season after season of Lucias and Toscas dying on the Colón's main stage, the character of Victoria Ocampo, by contrast, acquires a powerful voice that exalts her own life and passions as a woman of letters. Fictional Victoria—operatic Victoria—emerges as a living entity who reads and writes, and whose own oeuvre remains profoundly vital. Victoria Ocampo is a figure envoiced, to use Carolyn Abbate's term, by the work of opera.

Consider, for instance, the opening scene of *V.O.* As the libretto would have it, the audience listens to string music as these dramatic words are projected onstage and read by an actor:

> El último acorde es un ruido. La noche del estreno, nadie escuchó ese final, que se perdió entre los silbidos. En cambio, los primeros compases tienen la música que imaginaba: el timbre y la altura de ese fagot, la repetición de una frase insidiosa, que se mete en el oído y más abajo, más abajo. Un fagot agudo que contradice su madera. Esa es la cuestión: arrancar los sonidos de su costumbre. Lo que se bailó en ese escenario es un sueño pretérito: la muerte de una muchacha para celebrar la vida. El solo de fagot es una anticipación de la barbarie. ¿Quién no soñó esa muerte con horror e impaciencia? Victoria dijo: tiene el ritmo brutal de un cataclismo.[44]

> The last chord is noise. On the night of the premiere, no one listened to that finale, which became lost in the hissing. By contrast, the first bars have the music I imagined: the timbre and pitch of that bassoon, the repetition of that insidious phrase, which penetrates the ear and lower, lower. An acute bassoon, which gainsays the wood it's made of. That is the question: to snatch sounds from their custom. What they danced on that stage was a primeval dream: the death of a girl to celebrate life. The bassoon solo is the anticipation of barbarism. Who did not dream up that death with horror and impatience? Victoria said: it has the brutal rhythm of a cataclysm.

The musical event invoked here is the legendary premiere of Stravinsky's *The Rite of Spring* at the Théâtre des Champs-Elysées in Paris in May 1913. As is well known, the performance of Stravinsky's unconventional score for Diaghilev's Ballets Russes triggered riots and critical accusations of barbarism.

But as Sarlo puts it in *La máquina cultural*, this watershed moment in European music was also a revelation for Ocampo, who was in the audience. Later, she returns to the Ballets Russes—to a performance by Nijinsky and Tamara Karsavina of *Le Spectre de la rose*—in the company of her husband, Luis Bernardo de Estrada, and her husband's cousin, Julián Martínez, whom she had recently met in Rome and who would become her lover in Buenos Aires shortly thereafter. In her essay, Sarlo collapses the two events into one; in just over a week, she says, Ocampo falls in love with Stravinsky, whom she has never met, and with Julián Martínez.[45] To a large extent, the subject of *V.O.* is Ocampo's passion for modernity—in the arts as well as in personal life choices. What matters even as the opera starts are her own authoritative words, which Sarlo clearly labels a citation: "Victoria dijo: tiene el ritmo brutal de un cataclismo." Indeed, these words on *The Rite of Spring* appear more or less the same early on in *La rama de Salzburgo*, the third book of her autobiography: "Asistí, en primera fila de platea, al tumulto del *Sacre du Printemps*. Al final de la cuarta representación, creo (fui a todas), vi a Strawinsky, pálido, saludando a ese público que aplaudía *L'oiseau de feu* y silbaba despiadadamente el *Sacre*. Compré la partitura del *Sacre* y alquilé un piano para tocarla en mi salita del Meurice. No sabía bien que me atraía tanto en ese galimatías de notas y en ese ritmo brutal de cataclismo" (I attended, sitting in the front row of the orchestra, the tumult of the *Sacre du Printemps*. At the end of the fourth performance, I think [I went to all], I saw a pale Stravinsky, saluting that audience which applauded *L'Oiseau de feu* and mercilessly hissed the *Sacre*. I bought the score of the *Sacre* and rented a piano to play it on in the small salon of my suite at the Meurice. I didn't really know what attracted me so much in that chaos of notes and that brutal cataclysmic rhythm).[46]

The placement of Ocampo's words at the end of the libretto's description of the closing and opening of Stravinsky's score is doubly meaningful. Even as Sarlo's act of citation captures the sharpness of Ocampo's receptivity for modern forms, it suggests that all that follows in the opera should be interpreted through the prism of her perception. What matters most, again, is Ocampo's authorship—her ability to capture verbally a passionate engagement with art and people, an impulse that, after all, is at the core of her literary oeuvre. As *V.O.* begins, the sound of Stravinsky's music and the noise generated by the angry audience are turned into Victoria's words. Those attending the performance of *V.O.* hear sounds, but they also read a projected text in which those words are a valued record of Victoria's affects and a key to the opera about to unfold.

The first night of *The Rite of Spring* is variously recounted or alluded to through *V.O.* In the second scene, Victoria plays the "Spring Round Dance" on a gramophone and the stage designs by Nicholas Roerich are projected behind her, immersing the audience in the sounds and sights of *The Rite*. In the fifth scene, an actor playing Stravinsky, referred to as Igor, watches a dancer even as he recites his own version of the text first projected in the prologue: "Un ruido, / los silbidos, / frase insidiosa, / fagot agudo. / Anticipación de la barbarie, / sueño pretérito, / ritmo brutal de un cataclismo" (A noise / the hissing, / insidious phrase, / treble bassoon. / Anticipation of barbarism, / primeval dream, / brutal cataclysmic rhythm). That Igor should cite Victoria's already-cited words is a form of recitation, if you will, that highlights the value of Ocampo's musical judgments. In the next scene, Victoria looks at Igor as she recounts the momentousness of the work's premiere, a night that will change her life: "Una noche de primavera, a fin de mayo, / la noche del estreno. / Se consagra la primavera / esa noche a fin de mayo. / Yo, en la platea, / entre dos hombres, mi marido / y quien será mi amante. / Yo entre dos hombres, paralizada / de emoción y de miedo, / descubro mi futuro" (On a spring evening, in late May, / the night of the premiere. / Spring is to be consecrated / on that evening in late May. / Me, in the orchestra, / between two men, my husband / and the man who will be my lover. / Between two men, paralyzed / by emotion and fear, / I discover my future). At the end of this scene, Victoria collapses "como en un trance" (as if in a trance), while in the thirteenth scene, she plays the chord from the start of *The Rite* on the piano and later speaks to Igor, retelling once again her experience at the premiere: "Desde que era una niña, me preparé para esa noche, sin saber para qué me estaba preparando. Esperé como si me hubieran prometido que algo iba a suceder sobre ese escenario. No escuché los silbidos... Estaba encandilada como un gato" (Since I was a child, I was preparing for that evening, not knowing what I was preparing for. I waited, as if I had been promised that something would happen on that stage. I didn't hear the hissing. I was bedazzled like a cat). She adds, "La música era un animal. Nada más había en ese teatro" (Music was an animal. Nothing else existed in that theater). Finally, in the fourteenth and last scene, Victoria goes back once again to the famous evening in 1913:

> La noche del Sacre,
> con mi vestido de terciopelo azul
> y mi diadema de brillantes,
> bella como una sudamericana.
> La noche del Sacre olvidé mi cuerpo,
> como si me lo hubieran robado.
> Olvidé que era Victoria.
> Yo era sólo un espacio
> donde resonaba la música.
> No escuché los silbidos ni los gritos,
> solo vi a Igor, en una esfera de luz.
> La música caía como una lluvia.
> Y las noches siguientes,
> seguía cayendo.
> Se perdió mi diadema,
> mi vestido azul desapareció en la lluvia.

> On the evening of the *Sacre*
> in my blue velvet dress
> and my diamond diadem,
> as beautiful as a South American woman.
> On the evening of the *Sacre* I forgot my body,
> as if it had been stolen from me.
> I forgot I was Victoria.
> I was just a space
> where music resounded.
> I didn't hear the hissing or the screams,

I only saw Igor, in a sphere of light.
Music fell like rain.
And on the following evenings,
it kept falling.
My diadem was lost,
my blue dress vanished in the rain.

As the opera concludes, it returns to its own first scene—a metatheatrical experience whose comment on a legendary performance remains firmly mediated through Ocampo's perception, but now told in and amplified by Sarlo's own words.

Beyond the story of *The Rite of Spring*, the act of citation reappears powerfully in the libretto's account of Ocampo's thwarted acting career. As Ocampo tells it in her letters to her friend, Delfina Bunge, cited in full in *El imperio insular*, the second book of the autobiography, she was an eager and talented student of French diction and acting with Marguerite Moreno, the renowned actress. Her dream was to perform Jean Racine's princesses and Alfred de Musset's muses. In a letter dated September 6, 1908, in Paris, Victoria writes to Delfina that Moreno wants her to wear "una simple túnica blanca con muchos pliegues" (a simple white tunic with many pleats) for an amateur performance.[47] Sarlo's libretto invokes these words by having the character of Marguerite repeat them in a slightly changed form to Victoria: "Solo una túnica, simple y blanca, con muchos pliegues" (Just a tunic, white and simple, with many pleats). This, in a sense, is a multiple act of citation that also involves translation and performance. Moreno's original words, said in French, are written down in a letter composed also in French, which is in turn cited in Ocampo's autobiographical text, which in its turn written originally in French and translated into Spanish by the author herself—a text then cited by Sarlo's Marguerite as the opera stages Victoria's passion for acting. In this scene, the young woman says to her teacher, "Quisiera parecerme a usted" (I'd like to be like you), and then recites, in Spanish, the first three lines of Hermione's monologue in the fifth act of Racine's *Andromaque*: "¿Dónde estoy y qué hice? ¿Qué debo hacer ahora? / ¿Qué emoción me domina? ¿Qué pena me devora? / Errante y sin destino, perdida en el palacio" (Where am I, and what have I done? What should I do now? What emotion is gripping me? What grief is devouring me? Errant, without destiny, lost in the palace).[48]

In *La máquina cultural*, Sarlo analyzes Ocampo's writings on acting, which she then relates to the author's penchant for citing the words of others, often in foreign tongues. Just like an actor takes occupies someone else's text with her voice and body, Ocampo's writing is also an act of possession: "Este movimiento por el cual las palabras ajenas se convierten en palabras propias es el que Victoria Ocampo elige, más tarde, como movimiento típico de su escritura donde las citas y los *glissandos* al francés, el inglés y el italiano son tan importantes como el texto propio y la propia lengua" (This movement through which someone else's words become one's own is what Victoria Ocampo would later choose as the habitual movement of her writing, in which citations and glissandos into French, English and Italian matter as much as one's own text and tongue).[49] Notably, Sarlo herself engages in a similar act whereby someone else's words—Victoria's, Marguerite's, or even Racine's as recited by Victoria—become the fabric of her own libretto, a kind of mimicry or ventriloquism that serves to both represent and validate Ocampo's practice of writing. Once again imitating her diction, the libretto glides into English—this time in the words of María Inés, Victoria's servant—to tell a tale of longing: "Out from the pampas where grows the ombú / came a fair lady and clever too. / Her parents owned houses and lots of land / that stood out there right at hand, / with cows and horses, gardens and cars, / pesos and pounds and gold in bars. / But the lady only dreamed under the ombú / of music and travel and her Russian guru." In this story of linguistic diversity and transitions, it should be noted that Sarlo herself translated the passages by Racine. One can hear those words not only as an act of multiple citation but also as a prolongation of Ocampo's "máquina de traducir" (translation machine), Sarlo's phrase to describe both the author's practice and the work of *Sur* as a journal charged with the mission of translating foreign texts into Spanish—both a cosmopolitan and a democratizing endeavor.

In her critical analysis of Ocampo's corpus, Sarlo curiously employs the Italian word *glissando* yet a second time to refer to the author's effortless movement from one language to another: "Jamás se le ocurrió que la idea de que esa mezcla de lenguas, convocadas cada vez que las siente necesarias, no sea sólo un emblema de riqueza sino también la imposibilidad de decir las cosas de otro modo: una servidumbre al francés o al inglés, en lugar de una libertad de transitar *glissando* de uno al otro" (Never did it occur to her that her mixture of languages, brought together whenever she felt the need, could be not just an emblem of wealth, but also the impossibility of saying things in any other way: a servitude to French or English, instead of the freedom to transit *glissando* from one language to another).[50] Sarlo's use of a musical term retrieves Ocampo's style from accusations of linguistic inelegance or colonial dependence even as it appears to describe unwittingly the nature of *V.O.* as its own kind of opera. In Bauer and Sarlo's work, song and speech, or music and words, slide against and away from each other in an unconventional manner—a new and nuanced staging, arguably, of the old debate about the primacy of one code over the other in the operatic text. Not quite a *Singspiel*, say, in which song and spoken dialogue are alternated, *V.O.* does assert that operas come in many different forms. In this opera, singers and actors share the stage, the musical and the verbal work together in the act of singing, and a piano solo and a player's monologue harmoniously glide together. Through these fluctuations, one is reminded of the ardent interplay of literature and music in Ocampo's own autobiographical volumes. Even as she proclaims her devotion to the practices of reading and writing, Ocampo's words often engage in narratives about the affects triggered by music. Again in *La máquina cultural*, Sarlo contrasts Ocampo's reaction to *The Rite of Spring* with that of Carmen Peers de Perkins, another Argentine woman from the same privileged social class, who also happened to be there and wrote about the event. Peers de Perkins recalls the evening, rather detachedly, for its significance in the arch of European culture. Ocampo, by contrast, becomes obsessed with the work, attending every performance and playing a piano version of the score in her hotel suite. In Sarlo's words, she is ravished: "Para Victoria Ocampo, en cambio, fue un rapto" (For Victoria Ocampo, by contrast, it was a rapture).[51] This passionate reaction is hardly an exceptional affect. Ocampo herself, in various passages of her autobiography, repeatedly describes the transports of music, as when she listens to Mercedes, an aunt who had studied piano in Paris, playing Chopin: "Todo en esa música me llegaba al corazón. Me inundaba deliciosamente sin que llegara a hacer pie en ese mar. Ya no sabía dónde estaba la costa, por la marea de esa agua sonora. No sabía adónde me llevaba" (Everything in that music entered my heart. It flooded me with delight without my being able to reach the bottom of that sea. I didn't know where the shore was, so much like a tide was that sonorous water. I didn't know where it was carrying me).[52]

In this fervent engagement with music, it would not be true to claim that praise for opera consistently plays the most prominent role. Ocampo's writings often mention opera, operatic composers and nights at the opera, but these allusions tend to occur in passing. More often than not, the realm of opera appears simply as the background against which certain episodes of her life take place. Such is the case with a mention of Debussy's *Pelléas et Mélisande*, early in *El imperio insular*, as she recounts the death of Clara, her younger sister. The work comes up first as a date in her personal and family story; someone is said to have died in the same year that *Pelléas* was first performed in Buenos Aires. Likewise, in the same volume, she recalls home stagings of an English musical play, which she calls *opereta*, after the local engagement of a company from England.[53] Elsewhere, opera provides a useful metaphor, as when, also in *El imperio insular*, she invokes Puccini's "Coro a bocca chiusa" to describe an early kiss: "El beso que hubiera podido confesar, el único, fue un momentáneo y fugitivo apoyarse de dos bocas muy jóvenes, una sobre la otra (cerradas como para el coro de *Madame Butterfly*)" (The kiss to which I could have confessed was an instantaneous and fleeting coming together of two very young mouths, one on the other [closed, as if for the chorus in *Madama Butterfly*]).[54] On yet another occasion, again in the same book, she invokes the cliché of operatic singers as corpulent people when she describes her singing lessons with one Mme Sanderson in Paris: "Cuando cantaba el dúo de *Sansón y Delila* [. . .] le temblaba tanto la papada que parecía un budín de gelatina" (2:66; When she sang the duet from *Samson and Delilah* . . . her jowl shook so much that it resembled a gelatin pudding).

In a sense, these numerous allusions may be regarded as signs of class, yet occasionally, when it comes to some specific composers and performers, Ocampo's text underscores the transports of song and opera. Also in Paris, she admires a performance by Reynaldo Hahn, whose feeble voice was still capable of producing miracles. At times, her words reach the level of ravishment, as in the case of Wagner and one of his singers (2:67).[55] If Victoria and her sister, Clara, had fallen in love with Marguerite Carré when she performed the role of Mélisande at the Buenos Aires premiere of Debussy's opera, Ocampo's passion for the Wagnerian soprano appears to be boundless. Through Madame Sanderson's agency, she persuades her mother to have tea at the singer's house. Young Victoria is speechless, which impresses the singer, yet she is later capable of telling the event by resorting to two languages: "No pude articular palabra en su presencia. Esto al parecer conmovió a la Walkiria de mis sueños, porque me mandó una fotografía con esta dedicatoria: 'A V.O. la chère et charmante créature.' La alegría y la emoción fueron tales, que enseguida empecé a pensar que no era cierto; que había escrito eso no porque lo sintiera, sino como una *formule de politesse*" (I wasn't able to produce a word in her presence. This apparently moved the Walküre of my dreams because she sent me a photograph with this dedication: *"A V.O. la chère et charmante creature."* My happiness and feelings were such that I immediately started thinking that it wasn't true, that she had written that not because she felt it, but as a *formule de politesse*).[56] Be that as it may, Ocampo's passionate praise for the renowned singer foreshadow the role of opera in narrating the early stages of her love affair with Julián Martínez, with whom she would be romantically involved for well over a decade.

In yet another act of citation, Ocampo resorts to words from Stendhal's *De l'amour* to recount and scrutinize her feelings for

Martínez. The third volume of her autobiography, which narrates the affair, is titled *La rama de Salzburgo*, and the book also opens with an epigraph from Stendhal's famous text on the process of love as a form of crystallization. Ocampo's use of the French author's words and concepts alternates with her relentless invocation of operas by two composers, Wagner and Debussy—works that deal with what she calls, quoting Stendhal's phrase, *amor pasión*, even as they chronicle stories of forbidden love with tragic outcomes. As it happens, Ocampo and Martínez, both of whom have returned to Buenos Aires from Paris, first see each other by accident at a performance of *Parsifal* at the Colón. The event is told in the middle of a paragraph in which she describes in much detail the process of decorating her home on calle Tucumán. Suddenly, the narrative moves to the opera house and Ocampo's words accelerate passionately: "Una noche, inesperadamente, vi a J. en el Colón, en un palco bajo. Daban *Parsifal*. De nuevo me sentí limalla de hierro ante un imán. Las grandes oleadas de música me llevaban en su cresta y rompían allí donde él estaba. Las lágrimas me ardieron en los ojos. Estaba exasperada por mi estupidez y maravillada de encontrarla intacta" (One evening, unexpectedly, I saw J. at the Colón, in a lower box. They were doing *Parsifal*. Once again I felt like iron filings before a magnet. The great waves of music carried me in their crests and broke where he was. Tears burned in my eyes. I was frustrated by my foolishness and astounded to see that it was intact).[57] The quiet domestic space in which she immersed herself upon her return to the city vanishes in the heady realm of the opera house, where fictional and real stories of transports unfold before and inside her.

In Ocampo's account, allusions to *Parsifal* as well as *Tristan und Isolde* and *Pelléas et Mélisande* serve to explain various aspects of her relationship with Martínez. All three operas chronicle stories of sexual transgression, and, in the case of the latter two, each protagonist is a married woman who, like Ocampo, loves a man who is not her husband. Ocampo resorts to the *Tristan* prelude and the opera's motifs to capture the sense of dramatic expectation at the start of her affair with Martínez, seen also, as if in a time warp, from the vantage point of the author who poignantly recalls those days in her memoirs: "Porque lo nuestro fue fuga en la nave que bogaba, y boga siempre, en alta mar, hacia la península de Tristán. Nos habíamos evadido. Será ridículo o no, traer a colación la leyenda de la Edad Media. ¡Poco importa! Así fue. Este era el preludio. Tarde o temprano, y fatalmente, el telón se levantaría sobre la historia de un amor pasión" (Because our relationship was an escape on the ship that sailed, and still sails, in the high seas, toward Tristan's peninsula. We had escaped. It might be ridiculous to bring up that legend from the Middle Ages. But that doesn't matter much. That's how it was. This was the prelude. Sooner or later, and fatally, the curtain would rise over the story of a passionate love).[58] As she considers her parents' or her husband's potentially negative reaction to news of the affair, she cites the story of Pelléas and Mélisande, quoting Golaud's words and transposing the opera's plot to her present circumstances: "Si Dios existe y se mete en estas miserias (en ese caso mejor es que no exista), podría atestiguar que la violencia de M. era la de Golaud. Y yo había visto menos a mi Pelléas que la idénticamente inocente (e idénticamente culpable) Mélisande" (27; If God exists and buts into these miserable things [in that case it would be better if He didn't exist], I could testify that M.'s violence was akin to Golaud's. And I had seen my Pelléas less than the equally innocent [and equally guilty] Mélisande).

Throughout this part of the book, Ocampo also mentions a series of literary lovers, including Paolo and Francesca (who would be the subject of her first book) and the Princesse de Clèves, but she keeps returning to opera and its stories. She reads Amfortas's wound in *Parsifal* in the light of Stendhal: "La llaga de Amfortas es el amor pasión, no el placer, no la voluptuosidad de las *filles-fleurs*" (32; Amfortas's wound is passionate wound, not pleasure, not the voluptuousness of the flower maidens). Hiding in a taxi that drives them around Buenos Aires, she kisses Julián for the first time and remembers the life and works of Wagner—his famous affair with a married woman in Zurich, and the ravishing opera frequently linked with those emotions. Her focus is the thrill of physical contact: "Grito de ópera (se burlaba de mi espíritu crítico). Pero había sido el grito de Wagner y de Matilde Wesendonck, antes de ser el de Tristán e Isolda. La ópera nació de ese grito. (¡Qué mezquino y de bajo vuelo era el espíritu crítico!)" (34–35; An operatic scream [it mocked my critical spirit]. But it had been the scream of Wagner and Mathilde Wesendonck before it was Tristan and Isolde's. The opera was born from that scream [how mean and lowly critical spirit was!].

Some readers might be tempted to dismiss these operatic verbal flights merely as signs of Ocampo's European-inflected upbringing and affinities, about which much has been written. More specifically, they can also be read in the context of her love and knowledge of music, an aspect of her cultural endeavors and tastes that Sarlo, for one, elevates over the literary.[59] It is music, principally, that Ocampo chooses here as the best metaphor for speaking about the affects of love: "El amor, como la música, cambia los estados de ánimo. (Por eso Tolstoy, sensible a la música, temía sus efectos de droga.) Arrastrada por ese torrente, yo renegaba de 'mis principios' y buscaba justificación" (35; Love, like music, changes one's moods. [That's why Tolstoy, sensitive to music, feared its drug-like effects. Dragged by that torrent, I reneged on 'my principles' and sought justification]). Ambiguously, the syntax of the sentence appears to at least momentarily unite love and music as one natural force. Even if a second, more careful reading confirms that "the torrent" refers to the idea of love, one is still left with the impression that Ocampo's erotic passion is inextricably bound to the transits of music and her literary self-fashioning as an operatic heroine. Invoking yet again Tristan and Isolde, she reaffirms how that legend from the Middle Ages was still alive in her. In that regard, spectators of opera reading of Ocampo's travails, aware of the stories she repeatedly alludes to as well as other operatic plotlines, might expect a tragic denouement—one in which Victoria, like so many operatic heroines, is undone. The irrational, sometimes linked with music as well as madness and death, might point to a disastrous finale. But Ocampo, as the unfolding of her autobiography eventually reveals, is saved. Ultimately, all passion is spent, reason prevails and the text ends up chronicling the rise of a strong woman who becomes the publisher of a storied Latin American journal and the author of a compelling literary oeuvre as well.

In her libretto, too, Sarlo empowers the figure of Ocampo with the ability to verbalize and enact her own story and vision of things. Isolde exits the stage after her "Liebestod" and a heroine like Lucia di Lamermoor dies after her so-called Mad Scene; but the central event in *V.O.* is arguably Victoria's aria in the ninth scene—a perfect hendecasyllabic sonnet in which she invokes through music and words aspects of her erotic life even as she asserts a sense of victory over the social impediments of gender:

> Otros cuerpos nunca conocieron
> mayor entendimiento que los nuestros,
> mayor placer, tampoco más ternura,
> cuando el deseo, cumplido, se dormía.
> No dejes que me vaya, no me pierdas.
> No sé nada de vos. ¿De dónde viene
> esta locura? Restos del naufragio
> de un verde paraíso en la llanura.
> ¿Quién llora cuando yo estoy llorando?
> ¿El viento y los diamantes de la noche?
> ¿De quién es esta mano que me toca?
> Amor, voy a olvidarte y recordarte.
> Allá voy. Te doy la espalda y te miro.
> Fui Isolda y Melisande y fui Victoria.

> Other bodies never knew
> a greater understanding than our bodies,
> or greater pleasure, or tenderness,
> when desire, fulfilled, would fall asleep.
> Don't let me go, don't lose me.
> I haven't heard from you. Where does it come from,
> this madness? Residues of the shipwreck
> of a green paradise on the plain.
> Who cries when I cry?
> The wind and the night's diamonds?

Whose hand is this that touches me?
Love, I will forget and remember you.
I'm going there. I turn away and look at you.
I was Isolde and Mélisande and I was Victoria.

Unlike the "Liebestod" and the mad scene, Victoria's sonnet aria is performed not as the character's last number, but rather at the work's midpoint. Yet, like those two famous moments in opera, it defines her story most clearly. At first, the sonnet aria might be read as a response to the character of Pierre Drieu de la Rochelle, the author with whom Victoria was romantically involved, played by an actor (not a singer) in the opera. At the end of the previous scene, Drieu, identified in the libretto generically as "Hombre," addresses to her a series of denigrating phrases, ending thus: "Tan rica, tan pobre, tan colmada y vacía. Victoria, con esa tricota pareces un muchachito" (So rich, so poor, so satiated, so empty. Victoria, you look like a little boy in that sweater). Drieu's cruelty resounds with previous scenes in which she, or her name, is belittled. In the first scene, for instance, she says, "Victoria me llamo, por algo será" (My name is Victoria, there must be a reason), but the character of María Inés replies, "Tu nombre es nada, estás atrapada" (Your name is nothing, you're trapped). Later, in the third scene, she herself wonders about the appropriateness of her imperial appellation when she in fact wields little power. Others control her body and manage her readings, labeled unfit for girls, and impede her physical movement: "Me llamo Victoria, / por algo será. / Me encierran, / me mandan, / me visten, / me peinan, / me traen y llevan / de aquí / para allá" (My name is Victoria, / there must be a reason. / They don't let me go out, / they order me around, / they dress me, / they comb my hair, / they take me / from here / to there). Yet in the sonnet aria, as she rejoices in the pleasures of love and laments its sorrows, she proclaims the name Victoria, placed last, both as her ultimate identity and as the word that defines her best.[60]

Like much else in *V.O.*, the sonnet rests largely on the practice of citation. For one, its first two lines are Sarlo's version of a sentence from Ocampo's autobiography in which she openly extols her physical relationship with Julián Martínez: "Dudo que otros cuerpos hayan tenido, jamás, mayor entendimiento, mayor placer en tutearse y más ternura que prodigarse cuando el deseo saciado se alejaba" (I doubt that any other bodies could ever have had a better understanding, a bigger pleasure in treating each other with familiarity, or more tenderness to share after the fulfillment of desire).[61] Although neither Julián nor, for that matter, her husband are mentioned directly in the opera, the sonnet aria may nevertheless be read as a meditation on the intertwined stories of amatory liaisons and literary pursuits. Placed at the sonnet's center, two rather cryptic lines strike me as especially suggestive of this narrative of love and creation: "Restos del naufragio de un verde paraíso en la llanura." In the context of her romantic life, the phrase "verde paraíso" alludes to "Le vert paradis," the last section in the first volume of the autobiography, which in turn cites three nonsequential lines from Baudelaire's "Moesta et errabunda" as its epigraph: "Mais le vert paradis des amours enfantines, / [. . .] L'innocent paradis, plein de plaisirs furtifs, / Est-il déjà plus loin que l'Inde et que la Chine?"[62] ("But the green paradise of childhood loves . . . That sinless paradise, full of furtive pleasures, / Is it farther off now than India and China?").[63] In the pages of "Le vert paradis," Ocampo recounts her girlhood infatuation with a boy identified simply as L.G.F., whom she likes first and foremost for his physical beauty. Moreover, *Le vert paradis* is also the title of a French-language book, published during World War II, in which she collects four essays on her passionate feelings for England and France, especially their literary histories. The sonnet aria's invocation of *la llanura* both as a green paradise and as the site of metaphorical shipwrecks refers to the actual space of Argentina, where her tumultuous life as a reader, writer, and lover has unfolded. But that Baudelaire's phrase should be the title of two separate texts highlights Ocampo's accomplishment in the permutation of experience into literature, a process in which the practice of citation plays, again, a visible and endearing role. The sonnet aria, then, emerges as a story of survival full of pleasures, perils, and prohibitions not unlike what one finds in the tales of Isolde and Mélisande—except that

Victoria, in this opera of her own, comes out triumphant in the end.

Beyond words and music, opera is also about what audiences see onstage, and here too *V.O.* showcases Ocampo's passion for modernity. Although the plotline moves vertiginously across time and space, traversing decades and crossing the Atlantic Ocean on several occasions, the staging at the Centro de Experimentación depicts only one place: the very modern house Ocampo had built in Buenos Aires's Barrio Parque in the late 1920s and where she lived for just a few years. In the opera, Victoria plays Racine's Hermione and walks around an imaginary palace, and recalls many times *The Rite of Spring* at a theater in Paris, but the audience at the CETC sees just one structure, located in their own city: the living room of a house by means of which she contested the traditional styles of architecture prevailing in Buenos Aires at the time. Ocampo, who loved Le Corbusier's work, persuaded Alejandro Bustillo, an architect whose works until then had been classically conventional, to design a house that expressed her love for clean lines and minimal decor. Her well-heeled neighbors on calle Rufino de Elizalde were troubled as plain white cubes appeared amid their own Beaux Arts mansions, and Ocampo herself eventually sold the house to preserve her parents' villa in San Isidro, a far more traditional structure. For Sarlo, the audacious experiment in Barrio Parque remains an ambiguous accomplishment: a lesser act of imitation but also Ocampo's "primera gran traducción" (first great translation), the first link in what would become in *Sur,* founded shortly thereafter, a long chain of real and metaphoric transits and transports between languages and cultures.[64] Rebuilt on the stage of the CETC, the house may be seen, then, as the embodiment of Ocampo's aesthetic affinities and projects. If only temporarily and obliquely, it could also be interpreted as a visual commentary on the nature of opera in a city like Buenos Aires and a theater like the Colón. Ocampo's minimalist house may have risen in a peripheral site inside the grand old edifice, yet its presence there, along with the music and words of *V.O.*, could suggest only the design of another kind of opera for Latin America.

Afterword

Caliban at the Royal Opera House

THE STORY THIS BOOK has told is now ended, but let's return yet once again to a stage. This is London, but the opera is set on an island that has no name and no precise geographic location, yet occupies a vast space in transatlantic imaginings. In the history of fictional islands, it would be hard to find a more fruitful site than the speckle of land where Shakespeare set the tale of Prospero the magician and his daughter Miranda, a few shipwrecked Italians, a lofty spirit named Ariel, and the ferocious Caliban, called "this thing of darkness" (*The Tempest* 5.1.274). The island where *The Tempest* unfolds must be found somewhere in the Mediterranean, between Italy and North Africa, but it is often subject to radical displacements. At times, the island moves eastward to the mid-Atlantic (Bermuda, associated with angry storms, is referenced in act 1), or south of there, as an emblem of European conquests, to the Caribbean. In these various transports, Caliban is perhaps the most powerful actor. Not only is he physically different from the other characters, his very name conjures up *cannibal*, which in turn invokes the Caribs, those savage inhabitants of the region where the so-called Old and New Worlds encountered each other—well before the birth of opera and almost two centuries before any European composer could dream up any music drama set in the Americas.

Like the island itself, the story written by Shakespeare has undertaken its own journeys, inspiring multiple literary, musical, and cinematic adaptations in many parts of the world. A highly musical play, it may not come as a surprise that there have been as many as fifty music dramas based on it. They range from a semiopera in Restoration England, with words by John Dryden and others, to Andrew Porter's grand opera, premiered in Santa Fe in 1985, plus such odd works as Jan Sibelius's haunting incidental music for the play, which Alex Ross describes as a shadow opera, "perhaps the greatest Shakespeare opera never written."[1]

My focus is on an early twenty-first-century retelling: the opera composed by Thomas Adès, with a libretto by Meredith Oakes, premiered at London's Royal Opera House in 2004. Specifically, I am interested in this new engagement with Shakespeare's text for what it says about postcolonial readings and rewritings of the figure of Caliban and how these standpoints may permeate, or not, the creation of a new European opera.[2] That forceful corpus of works in which others write back to Shakespeare includes, to cite just a couple of examples from Latin America and the Caribbean, Aimé Césaire's play *Une tempête* (1969) and Roberto Fernández Retamar's essay "Calibán: Apuntes sobre la cultura en nuestra América" (1971). Both works, albeit in different genres and tones, propose readings of *The Tempest* as a kind of allegory of colonial relations in which Caliban stands as an enslaved and racialized other. He is the rebellious vassal of Prospero, the banished duke of Milan, who has taken possession of the island. Fernández Retamar transposes the story to the Antilles in a blunt narrative capsule: "Prospero invaded the islands, killed our ancestors, enslaved Caliban, and taught him his language to make himself understood."[3] Adès's and Oakes's opera, by contrast, appears to underplay the postcolonial viewpoint. In previous works, Adès had cast his eyes and ears to multiple forms of Latin American culture. Fragments of tango are heard in *Powder Her Face* (1995), his first opera; one of the movements of *America: A Prophecy,* a work for orchestra and mezzo-soprano, employed Maya poetry from the *Chilam Balam* (1999); and *The Exterminating Angel* (2016), his third opera, adapted the film Luis Buñuel made in Mexico, and takes place in a house on Calle de la Providencia in an unnamed Spanish-speaking city.[4] But Adès's opera, if anything, appears to shy away from any substantial thematic commitment to readings and re-creations of the play in other parts of the world conquered by European powers.[5]

Consider, for instance, the issue of race, central in postcolonial reformulations of the play. As Caliban returns from his tropical discourses to an opera stage in the British capital, his new avatar is still recognizable as a colonial subject, but he is no longer racially distinct. His darkness, at least at face value, is whitewashed by the pale visage of Ian Bostridge, the renowned English tenor who created the role at Covent Garden. Significantly, the word *darkness* itself does not appear in Oakes's libretto. Yet if we look, listen, and read closely, and if we ponder what Bostridge himself wrote about his role in the opera, this new and apparently postracial yet still postcolonial Caliban emerges as yet another emblem of the complex ties that bind the peoples of the Atlantic world. Consequently, Adès's opera too may be heard as a powerful, albeit cryptic text in the archive of Latin American and operatic convergences.

In this story of textual permutations, Shakespeare has the first word—a powerful eloquence that suggests and generates postcolonial readings. The terms used to describe Caliban, or the names that he is called to his face, make up a powerful catalog of slurs grounded on alterity. In act 1, Miranda designates the island native "a villain . . . I do not love to look on" (1.2.310–11), while Prospero taunts him by shouting "thou earth" (1.2.315) and "filth as thou art" (1.2.347); Caliban is nothing but a "poisonous slave" (1.2.320) in Prospero's eyes, or, to cite Miranda, an "abhorrèd slave" (1.2.351). He is also animalized—called "tortoise" *(*1.2.317), "moon-calf" (2.2.113), and "deboshed fish" (3.2.24)—or repeatedly called a monster, or a mixed creature made up of these things, as Trinculo would have it: "Wilt thou tell a monstrous lie, being but half a fish, and half a monster" (3.2.25–26). In this, Caliban resembles Calderón's Adonis in *La púrpura de la rosa*, who, as we saw, emerges as a hybrid creature—a "bastard embryo" or the "aborted offspring of a tree."

On one momentous occasion, Caliban's difference becomes a collective attribute as well. Reminding him that she taught him how to speak, Miranda accuses him and his ilk of ingratitude: "But thy vile race . . . had that in't which good natures could not abide to be with" (1.2.358–360). In a note for his edition of the play, David Lindley points out that race in seventeenth-century English did not signal ethnicity, as it has since the nineteenth century, but "its general sense in the period—of a grouping by descent or common characteristics—does not exclude the possibility of its carrying something of its current resonance."[6] As Kim F. Hall argues, Miranda's "language lessons" reveal "an epistemic 'difference' that serves only to heighten her sense of racial difference and her estrangement from Caliban."[7] In act 5, as the play reaches its denouement, Prospero calls Caliban his possession even as he defines him as a murky entity: "this thing of darkness, I acknowledge mine" (5.1.274–275)—an early figuration, perhaps, of the white man's burden. Like *race* before, the meaning of *darkness* is not altogether clear; as Lindley explains, the term "may allude to Caliban's colour (not elsewhere remarked) as well as to his diabolic status."[8] Whatever its signification at the time, Caliban's darkness—intended either as literally racial or as metaphorically evil, or both—has contributed to his status as a postcolonial icon with a formidable voice. Hall invokes the fact that he has been "read alternatively as black African, Afro-Caribbean and native American."[9] In this tale of local and global power relations, it matters that the island monster has learned to speak from his foreign masters and that he can deploy language to expose and combat his oppressors. But what happens what he sings the words Oakes wrote and the airs Adès composed?

When the opera was first performed, Oakes's libretto was praised for how it streamlined and modernized Shakespeare's complex diction. Ariel's song at the end of act 1, in which he tells Ferdinand that his father must have died at sea, is a good example; the original "Full fathom five thy father lies" becomes "Five fathoms deep your father lies."[10] Some aspects of the plot have been simplified too. Caliban remains the butt of cruel insults. He is called "Abhorrent slave . . . Lunatic . . . Serpent . . . devil's spawn" (28), and certainly "monster." But there are new elements not found in Shakespeare's text alluding to other geographic and cultural latitudes. When the island is described, one senses a space redolent of the tropics. There are mentions of "parrots" (28) and a dense "jungle" (39), and suggesting global tourism, Antonio describes their ocean voyage as a "holiday" (35). When Caliban first appears, the chorus—whose men, and also women, make up the king of Naples's court—exclaim, "A monster! A local!" and soon thereafter this native person is both "ugly" and "friendly" (36). Even the tempest that causes the shipwreck is called a "hurricane" (35), a word deriving from the Spanish *huracán*, which in turn stems from a word in Taino, an indigenous Caribbean language. The opera's first staging at Covent Garden illustrated this transatlantic turn by deploying palm trees and purple sunsets. Miranda was clad in an exotic colorful petticoat, and the storm-tossed vessel resembled a small cruise ship, all of which, again, points to postcolonial geographies and discourses. Further signaling the story's displacement from Europe, the opera's program included an excerpt from Sylvester Jourdain's *A Discovery of the Barmudas*, first published in 1610. What's more, unlike the original character in the play, Adès and Oakes's Caliban, a political creature, is fervently aware of his own royal status and deposed condition: "This island's mine / I am king / You treat me like nothing / . . . I took you for my brother" (27). He decries the absence of liberty, equality and fraternity in explicitly political speeches. Yet despite all these nods to Caliban's advent as a revolutionary icon, the libretto, as I said, eschews any reference to Caliban's darkness. In this, Adès and Oakes's operatic Caliban differs from his black-inflected counterpart in Porter's *The Tempest*, whose low-tessitura part, as Robert P. Morgan describes it, "is heavily influenced by traditional blues and is accompanied by a jazz trio"—musical forms easily housed in Carpentier's hybrid, baroque resonances.[11] Interpreted in the opera's invocation of the play's travels beyond England, one wonders, then, what meanings to attach to the elision of anything resembling race in Oakes's libretto. Why is Caliban, upon this new return to a stage in London, no longer a racial other?

A first thought concerns Bostridge's own background. If he, a white singer, was chosen to create the role, why bring up any potential allusion to race? Then again, the art of opera is assertively nonrealistic, and instances abound of singers of various colors performing roles that do not resemble them. Indeed, in many stagings of Shakespeare's play, actors who are not "dark" take on Caliban even as the word *darkness* is preserved. Nonetheless, the English tenor himself was aware of the obvious clash between Caliban's body and his own looks. In "Me and My Monster," a newspaper article that later became a chapter in *A Singer's Notebook*, Bostridge reflected on that visual discord. But he, like Oakes, eschews the subject of race: "As a singer at what you may call the highbrow end of the business, engaged in art-song and accustomed to singing princes or fresh-faced juveniles in opera, I'm hardly central casting for the hairy wild man to which audiences have long been accustomed."[12] Yet building on the aristocratic resonances of his theatrical persona, Bostridge insists on Caliban's own nobility, which was already present in Shakespeare but which, in his view, Adès and Oakes underwrite more poignantly. The opera emerges as a tale of restoration. Intelligently, Bostridge analyzes the changes in the famous passage in which Caliban extols the island's soundscape: "Be not afeared; the isle is full of noises, / Sounds, and sweet airs, that give delight and hurt not" (3.2.127). For the tenor, the play buries the speech in a comical scene, but it becomes "dramatically liberated and transformed" through Adès's music and Oakes's words.[13] Indeed, in the opera, Caliban sings a sweet, lofty melody that, as Bostridge would have it, amplifies the character's agency through "a vision of what the island could be like without Prospero's curdling rage":[14]

> Friends don't fear
> The island's full of noises
> Sounds and voices
> It's the spirits
> Sometimes they come
> After I've slept
> And hum me
> Back to sleep
> With a twanging

And a sweetness
Like playing
A thousand instruments
Then I dream
I'm seeing heaven
It's as if the clouds had opened
I see riches
Raining from them
Then I wake
And cry to dream again (38)

Indeed, as the opera concludes, the Europeans settle their quarrels and depart, restoring Caliban's dominion over the island: "Who was here? / Have they disappeared? / Were there others? / Were we brothers?" (52). His dream of a heavenly cloudless island appears to have become true, and the cruel colonial occupation just a vague memory.

But what about Caliban's original darkness? Beyond political values, Caliban is a compelling figure because he knows what he wants and does not shy from expressing it. This includes the thorny issue of his desire for Miranda, whom he imagines as the future mother of his children. In the opera, he sings about this royal progeny to Prospero: "Give me your daughter / We'll have Calibans / Many and strong / So my line goes on" (48). Heralded as the island's queen, the mother of mixed-race children, Miranda listens in and protests: "You and me. How could that be?" (48). She calls Caliban "alien," while Prospero brings up the subject of race, canceling the emergence of hybrid subjects and announcing a people's possible extinction: "Poor beast / Last in the race / Creature / You have no future" (49). What color, though, is Caliban's race? Much can be said about Prospero's words in the afterlife of empires, but the textual elision of *darkness* is critical. Race as a concept may still matter, but by choosing not to sing that word, the opera works to undo the linkage between skin color and moral flaws, thus canceling darkness as a sign of, or metaphor for, turpitude. Like the magical play upon which it is based, this is ultimately an opera about forgiveness and reconciliation—and one way to achieve this might be by banishing the sign of darkness and all the troubling intertwining of character and color. Just before the curtain falls, after Prospero and company exit the stage, Caliban, envoiced by the English tenor, keeps questioning the reality of his island's invasion: "Were there fires and ships? / They were human seeming / I was dreaming" (52). Opera cannot cancel history, but this work allows spectators to rethink the ways in which cultures transport one another to places that exist for now only in the future. Significantly, this may all just be opera's dream: to revise its own original darkness, as if making up for the past were just a matter of crafting a new libretto in search of benevolently colorblind reviews.

The curtain falls. Ambivalence reigns. As Caliban takes his bow at the Royal Opera House, operagoers, eyes wide open, may see a rich velvet curtain emblazoned with Queen Elizabeth II's initials, crowned by the royal coat of arms of the United Kingdom, a golden lion and silver unicorn and four imperious words, "Dieu et mon droit." But the spectacle of opera is larger and deeper than any one opera house, than any monarch, than the myths of Europe and Europa. Operagoers, readers all, may close their eyes and recall, vertiginously, the story of Caliban, enslaved by Europeans, just like Henze's Esteban and Gomes's Iberè had been, but all at last free to speak and sing, like Sarlo's Victoria and Catán's Florencia, or Vivaldi's Montezuma and Carpentier's Filomeno and even Calderón's mixed-up Adonis, through the power of opera.

NOTES

INTRODUCTION

1. Walt Whitman, *Complete Poetry and Collected Prose* (New York: Library of America, 1982), 523.
2. Writing partly from the viewpoint of literary authors such as Jorge Luis Borges and Alejo Carpentier as well as literary critics, especially Roberto González Echevarría, Malena Kuss amply discusses the multiple uses and meanings of Latin America in its relation to "the musical legacies of indigenous peoples, African descendants, Iberian colonizers and creoles, and other immigrants that met and mixed in the New World." Malena Kuss, prologue to *Music in Latin America and the Caribbean: An Encyclopedic History* (Austin: University of Texas Press, 2004), 1:ix.
3. An exception to centripetal forces is Ópera Latinoamericana (OLA). Founded in 2007 and headquartered in Santiago de Chile, this nonprofit organization reunites opera companies in ten Latin American countries (and Spain) with the goal of creating artistic and professional networks to support the performance of opera throughout the region. See OLA's website at https://www.operala.org/en.

CHAPTER 1

1. See Frances Aparicio, *Listening to Salsa: Gender, Latin Popular Music and Puerto Rican Cultures* (Middletown, CT: Wesleyan University Press, 1998); Florencia Garramuño, *Primitive Modernities: Tango, Samba, and Nation* (Stanford, CA: Stanford University Press, 2011); Idelber Avelar and Christopher Dunn, eds., *Brazilian Popular Music and Citizenship* (Durham, NC: Duke University Press, 2011); Kathryn Bishop-Sanchez, *Creating Carmen Miranda: Race, Camp and Transnational Stardom* (Nashville, TN: Vanderbilt University Press, 2016); and Manfred Engelbert, *Violeta Parra: Lieder aus Chile* (Frankfurt, Germany: Vervuert/Iberoamericana, 2017).
2. Mariano Siskind, *Cosmopolitan Desires: Global Modernity and World Literature* (Evanston, IL: Northwestern University Press, 2014), 10.

3. David Littlejohn, *The Ultimate Art: Essays Around and About Opera* (Berkeley: University of California Press, 1994), 69.
4. Cristina Magaldi, *Music in Imperial Rio de Janeiro: European Culture in a Tropical Milieu* (Lanham, MD: Scarecrow Press, 2004), xii.
5. Rogério Budasz, *Opera in the Tropics: Music and Theater in Early Modern Brazil* (Oxford: Oxford University Press, 2019), 3.
6. In a keynote speech delivered in Rio de Janeiro in 2013, Kuss defined the challenge of chronicling Latin American opera and other kinds of music within a discipline still dominated by European parameters—both a conceptual framework and a master story beholden to European culture to which a history of opera in Latin America would be hard-pressed to conform. "Opera in Latin America: Some Premises for a History" (lecture, IV Simpósio Internacional de Musicologia da UFRJ, Rio de Janeiro, August 15, 2013). Kuss has also considered the history of opera in Latin America side by side with literary works, a gesture this book adopts. See Kuss's prologue in which she cites Roberto González Echevarría on the difficulty of writing a history of the Latin American novel autonomous of European literary historiography, a predicament Kuss identifies also for writing the history of music in Latin America: "Likewise, when musicologists apply regulative concepts devised by Europeans for the European experience to compositions by Latin Americans—the simplest example of which is the indiscriminate transfer of style-period labels and/or aesthetic movements—they are dooming one historical experience and concomitant aesthetics to representation through the discursive modality of another" (xvii). Indeed, going further, it is not difficult to see how European literary and musical histories can also adversely affect the evaluation of European works too that for various reasons may not conform to their disciplinary parameters.
7. Carl Dahlhaus and Sieghart Döhring et al., eds., *Pipers Enzyklopädie des Musiktheaters*, 5 vols. (Munich: Piper, 1986); Stanley Sadie, ed., *History of Opera* (New York: W. W. Norton); Malena Kuss, "Das Lateinamerikanische Libretto," in *Die Musik in Geschichte und Gegenwart*, ed. Ludwig Finscher (Kassel, Germany: Bärenreiter-Verlag, 1994–2008), 5:1196–1203.
8. Donald J. Grout, *A Short History of Opera* (New York: Columbia University Press, 1954), 492–93.
9. Stanley Sadie, ed., *The New Grove Book of Operas* (New York: St. Martin's Press, 1997).
10. Carolyn Abbate and Roger Parker, *A History of Opera* (New York: W. W. Norton, 2012), 524.
11. Carol A. Hess, *Representing the Good Neighbor: Music, Difference, and the Pan American Dream* (Oxford: Oxford University Press, 2013), 140.
12. Hess, 142.
13. Gonzalo Aguilar, "The National Opera: A Migrant Genre of Imperial Expansion," *Journal of Latin American Cultural Studies* 12, no. 1 (2003): 84. As Hervé Lacombe notes, the spread of opera through the Americas was hardly a uniform process. Rather, its development depended on several

factors, such as the degree of Westernization or a country's wealth. Hervé Lacombe, *Géographie de l'opéra au XXe siècle* (Paris: Fayard, 2007), 188.
14. John Rosselli, "Latin America and Italian Opera: A Process of Interaction, 1810–1930," *Revista de Musicología* 16, no. 1 (1993): 139.
15. John Rosselli, "The Opera Business and the Italian Immigrant Community in Latin America 1820–1930: The Example of Buenos Aires," *Past and Present* 127 (May 1990), 165–67. See also Benjamin Walton's detailed study of how Italian opera came to acquire canonical status in the River Plate: "Canons of Real and Imagined Opera: Buenos Aires and Montevideo, 1810–1860," in *The Oxford Handbook of the Operatic Canon*, ed. Cormac Newark and William Weber (Oxford: Oxford University Press, 2020), 271–91.
16. Rosselli, "The Opera Business," 162.
17. Aníbal Enrique Cetrangolo, "Aida Times Two: How Italian Veterans of Two Historic Aida Productions Shaped Argentina's Music History," *Cambridge Opera Journal* 28, no. 1 (2016): 80.
18. See Josmar F. Lopes, who describes the actual event as well as its permutation into Franco Zeffirelli's film, *Il giovane Toscanini* (1988). Josmar F. Lopes, "Opera Personalities in Brazil—Part One: 'The Young Toscanini," *Curtain Going Up!* (blog), November 9, 2012, https://josmarlopes.wordpress.com/2012/11/09/opera-people-in-brazil-part-one-personalities.
19. John Dizikes, *Opera in America: A Cultural History* (New Haven, CT: Yale University Press, 1993), 124. For Dizikes, the Havana-based companies, besides staging a new repertory in the United States, played a role in developing a taste for excellent and exciting singing: "The new feature of the group that bowled over American audiences was its cluster of superior singers, America's introduction to star singers on a large scale. Everything else yielded to the excitement kindled by their presence" (123).
20. Rosselli, "Latin America and Italian Opera," 142.
21. Rosselli, 141.
22. See Robert Stevenson, "Buenos Aires," in *The New Grove Dictionary of Opera*, ed. Stanley Sadie (London: Macmillan Reference, 1997), 1:633–35.
23. "Caruso Returns with South American Gold," *New York Times*, November 5, 1917, https://www.nytimes.com/1917/11/05/archives/caruso-returns-with-south-american-gold-sang-in-forty-performances.html.
24. "Bomb Exploded at Caruso Performance; Six Injured in Havana Opera Panic," *New York Times*, June 14, 1920, https://www.nytimes.com/1920/06/14/archives/bomb-exploded-at-caruso-performance-six-injured-in-havana-opera.html.
25. Michael Scott, *Maria Meneghini Callas* (Boston: Northeastern University Press, 1991), 58.
26. Margarita Pollini, *Palco, cazuela y paraíso: Las historias más insólitas del Teatro Colón* (Buenos Aires: Sudamericana, 2001), 104–05.
27. For a sociological study of the "opera fanatic" at the Teatro Colón, see Claudio Benzecry, who views it as an obsession displayed not only in the hallowed spaces of the opera house, or the lines outside the theater

as fans wait to obtain tickets, but also in other practices and media "from Walkman CD players, background radio, specialized shows, and home listening to public DVD viewings, conferences, classes with music examples, amateur recitals, minor opera houses in and outside the city, crossover shows at sports stadiums, and trips to Europe and the United States with the sole aim of attending live opera." Claudio Benzecry, *The Opera Fanatic: Ethnography of an Obsession* (Chicago: University of Chicago Press, 2011), 12.

28. Joseph Kerman, *Opera as Drama* (Berkeley: University of California Press, 1988), 91.
29. David J. Levin, introduction to *Opera through Other Eyes*, ed. David J. Levin (Stanford, CA: Stanford University Press, 1993), 9. Citing the difficulty of understanding sung words, Paul Robinson argues against "the overevaluation of a textual approach to opera," in "A Deconstructive Postscript: Reading Libretti and Misreading Opera," in *Reading Opera*, ed. Arthur Groos and Roger Parker (Princeton, NJ: Princeton University Press, 1988), 329. Since then, supertitles at opera theaters and subtitles in video recordings have turned the act of reading into a meaningful aspect of the operatic experience for many.
30. Alicia Alonso, *Diálogos con la danza* (Buenos Aires: Galerna, 1988), 84–87.
31. Alonso's own career may denote a more complicated relationship between her rise as a practitioner of classical ballet and her status as a Cuban dancer. Lester Tomé quotes a review by Edwin Denby written at the onset of Alonso's career in New York in 1945 in which an ethnic prism invokes clichés about Cuba: "Alonso is a delightfully young and very Latin Giselle, quick, clear, direct in her relation to her lover. She is passionate rather than sensuous. She is brilliant in allegro, not so convincing in sustained grace. . . . She has little patience for those slow-moving, vaporous effects that we Northerners find so touching." Lester Tomé, "*Giselle* in a Cuban Accent," in *The Cambridge Companion to Ballet*, ed. Marion Kent (Cambridge: Cambridge University Press, 2007), 263–64. Tomé also notes that Alonso's version of *Giselle* would be incorporated into the repertoire of several theaters in Europe and elsewhere, including the Opéra National de Paris, where the ballet had been first performed.
32. Jorge Luis Borges, "El escritor argentino y la tradición," in *Discusión* (Buenos Aires: Emecé Editores, 1976), 162; Jorge Luis Borges, "The Argentine Writer and Tradition," in *Selected Non-Fictions*, ed. Eliot Weinberger, trans. Esther Allen (New York: Viking, 1999), 427.
33. José Martí, "Nuestra América," in *Obras completas* (Havana: Editorial Nacional de Cuba, 1963–1966), 6:20; "Our America," in *Selected Writings*, trans. Esther Allen (New York: Penguin, 2002), 293.
34. Theodor Adorno, "Bourgeois Opera," trans. and ed. David J. Levin, in *Opera through Other Eyes*, 29.
35. Hans Werner Henze, *Music and Politics: Collected Writings, 1953–81*, trans. Peter Labanyi (London: Faber and Faber, 1982), 201. Henze also comments on how the Cuban Revolution transformed the cultures of opera and ballet: "Now the mink coats have emigrated to Miami, and the opera house

has a different audience; . . . Alicia Alonso, a great ballerina returned from the United States and built up the national ballet company, which with its classical and modern repertoire enjoys international success" (201).

36. Quoted by Leonardo Depestre Catony, *Españoles en la memoria habanera* (Madrid: Verbum, 2021), 91. For Martí's reviews of concerts by José White, the Cuban violinist, in Mexico City in 1875, and performances by Patti in New York in 1884, see Robert Stevenson, "Musical Silhouettes Drawn by José Martí," *Inter-American Music Review* 14, no. 2 (1995): 21–37.

37. José Martí, "Los zapaticos de rosa," in *La Edad de Oro* (Miami: La Moderna Poesía, 1983), 188. Unless otherwise indicated, all translations are mine.

38. On the poem's possible settings, variously identified as beaches near Havana or New York, see Luisa Isabel Rodríguez Bello, "Estructuras ideológicas y estéticas en 'Los zapaticos de rosa' de José Martí," *Investigación y Postgrado* 28, no. 1 (2013): 19–20.

39. On the identity of Marie, often identified with Martí's daughter, María Mantilla, and with the poem's Pilar, see Rodríguez Bello, 20–21.

40. Roberto Fernández Retamar, "Introducción a *La Edad de Oro*," *Santiago* 87 (1999): link.gale.com/apps/doc/A146628762/IFME?u=usocal_main&sid=IFME&xid=b8465bae. To compensate for the dearth of Latin American subjects in the magazine, Fernández Retamar underscores the presence of Asia and Africa in two essays: "Un paseo por la tierra de los anamitas" (A Promenade through the Land of the Annamites) and "Cuentos de elefantes" (Elephant Stories). In the spirit of his canonical essay on Shakespeare's Caliban as a Third World emblem, Fernández Retamar retrieves *La Edad de Oro* for his own decolonial project sustained on Latin America's cultural autonomy.

41. José Martí, "Músicos, poetas y pintores," in *La Edad de Oro* (Miami: La Moderna Poesía, 1983), 158–78.

42. For an analysis of Martí's six translated texts as part of a "literary fraternity" that would contribute to beauty and harmony around the world, see María del Rocío García Rey, "Transpensar para la infancia," *Pacarina del Sur: Revista de Pensamiento Crítico Latinoamericano* 5, no. 17 (October–December 2013). On Martí's notions of translation versus those of George Steiner, see Beatriz Colombí, "José Martí: Traducir, transpensar," *Inti: Revista de Literatura Hispánica* 49–50 (1999): 60–69.

43. Martí, "La imagen del rey," in *Obras completas*, 16:105.

44. Estanislao del Campo, *Fausto y poesías completas* (Buenos Aires: Sopena, 1969), 13; Estanislao del Campo, *Faust,* trans. Walter Owen (Buenos Aires: Walter Owen, 1943), 13.

45. Enrique Anderson Imbert, "Formas del Fausto," *Revista Iberoamericana* 32, no. 61 (1966), 12.

46. Nancy Vogeley, "Italian Opera in Early National Mexico," *Modern Language Quarterly* 57, no. 2 (June 1996): 286.

47. Josefina Ludmer, *El género gauchesco: Un tratado sobre la patria* (Buenos Aires: Libros Perfil, 2000), 212.

48. Said refers to the renovation of Cairo under Khedive Ismail, the Ottoman viceroy, which needed "a new class of city-dwellers whose tastes and

requirements portended the expansion of a local market geared to expensive imported goods," which included "operas, composers, singers, conductors, sets, and costumes." Edward Said, *Culture and Imperialism* (New York: Vintage Books, 1994), 127.
49. Eugenio Cambaceres, *Sin rumbo* (Buenos Aires: Stock Cero, 2005), 42.
50. Rubén Darío, *Viajes de un cosmopolita extremo*, ed. Graciela Montaldo (Buenos Aires: Fondo de Cultura Económica, 2013).
51. Rubén Darío, "Sonatina," in *Prosas profanas y otros poemas* (Madrid: Castalia, 1983), 97; Rubén Darío, "Sonatina," in *Selected Poems of Rubén Darío*, trans. Lysander Kemp (Austin: University of Texas Press: 1965), 52. Kemp's translation does not include the word "unanimous".
52. Rubén Darío, "Divagación," in *Prosas profanas y otros poemas* (Madrid: Clásicos Castalia, 1983), 92.
53. Rubén Darío, "El cisne," in *Prosas profanas*, 134; Rubén Darío, "The Swan," in *An Anthology of Spanish American Modernismo: In English Translation, with Spanish Text*, ed. Kelly Washbourne, trans. Kelly Washbourne and Sergio Waisman (New York: Modern Language Association of America, 2007), 103.
54. Darío, *Prosas profanas*, 86–87.
55. Judging from the number of allusions to the composer in his works, Stevenson speculates that José Martí, also a towering figure of Spanish American *modernismo*, might have been a fervent admirer of Wagner. See Robert Stevenson, "Musical Silhouettes Drawn by José Martí (1853–1895)," *Inter-American Music Review* 14, no. 2 (Winter–Spring 1995): 24n25.
56. Cathy L. Jrade, *Modernismo, Modernity, and the Development of Spanish American Literature* (Austin: University of Texas Press, 1998), 105. On Wagner's *Oper und Drama,* which posits the ideal union of music and words in opera, and its possible influence in Darío and other poets, see André Fiorussi, "Preceitos poéticos-musicais de Wagner na poesia modernista hispano-americana," *ALEA* 21, no. 2 (May–August 2019): 173–89. On Darío's writing about the premiere of Wagner's *Die Walküre* in Madrid, see Almudena Mejías Alonso and Cristina Bravo Rozas, "Visiones teatrales de Rubén Darío," *Anales de Literatura Hispanoamericana* 46 (2017): 101–15.
57. Darío, *Prosas profanas*, 134.
58. Rubén Darío, "The Swan," in *Selected Poems of Rubén Darío*, trans. Lysander Kemp (Austin: University of Texas, 1965), 103.
59. Darío, *Prosas profanas*, 87. The ironic allusion to Whitman as the poet of "lo demás" (87; "all the rest") is, of course, emblematic of Darío's highly selective poetic vision in which not all themes are poetical subjects. The phrase "nuestra América" recalls "Nuestra América," discussed earlier.
60. Free from the facile exoticism of some European works, Darío later deploys, in "A Roosevelt," names from the pre-Hispanic past to signify Latin America's resistance to the United States, appearing side by side with a reverent invocation of Spain and the conquest. In an uncanny instance of *mestizaje*, Darío reunites the two sides in a declamation against a powerful neighbor that appears to be nothing short of operatic.

If Darío would grow to qualify the European embellishments of his first books, swans and monarchs are hardly absent from later poems, such as "Los cisnes" and "Al rey Oscar" in *Cantos de vida y Esperanza* (1904).
61. Benzecry summarizes the convergence of immigration—especially from Italy—and opera in Buenos Aires, including the periods when Darío lived there. See Benzecry, *The Opera Fanatic*, 28–30.
62. Ricardo Jaimes Freyre, *Castalia bárbara* (La Paz: Los Andes, 1918), 55.
63. For other poets in Latin America and Spain who wrote on Wagnerian motifs, see Alberto Acereda and Rigoberto Guevara, *Modernism, Rubén Darío, and the Poetics of Despair* (Dallas: University Press of America, 2024), 17–18.
64. Carlos Fuentes, *Instinto de Inez* (Buenos Aires: Aguilar, 2001), 24-25; Carlos Fuentes, *Inez: A Novel*, trans. Margaret Sayers Peden (Orlando, FL: Harcourt, 2002), 94.
65. Carlos Fuentes, "How I Wrote One of My Books," in *Myself with Others: Selected Essays* (New York: Noonday Press, 1988), 43.
66. Mentioned in Chapter 3, Hamel's *Caruso a Cuba*, an opera about opera inspired by *Como un mensajero tuyo*, simplifies Montero's tale of multiple ethnicities by erasing all references to the Chinese in Cuba and focusing exclusively on characters of African and European descent. For an analysis of Montero's novel, see Roberto Ignacio Díaz, "Silencios de Caruso o la ópera en La Habana," *América: Cahiers du CRICCAL* (Sorbonne Nouvelle) 31 (2004): 153–59.
67. Alejo Carpentier, *Concierto Barroco*, trans. Asa Zatz (Tulsa, OK: Council Oak Books, 1988), 114.

CHAPTER 2

1. Richard Leppert, "Opera, Aesthetic Violence, and the Imposition of Modernity: *Fitzcarraldo*," in *Beyond the Soundtrack: Representing Music in Cinema*, ed. Daniel Goldmark et al. (Berkeley: University of California Press, 2007), 102.
2. Eduardo Galeano, *Open Veins of Latin America: Five Centuries of the Pillage of a Continent*, trans. Cedric Belfrage (New York: Monthly Review Press, 1996), 102.
3. Alain Pacquier, *Les chemins du baroque dans le Nouveau Monde* (Paris: Fayard, 1996), 204.
4. Benjamin Ramm, "The Beautiful Theater in the Heart of the Amazon Rainforest," *BBC Culture*, https://www.bbc.com/culture/article/20170316-the-beautiful-theatre-in-the-heart-of-the-amazon-rainforest.
5. Derek Malcolm, "Les Blank: *Burden of Dreams*," *The Guardian*, January 12, 2000, https://www.theguardian.com/film/2000/jan/13/derekmalcolmscenturyoffilm.
6. In his critically informed biographical sketch of Fitzcarrald, Joshua Lund writes: "While I have found no evidence that he may have included opera among his passions for European culture, the meteoric trajectory of his

life and the poetic justice of his tragic death certainly had something operatic about it." Joshua Lund, *Werner Herzog* (Urbana: University of Illinois Press, 2020).

7. Mário Ypiranga Monteiro, *Teatro Amazonas* (Manaus: Editora Valer and Governo do Estado do Amazonas, 2003), 17. See also Daniel Balderston, who critiques Herzog's role in setting the default image of Latin America and opera. Daniel Balderston, "Opera," in *Encyclopedia of Contemporary Latin American and Caribbean Cultures*, ed. Balderston et al. (London: Routledge, 2001), 3:1076.

8. Lund, *Werner Herzog*, 104, 111.

9. The Teatro Amazonas is of course not the only opera house in Latin America whose architecture mimics Europe; Rio de Janeiro's Theatro Municipal, for instance, was inspired by the Palais Garnier, Paris's grand nineteenth-century theater. Conversely, Paris's Opéra Bastille was designed by Carlos Ott, the Uruguayan-Canadian architect..

10. José Seráfico, "Teatro Amazonas: Símbolo de quê?" *Ciência e Cultura* 61, no. 3 (2009): 37–38.

11. Ana Maria Daou, *A belle époque amazônica* (Rio de Janeiro: Jorge Zahar, 2004), 36–37, 53.

12. Elizabeth Bishop, "To Robert Lowell," in *Poems, Prose, and Letters*, ed. Robert Giroux and Lloyd Schwartz (New York: Library of America, 2008), 832.

13. Bishop.

14. The Teatro Amazonas was not the only opera house the Amazon, and not all operas staged in the region were European imports. See, for instance, Sarah J. Townsend, who analyzes José Cândido da Gama Malcher's *Iara* (1895), an opera composed for Belém's Theatro da Paz, sung not in Portuguese but in Italian interspersed with words from the indigenous Nheengatu language. Drawing on Marx's concept of commodity fetishism such as Theodor Adorno saw in Wagner's operas, Townsend's argument also connects the rubber trade and opera production. Sarah J. Townsend, "The Siren's Song; or, When an Amazonian Iara Sang Opera (in Italian) on a Belle Époque Stage," *Latin American Theatre Review* 52, no. 2 (2019): 149–67.

15. Julian Barnes, *Flaubert's Parrot* (New York: Vintage, 1990), 98.

16. On Barnes's passage in the context of magical realism, see Lois Parkinson Zamora and Wendy B. Farris, "Introduction: Daiquiri Birds and Flaubertian Parrot(ie)s," in *Magical Realism: Theory, History, Community*, ed. Zamora and Farris (Durham, NC: Duke University Press, 1995), 1–3.

17. Monteiro, *Teatro Amazonas*, 479.

18. Ralph P. Locke, *Music and the Exotic from the Renaissance to Mozart* (Cambridge: Cambridge University Press, 2015), 3.

19. Drawing on Bakhtin, Timothy D. Taylor calls opera "the polyglossic art" and views its origin and growth in the "jumble of different musics and musical practices, representations and representational practices, that facilitated the representation of new peoples and new social roles

and relationships in early modern Europe." Timothy D. Taylor, *Beyond Exoticism: Western Music and the World* (Durham, NC: Duke University Press, 2007), 34.

20. After analyzing several instances of Orientalism and other forms of "otherness" throughout the history of opera, Lindenberger concludes: "A genuine historically based aesthetics would encourage us to rethink the common wisdom that has accrued over the years about long-familiar works. It would ask us to reframe the questions we ask ourselves about these works, to attempt to locate the most appropriate contexts within which to ponder their meaning, their formal properties, and the power they exercise over us." Herbert Lindenberger, *Opera in History: From Monteverdi to Cage* (Stanford, CA: Stanford University Press, 1998), 189.

21. Michael V. Pisani, *Imagining Native America in Music* (New Haven, CT: Yale University Press, 2005), 30. Even earlier, *Le Grand Bal de la douairière de Billebahaut* (1626), a ballet performed for Louis XIII also at the Louvre, had a character named Atabalipa (a variant of Atahualpa, the last Inca ruler), played by a hydrocephalic dwarf (21). As Miriam K. Whaples would have it, this dwarf spoke "some particularly egregious inanities." Miriam K. Whaples, "Early Exoticism Revisited," in *The Exotic in Western Music*, ed. Jonathan Bellman (Boston: Northeastern University Press, 1996), 7.

22. Olivia Bloechl, *Native American Song at the Frontiers of Early Modern Music* (Cambridge: Cambridge University Press, 2008), 161. For a full list of extant works by Lully that feature "Indians," "savages" or "Americans," see Bloechl, 156–59. As Bloechl explains, the inhabitants of the New World in Lully's works were not always associated with exoticism, but deployed other colonial strategies, including mimicry as conceived by Homi Bhabha.

23. Richard Frohock, "Sir William Davenant's American Operas," *Modern Language Review* 96, no. 2 (April 2001): 324.

24. Curtis Price, *"The Indian Queen,"* in *The New Grove Book of Operas*, ed. Stanley Sadie (New York: St. Martin's Press, 1997), 2:797.

25. Jan Breslauer, "Into Uncharted Waters," *Los Angeles Times*, October 5, 1997, https://www.latimes.com/archives/la-xpm-1997-oct-05-ca-39314-story.html.

26. On Aguilar's feminist reworking of history, especially the Spanish conquest of Central America, see José María Mantero, "Hacia la interculturalidad: Rosario Aguilar y *La niña blanca y los pájaros sin pies*," *Romance Studies* 28, no. 4 (November 2010), 260. For an analysis of the musical, literary, and theatrical choices of what she calls Sellars's "Mayan passion," see Susan McClary, *The Passions of Peter Sellars: Staging the Music* (Ann Arbor: University of Michigan Press, 2019), 143–61.

27. Jürgen Maehder, "Alvise Giusti's Libretto *Motezuma* and the Conquest of Mexico in Eighteenth-Century Italian *Opera Seria*," in *Vivaldi, "Motezuma" and the Opera Seria: Essays on a Newly Discovered Work and Its Background*, ed. Michael Talbot (Turnhout, Belgium: Brepols, 2008), 63–80.

28. See, for instance, Bernardo Pasquini's *Il Colombo, overo l'India scoperta* (1690), an opera composed and performed in Rome. As Pisani notes, its

libretto, by Pietro Ottoboni, "unfolds in a series of ludicrous love intrigues between fictional characters of opposing sides" including an Indian king who falls in love with Columbus's wife. See Pisani, *Imagining Native America in Music* 32, 347n23.

29. Maehder cites Algarotti's description of the operatic potential of the subject of Moctezuma in the first edition of the *Saggio sopra l'opera in musica*, whose only surviving copy is housed in Venice's Biblioteca Marciana. In Algarotti's translated words, an opera on Moctezuma "would provide a fine opportunity for a capable *maestro di cappella* to transport us to music through a new world"; these transports would be achieved by the use of instruments little used in Europe, "or through certain melodic particulars; seeking out not new modes but strange cantilenas." Maehder, "Alvise Giusti's Libretto," 75.

30. Pierpaolo Polzonetti, "Opera as Process," in *The Cambridge Companion to Eighteenth-Century Opera*, ed. Anthony R. DelDonna and Pierpaolo Polzonetti (Cambridge: Cambridge University Press, 2009), 12.

31. On Frederick's identification with Montezuma, as well as his rich, long-standing relationship with Algarotti, see Pierpaolo Polzonetti, *Italian Opera in the Age of the American Revolution* (Cambridge: Cambridge University Press, 2011), 107–15. In 1753, Frederick wrote to Algarotti: "If the operas you are attending are bad, you will find a new one here that might surpass them. It is *Montezuma*. I chose this subject and I am working on it at the present moment. As you can well imagine, I take the part of Montezuma, Cortez will be the tyrant, and consequently [the opera] will likely discharge, in the music as well, some good jibes against the barbarity of the Ch[ristian] r[eligion]" (112). On the connection between Graun's opera and Voltaire's *Alzire,* which has a Peruvian theme and is the source for Verdi's *Alzira*, see Ernest Helm, *Music at the Court of Frederick the Great* (Norman: University of Oklahoma Press, 1960), 67–70.

32. Booklet in Carl Heinrich Graun, *Montezuma*, libretto by Frederick II, Deutsche Kammerakademie, Johannes Goritzki, with Encarnación Vázquez, María Luisa Tamez, et al., Capriccio 60 032-2, 1992, CD, 63, 65.

33. For dates and settings of these performances, see Maehder, "Alvise Giusti's Libretto," 76–77.

34. Polzonetti, "Opera as Process," 21.

35. See John A. Rice, "Montezuma at Eszterház: A Pasticcio on a New World Theme," in *Joseph Haydn & die "Neue Welt": Musik- und Kulturgeschichtliche Perspektiven*, ed. Walter Reicher and Wolfgang Fuhrmann (Vienna: Hollitzer, 2019), 231–42.

36. First performed at the Théâtre de l'Académie Impériale de Musique, the opera was originally conceived as propaganda to justify Napoleon's invasion of Spain. After Napoleon's fall, Spontini crafted new versions of the opera. See Anselm Gerhard, "*Fernand Cortez, ou La conquête du Mexique*," in *The New Grove Book of Operas*, ed. Stanley Sadie (New York: St. Martin's Press, 1997), 2:156.

37. Pisani, *Imagining Native America in Music,* 346n49.

38. Whaples, "Early Exoticism Revisited," 19.
39. Cecilia Ligoria, bonus material, *Fernand Cortez*, by Gaspare Spontini, Dynamic, 2019, Blu-ray disc.
40. W. Anthony Sheppard, "Exoticism," in *The Oxford Handbook of Opera*, ed. Helen M. Greenwald (Oxford: Oxford University Press, 2014), 806.
41. Martin Brody, "Sessions, Roger (Huntington)," in *The New Grove Dictionary of Opera*, ed. by Stanley Sadie (London: MacMillan Reference Limited, 1997), 4:333.
42. Andrea Olmstead, "The Plum'd Serpent: Antonio Borgese and Roger Sessions's 'Montezuma," *Tempo* 152 (March 1985): 16.
43. Alastair Williams, "Voices of the Other: Wolfgang Rihm's Music Drama *Die Eroberung von Mexico*," *Journal of the Royal Musical Association* 129, no. 2 (2004): 263–64.
44. W. Anthony Sheppard, "Exoticism," 807.
45. Williams, "Voices of the Other," 240.
46. Wolfgang Rihm, libretto to Rihm, *Die Eroberung von Mexico*, performed by Richard Salter, Renate Behle, the Chor der Hamburgischen Staatsorchester and the Philharmonisches Staatsorchester Hamburg, conducted by Ingo Metzmacher, NDR, 1992, p. 4.
47. In a serendipitous meeting of history-based opera and literary archeology, Rihm's libretto preserves for posterity the four stanzas of "Poema XV" in Paz's first version of *Raíz del hombre* (1937). Along with all other poems but three, "Poema XV" was excised from later versions of the text in *Libertad bajo palabra* and *Obra poética*. The libretto's last stanza reads thus in the original Spanish: "Bajo esta muerte, Amor dichoso y mudo, / no hay venas, piel ni sangre, / sino la muerte sola: / frenéticos silencios, / eternos, confundidos, / inacabable Amor manando muerte." Octavio Paz, *Obras completas* (Mexico City: Fondo de Cultura Económica, 1999), 13:69–70.
48. On the silent character of Malinche dressed like an actress from Japan's Noh drama, see Arturo Reverter, "La conquista a ambos lados del sueño," *Crítica*, October 10, 2013, https://www.beckmesser.com/la-conquista-a-ambos-lados-del-sueno/. On the interchangeability of exotic cultures, see Rubén Gallo on Marcel Proust's first draft of *À la recherche du temps perdu*, in which South America is replaced by Algeria. Rubén Gallo, *Proust's Latin Americans* (Baltimore: Johns Hopkins University Press, 2014), 10.
49. At the Teatro Real, *Die Eroberung von Mexico* was part of a season that also included Peter Sellars's staging of Purcell's *The Indian Queen* (1695), mentioned earlier. Gerard Mortier, the theater's new artistic director at the time, sought to confront Madrid opera audiences with the legacy of the Spanish conquest of the Americas within, and in contrast with, the larger history of European imperial endeavors. Gerard Mortier, *In audatia veritas: Reflexiones sobre la ópera, el arte y la política*, ed. Mar Fosca (Almería, Spain: Editorial Confluencias, 2015), 171.
50. William Ashbrook, "*Furioso nell'isola di San Domingo, Il*," in *The New Grove Dictionary of Opera*, ed. Stanley Sadie, 2:316.
51. Sylvie Bouissou, *Rameau: Musicien des Lumières* (Paris: Fayard, 2014), 370–73.

52. On *mestizaje* in *Les Indes galantes*, see Roberto Ignacio Díaz, "Rameau's Replay: The Reprise of Peru at the Opéra Bastille," *L'Esprit Créateur* 62, no. 2 (Summer 2022), 104–18.
53. For a comparative analysis of Voltaire's play and Verdi's opera, see Guido Paduano, *"Alzire* e *Alzira:* varietà di colonialismi," in *Le arti della scena e l'esotismo in età moderna,* ed. Francesco Cotticelli and Paologiovanni Maione (Naples: Turchini Edizioni, 2006), 531–53.
54. Pablo Macalupú-Cumpén, "Resignificación en la producción operística peruana: crítica social y política en *Alzira* de Verdi," *ANTEC Revista Peruana de Investigación Musical* 4, no. 1 (August 2020): 29.
55. Analyzing race in Rivas's *Don Álvaro o la fuerza del sino*, on which *La forza del destino* is based, Lisa Surwillo underscores Don Álvaro's racial otherness—his "paradoxical position as both Spanish and non-white"—in the context of Spain's myth of national homogeneity, an axiom shared with other European countries. Lisa Surwillo, "Speaking of Race in *Don Álvaro,"* *Revista Hispánica Moderna* 63, no. 1 (June 2010): 52.
56. Francesco Maria Piave, libretto to Giuseppe Verdi, *La forza del destino,* performed by Leontyne Price, Plácido Domingo, Sherrill Milnes and the London Symphony Orchestra conducted by James Levine, BMG Entertainment, 1998, CD, 38.
57. Malena Kuss, "Das lateinamerikanische Libretto," in *Die Musik in Geschichte und Gegenwart*, ed. Ludwig Finscher, trans. Thomas M. Höpfner (Kassel, Germany: Bärenreiter-Verlag, 1994–2008), 5:1200.
58. Robert Stevenson, "Pasta, Carlo Enrico," in *The New Grove Dictionary of Opera,* ed. Stanley Sadie, 3:906.
59. Antonio Ghislanzoni, *Atahualpa: Dramma lirico in quattro atti* (Milan: Tipografia A. Gattinoni, 1875), 41.
60. Kuss, "Das lateinamerikanische Libretto," 5:1200.
61. Antonio Ghislanzoni, *Atahualpa: Drama lírico en cuatro actos* (Lima: Imprenta de la Patria, 1877), 5.
62. Joseph Conrad, *Nostromo* (New York: Everyman's Library, 1992), 144.
63. O. Henry, *Cabbages and Kings* (New York: Doubleday, Page & Co., 1920), 132.
64. Pablo Neruda, "La United Fruit Co.," in *Canto general* (Barcelona: Seix-Barral, 1982), 214.
65. Discursive convergences of Latin America and some kind of comic opera come into the fore often in contrast with Europe. Consider a biography of Margot Fonteyn, by Meredith Daneman, in which the English dancer is said to dismiss an episode involving her Panamanian husband in his own country as "yet another comic scene from the long-running opera of Latin politics." Meredith Daneman, *Margot Fonteyn: A Life* (New York: Penguin, 2005), 369. In Joan Didion's short travel piece "In Bogotá" (1973), the author observes the servers at the Hostería del Libertador in Zipaquirá: "little boys, twelve or thirteen years old, dressed in tailcoats and white gloves and taught to serve as if this small inn on an Andean precipice were Vienna under the Hapsburgs." Didion's concluding description of the serving of wine suggests a performance as one might

find in an operetta: "I had never seen and would perhaps never see again the residuum of European custom so movingly and pointlessly observed." Joan Didion, "In Bogotá," in *The White Album* (New York: Farrar, Straus and Giroux, 2009), 196–97. Importantly, Latin America is not the only region in the Global South were opera and politics are linked. In a novel about Vietnam, the narrator observes: "Before us was the grand Grecian façade of the National Assembly, formerly the city's opera house. From here the politicians managed the shabby comic operetta of our country, an off-key travesty starring plump divas in white suits and mustachioed prima donnas in custom-tailored military uniforms." Viet Thahn Nguyen, *The Sympathizer* (New York: Grove Press, 2015), 23.

66. M. Elizabeth C. Bartlett defines the opéra bouffe as "a mid- to late-19th-century comic opera in which a witty spoken dialogue and sparkling, light music combine in a genre designed to entertain. . . . It differs from *opéra comique* of the same period in its more frankly humorous tone, often bordering on farce, and its use of parody and satire (literary, musical, social and sometimes political)." M. Elizabeth C. Bartlett, "Opéra bouffe," in *The New Grove Dictionary of Opera*, ed. Stanley Sadie, 3:684.

67. Georgine Maria-Magdalene Balk, *Militarismus in "La Grande Duchesse de Gerolstein" und Exotismus in "La Périchole" von Jacques Offenbach* (Munich: Der GRIN Verlag, 2004), 30.

68. Henri Meilhac and Ludovic Halévy, libretto to Jacques Offenbach, *La Périchole*, performed by Régine Crespin, Alain Vanzo, Jules Bastin, the Choeurs de l'Opéra du Rhin and the Orchestre Philharmonique de Strasbourg conducted by Alain Lombard, Erato, 1977, CD, 33.

69. Susan McClary explores the connections between the "Habanera," exoticism and the erotic. As she states, "it lends a touch of 'authentic' (rather than concocted) exoticism, even if its African-Latin origins scarcely seem appropriate for an opera set in Seville. Yet Bizet's lack of interest in imitating the 'correct' ethnic musics does not betray a lack of discrimination. He was concerned with the *aura* of exoticism and with the affective or rhetorical consequences of his choices." Susan McClary, *George Bizet, Carmen* (Cambridge: Cambridge University Press, 1992), 74–75. The "Habanera" also contributes to Carmen's physical eroticism: "An instrumental vamp sets up and maintains an African-Latin rhythmic impulse that engages the lower torso, inviting hip swings in response. She thus makes us aware of her body in the context of a genre—*opéra-comique*—that usually offers evidence of physicality only through highly sentimentalized guises" (75). See also Hervé Lacombe and Christine Rodriguez, *La Habanera de Carmen: Naissance d'un tube* (Paris: Fayard, 2014); Nelly Furman, *George Bizet's* Carmen (New York: Oxford University Press, 2020).

70. In yet another transatlantic fusion, it is worth recalling the character of Preziosilla in Verdi's *La forza del destino*, yet another gypsy girl whose ethnic otherness is mirrored by Don Alvaro, the Peruvian mestizo.

71. On the passage from an idea of Spain as hegemonic or dominant to marginal or exotic, see Jesús Torrecilla, *España exótica: La formación de la*

imagen española moderna (Boulder, CO: Society of Spanish and Spanish-American Studies, 2004), 11.

72. Komische Oper Berlin Spielplanheft 2012/2013, 36, https://issuu.com/komische_oper/docs/kop_spzh_2012_13_120216_final

73. Jürgen Schebera, "*Shady Dealing:* The Disadvantages of Exile," in *Der Kuhhandel*, by Kurt Weill, and performed by Lucy Peacock, Eberhard Büchner and the Kölner Rundfunk Orchester conducted by Jan Latham-König, Capriccio, 1992, CD, 30–31.

74. Robert Vambery, libretto to Kurt Weill, *Der Kuhhandel*, 68.

75. The ties that bind *Ciboulette* with French musical-theater history are even stronger if one considers, as Patrick O'Connor explains, that the work was "at once an innovation, the beginning of a long series of light operas written in a nostalgic vein for the Paris stage, and an homage to Offenbach, Hervé and Olivier Métra (who appears as a character)." Patrick O' Connor, "*Ciboulette*," in *The New Grove Dictionary of Opera*, ed. Stanley Sadie, 1:860. Indeed, Offenbach as well as his librettists, Meilhac and Halévy, are alluded to directly in the libretto; when a character enquires about "Monsieur Offenbach?" the answer is "Il est chez Meilhac" (9), thereby invoking a previous operatic culture (*Ciboulette* is set in 1867) in which a work about Latin America such as *La Périchole* shares the stage with works that take place elsewhere. Robert de Flers and François de Croisset, libretto to *Ciboulette*, https://reynaldo-hahn.net/Textes/livrets/ciboulette.pdf.

76. Rubén Gallo, *Proust's Latin Americans*, 69. Hahn's first opera, *L'Île du rêve* (1898), had flaunted a sense of the exotic; adapted from a text by Pierre Loti, it was set in Tahiti, not anywhere in the Americas.

77. Susan Graham, *French Operetta Arias*, City of Birmingham Symphony Orchestra, Yves Abel, recorded June 2001, Erato 0927-42106-2, 2002, CD.

78. For a podcast on the composition and performance of *Toi, c'est moi* in Paris, see Marcel Quillévéré, episode 33, "Moisés Simons et Joséphine Baker," *Carrefour des Amériques à Cuba*, Radio France, August 17, 2022.

79. By García Márquez's "polysemic manner" Eötvös means the possibility of interpreting the plot's events variously as miracles, the demon's work, or just natural phenomena. See Aurora Rivals, *Entretiens autour des cinq premiers operas de Peter Eötvös* (Nantes, France: Éditions Aedam Musicae, 2012), 45. One of the critics was Andrew Clements, who wrote: "By removing its 18th-century Latin American context almost entirely, the power of Márquez's magic realism is neutralized, leaving just an unsavoury story not far removed from Ken Russell's *The Devils*, with an ending that seems carelessly inconclusive." Andrew Clements, "*Love and Other Demons*," The Guardian, August 11, 2008, https://www.theguardian.com/music/2008/aug/12/classicalmusicandopera1.

80. For the Glyndebourne production, as Clements describes it, director Silviu Purcarete sought to exacerbate the outlandishness of the story through the "lavish use of video projections full of writhing bodies, insects and reptiles." (This production was also seen at Vilnius's Lithu-

anian National Opera in 2008.) Arguably heeding the music and libretto more closely, a later production in Chemnitz, Germany, in 2009 refrained from formulaic depictions.
81. None of the six composers is biographically connected with Latin America, whereas one of the six librettists, Janine Salinas Schoenberg, is partly of Peruvian descent.
82. Insofar as *Hopscotch*, as staged by Sharon, is an opera about Los Angeles, it may be productive to consider Jameson's analysis of John Portman's Westin Bonaventure Hotel in the city's downtown. If, in Jameson's eyes, the building's "glass skin repels the city outside," the opera, by contrast, forced audience members to undertake an ambitious, if safe, urban excursion through streets in various neighborhoods. Frederic Jameson, *Postmodernism, or, The Cultural Logic of Late Capitalism* (Durham, NC: Duke University Press, 1995), 42. For the program, see The Industry, *Hopscotch: A Mobile Opera* (Los Angeles: The Industry, 2015), 116.
83. While crediting Cortázar as his "inspiration," the director Sharon views the fact that permission was denied for an adaptation as an unexpectedly positive turn of events, as he tells Matthew Worley for an article in *Opera News*. Matthew Worley, "On the Road with The Industry," *Opera News*, August 2016, 17. As Worley would have it, "Instead, Sharon preserved only the format and title, reimagining *Hopscotch* as a mobile opera" (17). On audience engagement, see Megan Steigerwald Ille, "Live in the Limo: Remediating Voice and Performing Spectatorship in Twenty-First Century Opera," *Opera Quarterly* 36, nos. 1–2 (Winter-Spring 2020), 1–26.
84. Louise K. Stein believes that *La Parténope* was most likely performed in Mexico City between 1700 and 1711. Louise K. Stein, "How Opera Traveled," in *The Oxford Handbook of Opera*, ed. Helen M. Greenwald, 847–49.
85. Robert Stevenson, "Opera Beginnings in the New World," *Musical Quarterly* 45, no. 1 (January 1959): 8.
86. Performed in Germany, Spain, Britain, and Mexico itself, Valdés Kuri's production was assertively transatlantic, gathering soloists from various countries, a Mexican chorus, and a Geneva-based orchestra (the Ensemble Elyma) with an Argentine conductor, Gabriel Garrido, at the helm. At the Edinburgh Festival, the show was deemed problematic by most reviewers: "From the opening scene in which a loincloth-clad Montezuma performs a human sacrifice to the denouement, in which Mexican wrestlers do unmentionable things with bottles of Coke, director Claudio Valdés Kuri's vision of Montezuma is a surreal train wreck of a production, like a B-movie so awful it becomes rather watchable." Rowena Smith, "*Montezuma*," *The Guardian*, August 15, 2010, https://www.theguardian.com/culture/2010/aug/15/montezuma-edinburgh-opera. Ironically, the reviewer's description of the opera's extremism appears to mimic some of the reactions to aspects of indigenous cultures by the first European chroniclers of the Americas—or European composers of exoticist operas. In this regard, Valdés Kuri's plan for dialogue with Graun's opera came to fruition, if in a somewhat halting and uncomfortable manner.

87. Nancy Vogeley examines the dual status of performing Italian operas in newly independent Mexico. On the one hand, "Italian opera provided the new interests with the vocabulary they needed to state their difference from Spanish culture and to legitimate their control. Opera's physical appearance, by itself, was a decolonizing sign of cultural newness." Nancy Vogeley, "Italian Opera in Early National Mexico," *Modern Language Quarterly* 57, no. 2 (June 1996): 281. On the other, "in many ways Italian opera contained the seeds of further colonization and retarded decolonization in Mexico. . . . Performances that called for sitting through hours of incomprehensible Italian singing, for tolerance and appreciation of such oddities as a woman dressed as a man, and for a voyeuristic interest in the intimacies of others helped make the Mexican elite class more like audiences in non-Spanish Europe; yet cultivated taste, which ignored Mexican realities, deepened the split between this class and the rest of the nation" (286).
88. See Manuel Mañón, *Historia del viejo Gran Teatro Nacional de México* (Mexico City: Instituto Nacional de Bellas Artes and Consejo Nacional para la Cultura y las Artes, 2009), 1:174–75.
89. In Ochs's words, "the opera helped to demonstrate Mexico's potential as a budding 'European' nation. Perhaps such a composition could prove Mexicans' artistic and cultural legitimacy as a 'civilized; people in the eyes of Europe, if it received enough exposure in Mexico and abroad." Anna Ochs, "Opera in Contention: Social Conflict in Late Nineteenth-Century Mexico" (PhD diss., University of North Carolina at Chapel Hill, 2011), 54. On the interconnected operatic histories of Mexico, Brazil, and Italy, focused through Morales's *Ildegonda* and Gomes's *Il guarany*, see Verónica Zárate Toscano and Serge Gruzinski, "Ópera, imaginación y Sociedad: México y Brasil, siglo XIX. Historias conectadas: *Ildegonda* de Melesio Morales e *Il guarany* de Carlos Gomes," *Historia Mexicana* 58, no. 2 (2008): 803–60.
90. Ramón Pulido Granata, *La tradición operística en la ciudad de México (siglo XIX)* (Mexico City: Secretaría de Educación Pública, 1970), 170n24.
91. On the reception of Mexican operas in late-nineteenth-century English and French journals, see Anna Ochs, "Opera Achievements on the European Scale: French and English Correspondents in Late Nineteenth-Century Mexico," *Opera Journal* 44, nos. 1–2 (March 2011): 10.
92. Robert Stevenson, "Ortega del Villar, Aniceto," in *The New Grove Dictionary of opera*, ed. Stanley Sadie, 3:780.
93. Malena Kuss, "Identity and Change: Nativism in Operas from Argentina, Brazil, and Mexico," in *Musical Repercussions of 1492: Encounters in Text and Performance*, ed. Carol E. Robertson (Washington, DC: Smithsonian Institution Press, 1992), 325. Kuss describes and evaluates the uses of Amerindian, African American, and rural Ibero-American musical traditions in Latin American operas from 1854 to 1964. As the musicological analysis shows, Latin American composers in search of cultural identity could resort to any of these streams in works whose fabric essentially

corresponds to the patterns of European art music, resulting in "cases of acculturation proper" (301).
94. Pulido Granata, 185.
95. Malena Kuss, "The 'Invention' of America: Encounter Settings on the Latin American Lyric Stage," *Revista de Musicología* 16, no. 1 (1993): 201.
96. Durval Cesetti, "*Il guarany* for Foreigners: Colonialist Racism, Naive Utopia, or Pleasant Entertainment?," *Latin American Music Review* 31, no. 1 (2010): 102.
97. Cesetti, 104.
98. Maria Alice Volpe analyzes the history of *indianismo* in Brazilian arts and letters of the nineteenth century in the nation's official self-fashioning: "Emperor Pedro II systematically adopted Indianismo in the symbolic representation of the 'monarchy of the tropics,' including Imperial numismatic and vestments. D. Pedro II also fostered an official culture constructed by the literature and visual arts associated with Indianismo symbology and ideology." Maria Alice Volpe, "*Indianismo* and Landscape in the Brazilian Age of Progress: Art Music from Carlos Gomes to Villa-Lobos, 1870s–1930s" (PhD diss., University of Texas at Austin, 2001), 158.
99. Marcelo Góes questions the authenticity of the citation attributed to Verdi, giving more credence to a letter by the composer published in Rome's *Il Messaggero* in 1872, following a performance of *Il guarany* in Ferrara: "Ho assistito con grande viva soddisfazione all'opera del collega maestro Gomes, e posso affermarle che la medesima è di squisita fattura, e rivelatrice di un anima ardente, di un vero genio musicale" (I have attended the opera of our colleague maestro Gomes with very great pleasure, and I can assure you that it is exquisitely crafted and revealing of an ardent soul and true musical genius). Marcelo Góes, *Carlos Gomes: Documentos comentados* (São Paulo: Algol, 2008), 307.
100. The opera recalls those nineteenth-century fictional works analyzed by Doris Sommer in which love between characters of different ethnic backgrounds may also be read on a political key. For Sommer, the "most insistent message" in Alencar's *O Guaraní* is that "Brazilians are a coherent race produced long ago from the mutual love between native nobles and the best Portuguese." Doris Sommer, *Foundational Fictions: The National Romances of Latin America* (Berkeley: University of California Press, 1991), 161. Nonetheless, as Volpe argues, librettists Antonio Scalvini and Carlos d'Omerville transformed several key passages, which "disrupted the symbolic relationships that empowered the novel as a mythical narrative of national foundation." Volpe, "*Indianismo* and Landscape in the Brazilian Age of Progress," 172. These changes are seen as ultimately positive by Durval Cesetti: "The bowdlerization done in many elements of the story might have left us with a plot that is more innocuous and commonplace, but it also might have saved the opera from embracing a dated and pernicious ideology. Cesetti, "*Il guarany* for Foreigners: Colonialist Racism, Naive Utopia, or Pleasant Entertainment?," 117. On other changes, including Peri's language, who now sings eloquent Italian

instead of speaking simple and childlike Portuguese, see Jean Andrews, "Carlos Gomes' *Il guarany*: The Frontiers of Miscegenation in Nineteenth-Century Grand Opera," *Portuguese Studies* 16 (2000): 26–42.

101. Jorge Coli, *A paixão segundo a ópera* (São Paulo: Editora Perspectiva, 2003), 105.

102. Maria Alice Volpe, "Remaking the Brazilian Myth of National Foundation: *Il guarany*," *Latin American Music Review / Revista de Música Latinoamericana* 23, no. 2 (Autumn–Winter 2002): 179.

103. See Lund, *Werner Herzog*, 110.

104. Gerard Béhague, *"Guarany, Il,"* in *The New Grove Dictionary of Opera*, ed. Stanley Sadie, 2:559–60.

105. Malena Kuss, "Lenguajes nacionales de Argentina, Brasil y México en las óperas del siglo XX: Hacia una cronología comparativa de cambios estilísticos," *Revista Musical Chilena* 34, nos. 149–50 (1980): 76–77.

106. Ghislanzoni would also write the libretto for Melesio Morales's *Cleopatra*, staged at Mexico City's Gran Teatro Nacional in 1891.

107. For an analysis of Gomes's use of leitmotifs in *Fosca*, see Lindomar Linos Lerner, "A Study of the Systematic Use of Themes and Motives for Dramatic Effect and Coherence in the Opera *Fosca* by Antônio Carlos Gomes" (PhD diss., University of Arizona, 2008), 28.

108. Alluding to Maria Teresa's "interferência," Wilson Martins regrets Gomes's arrival in Italy at a time when Italian opera, albeit at its pinnacle, had inevitably begun its decline while the future of the art form was elsewhere. See Lutero Rodrigues, *Carlos Gomes: Um tema em questão* (São Paulo: Editora Unesp, 2011), 286. In his analysis of the reception of Gomes by Brazilian modernists, where he focuses on Mário de Andrade, Rodrigues refers to Oswald de Andrade's sarcastic judgment of the composer, who "nem imitar soube os grandes mestres sérios, preferindo filiar-se à decadência melódica italiana, seção cançoneta heroica" (qtd. by Rodrigues at 139; was not capable of imitating serious great masters, preferring to affiliate himself with Italian melodic decadence, heroic ditty section). On the initial, mostly adverse, reaction to Wagner's music in Rio de Janeiro, specifically around the premiere of *Lohengrin* in the city in 1883, see Cristina Magaldi, who cites the absence of large local orchestras and unfamiliarity with German as possible reasons for a delayed embrace of his operas. Cristina Magaldi, *Music in Imperial Rio de Janeiro: European Culture in a Tropical Milieu* (Lanham, MD: Scarecrow Press, 2004), 49–50.

109. Quoted by Gonzalo Aguilar, "The National Opera: A Migrant Genre of Imperial Expansion," *Journal of Latin American Cultural Studies* 12, no. 1 (2003): 90–91.

110. Aguilar, 91.

111. See the review in Buenos Aires's *La Revista Moderna* by Cravache, for whom the opera resembled any work imported from Italy and could be named *Il bandito della Calabria* "ó algo que lo equivaliera" (or something along those lines). At least for this critic, Berutti's attempt at capturing an Argentine *Volksgeist* came mostly to naught, largely due to its libretto. Cravache, "Los teatros: *Pampa*," *La Revista Moderna* 1 (May–July 1897), 365.

112. Claudio Benzecry also underscores the synchronicity of operatic culture in Argentina—or at least its capital—with that of Europe: "For instance, *La traviata* opened in Buenos Aires in 1856, just three years after its world premiere. This synchronicity accelerated with time, as evidenced by the premiere of *Pagliacci*, which appeared in Buenos Aires on February 28, 1891, only a few months after the work won an award by Ricordi in Italy. *La Bohème* premiered in Torino just four months before its Argentinean debut, and *Madame Butterfly* opened in Buenos Aires less than two months after its final revision in Brescia, on May 28, 1904. *Turandot* premiered in Buenos Aires on June 25, 1926, exactly two months after its world premiere at La Scala." Claudio Benzecry, *The Opera Fanatic: Ethnography of an Obsession* (Chicago: University of Chicago Press, 2011), 23. Indeed, eight of Puccini's twelve operas were first performed outside of Italy in Buenos Aires within months of their world premieres. See Gustavo Gabriel Otero and Daniel Varacalli Costas, *Puccini en la Argentina: junio–agosto de 1905* (Buenos Aires: Instituto Italiano de Cultura de Buenos Aires, 2006), 88.
113. See Kuss, "Lenguajes nacionales de Argentina, Brasil y México," 64.
114. See Malena Kuss's entries for each opera in *Pipers Enzyklopädie des Musiktheaters*, ed. Carl Dahlhaus et al. (Munich: Piper, 1986). For Boero, see also Kuss's "Identity and Change," where she describes *El matrero* as a "nativistic masterpiece" (303); and "Das lateinamerikanische Libretto," where she links the work's music and story to folklore and audience identification (5:1200–01).
115. Kuss, "Lenguajes nacionales de Argentina, Brasil y México," 64–67.
116. Octavio Sosa, "Catálogo de óperas mexicanas," in *La ópera mexicana, 1805–2002*, ed. Sosa et al. (Mexico City: Centro Universitario de Estudios Londres, 2022), 182–98.
117. Jorge Antonio González, *La composición operística en Cuba* (Havana: Letras Cubanas, 1986).
118. For detailed analyses of these heterogeneous works, see Gonzalo Cuadra, who also provides a register of several European (German, Italian, French, Dutch) composers who wrote operas in Chile (258–60). Gonzalo Cuadra, *Ópera nacional: Así la llamaron 1898–1950* (Santiago: Universidad Alberto Hurtado Ediciones, 2019).
119. Malena Kuss, "*Proserpina y el extranjero ('Proserpina and the Visitor')*," *Grove Music Online*, 1992, https://www-oxfordmusiconline-com.libproxy2.usc.edu/grovemusic/view/10.1093/gmo/9781561592630.001.0001/omo-9781561592630-e-5000005624?rskey=ABmXQs.
120. Carol A. Hess, *Representing the Good Neighbor: Music, Difference, and the Pan American Dream* (Oxford: Oxford University Press, 2013).
121. Kallman had collaborated with W. H. Auden on the libretto for Stravinsky's *The Rake's Progress* and would do so again in Henze's *Elegy for Young Lovers* and *The Bassarids*, but his work for Chávez's opera was problematic from the start, as a review of the first performance for the *New York Times* states: "Mr. Kallman's diction is often genuinely poetic. But there is too much talk for the sake of verbal imagery. In printed form this text might

be fine for the eye, but it poses an impossible problem for the composer, who must make it assimilable to the ear in a musical line." Taubman, "Opera: First by Chavez," *New York Times*, May 10, 1957, https://www.nytimes.com/1957/05/10/archives/opera-first-by-chavez.html.
122. Robert Stevenson, "Chávez (y Ramírez), Carlos (Antonio de Padua)," in *The New Grove Dictionary of Opera*, ed. Stanley Sadie, 1:826.
123. Lisa M. Peppercorn, "Villa-Lobos's Stage Works." *Revue Belge de Musicologie / Belgisch Tijdschrift voor Musikwetenschap* 36–38 (1982–1984): 175–84.
124. Peppercorn pieces together the probable composition history of *Izaht*, whose overture was conceived as early as 1915. Peppercorn, "Villa-Lobos's Stage Works," 176–77.
125. *Magdalena* invoked a series of stereotypes about Latin America, which Hess enumerates: "Appearing in quick succession are the Latin American dictator Carabaña, his voluptuous paramour Teresa, childlike Indians (the Muzos), a temperamental, violence-prone young man (Pedro), and, in contrast to the 'whore' lover, a docile young 'madonna' (predictably named Maria), who will convert the young man and the rest of the tribe to Christianity." Hess, *Representing the Good Neighbor*, 137.
126. Quoted by Peppercorn, "Villa-Lobos's Stage Works," 182.
127. Gilbert Chase and Lionel Salter, "Ginastera, Alberto," in *The New Grove Dictionary of Opera*, ed. Stanley Sadie, 2:421.
128. Hess, *Representing the Good Neighbor*, 159.
129. Quoted by Hess, 169.
130. As Buch explains, the history of the opera's censorship preceded the opera itself, and both stories, as it were, remain imbricated to a large extent. Esteban Buch, *The Bomarzo Affair: Ópera, perversión y dictadura* (Buenos Aires: Adriana Hidalgo, 2003), 17.
131. The prestige of Europe still informs much of the discourse built around opera in Latin America. Describing a new production of *A menina das nuvens*, staged in Belo Horizonte in 2009 and then in São Paulo and Rio de Janeiro, director William Pereira referred to the work in terms of Mozart's oeuvre, noting that it could be called Brazil's *Magic Flute* because of its fantasy and playfulness. "'A menina das nuvens' volta ao Municipal 55 anos após estreia," *O Globo*, October 23, 2015, https://oglobo.globo.com/cultura/teatro/a-menina-das-nuvens-volta-ao-municipal-55-anos-apos-estreia-17852699.
132. William Robin, "Protecting Alberto Ginastera from Oblivion," *New York Times*, March 2, 2016, https://www.nytimes.com/2016/03/06/arts/music/protecting-alberto-ginastera-from-oblivion.html.
133. Bernardo Illari, "*María de Buenos Aires*: el tango del eterno retorno," in *Estudios sobre la obra de Astor Piazzolla*, ed. Omar García Brunelli (Buenos Aires: Gourmet Musical Ediciones, 2014), 170, 186–87.
134. See Stephanie Minasian, "Long Beach Opera's 'Maria de Buenos Aires's Tells Story of Despair, Triumph," *Long Beach Press-Telegram*, January 24, 2012, https://www.presstelegram.com/2012/01/24/long-beach-operas-maria-de-buenos-aires-tells-story-of-despair-triumph/amp.

135. David Sawer, "Kagel, Mauricio," in *The New Grove Dictionary of Opera,* ed. Stanley Sadie, 2:941.
136. See Diego Fischerman, "Fuga y Vuelta," *Página 12*, July 9, 2008, https://www.pagina12.com.ar/diario/suplementos/radar/9-3113-2006-07-09.html.
137. Yayoi Uno Everett, *Reconfiguring Myth and Narrative in Contemporary Opera: Osvaldo Golijov, Kaija Saariaho, John Adams, and Tan Dun* (Bloomington: Indiana University Press, 2015), 59.
138. While praised by some critics, others disapproved of the work's inclusion in the Teatro Real season. Ironically (if unwittingly) recalling the early exchanges between Europeans and native Americans, Alberto González Lapuente faulted the company for searching abroad for precious stones that turn to be nothing but colorful glass beads. Alberto González Lapuente, "'Ainadámar,' la alargada sombra de un tópico universal," *ABC,* October 7, 2012, https://www.abc.es/cultura/musica/abci-critica-ainadamar-teatro-real-201207100000_noticia.html.
139. Like *Ainadámar*, *Alice in Wonderland* appeared early on as one of the most highly regarded operas of the twenty-first century. That it should be the work of a Korean composer and an Asian American playwright challenges the European dominance of opera, newly recast as a global practice in which Asia, like Latin America, can play an active role. Unsuk and Hwang's work, like that of Golijov and Hwang, can be read as a complex episode in the history of East-West relations. *Alice in Wonderland* reverses the traditional itineraries of opera in which European composers stereotypically depict others part of the world, very often Asia, for the sake of Western audiences—as is the case of Puccini's *Madama Butterfly*, famously questioned in Hwang's *M. Butterfly*.
140. Ann Patchett, *Bel Canto* (New York: Perennial, 2002), 105.
141. Maia Morgan, *"Bel Canto*: Opera Guide," Lyric Opera of Chicago, 8, http://lyricoperamedia.s3.amazonaws.com/_pdf/1516-publications/BelCantoOperaGuide.pdf.
142. In yet another sign of the rise of Latin America in the operatic culture of the United States, López's *Bel Canto* was the first commission proposed by Renée Fleming, the celebrated soprano, in her new role as creative consultant for the Lyric Opera. In an interview printed in the opera's program where she is described as the work's "curator," she chronicles her search for the ideal composer for Patchett's story: "I decided to focus on American composers, but then I thought, 'What if we focus on South America as a mine for a musical language that would lend itself geographically to this piece?'" While the word *mine* is full of imperial resonances, the creative latitude extended to López appears to tell a story of fruitful collaboration.
143. On the role of Hans Werner Henze in commissioning the opera, and León's search for a literary work to adapt, see Alejandro L. Madrid, *Tania León's Stride: A Polyrhythmic Life* (Urbana: University of Illinois Press, 2021), 85–87.
144. See Naomi André, *Black Opera: History, Power, Engagement* (Urbana: University of Illinois Press, 2018), 12.

CHAPTER 3

1. Margaret Lindauer describes the "cult" status of Kahlo in culture and commerce: "The so-called Frida-look was copied in high fashion magazines and look-alike contests; museum gift shops offered postcards, T-shirts, and jewelry incorporating Kahlo's self-portraits; and specialty shops commemorating Kahlo's life and work sold Frida nail polish, Frida shoes, and Frida clothing." Margaret A. Lindauer, *Devouring Frida: The Art History and Popular Celebrity of Frida Kahlo* (Middletown, CT: Wesleyan University Press, 1999), 1. I am thankful to Leo Cabranes-Grant for first pointing to me the Kahlo connection on the CD's cover. Kahlo herself has been the subject of operas, including Robert Xavier Rodriguez's *Frida* (1991), staged in various cities around the world, and Gabriela Lena Frank's *El último sueño de Frida y Diego* (2022), mentioned in Chapter 2.
2. Robert Stevenson, "Opera Beginnings in the New World," *Musical Quarterly* 45, no. 1 (January 1959): 25.
3. Louise K. Stein, "'*La música de dos orbes*': A Context for the First Opera of the Americas," *The Opera Quarterly* 2, nos. 3–4 (Summer–Autumn 2006): 441.
4. Bernardo Illari, "La obra y nuestra reconstrucción," in Tomás de Torrejón y Velasco, *La púrpura de la rosa*, performed by Isabel Monar, Graciela Oddone, Cecilia Diaz and the Ensemble Elyma conducted by Gabriel Garrido, K617, 1999, CD, 88.
5. Stein underscores the autonomy of Juan Hidalgo's *Celos aun del aire matan* (1660) and Torrejón y Velasco's *La púrpura de la rosa*, the only two extant works from before the arrival of Italian opera in Spain in the early eighteenth century. Both adopted Spanish theatrical conventions without resorting to foreign models. Louise K. Stein, "De la contera del mundo: Las navegaciones de la ópera entre dos mundos y varias culturas," in *La ópera en España e Hispanomérica*, ed. Emilio Casares Rodicio and Álvaro Torrente (Madrid: Instituto Complutense de Ciencias Musicales, 2001), 79.
6. Stein also analyzes the possible roles of both Hidalgo and Torrejón y Velasco as composers of the Lima opera: "The score to *La púrpura de la rosa* is the only profane music attributed to Torrejón y Velasco.... Its close musical relationship with Hidalgo's theatrical music casts doubt on Torrejón's sole authorship, though its extraordinary lyricism and strikingly pan-consonant harmony are characteristic of his vernacular sacred pieces. Torrejón surely 'compiled' the Lima manuscript and was the composer most likely to 'compose' the viceroy's opera in 1701." Louise K. Stein, "Opera," in *Lexikon of the Hispanic Baroque: Transatlantic Exchange and Transformation*, ed. Evonne Lewis and Kenneth Mills (Austin: University of Texas Press, 2013), 254–55.
7. My discussion builds on the work of Stein, who underscores the bonds that tie the opera's story and music to Peruvian elite criollo culture: "Its tragic mythological plot and performance history were well adapted to the political situation and to the taste of the audience. Classical European

myths and emblematic literature were drawn upon quite consistently by writers of plays, official histories, and chronicles in the late years of the seventeenth century and in the early eighteenth century, to exalt the sovereign and his representatives in Peru, entertain the educated minority, and sustain the notion of the '*sabio criollo*' (the enlightened Spaniard born in the colonial Americas), while distinguishing Peru as a place capable of an extreme refinement and elegance that could surpass even that of the great European courts. Classical mythology and the elegant, fully sung performance of opera served not only as a link to the vastness and antiquity of the European cultural heritage, but as a hedge against perceived provincialism and barbarism in the colony. Certainly the extreme lyricism of this music (striking even by European standards) might be heard as analogous to the extreme poetic lyricism cultivated by criollo poets, who had also shown a taste for violent fables with bloody episodes and tragic endings—precisely what *La púrpura de la rosa* offered in 1701." Stein, "'*La música de dos orbes*,'" 449.

8. David J. Levin, introduction to *Opera through Other Eyes*, ed. David J. Levin (Stanford, CA: Stanford University Press, 1993), 9.
9. Lois Parkinson Zamora and Monika Kaup, eds., *Baroque New Worlds: Representation, Transculturation, Counterconquest* (Durham, NC: Duke University Press, 2010), 8. On the programmatic uses of European art history for creating a syncretic esthetics in Latin America, see Tristan Weddigen, "Hispano-Incaic Fusions: Ángel Guido and the Latin American Reception of Heinrich Wölfflin," *Art in Translation* 9, no. S1 (2017): 92–120.
10. Parkinson Zamora and Kaup.
11. On Calderón's status in Lima as the perfect author for the imperial festivity, see José Antonio Rodríguez Garrido, who also analyzes in great detail the theatrical history and political underpinnings that led to various performances of *La púrpura de la rosa* in 1701 and 1702 as the commemorative pinnacle of the dynastic transition. José Antonio Rodríguez Garrido, "Teatro y poder en el palacio virreinal de Lima (1672–1707)" (PhD diss., Princeton University, 2003), 193.
12. Another kind of rereading—indeed, slight rewriting—concerns the libretto of Bellini's *Norma* published in Buenos Aires in 1849, whose subtle differences with the Italian original suggest, as Vera Wolkowicz shows, a political reinterpretation of the opera in the context of Camila O'Gorman's elopement with a Catholic priest at the time of Juan Manuel de Rosas's rule over the Argentine Confederation. Vera Wolkowicz, "Opera as a Moral Vehicle: Situating Bellini's *Norma* in the Political Complexities of Mid-Nineteenth-Century Buenos Aires," *Nineteenth-Century Music Review* (2021): 1–23.
13. On the rich musical cultures of the Guarani, Moxo, and Chiquito peoples that emerged from the contact with Jesuit missionaries, including operas often performed in indigenous languages by native musicians and singers, see Piotr Nawrot, *Indígenas y cultura musical de las reducciones jesuíticas* (La Paz: Editorial Verbo Divino, 2000), 29. All in all, it was a

hybrid spectacle, as Nawrot concludes elsewhere: "The music of the missions is different from the music of the indigenous peoples of these regions, which is not to say that it is the same as the music brought by missionaries and colonizers. Rather, it has features from both worlds." Piotr Nawrot, "Music: Missions," in *Lexikon of the Hispanic Baroque: Transatlantic Exchange and Transformation*, ed. Evonne Lewis and Kenneth Mills (Austin: University of Texas Press, 2013), 252.

14. Bernardo Illari, *"San Ignacio de Loyola:* Una ópera de la alteridad en las reducciones jesuíticas," in *San Ignacio: L'Opéra perdu des missions jésuites de l'Amazonie*, performed by Rosa Dominguez et al., the Ensamble Luis Berger and the Ensemble Elyma conducted by Gabriel Garrido, K617, 1996, CD, 35. Illari develops this idea in a book on Domenico Zipoli, the Italian composer who became a Jesuit missionary in South America. Bernardo Illari, *Domenico Zipoli: Para una genealogía de la música "clásica" latino-americana* (Havana: Fondo Editorial Casa de las Américas, 2011).

15. Illari argues that Zipoli wrote the third, fourth and sixth scene of *San Ignacio*. See Illari, *Domenico Zipoli*, 450–451. According to Illari, Zipoli also composed *La renuncia de Felipe V en Luis I*, a lost opera that may have been performed in Córdoba, present-day Argentina, in 1725.

16. The festival is held every two years in Santa Cruz and small towns such as San Ignacio and San Javier, where the eighteenth-century works were carefully preserved and transcribed from one generation to another. The festival's concerts are required to feature both European and Latin American music, and performers hail from various parts of the world—yet another story of transports that stresses the transatlantic status and present-day circulation of these works. The Geneva-based Elyma Ensemble, conducted by Gabriel Garrido, recorded *San Ignacio* in the cathedral of Concepción, Bolivia, in 1996; the opera's score was reconstituted by Illari.

17. Lorenzo Da Ponte, Libretto for Wolfgang Amadeus Mozart, *Così fan tutte*, performed by Carol Delores Ziegler, Dale Duesing, John Aler and the London Philharmonic Orchestra conducted by Bernard Haitink, EMI Classics, 1993, CD, 74.

18. Stevenson mentions Lorenzo de las Llamosas's *También se vengan los dioses* (1689), a zarzuela also performed in a viceregal context. Its music, now lost, may have been composed by Torrejón y Velasco. Robert Stevenson, "Estudio preliminar," in *La púrpura de la rosa*, by Tomás de Torrejón y Velasco (Lima: Instituto Nacional de Cultura, 1976), 51. See also Chad M. Gasta, *Transatlantic Arias: Early Opera in Spain and the New World* (Madrid: Iberoamericana, 2013), 25–28.

19. See Don Cruickshank, "Estudio crítico," in *La púrpura de la rosa*, by Pedro Calderón de la Barca and Tomás de Torrejón y Velasco (Kassel, Germany: Reichenberg, 1990), 70; Rodríguez Garrido, "Teatro y poder," 221–23.

20. The ties that bind Calderón's mythological plays, of which *La púrpura de la rosa* is one, to royal authority has negatively impacted their reception, as Margaret Greer explains: "The discomfort of succeeding generations with

the apparent subservience of the creative mind to the uses and pleasures of absolute monarchs has been a primary factor in the neglect of the mythological plays." Margaret Greer, *The Play of Power: Mythological Court Dramas of Calderón de la Barca* (Princeton, NJ: Princeton University Press, 1991), 5.
21. Tomás de Torrejón y Velasco, *La púrpura de la rosa*, performed by Judith Malafronte, Ellen Hargis, María del Mar Fernández Doval and the Harp Concert conducted by Andrew Lawrence-King, Deutsche Harmonia Mundi, 1999, CD, 44. Citations and translations of Calderón's libretto are taken from the Deutsche Harmonia Mundi recording.
22. Although no evidence can be cited, Gasta speculates that Torrejón y Velasco himself may be the author of the loa or that he extensively reworked it. Gasta, *Transatlantic Arias*, 83, 127n10.
23. Stein views the performance of the opera in the context of the viceroy's need to publicly assert his loyalty to the new king and dynasty. Stein, "'*La música de dos orbes*,'" 436–37). See also Stein, "The First Opera of the Americas and Its Contexts."
24. Mieke Bal, *Quoting Caravaggio: Contemporary Art, Preposterous History* (Chicago: University of Chicago Press, 1999), 1.
25. Stevenson, "Estudio preliminar," 77, 90.
26. Louise K. Stein, "The 'Blood of the Rose' and Opera's Arrival in Lima," in *La púrpura de la rosa*, by Tomás de Torrejón y Velasco. Deutsche Harmonia Mundi, 1999, CD, 9, 14.
27. Stein, 14.
28. As Baker explains, "If the Renaissance urban ideal transplanted to the Americas was abstract, intellectualized, and clean-cut, its baroque progeny was a more amorphous, chaotic, polysemic city of the senses, just as the abstract perfection of a musical work on the page is transformed in performance." Geoffrey Baker, "The Resounding City," in *Music and Urban Society in Colonial Latin America*, ed. Geoffrey Baker and Tess Knighton (Cambridge: Cambridge University Press, 2011), 18.
29. Andrew Lawrence-King, program notes to Tomás de Torrejón y Velasco, *La púrpura de la rosa*, Deutsche Harmonia Mundi, 1999, CD, 4.
30. Gabriel Garrido, interview by Pierre Michot, in Tomás de Torrejón y Velasco, *La púrpura de la rosa*, K617, 1996, CD, 95.
31. Garrido.
32. Garrido.
33. Jane W. Davidson and Anthony Trippett, eds., *Bringing the First Latin-American Opera to Life: Staging* La púrpura de la rosa *in Sheffield* (Manchester, UK: Durham Modern Language Series). Trippett, subtly alluding to the opera's transatlantic location, refers to it as "a Spanish opera" (7), while Andrew Lawrence-King, in one of his two essays in the volume, calls it "a Spanish baroque opera" (127) even as he writes about "Hispanic baroque music" (130).
34. Stein, "The 'Blood of the Rose' and Opera's Arrival in Lima," 14.
35. Although F. W. Sternfeld does not mention this libretto by Calderón in *The Birth of Opera*, *La purpura de la rosa* would be one in a long series of operas

derived from Ovid's *Metamorphoses* featuring a lament. F. W. Sternfeld, *The Birth of Opera* (Oxford, UK: Clarendon Press, 1995), 5.

36. Stevenson contrasts what he views as the literary mediocrity of early Italian, French and English operatic works, including John Blow's *Venus and Adonis*, with the librettos by Lope de Vega and Calderón de la Barca, who wrote the words of the first Hispanic operas. Stevenson, "Estudio preliminar," 15.
37. Roberto González Echevarría, *Celestina's Brood: Continuities of the Baroque in Spanish and Latin American Literature* (Durham, NC: Duke University Press, 1993), 86.
38. González Echevarría, 93.
39. Sor Juana Inés de la Cruz, *Poems, Protest, and a Dream*, trans. Margaret Sayers Peden (New York: Penguin Books, 1997), 212–13.
40. Informed by Margaret Greer's analysis of Calderón's invocations of Apollo as comparable to the Spanish king, Gasta persuasively suggests that Apollo's absence as a character in the loa is actually "a form of presence": "His forever youthful and graceful countenance is presented as a mirror image of the young and beautiful eighteen-year-old Philip V. The new King, like Apollo, is the benefactor and patron of the arts across the Spanish empire." Gasta, *Transatlantic Arias*, 133.
41. Rolando Pérez, *Severo Sarduy and the Neo-Baroque Image of Thought in the Visual Arts* (West Lafayette, IN: Purdue University Press, 2012), 26. Pérez argues that his duplication of the center—which is also a decentering—"will find expression in the symbolic imaginary of Mannerist or Baroque art" (26). It is not difficult to conceive of a production of *La púrpura de la rosa* in which this line of thought could be apprehended visually onstage.
42. Alain Pacquier, who founded K617, intended the collection to record—quite literally—baroque musical works that reflected the cultural contacts between Europeans and the indigenous peoples of the Americas.
43. Theodor Adorno, "Opera and the Long-Playing Record," in *Essays on Music* (Berkeley: University of California Press, 2002), 284.
44. Pedro Calderón de la Barca, "Deposición en favor de los profesores de la pintura," in Edward M. Wilson, "El texto de la 'Deposición a favor de los profesores de la pintura' de don Pedro Calderón de la Barca," *Revista de Archivos, Bibliotecas y Museos* 72, no. 2 (July–December 1974): 721–22. On the "Deposición" and its centralidad a Calderón's poetics, see Maria Alicia Amadei-Pulice, *Calderón y el barroco: Exaltación y engaño de los sentidos* (Amsterdam: John Benjamins, 1990), 122–24.
45. Philip IV also possessed other paintings of the same subject by Titian and Annibale Carracci.
46. In dialogue with Cherríe Moraga's interpretation of Kahlo's painting, Lindauer remarks on the red shawl's association with lesbian sexuality—"the barrenness of the lesbian womb as it drips blood into a dry riverbed"—as well as with "the brutality of the conquest that led to

obstructing pre-Columbian cultural practices, the intent being to eradicate indigenous culture." Margaret A. Lindauer, *Devouring Frida*, 48.

47. See, for instance, the overstated sexuality from the *Boston Globe* on María Luisa Bemberg's *Yo, la peor de todas* (1990), a film about Sor Juana Inés de la Cruz: "Lesbian passion seething behind convent walls... engrossing, enriching, and elegant!"

48. Garcilaso de la Vega, *Royal Commentaries of the Incas and General History of Peru*, trans. Harold V. Livermore (Austin: University of Texas Press, 1994), 132.

49. Garcilaso de la Vega, *Comentarios reales de los incas*, ed. Carlos Araníbar (Lima: Fondo de Cultura Económica, 1991), 1:4.

50. Alessio Cervelli cites the words of Pope Benedict XIV, who in 1749 praises missionaries in Paraguay for making good use of the natural musical skills of indigenous peoples, equal to those of Europeans in the process of evangelization. Alessio Cervelli, *Domenico Zipoli: "Amo Dunque Sono"* (Streetlib, 2016), 54.

51. Nawrot, *Indígenas y cultura musical de las reducciones jesuíticas*, 32.

52. Leonardo J. Waisman, "Urban Music in the Wilderness: Ideology and Power in the Jesuit *Reducciones*, 1609–1767," in *Music and Urban Society in Colonial Latin America*, ed. Geoffrey Baker and Tess Knighton (Cambridge: Cambridge University Press, 2011), 217.

53. Illari, "San Ignacio de Loyola," 39.

54. Illari, 38–39, 53–54.

55. Illari, 54.

56. Libretto to *San Ignacio: L'Opéra perdu des missions jésuites de l'Amazonie*, performed by Rosa Domínguez, Silvia Pérez Monsalve, Alicia Borges, Fabian Schofrin, Gustavo Báez, Fabián Neira, Furio Zanasi, and Ensemble Elyma conducted by Gabriel Garrido, K617 France, 1996, CD, 24.

57. Orazio Grassi, libretto to Johannes Hieronymus Kapsberger, *Apotheosis sive Consecratio Sanctorum Ignatii et Francisci Xaverii*, performed by Ellen Hargis, Ryan Turner, et al., and the Ensemble Abendmusik conducted by James David Christie, in *The Jesuit Operas by Kapsberger & Zipoli*, Dorian, 1999, CD, 15.

58. Victor Anand Coelho, "Kapsberger's *Apotheosis... of St. Francis* (1622) and the Conquering of India," in *The Work of Opera: Genre, Nationalism, and Sexual Difference*, ed. Richard Dellamora and Daniel Fischlin (New York: Columbia University Press, 1997), 32.

59. Ralph P. Locke, "Exotic Elements in Kapsberger's Jesuit Opera (Rome, 1622) Honoring Saints Ignatius and Francis Xavier," in *A Festschrift for Prof. Kerala J. Snyder*, ed. Johann Norrback and Joel Speerstra (Gothenburg: Göteborgs Universitetsbibliotek, 2016), 16, http://hdl.handle.net/2077/54931.

60. Libretto to *Mission San Francisco Xavier: Ópera y Misa de los Indios*, performed by the Coro de Niños Cantores de Córdoba and Ensemble Elyma conducted by Gabriel Garrido, K617 France, 2000, CD, 14–15.

CHAPTER 4

1. Mary Ellen Miller links the chacmool and human sacrifices to Tlaloc, the "god of rain" and a deity of the earth, at the Templo Mayor in Mexico City: "These Tlaloc-associated sculptures not only receive the blood of captives but also commemorate them, the single, humiliated, recumbent figure perhaps recalling many." Mary Ellen Miller, "A Re-examination of the Mesoamerican Chacmool," *Art Bulletin* 67, no. 1 (March 1985), 15. In "El *chacmool* mexica," Alfredo López Austin and Leonardo López Luján discuss the chacmool as a possible representation of a sacrificial victim, a military figure, a priest, a historical character, a man-god, a divine messenger or a specific deity; and as a functional object—a table used for offerings, a recipient for hearts, or a stone on which sacrifices were performed. Alfredo López Austin and Leonardo López Luján, "El *chacmool* mexica," *Caravelle: Cahiers du Monde Hispanique et Luso-brésilien* 76–77 (2001): 59–84.
2. See the website Mark Lewis Photography, https://markpix.com/galleries/time.
3. Adorno, "Bourgeois Opera," 37. On Adorno's dictum as its link with the idea of opera as a field where "not much critical reading gets done," see David J. Levin's introduction to *Opera through Other Eyes*, ed. David J. Levin (Stanford, CA: Stanford University Press, 1993), 1.
4. On operatic singing as "the most intractable element of intelligibility in opera" presented as part of an argument against the importance of words in the art form, see Paul Robinson, "Reading Libretti and Misreading Opera," 33. For a counterargument, see Levin, *Opera through Other Eyes*, 5–7.
5. Quoted by Carolyn Abbate and Roger Parker, *A History of Opera* (New York: W. W. Norton, 2012), 117.
6. In this regard, I ascribe to Cameron Fae Bushnell's analysis of representations of Western classical music in postcolonial fiction. As he observes, these works "create or highlight tensions in protagonists' social circumstances in referring to an extensive, disseminated colonial history" and "pose analogies for literary consciousness and suggest alternative processes of thought both for characters and for readers in facing intransigent social and political problems." Cameron Fae Bushnell, *Postcolonial Readings of Music in World Literature: Turning Empire on Its Ear* (New York: Routledge, 2013), 6. See also Malena Kuss, who highlights *Concierto barroco* as an ideal site for viewing literature's engagement with music in the context of Carpentier's career as music critic, amateur ethnographer, music historiographer, opera librettist, and cultural critic. Malena Kuss, prologue to *Music in Latin America and the Caribbean: An Encyclopedic History*, ed. Malena Kuss (Austin: University of Texas Press, 2004), xvi.
7. Catherine Clément, *Opera, or the Undoing of Women*, trans. Betsy Wing (Minneapolis: University of Minnesota Press, 1988), 22.

8. David Vickers, "Unearthing a Treasure: The Rediscovery of 'Motezuma,'" program notes to Antonio Vivaldi, *Motezuma*, Archiv Produktion, 2006, CD, 12.
9. Steffen Voss, "Antonio Vivaldi's Dramma per Musica *Motezuma:* Some Observations on Its Libretto and Music," in *Vivaldi, "Motezuma" and the Opera Seria: Essays on a Newly Discovered Work and Its Background*, ed. Michael Talbot (Turnhout, Belgium: Brepols, 2008), 16–17, 18.
10. Clément, *Opera, or the Undoing of Women.*
11. Clément, 22–23.
12. Alejo Carpentier, *Concierto barroco* (Madrid: Siglo XXI, 1982), 36.
13. Alejo Carpentier, *Concierto barroco*, trans. Asa Zatz (Tulsa, OK: Council Oak Books, 1988), 70.
14. Ireri E. Chávez-Bárcenas investigates the links between both places and their possible effect in Giusti's libretto: "Venetian printers and editors had long disseminated images of ancient Tenochtitlan as a civilized urban center that physically and intellectually resembled their own *Repubblica*. Early modern images of Moctezuma influenced by discussions of the Noble Savage such as those by André Thevet and Piccini . . . had suggested his potential to be a respectable emperor, and Cortés and other conquistadors were considered tyrants by Venetian intellectuals and diplomats influenced by Las Casas. Perhaps for all these reasons, Giusti decided to balance Solís's chronicle to reflect traditional Venetian representations of Tenochtitlan and its ruler. Venetian sympathy with the Aztec Empire, as well as historic Venetian criticism of Spanish imperialism, also prompted Giusti to supplement his libretto with dialogues inspired by alternative historical sources; perhaps not surprising in a period in which Venetians were debating a new European order in the aftermath of the War of Spanish Succession. Even further, it is possible that Giusti used the fall of Tenochtitlan as a reflection of the Venetian nostalgia for the loss of the overseas empire that, just like Motezuma's, would never be recovered." Ireri E. Chávez Bárcenas, "Vivaldi's *Motezuma*: The Conquest of Mexico on the Venetian Operatic Stage," in *The New World in Early Modern Italy*, ed. Elizabeth Horodowich and Lia Markey (New York: Cambridge University Press, 2017), 306–7.
15. In Giusti's libretto, the name is actually rendered as Uccilibos.
16. Carpentier's Vivaldi is, of course, wrong. See, for instance, Gabriel Pareyón's *Xochicuicatl cuecuechtli* (Ribald Flower Song), an opera with a libretto in Nahuatl, which was premiered in Arcelia, Mexico, in 2014 and revived in Guanajuato in 2018. Yet another music drama, *Cuitlahuatzin*, with music by Samuel Máynez and a libretto by Samuel Zyman, was sung in Nahuatl at Mexico City's Palacio de Bellas Artes in 2023.
17. See Roberto González Echevarría, *Alejo Carpentier: The Pilgrim at Home* (Ithaca, NY: Cornell University Press, 1977).
18. Francesco Algarotti, *Saggio sopra l'opera in musica* (Leghorn: Marco Coltellini, 1763), 20–21.
19. Whaples, "Early Exoticism Revisited," 3.

20. Whaples.
21. See also Tzvetan Todorov, who views exoticism as commendation without knowledge, in *Nous et les autres: La réflexion française sur la diversité humaine* (Paris: Seuil, 1989), 356.
22. In the afterword to *M. Butterfly*, Hwang explains such gendered views on historical grounds: "Now our considerations of race and sex intersect the issue of imperialism. For this formula—good natives serve Whites, bad natives rebel—is consistent with the mentality of colonialism. Because they are submissive and obedient, good natives of both sexes necessarily take on 'feminine' characteristics in a colonialist world. Gunga Din's unfailing devotion to his British master, for instance, is not so far removed from Butterfly's slavish faith in Pinkerton." David Henry Hwang, *M. Butterfly* (New York: Plume Book, 1989), 99.
23. Margarita Zamora, *Reading Columbus* (Berkeley: University of California Press, 1993), 157.
24. Jean-Claude Malgoire, program notes to Antonio Vivaldi, *Montezuma*, Astrée, 1992, CD, 59.
25. Alvise Giusti, libretto for Antonio Vivaldi, *Motezuma*, performed by Vito Priante, Marijana Mijanovic, Maite Beaumont and Il Complesso Barocco conducted by Alan Curtis, Archiv Produktion, 2006, CD, 91.
26. Pierpaolo Polzonetti, "Opera as Process," 14.
27. Martha Feldman, *The Castrato: Reflections on Nature and Kinds* (Oakland: University of California Press, 2015), 45.
28. Roger Covell, "Voice Register as an Index of Age and Status in Opera Seria," in *Opera & Vivaldi*, ed. Michael Collins and Elise K. Kirk (Austin: University of Texas Press, 1984), 194.
29. Ulrich Linke, "Vokaler Gender Trouble: Wie queer sind sehr hohe Männerstimme?," in *Der Countertenor: Die männliche Falsettstimme von Mittelalter zum Gegenwart*, ed. Corinna Herr et al (Mainz, Germany: Schott, 2012), 215–50.
30. Polzonetti, "Opera as Process," 14–15.
31. Linke, "Vokaler Gender Trouble," 234.
32. Perhaps classical music's response to high voices in popular music (see Linke 239–47), the countertenor from at least the 1990s, when Malgoire resets Giusti's libretto, is no longer a marginal phenomenon. The countertenor's androgyny is often at play; in a staging of Monteverdi's *L'incoronazione di Poppea* in 2000 at the English National Opera, one scene featured a countertenor singing the role of Nerone in the nude—a gendered clash of body and voice.
33. Blas Matamoro, "El neobarroco: Diferencias, tientos y ensaladas," *América: Cahiers du CRICCAL* (Sorbonne Nouvelle) 20 (1998), 19.
34. Malgoire, program notes to Antonio Vivaldi, *Montezuma*, 59.
35. Serge Gruzinski, "The Spanish Invasion: The Mexican Version," program notes to Antonio Vivaldi, *Montezuma*, Astrée, 1992, CD, 72.
36. Carpentier postulates his vision of the marvelous real as a specific condition of Latin American history in "Lo real maravilloso de América,"

an essay first published in 1948 that later became the preface of his novel, *El reino de este mundo*, set mostly in eighteenth- and nineteenth-century Haiti. The marvelous real has been critically linked with magical realism since the 1950s. For an analysis of magical realism and world literature, including Carpentier's important role, see Mariano Siskind, *Cosmopolitan Desires: Global Modernity and World Literature in Latin America* (Evanston, IL: Northwestern University Press, 2014), 59–100.

37. Sir Philip Sidney, "The Defence of Poesy," in *Sir Philip Sidney*, ed. Katherine Duncan-Jones (Oxford: Oxford University Press, 1989).
38. Patrick Barbier, *The World of the Castrati: The History of an Extraordinary Operatic Phenomenon* (London: Souvenir Press, 1996), 3.
39. For an analysis of the various modes in which Vivaldi's operas have been produced in the twentieth century—transposition, adaptation, reconstitution—as well as what we might know about the first staging of *Motezuma*, see Frédéric Delaméa, "*Vivaldi in scena:* Thoughts on the Revival of Vivaldi's Operas," in *Vivaldi, "Motezuma" and the Opera Seria: Essays on a Newly Discovered Work and Its Background*, ed. Michael Talbot (Turnhout, Belgium: Brepols, 2008), 169–85.
40. Matthew Restall, *When Montezuma Met Cortés: The True Story of the Meeting That Changed History* (New York: HarperCollins, 2018), 353.
41. Restall, *When Montezuma Met Cortés*, 352.
42. Malena Kuss analyzes Carpentier's meditation on music in the Americas, delineated in his essay "América Latina en la confluencia de coordenadas históricas y su repercusión en la música," in the context of both *Eurindia: Ensayo de estética fundado en la experiencia de las culturas americanas* (1924), by the Argentine writer Ricardo Rojas, and of Gilbert Chase's music historiography: "Far less systematic but equally compelling is Carpentier's vision of the new world. Adducing the musical instruments that already meet in Silvestre de Balboa's poem *Espejo de paciencia* (1608), he speaks of the New World as a 'prodigious crucible of civilizations, planetary crossroads, place of syncretisms, transculturations, symbioses of musics still primeval or already very elaborate.'" Malena Kuss, "The Confluence of Historical Coordinates in Carpentier/Caturla's Puppet Opera *Manita en el Suelo*," in *Musical Repercussions of 1492: Encounters in Text and Performance*, ed. Carol E. Robertson (Washington, DC: Smithsonian Institution Press, 1992), 356.
43. González Echevarría, *Alejo Carpentier*, 266.
44. Alejo Carpentier, *Cartas a Toutouche* (Mexico City: Lectorum, 2011), 163, emphasis in original.
45. Malena Kuss, "Modernismo Rumbero in Carpentier's and Caturla's Puppet Opera *Manita en el Suelo* (1931–34)," *Review: Literature and Arts of the Americas* 44, no. 1 (2011): 140.
46. For a comparison of *Manita en el suelo* with Boero's *El matrero*, see Kuss, "Das lateinamerikanische Libretto," 5:1200–1201.
47. Voss, "Antonio Vivaldi's Dramma per Musica *Motezuma*," 7.
48. Voss, "Antonio Vivaldi's Dramma per Musica *Motezuma*," 5.

49. Chávez-Bárcenas, however, also views Mitrena as modeled upon Malintzin, Cortés's native translator, also known as Doña Marina or Malinche. Chávez-Bárcenas, "Vivaldi's *Motezuma*," 303.

CHAPTER 5

1. Lorenzo Da Ponte, libretto to Wolfgang Amadeus Mozart, *Le nozze di Figaro*, performed by Simon Keenlyside, Véronique Gens, Patrizia Ciofi, Lorenzo Regazzo and the Concerto Köln conducted by René Jacobs, Harmonia Mundi, 2004, CD, 120–23.
2. As Paul Robinson argues, Mozart is the "musical embodiment" of the values of the Enlightenment, which he shared with Voltaire, Rousseau, and Kant. Paul Robinson, *Opera and Ideas: From Mozart to Strauss* (Ithaca, NY: Cornell University Press, 1985), 14.
3. On the anthem's music, including the Mozart connection, see Cristóbal Díaz Ayala, *Música cubana: Del areyto a la nueva trova* (Miami: Universal, 1993), 70–72. By contrast, nothing of the sort is mentioned by Jesús Guanche, "Himno VII: Cuba," in *Diccionario de la música española e hispanoamericana*, ed. Emilio Casares Rodicio et al. (Madrid: Sociedad General de Autores y Editores, 2000), 10:318–19. My gratitude to James Walker for his careful and suggestive comparison of the scores of "Non più andrai" and "La bayamesa" in the context of martial music.
4. William Finnegan describes listening to "La bayamesa" at a political meeting of exiled Cubans in the United States; dumbfounded, but perhaps not far from the truth, he writes, "After an overloud recording of 'The Star-Spangled Banner' came an even louder rendition of the strangely Germanic Cuban national anthem." William Finnegan, "Letter from Miami: The Cuban Strategy," *New Yorker* (March 15, 2004), 77.
5. Jesús Gómez Cairo, "La marsellesa cubana," interview by Andrés Machado Conte, Radio Rebelde, February 1, 2018, https://www.radiorebelde.cu/noticia/la-marsellesa-cubana-20180201. See also Jesús Gómez Cairo, *Creación, realización y desarrollo de* La bayamesa, *Himno de Bayamo, Himno Nacional de Cuba* (Havana: Ediciones Museo de la Música, 2013), which does not refer to Mozart.
6. Jorge Mañach, *An Inquiry into Choteo*, trans. Jacqueline Loss (Barcelona: Red Ediciones, 2018), 82.
7. Guillermo Cabrera Infante, *Tres tristes tigres* (Barcelona: Biblioteca de Bolsillo, 1983), 294.
8. Guillermo Cabrera Infante, *Three Trapped Tigers*, trans. Donald Gardner and Suzanne Jill Levine (New York: Marlowe & Co., 1971), 318.
9. "La bayamesa" is not the only Latin American national anthem where opera plays an audible role. As we saw, the overture to Gomes's *Il guarany*, the "Protofonia," has achieved iconic status in Brazil, but the country's actual anthem, too, is often linked with opera. Osvaldo Colarusso relates it to Rossini's *Cenerentola* for its ornaments, appoggiaturas and trills. Osvaldo Colarusso, "Hino Nacional—Motivo de orgulho num país

corrupto," in *Falando de musica*, https://www.gazetadopovo.com.br/vozes/falando-de-musica/hino-nacional-motivo-de-orgulho-num-pais-corrupto. Louis Moreau Gottschalk, who died in Rio de Janeiro, composed two pieces based on it: the *Brazilian Solemn March* and the *Great Triumphal Fantasy on the Brazilian National Anthem*. Uruguay's national anthem, in its turn, has been connected with Donizetti's *Lucrezia Borgia*, yet another bel canto work.

10. As Emilio Bejel states, one can observe "the construction of a nationalist discourse in which the homosexual is perceived as a corrupter of the national body for having transgressed gender roles." Emilio Bejel, *Gay Cuban Nation* (Chicago: University of Chicago Press, 2001), xxii.
11. See, for instance, Wayne Koestenbaum's groundbreaking *The Queen's Throat: Opera, Homosexuality, and the Mystery of Desire* (New York: Vintage, 1994); and, for the Hispanic context, Adolfo Planet, *Del armario al escenario: la ópera gay* (Barcelona: Ediciones la Tempestad, 2003).
12. In this I am persuaded by Kristeva, who calls for nations in which diverse elements can coexist without fear of each other, extending Freud's acceptance of one's own strangeness to national communities. Julia Kristeva, *Étrangers à nous-mêmes* (Paris: Seuil, 1988), 87.
13. Senel Paz, *El lobo, el bosque y el hombre nuevo*, (Mexico City: Era, 2000), 46.
14. Enrique Río Prado, *Pasión cubana por Giuseppe Verdi* (Havana: Unión, 2001), 44.
15. Río Prado, 9.
16. Río Prado, 19.
17. Quoted by John Dizikes, *Opera in America*, 123. For the history of Havana-based Italian opera companies and their performance in the United States, see Dizikes 122–25. See also Katherine K. Preston, *Opera on the Road: Traveling Opera Troupes in the United States, 1825–60* (Urbana: University of Illinois Press, 1993), 113–22. The US premieres of such operas as Rossini's *Semiramide* and Bellini's *Norma* were undertaken by these Havana companies as they toured such cities as New Orleans; see Preston 114, 394n58.
18. See Díaz Ayala, *Música cubana*, 111. As mentioned in Chapter 1, Caruso's visit to Havana is the subject of *Como un mensajero tuyo*, a novel by Mayra Montero; see Roberto Ignacio Díaz, "Silencios de Caruso o la ópera en La Habana," *América: Cahiers du CRICCAL* (Sorbonne Nouvelle) 31 (2004): 153–59.
19. See Chapter 2, note 69.
20. See, for instance, the *cantades* of habaneras on Spain's Costa Brava—in Catalan yet—examined by Galina Bakhtiarova, "A Tale of Two Habaneras: Transatlantic Journeys of a Cultural Sign," *Journal of Transatlantic Studies* 1, no. 2 (2003): 117–30.
21. Pierre-Augustin Caron de Beaumarchais, *Théâtre* (Paris: Garnier-Flammarion, 1965), 155; the translation is from Pierre-Augustin Caron de Beaumarchais, *The Barber of Seville / The Marriage of Figaro*, trans. John Wood (London: Penguin, 1964), 126.

22. Beaumarchais, 155.
23. Da Ponte, 123.
24. Pitts Sanborn and Emil Hilb, *The Metropolitan Book of the Opera* (Garden City, NY: Garden City Publishing, 1942), 281.
25. In Paz's *El lobo, el bosque y el hombre nuevo* (1991), David cites Diego's less subversive, yet fervent and cultish, words about a Callas recording of *La Traviata* at La Scala in 1955, which Diego will have the honor of being the first person to listen to (23).
26. Koestenbaum, 147.
27. See Emilio Bejel, *Gay Cuban Nation*, 95-112; Brad Epps, "Proper Conduct: Reinaldo Arenas, Fidel Castro, and the Politics of Homosexuality," *Journal of the History of Sexuality* 6.2 (1995): 231-83.
28. Koestenbaum, 144-45.
29. See Charles I. Nero, "Diva Traffic and Male Bonding in Film: Teaching Opera, Learning Gender, Race, and Nation," *Camera Obscura* 56, no. 19 (2004): 46-73.
30. Enrico Mario Santí, *"Fresa y chocolate:* La retórica de la reconciliación," in *Por una politeratura: literatura hispanoamericana e imaginación política* (Mexico City: Consejo Nacional para la Cultura y las Artes, 1997), 301; Paul Julian Smith, *Vision Machines: Cinema, Literature, and Sexuality in Spain and Cuba, 1983-1993* (London: Verso, 1996), 95.
31. For a feminist and psychoanalytic reading that retrieves Merlin for the Cuban literary canon, see Adriana Méndez Rodenas, *Gender and Nationalism in Colonial Cuba: The Travels of Santa Cruz y Montalvo, Condesa de Merlin* (Nashville, TN: Vanderbilt University Press, 1998).
32. See April Fitzlyon, *Maria Malibran: Diva of the Romantic Age* (London: Souvenir, 1987), 250.
33. For Merlin's reincarnation in Arenas's fiction seen from different angles, see Méndez Rodenas, *Gender and Nationalism in Colonial Cuba*, which places Merlin's characterization within the "consistently devalued position which all female characters occupy in [Arenas'] fiction" (291); and Jorge Olivares, who reads Merlin within Arenas's profound inquiry into sexual desire, exile, and the elusive idea of Cuba. Jorge Olivares, *Becoming Reinaldo Arenas* (Durham, NC: Duke University Press, 2013), 88-90.
34. Reinaldo Arenas, *El color del verano* (Miami: Ediciones Universal, 1991), 236; Reinaldo Arenas, *The Color of Summer*, trans. Andrew Hurley (New York: Penguin, 2000), 239.
35. Felice Romani, libretto to Vincenzo Bellini, *Norma*, performed by Maria Callas, Franco Corelli, Christa Ludwig, and the Orchestra e Coro del Teatro alla Scala di Milano conducted by Tullio Serafin, EMI Classics, 1997, CD, 64.
36. Malibran's father, Manuel García, the tenor and composer, did work for two years in Mexico; Merlin studied singing with García.
37. Gastón Baquero, "Introducción a la novela," in *La Enciclopedia de Cuba* (San Juan: Playor, 1975), 3:8.
38. Mercedes Merlin, *La Havane* (Paris: Librairie d'Amyot, 1844), 1:23-24.
39. For an analysis of this passage in the context of translingual writing, see Díaz, *Unhomely Rooms*, 92-93.

40. See Dizikes, *Opera in America*, 3–11.
41. Dizikes, 3.
42. Edgar Allan Poe, Review of *Memoirs and Letters of Madame Malibran. By the Countess de Merlin. With Notices of the Progress of the Musical Drama in England. Burton's Gentleman's Magazine* (Philadelphia), 6 (May 1840): 238–39.
43. Ernesto Lecuona's *Sor Inés* (1937) is a zarzuela based on Merlin's *Histoire de sœur Inès* (1832), a Romantic tale set mostly in Havana. See Marcel Quillévéré, *Cuba: Une histoire de l'île par sa musique et sa littérature* (Paris: Albin Michel, 2022), 116.
44. Claire Martin delves into the various interrelated modalities and themes of Merlin's book, including the singer's hagiography, and the customs and manners of European societies at the time. Claire Martin, "Las múltiples voces de Merlin: del *bel canto* a la escritura," in *Fronteras de la literatura y la crítica*, Actas del XXXV Congreso del Instituto de Literatura Iberoamericana, Université de Poitiers, ed. Fernando Moreno, Sylvie Josserand, and Fernando Colla (Poitiers, France: Centre de Recherches Latino-Américaines, 2006), CD-ROM.
45. Mercedes Merlin, *Les loisirs d'une femme de monde* (Paris: Librairie de l'Advocat, 1838), 1:56, her italics.
46. In Catherine Clément's retelling of this episode, presented as real or as a dream, García warns his daughter that he will kill her unless her performance in the role of Desdemona is impeccable; as he strangles her, she bites his hand until it bleeds. Catherine Clément, *Opera, or the Undoing of Women*, 59–60.
47. Fitzlyon, *Maria Malibran*, 28.
48. Poe, 238.
49. Following Bartoli, whom he credits for her efforts, Mexican tenor Javier Camarena devoted an entire recording, *Contrabandista*, in 2018 to the mostly forgotten opera and zarzuela repertoire by Manuel García, whom he compares with the great bel canto composers. See Gonzalo Lahoz, "Javier Camarena: 'Manuel García está a la misma altura que Bellini, Rossini o Donizetti," *Platea Magazine*, August 13, 2018, https://www.plateamagazine.com/entrevistas/5151-javier-camarena-manuel-garcia-esta-a-la-misma-altura-que-bellini-rossini-o-donizetti.
50. Book for *Maria*, performed by Cecilia Bartoli, Decca, 2007, CD, 8.
51. Book for *Maria*, 22.
52. Book for *Maria*, 24.
53. Mercedes Merlin, *Memoirs of Madame Malibran, by the Countess de Merlin and Other Intimate Friends* (London: Henry Colburn, 1840), 1:279.
54. Pauline Viardot, Malibran's younger sister, is one of the subjects treated by Orlando Figes in his chronicle of the rise of a cosmopolitan European culture in the nineteenth century, in which opera plays a salient role. Figes notes that it was through Viardot that Georges Bizet became acquainted with "El arreglito," the work by Sebastián Iradier from which he borrowed to compose Carmen's "Habanera." Orlando Figes, *The Europeans: Three Lives and the Making of a Cosmopolitan Culture* (New York: Metropolitan Books, 2019), 365.

55. The Catalan slaver Francesc Martí i Torrents owned the Teatro Tacón, Havana's grand opera house, where, incidentally, an Italian theater engineer, Antonio Meucci, discovered the principles of telephonic communication. On this episode and its links with opera, see Rachel Price, "Between an Angel's Cry and a Murmur: The Invention of the Telephone in Colonial Havana," *Discourse* 36, no. 3 (Fall 2014), 340–46. See also Marcelo Diego, "'Corramos un velo sobre esta escena tan triste': Ópera e escravidão na Havana do século XIX," *Alea* 23, no. 2 (May–August 2021), https://go-gale-com.libproxy1.usc.edu/ps/i.do?p=IFME&u=uso-cal_main&id=GALE%7CA682702801&v=2.1&it=r.
56. Writing before Vilar's downfall, Norman Lebrecht praised his donations—$250 million for organizations that included the Kennedy Center, the Metropolitan Opera House, the Royal Opera House, the Kirov, the Los Angeles Opera, and more—and described him as "the biggest opera buff since King Ludwig of Bavaria, Wagner's patron." Norman Lebrecht, "Alberto Vilar: The Benefactor and His Wife," *Lebrecht Weekly*, August 14, 2002, http://www.scena.org/columns/lebrecht/020814-nl-bride.html. On his numerous gifts and pledges not related to the arts, see James B. Stewart, "The Opera Lover: How Alberto Vilar's Passion for Philanthropy Landed Him in Jail," *New Yorker*, February 13, 2006, 117.
57. On the Royal Opera House renovation project, in which the Floral Hall, the old Covent Garden floral market, occupies a central position, see Kenneth Powell, *New London Architecture* (London: Merrell, 2001), 112–13.
58. The press release from the Royal Opera House read: "We will cease to use Mr. Vilar's name on printed material and programmes, and the signage in the public areas will be altered over the next few months in no particular order or time-scale. However, in recognition of his generous donation of approximately £4.4m to the Royal Opera House since 1999, he will remain listed on the Donor and Benefactors Board." "Covent Garden Removes Vilar's Name from Floral Hall Citing Failure to Make Good on Promised Payments," *Opera News*, September 19, 2005, https://www.operanews.com/Opera_News_Magazine/2005/9/News/Covent_Garden_Removes_Vilar_s_Name_from_Floral_Hall_Citing_Failure_to_Make_Good_on_Promised_Payments.html.
59. Vilar's real-life actions resound with Newman's malevolent entrepreneurship in the novel, as analyzed by John Carlos Rowe: "Newman announces to the reader that the legacy of Eurocolonialism is not only alive and well in his New World, but it is morphing into a new, potentially even more poisonous version in the figure of the cosmopolitan capitalist." John Carlos Rowe, "Henry James and Globalization," *Henry James Review* 24, no. 3 (Fall 2002): 206.
60. Allan Kozinn, "So You Can Buy Love after All," *New York Times*, October 8, 2000, https://www.nytimes.com/2000/10/08/arts/music-so-you-can-buy-love-after-all.html.
61. Norman Lebrecht, *Covent Garden: The Untold Story: Dispatches from the English Culture War, 1945–2001* (London: Pocket, 2000), 4.

62. Quoted by Kozinn, "So You Can Buy Love after All."
63. John Allison, "Opera Moneybags Faces the Music," *The Telegraph*, February 19, 2006, https://www.telegraph.co.uk/culture/3650295/Opera-moneybags-faces-the-music.html.
64. Robert Hilferty, "A Knight at the Opera," *New York*, January 21, 2002, https://nymag.com/nymetro/arts/music/features/5616.
65. Dalya Alberge and Helen Rumbelow, "Rich Told: Get Your Hand in Your Pocket," *The Times*, February 6, 2003, https://www.thetimes.co.uk/article/rich-told-get-your-hand-in-your-pocket-dqqch76tj57. Sarah Gaines, "Britain's Super-Rich Are Miserly, Says Philanthropist," February 6, 2003, https://www.theguardian.com/society/2003/feb/06/fundraising.uknews.
66. In May 2007, in a denouement of sorts that seems to belie Vilar's claims about European millionaires, the Royal Opera House announced the renaming of its atrium as the Paul Hamlyn Hall, in recognition of the many contributions of the foundation created by the German-born British publisher and philanthropist.
67. James B. Stewart, "The Opera Lover: How Alberto Vilar's Passion for Philanthropy Landed Him in Jail," *New Yorker*, February 13, 2006, 108.
68. David Remnick, "The Imperial Stagehand," *New Yorker*, February 22, 1999, https://archives.newyorker.com/newyorker/1999-02-22/flip112.
69. Johanna Fiedler, *Molto Agitato: The Mayhem behind the Music at the Metropolitan Opera* (New York: Anchor, 2003), 337.
70. Norman Lebrecht, "A New Future for Opera?," *Lebrecht Weekly*, May 23, 2001, http://www.scena.org/columns/lebrecht/010523-NL-vilar.html.
71. Hilferty, "A Knight at the Opera."
72. Fiedler, *Molto agitato*, 334.
73. Hilferty, "A Knight at the Opera."
74. Stewart, 120.
75. Stewart, 120.
76. Allison, "Opera Moneybags Faces the Music."
77. Robinson writes: "Like the *philosophes*, Mozart believes that we have within us the intellectual and emotional resources to transcend our hostilities. To put the matter in a word, he believes in the possibility of reconciliation." Robinson, *Opera and Ideas*, 14.
78. As Robinson explains, the aria's text is ambiguous—hope is not self-evident—but the music anticipates a possible happy ending. Robinson, *Opera and Ideas*, 31. See also Koestenbaum, who states, "Listen to the Countess sing sweetly about events that usually provoke anger, and learn to forgive history's mutations, domesticity's interruptions." Wayne Koestenbaum, *The Queen's Throat*, 212.
79. Kerman criticizes Da Ponte's libretto even as he praises Mozart's art: "With this miserable material before him, Mozart built a revelation, and saw how it could be supported by other elements in Beaumarchais's scaffolding." Kerman, *Opera as Drama*, 91.
80. Julian Rushton, "Nozze di Figaro, Le," in *The New Grove Book of Opera*, ed. Stanley Sadie (New York: St. Martin's Press, 1997), 450.

CHAPTER 6

1. Booklet to Hans Werner Herzog, *El Cimarrón*, performed by Angelo De Leonardis, Gundl Aggermann, Christina Schorn, and Ivan Mancinelli, Wergo, 2007, CD, 19.
2. Henze's *El Cimarrón* was not the first musical stage work about slavery in Cuba. First staged at Havana's Teatro Nacional in 1921, José Mauri Esteve's *La esclava* chronicles the complicated story of Matilde. For an analysis of the opera, including its performance history to 1980, see Jorge Antonio González, *La composición operística en Cuba*, 482–523.
3. Naomi André, *Black Opera: History, Power, Engagement* (Urbana: University of Illinois Press, 2018), 10.
4. André, 5–6.
5. André, 20.
6. "The History of the Royal Danish Theatre," Royal Danish Theater, https://kglteater.dk/en/about-us/about-the-theatre/the-history-of-the-royal-danish-theatre.
7. See Pablo Calvi, who, like other critics, places Barnet's text in the larger context of works by Truman Capote and Norman Mailer and, more specifically, Latin American authors such as Rodolfo Walsh and Gabriel García Márquez. Pablo Calvi, "Latin America's Own 'New Journalism,'" *Literary Journalism Studies* 2, no. 2 (Fall 2010): 75.
8. Henry James, "The Art of Fiction," in *Major Stories and Essays* (New York: Library of America, 1999), 577.
9. James, 577.
10. Abraham Acosta, *Thresholds of Illiteracy: Theory, Latin America, and the Crisis of Resistance* (New York: Fordham University Press, 2014),
11. Miguel Barnet, *Biography of a Runaway Slave: Fiftieth Anniversary Edition*, trans. W. Nick Hill (Evanston, IL: Northwestern University Press, 2016), 16.
12. Elzbieta Sklodowska, "Testimonio mediatizado: ¿Ventriloquía o heteroglosia? (Barnet/Montejo; Burgos/Menchú)," *Revista de Crítica Literaria Latinoamericana* 38 (1993): 86. For a metacritical analysis of *testimonio*, including the tensions between the literal and the literary, see Acosta, *Thresholds of Illiteracy*, 121–63.
13. Sklodowska.
14. Roberto González Echevarría, *Myth and Archive: A Theory of Latin American Narrative* (Cambridge: Cambridge University Press, 1990), 168.
15. Stephan Palmié, "Slavery, Historicism, and the Poverty of Memorialization," in *Memory: History, Theory, Debates*, ed. Susannah Radstone and Bill Schwarz (New York: Fordham University Press, 2010), 365.
16. Palmié, 363.
17. Palmié, 364.
18. Jorge Luis Borges, "The Witness," in *Dreamtigers*, trans. Mildred Boyer and Harold Morland (Austin: Texas University Press, 1964).
19. Hans Werner Henze, *Music and Politics: Collected Writings, 1953–81*, trans. Peter Labanyi (London: Faber and Faber, 1982), 199.

20. Henze, 181.
21. Henze, 174.
22. Carlos Barral et al., "Primera carta de los intelectuales a Fidel Castro," *Rialta*, https://rialta.org/primera-carta-de-los-intelectuales-a-fidel-castro.
23. Hans Magnus Enzensberger, "Der Cimarrón: Angaben über eine Handlung," in *El cimarrón: Ein Werkbericht*, Enzensberger et al., ed. Claus H. Henneberg (Mainz: Edition Schott, 1971), 33.
24. Ivanka Stoianova, "'Music Becomes Language': Narrative Strategies in *El Cimarrón* by Hans-Werner Henze," in *Musical Signification: Essays in the Semiotic Theory of Music*, ed. Eero Tarasti (Berlin: Mouton de Gruyter, 1995), 511.
25. Stoianova.
26. Stoianova, 512.
27. By comparing the libretto to the German translation of *Biografía de un cimarrón* made by Hildegard Baumgart, Enzensberger defends how his streamlined reworking thereof can still be regarded as "authentic." See Hans Magnus Enzensberger, "Der Cimarrón: Angaben über eine Handlung," 34–37.
28. Booklet to Hans Werner Henze, *El Cimarrón*, 18–19.
29. Wolfgang Becker-Carsten, "Current Chronicle: Berlin," *Musical Quarterly* 57, no. 2 (April 1971): 315.
30. Edward Greenfield, "Festivals: Aldeburgh," *Musical Times* 111, no. 1530 (August 1970): 819.
31. Stomu Yamashta, "Berichte über die Ausführung," in *El Cimarrón: Ein Werkbericht*, ed. Claus H. Henneberg, 52. Yamashta nonetheless underscores the sense of friendship among the four original performers, who came from different parts of the world: William Pearson, the baritone, an American; Leo Brouwer, the guitarist, Cuban; Karlheinz Zöller, the flutist, German; and Yamashta himself, Japanese.
32. Miguel Barnet, *Biography of a Runaway Slave*, trans. W. Nick Hill (Evanston, IL: Curbstone Books, 2004), 17–18.
33. For a singer's perspective on race and opera, see George Shipley's "Il Rodolfo Nero, or the Masque of Blackness," in André, Bryan, and Saylor, *Blackness in Opera*, 260–74. See also André, *Black Opera*, 13–20, and John Graziano's "Race and Racism" in *The Oxford Handbook of Opera*, ed. Helen M. Greenwald, 754–73.
34. William Pearson, the African American baritone born in Tennessee who created the role of Esteban, recalled discussing with Henze his vocal possibilities, which included rapid staccatos, falsettos, coloraturas, trills, and gutturals, as well as his personal memories of the "Tonfall und Singweise" (tone of voice and way of singing) of black people in the southern United States. William Pearson, "Berichte über die Ausführung," in *El Cimarrón: Ein Werkbericht*, ed. Claus H. Henneberg, 44.
35. Brouwer praises Henze for exploring the acoustic world of Cuba: its multiple voices; Yoruba rituals; people singing in streets and villages; dance music; and local music, with its African and Spanish origins. Leo

Brouwer, "Berichte über die Ausführung," in *El Cimarrón: Ein Werkbericht*, ed. Claus H. Henneberg, 49.

36. Gregers Dirckinck-Holmfeld, "Forførende!," review of *El cimarrón*, by Hans Werner Henze, Royal Danish Theater, Copenhagen, *GregersDH* (blog), September 27, 2009, http://gregersdh.dk/el-cimarron-kgl-teater-gl-scene-26-9-09-anm.

37. William Morton Payne, an American educator and critic of Scandinavian literatures, seeks to explain the meaning of the phrase in a sonnet titled "Ej Blot Til Lyst": "Not merely for our pleasure, but to purge / The soul from baseness, from ignoble fear, / And all the passions that make dim the clear / Calm vision of the world." William Morton Payne, "Ej Blot Til Lyst," Bartleby.com: Great Books Online, https://www.bartleby.com/248/1303.html.

38. On the links between slavery and opera in Brazil, see, for instance, Marcelo Diego, "O escravo vai à ópera: Ópera e escravidão no Rio de Janeiro ao redor de 1850," *Sociologia & Antropologia* 9, no. 2 (2019): 597–613.

39. Luis Gonzalo de Aguiar, "Lo schiavo," program notes to Carlos Gomes, *Lo schiavo*, Sonopress Rimo, 1997, CD, 16.

40. Alfredo d'Escragnolle Taunay, quoted by César de Carvalho Ismael, "O 'maestro' da abolição e sua ópera *O escravo*: dilemas do pensamento social na transição para a República" (PhD diss., Universidade Federal Rural do Rio do Janeiro, 2014), 105.

41. For a detailed study of Taunay's reactions to Paravicini's libretto, see César de Carvalho Ismael, "O 'maestro' da abolição e sua ópera *O escravo*," which reproduces Taunay's sketch on pages 65–68. For other influences in *Lo schiavo* besides Taunay's work, including a play by Alexandre Dumas, see Marcus Góes, *Carlos Gomes: Documentos comentados* (São Paulo: Algol, 2008), 97.

42. Carlos Gomes, quoted by Ismael, "O 'maestro' da abolição e sua ópera *O escravo*," 94–95.

43. The imperial family had just received news of the death of a relative in Lisbon. Instead of attending the opera, Isabel had a messenger report to her after each act. See Lutero Rodrigues, *Carlos Gomes: Um tema em questão* (São Paulo: Editora Unesp, 2011), 85–87. The dedication is also cited in Rubem Fonseca's *O selvagem da ópera,* his cinematic novel on the life of Gomes (211).

44. The most prominent figure in the history of operatic rapture in Latin America may well be Pedro II, an ardent patron and lover of the genre, who famously attended the inaugural performances of *Der Ring des Nibelungen* at Bayreuth—at the hotel register, he signed his profession as Emperor—and may have even tried to lure Richard Wagner to settle permanently in Rio de Janeiro. Indeed, Pedro II's passion for Wagner was the stuff of legend. As early as 1886, Adolphe Jullien reports on an imperial envoy charged with visiting the composer in Zürich. Adolphe Jullien, *Richard Wagner: Sa vie et ses œuvres* (Paris: Librairie de l'Art, 1889), 114.

Jullien adds that the offer may have been real, since Pedro II later became one of the patrons of Bayreuth.
45. Gérard Genette, *Paratexts: Thresholds of Interpretation* (Cambridge: Cambridge University Press, 1997), 136, emphasis in original.
46. Rodolfo Paravicini, libretto for Carlos Gomes, *Lo schiavo*, performed by Ida Miccolis, Lourival Braga, Alfredo Colosimo, Luiz Nascimento, Antea Claudia and the Orquestra e Coro do Teatro Municipal do Rio de Janeiro conducted by Santiago Guerra, Sonopress Rimo, 1997, CD, 38.
47. Volpe, "*Indianismo* and Landscape in the Brazilian Age of Progress," 247.
48. Volpe, 246.
49. Quoted by Volpe, 261.
50. Márvio dos Anjos, "Teatro Municipal Celebra os 180 anos de Carlos Gomes com 'Lo schiavo,'" *O Globo*, October 21, 2016, https://extra.globo.com/tv-e-lazer/teatro-municipal-celebra-os-180-anos-de-carlos-gomes-com-lo-schiavo-20326478.html.

CHAPTER 7

1. D. L. Groover, "Mild *Salsipuedes*," *Houston Press*, November 4, 2004, https://www.houstonpress.com/arts/mild-salsipuedes-6551409; "Love and Anchovies: Catán's 'Salsipuedes' from Houston Grand Opera," NPR, June 13, 2008, https://www.npr.org/2008/06/13/91309131/love-and-anchovies-catans-salsipuedes
2. In Latin American history, the name Salsipuedes is tragically linked to the massacre of Charrúa people that took place in Uruguay in 1831, after which, in a kind of Latin American display altogether different from that of Catán's opera, four survivors were taken to Paris and exhibited in a human zoo. It is also a song performed by Celia Cruz in which the place is defined as a "tierra de ilusión donde el amor nunca se muere" (land of hope where love never dies).
3. Ironically, Samuel Barber's *Vanessa* (1958), with a libretto by Gian-Carlo Menotti, "draws inspiration," as Logan Martell puts it, from Isak Dinesen's *Seven Gothic Tales*. While praised at its premiere as "a grand opera penned by an American composer," later critics, "insist that the work is American only insofar as Barber himself was born in the country"—as if questioning the notion that American composers should fe free to write on any topic. Logan Martell, "Opera Profile: Barber's *Vanessa*," *Operawire*, January 15, 2018, https://operawire.com/opera-profile-barbers-vanessa. On the actual contacts between *Vanessa* and "The Monkey," a story in *Seven Gothic Tales*, see Rachel Golden Carlson, "'As We Were Born Today: Characterization and Transformation in Samuel Barber's *Vanessa*," *Opera Quarterly* 17, no. 2 (Spring 2021), 235–49.
4. For a brief account of Catán's commission from the Houston Grand Opera, see Jan Breslauer, "Into Uncharted Waters," *Los Angeles Times*, October, 5, 1997, https://www.latimes.com/archives/la-xpm-1997-oct-05-ca-39314-story.html; and Steven Rosen, "Opera Ahoy! Climbing Aboard

Cincinnati Opera's Production of *Florencia en el Amazonas*," *City Beat*, July 9, 2008, https://www.citybeat.com/news/cover-story-opera-ahoy--12214957. According to Francesca Zambello, the opera's first director, Catán passionately embraced the challenge of composing a magic realist work. She also recounts briefly a visit to García Márquez's compound "deep in the jungle near Cartagena." Francesca Zambello, "A Note from Francesca Zambello," Wise Music Classical, https://www.wisemusicclassical.com/work/26750/Florencia-en-el-Amazonas--Daniel-Catán/. In a videotaped interview, Catán recounts speaking with García Márquez after the premiere of *La hija de Rappaccini* in Mexico City, a conversation during which the novelist said, "Next time you write an opera, I'll help you find a libretto." See Lorena Mora-Mowry, "Mexican Opera Composer Daniel Catán at Cincinnati Opera," June 15, 2008, YouTube video, https://www.youtube.com/watch?v=adoDkwvVO5g. On Catán's and Fuentes-Berain's process of collaboration with García Márquez (as well as Álvaro Mutis), see Catán's interview with María Josefa Velasco, "L'opéra et le réalisme magique: *Florencia en el Amazonas* de Daniel Catán (1996)" (master's thesis, Université Rennes II, 2009), 165–66.

5. Mark Swed, "A Savvy but Sketchy *Florencia*," *Los Angeles Times*, October 7, 1997, https://www.latimes.com/archives/la-xpm-1997-oct-07-ca-39998-story.html. See also Anthony Tommasini's review of the Houston premiere for the *New York Times*: "*Florencia en el Amazonas*', which draws its inspiration from the ruminative writings of Gabriel Garcia Marquez, was disappointing. While much modern opera is melodically stingy, Mr. Catan's writing for the voice is luxuriously lyrical; and he orchestrates with skill. But as musical drama, the opera is derivative and almost sunk with symbolism." Anthony Tommasini, "In Houston, a Premiere of a Mexican's Work," *New York Times*, October 29, 1996, https://www.nytimes.com/1996/10/29/arts/in-houston-a-premiere-of-a-mexican-s-work.html. On the uses and abuses of magical realism and related concepts in the discussion about *Florencia en el Amazonas*, see Velasco, "L'opéra et le réalisme magique."

6. On the relationship between Herzog and García Márquez, see Lund, *Werner Herzog*, 119, 205n117.

7. Siskind, *Cosmopolitan Desires*, 51, his emphasis.

8. Siskind, 54. For a Latin American author's protest against the exigencies of magical realism written around the time when *Florencia en el Amazonas* was first staged, see Alberto Fuguet's "I Am Not a Magic Realist," *Salon*, June 11, 1997, https://www.salon.com/1997/06/11/magicalintro.

9. In an essay, Catán explains that composing operas with Spanish-language librettos is first and foremost about representing the supranational culture shared by all Spanish speakers, including those who live in Spain and the United States. Daniel Catán, "Ópera en español," *Revista de Musicología* 31, no. 1 (2008): 251. Regarding his own work, Catán wistfully reflects on the fact that his *Il Postino* rescued Neruda's poetry—and, by extension, Skármeta's novel—via an Italian film; Catán, 254.

10. George Loomis, "Pablo Neruda and His Mailman, This Time Sung," *New York Times*, December 14, 2010, https://www.nytimes.com/2010/12/15/arts/15iht-loomis15.html.
11. Loomis.
12. For the process of adapting Paz's play into the opera, see Catán's fascinating series of letters—never mailed—to the poet discussing such creative issues as changing the name of Juan to Giovanni (a polysyllabic name is easier to sing) to his appreciation of the *shakuhachi* flute, which for Japanese poets is the sound of the wind as it traverses bamboo fields. Daniel Catán, "La música de *La hija de Rappaccini:* Cartas no echadas a Octavio Paz," *Vuelta* 173 (April 1991): 28–31. The letters reveal Catán as a composer at home in the world beyond the Americas and Europe; like Paz, who was Mexico's ambassador to India, Catán lived in Asia—Japan and Indonesia—for a year and a half.
13. Martin Bernheimer praised both the production's "modernism" and the director's "knowing eye for abstraction," yet more elements devoid of Latin American signs. Martin Bernheimer, "Opera: 'La Hija de Rappaccini': Venturing a Mexican Fantasy," *Los Angeles Times*, March 7, 1994, https://www.latimes.com/archives/la-xpm-1994-03-07-ca-31172-story.html. Reviewing the East Coast premiere at the Manhattan School of Music in 1997, Anthony Tommasini began by commenting on demography and opera in America: "The influence of Hispanic culture in the United States has been so pervasive for so long it is no longer remarkable. Yet the opera world has been surprisingly untouched by this development, for when Daniel Catan's opera 'Hija de Rappaccini' ('Rappaccini's daughter') was produced in San Diego three years ago, it was the first time an opera by a Mexican composer was presented by a professional company in the United States." Anthony Tommasini, "A Mad Botanist's Idea of Fathering," *New York Times*, April 25, 1997, https://www.nytimes.com/1997/04/25/arts/-mad-botanist-s-idea-of-fathering.html.
14. Mark Swed calls attention to Catán's various influences, including those from Asia, in a review of *La hija de Rappaccini* performed in 2013 in the gardens of Greystone Mansion, Beverly Hills: "The orchestra is a field of ravishing exotica, which alludes to the sinuous call of the Japanese flute and the glamorous clangor of the gamelan." Mark Swed, "Review: 'La Hija de Rappaccini's Passionate Exoticism," *Los Angeles Times*, July 22, 2013, https://www.latimes.com/entertainment/arts/culture/la-et-cm-rappaccinis-daughter-review-20130721-story.html.
15. Based on the number of his operas performed worldwide for five seasons (2013–2014 to 2017–2018), the website Operabase.com ranked Adams sixth among living composers. Only two Americans, Leonard Bernstein and Philip Glass, were ranked among all composers for the same period, at 39 and 41 (all other composers were European).
16. John Adams, *Hallelujah Junction: Composing an American Life* (New York: Picador, 2008), 253.

17. Adams, 245.
18. Erwan Dianteill, "Contrepoint américain de la Nativité et de la Passion du Christ: *La Pasión según San Marcos* d'Oswaldo Golijov et *El Niño* de John Adams, deux opéras de la fin du millénaire," *Nuevo Mundo, Mundos Nuevos*, January 2014, https://journals.openedition.org/nuevomundo/66312.
19. Susan McClary, *The Passions of Peter Sellars*, 65.
20. Cervántez's image also appears on the cover of Lara Medina's book, *Las Hermanas: Chicana/Latina Political Activism in the US Catholic Church* (Philadelphia: Temple University Press, 2004). Her slightly revised essay on the image, to which I allude here, is also included in Medina's book (x–xii).
21. In an interview, Sellars rightly explains why "CNN opera" is a misnomer for Adams's works, including *The Death of Klinghoffer*: "I don't even see how you could get that, when the opera itself is a million miles from anything you would ever see on CNN! . . . Opera is able to go inside to a place where the headlines aren't going." Thomas May, "Creative Contexts: Peter Sellars on Working with Adams," in *The John Adams Reader: Essential Writings on an American Composer*, ed. Thomas May (Pompton Plains, NJ: Amadeus Press, 2006), 241–42, his italics.
22. Yreina Cervántez, "'Mujer de Mucha Nnagua,' Pa'ti Xicana," in John Adams, *El niño*, Deutsches Symphonie-Orchester, Kent Nagano, with Lorraine Hunt Lieberson, Dawn Upshaw, Willard White, et al., recorded December 2000, Nonesuch 79634-2, two CDs, 31.
23. Cervántez, 33.
24. Cervántez.
25. For an analysis of Cervántez's serigraph and, specifically, "Tla ya timohuica," the Nahuatl *villancico* written on Sor Juana's habit, see Mario A. Ortiz, "Sor Juana en *El Niño* de John Adams y *Óyeme con los ojos* de Allison Sniffin," *Cuadernos de Música, Artes Visuales y Artes Escénicas* (2008): 207–34.
26. May, "Creative Contexts," 246. On the effect of texts originally written in English, Spanish and medieval Latin alongside English-language translations of texts by Hildegarde von Bingen and others, see Mathieu Duplay, *Les œuvres scéniques de John Adams: L'opéra et les frontières de la littérature* (Paris: Honoré Champion, 2023), 182-83.
27. Even as he praises Golijov's *La Pasión según San Marcos* for its use of musical elements derived from various cultures, including popular Latin American rhythms sung and played by nonclassical artists, Dianteill questions the search for diversity in *El Niño*, deeming the onscreen depiction of Chicanos and the employment of a partly Spanish libretto as insufficient to make it a multicultural work. Erwan Dianteill, "Contrepoint américain de la Nativité et de la Passion du Christ."
28. Michael Steinberg, "*El Niño:* A Nativity Oratorio," in Thomas May, ed., *The John Adams Reader* (Pompton Plains, NJ: Amadeus Press, 2006), 173. Adams expands on the experience in his autobiography, *Hallelujah Junction*, 239–40.
29. Bernard Holland, "With Ears and Eyes in Fierce Competition, the Eyes Have It," *New York Times*, January 15, 2001, https://www.nytimes.

com/2001/01/15/arts/music-review-with-ears-and-eyes-in-fierce-competition-the-eyes-have-it.html.
30. McClary describes Sellars's process to craft what she terms "a libretto of one's own": "he culls materials from a wide range of historical and international sources and patches them together to create his music-theater pieces in keeping with his particular aesthetic and critical priorities." McClary, *The Passions of Peter Sellars*, 87.
31. Mathieu Duplay, "'Alta, desnuda, única. Poesía': Échos de la poésie mexicaine dans les opéras de John Adams," *Amerika* 4 (2011): 7.
32. Duplay, *Les œuvres scèniques de John Adams*, 178.
33. Writing about the use of Spanish in *A Flowering Tree* (2006), an opera by Adams set in India, Duplay detects in the interpolation of Castellanos's text with the ancient Middle Eastern fragment a meaningful convergence of various geographical and cultural regions as well. These various places—Southern India, Bethlehem and Palestine, the Egyptian oasis where the Holy Family seeks rest, the mountains of California, and Castellanos's rural Mexico—incarnate a bright southern world set in opposition to the dark land alluded to in "Poesía." Duplay, "'Alta, desnuda, única. Poesía,'" 16.
34. Ken Ueno, "John Adams on *El Niño* and Vernacular Elements," in *The John Adams Reader: Essential Writings on an American Composer*, ed. Thomas May, 185.
35. In his autobiography, Adams narrates in detail the process, prompted by Sellars, of learning Spanish and reading authors such as Cervantes and García Márquez in the original, which he views both as an aesthetic and political experience: "But of all the languages that I have learned, Spanish has afforded me the greatest enchantment and was the one that most radicalized my worldview. It unlocked for me the cultures, sensibilities, and long histories of Latin America, making me more aware and more sensitive to what it means to *not* be a part of the dominant culture." John Adams, *Hallelujah Junction*, 241, his italics.
36. Adams underscores the lack of correspondence between the music and the film ("like a John Cage-Merce Cunningham collaboration"), which was shot before most of the score had been composed—a "competition and sensory discord" similar to what he later experienced while watching Bill Viola's video for *Tristan and Isolde* as the opera was performed (249–50).
37. Bernard Holland, "With Ears and Eyes in Fierce Competition, the Eyes Have It."
38. Holland.
39. Adams, *Hallelujah Junction*, 242. On Adams's optimistic view of the planet's environment at the time, see Duplay, *Les œuvres scéniques de John Adams*, 168–69.
40. For a detailed review of the opera's performance history through 2008, see Maria Josefa Velasco, "L'opéra et le réalisme magique: *Florencia en el Amazonas* de Daniel Catán (1996)," 61.
41. Virginia Woolf, *The Diary of Virginia Woolf*, ed. Anne Olivier Bell (New York: Harcourt Brace Jovanovich, 1977–1984), 5:438–39.

42. For Woolf's influence on García Márquez, for instance, through Borges's translation of *Orlando*, see Suzanne Jill Levine, "A Second Glance at the Spoken Mirror: Gabriel García Márquez and Virginia Woolf," *Inti: Revista de Literatura Hispánica* 16 (1983): 53-60; Alexander Coleman, "Bloomsbury in Aracataca," *World Literature Today* 59, no. 4 (1985): 543-49. For Borges's problematic translation of *A Room of One's Own*, see Lea Leone, "A Translation of His Own: Borges and *A Room of One's Own*," *Woolf Studies Annual* 15 (2009): 47-66.

43. See Fiona G. Parrott, "Friendship, Letters and Butterflies: Victoria Ocampo and Virginia Woolf," *STAR (Scotland's Transatlantic Relations) Project Archive* (April 2004): 3-4. See also Alicia Salomone, "Virginia Woolf en los *Testimonios* de Victoria Ocampo: Tensiones entre feminismo y colonialismo," *Revista Chilena de Literatura* 69 (November 2006): 69-87; and Gayle Rogers, *Modernism and the New Spain: Britain, Cosmopolitan Europe, and Literary History* (Oxford: Oxford University Press, 2014), the fourth chapter of which deals with Ocampo as Woolf's "primary Hispanic interlocutor, translator, and publisher," and with their "shared antifascisms" (126).

44. Virginia Woolf, *The Letters of Virginia Woolf*, ed. Nigel Nicolson and Joanne Trautmann. (New York: Harcourt Brace Jovanovich, 1975–1980), 5:438-39.

45. Charles Darwin, *The Voyage of the Beagle* (New York: Modern Library, 2001), 141.

46. Hudson writes to Edward Garnett: "Somewhere in S. America it is supposed to be and once or twice 'natives' are mentioned. The scene might just as well have been in some hotel on the south coast of England." W. H. Hudson, *Letters from W. H. Hudson to Edward Garnett* (London: J. M. Dent, 1925), 147-48.

47. Rachel observes "a great yellow butterfly, which was opening and closing its wings very slowly on a little flat stone." The sight of the butterfly seems to trigger a momentous question never before verbalized: "'What is it to be in love?' she demanded, after a long silence; each word as it came into being seemed to shove itself out into an unknown sea." Virginia Woolf, *The Voyage Out* (New York: Modern Library, 2001), 179.

48. Victoria Ocampo, "Reencuentro con Virginia Woolf," in *Testimonios: Novena Serie* (Buenos Aires: Sur, 1975), 43.

49. Quentin Bell, "An Interview with Quentin Bell," by Antonio Bivar, 1993, https://www.ibiblio.org/sally/Bellinterview.html.

50. Woolf, *The Diary of Virginia Woolf*, 4:263.

51. Parrott, "Friendship, Letters and Butterflies," 2.

52. Woolf, *The Letters of Virginia Woolf*, 5:348-49. On the pattern of misunderstanding Victoria Ocampo by her foreign friends and acquaintances, see Beatriz Sarlo, *La máquina cultural: Maestras, traductores y vanguardistas* (Buenos Aires: Seix Barral, 2007), 106-25.

53. The last sentence in Rivera's novel is well known among readers of Latin American literature: "¡Los devoró la selva!" (The jungle devoured them). José Eustasio Rivera, *La vorágine* (Madrid: Cátedra, 1990), 385.

54. Carlos Fuentes, *La nueva novela hispanoamericana* (Mexico City: Cuadernos de Joaquín Mortiz, 1980), 9–10.
55. Marcela Fuentes-Berain, Libretto to Daniel Catán, *Florencia en el Amazonas*, Houston Grand Opera Orchestra and Chorus, Patrick Summers, with Mark S. Doss, Ana María Martínez, et al., Albany Records 531/32, 2002, two CDs, 17.
56. Darwin, *The Voyage of the Beagle*, 12.
57. Darwin, 29–30.
58. Darwin, 288.
59. See Jacques Joset, "Un sofocante aletear de mariposas amarillas: Lectura de un episodio de *Cien años de soledad*," *Actas del Simposio Internacional de Estudios Hispánicos*, ed. Mátyás Horányi (Budapest: Akadémiai Kiadó, 1978), 421–27.
60. Catán himself invokes a similar mythology as he recounts the history of the Manaus opera house: "Siempre me ha fascinado la historia del teatro de Manaus, porque es una historia de *locura*. [. . .] Sabía que de repente lo echaban a andar y pues a los pocos meses la selva devoraba otra vez el lugar" (The story of the Manaus theater has always fascinated me because it's a story of *madness*. . . . I knew that all of a sudden they would make it run, but within a few months the jungle would again devour the place). María Josefa Velasco, "L'opéra et le réalisme magique," 170, Catán's emphasis.
61. Velasco, "L'opéra et le réalisme magique," 171.
62. Efraín Kristal, "Literary Anecdotes," in Daniel Catán, *Florencia en el Amazonas*, 8.
63. Giuseppe Giacosa and Luigi Illica, libretto to Giacomo Puccini, *Madama Butterfly*, performed by Maria Callas, Nicolai Gedda and the Orchestra e Coro del Teatro alla Scala di Milano, conducted by Herbert von Karajan, EMI Classics, 1987, CD.
64. Synopsis in Daniel Catán, *Florencia en el Amazonas*, Albany Records, 2002, CD, 15.
65. Charles H. Parsons, "Florencia en el Amazonas." *Opera News* 73, no. 4 (October 2008), 50.
66. It also recalls the title of Joscelyn Godwin's *Athanasius Kircher's Theatre of the World: The Life and Work of the Last Man to Search for Universal Knowledge*, which closely examines Kircher's writings, including his music theory, and visual works.
67. See Paula Findlen, *Athanasius Kircher: The Last Man Who Knew Everything* (New York: Routledge, 2004), 329–64.
68. Octavio Paz, *Sor Juana, or, The Traps of Faith*, trans. Margaret Sayers Peden (Cambridge, MA: Harvard University Press), 177.
69. Sor Juana Inés de la Cruz, *Poems, Protest, and a Dream*, trans. Margaret Sayers Peden (New York: Penguin Books, 1997), 78, 79.
70. Helmut Krausser, libretto to Louis Andriessen, *Theater of the World*, performed by Leigh Melrose, Cristina Zavalloni and the Los Angeles

Philharmonic conducted by Reinbert de Leeuw, Nonesuch Records, 2017, CD, n.p.
71. Paz, 175.
72. John Henken, "About the Program: *Theater of the World*," *Performance* (May 2016): P2.
73. Damjan Rakonjac, "Louis Andriessen's *Theatre of the World*." *Music & Literature*, June 23, 2016, https://www.musicandliterature.org/reviews/2016/6/23/louis-andriessens-theatre-of-the-world. Mark Swed, "Why Andriessen's Daring and Difficult 'Theater of the World' Will Stand the Test of Time," *Los Angeles Times*, May 9, 2016, https://www.latimes.com/entertainment/arts/la-et-cm-la-phil-andriessen-review-20160509-snap-story.html.
74. Krausser, libretto to Andriessen, *Theater of the World*, n.p.
75. Krausser.

CHAPTER 8

1. Writing about the business of opera in Argentina, Aníbal Enrique Cetrangolo underscores two kinds of audiences: members of the upper classes, who sought to imitate Europe by means of its theaters; and more modest operagoers, often Italian migrants from remote villages who could now have easy access to operahouses. Aníbal Enrique Cetrangolo, *Ópera, barcos y banderas: El melodrama y la migración en Argentina (1880–1920)*, (Madrid: Biblioteca Nueva, 2015).
2. Alan Gilbert, "Latin America," in *The Oxford Handbook of Cities in World History*, ed. Peter Clark (Oxford: Oxford University Press, 2015), 485.
3. Beatriz Sarlo, *Una modernidad periférica: Buenos Aires 1920 y 1930* (Buenos Aires: Ediciones Nueva Visión, 1988), 15, her italics.
4. Pablo Gianera, *La música en el grupo Sur: Una modernidad inconclusa* (Buenos Aires: Eterna Cadencia Editora, 2011).
5. Gonzalo Aguilar, *Episodios cosmopolitas en la cultura argentina* (Buenos Aires: Santiago Arcos, 2009). See esp. pp. 29–33, 37–51, and 211–31, on Ocampo's literary relations with T. E. Lawrence.
6. Michael Scott, *Maria Meneghini Callas* (Boston: Northeastern University Press, 1991), 48–49. As Scott recounts, Callas's letters to her husband, Giovanni Battista Meneghini, touch on the city's modernity and wealth. Pablo D. Berruti underscores the place of the Colón in Callas's career: "The Teatro Colón of Buenos Aires has the double privilege of having been both the site of Maria Callas's début in America and of having made the first recording of her in a live performance on May 20, 1949, when the season was officially opened with *Turandot* starring Mario del Monaco and Maria Callas under the direction of Tullio Serafin, in what was to be Callas' last performances of this opera." Pablo D. Berruti, program notes to *Maria Callas: The Unknown Teatro Colón Recordings*, Divina Records, 1999, CD, 4. On July 9, 1949, Callas also sang excerpts from *Norma* and *Turandot* at the Colón's "Velada de Gala en Celebración del 133º Aniversario de

la Jura de la Independencia," the soiree commemorating Argentina's independence, attended by President Juan Perón and his wife Eva.

7. For a full roster of singers and conductors who performed at the Colón from 1908 to 1999, see Leonor Plate, *Óperas, Teatro Colón: Esperando el centenario* (Buenos Aires: Editorial Lunken, 2006), 1:147–285. On performances by the European visitors as "the major events of the year," see Enzo Valenti Ferro, "Ópera / Opera," in *Teatro Colón: A telón abierto / In Full View*, ed. Jorge Aráoz Badí (Buenos Aires: Julio Moyano, 2000), 158. In 1923, Strauss conducted both *Elektra* and *Salomé* with the Vienna Philharmonic Orchestra. Even before the new Teatro Colón opened its doors, Puccini spent several weeks in Buenos Aires in the austral winter of 1905. The Teatro de la Ópera (the major house in the city) scheduled nineteen performances of his works; after the first staging of *La Bohème*, the audience was transported, applauding enthusiastically and making Puccini take twenty bows. Gustavo Gabriel Otero and Daniel Varacalli Costas, *Puccini en la Argentina: Junio–agosto de 1905* (Buenos Aires: Instituto Italiano de Cultura de Buenos Aires, 2006), 35. While in Argentina, Puccini worked on the final version of *Edgar*, which premiered on July 8, 1905, at the Teatro de la Ópera (78–79); went hunting outside the city; and was financially well compensated, as this verse reflects: "Si sólo de una tan corta jira / se va Puccini con tanta lira, / reconozcamos que no es satírico / llamarle tigre del arte lírico" (qtd. by Otero and Varacalli Costa, 31; If after such a short tour, Puccini can leave with so many liras, let's acknowledge that it's no joke to call him the tiger of lyrical art).

8. Quoted by Aráoz Badí, *Teatro Colón*, 32.

9. Analyzing a plethora of subjects related to the city's cultural history, the book includes an essay on the Colón and its ties with Europe, as well as its enduring status, at least through the 1980s, as a stage for Argentina's mightiest. See Béatrice Muterel-Echo, "Al Colón!" in *Buenos Aires: Port de l'Extrême-Europe* ed. Graciela Schneider-Madanes (Paris: Autrement, 1987), 173.

10. Alberto Bellucci summarizes the eclectic nature of the various architectural styles: "So then, touring the Colón we are making a stylistic journey of almost four centuries, beginning in the Renaissance Rome of Bramante and Bernini, a free passage through Palladian Vicenza with an obligatory stopover in the Paris of Louis XIV, all seen, designed and certified in the vision of the Nineties and with a final diploma from the Academy of Beaux Arts. A reason for which, if indeed academic design grows progressively more French, we have the right here to baptise this child with so many fathers with the stylistic tag which suits it best: eclectic." Alberto Bellucci, "Arquitectura / Architecture," in *Teatro Colón: A telón abierto / In Full View*, ed. Jorge Aráoz Badí, 422. As if the Colón's architectural mélange needed validation several decades after its opening, Bellucci quotes Sir Norman Foster's words upon seeing the main auditorium in 1997: "incredible, amazing space" (434).

11. See Robert Stevenson, "Buenos Aires," in *The New Grove Dictionary of Opera*, ed. Stanley Sadie, 1:634.
12. Edward Said, *Culture and Imperialism* (New York: Vintage, 1994), 112.
13. Bellucci, "Arquitectura / Architecture," 420.
14. Enzo Valenti Ferro, "Ópera / Opera," in *Teatro Colón*, ed. Jorge Aráoz Badí, 138.
15. See María Cristina Pons and Claudia Soria, eds., *Delirios de grandeza: Los mitos argentinos; memoria, identidad, cultura* (Rosario: Beatriz Viterbo, 2005).
16. Deutsche-Welle's coverage of the production includes a documentary titled *The Colón Ring: Wagner in Buenos Aires*, https://www.dw.com/en/the-colón-ring-wagner-in-buenos-aires/a-16745392. Katharina Wagner explained to Buenos Aires's *La Nación* that she viewed the Colón as the ideal venue for the new version because of its architectural glamour and the technological update it underwent during its renovation. See Cecilia Scalisi, "La bisnieta de Wagner," *La Nación*, September 20, 2011, https://www.lanacion.com.ar/lifestyle/la-bisnieta-de-wagner-nid1409002.
17. Pablo Bardin, "The Colón-Ring, A Sorry Fiasco," *Buenos Aires Herald*, December 1, 2012. The review can be accessed on *Tribuna Musical*, the author's blog, https://tribunamusical.blogspot.com/2012/12/the-colon-ring-sorry-fiasco-i.html.
18. Barnard L. Collier, "Pinter Banned? Antonioni Banned? But Why?," *New York Times*, September 10, 1967, https://timesmachine.nytimes.com/timesmachine/1967/09/10/94889968.html?pageNumber=125. This article, to which I return, is analyzed by Enrique Buch, whose critical gesture of reading *El gran teatro* in the context of the opera's banning I follow here. Enrique Buch, *The Bomarzo Affair: Ópera, perversión y dictadura* (Buenos Aires: Adriana Hidalgo, 2003), 179–83.
19. Aráoz Badí, *Teatro Colón*, 35–36.
20. Manuel Mujica Lainez, *El gran teatro* (Buenos Aires: Debolsillo, 2010), 15.
21. For a description of the musical life of that bygone era, see Daniel Barenboim, *My Life in Music* (New York: Arcade Publishing, 2013), 3.
22. The performance during which the novel takes place appears to be one of five conducted by Fritz Busch between August and September 1942. Before the publication date of *El gran teatro*, there were stagings of *Parsifal* again in the 1946, 1955, 1961, and 1969 seasons. See Leonor Plate, *Óperas, Teatro Colón*, 213–14. On Mujica Lainez's general fear of anachronism in *El gran teatro*, especially regarding the possibility of *Parsifal* never having been performed in the evening at the Colón, see Buch, *The Bomarzo Affair*, 182–83.
23. Jorge Luis Borges, "A Manuel Mujica Lainez" and "To Manuel Mujica Lainez," in *Selected Poems*, ed. Alexander Coleman, trans. Eric McHenry (New York: Penguin, 2000), 374–75.
24. Benzecry, *The Opera Fanatic*, 26.
25. Quoted by Bellucci, "Arquitectura / Architecture," 393–94.

26. Adorno underscores the centrality of costume for opera's theatricality, which he also views in the context of the voice: "Costume is essential to opera: in contrast to a play, an opera without costume would be a paradox. If the gestures of singers—which they often bring along as if straight from the prop room—are themselves already part costume, then their voices—which natural people, as it were, don as soon as they step on the operatic stage—are entirely put on." Adorno, "Bourgeois Opera," 25–26.
27. For a study of opera and the Italian diaspora in Buenos Aires with a focus on ideas of *italianità* in the double programming of *Cavalleria rusticana* and *Pagliacci*, see Ditlev Rindom, "Bygone Modernity: Re-Imagining Italian Opera in Milan, New York and Buenos Aires, 1887–1914" (PhD diss., University of Cambridge, 2019), 93–142. Mujica Lainez himself preferred Italian to German opera. Originally, the novel was to take place during a performance of *Madama Butterfly*, but the author ultimately opted for *Parsifal*, which he viewed as a good musical example of boredom. See Buch, *The Bomarzo Affair*, 180.
28. Adorno, "Bourgeois Opera," 40.
29. Adorno.
30. Adorno.
31. Adorno, 41.
32. If the novel takes place in 1942, the presence of these instruments at the theater may be considered an anachronism. The Colón's Museo de los Instrumentos was established in 1949 to house the collection of old instruments belonging to the Museo de Arte Hispanoamericano Isaac Fernández Blanco. The instruments have been shown at the Fernández Blanco since 2007; see María Elena Polack, "Notable colección de cuerdas en el Museo Isaac Fernández Blanco," *La Nación*, December 16, 2013, https://www.lanacion.com.ar/sociedad/notable-coleccion-de-cuerdas-en-el-museo-isaac-fernandez-blanco-nid1648065/.
33. The poem was written by Oscar Monesterolo, a friend of the author. See Buch, *The Bomarzo Affair*, 181.
34. On the sexual dimensions of Amfortas's sin in *Parsifal*, see Linda Hutcheon and Michael Hutcheon, *Opera: Desire, Disease, Death* (Lincoln: University of Nebraska Press, 1996), 61–93.
35. As Buch argues, the decadent members of the Buenos Aires bourgeoisie may recall the suffering Knights of the Grail, but Salvador is far from being Wagner's hero. Buch, *The Bomarzo Affair*, 180.
36. In the article by Barnard Collier, Borges offers a defense of censorship as a beneficial practice for writers. Describing the novel on which the opera is based as "just an exaltation of homosexuality" having "no finesse," he asks Argentine writers to "learn to use the oblique attack" and imitate Voltaire's irony or Whitman's periphrases: "And there are abrupt Anglo-Saxon words Walt Whitman could have used, to less effect, when he said 'Love-flesh swelling and deliciously aching. . . . But he limited himself. Now I know that is far out, but it's true. Censorship can be discipline." Barnard L. Collier, "Pinter Banned? Antonioni Banned? But Why?"

37. Rubén Darío, "Parsifal," in *Poesías completas*, ed. A. Méndez Plancarte (Madrid: Aguilar, 1975), 963.
38. Yet another sonnet on Wagner's opera is Verlaine's "Parsifal," recalled in its entirety in *El gran teatro* by Mademoiselle Yvette Truc, a teacher at the Institut Français. Displeased by the opera's German origin as the war rages on, she is comforted by how its French literary connections—Chrétien de Troyes and Verlaine—protect her from devilish swastikas (193). In a letter to Oscar Monesterolo partly reproduced in the 2011 illustrated edition of the novel, Mujica Lainez mentions a letter by Victoria Ocampo containing a transcription of Verlaine's sonnet done by Ocampo's secretary. Manuel Mujica Lainez, *El gran teatro* (La Cumbre, Argentina: Fundación Manuel Mujica Lainez, 2011), 224.
39. Interestingly, the lexicon and images of Darío's "Parsifal" may have been inspired by João da Cruz e Sousa's sonnets. The preeminent Brazilian symbolist and an Afro-descendant, Cruz e Sousa is known as the Cisne Negro (Black Swan), a transethnic nod to Wagnerian motifs. See André Fiorussi, "Rubén Darío, leitor de Cruz e Sousa? Uma hipótese menosprezada de Andrade Muricy," *Caracol* 4 (2013): 82–85. On the sexual ambiguity of Darío's Parsifal, see Blas Matamoro, *Rubén Darío* (Madrid: Espasa Calpe, 2002).
40. Mujica Lainez takes this idea further in one of the novel's few self-reflexive moments, in which the narrator ironically retraces the sources of Parsifal's story of self-emasculation even as he appears to parody the cultural enumerations in which his own text routinely engages (161).
41. Sarlo, *Una modernidad periférica*, 87.
42. Pablo Gianera, "Amor por Victoria Ocampo," *La Nación*, July 6, 2013.
43. See Molloy on Ocampo's "theatrics of reading." Sylvia Molloy, *At Face Value: Autobiographical Writing in Spanish America* (Cambridge: Cambridge University Press, 1991), 55–56.
44. Beatriz Sarlo, "V.O.," unpublished libretto for *V.O.*, opera with music by Martín Bauer, 2013.
45. Beatriz Sarlo, *La máquina cultural: Maestras, traductores y vanguardistas* (Buenos Aires: Seix Barral, 2007), 80.
46. Victoria Ocampo, *Autobiografía III: La rama de Salzburgo* (Buenos Aires: Sur, 1982), 21.
47. Victoria Ocampo, *Autobiografía II: El imperio insular* (Buenos Aires: Sur, 1982), 107.
48. What Sarlo renders as *emoción* is actually *transport* in Racine's original text: "Quel transport me saisit?" Jean Racine, *Andromaque* (Paris: Larousse, 2008), 105.
49. Sarlo, *La máquina cultural*, 99.
50. Sarlo, 100.
51. Sarlo, 78.
52. Victoria Ocampo, *Autobiografía I: El archipiélago* (Buenos Aires: Sur, 1982), 136.
53. The work is *A Country Girl, or, Town and Country* (1902), a musical play by James T. Tanner with the collaboration of others.

54. Ocampo, *Autobiografía II: El imperio insular*, 70.
55. Ocampo refers to Salomea Krusceniski, a Ukrainian soprano who was later naturalized Italian. Rodolfo Celletti and Valeria Pregliasco Gualerzi underscore her physical attractiveness and theatrical gifts, which must have been at the heart of young Ocampo's attraction for her. Rodolfo Celletti and Valeria Pregliasco Gualerzi. "Krusceniski, Salomea," in *The Grove Book of Opera Singers*, ed. Laura Macy (Oxford and New York: Oxford University Press, 2008), 258.
56. Ocampo, *Autobiografía II: El imperio insular*, 68.
57. Ocampo, *Autobiografía III: La rama de Salzburgo*, 23.
58. Victoria Ocampo, *Autobiografía III: La rama de Salzburgo*, 24.
59. For Sarlo's view of Ocampo's musical culture, see *La máquina cultural*, 126.
60. In this tale of averted undoing and ultimate envoicing, Sarlo's encapsulation of Ocampo's life and works in the form of a sonnet might unwittingly invoke the old debate on the primacy of words or music in opera. Sonnets in opera are rare, but there is one example that might be pertinent here. In *Capriccio*, Richard Strauss's last opera, a poet writes and recites a sonnet in order to display the superiority of words, while a composer sets it to music and plays it on the piano to showcase the musical art. In *V.O.*, Victoria's sonnet is not about that dispute, but rather about the power of a consecrated literary form to reimagine Ocampo as a figure in possession of the attributes denied to her younger self..
61. Ocampo, *Autobiografía III: La rama de Salzburgo*, 39.
62. Charles Baudelaire, "Moesta et errabunda," in *Les fleurs du mal*, ed. Claude Pichois (Paris: Gallimard, 1996), 101.
63. Charles Baudelaire, "Grieving and Wandering," in *The Flowers of Evil / Les Fleurs du Mal*, trans. William Aggeler (Fresno, CA: Academy Library Guild, 1954).
64. Sarlo, *La máquina cultural*, 137.

AFTERWORD

1. Alex Ross, "This Rough Magic," *Alex Ross: The Rest Is Noise* (blog), September 17, 2004, https://www.therestisnoise.com/2004/09/this_rough_magi.html.
2. See, for instance, the essays collected in "Transatlantic Routes," in *"The Tempest" and Its Travels*, ed. Peter Hulme and William H. Sherman (London: Reaktion Books, 2000).
3. Roberto Fernández Retamar, *Caliban and Other Essays,* trans. Edward Baker (Minneapolis: University of Minnesota Press, 2005), 14.
4. When asked whether the tango heard in *Powder Her Face* was a quotation, Adès replies: "Quotation is the wrong word. It's robbery." Thomas Adès, *Thomas Adès: Full of Noises: Conversations with Tom Service* (New York: Farrar, Straus and Giroux, 2012), 152. He then goes on to explain how the "expanding harmony" (153) informs much of the opera.
5. As Jane Forner notes, Adès himself avoids discussing his work's "political significance," and views British colonialism as a nineteenth-century phenomenon and not the proper "historical context" for Shakespeare's

play. Jane Forner, "'O brave new Caliban': Postcolonial Perspectives on Adès's *The Tempest*," in *Thomas Adès Studies*, ed. Edward Venn and Philip Stoecker (Cambridge: Cambridge University Press, 2022), 72. Nonetheless, Forner persuasively places the opera's music and libretto in dialogue with postcolonial readings of the play, concluding that "its many ambiguities—especially the open horizon of the ending—reflect . . . a potentially productive, unstable space in which we might probe the symbolic, legal, psychological and physical violences that the 'colonial project' continues to exert today" (92). For a related context, see Ian Smith, who views "scholarly hesitations about race" in Shakespeare and early modern studies as "rooted in an anxious defense of whiteness often fashioned in the cool language of scholarly rigor and historical precision." Ian Smith, *Black Shakespeare: Reading and Misreading Race* (Cambridge: Cambridge University Press, 2022), 19.

6. David Lindley, introduction to *The Tempest*, by William Shakespeare (Cambridge: Cambridge University Press, 2002), 119.
7. Kim F. Hall, *Things of Darkness: Economies of Race and Gender in Early Modern England* (Ithaca, NY: Cornell University Press, 1995), 143.
8. Lindley, introduction to *The Tempest*, 215.
9. Hall, *Things of Darkness*, 142.
10. Meredith Oakes, libretto to Thomas Adès, *The Tempest*, Orchestra of the Royal Opera House, Thomas Adès, with Simon Keenlyside, Cynthia Sieden, Ian Bostridge, et al., EMI Classics, 6 95234 2, 2009, 2 CDs, 30.
11. Robert P. Morgan, "Tempest, The," in *The New Grove Dictionary of Opera*, ed. Stanley Sadie, 4:685.
12. Ian Bostridge, *A Singer's Notebook* (London: Faber and Faber, 2011), 247. Forner notes that productions of the opera (London, New York, Santa Fe and Budapest) have focused on "the strangeness" of both Ariel's and Caliban's bodies, but not engaged with the opera's "political potential." Jane Forner, "'O brave new Caliban,'" 85.
13. Bostridge, 248. See also Forner, whose "appraisal of the aria's effect admittedly rests on valorising standards of 'beautiful' sound in which conventional Western tonality is associated with positive qualities." Forner, "'O brave new Caliban,'" 84.
14. Bostridge, *A Singer's Notebook*.

BIBLIOGRAPHY

Abbate, Carolyn, and Roger Parker. *A History of Opera*. New York: W. W. Norton, 2012.
Acosta, Abraham. *Thresholds of Illiteracy: Theory, Latin America, and the Crisis of Resistance*. New York: Fordham University Press, 2014.
Adams, John. *The Gospel according to the Other Mary*. Libretto by Peter Sellars, based on Old and New Testament sources and with texts by Hildegard von Bingen, Rosario Castellanos, et al. Los Angeles Philharmonic. Gustavo Dudamel. With Kelley O'Connor, Tamara Mumford, Russell Thomas, et al. Recorded March 2013. Deutsche Grammophon 479 2243, 2014. 2 CDs.
———. *Hallelujah Junction: Composing an American Life*. New York: Picador, 2008.
———. *El Niño*. Libretto by Peter Sellars, adapted from poems by Rosario Castellanos, Sor Juana Inés de la Cruz, et al., and from texts from the Wakefield Mystery Plays, Martin Luther, et al. Deutsches Symphonie-Orchester Berlin. Kent Nagano. With Lorraine Hunt Lieberson, Dawn Upshaw, Willard White, et al. Recorded December 2000 and January 2001. Nonesuch 79634-2, 2000. 2 CDs.
Adès, Thomas. *The Tempest*. Libretto by Meredith Oakes. Orchestra of the Royal Opera House, Covent Garden. Thomas Adès. With Simon Keenlyside, Cynthia Sieden, Ian Bostridge, et al. Recorded March 2007. EMI Classics, 6 95234 2, 2009. 2 CDs.
———. *Thomas Adès: Full of Noises: Conversations with Tom Service*. New York: Farrar, Straus and Giroux, 2012.
Adorno, Theodor. "Bourgeois Opera." In Levin, *Opera through Other Eyes*, 25–43.
Aguilar, Gonzalo. *Episodios cosmopolitas en la cultura argentina*. Buenos Aires: Santiago Arcos, 2009.
———. "The National Opera: A Migrant Genre of Imperial Expansion." *Journal of Latin American Cultural Studies* 12, no. 1 (2003): 83–94.
Algarotti, Francesco. *Saggio sopra l'opera in musica*. Leghorn: Marco Coltellini, 1763.
Alonso, Alicia. *Diálogos con la danza*. Buenos Aires: Galerna, 1988.

André, Naomi. *Black Opera: History, Power, Engagement.* Urbana: University of Illinois Press, 2018.

André, Naomí, Karen M. Bryan, and Eric Saylor, ed. *Blackness in Opera.* Urbana: University of Illinois Press, 2014.

Andrews, Jean. "Carlos Gomes' *Il guarany:* The Frontiers of Miscegenation in Nineteenth-Century Grand Opera." *Portuguese Studies* 16 (2000): 26–42.

Andriessen, Louis. *Theatre of the World: A Grotesque Stagework in Nine Scenes.* Libretto by Helmut Krausser. Los Angeles Philharmonic. Reinbert de Leeuw. With Leigh Melrose, Lindsay Kesselman, Marcel Beekman, Cristina Zavalloni, et al. Recorded May 2016. Nonesuch 7559-79361-8, 2016. 2 CDs.

Aráoz Badí, Jorge, ed. *Teatro Colón: A telón abierto / In Full View.* Buenos Aires: Julio Moyano, 2000.

Arenas, Reinaldo. *El color del verano.* Miami: Ediciones Universal, 1991.

———. *The Color of Summer.* Translated by Andrew Hurley. New York: Penguin, 2000.

Baker, Geoffrey. "The Resounding City." In *Music and Urban Society in Colonial Latin America*, edited by Baker and Tess Knighton, 1–20. Cambridge: Cambridge University Press, 2011.

Bakhtiarova, Galina. "A Tale of Two Habaneras: Transatlantic Journeys of a Cultural Sign." *Journal of Transatlantic Studies* 1, no. 2 (2003): 117–30.

Barbier, Patrick. *The World of the Castrati: The History of an Extraordinary Operatic Phenomenon.* London: Souvenir Press, 1996.

Barnet, Miguel. *Biography of a Runaway Slave: Fiftieth Anniversary Edition.* Translated by W. Nick Hill. Evanston, IL: Northwestern University Press, 2016.

Bartoli, Cecilia, singer. *Maria.* Recorded August, September, and October 2007. Decca 475 9082, 2007. CD and DVD.

Bejel, Emilio. *Gay Cuban Nation.* Chicago: University of Chicago Press, 2001.

Benzecry, Claudio E. *The Opera Fanatic: Ethnography of an Obsession.* Chicago: University of Chicago Press, 2011.

Bloechl, Olivia. *Native American Song at the Frontiers of Early Modern Music.* Cambridge: Cambridge University Press, 2008.

Bostridge, Ian. *A Singer's Notebook.* London: Faber and Faber, 2011.

Bouissou, Sylvie. *Rameau: Musicien des Lumières.* Paris: Fayard, 2014.

Buch, Esteban. *The Bomarzo Affair: Ópera, perversión y dictadura.* Buenos Aires: Adriana Hidalgo, 2003.

Budasz, Rogério. *Opera in the Tropics: Music and Theater in Early Modern Brazil.* Oxford: Oxford University Press, 2019.

Bushnell, Cameron Fae. *Postcolonial Readings of Music in World Literature: Turning Empire on Its Ear.* New York: Routledge, 2013.

Calderón de la Barca, Pedro, and Tomás de Torrejón y Velasco. *La púrpura de la rosa.* Edited by Ángeles Cardona, Don Cruickshank, and Martin Cunningham. Kassel, Germany: Reichenberg, 1990.

Cambaceres, Eugenio. *Sin rumbo.* Buenos Aires: Stock Cero, 2005.

Campo, Estanislao del. *Faust.* Translated by Walter Owen. Buenos Aires: Walter Owen, 1943.

———. *Fausto y poesías completas.* Buenos Aires: Sopena, 1969.

Carpentier, Alejo. *Cartas a Toutouche*. Mexico City: Lectorum, 2011.
———. *Concierto barroco*. Madrid: Siglo XXI, 1982.
———. *Concierto Barroco*. Translated by Asa Zatz. Tulsa, OK: Council Oak Books, 1988.
Casares Rodicio, Emilio, and Álvaro Torrente, eds. *La ópera en España e Hispanomérica*. 2 vols. Madrid: Instituto Complutense de Ciencias Musicales, 2001.
Catán, Daniel. *Florencia en el Amazonas*. Libretto by Marcela Fuentes-Berain. Houston Grand Opera Orchestra. Patrick Summers. With Patricia Schuman, Oren Gradus, Mark S. Doss, Ana María Martínez, et al. Albany Records 531/31, 2002. 2 CDs.
———. "La música de *La hija de Rappaccini:* Cartas no echadas a Octavio Paz." *Vuelta* 173 (April 1991): 28–31.
———. "Ópera en español." *Revista de Musicología* 31, no. 1 (June 2008): 249–54.
Cesetti, Durval. "*Il guarany* for Foreigners: Colonialist Racism, Naive Utopia, or Pleasant Entertainment?" *Latin American Music Review* 31, no. 1 (2010): 101–21.
Cetrangolo, Aníbal Enrique. "*Aida* Times Two: How Italian Veterans of Two Historic *Aida* Productions Shaped Argentina's Music History." *Cambridge Opera Journal* 28, no. 1 (2016): 79–105.
———. *Ópera, barcos y banderas: El melodrama y la migración en Argentina (1880–1920)*. Madrid: Biblioteca Nueva, 2015.
Chávez Bárcenas, Ireri E. "Vivaldi's *Motezuma:* The Conquest of Mexico on the Venetian Operatic Stage." In *The New World in Early Modern Italy*, edited by Elizabeth Horodowich and Lia Markey, 288–308. New York: Cambridge University Press, 2017.
Clément, Catherine. *Opera, or the Undoing of Women*. Minneapolis: University of Minnesota Press, 1988.
Coelho, Victor Anand. "Kapsberger's *Apotheosis . . . of St. Francis* (1622) and the Conquering of India." In *The Work of Opera: Genre, Nationalism, and Sexual Difference*, edited by Richard Dellamora and Daniel Fischlin, 27–47. New York: Columbia University Press, 1997.
Coli, Jorge. *A paixão segundo a ópera*. São Paulo: Editora Perspectiva, 2003.
Colombí, Beatriz. "José Martí: Traducir, transpensar." *INTI: Revista de Literatura Hispánica* 49–50 (1999): 59–69.
Conrad, Joseph. *Nostromo*. New York: Everyman's Library, 1992.
Cotticelli, Francesco, and Paologiovanni Maione, eds. *Le arti della scena e l'esotismo in età moderna / The Performing Arts and Exoticism in the Modern Age*. Naples, Italy: Turchini Edizioni, 2006.
Covell, Roger. "Voice Register as an Index of Age and Status in Opera Seria." In *Opera & Vivaldi*, edited by Michael Collins and Elise K. Kirk, 193–210. Austin: University of Texas Press, 1984.
Cruz, Sor Juana Inés de la. *Poems, Protest, and a Dream*. Translated by Margaret Sayers Peden. New York: Penguin Books, 1997.
Cuadra, Gonzalo. *Ópera nacional: Así la llamaron 1898–1950*. Santiago: Universidad Alberto Hurtado Ediciones, 2019.
Daou, Ana Maria. *A belle époque amazônica*. Rio de Janeiro: Jorge Zahar, 2004.

Dahlhaus, Carl, and Sieghart Döhring, ed. *Pipers Enzyklopädie des Musiktheaters: Oper, Operette, Musical, Ballett*. 7 vols. Munich: Piper, 1986.
Darío, Rubén. *Poesías completas*. Edited by A. Méndez Plancarte. Madrid: Aguilar, 1975.
———. *Prosas profanas y otros poemas*. Madrid: Castalia, 1983.
———. *Selected Poems of Rubén Darío*. Translated by Lysander Kemp. Austin: University of Texas Press, 1965.
———. *Viajes de un cosmopolita extremo*. Edited by Graciela Montaldo. Buenos Aires: Fondo de Cultura Económica, 2013.
Davidson, Jane W., and Anthony Trippett, eds. *Bringing the First Latin-American Opera to Life: Staging* La púrpura de la rosa *in Sheffield*. Manchester, UK: Durham Modern Language Series, 2007.
Delaméa, Frédéric. "*Vivaldi in scena:* Thoughts on the Revival of Vivaldi's Operas." In *Vivaldi, "Motezuma" and the Opera Seria*, edited by Michael Talbot, 169–85.
DelDonna, Anthony R., and Pierpaolo Polzonetti, eds. *The Cambridge Companion to Eighteenth-Century Opera*. Cambridge: Cambridge University Press, 2009.
Dianteill, Erwan. "Contrepoint américain de la Nativité et de la Passion du Christ: *La Pasión según San Marcos* d'Oswaldo Golijov et *El Niño* de John Adams, deux opéras de la fin du millénaire." *Nuevo Mundo, Mundos Nuevos* (January 2014). https://journals.openedition.org/nuevomundo/66312.
Díaz, Roberto Ignacio. "Silencios de Caruso o la ópera en La Habana." *América: Cahiers du CRICCAL* (Sorbonne Nouvelle) 31 (2004): 153–59.
Díaz Ayala, Cristóbal. *Música cubana: Del areyto a la nueva trova*. Miami: Universal, 1993.
Dizikes, John. *Opera in America: A Cultural History*. New Haven, CT: Yale University Press, 1993.
Duplay, Mathieu. "'Alta, desnuda, única. Poesía': Échos de la poésie mexicaine dans les opéras de John Adams." *Amerika* 4 (2011). https://journals.openedition.org/amerika/2141?lang=es.
———. *Les œuvres scéniques de John Adams: L'opéra et les frontières de la littérature*. Paris: Honoré Champion, 2023.
Eötvos, Peter. *Love and Other Demons*. Libretto by Kornél Hamvai. London Philharmonic Orchestra. Vladimir Jurowski. With Allison Bell, Nathan Gunn, Mats Almgren, and Felicity Palmer, et al. Recorded 2008. Presto Classical GFOCD020-08, 2013. 2 CDs.
Epps, Brad. "Proper Conduct: Reinaldo Arenas, Fidel Castro, and the Politics of Homosexuality." *Journal of the History of Sexuality* 6, no. 2 (1995): 231–83.
Everett, Yayoi Uno. *Reconfiguring Myth and Narrative in Contemporary Opera: Osvaldo Golijov, Kaija Saariaho, John Adams, and Tan Dun*. Bloomington: Indiana University Press, 2015.
Farret, Georges. *Luigi Alva: El Almaviva de La Scala*. Lima: Pontificia Universidad Católica del Perú, 2008.
Feldman, Martha. *The Castrato: Reflections on Nature and Kinds*. Oakland: University of California Press, 2015.

Fernández Retamar, Roberto. *Caliban and Other Essays*. Translated by Edward Baker. Minneapolis: University of Minnesota Press, 2005.

Fiedler, Johanna. *Molto Agitato: The Mayhem behind the Music at the Metropolitan Opera*. New York: Anchor, 2003.

Fitzlyon, April. *Maria Malibran: Diva of the Romantic Age*. London: Souvenir, 1987.

Fonseca, Rubem. *O selvagem da ópera*. São Paulo: Companhia das Letras, 1994.

Forner, Jane. "'O brave new Caliban': Postcolonial Perspectives on Adès's *The Tempest*." In *Thomas Adès Studies*, edited by Edward Venn and Philip Stoecker, 72–92. Cambridge: Cambridge University Press, 2022.

Frohock, Richard. "Sir William Davenant's American Operas." *Modern Language Review* 96, no. 2 (April 2001): 323–33.

Fuentes, Carlos. "How I Wrote One of My Books." In *Myself with Others: Selected Essays*, 28–45. New York: Noonday Press, 1988.

———. *Instinto de Inés*. Madrid: Alfaguara, 2001.

———. *Inez: A Novel*. Translated by Margaret Sayers Peden. Orlando, FL: Harcourt, 2002.

Gallo, Rubén. *Proust's Latin Americans*. Baltimore: Johns Hopkins University Press, 2014.

García Rey, María del Rocío. "Transpensar para la infancia: Las traducciones de José Martí." *Pacarina del Sur: Revista de Pensamiento Crítico Latinoamericano* 5, no. 17 (October–December 2013): http://pacarinadelsur.com/nuestra-america/abordajes-y-contiendas/818-transpensar-para-la-infancia-las-traducciones-de-jose-marti.

Gasta, Chad M. *Transatlantic Arias: Early Opera in Spain and the New World*. Madrid: Iberoamericana, 2013.

Ghislanzoni, Antonio. *Atahualpa: Drama lírico en cuatro actos*. Lima: Imprenta de la Patria, 1877.

———. *Atahualpa: Dramma lirico in quattro atti*. Milan: Tipografia A. Gattinoni, 1875.

Gianera, Pablo. *La música en el grupo Sur: Una modernidad inconclusa*. Buenos Aires: Eterna Cadencia Editora, 2011.

Góes, Marcus. *Carlos Gomes: Documentos comentados*. São Paulo: Algol, 2008.

Gólijov, Osvaldo. *Ainadámar*. Libretto by David Henry Hwang. Performed by Dawn Upshaw and Kelley O'Connor. Atlanta Symphony Orchestra. Conducted by Robert Spano. Deutsche Grammophon, 2006. CD.

Gomes, Carlos. *Lo schiavo*. Libretto by Rodolfo Paravicini. Orquestra e Coro do Teatro Municipal do Rio de Janeiro. Santiago Guerra. With Ida Miccolis, Lourival Braga, Alfredo Colosimo, Luiz Nascimento, Antea Claudia, et al. Recorded June 1959. Sonopress Rimo, 1997. 2 CDs.

González, Jorge Antonio. *La composición operística en Cuba*. Havana: Letras Cubanas, 1986.

González Echevarría, Roberto. *Alejo Carpentier: The Pilgrim at Home*. Ithaca, NY: Cornell University Press, 1977.

———. *Celestina's Brood: Continuities of the Baroque in Spanish and Latin American Literature*. Durham, NC: Duke University Press, 1993.

———. *Myth and Archive: A Theory of Latin American Narrative*. Cambridge: Cambridge University Press, 1990.

Graun, Carl Heinrich, *Montezuma*. Libretto by Frederick II. Deutsche Kammerakademie. Johannes Goritzki. With Encarnación Vázquez, María Luisa Tamez, et al. Recorded June 1992. Capriccio 60 032-2, 1992. 2 CDs.

Greenwald, Helen M., ed. *The Oxford Handbook of Opera*. Oxford: Oxford University Press, 2014.

Greer, Margaret R. *The Play of Power: Mythological Court Dramas of Calderón de la Barca*. Princeton, NJ: Princeton University Press, 1991.

Grout, Donald Jay. *A Short History of Opera*. New York: Columbia University Press, 1954.

Gutiérrez Alea, Tomás, and Juan Carlos Tabío, dir. *Fresa y chocolate*. Henstooth Video, 2017. DVD.

Hahn, Reynaldo. *Ciboulette*. Libretto by Francis de Croisset and Robert de Flers. Orchestre Philarmonique de Monte-Carlo. Cyril Diederich. With Mady Mesplé, José Van Dam, and Nicolaï Gedda. Recorded June 1982. EMI Classics 66159-2, 2002. 2 CDs.

Hall, Kim F. *Things of Darkness: Economies of Race and Gender in Early Modern England*. Ithaca, NY: Cornell University Press, 1995.

Henneberg, Claus H., ed. *El Cimarrón: Ein Werkbericht*. Mainz, Germany: B. Schotts Söhne, 1971.

Henry, O. *Cabbages and Kings*. New York: Doubleday, Page & Co., 1920.

Henze, Hans Werner. *El Cimarrón*. Libretto by Hans Magnus Erzensberger. El Cimarrón Ensemble. Recorded August 2005. Wergo 6710 2, 2007. CD.

———. *Music and Politics: Collected Writings, 1953–81*. Translated by Peter Labanyi. London: Faber and Faber, 1982.

Herzog, Werner, dir. *Fitzcarraldo*. Werner Herzog Filmproduktion and Pro-Ject Film Produktion. 1982. DVD.

Hess, Carol A. *Representing the Good Neighbor: Music, Difference, and the Pan American Dream*. Oxford: Oxford University Press, 2013.

Hulme, Peter, and William H. Sherman, ed. *"The Tempest" and Its Travels*. London: Reaktion Books, 2000.

Hutcheon, Linda, and Michael Hutcheon. *Opera: Desire, Disease, Death*. Lincoln: University of Nebraska Press, 1996.

Illari, Bernardo. "*María de Buenos Aires*: El tango del eterno retorno." In *Estudios sobre la obra de Astor Piazzolla*, edited by Omar García Brunelli, 157–97. Buenos Aires: Gourmet Musical Ediciones, 2014.

———. "La obra y nuestra reconstrucción." In Torrejón y Velasco, *La púrpura de la rosa*, K617, CD booklet, 88–91.

———. "*San Ignacio de Loyola*: Una ópera de la alteridad en las reducciones jesuíticas." In *San Ignacio: L'Opéra perdu des missions jésuites de l'Amazonie*, K617, CD booklet, 35–41.

Ismael, César de Carvalho. "O 'maestro' da abolição e sua ópera *O escravo*: Dilemas do pensamento social na transição para a República." PhD diss., Universidade Federal Rural do Rio do Janeiro, 2014. https://tede.ufrrj.br/jspui/handle/jspui/1813.

Jrade, Cathy L. *Modernismo, Modernity, and the Development of Spanish American Literature*. Austin: University of Texas Press, 1998.
Jullien, Adolphe. *Richard Wagner: Sa vie et ses œuvres*. Paris: Librairie de l'Art, 1889.
Kapsberger, Johannes Hieronymus, and Domenico Zipoli. *The Jesuit Operas by Kapsberger & Zipoli*. Ensemble Abendmusik. James David Christie. Recorded December 1998 and January 1999. Dorian Recordings 93246, 2002. 2 CDs.
Kerman, Joseph. *Opera as Drama*. Berkeley: University of California Press, 1988.
Koestenbaum, Wayne. *The Queen's Throat: Opera, Homosexuality, and the Mystery of Desire*. New York: Vintage, 1994.
Kristal, Efraín. "Literary Anecdotes." In Daniel Catán, *Florencia en el Amazonas*. Albany Records, CD booklet, 6–9.
Kristeva, Julia. *Étrangers à nous-mêmes*. Paris: Seuil, 1988.
Kuss, Malena. "Carlos López Buchardo." In Dahlhaus and Döhring, eds., *Pipers Enzyklopädie des Musiktheaters*, vol. 3, 549–50.
———. "Felipe Boero." In Dahlhaus and Döhring, eds., *Pipers Enzyklopädie des Musiktheaters*, 1:377–78.
———. "Identity and Change: Nativism in Operas from Argentina, Brazil, and Mexico." In *Musical Repercussions of 1492: Encounters in Text and Performance*, edited by Carol E. Robertson, 299–335. Washington, DC: Smithsonian Institution Press, 1992.
———. "The 'Invention' of America: Encounter Settings on the Latin American Lyric Stage." *Revista de Musicología* 16, no. 1 (1993): 185–204.
———. "Das lateinamerikanische Libretto." In *Die Musik in Geschichte und Gegenwart*, edited by Ludwig Finscher and translated by Thomas M. Höpfner, 5:1196–1203. Kassel, Germany: Bärenreiter-Verlag, 1994–2008.
———. "Lenguajes nacionales de Argentina, Brasil y México en las óperas del siglo XX: Hacia una cronología comparativa de cambios estilísticos." *Revista Musical Chilena* 34, nos. 149–50 (1980): 61–79.
———. "Modernismo Rumbero in Carpentier's and Caturla's Puppet Opera *Manita en el Suelo* (1931–34)." *Review: Literature and Arts of the Americas* 44, no.1 (2011): 136–42.
———. "Opera in Latin America: Some Premises for a History." Keynote address at the IV Simpósio Internacional de Musicologia da Universidade Federal do Rio de Janeiro, Rio de Janeiro, August 2013.
———. Prologue to *Music in Latin America and the Caribbean: An Encyclopedic History*, 1:ix–xxvi. Edited by Malena Kuss. Austin: University of Texas Press, 2004.
Lacombe, Hervé. *Géographie de l'opéra au XXe siècle*. Paris: Fayard, 2007.
Lawrence-King, Andrew. Program liner in Torrejón y Velasco, *La púrpura de la rosa*. Deutsche Harmonia Mundi, CD booklet, 4–8.
Leppert, Richard. "Opera, Aesthetic Violence, and the Imposition of Modernity: *Fitzcarraldo*." In *Beyond the Soundtrack: Representing Music in Cinema*, edited by Daniel Goldmark et al., 99–119. Berkeley: University of California Press, 2007.

Levin, David J., ed. *Opera Through Other Eyes*. Stanford, CA: Stanford University Press, 1993.
Lewis, Evonne, and Kenneth Mills, eds. *Lexikon of the Hispanic Baroque: Transatlantic Exchange and Transformation*. Austin: University of Texas Press, 2013.
Lindenberger, Herbert. *Opera in History: From Monteverdi to Cage*. Stanford, CA: Stanford University Press, 1998.
Linke, Ulrich. "Vokaler Gender Trouble: Wie queer sind sehr hohe Männerstimme?" In *Der Countertenor: Die männliche Falsettstimme von Mittelalter zum Gegenwart*, edited by Corinna Herr et al., 215–50. Mainz, Germany: Schott, 2012.
Littlejohn, David. *The Ultimate Art: Essays around and about Opera*. Berkeley: University of California Press, 1994.
Locke, Ralph P. "Exotic Elements in Kapsberger's Jesuit Opera (Rome, 1622) Honoring Saints Ignatius and Francis Xavier." In *A Festschrift for Prof. Kerala J. Snyder*, edited by Johann Norrback and Joel Speerstra, 1–28. Gothenburg: Göteborgs Universitetsbibliotek, 2016. http://hdl.handle.net/2077/54931.
———. *Music and the Exotic from the Renaissance to Mozart*. Cambridge: Cambridge University Press, 2015.
Ludmer, Josefina. *El género gauchesco: Un tratado sobre la patria*. Buenos Aires: Libros Perfil, 2000.
Lund, Joshua. *Werner Herzog*. Urbana: University of Illinois Press, 2020.
Macalupú-Cumpén, Pablo. "Resignificación en la producción operística peruana: Crítica social y política en *Alzira* de Verdi." *ANTEC Revista Peruana de Investigación Musical* 4, no. 1 (August 2020): 14–41.
Macy, Laura, ed. *The Grove Book of Opera Singers*. Oxford: Oxford University Press, 2008.
Madrid, Alejandro L. *Tania León's Stride: A Polyrhythmic Life*. Urbana: University of Illinois Press, 2021.
Maehder, Jürgen. "Alvise Giusti's Libretto *Motezuma* and the Conquest of Mexico in Eighteenth-Century Italian *Opera Seria*." In Talbot, *"Motezuma" and the Opera Seria*, 63–80.
Magaldi, Cristina. *Music in Imperial Rio de Janeiro: European Culture in a Tropical Milieu*. Lanham, MD: Scarecrow Press, 2004.
Mantero, José María. "Hacia la interculturalidad: Rosario Aguilar y *La niña blanca y los pájaros sin pies*." *Romance Studies* 28, no. 4 (November 2010): 259–67.
Mañach, Jorge. *An Inquiry into Choteo*. Translated by Jacqueline Loss. Barcelona: Red Ediciones, 2018.
Mañón, Manuel. *Historia del viejo Gran Teatro Nacional de México*, 2 vols. Mexico City: Instituto Nacional de Bellas Artes and Consejo Nacional para la Cultura y las Artes, 2009.
Martí, José. *La Edad de Oro*. Miami: La Moderna Poesía, 1983.
———. *Obras completas*, 26 vols. Havana: Editorial Nacional de Cuba, 1963–1966.

———. "Our America." In *Selected Writings*, 288–95. Translated by Esther Allen. New York: Penguin, 2002.

Martin, Claire. "Las múltiples voces de Merlin: del *bel canto* a la escritura." In *Fronteras de la literatura y la crítica* (Actas del XXXV Congreso del Instituto de Literatura Iberoamericana, Université de Poitiers), edited by Fernando Moreno, Sylvie Josserand, and Fernando Colla. Poitiers, France: Centre de Recherches Latino-Américaines, 2006. CD-ROM.

Martin, George. *Verdi at the Golden Gate: Opera and San Francisco in the Gold Rush Years*. Berkeley: University of California Press, 1993.

Matamoro, Blas. "El neobarroco: Diferencias, tientos y ensaladas." *América: Cahiers du CRICCAL* (Sorbonne Nouvelle) 20 (1998): 13–21.

———. *Rubén Darío*. Madrid: Espasa Calpe, 2002.

May, Thomas, ed. *The John Adams Reader: Essential Writings on an American Composer*. Pompton Plains, NJ: Amadeus Press, 2006.

McClary, Susan. *George Bizet, Carmen*. Cambridge: Cambridge University Press, 1992.

Méndez Rodenas, Adriana. *Gender and Nationalism in Colonial Cuba: The Travels of Santa Cruz y Montalvo, Condesa de Merlin*. Nashville: Vanderbilt University Press, 1998.

Merlin, María de las Mercedes Santa Cruz y Montalvo, comtesse. *La Havane*. 3 vols. Paris: Librairie d'Amyot, 1844.

———. *Les loisirs d'une femme de monde*. 3 vols. Paris: Librairie de l'Advocat, 1838.

Mission San Francisco Xavier: Ópera y Misa de los Indios. Ensemble Elyma. Gabriel Garrido. With Coro de Niños Cantores de Córdoba. Recorded August 2000. K617 111, 2000. CD.

Molloy, Silvia. *At Face Value: Autobiographical Writing in Spanish America*. Cambridge: Cambridge University Press, 1991.

Mortier, Gerard. *In audatia veritas: Reflexiones sobre la ópera, el arte y la política*. Edited by Mar Fosca. Almería: Editorial Confluencias, 2015.

Mozart, Wolfgang Amadeus. *Le nozze di Figaro*. Libretto by Lorenzo Da Ponte. Concerto Köln. René Jacobs. With Simon Keenlyside, Véronique Gens, Patrizia Ciofi, Lorenzo Regazzo, Angelika Kirschlager, et al. Harmonia Mundi B0001HZ8X6, 2004. 3 CDs.

Mujica Lainez, Manuel. *El gran teatro*. Buenos Aires: Debolsillo, 2010.

———. *El gran teatro*. La Cumbre, Argentina: Fundación Manuel Mujica Lainez, 2011.

Nawrot, Piotr. *Indígenas y cultura musical de las reducciones jesuíticas*. La Paz: Editorial Verbo Divino, 2000.

———. "Music: Missions." In Levy and Mills, *Lexikon of the Hispanic Baroque*, 249–52.

Nero, Charles L. "Diva Traffic and Male Bonding in Film: Teaching Opera, Learning Gender, Race, and Nation." *Camera Obscura* 56, no. 19 (2004): 46–73.

Ocampo, Victoria. *Autobiografía I: El archipiélago*. Buenos Aires: Sur, 1982.

———. *Autobiografía II: El imperio insular*. Buenos Aires: Sur, 1980.

———. *Autobiografía III: La rama de Salzburgo*. Buenos Aires: Sur, 1981.
———. "Reencuentro con Virginia Woolf." In *Testimonios: Novena Serie*, 40–52. Buenos Aires: Sur, 1975.
Ochs, Anna. "Opera Achievements on the European Scale: French and English Correspondents in Late Nineteenth-Century Mexico." *Opera Journal* 44, nos. 1–2 (March 2011): 3–11.
———. "Opera in Contention: Social Conflict in Late Nineteenth-Century Mexico City." PhD diss., University of North Carolina at Chapel Hill, 2011.
Offenbach, Jacques. *La Périchole*. Libretto by Henri Meilhac and Ludovic Halévy. Orchestre Philharmonique de Strasbourg. Alain Lombard. With Régine Crespin, Alain Vanzo, Jules Bastin, et al. Recorded February 1976. Erato 2292-45686-2, 1991. 2 CDs.
Olivares, Jorge. *Becoming Reinaldo Arenas*. Durham, NC: Duke University Press, 2013.
———. "Otra vez *Cecilia Valdés:* Arenas con(tra) Villaverde." *Hispanic Review* 62, no. 2 (Spring 1994): 169–84.
———. "¿Por qué llora Reinaldo Arenas?" *MLN* 115, no. 2 (March 2000): 268–98.
Ortiz, Mario A. "Sor Juana en *El Niño* de John Adams y *Óyeme con los ojos* de Allison Sniffin." *Cuadernos de Música, Artes Visuales y Artes Escénicas* (2008): 207–34.
Otero, Gustavo Gabriel, and Daniel Varacalli Costas. *Puccini en la Argentina: Junio-agosto de 1905*. Buenos Aires: Instituto Italiano de Cultura de Buenos Aires, 2006.
Paduano, Guido. *"Alzire* e *Alzira*: Varietà di colonialismi." Cotticelli and Maione, eds., *Le arti della scena e l'esotismo in età moderna*, 531–53.
Palmié, Stephan. "Slavery, Historicism, and the Poverty of Memoralization." In *Memory: History, Theory, Debates*, edited by Susannah Radstone and Bill Schwarz, 363–75. New York: Fordham University Press, 2010.
Parrott, Fiona G. "Friendship, Letters and Butterflies: Victoria Ocampo and Virginia Woolf." *STAR (Scotland's Transatlantic Relations) Project Archive* (April 2004): 3–4.
Patchett, Ann. *Bel Canto*. New York: Perennial, 2002.
Paz, Octavio. "Raíz del hombre (1935–1936)." In *Obras completas*, 13:57–70. Mexico City: Fondo de Cultura Económica, 1999.
———. *Sor Juana Inés de la Cruz o las trampas de la fe*. Mexico City: Fondo de Cultura Económica, 1988.
———. *Sor Juana, or, The Traps of Faith*. Translated by Margaret Sayers Peden. Cambridge, MA: Harvard University Press, 1988.
Paz, Senel. *El lobo, el bosque y el hombre nuevo*. Mexico City: Era, 2000.
Peppercorn, Lisa M. "Villa-Lobos's Stage Works." *Revue Belge de Musicologie / Belgisch Tijdschrift voor Musikwetenschap* 36–38 (1982–84): 175–8
Pérez, Rolando. *Severo Sarduy and the Neo-Baroque Image of Thought in the Visual Arts*. West Lafayette, IN: Purdue University Press, 2012.
Pisani, Michael V. *Imagining Native America in Music*. New Haven, CT: Yale University Press, 2005.
Planet, Adolfo. *Del armario al escenario: La ópera gay*. Barcelona: Ediciones La Tempestad, 2003.

Plate, Leonor. *Óperas, Teatro Colón: Esperando el centenario*. 2 vols. Buenos Aires: Editorial Lunken, 2006.
Poe, Edgar Allan. Review of *Memoirs and Letters of Madame Malibran. By the Countess de Merlin. With Notices of the Progress of the Musical Drama in England*. Burton's Gentleman's Magazine (Philadelphia) 6 (May 1840): 238–39.
Pollini, Margarita. *Palco, cazuela y paraíso: Las historias más insólitas del Teatro Colón*. Buenos Aires: Sudamericana, 2001.
Polzonetti, Pierpaolo. *Italian Opera in the Age of the American Revolution*. Cambridge: Cambridge University Press, 2011.
———. "Opera as Process." In DelDonna and Polzonetti, *The Cambridge Companion to Eighteenth-Century Opera*, 3–23.
Preston, Katherine K. *Opera on the Road: Traveling Opera Troupes in the United States, 1825–60*. Urbana: University of Illinois Press, 1993.
Price, Curtis. "*The Indian Queen*." In Sadie, *The New Grove Dictionary of Opera*, 2:797–98.
Puccini, Giacomo. *Madama Butterfly*. Libretto by Giuseppe Giacosa and Luigi Illica. Orchestra e Coro del Teatro alla Scala di Milano. Herbert von Karajan. With Maria Callas, Nicolai Gedda, et al. Recorded 1955. EMI Classics B000002RXX, 1987. 2 CDS.
Pulido Granata, Ramón. *La tradición operística en la ciudad de México (Siglo XIX)*. Mexico City: Secretaría de Educación Pública, 1970.
Restall, Matthew. *When Montezuma Met Cortés: The True Story of the Meeting That Changed History*. New York: HarperCollins, 2018.
Rice, John A. "Montezuma at Eszterház: A Pasticcio on a New World Theme." In *Joseph Haydn & die "Neue Welt": Musik- und Kulturgeschichtliche Perspektiven*, edited by Walter Reicher and Wolfgang Fuhrmann, 231–42. Vienna: Hollitzer, 2019.
Rihm, Wolfgang. *Die Eroberung von Mexico*. Libretto by Rihm. Philharmonisches Staatsorchester Hamburg. Ingo Metzmacher. With Renate Behler, Richard Salter, et al. Recorded February 1992. CPO 999 185-2, 1992. 2 CDs.
Rindom, Ditlev. "Bygone Modernity: Re-Imagining Italian Opera in Milan, New York and Buenos Aires, 1887–1914." PhD diss., University of Cambridge, 2019.
Río Prado, Enrique. *Pasión cubana por Giuseppe Verdi*. Havana: Unión, 2001.
Rivals, Aurore. *Entretiens autour des cinq premiers operas de Peter Eötvös*. Nantes, France: Éditions Aedam Musicae, 2012.
Robinson, Paul. "A Deconstructive Postscript: Reading Libretti and Misreading Opera." In *Reading Opera*, edited by Arthur Groos and Roger Parker, 328–46. Princeton, NJ: Princeton University Press.
———. *Opera and Ideas: From Mozart to Strauss*. Ithaca, NY: Cornell University Press, 1985.
Rodrigues, Lutero. *Carlos Gomes: um tema em questão*. São Paulo: Editora Unesp, 2011.
Rodríguez Bello, Luisa Isabel. "Estructuras ideológicas y estéticas en 'Los zapaticos de rosa' de José Martí." *Investigación y Postgrado* 28, no. 1 (2013): 9–44.

Rodríguez Garrido, José Antonio. "Teatro y poder en el palacio virreinal de Lima (1672–1707)." PhD diss., Princeton University, 2003.

Rosselli, John. "Latin America and Italian Opera: A Process of Interaction, 1810–1930." *Revista de Musicología* 16, no. 1 (1993): 139–45.

———. "The Opera Business and the Italian Immigrant Community in Latin America 1820–1930: The Example of Buenos Aires." *Past and Present* 127 (May 1990): 155–82.

Sadie, Stanley, ed. *History of Opera*. New York: W. W. Norton, 1989.

———. *The New Grove Book of Operas*. New York: St. Martin's Press, 1997.

———. *The New Grove Dictionary of Opera*. 4 vols. London: Macmillan Reference, 1997.

Said, Edward. *Culture and Imperialism*. New York: Vintage Books, 1994.

Salomone, Alicia. "Virginia Woolf en los *Testimonios* de Victoria Ocampo: Tensiones entre feminismo y colonialismo." *Revista Chilena de Literatura* 69 (November 2006): 69–87.

Sanborn, Pitts, and Emil Hilb. *The Metropolitan Book of the Opera*. Garden City, NY: Garden City Publishing, 1942.

Santí, Enrico Mario. "*Fresa y chocolate*: La retórica de la reconciliación." In *Por una politeratura: literatura hispanoamericana e imaginación política*, 286–302. Mexico City: Consejo Nacional para la Cultura y las Artes, 1997.

Sarlo, Beatriz. *La máquina cultural: Maestras, traductores y vanguardistas*. Buenos Aires: Seix Barral, 2007.

———. *Una modernidad periférica: Buenos Aires 1920 y 1930*. Buenos Aires: Ediciones Nueva Visión, 1988.

———. "V.O." Unpublished libretto for *V.O.*, opera with music by Martín Bauer. 2013.

Sellars, Peter. "Creative Contexts: Peter Sellars on Working with Adams." Interview by Thomas May. In May, *The John Adams Reader*, 238–48.

Seráfico, José. "Teatro Amazonas: Símbolo de quê?" *Ciência e cultura* 61, no. 3 (2009): 37–40.

Shakespeare, William. *The Tempest*. Edited by David Lindley. Cambridge: Cambridge University Press, 2002.

Siskind, Mariano. *Cosmopolitan Desires: Global Modernity and World Literature in Latin America*. Evanston, IL: Northwestern University Press, 2014.

Sklodowska, Elzbieta. "Testimonio mediatizado: ¿ventriloquía o heteroglosia? (Barnet/Montejo; Burgos/Menchú)." *Revista de Crítica Literaria Latinoamericana* 38 (1993): 81–90.

Smith, Paul Julian. *Vision Machines: Cinema, Literature, and Sexuality in Spain and Cuba, 1983–1993*. London: Verso, 1996.

Sommer, Doris. *Foundational Fictions: The National Romances of Latin America*. Berkeley: University of California Press, 1991.

Soublette, Ned. *Cuba and Its Music: From the First Drums to the Mambo*. Chicago: Chicago Review Press, 2004.

Sosa, Octavio, et al. *La ópera mexicana, 1805–2002*. Mexico City: Centro Universitario de Estudios Londres, 2002.

Stein, Louise K. "The 'Blood of the Rose' and Opera's Arrival in Lima." In Torrejón y Velasco, *La púrpura de la rosa*. Deutsche Harmonia Mundi, CD booklet, 9–15.

———. "De la contera del mundo: Las navegaciones de la ópera entre dos mundos y varias culturas." In Casares Rodicio and Torrente, *La ópera en España e Hispanomérica*, 1:79–94.

———. "How Opera Traveled." In Greenwald, *The Oxford Handbook of Opera*, 843–61.

———. "'La música de dos orbes': A Context for the First Opera of the Americas." *Opera Quarterly* 2, nos. 3–4 (Summer–Autumn 2006): 433–58.

———. "Opera." In Levy and Mills, *Lexikon of the Hispanic Baroque*, 253–55.

Stein, Louise K., and José Máximo Leza. "Opera, Genre, and Context in Spain and Its American Colonies." In DelDonna and Polzonetti, eds. *The Cambridge Companion to Eighteenth-Century Opera*, 244–69.

Sternfeld, F. W. *The Birth of Opera*. Oxford, UK: Clarendon Press, 1995.

Stevenson, Robert. "Buenos Aires." In Sadie, *The New Grove Dictionary of Opera*, 1:633–35.

———. "Chávez (y Ramírez), Carlos (Antonio de Padua)." In Sadie, *The New Grove Dictionary of Opera*, 1:826.

———. "Estudio preliminar." In *La púrpura de la rosa*, by Tomás de Torrejón y Velasco, edited by Stevenson, 15–132. Lima: Instituto Nacional de Cultura, 1976.

———. "Musical Silhouettes Drawn by José Martí (1853–1895)." *Inter-American Music Review* 14, no. 2 (Winter–Spring 1995): 21–37.

———. "Opera Beginnings in the New World." *Musical Quarterly* 45, no. 1 (January 1959): 8–25.

———. "Pasta, Carlo Enrico." In Sadie, *The New Grove Dictionary of Opera*, 3:906.

Stewart, James B. "The Opera Lover: How Alberto Vilar's Passion for Philanthropy Landed Him in Jail." *New Yorker*, February 13, 2006, 108–22.

Stoianova, Ivanka. "'Music Becomes Language': Narrative Strategies in *El Cimarrón* by Hans-Werner Henze." In *Musical Signification: Essays in the Semiotic Theory of Music*, edited by Eero Tarasti, 511–34. Berlin: Mouton de Gruyter, 1995.

Surwillo, Lisa. "Speaking of Race in *Don Álvaro*." *Revista Hispánica Moderna* 63, no. 1 (June 2010): 51–67.

Talbot, Michael, ed. *Vivaldi, "Motezuma" and the Opera Seria: Essays on a Newly Discovered Work and Its Background*. Turnhout, Belgium: Brepols, 2008.

Taylor, Timothy D. *Beyond Exoticism: Western Music and the World*. Durham, NC: Duke University Press, 2007.

Tomé, Lester. "*Giselle* in a Cuban Accent." In *The Cambridge Companion to Ballet*, edited by Marion Kent, 263–71. Cambridge: Cambridge University Press, 2007.

Torrejón y Velasco, Tomás de. *La púrpura de la rosa*. Libretto by Pedro Calderón de la Barca. The Harp Concert. Andrew Lawrence-King. With

Judith Malafronte, Ellen Hargis, María del Mar Fernández Doval, et al. Deutsche Harmonia Mundi, 1999. CD.

———. *La púrpura de la rosa*. Libretto by Pedro Calderón de la Barca. Ensemble Elyma. Gabriel Garrido. With Isabel Monar, Graciela Oddone, Cecilia Díaz, et al. Recorded December 1999. K617 108/2, 1999. 2 CDs.

Townsend, Sarah J. "The Siren's Song; or, When an Amazonian Iara Sang Opera (in Italian) on a Belle Époque Stage." *Latin American Theatre Review* 52, no. 2 (2019): 149–67.

Velasco, Maria Josefa. "L'opéra et le réalisme magique: *Florencia en el Amazonas* de Daniel Catán (1996)." Master's thesis, Université Rennes II, 2009.

Verdi, Giuseppe. *La forza del destino*. Libretto by Francesco Maria Piave. London Symphony Orchestra. James Levine. With Leontyne Price, Plácido Domingo, Sherrill Milnes, et al. Recorded 1976. BMG 74321-39502-2, 1998. 3 CDs.

Vivaldi, Antonio. *Montezuma*. Libretto by Girolamo Giusti. Pasticcio by Jean-Claude Malgoire. La Grande Écurie et la Chambre du Roy. Jean-Claude Malgoire. With Dominique Visse, Danielle Borst, Nicolas Rivenq, et al. Recorded May 1992. Astrée E 8501, 1992. 2 CDs.

———. *Motezuma*. Libretto by Alvise (Girolamo?) Giusti. Musical reconstruction of the missing parts by Alessandro Ciccolini. Il Complesso Barocco. Alan Curtis. With Vito Priante, Marijana Mijanovic, Maite Beaumont, et al. Recorded November 2005. Archiv Produktion 28947 75996, 2006. 3 CDs.

Vogeley, Nancy. "Italian Opera in Early National Mexico." *Modern Language Quarterly* 57, no. 2 (June 1996): 279–88.

Volpe, Maria Alice. "*Indianismo* and Landscape in the Brazilian Age of Progress: Art Music from Carlos Gomes to Villa-Lobos, 1870s–1930s." PhD diss., University of Texas at Austin, 2001.

———. "Remaking the Brazilian Myth of National Foundation: *Il guarany*." *Latin American Music Review / Revista de Música Latinoamericana* 23, no. 2 (Autumn–Winter 2002): 179–94.

Voss, Steffen. "Antonio Vivaldi's Dramma per Musica *Motezuma:* Some Observations on Its Libretto and Music." In Talbot, *"Motezuma" and the Opera Seria*, 1–18.

Waisman, Leonardo J. "Urban Music in the Wilderness: Ideology and Power in the Jesuit *Reducciones*, 1609-1767." In *Music and Urban Society in Colonial Latin America*, edited by Baker and Tess Knighton, 208–29. Cambridge: Cambridge University Press, 2011.

Walton, Benjamin. "Canons of Real and Imagined Opera: Buenos Aires and Montevideo, 1810–1860." In *The Oxford Handbook of the Operatic Canon*, edited by Cormac Newark and William Weber, 271–91. Oxford: Oxford University Press, 2020.

Weddigen, Tristan. "Hispano-Incaic Fusions: Ángel Guido and the Latin American Reception of Heinrich Wölfflin." *Art in Translation* 9, no. S1 (2017): 92–120.

Weill, Kurt. *Der Kuhhandel*. Libretto by Robert Vambery. Kölner Rundfunkchor. Jan Latham-König. With Lucy Peacock, Eberhard Büchner, et al. Recorded March 1990. Capriccio 60 013-1, 1992. CD.

Whaples, Miriam K. "Early Exoticism Revisited." In *The Exotic in Western Music*, edited by Jonathan Bellman, 3–25. Boston: Northeastern University Press, 1996.

Williams, Alastair. "Voices of the Other: Wolfgang Rihm's Music Drama *Die Eroberung von Mexico*." *Journal of the Royal Musical Association* 129, no. 2 (2004): 240–71.

Wilson, Edward M. "El texto de la 'Deposición a favor de los profesores de la pintura' de don Pedro Calderón de la Barca." *Revista de Archivos, Bibliotecas y Museos* 72, no. 2 (July–December 1974): 709–27.

Wolkowicz, Vera. "Opera as a Moral Vehicle: Situating Bellini's *Norma* in the Political Complexities of Mid-Nineteenth-Century Buenos Aires." *Nineteenth-Century Music Review* (2021): 1–23.

Ypiranga Monteiro, Mário. *Teatro Amazonas*. Manaus: Editora Valer and Governo do Estado do Amazonas, 2003.

Zamora, Lois Parkinson, and Wendy B. Farris. "Introduction: Daiquiri Birds and Flaubertian Parrot(ie)s." In *Magical Realism: Theory, History, Community*, edited by Lois Parkinson Zamora and Wendy B. Farris, 1–11. Durham, NC: Duke University Press, 1995.

Zamora, Lois Parkinson, and Monika Kaup, eds. *Baroque New Worlds: Representation, Transculturation, Counterconquest*. Durham, NC: Duke University Press, 2010.

Zárate Toscano, Verónica, and Serge Gruzinski. "Ópera, imaginación y sociedad: México y Brasil, siglo XIX. Historias conectadas: *Ildegonda* de Melesio Morales e *Il guarany* de Carlos Gomes." *Historia Mexicana* 58, no. 2 (2008): 803–60.

Zipoli, Domenico, Martin Schmidt, et al. *San Ignacio: L'Opéra perdu des missions jésuites de l'Amazonie*. Ensemble Elyma. Gabriel Garrido. With Rosa Domínguez, Silvia Pérez Monsalve, Furio Zanasi, et al. Recorded April 1996. K617, 1996. CD.

INDEX

Abbate, Carolyn, 139, 310
Acosta, Abraham, 216, 372n12
Adams, John, 245
   El Niño, 10, 71, 251–65
   The Gospel according to the Other Mary, 71
Adès, Thomas
   and Latin America, 328–29, 387n4
   The Exterminating Angel, 71
   The Tempest, 11–12, 327–34
Adorno, Theodor, 342n14
   "Bourgeois Opera," 24–25, 136, 200, 301, 362n3, 385n24
   "Opera and the Long-Playing Record," 124, 224
Afro-Cuban culture, 22, 157–159. *See also* Cuba; Barnet, Miguel: *Biografía de un cimarrón*; Henze, Hans Werner: *El Cimarrón*
Aguilar, Gonzalo, 18, 81–83
Aguilar, Rosario, 50, 343n26
Aldeburgh Festival, 220, 224, 228
Algarotti, Francesco, 50–51, 144, 344n31
Alonso, Alicia, 5, 21–23, 338n31
Altmann, Charlotte, 95
Alva, Luigi, 29
Alves, Antônio de Castro, 242
Anderson Imbert, Enrique, 32
Andrade, Oswald de, 352n108
André, Naomi, 211–13, 242–43
Andriessen, Louis, 11, 70, 279–82
Arenas, Reinaldo, 150, 177, 191
   Antes que anochezca, 71
   El color del verano, 8, 41, 176, 185
   La loma del Ángel, 185

Argentina, 30–33, 71, 81–83, 84–91, 267–71, 357n12. *See also* Buenos Aires; Teatro Colón (Buenos Aires)
Armstrong, Louis, 158, 160
Artaud, Antonin, 6, 54
Audi, Pierre, 56, 88

Bach, Johann Sebastian, 174, 238
Baker, Geoffrey, 108, 130–131, 359n28
Bakhtiarova, Galina, 367n20
Bal, Mieke, 106–107
Balboa, Silvestre de, 157–158, 365n42
Balderston, Daniel, 342n7
ballet, 21–22
banana republics, 64–65, 67–68, 246
Barber, Samuel, 375n3
Barnes, Julian, 46, 273
Barnet, Miguel, 9, 70, 221, 239, 257
   Biografía de un cimarrón, 210, 212–13, 215–27
baroque, 99–100, 105–122, 161–2, 262, 360n42. *See also mestizaje* and hybridity
Bartoli, Cecilia, 195–97
Bauer, Martín, 11, 95, 307, 309
Beaumarchais, Pierre-Augustin Caron de, 169, 177, 179–80
Béhague, Gerard, 80
Bejel, Emilio, 367n10
Bellatin, Mario, 94
Bellini, Vincenzo, 2, 41, 196
   Norma, 182, 184–86, 195, 357n12, 367n17, 382n6
   Pirata, Il, 199

Benzecry, Claudio, 38, 295, 337n27, 341n61, 353n112
Berlioz, Hector, 39
Berhardt, Sarah, 43
Bernstein, Leonard, 17, 377n15
Berutti, Arturo, 19, 81–83, 352n111
Bishop, Elizabeth, 45
Bizet, Georges, 67, 194, 231, 347n69, 369n54
blackness, 9–10, 57, 80, 126, 157, 165, 197–99, 330–31. See also André, Naomi; Gomes, Carlos: *Lo schiavo*; Henze, Hans Werner: *El Cimarrón*; race and ethnicity
Blank, Les, 44
Bloechl, Olivia, 49, 343n22
Boero, Felipe, 83, 353n114
Bolivia, 8, 101. See also mission operas (Jesuit)
Borges, Jorge Luis, 17, 87, 268, 385n34
  "A Manuel Mujica Lainez," 294–95
  "La biblioteca de Babel," 70
  "El escritor argentino y la tradición," 5, 23, 78
  "El milagro secreto," 94
  "El testigo," 219
Bostridge, Ian, 329, 331–32
Bouissou, Sylvie, 57
Brazil, 10, 78–81, 374n38. See also Gomes, Carlos; Manaus, Rio de Janeiro,
Brouwer, Leo, 373n35
Buch, Esteban, 87, 354n130, 384n16, 385n34
Budasz, Rogério, 15–16
Buenos Aires, 18, 178. See also Argentina; Teatro Colón (Buenos Aires)
  and cosmopolitanism, 284–85, 287
  and modernity, 33, 37–38, 82, 284–5, 292, 325
  as periphery or center, 286–87
Burgtheater (Vienna), 169, 207
Burgos, Elisabeth, 218
butterflies. See Lepidoptera

Cabrera, Lydia, 84
Cabrera Infante, Guillermo, 174–175, 185
Cairo, 2, 339n48
  premiere of Giuseppe Verdi's *Aida*, 18–19, 32–33, 288–89
Calderón de la Barca, Pedro, 279
  La aurora en Copacabana, 114–115
  "Deposición en favor de los profesores de pintura," 125, 126–127
  libretto for Tomás de Torrejón y Velasco's *La púrpura de la rosa*, 7, 73–74, 96–129, 329
Callas, Maria, 20, 40–41, 183–84, 205, 227, 286, 368n25, 382n6
  in Latin America
Camarena, Javier, 369n49
Cambaceres, Eugenio, 32–33
Cammarano, Salvatore, 58
Campo, Estanislao del, 5, 30–32, 39, 293
Carpentier, Alejo, 99, 164–65, 364n36
  El arpa y la sombra, 147
  Cartas a Toutouche, 163–164
  Concierto barroco, 7, 8, 21, 42, 54, 140–163
  libretto for *Manita en el suelo*, 165
  La música en Cuba, 165
Caruso, Enrico, 71, 241
  in Latin America, 19–20, 41, 286, 299
  in Werner Herzog's *Fitzcarraldo*, 43–44, 274
Castellanos, Rosario, 379n33
  in John Adams's *El Niño*, 245, 252, 254, 256, 258–62
  in John Adams's *The Gospel according to the Other Mary*, 265
Castro, Juan José, 84
Catán, Daniel, 245–251
  Encuentro en el ocaso, 250
  Florencia en el Amazonas, 10–11, 90, 245–48, 266–79, *278*
  La hija de Rappaccini, 250–51, 375n4, 377n12, 377n13, 377n14
  Il Postino, 249–50, 376n9.
  Salsipuedes: A Tale of Love, War and Anchovies, 246–47
Centro de Experimentación del Teatro Colón (Buenos Aires), 95, 308
Cervántez, Yreina D., 252–58, *253*, 262

Césaire, Aimé, 328
Céspedes, Carlos Manuel de, 171–172
Cetrangolo, Aníbal Enrique, 18–19, 382n1
chacmool, 136–138, 137, 362n1
Charlotte of Belgium (empress), 76
Chávez, Carlos, 85, 353n121
Chávez Bárcenas, Ireri E., 363n14, 366n49
Chile, 84, 353n118
Chin, Unsuk, 92–93, 355n139
Cigna-Santi, Vittorio Amedeo, 52
Ciccolini, Alessandro, 167
Clément, Catherine, 140–142, 166, 167, 309, 369n46
Coelho, Victor Anand, 133
Colectivo de Ópera Nacional (Chile), 84
Columbus, Christopher, 2, 50, 146, 276, 288, 343n28
comicality and politics, 6, 63–69, 346n65
Comisión de la Verdad y Reconciliación (Peru), 58
compact disc covers, 96–98, 136–138, 252–57. *See also* Cervántez, Yreina D.; Kahlo, Frida
Conrad, Joseph, 63–64, 65, 246
Cortázar, Julio, 72–73, 89, 349n83
Cortés, Hernán, 150, 156
cosmopolitanism, 8, 14, 21–28, 37–41, 94, 188, 211, 305. *See also* Buenos Aires; Darío, Rubén; Fuentes, Carlos; Malibran, Maria; Merlin, Mercedes; Mujica Lainez, Manuel; Ocampo, Victoria
countertenors, 140, 149–151, 154–156, 364n32
criollos and *criollismo*, 42, 83, 98, 142, 144, 167, 356n7
Cruz, Nilo, 71, 93.
Cruz, Sor Juana Inés de la, 71, 98, 105
    El divino Narciso, 111, 115, 122–123
    in John Adams's *El Niño*, 253–54, 253, 256, 258
    in Louis Andriessen's *Theater of the World*, 11, 279–82
Cuadra, Gonzalo, 84, 353n118
Cuba, 8–9, 24, 84. *See also* Cuban Revolution; Figueredo, Pedro; Havana; nation and nationalism

Cuban Revolution, 41, 174, 219–221
Curtis, Alan, 137, 155

Da Ponte, Lorenzo, 189–90
    libretto for Wolfgang Amadeus Mozart's *Così fan tutte*, 102, 189
    libretto for Wolfgang Amadeus Mozart's *Le nozze di Figaro*, 169–171, 179, 180, 189, 371n79
Darío, Rubén, 5, 14, 33, 258, 262, 340n59
    Prosas profanas, 33–38
    and race, 33–36
    and Richard Wagner, 33–37, 304–5, 340n56, 386n37
Darwin, Charles, 269, 272–274
Debussy, Claude, 317, 319–20, 322, 325
decolonial, decolonization, 48, 147, 339n40, 350n87
Deutsche Harmonia Mundi, 97, 103, 106, 108, 124, 126
Dianteill, Erwan, 252, 257, 378n27
Díaz Ayala, Cristóbal, 366n3
Didion, Joan, 346n65
Dinesen, Isak (Karen Blixen), 10, 247, 375n3
Dizikes, John, 19, 190, 337n19
Domingo, Plácido, 80, 203, 227, 249, 286
Donizetti, Gaetano, 2, 366n9
    L'elisir d'amore, 3, 195
    Il furioso all'isola di San Domingo, 56–57
    Lucia di Lammermoor, 139, 182–83, 322
Dryden, John, 49, 50, 328
Duplay, Mathieu, 259, 379n33
Dutch National Opera, 71, 88, 279

elites and elitism, 14, 22, 31–32, 83, 283–84, 350n87, 367n7. *See also* Mujica Lainez, Manuel: *El gran teatro*; Ocampo, Victoria
Elizabeth (Queen Mother), 199, 200–201
El Niño Southern Oscillation, 264
Enzensberger, Hans Magnus, 9, 210, 215, 221–24, 233, 239, 373n27
Eötvös, Peter, 70, 93, 348n79
Errázuriz, Sebastián, 94
Esménard, Joseph-Alphonse, 52
Estrada, Julio, 84

Europa, myth of, 12, 334
European operas about Latin America, 47–63, 65–71; *see also* US American operas about Latin America; *names of individual composers*
Exoticism, 6, 47–63, 268–71, 273, 347n69, 348n76, 349n86, 363n21
Eszterháza Palace, 52
Everett, Yayoi, 91–92

Feldman, Martha, 149
Fernández Retamar, Roberto, 28, 328, 339n40
Ferrer, Horacio, 88
Ferrero, Lorenzo, 54
Ferretti, Jacopo, 56
Festival Internacional de Música Renacentista y Barroca Americana, 101, 358n16
Festival Internacional Cervantino (Guanajuato), 94
Figueredo, Pedro, 8, 172–6, 180–1, 204, 206–8
Fitzcarrald, Carlos Fermín, 44, 341n6
Flagstad, Kirsten, 286, 291
Fleming, Renée, 355n142
Fonseca, Rubem, 41, 374n43
Forner, Jane, 387n5, 388n12, 388n13
Forrest, George, 85
Fort Worth Opera, 71
Frank, Gabriela Lena, 71, 356n1
Frederick II of Prussia (king), 6, 51–52, 344n31
Freud, Sigmund, 176
Friis-Hansen, Mathias, 215, 227–231, 229, *230*
Fuentes, Carlos, 39–40, 262, 272
Fuentes-Beráin, Marcela, 247, 276
Fuzelier, Louis, 57–58

Galeano, Eduardo, 43–44
Gallo, Rubén, 69
Gamarra, Jean Pierre, 58
Garaviglia, Margherita, 18, 19
García, Manuel, 189–90, 191–92, 195, 368n36, 369n46, 369n49

García Caturla, Alejandro, 165
García Lorca, Federico
 and Heitor Villa-Lobos's *Yerma*, 85–86
 and Osvaldo Golijov's *Ainadámar*, 6, 91–92, 355n138
García Márquez, Gabriel, 17, 248, 375n4, 379n35
 and Daniel Catán's *Florencia en el Amazonas*, 247, 262, 273, 274
 and Peter Eötvös's *Love and Other Demons*, 70, 348n79
 See also magical realism
Garcilaso de la Vega, el Inca, 105, 129
Garrido, Gabriel, 108–109, 130, 358n16
Gasta, Chad M., 359n22, 360n40
gender and sexuality, 11, 54, 140–42, 145–46, 149–151, 181–86, 204–5
 in Antonio Vivaldi's *Motezuma*, 154–156
 in Manuel Mujica Lainez's *Bomarzo*, 300, 302–5, 386n38
 in Martín Bauer and Beatriz Sarlo's *V.O.*, 307–325
 See also Castellanos, Rosario; Clément, Catherine; Ocampo, Victoria; homosexuality, masculinity
Genette, Gérard, 238–39
Giacosa, Giuseppe, 288
Gigli, Beniamino, 241
Ghislanzoni, Antonio, 352n106
 libretto for Giuseppe Verdi's *Aida*, 61, 79, 81
 libretto for Carlo Enrico Pasta's *Atahualpa*, 61–63
 libretto (revision) for Giuseppe Verdi's *La forza del destino*, 59, 61
 libretto for Carlos Gomes's *Fosca*, 81, 352n107
 libretto for Carlos Gomes's *Salvator Rosa*, 81
Gianera, Pablo, 285, 308
Ginastera, Alberto, 6, 17, 85
 Beatrix Cenci, 87, 88
 Bomarzo, 16, 17, 86–87, 292, 354n130
 Don Rodrigo, 16, 86
Girri, Alberto, 87

Giusti, Alvise, 51, 52, 54, 55,
  libretto for Antonio Vivaldi's
  Motezuma, 139–147
Glyndebourne Festival Opera, 348n80
Góes, Marcelo, 351n99
Golijov, Osvaldo, 6, 90, 91–93, 378n27
Gomes, Carlos, 6, 17, 41, 78–81, 90,
  348n80
  Il guarany, 78–80, 350n89, 366n9
  Lo schiavo, 9–10, 79, 209, 210, 212,
    233–44
Gómez Cairo, Jesús, 173
Gómez-Peña, Guillermo, 49–50
González Echevarría, Roberto, 114–115,
  159, 218, 226, 335n2, 336n6
Gounod, Charles, 5, 30–31, 292
Graham, Susan, 69
Gran Teatro Imperial (Mexico City),
  76. *See also* Gran Teatro Nacional
  (Mexico City)
Gran Teatro Nacional (Lima), 58
Gran Teatro Nacional (Mexico City),
  77. *See also* Gran Teatro Imperial
  (Mexico City)
Grand Théâtre de Genève, 94, 123
Grassi, Orazio, 133
Graun, Carl Heinrich, 6, 51–52, 344n31,
  349n86
Greene, Graham, 215
Greer, Margaret, 358n20
Gronk, 50, 92, 257
Gruzinski, Serge, 151-2, 350n89
Guevara, Ernesto "Che," 94, 176–77
Gutiérrez Alea, Tomás, 8, 41, 176, 181–83

"Habanera." *See* Bizet, Georges
Hahn, Raynaldo, 69, 318, 348n75, 348n76
Halévy, Ludovic, 65–67
Hamel, Micha, 71, 341n66
Hamvai, Kornél, 70
Handel, George Frideric, 74, 148, 151, 152
  Messiah, 158–159
Havana, 8, 18, 19, 20, 41, 177, 367n17. *See
  also* Cuba
Hawthorne, Nathaniel, 250
Haydn, Joseph, 29, 52

Henry, O. (William Sydney Porter),
  64–65, 246
Henze, Hans Werner, 24, 239, 338n35,
  353n121, 355n143
  El Cimarrón, 9, 70, 210, 211, 213–33, 243
Herzog, Werner, 80
  Fitzcarraldo, 6, 43–47, 90, 95, 101,
    273–74
Hess, Carol A., 17, 85, 87, 354n125
Hidalgo, Juan, 73–74, 102–103, 117, 356n5,
  356n6
Holdridge, Lee, 70
homosexuality, 87, 175–185, 300, 302–4,
  367n10, 385n34. *See also* gender and
  sexuality; masculinity
Hopscotch. *See* Sharon, Yuval
Houston Grand Opera, 10, 245–48. *See
  also* Catán, Daniel
Howard, Sir Robert, 49, 50
Hudson, W.H., 269, 380n46
Hunt Lieberson, Lorraine, 254, 259
Hutcheon, Linda, 385n32
Hutcheon, Michael, 385n32
Hwang, David Henry, 146, 364n22
  libretto for Osvaldo Golijov's
    Ainadámar, 91–93
  libretto for Unsuk Chin's *Alice in
    Wonderland*, 92–93, 355n139
Humphrey, Hubert, 17
hybridity, *see mestizaje* and hybridity

Illari, Bernardo, 88, 98–99, 101, 130,
  358n14, 358n15
Illica, Luigi, 288
immigration, *see* migration
imperialism, 2, 12, 21–22, 45, 67, 238,
  345n49, 364n22
  and Tomás de Torrejón y Velasco's *La
    púrpura de la rosa*, 101, 103–4, 357n11,
  and mission operas, 130, 134
  and Alejo Carpentier's *Concierto
    barroco*, 143, 152, 163, 168
  and Antonio Vivaldi's *Motezuma*, 162,
    363n14
  See also Orientalism; Said, Edward;
    Giuseppe Verdi's *Aida*

410   *Index*

indianismo, 79
indigenous languages, 14, 53–54, 101, 134–35, 143, 144, 156, 363n16
Insinger, Esteban, 95
Isabel, Princess Imperial of Brazil, 10, 80, 236–39, 374n43
Ismael, César de Carvalho, 374n41
Ismail Pasha (Khedive of Egypt), 288–89, 339n48

Jaimes Freyre, Ricardo, 38
James, Henry, 200, 215–16
Jameson, Fredric, 72, 349n82
Jesuit mission operas. *See* mission operas (Jesuit)
Jobim, Antônio Carlos, 17
Jouy, Étienne de, 52
Jrade, Cathy L., 36–37, 340n56
Juárez, Benito, 76

Kaalund, Lars, 9, 215, 227–31, 232
Kagel, Mauricio, 89–90
Kahlo, Frida, 71, 96–98, 124–127, 255, 356n1, 360n46
Kallman, Chester, 85, 353n121
Kapsberger, Johannes Hieronymus, 133–134
Kaup, Monica, 100
Kennedy Center for the Performing Arts (Washington), 87
Kerman, Joseph, 20, 371n79
Khedivial Opera House (Cairo), 289. *See also* Cairo
Kircher, Athanasius, 279–82
Komische Oper (Berlin), 67
Koestenbaum, Wayne, 182
Krausser, Helmut, 280–81
Kristal, Efraín, 275
Kristeva, Julia, 367n12
Krozier, Daniel, 70
Kuss, Malena, 16, 61, 77–78, 80–81, 83, 165, 336n6, 350n93
  on opera and Latin American literature, 335n2, 362n6, 365n42

La Scala. *See* Teatro alla Scala (Milan)
Lang, Bernhard, 150

Latin America as operatic subject, *see* European operas about Latin America, US American operas about Latin America; *names of individual composers*
Latin American literature on opera, 5–6, 30–42. *See also* librettos, reading of; magical realism; marvelous real; *names of individual authors*
Latin American operas, 6, 73–95. *See also names of individual composers*
Lawrence-King, Andrew, 108, 109, 124
Lebrecht, Norman, 201
Lecuona, Ernesto, 369n43
Lehár, Franz, 64
Lei Áurea, 80, 236, 239
León, Tania, 94, 212, 355n143
León-Portilla, Miguel, 157
Leoncavallo, Ruggero, 299, 353n112
Lepidoptera, 246, 267–271, 275–79, *278*, 380n47
Leppert, Richard, 43, 46
Levin, David J., 20, 99.
Levine, Suzanne Jill, 380n42
Lewis, Mark, 136
Leza, José Máximo, 74
Lezama Lima, José, 7, 99
librettos, 14, 16, 106
  as "erratic players," 20–21, 99–100
  in indigenous languages, 53, 54, 134–135, 156, 363n16
  in Spanish, 249, 376n9, 379n33
  in Italian for Latin American operas, 75, 78, 83, 233–34, 351n100
  multilingual, 50, 53–54, 70, 83, 93, 280, 315,
  resignification, 6, 58–59, 96, 102–129, 357n12
  See also indigenous languages; reading; *names of individual composers and librettists*
Ligorio, Cecilia, 52
Lima, 93, 99, 103. *See also* Peru
Lindauer, Margaret, 356n1, 360n46
Lindenberger, Herbert, 48, 185, 343n20
Linke, Ulrich, 150
Lispector, Clarice, 3

literary studies and opera, 13–14, 23–42, 87–88. *See also* Latin American literature on opera; librettos, reading
Littlejohn, David, 15
Locke, Ralph P., 48, 97
Long Beach Opera, 49–50, 89, 94, 156
López, Jimmy, 6, 90, 93, 355n142
López Austin, Alfredo, 157
López Buchardo, Carlos, 83
Los Angeles, 85, 203, 257, 266. *See also* Los Angeles Opera, Los Angeles Philharmonic
Los Angeles Opera, 247, 249, 266
Los Angeles Philharmonic, 71, 265, 279
Lucas, Marcos, 95
Ludmer, Josefina, 32
Ludwig II of Bavaria (king), 203, 370n56
Lully, Jean-Baptiste, 49, 343n22
Lund, Joshua, 44–45, 341n6, 376n6
Lyric Opera of Chicago, 91, 266, 355n142

Macalupú-Cumpén, Pablo, 58–59
Maehder, Jürgen, 50, 344n29
Magaldi, Cristina, 14–16, 352n108
Maggio Musicale Fiorentino, 52
magical realism, 10, 46, 70, 245–48, 273, 348n79, 348n80, 376n5. *See also* marvelous real
Maiguashca, Mesías, 94
Malgoire, Jean-Claude, 148–152, 154, 364n32
Malibran, Maria, 184, 189, 192–97, 198, 205–6
Malinche (Malintzin), 54, 56, 145, 147, 345n48, 366n49
Manaus, 43–47. *See also* Teatro Amazonas (Manaus)
Mañach, Jorge, 174–175, 206
Martí, José, 5, 23–29, 181, 340n55
Martí i Torrents, Francesc, 370n55
Martin, Claire, 191, 369n44
Martín, Jorge, 70
Martínez, Julián, 311, 318–20, 324
marvelous real, 153, 164, 364n36. *See also* Carpentier, Alejo; magical realism
Mascagni, Pietro, 82, 287, 299

masculinity, 8, 146, 149–151, 155–56, 171–79, 204–5. *See also* countertenors; gender and sexuality
Matamoro, Blas, 151
Mauri Esteve, José, 372n2
Maximilian I of Mexico (emperor), 76
Máynez Champion, Samuel, 156, 363n16
McClary, Susan, 252, 343n26, 347n69, 379n30
Meano, Vittorio, 295
Meilhac, Henri, 65–67, 348n75
Menchú, Rigoberta, 218
Méndez Rodenas, Adriana, 368n31, 368n33
Mendieta, Ana, 107
Menotti, Gian-Carlo, 375n3
Mérimée, Prosper, 67
Merlin, Mercedes, 41, 177, 212
  La Havane, 187–89
  Les Loisirs d'une femme du monde, 190
  Maria Malibran, 8–9, 186–87, 192–97, 198
Messiaen, Olivier, 214, 227
mestizaje and hybridity, 22, 57–61, 78, 98, 230–31, 256–57, 340n60, 346n55
  and Frida Kahlo, 126–127
  and the baroque, 100, 106–109, 157–158, 357n9, 357n13
  and the neobaroque, 168
  See also baroque; race and ethnicity; Verdi, Giuseppe: *La forza del destino*
Metastasio, Pietro, 51
Metropolitan Opera House (New York), 3, 87, 148, 200, 204, 245
Mexico, 75–79, 83–84, 350n87, 350n89. *See also* Mexico City
Mexico City, 39–40. *See also* Mexico
migration, 4, 92, 189, 204–5, 208, 355n139
  Chinese in Cuba, 226, 341n66,
  Europeans in Latin America, 2, 4, 18–19, 38, 298–99, 341n61, 382n1, 385n25
  Latin American composers in the United States, 84–88, 90–93
  See also Adams, John: *El Niño;* Catán, Daniel; Gomes, Carlos; Henze, Hans Werner mission operas (Jesuit), 7–8, 75, 101, 129–135
Mistral, Gabriela, 258, 262
Mitisek, Andreas, 89

Moctezuma, 37, 77, 147
  as operatic subject, 50–56
  See also Carpentier, Alejo: *Concierto barroco*; Malgoire, Jean-Claude; Rihm, Wolfgang: *Die Eroberung von Mexico;* Vivaldi, Antonio: *Motezuma*
modernismo, 23–29, 33–38, 262, 304–5
Monesterolo, Oscar, 307, 385n31
Montale, Eugenio, 84
Montaldo, Graciela, 33
Monteiro, Mário Ypiranga, 44, 46–47
Montejo, Esteban, 9, 210, 212, 214–33
Montero, Mayra, 41, 70, 341n66
Monteverdi, Claudio, 4, 110, 165, 364n32
Montevideo, 18, 70, 91, 92
Moraes, Vinícius de, 17
Morales, Melesio, 76, 350n89
Mortier, Gerard, 345n49
Mozart, Wolfgang Amadeus, 24, 179, 204
  Così fan tutte, 102
  Don Giovanni, 173, 204
  Die Entführung aus dem Serail, 48
  Le nozze di Figaro, 8, 124, 139, 169–171, 173, 180, 206–8, 371n79
Mujica Lainez, Manuel, 284–85
  Bomarzo, 86
  El gran teatro, 11, 38,
  libretto for Alberto Ginastera's *Bomarzo*, 86–87, 286–307
multilingual librettos. *See* librettos, multilingualism in
musicology and opera, 14–17, 20
Musikfestspiele Potsdam, 123

Nagano, Kent, 92–93, 254, 255
nationalism and nationhood, 21–30, 63, 146, 159, 171–176, 206–8. *See also* Figueredo, Pedro
Nawrot, Piotr, 75, 130, 357n13
neobaroque, 99, 146–148, 162, 168
Neruda, Pablo, 65, 87, 262, 376n9
New York City Opera, 86, 266
novela testimonio or *testimonial, see* testimonio
Nguyen, Viet Thahn, 347n65

Oakes, Meredith, 11, 328–34
Ocampo, Victoria, 284–86, 386n36
  and Virginia Woolf, 267–71
  Autobiografía II: El imperio insular, 314, 317–18
  Autobiografía III: La rama de Salzburgo, 11, 38, 311, 319–22
  in Martín Bauer and Beatriz Sarlo's *V.O.*, 307–25
Ochs, Anna, 76, 350n89
Offenbach, Jacques, 64–69, 102, 348n75
Olivares, Jorge, 368n33
Olmstead, Andrea, 53–53
Oloixarac, Pola, 95
opera companies and theaters
  tours in the Americas, 18–19, 189–90, 337n19, 367n17
  See also names of individual companies and theaters
Ópera Latinoamericana (OLA), 335n3
Opera Society of Washington, 86
operetta, 64–70
Operettenstaat, 64, 66, 246
Orientalism, 32–34, 41, 194, 289, 343n20. *See also* Said, Edward
Ortega del Villar, Aniceto, 77–78
Ortiz, Gabriela, 94
Ott, Carlos, 342n9

Pacquier, Alain, 44, 360n42
Padilla, Heberto, 221
Palacio de Bellas Artes (Mexico City), 39–40, 156–157, 363n16
Palacio del Buen Retiro (Madrid), 102
Palais Garnier (Opéra national de Paris), 295, 342n9
Palma, Ramón de, 84
Palmié, Stephan, 218–19, 232
Pålsson, Per, 215, 229–31, 229
Panizza, Héctor
Paoli, Antonio, 29
Paravicini, Rodolfo, 79, 234–36, 243
Parker, Roger, 139
Parkinson Zamora, Lois, 100
Pasta, Carlo Enrico, 61–63, 102
Pasta, Giuditta, 196

Patchett, Ann, 93
Patti, Adelina, 25
Paz, Octavio, 6, 98, 250, 280, 377n12
   and Wolfgang Rihm's *Die Eroberung von Mexico*, 54–56, 345n47
Paz, Senel, 41, 176–177, 368n25
Pearson, William, 373n34
Pedro II of Brazil (emperor), 79, 81, 351n98, 374n44
Peppercorn, Lisa M., 85, 87–88
Peralta, Ángela, 29
Pérez, Rolando, 120, 360n41
Peru, 57–63, 65–67, 101–102, 111. *See also* Lima
Philip V of Spain (king), 73, 74, 103–105, 117, 237
Piave, Francesco Maria, 59–61
Piazzolla, Astor, 88–89
Pisani, Michael V., 48, 52, 343n21, 343n28
Pizarro, Francisco, 61, 103
Plate, Leonor, 383n7, 384n20
Poe, Edgar Allan, 190–91, 195
Polzonetti, Pierpaolo, 51, 52, 149, 344n31
Ponchielli, Amilcare, 44
Popol Vuh, 256
popular music, 13, 17
Porro, Ricardo, 94
Porter, Andrew, 328, 331
Portocarrero Lasso de la Vega, Melchor (viceroy), 103
Portugal, 15, 45, 290, 293
Price, Leontyne, 213, 227
Price, Rachel, 370n55
Puccini, Giacomo, 249, 250, 288
   in Argentina, 353n112, 383n7
   Madama Butterfly, 48, 146, 227, 231, 275, 278, 288, 317–18
   Tosca, 41, 249, 278, 288
Pulido Granata, Ramón, 76
Purcell, Henry, 49–50

Quesada, Héctor, 288
Quillévéré, Marcel, 348n78, 369n43

race and ethnicity, 22, 33–36, 194, 197–99, 386n37. *See also* blackness; Gomes, Carlos: *Lo schiavo*; Henze, Hans Werner: *El Cimarrón* mestizaje and hybridity
Racine, Jean, 23, 315
Radford, Michael, 249
Rama, Ángel, 108
Rameau, Jean-Philippe, 4, 57–58, 102, 148
reading, 1, 48, 106, 138–140, 153–154. *See also* librettos
real maravilloso, *see* marvelous real
Restall, Matthew, 156–157
Rihm, Wolfgang, 6, 54–56, 345n47, 345n49
Rindom, Ditlev, 385n25
Rio de Janeiro, 15, 19, 178, 352n108. *See also* Teatro Imperial Dom Pedro II; Teatro Lírico Fluminense
Río Escalante, Gustavo, 83–84
Río Prado, Enrique, 178
Robinson, Paul, 138, 338n29, 362n4, 366n2, 371n77, 371n78
Rodríguez, Marcela, 94
Rodríguez, Yelaine, 94
Rodríguez Garrido, José Antonio, 357n11
Rohloff, Steingrímur, 70
Romani, Felice, 185–86
Ross, Alex, 328
Rosselli, John, 18–19
Rossini, Gioachino, 27, 191, 192, 196, 366n9, 367n17
Rowe, John Carlos, 370n59
Royal Danish Theater (Copenhagen), 9, 209, 210, 213–14, 224, 225, 228–33
Royal Opera House (London), 370n57, 371n66
   and Thomas Adès's *The Tempest*, 11
   and Alberto Vilar, 9, 199–203, 370n58

Said, Edward, 32–33, 52, 142, 152, 211, 259, 288–89, 339n48. *See also* Orientalism
Saint-Saëns, Camille, 287
Salkey, Andrew, 219
Salzburg, 39, 42
San Francisco, 18, 258
San Francisco Opera, 71, 214

San Francisco Xavier (mission opera), 130, 134–135. *See also* mission operas (Jesuit)
San Ignacio (mission opera), 130–133, 134. *See also* mission operas (Jesuit)
Santa Fe Opera, 92
Santí, Enrico Mario, 184
Sarah Lawrence College, 86
Sarduy, Severo, 7, 99, 120
Sarlo, Beatriz, 11, 95, 284, 307–25, 380n52
Scarlatti, Domenico, 152
Schebera, Jürgen, 68
Schieroni, Teresa, 18, 19
Schwarzkopf, Elisabeth, 20, 286
Seattle Opera, 247, 266
Sellars, Peter, 49–50, 92, 343n26, 345n49, 378n21, 379n30
  libretto for John Adams's *El Niño*, 10, 252, 255–58, 263–65
  libretto for John Adams's *The Gospel according to the Other Mary*, 265
Sessions, Roger, 53, 93
Shakespeare, William, 23
  Hamlet, 153
  The Tempest, 11, 148, 327–34, 339n40
Shand, William, 87
Sharon, Yuval, 72–73, 349n82, 349n83
Sheffield, University of, 109, 123
Sheppard, W. Anthony, 53, 54, 56
Sibelius, Jan, 328
Sidney, Sir Philip, 154
Sigüenza y Góngora, Carlos de, 105
Simonetti, Pablo, 41
Simons, Moisés, 69–70
singers, 3–4, 12, 18–20, 29–30, 138–39, 189, 211–12, 286–87. *See also names of individual singers*, Teatro Colón
Siskind, Mariano, 14, 248, 364n36
Skármeta, Antonio, 249
Sklodowska, Elzbieta, 217–18
slavery, 9–10, 209, 211–13, 225, 231–32, 372n2, 374n38. *See also* Carlos Gomes's *Lo schiavo*; Hans Werner Henze's *El Cimarrón*; Lei Áurea
Smith, Paul Julian, 184
Soldi, Antonio, 295
Solera, Temistocle, 76
Solís, Antonio de, 55
Sommer, Doris, 351n100
Søndergaard, Morten, 70
Sousa, João da Cruz e, 386n37
Soyinka, Wole, 94
Spivak, Gayatri Chakravorty, 218–19
Spontini, Gaspare, 52–53, 344n36
staging of opera, 365n39***
Steen-Ardensen, Simon, 71
Stein, Louise K., 73, 74, 98, 104, 108, 109, 349n84, 359n5, 359n6, 359n7
Stendhal (Marie-Henri Beyle), 319
Stensgaard, Mia, 9, 215, 225, 227–31
Stevenson, Robert, 83, 85, 130, 340n55, 358n18
  on Tomás de Torrejón y Velasco's *La púrpura de la rosa*, 61, 98, 107–8, 360n36
Stoianova, Ivanka, 221–22
Strauss, Richard, 287, 382n6, 387n58
Stravinsky, Igor, 84, 165, 311, 316–17
  in Alejo Carpentier's *Concierto barroco*, 152
  in Martín Bauer and Beatriz Sarlo's *V.O.*, 309–10, 312–14
Su, Cong, 71, 150
Surwillo, Lisa, 346n55
Swed, Mark, 247, 281, 377n14

Tabío, Juan Carlos, 8, 41, 176
Tanglewood Music Festival, 90
Tamburini, Francesco, 295–96
Taunay, Alfredo d'Escragnolle, 80, 209–10, 234–36, 239, 242, 374n41
Taylor, Timothy D., 342n19
Tchaikovsky, Pyotr Ilyich, 4
Teatro alla Scala (Milan), 10, 33, 79, 84, 88, 90, 266
Teatro Amazonas (Manaus), 10, 43–47, 90, 243, 248, 266, 276, 342n9, 381n60
  in Werner Herzog's *Fitzcarraldo*,
Teatro Colón (Buenos Aires), 2, 4, 38, 46
  and Alberto Ginastera's *Bomarzo*, 87
  and Argentine composers, 83, 84, 86, 288
  and Verdi's *Aida* in 1908, 2, 283

Teatro Colón (*continued*)
  architecture, 290, 292–94, 383n8
  singers and conductors, 286–87, 290–91, 382n6, 383n7
  See also Centro de Experimentación del Teatro Colón (Buenos Aires); Wagner, Richard
Teatro Colón (Buenos Aires, until 1888), 30, 32, 287–88
Teatro Comunale di Ferrara, 155
Teatro de la Ópera (Buenos Aires), 19, 81, 383n7
Teatro de la Zarzuela (Madrid), 123
Teatro Imperial Dom Pedro II (Rio de Janeiro), 19, 209, 210, 237
Teatro Lírico Fluminense (Rio de Janeiro), 79
Teatro Municipal (Rio de Janeiro), 85, 235, 243, 342n9
Teatro Municipal (Santiago de Chile), 94
Teatro Principal (Lima), 58
Teatro Real (Madrid), 49, 56, 92, 345n49, 355n138
Teatro San Carlo (Naples), 52
Teatro Solís (Montevideo), 91
Teatro Tacón (Havana), 178, 370n55
Tebaldi, Renata, 88, 205, 227, 286
testimonio, 215–19
Theater an der Wien (Vienna), 249
Théâtre des Champs-Elysées (Paris), 310
Théâtre du Châtelet (Paris), 245, 249, 251, 252
Thiele, Kerstin, 215, 229–31, 229
Todorov, Tzvetan, 364n21
Tomé, Lester, 338n31
Torrejón y Velasco, Tomás, 7, 73–74, 96–129, 133, 255
Townsend, Sarah J., 342n14
Toscanini, Arturo, 19
Trippett, Anthony, 359n33

US American operas about Latin America, 53–54, 70–73
Upshaw, Dawn, 254, 259–60

Valdés Kuri, Claudio, 74, 349n86
Valera, Roberto, 94

Valmont, Lina (Toutouche), 161–162
Vambery, Robert, 68–69
Vargas Llosa, Mario, 216
Velasco, María Josefa, 375n4, 381n60
Verdi, Giuseppe, 348n80, 353n112
  Aida, 16, 32, 41, 48, 60–61, 71, 79, 211–12
  Alzira, 58–59, 102
  Un ballo in maschera, 76
  Ernani, 19, 43, 178
  La forza del destino, 59–61, 66, 102, 227, 347n70
  Otello, 211–12
  Il trovatore, 182
  See also Cairo; Teatro Colón (Buenos Aires)
verismo, 82–83
Verlaine, Paul, 386n36
Verne, Jules, 188
Veronese, Paolo, 125–126, 127
Viardot, Pauline, 196, 369n54
Vickers, David, 141
Vilar, Alberto, 9, 177, 199–205
Villa-Lobos, Heitor, 85
  A menina das nuvens, 85, 87–88, 354n131
  Yerma, 16, 85–86
Villazón, Rolando, 41–42
Villegas, Micaela, "la Perricholi," 65
Vinay, Ramón, 29
Viola, Bill, 379n36
Visse, Dominique, 149
Vivaldi, Antonio, 7, 8, 21, 51, 92, 148, 175, 365n39
  Farnace, 167
  Motezuma, 136–163, 255
Vogeley, Nancy, 32, 77, 350n87
Volpe, Maria Alice, 80, 235–36, 240–43, 351n98
Volpi, Jorge, 38–39
Voltaire (François-Marie Arouet), 58, 344n31
Voss, Steffen, 141, 167

Wagner, Katharina, 291
Wagner, Richard, 4, 5, 24, 81, 352n107, 352n108, 370n56
  and Bayreuth, 29

Wagner, Richard (*continued*)
  and Latin American literature, 33–39,
    340n55, 340n56, 341n63
  at the Teatro Colón, 290–91, 384n14,
    384n20
  in Alejo Carpentier's *Concierto barroco*,
    152–153
  Parsifal, 11, 38, 293–95, 299–306, 319–20,
    385n32
  Tristan und Isolde, 319–22, 325
  See also Mujica Láinez, Manuel
Waisman, Leonardo J., 130
Walt Disney Concert Hall (Los Angeles), 265
Walton, Benjamin, 337n15
Washington National Opera, 80
Weddigen, Tristan, 357n9
Weill, Kurt, 67–69
Wesendonck, Mathilde, 321
Whaples, Miriam K., 52, 144–145, 343n21
White, Sir Willard, 10, 214–15, 217, 227–32, 229, 230, 233, 254
Whitman, Walt, 37, 340n59
  "Italian Music in Dakota," 2–3, 5, 32
Williams, Alan Edward, 95
Williams, Alastair, 54, 55
Wolkowicz, Vera, 357n12
Woolf, Virginia, 267–71
Wright, Robert, 85

Xirgu, Margarita, 91–92

Yamashta, Stomu, 373n31

Zambello, Francesca, 266, 267, 279, 375n4
Zárate Toscano, Verónica, 350n89
Zentrum für Kunst und
  Medientechnologie (Karlsruhe), 94
Zingarelli, Niccolò, 52
Zipoli, Domenico, 101, 129–130, 132, 358n14, 358n15
Zumaya, Manuel de, 74, 83
Zweig, Stefan, 95
Zyman, Samuel, 363n16

www.ingramcontent.com/pod-product-compliance
Lightning Source LLC
Chambersburg PA
CBHW051203300426
44116CB00006B/420